A LEAP IN THE DARK

A Leap

in the

Dark

→

The Struggle to Create the
American Republic

John Ferling

OXFORD
UNIVERSITY PRESS

2003

OXFORD
UNIVERSITY PRESS

Oxford   New York
Auckland   Bangkok   Buenos Aires   Cape Town   Chennai
Dar es Salaam   Delhi   Hong Kong   Istanbul   Karachi   Kolkata
Kuala Lumpur   Madrid   Melbourne   Mexico City   Mumbai   Nairobi
São Paulo   Shanghai   Taipei   Tokyo   Toronto

Copyright © 2003 by John Ferling

Published by Oxford University Press, Inc.
198 Madison Avenue, New York, New York 10016
www.oup.com

Oxford is a registered trademark of Oxford University Press.

Library of Congress Cataloging-in-Publication Data
Ferling, John E.
A leap in the dark : the struggle to create the American republic /
    John Ferling.
p. cm.   Includes bibliographical references.
ISBN 978-0-19-517600-1
1. United States—History—Colonial period, ca. 1600-1775.
2. United States—History—Revolution, 1775-1783.
3. United States—History—1783-1815. I. Title.
E195 .F47 2003 973.3—dc21
2003001212

To
Josh Raskob,
Paul Miller,
and
Michael Miller

Contents

Illustrations and Maps

Illustrations

Maps

Preface

W hile a college student, I read *The Crisis of the Old Order,* the first volume in Arthur M. Schlesinger's history of the New Deal. Like most youngsters, I had thought that what occurred before my birth was ancient history and therefore unrelated to my world. Instead, I was amazed to discover in Schlesinger's history that much of the politics of my time had roots extending back a couple of generations or more. As I began to study history with wonderful teachers and scholars such as William Painter, E. Bruce Thompson, Kurt Rosenbaum, and Elizabeth Cometti, I grew steadily more aware that the past is prologue to the future.

Somewhat like Professor Schlesinger, my objective with this book was to write a political history. I wanted to explore the age of the American Revolution—which I generously defined as spanning the years of 1750 to 1800—in search for links that connected the political ideas of one generation to those of another. First, I wished to focus on the establishment of the American Union. To one degree or another, nearly everyone saw advantages to confederating, but all perceived dangers as well. This book, therefore, has sought to inquire into who desired a Union? What did they seek from a Union? What were they prepared to do to maintain a Union? Just as crucial to my inquiry, of course, was the shape of the national government that would exist when the Union came into being. What were the choices? What led one faction to seek a strong central government? What caused another to resist centralization? Who won the battle? Why? And in probing these matters, other questions came front and center. Did the politics of the American Revolution spring newly born after 1763 when the imperial government in London sought to implement a new colonial policy? Did the political struggles that preceded independence have roots in the long colonial past? How did the factional, and later party, battles that followed the War of Independence fit within this long transitional era? Did the parties in the 1790s, the Federalists and Republicans, have a lineage that stretched back to prerevolutionary America? How did the colonists' hopes, dreams, and fears of independence fit into the politics of postwar America? How did the protracted war, and the changes that resulted from war and revolution, shape the politics of the Early Republic?

Furthermore, during much of my career I have been intrigued with problems of leadership, and especially with those who led, or sought to lead, during the era of the American Revolution. In recent years, that interest has prompted me to structure a couple of seminars around questions of leadership in the American Revolution and Early Republic, and my students and I have attempted to understand history and this age through biography. So, in this work, I have sought to explore the origin and shaping of political movements and to explain the role of leaders in creating and giving shape to those endeavors.

Another matter gave birth to this endeavor. Perhaps most historians who have written about the eighteenth century have stressed that the political practices of that time were quite unlike those of today. But in the course of my teaching and scholarly work, I have been struck by the profound similarities in the politics and political practices of then and now. Differences existed, of course, but I found it striking that while so much about life in that earlier time had a distinctly premodern ring, many of the politicians seem surprisingly modern. Some in public life appeared to be as opportunistic as today's most unabashedly opportunistic politicians. Ambition led cunning individuals down disingenuous paths. Parties and politicians sometimes shaded the truth in self-serving pronouncements. Some activists conspired to deceive the public. And politics could be just as nasty as it is today, as parties heaped abuse on adversaries and searched the behavior of their foes for evidence of scandal, whether sexual misconduct or economic malfeasance.

Finally, when I was in graduate school, it was all the rage to believe that ideas shaped political behavior, and my earliest writings, which focused on the behavior of the Loyalists in the American Revolution, stressed that outlook. Over the years I have become convinced that political behavior usually owes more to economic considerations and that most people customarily embrace ideas that tally with their personal interests, especially their pecuniary considerations. However, this is not to say that I regard ideas as unimportant. Ideas, in fact, may never have been more crucial than in the struggle to create the United States, for the passionate factional battles of that day were fought over the shape and fabric of the new nation. Indeed, following independence, the primal question that confronted political activists and an engaged public was just how revolutionary the break with the Anglo-American past would be. In most instances, the answer lay at the very heart of one's ideology.

The title of this book was taken from a line in a newspaper essay written in 1776 by a Pennsylvanian who opposed American independence. To separate from the mother country, he cautioned, was to make "a leap in the dark," to jump into an uncertain future. Time and again in the course of the half century spanned by this book, political activists confronted the reality that their actions would catapult them onto amorphous terrain. In every instance, there were those who were ready to take the chance. Always, too, there were those who resisted approaching the abyss that would be ushered in by breaking with the past. Twenty years before independence, it would have been a leap in the dark for the individual colonies to surrender their autonomy and consent to a national confederation of thirteen provinces or for the imperial government in London to countenance such a union. Subsequently, it was a leap into an unpredictable place to resist British policies, go to war, declare independence, embrace republicanism, ratify the Constitution, enfranchise additional citizens, permit those who had never been trusted with public office to be elected as public officials, or to cast aside the habits of the Anglo-American colonial past.

Each step was uncertain and chancy. The success of the American Revolution was far from inevitable. Years were required to forge an effective opposition to British imperial policies, and that was followed by a protracted war to bring about separation from the empire. Militarily, of course, an American victory was not assured. That has been well remembered by subsequent generations. However, the labyrinthian political struggles that accompanied the war and persisted in its aftermath have been long forgotten, save by a few scholars. When in 1780 General George Washington said that the peril was greater than in the dark days of 1776, and he despaired that the American Revolution might be lost, he did not fear military defeat so much as he believed the effort to attain independence might fail due to political shortcomings. Later, in 1786, after the war had been won, many feared that seemingly insoluble political and economic problems doomed the Union. Still later, in the passionate partisanship of the 1790s, the fate of the Union remained uncertain as two factions with competing visions of the American future and clashing understandings of the meaning of the American Revolution battled for control of the new national government. Only with the presidential election of 1800 was it clear which vision of the American Revolution had at last prevailed. This book, ultimately a political history of the era of the American Revolution, explores these matters. It finds roots to that revolution entangled in the colonial past, and it sees the resolution of what the American Revolution was to mean occurring both on blood-soaked battlefields between 1775 and 1783 and in innumerable, and often desperate, political battles that ensued over the next twenty years, down to Inauguration Day, 1801.

The past half century has witnessed the creation of innumerable new nations. Not all have survived, and some have made it—at least for a few decades—only by surviving violent and bloody civil upheavals or after falling into the clutches of despots. In almost every instance, great powers, or at least more powerful neighbors, have sought to exploit these weak new nations for their own gain. Some of this sounds distressingly similar to the experience of the United States between 1776 and 1801. When American political leaders spoke of "tyranny," their utterances were more than hyperbolic rhetoric. They coped with insurrections, found their aspirations thwarted at times by great powers half a world away, and debated America's relationship with monarchies and revolutionary regimes across the sea. They expressed bona fide fears for political institutions that we take for granted, and dreamed seemingly unrealizable dreams that long ago were fulfilled but that today we accept unthinkingly.

When more than five years are consumed in the completion of a book, numerous debts of gratitude mount up. I was assisted by two research grants provided by the Learning Resources Committee at the State University of West Georgia. Most of my research was undertaken in the Ingram Library at the State University of West Georgia, where I teach. Day in and day out, I found the librarians and staff of that facility to be unfailingly helpful and cooperative. I especially appreciated the efforts of Angela Mehaffey and her staff in the interlibrary loan office of the Ingram Library to meet my rapacious requests. I also worked for several weeks in the Massachusetts Historical Society in Boston, and I am grateful to its staff and librarians for their generous and always cordial assistance. I am grateful, too, to William Fowler for granting permission to use numerous quotations from unpublished manuscripts in the Massachusetts Historical Society and to the staff of the Adams Family Papers for permission to utilize unpublished materials pertaining to John Adams. John Alexander, who has written a wonderful biography of Samuel Adams, corresponded with me via email, and we discussed and debated too many issues to enumerate. In the end, he enriched my understanding of the period, especially my sense of the battle in Massachusetts to ratify the Constitution in 1787–88. For a second time now, Peter Ginna at Oxford University Press has encouraged and guided me through the travail of bringing a manuscript to completion, and I appreciate his care, cheer, courtesy, and ready helpfulness. I am grateful to Elaine Otto, Helen Mules, and Furaha Norton for their care and assistance in the completion of this endeavor. And lastly, Carol, as always, was supportive and understanding of a distracted husband who was preoccupied with long ago events and personalities that continue to shape life in our time.

October 2002   JF

A LEAP IN THE DARK

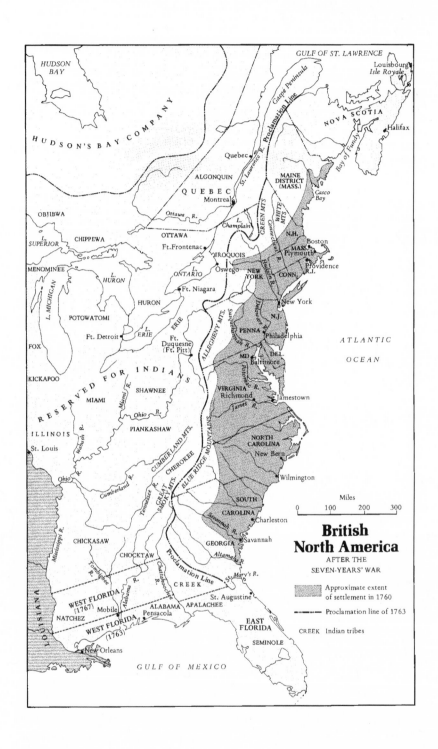

HUDSON BAY

GULF OF ST. LAWRENCE

Louisbourg
Isle Royale

HUDSON'S BAY COMPANY

Gaspe Peninsula

Proclamation Line

NOVA SCOTIA

Halifax

Quebec

ALGONQUIN

QUEBEC
Montreal

MAINE
DISTRICT
(MASS.)

St. Lawrence R.

Bay of Fundy

OBJIBWA

Ottawa R.

Casco
Bay

CHIPPEWA

L.
SUPERIOR

OTTAWA

Ft. Frontenac

Champlain

L.

GREEN MTS

WHITE
MTS.

N.H.

Boston

MENOMINEE

L.
HURON

IROQUOIS

Oswego

NEW
YORK

Connecticut R.

Hudson R.

MASS.
Plymouth

Providence
R.I.

CONN.

L.
ONTARIO

Ft. Niagara

HURON

New York

POTOWATOMI

L.
MICHIGAN

L.
ERIE

ERIE

Ft. Detroit

Ft.
Duquesne
(Ft. Pitt)

ALLEGHENY MTS.

N.J.

PENNA

Philadelphia

Delaware R.

ATLANTIC

OCEAN

FOX

MD.

DEL.

Baltimore

Potomac R.

KICKAPOO

RESERVED FOR INDIANS

SHAWNEE

MIAMI

Miami R.

Ohio R.

VIRGINIA
Richmond

Jamestown

James R.

ILLINOIS

St. Louis

PIANKASHAW

Wabash R.

Ohio R.

Cumberland R.

CUMBERLAND MTS.

Tennessee R.

CHEROKEE

GREAT
SMOKY MTS.

BLUE RIDGE MOUNTAINS

NORTH
CAROLINA

New Bern

Wilmington

Miles

0   100   200   300

SOUTH
CAROLINA

Charleston

CHICKASAW

GEORGIA

Savannah

Savannah R.

**British
North America**

AFTER THE
SEVEN-YEARS' WAR

CHOCKTAW

Proclamation Line

Altamaha R.

CREEK

Mary's R.

Mississippi R.

Tombigbee R.

WEST FLORIDA
(1767)   Mobile

Alabama R.

St. Augustine

Chattahoochee R.

ALABAMA

APALACHEE

Approximate extent
of settlement in 1760

Proclamation line of 1763

LOUISIANA

NATCHEZ

WEST FLORIDA
(1763)

Pensacola

EAST
FLORIDA

CREEK   Indian tribes

New Orleans

SEMINOLE

GULF OF MEXICO

1

1754–1763

"Join, or Die"

Benjamin Franklin stood on a bobbing ship, bathed in a warm summer sun. On this golden morning in June 1754, he was sailing north on the blue-green Hudson River, past dusty little villages and seemingly endless grand estates, beyond the gently rolling wooded terrain just north of Manhattan and into the New York Highlands, where tall hills hovered above emerald meadows. Franklin had retired as a printer and publisher, but this was not a pleasure cruise. He was on a mission. Pennsylvania had selected him as a representative to meet in Albany with commissioners from other British colonies. They were to search for a means by which the provinces, and their Native American allies, could cooperate in the likely event that war erupted with France.

Franklin, who strained for a glimpse of Albany through the mottled summer haze, bore little resemblance to the plainly dressed, stout, avuncular, older man that we usually imagine from the numerous portraits and sculptures produced a quarter century or so later. In 1754 Franklin, who was not yet fifty, was physically trim, with the thick neck and sinewy arms of a swimmer, for in fact he began most days with a lengthy swim (the best workout, he thought, for maintaining one's physical fitness). If he was dressed as normal, Franklin wore an expensive lace shirt, silver buckled shoes, and a wig with long brown curls, which lent an air of priggishness, if not unctuousness, to his appearance.

Suddenly, not far ahead, and on his left, Franklin spotted Albany. This was his first trip to what, by American standards, was a very old town. The French had established a settlement here more than 200 years before, then came the Dutch, and finally the English, who named the place Albany, or Albainn, the ancient name for the Scottish Highlands,

to which this region bore a resemblance. The English, like their predecessors, had erected a fort that served as a fur emporium, a venue for
commerce with the Mohawk Indians, whose villages and verdant fields
of corn dotted the landscape along this stretch of the Hudson Valley. As
Franklin's vessel drew near the surprisingly busy Albany pier, he glimpsed
reminders that he was on the exposed frontier, far removed from the
protective arm of a strong central government. This town of 2,000 inhabitants stood entirely enclosed within a wooden palisade, and on a
steep hill on the far side of town, Franklin spotted the old fort, still formidable with high, thick, grey stone walls.[1]

Franklin had come to Albany to prepare for war. King George's War,
Great Britain's third war with France since 1689, had ended six years
earlier without a clear victor, and most leaders in London, as well as the
colonies, feared that hostilities would soon resume. Once before, when
the first Anglo-French war of the series, King William's War, had ended
inconclusively, the fragile peace that followed lasted only four years. Besides, a new source of tension was apparent. Peace had hardly come in
1748 before Versailles sent a modest military detachment to what the English called the Ohio Country, a region bounded by the Mississippi River,
the Great Lakes, the Ohio River, and the Appalachian Mountains. France,
like Great Britain, claimed this area. It regarded the trans-Appalachian
West to the Mississippi River—together with Canada—as part of New
France, its colonial domain in North America. When it dispatched its
white clad soldiery to the Ohio Country, France had acted to woo the
Indian inhabitants and select sites for the eventual construction of fortifications. British officials, both in America and London, were immediately concerned. With crystal clarity, they saw that if the French won
control of the Ohio Country, the English would be hemmed in between
the Atlantic and the Appalachians, caught between New France to the
north and west, and Spanish Florida to the south. Opportunities for
colonists who aspired to own land would vanish, fortunes sunk in western land speculation would be lost, and the dream of a mighty and ex-
pansive British empire would die.

Robert Dinwiddie, the crown-appointed governor of Virginia, was
the first American official to alert London to the danger. It was logical
that he would act swiftly. Not only did Virginia claim the Ohio Country
through grants made a century and a half earlier in its initial charters,
but Dinwiddie was a stockholder in the Ohio Company, an enterprise
that had been awarded title by the Crown to hundreds of thousands of
acres in the disputed region. It took little imagination for Dinwiddie to
guess that the French soldiers had been sent to take control of the head
of the Ohio River, Anglo-America's access route to the Ohio Country.

He wanted guidance from London about how to respond. Before the year was out, he was advised to send a messenger to the French army in the Ohio Country informing them that the region belonged to Virginia. He selected young George Washington for the mission.

Washington was just twenty-one years old and militarily inexperienced. A few months before, he had been appointed Virginia's adjutant general for the southern portion of the province, but he had no military training and had never been in combat. However, he was a rugged outdoors type with a bit of polish to his behavior. He also was ambitious, eager to carry the message, and backed by influential patrons who urged Dinwiddie to select him. The son of a wealthy planter-businessman, Augustine Washington, young George should have had a promising future, but at age eleven he had lost his father to one of the virulent fevers that preyed on residents of the Chesapeake. Thereafter, doors seemed to close in his face. As a third son, George inherited little more from his father's estate than a small, spent farm. Suddenly, the best he could hope for appeared to be a life as a middling planter. With a bit of luck, he might someday be a man of consequence locally, but without great wealth and the power it could muster, and devoid of a formal education—the opportunity for extended schooling had vanished with his father's demise—Washington's prospects of ever being an important figure in Virginia were slim.

George was about twelve when he first saw Mount Vernon, the estate of his half-brother Lawrence. Although not much more than a country farmhouse standing on jade green land high above the Potomac River, it—and Lawrence—opened a new world to him. Lawrence not only had been educated in England prior to Augustine's death, but he had soldiered in the Caribbean and South America during King George's War. When he returned to the Northern Neck of Virginia, the region between the Potomac and the Rappahannock Rivers, he had married into the Fairfax family, the most powerful clan in that part of Virginia, and soon was elected to the colonial assembly. At Mount Vernon, and neighboring Belvoir, a stately Fairfax plantation, young George discovered a world of wealthy, powerful, urbane men and women. He wanted to be like them. Cosmopolitanism, he thought, would come from listening to their conversations, reading what they read, and modeling his behavior on what he observed. Soon he was taking fencing and dancing lessons, and poring over guidebooks on etiquette and comportment. But formidable obstacles lay in his path. While he might acquire the trappings of urbanity, gaining wealth and power were more problematical. Nevertheless, at about age sixteen he acquired the skills of a surveyor, a craft that paid well and offered those who dared an opportunity to speculate in frontier lands. But he found soldiering even more alluring. He noticed the deference that others extended to Lawrence and the esteem with which he was held for having risked his life for the common good. George Washington wanted that respect as well, but martial adventures seemed unlikely until he learned that Dinwiddie was searching for an intrepid soul to carry his message to the French. Washington knew that if he served as the governor's messenger, he would be in an excellent position to acquire an important post in any army that Virginia might create. Washington hurried to Williamsburg to volunteer.

Seven months before Franklin's arrival in Albany, in November 1753, Washington departed for the Ohio Country. He was a sturdy young man in excellent physical condition. Observers described him as about 6'4" in height, with broad shoulders, a narrow waist, and remarkable upper body strength. Several mentioned his agility and grace, and some thought him the finest equestrian they had ever observed. Furthermore, after five years of hacking his way through dense, mountainous forests and lugging heavy surveying instruments up and down Virginia's western hills, he exuded stamina and endurance and long since had evinced the mettle for coping with the hazards of the mountain wilderness. Young Washington was accompanied by a party of six, all of whom were accustomed to physical labor and experienced in the vicissitudes of the wilderness. Two were Indian traders, one a gunsmith, one had frequently carried messages for Governor Dinwiddie, and one was to serve as a translator. The sixth was Christopher Gist, a tough frontiersman, whose job was to serve as a guide and get Washington home alive.

Washington's party set out from Virginia under a flawless blue sky on the final day of October. As the men started their ascent into the barren mountains northwest of the Shenandoah Valley, entering western Maryland and eventually southern Pennsylvania, the lush days gave way to cold autumn rains. The party moved relentlessly up steep wooded slopes and down into cheerless hollows half obscured by gloomy fog. They observed no sign of human life, save for the trails they rode, carved through the wilderness by generations of Indians who now—menacingly—remained hidden. When they reached the Monongahela River, about thirty miles below the Ohio, they spotted the log cabin of an English Indian trader. Washington paused only long enough to learn what the trader knew of recent Indian activities in the region. From there the men pressed on, traversing one brown ridgeline after another, until three weeks out from Alexandria, Virginia, they at last reached the Forks of the Ohio, the site of the confluence of the Monongahela, Allegheny, and Ohio Rivers at present-day Pittsburgh. The men explored the Forks for a possible site upon which Virginia could someday erect a fort that would command the Ohio Country. Washington paddled about in a canoe near the shoreline straining to see, and at times alighted to walk the terrain, until he found what he believed was the perfect spot that "Nature has contriv'd" for building the installation. Soon the party was on the move again, traveling almost straight north, for the most part hugging the banks of the fast flowing Ohio River. Now they rode full into a remorseless northern wind, often accompanied by snow, and in the evening, as the dark tightened around a landscape that was snowbound and silent, the men shivered in their tents.

At Logstown, a couple days above the Forks, Washington was greeted by Half King, an envoy sent by the Six Nations Confederacy, which included the Mohawk and Iroquois. Dispatched to negotiate with the French, Half King repeated to Washington the truculent address he said that he had given earlier to the French commander in the Ohio Country: He accused the French of being "the Disturber in the Land, by coming & building your Towns, and taking it away unknown to us & by Force." To this, the French commander had rejoined that his nation possessed the Ohio Country and intended to repulse any English, or Indians, so brazen as to invade the region. Washington, who was unauthorized to negotiate, listened in silence, promising only to relate to Virginia's governor what he had heard.

On November 30, a month out from Alexandria, Washington began the final, most arduous leg of his journey. Alternately traveling on foot and horseback in temperatures that seldom rose above freezing, the men climbed hills with old snow that barely remained white, slogged through thick, black bogs, and from time to time used hastily built log rafts to make their way through seemingly impenetrable swamps. Finally, nearly 100 miles north of the Forks of the Ohio, and just south of Lake Erie, their destination came into view: Fort Le Boeuf, a small rectangular French post that bristled with artillery and was garrisoned by nearly 100 French soldiers.

Changing from the buckskin and moccasins he had worn during his journey, Washington donned attire more suitable for a gentleman and royal messenger, and hurried to the fort amid swirling gusts of snow. The French received him hospitably, and soon the young Virginian was dining with his hosts, enjoying perhaps his first good meal in six weeks, replete with excellent French wine. Afterwards, Washington got down to business. Preeningly tough, he presented Dinwiddie's message. The French response was no less emphatic: France was not encroaching on British soil; the Ohio Country belonged to France by the right of discovery and exploration. Throughout, the French officers and Washington remained cordial, but all knew that what had been said meant that war was on the horizon. Forty-eight hours later, Washington—rested, clad again in buckskin and furs, and carrying food and liquor provided by his generous hosts—departed under shifting grey clouds to return across the Appalachians in the dead of winter.

Washington barely survived the trip home. First, he was fortunate to escape harm when a brave who had fallen in with him and Gist somewhere between the Allegheny and the Ohio—near what the English traders disquietingly called Murthering Town—tried to kill him. The Indian, who was walking about fifteen paces ahead of the two Englishmen, abruptly wheeled about brandishing a single-shot handgun and fired. His shot missed. Thereafter, Washington and Gist disarmed the Indian and sent him on his way unharmed, or so Washington later claimed. Later, Washington might have drowned, or died from hypothermia, when he fell from his raft into the swirling Allegheny River, whose temperature, he later said, was "extream severe." He was rescued by Gist, who got him ashore, built a fire, and tended his frostbitten extremities. Thereafter, the journey was largely uneventful, and it was speedier than the outbound trek. Making about ten miles a day under the paltry winter sun, Washington came down out of the mountains only three weeks after leaving Fort Le Boeuf. A few days later he reached Williamsburg.[2]

When Washington was received by Dinwiddie, he made his report: the French denied Virginia's claims to the Ohio Country. The governor wasted no time asking the assembly to raise an army, which in turn acted rapidly to create the Virginia Regiment. Washington was rewarded with the post of second in command, but soon was named commander of Virginia's army when his superior died in an accident. Recruiting proceeded through the damp, chilly spring, and as Franklin and the other commissioners started their journeys to Albany, Lieutenant Colonel Washington, now all of twenty-two years old and wearing a blue and red uniform of his own design (it was the exact reverse of the redcoat uniform worn by British regulars), marched his men toward the area in dispute. His orders were to proceed to the forks of the Ohio River, where he was to build a fort. If the French had already arrived, he was to drive them away.

Late in May 1754, as Washington's ragged, ill-trained force of fewer than 150 men advanced through the tangled Pennsylvania forests to within forty miles of the forks of the Ohio, intelligence arrived that a party of French soldiers had been spotted. Washington moved quickly to intercept them. Indian guides led him, with about forty men, deeper into the dark wilderness. After a few hours they found their prey. There were thirty-five French soldiers. Having only a slight numerical advantage, Washington decided on a surprise attack. With stealth, he moved forward, until his men encircled the adversary. At the right moment,

Washington screamed the order to open fire. A volley of shots poured down on the unsuspecting French. Some were hit. The others fought back, but the firefight was brief. Caught off guard, and without adequate cover, the overpowered French surrendered. Washington's Indian allies then went to work, and the young Virginian was unable, or unwilling, to stop them. In all likelihood Washington, who never before had experienced combat, was "unmanned," as the historian Fred Anderson has observed, possibly by the shocking carnage that he had just unleashed, including the realization that he had just killed, or mortally wounded, another man. Momentarily disoriented, or perhaps in a rush of blood lust, Washington stood aside while the Indians massacred several of the French, together with their commander, Ensign Joseph Coulon de Villiers de Jumonville. Ensign Jumonville was tomahawked and scalped, after which Half King, the leader of Washington's Indian allies, scooped out the Frenchman's still warm brain and squeezed it in his hands.[3] What Washington did not know before he ordered the attack was that Jumonville was on a peaceful mission, not unlike that which had taken him to Fort Le Boeuf six months earlier.

Long before Washington opened fire on the French in that thick American forest, imperial authorities in London had recognized the gathering war clouds. Not only was trouble brewing in the Ohio Country, but evidence existed that France was considering an attempt to retake Nova Scotia, which it had lost to Great Britain forty years before. In August 1753, the Board of Trade directed all colonial governors to use force if necessary to resist French encroachments on their frontiers. A month later, it instructed the governors of New York to call an intercolonial conference. London had several things on its mind. It wished to restore friendship with the Indians of the Six Nations Confederacy, an alliance of tribes that inhabited the vast area stretching from the Hudson Valley deep into the western regions of the Ohio Country. It wanted the colonies to find a way to build a string of forts across the vulnerable frontier, and to act cooperatively in supplying the forces that were raised to deal with the French.[4] Lieutenant Governor James De Lancey of New York quickly invited eight colonies to send delegates to Albany—he chose that site because of its proximity to the Iroquois homeland in what now is upstate New York—to treat with the Indians and to seek ways in which the provinces might cooperate against the French. Virginia, which had already been promised aid by London, declined, as did New Jersey, which was far from New France and had no land claims in the West. However, the six other provinces—the New England colonies, as well as Maryland and Pennsylvania—joined New York in sending delegations of varying size. Some of the twenty-five commissioners came quite eagerly, seeing the conference not merely as useful in the event of hostilities with France but as a golden opportunity to fulfill a long cherished dream. They planned to seek a union of the colonies under British control.[5] Benjamin Franklin was one such delegate.

Though middle-aged, Franklin was new to politics. Raised in Boston and trained as a printer, he had left in his late teenage years to make his way in the world. He explored opportunities in New York and London, but finally settled in Philadelphia—the city, in his estimation, in which an industrious go-getter might have the best shot at success. "All his surviving papers," the historian Edmund S. Morgan has written, "testify to his lifelong wish to be useful to his friends, to his countrymen, and to mankind in general."[6] His voluminous writings also unmistakably reveal a man of insatiable ambition who was incapable of realizing all his aspirations, for each new success only whet his appetite to achieve even more. He began his dizzying arc of assent as a clerk in a print shop, earning a meager but

Benjamin Franklin at age fifty-four. Engraving by James McArdell after painting by Benjamin Wilson.

livable income. Soon he was the foreman of the shop. After three years, he and a partner purchased their own newspaper. Twelve months later, Franklin bought out his business associate. Sometime thereafter he opened a stationer's shop, which quickly flourished. He now was earning money as a shopkeeper and the publisher of a newspaper, magazine, and almanac. Within a short time, additional income rolled in from partnerships that he entered into with several former apprentice printers. In addition, like many others with a discretionary income, Franklin speculated in real estate, some of it in the trans-Appalachian West. Nineteen years after taking the clerking job in Philadelphia, and at a time when the most successful skilled craftsman could hardly hope to earn more than £30 a year, Franklin enjoyed an annual income in excess of £2,000.

He had been inordinately successful, and not just in material terms. He had become a leading figure in Philadelphia. He not only impressed people with his assertive intelligence; he was an activist who had been instrumental in creating a police force, firefighting units, a library, hospital, college, and a scientific society in his adopted hometown. He had also acquired a reputation throughout the empire for his inventions—which by this time included improved stoves, candles, and lamps, as well as the lightning rod—and scientific experiments. By mid-century Franklin was the best-known person in the colonies. Wishing for free time "during the rest of my Life for Philosophical Studies and Amusements," Franklin retired. He was forty-two years old. He lived for another forty-two years and more. He never resumed a business career, but three years after retiring he embarked on a new endeavor. He entered politics and was elected to the Pennsylvania Assembly in 1751.[7]

Franklin did not turn to politics merely to dabble now that he had time on his hands. Terribly ambitious, he sought to scale new heights. Moreover, he was a British nationalist who chafed at the prospect that France and Spain might dominate the region beyond the mountains and someday perhaps all of North America. Nor was he disinterested. Franklin owned land in the Ohio Country. Just as he entered the assembly, Franklin published an essay entitled *Observations concerning the Increase of Mankind*, his most complete public statement concerning Anglo-American expansionism. Should the British lose the American West, he cautioned, the inhabitants of the thirteen mainland colonies would in no time be "crowded together in a barren Country insufficient to support such great Numbers." They would be too poor to consume British manufactures and perhaps even incapable of feeding themselves. The available land would be insufficient for all who wished to become property-owning yeomen. Most Americans would be no better off than the multitudes who inhabited the mother country. The only hope of avoiding the fate of those in the old country, he said, was to wrest control of trans-Appalachia from its rivals, then remove the Indians. Franklin's object was to make the British Empire the world's largest and most powerful. But he also hoped to make Philadelphia its American center, and "in another Century . . . [when] the greatest Number of Englishmen will be on this Side of the Water," to see that it was the capital of the Anglo-American empire.[8] And expansion beyond the mountains was but the first—or next—step that Franklin envisioned for the Anglo-American empire. A "great empire, like a great cake, is most easily diminished at the edges," he warned, as he dilated about the necessity for London to spread, and strengthen, its jurisdiction over America's borderlands.[9] Franklin, who seemed to say that the moment had arrived for

Quaker Pennsylvania to take on a character of unyielding, militant tough-ness required for imperial greatness, also appeared to be offering him-self as the tenacious visionary who could transform the province's dreams of expansion into reality.

During King George's War, which ended three years before Franklin assumed public office, Pennsylvania's Quaker-dominated assembly had refused to enact a militia bill. Franklin, a private citizen, had been in-strumental in the movement to have his colony play a substantive role in the conflict. His motto had been the "Way to secure Peace is to be pre-pared for War." He helped raise a volunteer military force, proposed a lottery that ultimately provided money for the purchase of arms from Massachusetts and the fortification of the Delaware River, and served as an envoy to New York to borrow cannon. He also used his printing press to rally the population to take up arms, sometimes appealing to the anti-Catholic prejudices of many inhabitants to arouse fear and hatred of the French. In the most lurid terms he described to Philadelphians what might occur if the city was sacked by a French army. Wives, children, and aged parents would be its prey, businesses would be laid waste, homes would be plundered, and only too late would the city's inhabitants learn "what Misery and Confusion, what Desolation and Distress" had befallen them because they were unprepared for war. Franklin additionally printed essays by others that warned of French and Spanish encirclement of the British colonies, denying future generations access to the bucolic farm-land beyond the mountains. He authored muscular tracts that advo-cated a steady push westward, arguing that the best means of conquering the vast frontier was through the succor and direction of a union of the colonies. If "ignorant Savages" were capable of forming the Six Nations Confederacy, Franklin added, surely the thirteen English colonies should be able to do the same. The leaders responsible for creating such a union, he went on, "may be properly called *Fathers* of their Nation."[10]

Franklin preferred that the colonists take the lead in creating an American union, as he believed that the inhabitants of America would be more receptive to a plan that was hatched on their side of the Atlan-tic. He also knew that it would be easier to correct any flaws in the scheme if it were a homegrown invention. About three weeks before he left Phila-delphia for Albany, Franklin published a story in his newspaper, the *Penn-sylvania Gazette*, about the menacing French activities in the Ohio Country. Accompanying the account was a drawing of a snake severed into several sections, each identified as a separate colony, and beneath the caption: "JOIN, or DIE." The illustration soon appeared in several colonial newspapers.[11]

Franklin's colleagues slowly drifted into Albany. Considering the adversities that confronted all travelers in early America, it was hardly surprising that not a single commissioner had reached the village by June 14, the date that De Lancey had set for the opening session. Nor had the Iroquois arrived. Finally, five days late, enough delegates were on hand to begin. As all the delegates were committed to establishing good relations with the Iroquois Confederacy, their first important business was to prepare a cordial address to the Indians. Chief Hendrick, speaking for the 150 tribesmen who by now were encamped in and about Albany, replied on July 2. He minced no words. "Look at the French," he cried. "They are men. They are fortifying everywhere. But—we are ashamed to say it—you are like women." Furthermore, he castigated the English for having ignored the Iroquois for too long. He had a point. Since Queen Anne's War at the beginning of the century, the English in New York, who steadfastly evinced an interest in landjobbing the Iroquois, had displayed little concern for their plight when they were threatened by the French and their Indian allies. He punctuated his remarks by picking up a stick and throwing it behind him, after which he acrimoniously declared: "You have thus thrown us behind your back and disregarded us."[12]

The delegates were quick to mollify him. They promised to stand by the Six Nations and gave their sachems so many gifts that thirty wagons were required to transport the booty. Meanwhile, the British uncorked the rum pot and proceeded to fleece their inebriated new friends. A representative of the Penn family—the proprietary family in Pennsylvania—and commissioners from Connecticut negotiated separate land deals with the Iroquois. The latter paid the Iroquois £2,000 in New York currency for 5,000,000 acres on the upper Susquehanna River, while Pennsylvania induced them to sign away their title to an even greater amount of land west of the Susquehanna for £400.[13]

The delegates then turned to how they might further cope with the French threat. De Lancey, who had called the meeting, delivered what in effect was a keynote address in which he raised the issue of a mutual assistance pact between the colonies. The delegates, knowing already that several in attendance had brought proposals for intercolonial cooperation, debated the matter only briefly before creating a committee to craft a "general plan" from among the "Schemes" that were introduced. Several propositions were offered. A representative of the proprietors of Pennsylvania urged the creation of an army, called the "Union regiment," that was to consist of companies of 100 men from each colony. It was to be financed by excise taxes and commanded by officers appointed by the Crown. This scheme not only failed to address issues of governance, but it would have compelled colonial soldiers to serve under British regulars. This plan went nowhere.

De Lancey, who was not well liked, then offered New York's plan. Though the competition would have been stiff, he might have edged out all rivals for the title of the most unpopular royal official in America. Virtually everyone who met De Lancey concluded that he looked with contempt on all whom he regarded as his inferiors, and that he judged almost everyone to be in that category. If his supercilious manner was not bad enough, he also struck a considerable number of acquaintances as an ambitious, cunning, scheming backstabber. De Lancey's plan would have compelled each colony to contribute to the establishment of forts and fleets on Lake Erie and Lake Ontario. It required little perceptivity for these worldly men to see that the chief beneficiaries of De Lancey's scheme would be De Lancey himself, as his commercial dealings with the Iroquois would flourish through the protection provided by other colonies, and New York, whose defense expenditures henceforth would be borne in large measure by other colonies. Nevertheless, there was a meritorious aspect of the plan. If successful, it would have severed all links between French holdings in the Ohio Country and Canada, and thus might have pacified the New York frontier while simultaneously opening Anglo-America's access to the Ohio Valley. Nevertheless, most delegates thought it self-serving and likely to hurt their interests as much as it helped New York's cause. It was rejected out of hand.[14]

Thomas Hutchinson, a Massachusetts representative, also put forward a plan. Born in 1711, just five years after Franklin, and only a couple of blocks away from the modest cottage in Boston's North End where young Benjamin was growing up, Hutchinson knew quite different surroundings. The scion of a wealthy and influential family prominent for producing powerful merchants, shipbuilders, and public officials, he was raised in one of the city's most fashionable mansions. A precocious youngster, he had entered Harvard College at twelve, matriculating with a little money in his pocket provided by his father, who had urged him to invest it and make it grow. Four years later, when he graduated at sixteen, Hutchinson's little nest egg had grown by quantum leaps and was worth perhaps ten times the annual income that most workers could anticipate. His fortune continued to grow, and by the time he turned twenty-one, Hutchinson owned eight houses, including a 100-acre estate in suburban Milton, and several lots and buildings in Boston. He married well two years later, increasing his net worth to £6,000. The only surviving portrait of Hutchinson, painted in 1741, when he was thirty, reveals a mature man who looked youthful as a teenager. Tall and slender, with a fair complexion, he appeared soft and effete. By the time he sat for the artist, Hutchinson had been in politics for a few years. After serving in the Massachusetts assembly for a dozen years, he secured an appointment as a Judge of Probate and Common Pleas, despite never having studied or practiced law. This suggests that he was well connected politically. In fact, almost immediately upon entering public life, Hutchinson had joined with what contemporaries called the "hard money" faction in the assembly. An anti-inflationary element that represented the greatest merchants and money-lenders, these legislators embraced economic stability. Their stance, however, was unpopular with the general public, many of whom were in debt, or hovered about its fringes, and who relished the additional money in their pay-

Thomas Hutchinson, age thirty. Oil on canvas by Edward Truman, 1741.

checks that accompanied an inflationary currency. As Hutchinson's unpopularity grew, and it became evident that there was little likelihood that he would ever wield much power in the assembly; he linked up with what the residents of Massachusetts called the Court Party, the circle around the governor, an official who was appointed by authorities in London.[15]

Hutchinson's patron in 1754, when he was sent to Albany, was Governor William Shirley. The governor, like Franklin, thought a union of the colonies was desirable, but not for the same reason. Shirley wanted to see America brought more fully under Great Britain's control. Like many officials in London, Shirley feared that the colonies, separated from the mother country by the 3,000 miles of blue Atlantic, were drifting apart from England. Imperial administrative machinery was lacking for the proper enforcement of imperial policies, especially the maritime regulations, and the colonial assemblies had grown disturbingly more powerful in their battles with royal governors. He thought it was time that more rigid controls should be implemented. A union of the colonies, properly subservient to Parliament and the Crown, yet draining power away from the local provinces, was just the vehicle for accomplishing these ends. Hutchinson was sent to Albany to pursue this goal.[16]

Hutchinson, like Shirley, favored an American union, but not for the reasons that moved the governor or Franklin. His objective, as had been the case with many in Massachusetts during the past half century, was the utter destruction of New France. In 1691, in the first of the inter-colonial wars with France, waged two decades prior to Hutchinson's birth, Massachusetts had sent an armada of thirty-four vessels and 2,200 men to take Quebec. Its leadership had reckoned that only the expulsion of the French, who armed the Native Americans all along Massachusetts's extensive frontier, could bring true peace and security to the province. The attempt failed. Not only was the attack on Quebec repulsed, but only about half the colony's soldiery survived the campaign. Thereafter, Massachusetts understood that it could eliminate the French only with help both from the other colonies and Great Britain. Hutchinson came to Albany to fashion a union of provinces that would help secure Massachusetts's ends. He unveiled a plan that urged Parliament to form two confederations, one of the eight northern colonies, and a separate union consisting of the southern provinces. The two were to be created "for their Mutual Defence & Security & for extending the British Settle-ments Northward & Westward." In the event of war, the Southern union would cope with the overextended French in the Ohio Country, while the Northern union would invade New France.[17]

Benjamin Franklin arrived in Albany with a paper he had drafted during his brief stay in Manhattan en route to the conference. He titled it "Short Hints towards a Scheme for a General Union of the British on the Continent." Unlike Hutchinson, he proposed one union that would consist of all thirteen mainland colonies, and he recommended that it be created by the colonists, rather than by Parliament. The government of the American confederation was to include a chief executive, who was to be "a Military man" appointed by the Crown, and an elected assembly in which the number of representatives allotted each colony was to be determined by the size of its population. The powers of this national government would be limited to matters of Indian diplomacy and na-tional defense, and would include "every thing that shall be found nec-essary for the defence and support of the Colonies in General, and encreasing and extending their settlements." Franklin closed with the recommendation that the Albany Congress adopt the plan, after which it would "be sent home" for the consideration of Parliament.[18]

The various plans introduced at Albany were not the first instances when American colonists had contemplated acting in concert or had consid-ered the establishment of a political confederation. However, only the Puritan colonies in seventeenth-century New England had succeeded in actually forming a federation of sorts, and in reality it was never more than a defensive league against regional Indian tribes. Outside New England, each province dealt unilaterally with nearby Native Americans, but when Britain's struggles with France and Spain began, plans of union and calls for a greater centralization of authority mushroomed. At least eleven plans of union are known to have been concocted after 1689, pouring forth from essayists, merchants, a founder of a colony, a governor, colonial officeholders—especially those whose responsibilities included Indian concerns—and imperial officials, including a member of the Board of Trade. The goal of military coordination lurked behind every plan, if in fact defense was not the sole reason for every proposed super-government. Most contemplated a national union, one that could set quotas for men and revenues in wartime, raise armies, and dispatch militia units from one colony to another, an act that was prohibited by the laws of most provinces.[19]

None of these plans came into being. Each colony had a long, unbroken history as a separate entity. Each had its own charter, institutions, history, statutes, and identity. Each was independent of the others, generally liked it that way, and hoped to remain unfettered by ties to anyone, save the mother country. The provincials saw dangers in each proposed scheme. The smaller colonies always chafed at the prospect of being underrepresented in a national congress dominated by the largest colonies. Men with influence in the provincial government feared losing their clout in a large confederation. Provincial taxpayers were loath to pay additional duties to still another government, especially to a central government over which they might exercise little leverage with regard to who was taxed and how the tax dollars were spent. Among a people who had fled Europe to escape tyranny, civil and religious, it was unnerving to consider the prospect of surrendering local autonomy and leaping into a strange new union, in which distant provinces, and faraway London, would exercise formidable power. Insularity prevailed. Each colony cried out for its security and sought to protect and further its vital interests, but few conceived a common bond with all, or even many, other British provinces in North America. Historically, they had looked across the Atlantic to the parent state, not across the borders to their neighboring American provinces. Indeed, the colonies often had strikingly different interests. Some traded with the Indians to a far greater degree than others. Some had extensive claims to western lands; others had none. Massachusetts at times wished to fight to secure fishing rights off Newfoundland, or coal deposits in Nova Scotia, or timberlands in Maine whose products were essential in its ship construction yards. Those were not burning issues in the Carolinas or Georgia, which were preoccupied with trade with the Indians in the Southern backcountry, while they kept a wary eye on the Spanish in nearby Florida.[20] Nor did every colony always feel threatened, even in the midst of war. Massachusetts, New York, and Connecticut had the misfortune to be hit hard by each of the previous intercolonial wars, but Maryland and New Jersey were hardly scathed, and before the 1740s Virginians were barely aware that the European powers were fighting one another in North America.

At times, the imperial government attempted to induce the colonies to act in concert, but it too had little success. Aware that some colonies neither defended themselves nor provided aid to their neighbors during wartime, the Board of Trade—the British government body that supervised colonial affairs—had longed to royalize each province, in which case all governors would be appointed by the Crown and all would be made to march to the same drummer. During a period of twenty years, into the 1720s, it repeatedly sought Parliament's endorsement for altering the colonial charters. It always failed, due to opposition from the colonial governments and vested interests in Britain itself. The Board even tried to accomplish its ends through the judicial process, but that failed as well. Defeated at every turn, the Board in 1721 simply proposed the construction of a string of frontier forts "at the two heads of the Colonies, North and South," and the reassignment of eight regiments of British regulars to America to guard those outposts. Little came of either recommendation.[21]

In the absence of any confederation, desperate colonial leaders sometimes had attempted to orchestrate collaborative military initiatives with their neighbors, but those efforts rarely succeeded. In 1690 during King William's War, New York and the New England colonies, each of which possessed a vast frontier that was vulnerable to French and Indian attacks, had eagerly sought to coordinate their military strategies, but the partners soon were torn asunder by conflicting interests. New England wished to strike at Quebec, the heart of New France. New York favored a more modest objective, the pacification of its Champlain Valley, through which its enemies often debouched. The two parties eventually compromised on a two-pronged offensive, with one force, assisted by their Iroquois allies, campaigning in the West, the other striking down the St. Lawrence at the capital. Weak and divided, both campaigns failed.

Outraged New Englanders blamed the failure on New York. In fact, when the governor of the latter province subsequently proposed the creation of an intercolonial defense fund for fighting the French, Massachusetts's governor roared that he would "not send a man or a farthing of money to the assistance of New York." It soon was New York's turn to fume. When the French in 1693 took advantage of New York's weakness and struck through the Champlain Valley, destroying frontier settlements, New England refused its neighbor's entreaties for a helping hand. Moreover, when London subsequently directed several colonies to contribute men to an American army that was to be established to defend the New York frontier, not one colony obeyed.[22]

Despite this long-standing indifference, or hostility, to cooperative endeavors, signs abounded that a new spirit existed in 1754. In part this was due to the realization that the colonists' most spectacular military successes had always grown out of joint endeavors between several provinces and Great Britain. Nova Scotia had been captured in Queen Anne's War when the four New England colonies raised an army of 3,500 men and the imperial government furnished a powerful naval arm. In King George's War, Louisbourg, which guarded the approaches to the St. Lawrence, had been taken by a New England army of over 3,000 men that acted in concert with a royal fleet of nearly 100 vessels. In addition, as Franklin later remarked, many suddenly wished for a confederation now that hopes for westward expansion were imperiled, as never before, by a formidable enemy. Some among the delegates at Albany saw an American union as a deterrent to war and believed, as did Franklin, that the "disunited state" of the colonies encouraged French aggression.[23] Experience also taught these delegates that little hope existed of the provinces acting in concert to overcome the common threat unless a confederation existed to provide central guidance. That very spring, in fact, as these delegates well knew, only South Carolina had responded with troops to Virginia's entreaties for help when the Virginia Regiment marched to the disputed lands at the head of the Ohio River. One additional point was crucial in shaping the thinking of those at Albany. At some point in their deliberations, perhaps when the committee cobbled together a plan from the many that had been introduced, word arrived of Colonel Washington's bloody ambush of the French party at Jumonville's Glen. Now that French blood had been spilled, what previously had been a prospect of war changed immediately to the reality of war.

Four days after the committee heard the first plan of union, on June 28, it proposed a scheme for the consideration of the Albany Congress. Although some changes had occurred in committee, the final product closely resembled Franklin's sketchy plan, and like Franklin's it too was entitled "Short Hints." The Congress debated the proposal for ten days. Some discussion revolved about the limits of London's power over an American confederation, or "Their power of hurting us," as one delegate candidly remarked. Most, like Franklin, thought America's security so gravely threatened that the colonists had no choice but to act and hope for the best. Form a union, Franklin said, extend greater sway to London than ever before, and "make as good a night of it as we can."[24] Some deliberation also took place over the colonists' freedom of trade with other imperial powers. Even the utilization of the Mississippi River, far, far to the west, crept into the discussion. Congress made additional changes, particularly with regard to the proposed sections concerning taxation, representation, and land policies. Nevertheless, the final product was sufficiently similar to Franklin's original proposal that he might fairly be thought the father of the Albany Plan of Union.[25]

This plan urged that Parliament sanction a union of eleven mainland colonies. Georgia, founded only twenty years before and still in a primitive state, and tiny Delaware, which many yet thought of as part of Pennsylvania, as in fact it had been until recently, were excluded. The government was to include a President General appointed by the Crown and a Grand Council, the national legislature, which was to consist of forty-eight members elected for three-year terms by whomever each province designated as qualified voters. Representation and taxation were initially to be based on population. Massachusetts and Virginia, for instance, were each to have seven representatives, and New Hampshire and Rhode Island would have two apiece; the others were to fall somewhere in between. In time, however, the number of representatives allotted to each colony was to be made proportional to the amount of taxes paid. The Council was to meet annually in Philadelphia, but could be summoned to emergency meetings by the executive. It could elect its speaker and could be dissolved, or prorogued, by the executive.

The Albany Plan proposed that the President General, with the advice and consent of the assembly, could declare war and make peace, negotiate treaties, regulate trade, and arrange land transactions. The central government was authorized to equip vessels of war and raise armies, but it could only conscript men with the consent of the colonial assemblies. It could build forts, administer territorial expansion, and regulate new western settlements. The assembly could levy taxes that "to them shall appear most equal and Just," but in so doing it was not only to consider the citizenry's ability to pay but also to focus as much as possible on luxury items. All legislative enactments required the assent of the executive and could be invalidated within three years by the Privy Council in London.[26] The Albany Plan was adopted unanimously and sent to London and to each colony for approval.

The plan did not fare well on either side of the Atlantic. The prime minister and his cabinet, or ministry, having learned of the firefight at Jumonville's Glen, had committed two regiments of British regulars to North America just ten days before the Albany Plan reached London.

This force was to clear the head of the Ohio of all enemy personnel. London also had ordered the colonies to raise up to 3,000 men to augment the redcoats, directed the colonial governors to make available supplies, transportation, and quarters for the soldiery, and commanded that the provinces establish a common defense fund for covering a part of the cost of this initiative. Word of the Albany Plan did not cause the imperial officials to reconsider their earlier steps. Many powerful figures, such as the Speaker of the House of Commons, fretted that "an Independency upon this country [is] to be feared from such an union" of the colonies. Although more the product of ruffled paranoia than cold reason, there were those who suspected that an American revolt to separate from the empire had long been in gestation, especially in New England, home to the descendants of the Puritans, and that a union of the colonies would only facilitate such treachery. Even with a cataclysmic war apparently under way in America's dark, tangled interior, London superciliously concluded—as Franklin put it—that an American "Union might make the Colonies in some degree [as] formidable to the Mother Country . . . as to the Enemy."[27]

The Albany Plan foundered in America as well, smashed by the age-old fears that had wrecked so many previously proposed schemes of union. The Massachusetts assembly obsessed that Parliament would use the American government for "gaining power over the Colonies." Governor Shirley had a different take. The legislators, he said, "don't like the plan . . . which all of 'em conceive to infringe upon the Colony-liberties & privileges." Rhode Island worried that it might ultimately destroy the existing colonial charters. Connecticut declared that to grant revenue-raising powers to a central government was "a very extraordinary thing, and against the rights and privileges of Englishmen." Likewise, Pennsylvania's assembly, acting on a day when Franklin was not in attendance, rejected the proposed union. Powerful men in Virginia, fearful that a national congress dominated by populous northern colonies might scuttle their province's title to western lands, blocked the House of Burgesses from even considering the proposed union. Although in a couple of instances one house of an assembly endorsed the proposal, not a single colony approved the Albany Plan of Union.[28]

Although the push for an American union with central authority over colonial affairs had been a chimerical quest, Great Britain sought to win the French and Indian War—as the conflict that was officially declared two years after the Albany Congress often has been called—through centralized direction. Imperial officials were always in charge. General Edward Braddock, who led the regiments sent across the Atlantic soon after the meeting in Albany, was initially in overall command

and in charge of the common defense fund. Following Braddock's death in battle on the Monongahela in July 1755, Governor Shirley was named the commander-in-chief of Anglo-American operations. Military figures ultimately succeeded him, beginning with John Campbell, the fourth earl of Loudoun, who took charge late in 1756. Loudoun sought to bring order and efficiency into the colonists' war effort. To remedy a chaotic logistical situation, he hired crews and set them to work widening roads, improving portages, and constructing way stations, and he even standardized the size of bateaux and scows used in supplying the Anglo-American armies. Loudoun was outraged to find that merchants in many colonies were trading with the enemy and that corrupt, or inept, royal governors often did nothing to stop them. Nor did Loudoun shrink from using his powers to attempt to stamp out the illicit commerce. In fact, in short order Loudoun reached the identical conclusion that Franklin and Hutchinson, and others at Albany, had mooted following King George's War. The provincials, Loudoun came to believe, were so divided by their multitudinous selfish interests that they were incapable of waging an intercolonial war with any degree of efficiency. By 1757 he had marched step-by-step in the same direction that the Albany Congress had longed to go: toward greater centralized control of the war effort.[29]

Loudoun's cranky dislike of the Americans hardened into contempt as the British and their colonists suffered a nearly unbroken chain of disasters in the first years of hostilities. Braddock's force was decimated in an encounter on the Monongahela River, near the Forks of the Ohio, in July 1755. The following year Colonel Washington's Virginia Regiment, which no longer received any assistance from its neighbors, lost one-third of its men in the ghastly frontier fighting. Indeed, by the end of 1756 Washington, flailed with agitation, acknowledged the loss of the Shenandoah Valley. That was the story throughout America. Georgia's lieutenant governor reported that the "frontier, instead of being covered by Forts, is entirely destitute of any, at least, that are not in ruins." According to a Philadelphia newspaper, "nothing but Murdering and Captivating . . . by Indians" prevailed on the Pennsylvania frontier. A royal official in Rhode Island, with lancing invective, attributed the colonists' dire predicament to their excessive individualism. In America, he said, "all seek their own, every Man his private Gain, pursuing a distinct and separate Interest from that of his Majesty and the public." No one understood this better than young Colonel Washington. Lamenting the lack of cooperation, he predicted that "without a much greater number of Men than we have a visible prospect of getting," conditions inevitably would "assume a more melancholy appearance."[30]

But steadily larger numbers of men arrived from Great Britain in 1758 and thereafter. They crossed the Atlantic, sent by a new prime minister, William Pitt, who understood that conditions had to be changed. Pitt secured new allies in Europe, whose armies took on the fight against the French on the continent. This enabled him to send 20,000 British regulars across the Atlantic, more than ten times the number that Braddock had brought, to fight in the American theater. He asked the colonies to raise nearly an equal number of men, and established manpower quotas for each colony. He also promised to reimburse each province at war's end for supplying and paying its soldiers. In 1758 Massachusetts raised an army of 7,200 men, Connecticut put 5,000 under arms, and tiny Rhode Island and New Hampshire each fielded armies of 300 men. Altogether, the Northern colonies alone raised 16,300 men that year, a total that nearly exceeded the number raised by these colonies in the two previous years combined. Overall strategy was planned in London, and troop allocation decisions were generally made in Whitehall, the seat of the ministry, as well.[31]

Pitt never set out to unify the colonies, and the provinces did not fight in 1758 or thereafter, in a unified manner. However, joint Anglo-American operations, a rare occurrence in the earlier wars, became commonplace. In the crucial struggles between 1758 and 1760, several Northern provinces contributed men who served alongside British regulars at the front in New York and New France, while many Southern provinces sent troops to campaign with His Majesty's regiments in the battle for the Ohio Country. In the climactic campaigns for New France, up to half the soldiery consisted of colonials, and even more when it is remembered that thousands of militiamen were simultaneously summoned to duty to guard the frontier nearer the home front. Pitt's central leadership resulted in a greater coordination and cohesion of the colonial war effort, not least in acting on his conviction that victory hinged on "carrying War into the Heart of the Enemy's Possessions." Principally, this meant that Quebec must be the primary objective in securing victory. It was an axiom that generations of New England's leaders had carried to London, which Hutchinson had conveyed at Albany, and which one ministry after another had largely ignored.[32] But when Quebec fell in 1759, New France was doomed.

News of the capture of Quebec triggered a jubilee in the northern provinces. Philadelphians put candles in their windows, and New Yorkers built a great bonfire. Bostonians outdid both. After three-quarters of a century of failed attempts to take the capital of New France, Boston's militia paraded and fired artillery, churches throughout the city rang their bells from sunrise to sunset, special worship services were conducted, and the elite celebrated at a festive banquet at Faneuil Hall.[33]

Anglo-America was victorious, and the joint operations of British redcoats and the American soldiery had been crucial in securing that victory. Nevertheless, joint operations were not the same as unity. The war had ended satisfactorily for the provinces, yet as time passed, some saw clearly how the creation of an American national government during this war might have changed the course of history. Franklin understood. Reminiscing on the Albany Plan in his memoirs, he wrote with dismay: "I am still of opinion it would have been happy for both sides of the water if it had been adopted. The colonies, so united, could have been sufficiently strong to have defended themselves; there would then have been no need of troops from England." London would neither have been driven deeply into debt by this war, he added, nor would it have felt the necessity afterwards to tax the provinces, which helped trigger the American Revolution. "But such mistakes are not new," Franklin added. Most leaders do not like to contemplate change. "The best public measures are therefore seldom *adopted from previous wisdom but forc'd by the occasion.*"[34] Left unsaid, but implied as a disquieting reality in Franklin's reminiscence, was his conviction that had the Albany Plan been adopted, the American Revolution would not have occurred, at least not in his lifetime.

2

"A Loss of Respect and Affection"

Late in life Andrew Oliver resembled the type that Hollywood once selected to portray a pernicious big businessman. He stares out from his sole surviving portrait as hard-bitten, perhaps not quite malevolent, but unappealing nonetheless. Residents of colonial Boston knew him as a pillar of society and a force in Massachusetts Bay politics. There seemed to be an inextricable link between the Oliver family and political power in the colony. In 1765 Oliver, then fifty-nine years of age, served as the secretary of the colony and, like his father before him, he too sat in the upper house of the assembly. His younger brother, Peter, was the Chief Justice of Massachusetts, though he had not been trained as a lawyer.

Close acquaintances thought Oliver a man of many admirable traits. They described him as industrious, perceptive, sober, pious, reasonable, humble, bright, and cultivated.[1] The general public held another view and never displayed much affection for him. The residents of Boston, a city of 15,000, looked on Oliver as imperious and unapproachable, a man of great wealth who lived like a grandee and utilized his influence as a public official—including his serviceable ties with authorities in England—in a never ending quest for even greater wealth. The Crown paid him £300 annually, roughly ten times the income of most artisans, to do a bit of clerical work as provincial secretary. He derived additional income as a landlord and through numerous investments. At a time when one in three inhabitants of Boston was too poor to own property, and when the lower half of the propertied population possessed just 10 percent of the taxable wealth, Oliver amassed property worth an assessed value of £9,121. His holdings included seven buildings on Oliver Dock, a

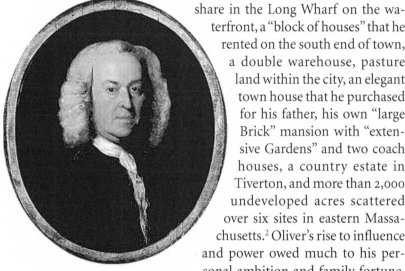

share in the Long Wharf on the waterfront, a "block of houses" that he rented on the south end of town, a double warehouse, pasture land within the city, an elegant town house that he purchased for his father, his own "large Brick" mansion with "extensive Gardens" and two coach houses, a country estate in Tiverton, and more than 2,000 undeveloped acres scattered over six sites in eastern Massachusetts.[2] Oliver's rise to influence and power owed much to his personal ambition and family fortune, but like Hutchinson, he flourished in public life through a cozy relationship with a string of royal governors.

Andrew Oliver. Oil on copper by John Singleton Copley, about 1758.

In the late 1740s, for instance, when Oliver was defeated in his bid to be reelected to the lower house of the assembly, the governor simply appointed him to a seat in the upper chamber.

Oliver's wealth and manner, and his close ties with royal officials, did not win him many friends. Nor did the policies that he embraced. Although he tried to introduce manufacturing to Boston, and worked for town markets that might have lowered consumer prices, his fiscal conservatism helped keep money in short supply. Farmers, many of whom habitually faced the prospect of indebtedness, were foes of tight money policies. So, too, were laborers, who struggled in the best of times to climb above the margins of poverty. They were further alienated in 1747 when Oliver used his influence to suppress the Knowles Riot, a workers' uprising that sought to prevent the Royal Navy from dragooning the city's longshoremen, stevedores, and merchant marine into military service during King George's War. Subsequently, while a Massachusetts army sustained appalling casualties in the Louisbourg campaign in that war, Oliver and his sons, who remained safely at home, reaped the benefits of one generous defense contract after another. In the French and Indian War, while thousands more men from New England bore arms, he grew still richer as a war contractor, a sideline that earned some well-connected Boston merchants as much as £12,000 in two or three years. Soon after peace came in 1763, Oliver aided the governor in stripping the govern-

ment printing contract from a popular newspaper editor and openly denigrated such emerging democratic practices as soliciting votes by providing the electorate with free beer and rum. Earlier, he had been part of an
unsuccessful movement, supported by royal governors, to terminate the
popular town meeting system of governance in Boston.[3]

If John Adams, an ambitious, struggling young attorney was typical,
workers were not alone in scorning Oliver: up and coming young professionals were not enamored with him either. In the early 1760s, Adams
complained that Oliver held more than one public office. He chafed at
the royal system in Massachusetts that enabled Lieutenant Governor
Hutchinson to simultaneously hold four offices, while Oliver, his brother-
in-law, held two, one of which, Adams railed, was among the "greatest
places in government." Nor was that all, for Oliver's brother was an important magistrate; his son, who was married to the daughter of a judge
of the Superior Court, sat in the assembly, as did his nephew. Hutchinson,
meanwhile, had a brother who was a high judge and three close relatives
who also sat on the bench, or served as deputy secretary of the province,
or acted as clerk of the legislature. What "an amazing ascendancy of one
family.... Is it not enough to excite Jealousies among the People?" Adams
wondered. It was.[4]

Yet, while Oliver was unpopular, even hated by some, his political
prominence was never threatened during a stretch of twenty years or
more. He accumulated new offices and steadily greater power, which he
often utilized to enhance his already inordinate wealth. But his life, and
that of many Americans, changed dramatically in 1765, the year of the
Stamp Act.

While most colonists in 1763 were the descendants of those who had left
the British homeland for America, they nevertheless happily thought of
themselves as British who by happenstance lived in America. Well they
might, too, for life in the colonies often resembled life at home. Accents
might differ, but English was the "official" language in the colonies. The
legal system in America rested comfortably on English common law. The
provincial governments were modeled on that at home, as governors and
bicameral assemblies were minuscule versions of king and Parliament,
and in the towns and counties sheriffs and justices of the peace were familiar figures, as they were in the English countryside. Innumerable villages were named after hamlets in England, if they were not named in
honor of a British monarch. The diet and dress of a large portion of the
population resembled that of the English at home, the colonists celebrated the same national holidays and enjoyed similar pastimes, and

on Sunday mornings perhaps a majority in the provinces worshiped in the same churches—be it Anglican, Presbyterian, Methodist, or Quaker.

Differences of course existed between the homeland and colonies, and to some contemporaries they must have seemed considerable. For instance, Michel-Guillaume Jean de Crèvecoeur, who immigrated from France to New France, and finally in 1765 to New York, concluded after a brief residence in the British colonies that the "American is a new man," transformed by his distance from Europe, and shaped by his new environment and the intermingling of diverse cultures, which included divergent customs brought over by German, Dutch, Swiss, French, Scotch-Irish, and African immigrants. The result, said Crèvecoeur, was "a new race of men" who for the most part enjoyed a more exalted rank in society than would have been true had they, or their ancestors, never left the homeland, and who were busily reshaping the Old World culture that had initially been brought across the Atlantic. This new American, Crèvecoeur added, acted "upon new principles; he must therefore entertain new ideas and form new opinions."[5]

While Crèvecoeur penned his thoughts in the course of the War of Independence, which doubtless colored his perspective and caused some exaggeration, he was correct that in some ways life in the provinces was profoundly dissimilar to that in the imperial metropolis. America had its elite, but there was no titled nobility, and no one inherited a position of power. One could rise more easily in America's fluid social structure, but one could fall more quickly, and much further, for station and rank hinged almost solely on wealth, and pedigree counted for little. By old country standards, unheard of numbers could vote in the colonial elections. More than 90 percent of freemen possessed suffrage rights in New England, while half or more of the free, adult, white males in the mid-Atlantic and South voted. Opportunities were better in America for young men from humble backgrounds who were ambitious and industrious. They too could rise to be part of the "middling sort" of society—as the provincials referred to small farmers and tradesmen who owned a modest amount of property—and if they reached that level, they might someday hold public office or serve as an officer in a militia company. Now and then, someone—such as Benjamin Franklin—rose even higher, growing wealthy and powerful. It was the exception, not the rule, but it was more likely to occur in America than in England.

The differences notwithstanding, little evidence can be found that at the end of the French and Indian War the colonists chafed at being part of the British Empire or at living with governmental policies made faraway and across the sea. Just the opposite. Benjamin Franklin, fluent and persuasive, claimed in 1766 that at the close hostilities the American colonists "submitted willingly to the government of the Crown." Its authority, he went on, had traditionally rested lightly on the shoulders of the provincials. London had governed America "at the expense only of a little pen, ink and paper. They [the colonists] were led by a thread." He added that the Americans "had not only a respect, but an affection, for Great-Britain." Their warm-heartedness was palpable, he said, when visitors or immigrants from England arrived on their shores. In America, "an Old England-man was . . . a character of some respect" who was given "a kind of rank among us" by the deferential colonists. Franklin additionally claimed that the colonists viewed Parliament "as the great bulwark and security of their Liberties and privileges" and as its protector against the occasional misguided ministerial official. He was more accurate when he suggested that the colonists' ties to the empire had resulted in considerable prosperity. Although not every free citizen flourished, and some regions and cities were economically healthier than others, the American economy grew in the third quarter of that century. By the early 1770s, the exports of the mainland colonies—chiefly tobacco, rice, grains, indigo, forest products, fish, whale oil, rum, and oceangoing vessels—annually averaged nearly £3,000,000 and the value of their imports were nearly identical, resulting in a negligible deficit. Per capita incomes rose by 0.5 percent per year after 1750, and with it the population grew at a rate unimaginable throughout Europe. The middle colonies—which Franklin represented—did better than the rest, but overseas trade was brisk in New England and the South, and the merchants and planters in those sections benefited from the protection given by the Royal Navy and the easy credit extended by English financial houses. Thus Franklin only slightly exaggerated when he added that the Americans "consider themselves as a part of the British empire, and as having one common interest with it; they may be looked on here [in London] as foreigners, but they do not consider themselves as such. They are zealous for the honour and prosperity of this nation, and . . . will always be ready to support it."[6]

Yet as Franklin spoke of prosperity, austere times commenced in the immediate postwar era for many tradesmen and unskilled workers in America's cities. When the French and Indian War drew to a close, redcoat regulars and Royal sailors—together with the money they had spread around as consumers—disappeared, war contracts dried up, credit contracted, and trade suddenly languished. Workers everywhere were soon distressed, but they were particularly hard hit in New York and Philadelphia, as European immigrants flooded into those cities the moment the peace treaty was signed, deluging a labor market already in the morass of despair. In the best of times, workers struggled to find a way to pay for necessities, including food, clothing, rent, firewood, and taxes. In the worst of times that set in with the peace, many were without work, and others fortunate enough to keep their jobs often were driven to adopt strategies for "living in the most frugal Way," as a distressed New York artisan put it. Sometimes, even the best laid plans were unavailing, he added, leaving the workers and their families to fall "every Day more and more behind." Nor was the misery confined to those at the bottom of the working class. Many property owners in the cities were forced to sell soon after the war, and in Philadelphia foreclosures nearly tripled in the course of the first five years after fighting in the French and Indian War ended in North America.[7]

Nevertheless, Great Britain's stunning victory over France in 1763 quickened the colonists' pride in being part of such a great and noble empire, one with a reputation for being the most religiously tolerant and enlightened of the great powers. "I am a BRITON," Franklin rejoiced at his good fortune to reside in a British province, and many shared his exuberance.[8] After Quebec's fall, colonists erected memorials to the British regulars who had perished in defense of the colonies, named new towns for them, listened with satisfaction as their pastors preached sermons extolling the quality of life in the British provinces, and spontaneously celebrated the news of the coronation of the new monarch, George III, in 1760. When the hard-earned victory was behind them, the colonists hoped to get on with their lives, which for many included plans for settling in the newly won trans-Appalachian West. Most Americans anticipated that the imperial government seldom would be seen or heard from, except to nurture and protect the provinces. That had been the custom throughout most of the colonial years. Some provincials even believed that America's reward for its contribution to the recent victory over France would be an enhanced status within the empire, including a greater voice in making policy for Anglo-America. The pastor of the First Congregational Church in Salem, Massachusetts, expressed both sentiments:

Now commences the Era of our quiet Enjoyment of those Liberties, which our Fathers purchased with the Toil of their whole Lives. . . . Here shall be the late founded Seat of Peace and Freedom. Here shall our indulgent Mother, who has most generously rescued and protected us, be served and honoured by growing Numbers, with all Duty, Love and Gratitude, till time shall be no more.[9]

Things did not go as the parson anticipated.

In large measure, this was because the parson, together with the great majority of the colonists, was unaware of the agenda with which the imperial government entered the postwar era. Large numbers of Royal officials, including British regulars, had come to wartime America after 1756, and many had been struck, even alarmed, by the differences they found between the Britons in America and the Britons living at home. Many words commonly in use in England had been abandoned in much of America (such as fen, wold, and moor), and Americans sometimes spoke a strange language that incorporated terms derived from the Dutch or the Indians (porch, stoop, rattlesnake). Sometimes the words used by Americans meant something quite different than in England; corn in America was maize in England, while what the colonists called wheat was termed corn by the inhabitants of the mother country.[10] Inconsequential as these differences were, some visitors from England concluded they were signs that America was drifting apart from England. These visitors from the metropolis also found a population that consisted of significant numbers without long-standing ties to Great Britain and its ways. Massive immigration of non-English settlers after 1715, especially among Germans and Scotch-Irish, had brought to about one in three the number of free inhabitants who were non-English and whose loyalty was doubted by some in London.

To this mistrust was added suspicions that had been aroused by American behavior during the two final intercolonial wars. There had been times when some colonies had not fulfilled their manpower quotas, their armies had performed inadequately, colonists fleeced the redcoat soldiery, or merchants had traded with the enemy in wartime, perhaps prolonging hostilities. In the eyes of many in the seat of empire, the infidelity of the American merchants hardly differed from their behavior in peacetime. There was some truth to this. American merchants often conducted business with a wink and a nod toward imperial restrictions. It was an old habit. Trade with foreign ports in the West Indies and southern Europe was legal so long as the imperial duties were paid, but American merchants were not always keen on paying those tariffs.[11] Many in London concluded that the colonists, separated from the homeland by the Atlantic, were drifting apart, hastening the day when America might go its separate way. The British government had long known much of this, and it had been a factor in London's repudiation of the Albany Plan of Union. For some time before the French and Indian War, various ministries had contemplated the need to exercise greater control over its colonies. Always, however, the wars had stayed their hand. They had needed America's goodwill and assistance. Peace changed matters.

In 1763, London at last saw an opportunity to enforce its authority, including what Francis Bernard, the Royal governor of Massachusetts between 1761 and 1769, called the "necessary Work" of the "Regulation & Reformation" of imperial control.[12] It also had a new reason for doing so. Britain had achieved its military glory at a high price. Four long, costly wars since 1689 had left Britain deeply in debt. The last war alone had nearly doubled the debt. The imperial government thought it only fair—essential, even—that the colonists help with imperial expenses. After all, Great Britain had been instrumental in purging North America of the French. Not only was encirclement by foreign powers no longer a concern, but Canada and the West soon would be opened for settlement. The colonists profited in other ways as well. The Crown not only had awarded bountiful defense contracts to colonists, but it had reimbursed the provincial governments to help defray the costs of the war, a step that made colonial taxation less onerous. The result had been a decade of nearly unprecedented prosperity for many in the colonies. Now, London thought, the colonists should assume responsibility for a share of the postwar economic obligations. It wanted the colonists to help pay for the seven regiments of infantry, about 8,500 men, that it had decided to post in Canada and the West to help pacify those regions.[13]

Piecemeal, Great Britain's new colonial policy—a policy that aimed at enhanced regulation of imperial commerce, greater control of the provinces in general, and the collection of revenue—unfolded during the initial eighteen months of peace. The army left in America was to serve as a lever to induce the Indians to relinquish their lands. But London hoped to accomplish its ends bloodlessly, and it issued the Proclamation of 1763, which temporarily closed the region beyond the Appalachian ridge to settlement. It wanted the expected floodtide of western migration to be gradual and orderly, and to flow into designated areas that the Indians had ceded in solemn treaties. Above all else it wished for peace. It sought to avoid being driven more deeply into debt by having to help the colonists wage a bloody war with the Native Americans. More legislation followed. Whitehall soon moved to eradicate the rot in its customs service and to dramatically increase the number of agents that patrolled provincial wharves. It additionally erected an Admiralty Court in Halifax, where mobs were unlikely to intimidate magistrates, and gave it original jurisdiction in cases involving violations of imperial trade laws. By the Currency Act of 1764, it restricted the issuance of paper money by the colonies. This act was designed largely to protect British creditors from Virginia's debtors, by preventing the planters in that province from retiring debts with inflated paper currency.[14] Henceforth, American money had to be based on gold and silver and was to have the same value as the pound that circulated in the mother country.

London increased taxes on the citizenry in the home islands and introduced new measures to secure revenues in the colonies. The Sugar Act, which candidly acknowledged in its preamble that its intent was to raise revenue, reduced duties on heavily consumed products imported from the foreign islands in the Caribbean. Hoping to eliminate the smuggling of French and Spanish sugar, Parliament envisioned a plentiful trade and bountiful financial returns. The Mutiny Act—or Quartering Act, as the provincials habitually referred to it—was enacted in the spring of 1765 to deal with the large British army that remained in America. This legislation permitted troops to be housed in public buildings and compelled the colonists to pay for their food, cider, beer, firewood, and candles.[15] Finally, Parliament enacted the Stamp Act of 1765, the first time it had attempted to directly tax the colonists. Intended to be the greatest revenue producer, the Stamp Act imposed duties on most court-sanctioned documents, licenses, contracts, commissions, wills, and mortgages, as well as on playing cards, dice, and published materials, including newspapers, calendars, pamphlets, and almanacs.

Every aspect of the new policy aroused anger in America. Although the Proclamation of 1763 was understood to be a temporary expedient, speculators were unable to sell land unless they possessed clear title to it, and for the most part land-hungry settlers were reluctant to move west without a deed in hand.[16] Merchants objected to the new Admiralty Court. Not only was standing trial in faraway Halifax a costly proposition, but an accused smuggler stood a far greater likelihood of conviction by a panel of naval officers than by a jury of his peers at home. Customs agents had never been well liked by American merchants, and an increase in their numbers and their effectiveness aroused great concerns over profit margins in America's countinghouses. No one suffered more than Chesapeake planters from the restrictions on colonial currency. As tobacco prices had declined over the past generation, a tight money policy confronted many planters with the all-too-real likelihood of a perilous indebtedness. The Mutiny Act caused many colonial assemblymen to believe that orders to provide billeting and supplies for the British army was in no wise different from facing a tax imposed by London. But no aspect of the new policy—nothing in fact that the parent state had ever done in 150 years—provoked such widespread fury as the Stamp Act.

When this tax bill was introduced in Parliament, a New Englander in London predicted that it "would go down with the people [in America] like chopt hay." Similarly, Governor Bernard foresaw problems. The tax, he said, "would cause a great Alarm & meet much Opposition." For one thing, he said, the timing was bad, as the tax came on the heels of a war that had witnessed dramatic sacrifices and skyrocketing taxes in the colonies. In addition, Bernard expressed concern both because parliamentary taxation "was quite new to the People" and as the employment of parliamentary authority came with "no visible Bounds set to it."[17] Both observers were prescient. While in theory this tax was to fall most heavily on printers and lawyers, it was widely expected that, in the time-honored tradition of businessmen everywhere, they would simply pass along the costs to their customers and clients. Every American who purchased a newspaper, bought or sold real estate, or was involved in probate following the demise of a loved one would pay stamp taxes. The colonists' outrage was palpable. It is amazing that London did not foresee the firestorm it was about to ignite. It deluded itself into believing that problems would not ensue because the tax was small. Some myopically thought that appreciative Americans, grateful that Great Britain had made monumental sacrifices to secure them from New France, would quietly, if not cheerfully, pay the duties. In addition, when the provinces were not seized with organized protest after the ministry announced in 1764 that it was considering a stamp tax, the imperial government concluded that the colonists would acquiesce. Nevertheless, there were signs of discord that London should have discerned. When the stamp legislation was in gestation, six colonial assemblies petitioned against the proposed tax, leaving no doubt that they believed that Parliament had no right to tax the colonies.[18]

Word reached America in April that the Stamp Act had passed Parliament, but it was another thirty days, and sometimes sixty or more, before some colonies received the text of the legislation. Nevertheless, protests began immediately. The act was denounced in pamphlets, the most significant of which was authored by Daniel Dulany, a Maryland lawyer. In *Considerations on the Propriety of imposing Taxes in the British Colonies*, he argued that as the colonists were unrepresented in the imperial legislature, Parliament had overstepped its bounds. Essayists in newspapers also soon opened fire, and many were far more radical than Dulany's legalistic tome. Some of these writers openly discussed the notion of American independence, although all stopped short of calling on the colonies to break away from the parent state.[19] Legislative resistance followed.

The Virginia House of Burgesses was first to act. By the time the assembly session was called to order early in May, newspapers throughout the colonies had published word that the Stamp Act had been enacted. Nevertheless, the Burgesses devoted its initial three weeks to routine business. It considered road bills, issued licenses to ferry operators, and voted bounties for wolves. Toward the end of May, some deputies, including George Washington, now an assemblyman from Fairfax County, started home, convinced that the legislature's leadership would not bring up the new tax. The Speaker's disinclination to act may have arisen because only five months had passed since the Burgesses sent a remonstrance against the proposed stamp duties to London. In December 1764, it had argued that too little specie existed in Virginia to pay the projected tax, and it maintained as well that the province had borne extraordinarily heavy costs—perhaps more, proportionately, than any other colony—during the recent war.[20] The leadership had its way of doing things. The Burgesses had a long history of beseeching London to make changes, but it did not have a history of protest, and it is likely that the leadership was uncomfortable with such action. It may also have feared that an intemperate petition would be sent to London. What does seem clear is that Patrick Henry, almost single-handedly, changed the tempo of this session. On May 30, with a bare majority still in attendance, Henry galvanized his colleagues into action.

Henry was a newcomer. He had entered the Burgesses only nine days earlier. He hailed from a family that enjoyed considerable influence within a relatively new county in the Virginia piedmont, but his kin were neither especially wealthy nor among the province's social or political elite. He had little formal education. Indeed, at an age when many of the colony's leaders were studying in England or at William and Mary College, Henry was clerking in a country store. He failed at everything he tried until, in his midtwenties, he took up the law, studying for only six weeks before he opened his practice. Henry succeeded at once in his new career. He understood intuitively how to awe rustic jurors. Combining silver-tongued oratory with the dramatic flair of an actor, Henry found the means of winning over one jury after another. His success convinced him that he could branch out from the law to politics, and at age twenty-nine he was elected to the assembly. When he took his seat in the House of Burgesses, Henry was lithe and trim, with flowing brown hair, deep-set flashing eyes, and an expressive mouth. He conveyed the self-assured air of a man in the habit of leading.[21]

Henry had watched with impatience for several days as the Speaker of the House, and the old guard within his orbit, avoided taking action on the Stamp Act. Finally, acting with the verve of an arriviste who refused to be shackled by tradition or a stodgy elite, and with an incandescence born of outrage at London's new intrusiveness in Virginia's affairs, Henry was on his feet and making the sort of speech that had dazzled many a backwoods jury. His magic worked here as well. Thomas Jefferson, only twenty-two, a tall, gangly, red-haired, freckled law student in Williamsburg, stood in a hallway and listened through an open door as Henry played his fellow Burgesses with virtuosity. Jefferson later said that Henry was the greatest orator he ever heard. His remarks were "impressive and sublime" and delivered in a "voice free and manly." Henry's speech built to a crescendo that in myth has been remembered as "Give me liberty or give me death." In reality, he was somewhat less eloquent. A French visitor to Williamsburg, who took notes during the speech, wrote that

Shortly after I Came in one of the members stoop up and said he had read that in former times tarquin and Jules had their Brutus, Charles had his Cromwell, and he Did not Doubt but that some good american would stand up, in favour of his Country, but (says he) in a more moderate manner, and was going to Continue, when the speaker of the house rose and Said, he, the last that stood up had spoke traison, and was sorey to see that not one of the members of the house was loyal Enough to stop him, before he had gone so far, upon which the Same member stood up again (his name is henery) and said that if he had afronted the speaker, or the house, he was ready to ask pardon, and he would shew his loyalty to his majesty King G. the third, at the expense of the last Drop of his blood, but what he had said must be atributed to the Interest of his Countrys Dying liberty which he had at heart, and the heat of passion might have lead him to have said something more than he intended.[22]

Nevertheless, the legislators who had chafed at the leadership's restraint, had found a new leader, a man who—as Jefferson remarked a half century later—was far ahead of most Virginians in having embraced "the spirit of the Revolution." The assembly immediately passed the Virginia Resolves, culled from among the resolutions that Henry introduced and not unlike the remonstrance adopted the previous December. However, the language of the Resolves was less obsequious, and it was unmistakable that the Resolves pressed the argument that the Burgesses "HAVE the Sole Right and Authority to lay Taxes and Impositions" on the citizenry of Virginia.[23]

No other assembly took a stand that spring or summer. Poorly led and unwilling to act alone, the Massachusetts legislature initially sat mutely while Governor Bernard insisted on a "respectful submission" to the Stamp duties. It was a Boston town meeting that took the first resolute step. A year earlier, when word of the Sugar Act arrived, a town meeting had warned that once parliamentary taxation was permitted, it could never be stanched. It also declared that "if Taxes are laid upon us in any shape without our having a legal Representative where they are laid, are we not reduced from the Character of free Subjects to the miserable State of tributary Slaves?"[24] Now, in mid-1765 it struck again. The Boston town meeting urged the Massachusetts lawmakers to seek an intercolonial conclave to respond in concert to the Stamp Act. Consideration of such a step provoked lengthy debate, but the assembly eventually appealed to every other colony to appoint delegates to meet in New York in October for the purpose of adopting "a dutiful, loyal and humble" petition to London urging the repeal of the Stamp Act. The delegation that it sent was composed largely of men who could be expected to approach Parliament with deference. Many radicals in Boston were disappointed and one, in a vitriolic newspaper essay, labeled the assembly's action a "tame, pusillanimous, daubed, insipid thing" voted by men who feared offending "the tools of corruption" in London.[25]

By late summer, the most zealous foes of the Stamp Act could point to few victories. Most assemblies had not yet acted. Furthermore, no one imagined that the national congress would do more than adopt a resolution or two, likely a meaningless gesture inasmuch as the remonstrances adopted by several assemblies in 1764 had never received a hearing in Parliament. It was at this moment that the protest took a new, violent direction. In Newport, Rhode Island, crowds of protestors tore down property belonging to those who openly defended the Stamp Act. That city's stamp collector was hanged in effigy, and affixed to the body was a placard labeling him an "INFAMOUS, MISCREATED, LEERING JACOBITE." A Newport pamphleteer who not only had championed the Stamp Act but urged Royal government for Rhode Island, was also hanged in effigy; a sign was pinned to one of the arms that read "CURS'D AMBITION," while to the other a note was affixed declaring "POSTERITY WILL CURSE MY MEMORY." In Annapolis a mob destroyed a warehouse owned by a stamp collector. A New York crowd, led by two carpenters in the ship construction yards, wrecked some property and hanged the governor in effigy, using an elaborately prepared dummy that included Satan whispering in the chief executive's ear. Some in the mob stole the lieutenant governor's elegant carriage and drove it about the streets of Manhattan before setting it ablaze, while their comrades jeered at Royal officials and their sympathizers "with all the insulting ribaldry that malice could invent." The homes of two of South Carolina's stamp collectors were invaded, and damaged, by a Charleston mob. The lieutenant governor of that colony wrote London about the "infection," the "fury," and the "madness" of the activists. In each of these cities the crowd actions had been undertaken by workers and merchants. Symbiotically linked economically, and sharing similar concerns about new taxes, they combined in associations to adopt, then enforce, embargoes of British trade that were designed to force Parliament to repeal the Stamp Act. In Philadelphia, for instance, a merchants' committee kept an eye on importers while an artisans' committee ascertained that shopkeepers observed the boycott.[26]

Boston also boiled over late in the summer. Indeed, the most violent, and destructive, provincial riots occurred in that city in August. Numerous scholars have pretended to know who orchestrated the mob action that followed. In fact, no one knows precisely. Many have suspected that the Loyal Nine, an artisan's club, planned the protest and, like a puppeteer, manipulated the crowds that carried out the riots. But laborers on the waterfront, and other workers whose well-being hinged on maritime prosperity, already were well aware of the stakes posed by imperial taxation and commercial regulation. As is always the case in a complex economic system, the welfare of many throughout society was inextricably linked to those at the top. If merchants suffered, dockhands, sailors, shipyard workers, teamsters, and craftsmen inevitably faced distress. Prosperity seeped down through society, but so did adversity; its descent was quick and certain and very much feared along the wharves at Boston harbor and in the shops off the city's cobblestone streets. Workers feared that overzealous, and unrestrained, customs officers would adversely affect commerce and that it would be their jobs that were lost if traffic in the port of Boston slowed. Underpaid, and faced with an enduring struggle to make ends meet, they knew, too, that they could ill-afford to pay additional taxes.

Those who worked with their hands in Boston had a long record of public action. They composed the lion's share of the city's nine fire companies, and on many occasions during the previous two decades they had taken to the streets to demonstrate for or against social and political causes. They were not leaderless. They looked to other workers for direction, to men in their neighborhood who spoke their language and also worked with their hands, men with a keen sense of the interest of hardworking laborers. Ebenezer MacIntosh, a twenty-eight-year-old shoemaker, is to us the most visible of these working-class leaders, but there were others. Years after the American Revolution, a Tory historian conjectured that MacIntosh had been a pawn of smarter, more affluent dissidents, and many modern scholars have been inclined to agree with that judgment.[27] But that was not the case. Boston's workers understood the issues and their self-interest and were capable of acting without guidance from the elite. MacIntosh was no one's tool, and the workers would not have followed him had he been. They knew that he had an intimate knowledge of hard times. Not only had he been the child of an often unemployed and sometimes indigent father, but his craft, cordwaining, was the lowest paid of the trades. MacIntosh and the workers he led never had to be told that new taxes would drain away their sparse earnings. What they did need, however, were allies to resist the taxes, and in the Stamp Act episode, as rarely before, the city's laborers, artisans, and many from the commercial elite—all of whom were in some way threatened by Britain's new imperial policy—acted to some degree in concert in defiance of the measure. It appears likely that there was some central direction to the events that unfolded in August, and the best guess is that those who planned and managed the tactics of protest included men from the Loyal Nine, some merchants, disparate activists, and assemblymen who had failed to achieve their ends through the normal political process.[28]

Some who planned the street violence probably acted to frighten the pending national congress—and especially the more conservative congressmen, who might fear that additional insurrections would occur if the Stamp Act remained in effect—into taking a more intrepid stand. That would explain the timing of the events in Boston, as news of August riots would have time to eddy through all America by the time the congress convened in October. The protesters needed only to settle on their targets. That was easy. During the summer, word arrived that Andrew Oliver had been designated distributor of stamps for Massachusetts. It was also well known that Lieutenant Governor Hutchinson had counseled compliance with the taxation. A venomous hatred of both men long had pulsated among many who engaged in physical labor, and nothing aroused their visceral loathing of Hutchinson and Oliver more than the notion that these American-born officials were serving a foreign master rather than their brethren in Boston.

Despite his habitual eagerness for new posts, Oliver had not sought to be a stamp distributor. His name was probably communicated to London by the governor, as a favor for past services, for it was assumed that a stamp distributorship would be a lucrative position. Oliver, in fact, was congratulated by a ministerial official for the "private Benefit" he would derive from the post. But Oliver envisaged problems. So did Hutchinson, who bore responsibility for enforcing what Oliver referred to as "a measure at present so unpopular." In the spring Hutchinson anguished that there were those in Boston "who will stick at nothing to inflame the people. I have always been more or less their butt," he added. Threatening newspaper essays in the course of the summer provoked additional concern on his part, and doubtless Oliver's as well. "I hope we shall be able to keep the peace," Hutchinson told London on August 6, and he pleaded with the ministry "not to be in great haste with more of the same sort" of legislation. One week later, Boston exploded.[29]

The city awakened on August 14 to discover effigies hung from an elm—newly named the "Liberty Tree"—near Boston Common. One was that of the earl of Bute, a confidant of the monarch and head of the ministry that first had bruited Britain's new colonial policy. The other effigy was that of Oliver, who was about to reap the rewards of years of sycophancy toward royal authority, as well as his advocacy of policies that distressed Boston's workers. Pinned to Oliver's effigy was a note that read:

Fair Freedoms glorious Cause I meanly Quitted &
Betrayed my Country for the Sake of Pelf
But ah! At length what evil hath me willed,
Instead of Stamping others have hanged myself.[30]

During the morning a crowd gathered, some even from surrounding towns, anxious to witness the spectacle. Samuel Adams was one of the onlookers. When someone asked him about the effigies, he professed ignorance and promised to make inquiries, although it is unlikely that he was as surprised at these activities as were the other gawkers. Late in the morning a band of nearly 300 children, carrying a flag emblazoned with the motto "King, Pitt, & Liberty," paraded around the Liberty Tree. Oliver, an observer said, was ridiculed by "all Collours." The crowd had grown quite large by early afternoon and showed no sign of dispersing. After meeting with his council, Governor Bernard ordered the sheriff to cut down the effigies and disperse the crowd. The peace officer demurred. Such an assignment was tantamount to a suicide mission, he thought. Still later, under a warm setting sun, the boisterous crowd at the elm took down the effigy of Oliver and carried it to the front door of his mansion. There it was decapitated.

As night approached, this capricious mob, now caught up in the carnival spirit of the moment, dragged Oliver's effigy to one of the many buildings he owned in Boston, a handsome red brick office on the South End wharves. In the half light of early evening, the crowd promptly tore down the structure, then tossed the effigy on a bonfire built from the debris, a blaze that cast a ruddy light over Boston harbor. By the time the fire burned itself out, night had settled over the city, and the mob, exhilarated and restless for yet more action, surged in the starry darkness to Oliver's residence. Oliver subsequently claimed that to protect his dwelling he "stood alone, a single man against a whole People." Hutchinson recollected differently: He said Oliver and his family had fled "in terror" and that he, the sheriff, and a royal officer from the admiralty court stayed on and sought to restrain the crowd. While it is not clear whose memory was most accurate, it is known that no peacekeeping force was present to protect the mansion. The governor had called on the leaders of Boston's militia to disperse the crowd, but was told that most of the city's militiamen were members of the mob. Thus unrestrained, the crowd pelted the house with stones, breaking several windows, then muscled its way into the residence and looted Oliver's wine cellar. Near midnight, worn out by hours of frenetic activity, the crowd finally dispersed, but not until it had caused enormous damage to the house and furnishings. A fifteen-foot-tall fence that surrounded the residence had been pulled down, stacked up, and set afire. Oliver's privy, carriage house, phaeton, and a gazebo in his lovingly-tended garden were likewise destroyed and thrown into the fire. Soon after sunrise the next day, with Boston buzzing that another mob would gather at twilight, Oliver announced that he "would not exercise the Functions of my Office." He had no choice but to issue the disclaimer, he lugubriously told London, as "I could expect no aid from the Government."[31]

Another crowd did gather that evening and marched on the lieutenant governor's residence, but it dispersed when assurances were given that Hutchinson had played no role in the enactment of the Stamp Act. Eleven days later another throng gathered. It was summoned by a bonfire set ablaze in front of the town hall, the "usual signal for a mob," according to a subsequent statement of the governor. Early in the evening, just after sunset, the crowd visited the homes of the marshal of the admiralty court and the comptroller of the customs, causing considerable damage. Worked up to a fever pitch, and fueled by a barrel of punch provided by a tavern keeper, the mob, chanting "liberty and property," set out for Hutchinson's six-pilastered brick mansion just after 9 o'clock. Hutchinson had long since been warned that he too was likely to be victimized, and he had sent his children away, although he stayed behind to defend his house. He did not linger long. The arrival of the liquor-soaked mob led him to see things in a clearer light. This crowd, at least according to Hutchinson's later testimony, was bent on finding and murdering him. As soon as it arrived, that "hellish crew fell upon my house with the rage of devils," Hutchinson said a few days later. In only a moment, they "split down the door and entered," and he "was obliged to retire thro yards and gardens to a house more remote where I remained until 4 o'clock." The mob worked until the wee hours of the morning, smashing furniture, stealing what could be taken, and throwing much that remained—including the manuscript for a history of the colony that he had been writing—into the muddy front yard. When Hutchinson returned he discovered that £900 in cash, as well as books, clothing, china, and the family silver had been stolen. Portraits of family members had been torn to shreds, and every tree on the property had been cut down. "Nothing remained but the bare walls and floors," Hutchinson despaired. Even the cupola had been torn from the roof. Estimates of the total loss ranged up to £25,000.[32]

No further mob violence occurred that year in Boston, but in December, when Oliver's commission at last arrived from London, another mob compelled him to appear in a cold rain at the foot of the Liberty Tree and—after it had first hanged effigies of the pope and the devil—made him formally renounce his post as stamp collector. Collectors elsewhere also resigned when confronted by crowds of protesters, some like the stamp collector in Wethersfield, Connecticut, who bowed to threats of lynching, after which he was forced to throw his hat in the air and cheer for liberty. Generally, however, collectors and distributors prudently stepped down long before hordes mobilized. By the fall, in fact, no tax collectors were to be found in the colonies. All had resigned or fled for their lives.[33]

The crowd actions in 1765 were accompanied by an astonishing intellectual ferment. Between May and November, town meetings in New England, as well as essayists and assemblies from one end of America to the other, took pains to define the rights of the colonists within the empire. The impact on some colonists was electrifying. John Adams believed that he and many others had been transformed by the events of that frantic year. The people in all social classes, he ruminated, had become "more attentive to their liberties, more inquisitive about them, and more determined to defend them." Many years later, he reflected that the "child Independence" was born in the minds of the colonists during the Stamp Act crisis.[34]

Nonetheless, Americans did not advocate independence in 1765, and indeed they were not yet revolutionaries. Many were not yet even radicals, but as never before they had begun to contemplate their position within the empire. During that year a consensus crystallized that Parliament's power over the colonies was limited and did not include the authority to tax the provinces. But few Americans, and still fewer public officials—by and large pragmatic men who dealt in the hard realities of governance—were willing to explore just how far Parliament's authority stretched. Their object was the repeal of the Stamp Act, not the promulgation of treatises on political theory. Some issues, most believed, were better left unaddressed, including the full extent of colonial liberties. The provincial assemblies, therefore, ignored London's multifaceted new colonial policy and pretended not to see a pattern in the striking array of American legislation that poured from Parliament between 1763 and 1765. Instead, they focused almost entirely on the Stamp Act. Nine colonial assemblies took a stand. Their remonstrances were strikingly similar. They not only attacked Parliament's right to tax the colonies but for the most part grounded their declarations on the premise that the colonists were not, and could not be, represented in Parliament and that

"Taxation . . . by Persons chosen to represent them" was a right of all Englishmen.[35]

A similar position was taken by the Stamp Act Congress, as the body that the Massachusetts assembly had proposed came to be called. Nine colonies, mostly those that had sent representatives to the Albany Congress a decade earlier, dispatched twenty-seven delegates to the meeting, which convened in New York's city hall early in October. All the delegates were political activists, and all were drawn from among the social elite. Though some of them would support separation from the parent state in 1776, most resisted dramatic domestic changes in American life. Some, including Timothy Ruggles, a Massachusetts judge who had been handpicked by Governor Bernard for inclusion in the colony's delegation, and who was elected president of this Congress, never embraced American independence, and a few never wavered in their open loyalty to Great Britain.

Only a handful of these delegates wished to take a muscular stand. One was Christopher Gadsden of South Carolina, a wealthy planter and merchant who owned stores and a wharf in Charleston. Gadsden had become prominent politically in his colony three years earlier by successfully resisting an attempt by the royal governor to appropriate the assembly's traditional authority to decide disputed legislative elections. During that contest Gadsden had boldly told Governor Thomas Boone that his actions threatened "to destroy the most essential and inviolable rights of the people." At the Stamp Act Congress he fought to base America's opposition to parliamentary taxation "on those natural and inherent rights all feel and know, as men and as descendants of Englishmen." What he meant was that the colonists' rights transcended Crown-granted charters, as they were derived from God and affirmed in the Magna Carta.[36] James Otis Jr., a prominent Boston lawyer and assemblyman who hailed from a politically influential Cape Cod family, likely took a similar position. Although erratic, Otis earlier had fought against Hutchinson's multiple officeholding practices and led a battle to prevent the royal governor from gaining greater authority in enforcing imperial commercial restrictions. In those struggles, Otis had questioned the limits of monarchical and parliamentary powers, urged the citizenry to courageously resist "blind, slavish submission" to those in power, and portrayed royal officials as "a little dirty, drinking, drabbing, contaminated knot of thieves [and] beggars." He also had authored *The Rights of the British Colonies Asserted and Proved*, a constitutional treatise that John Adams subsequently called the foremost statement on American rights and the legal limits of British authority that appeared before 1776. Otis cooly opened his tract with a synopsis of John Locke's conditions under which revolution was justified, then—in an argument that presaged later American federalism—he maintained that while Parliament was sovereign, it was not all powerful. For instance, it lacked the authority to levy taxes on the colonists without their consent.[37]

Ultimately, the Congress rebuffed those delegates who wished to ground America's opposition to parliamentary taxation on the premise that it violated the natural rights of humankind. That sounded too much as if they wished to say that all people possessed a God-given right to self-government, a notion that for the most conservative delegates was disturbingly open-ended. Instead, after two weeks of wrangling, the Stamp Act Congress produced a set of resolutions that rejected Parliament's authority to levy taxes in America on the grounds that it violated the colonists' rights as Englishmen. It was the "undoubted right of *Englishmen*, that no Taxes be imposed on them, but with their own Consent, given personally, or by their Representatives," the Congress stated. To that was appended the sort of utilitarian statement that politicians find attractive. Taxation, one resolution insisted, would reduce the ability of Americans to purchase manufactured goods from the mother country. Other resolutions were at pains to demonstrate the colonists' deference. Americans owed "all due Subordination to that August Body the Parliament," one stated, and another, in penitent language, humbly petitioned king and Parliament to repeal the taxes.[38]

Politicians might have wanted a quick, simple, pacific solution—repeal, followed by a restoration of normality—but powerful forces had been unleashed. Many people, as John Adams observed, had been set to thinking about America's place and its rights within the empire. Governor Bernard saw the same thing and remarked that the crisis had been like "an alarm bell to the disaffected."[39] Charges of "Tyranny and Oppression" in London were heard, and some warned that the colonists faced the danger of being "crush'd by the iron rod of power," even of being reduced to abject "Slavery" by their imperial masters. Suddenly there was talk of how Great Britain had plundered Ireland for 200 years. Some asked if avaricious London was now about to attempt to "drink . . . your vital blood." For the first time, too, there was the barest hint that the colonists would use force to protect their rights. It was promised that this tax would "rouse the most indolent of us . . . and make us use our strongest Efforts to be free."[40]

As 1765 passed into history, it was clear that three discernible factions had emerged during the agitation and violence of that year. One bloc—soon it would be clear that it was the largest element among the articulate—wished to resist the Stamp Act by forthrightly asserting that Parliament had overstepped its boundaries. A second faction, large and powerful, opposed the act, yet feared opening the Pandora's Box that contained questions of parliamentary limits or the colonists' rights. Some in this group embraced the rapturous illusion that London had plotted nothing sinister, but had innocently blundered by thinking that the colonists would not object terribly to the duties. Hoping to make it easier for their friends in the seat of empire to repeal the tax, and believing that no new taxes would follow, this faction preferred the safer ground of objecting to imperial taxation because the duties would be harmful to commerce in both America and Great Britain. The smallest faction, described by one observer as "more inclined . . . to Great Britain than to [their] own Country," believed that British law was supreme and must be adhered to in all cases whatsoever.[41]

A combustible tension suffused the provinces in 1765, and sometimes burst into brief episodes of unbridled violence. But the convulsions could have been worse, and the rhetoric might have been more strident. The popular response was muted by several factors. As Britain's policies were unprecedented, many were convinced that the mother country had stumbled accidentally into this mess and soon would rectify its error. Furthermore, the protestors, and protest leaders, were new at this business. These unpracticed dissidents anticipated a swift capitulation by an imperial government still widely perceived to be friendly and benevolent. Both assumptions discouraged vitriolic outbursts that might only have proven counterproductive. In addition, although their authority was challenged, and in some places weakened, the old elite generally remained sufficiently powerful to muffle the vehemence of the protest. For instance, Governor Bernard had a hand in the selection of Massachusetts' moderate delegation to the Stamp Act Congress, and instructed those delegates to prevent the meeting from articulating colonial rights or spelling out the specific powers of the imperial government.

Even so, 1765 was a "most remarkable" year, as John Adams remarked in December, for during that momentous year the colonists had begun to reflect on their rights and their relationship to Great Britain.[42] It was even more remarkable, perhaps, that such a groundswell of protest had erupted from within a system that was so hierarchically structured. Although the electorate in the colonies was huge by comparison with that of England, the presumption throughout America, as in the parent state, remained that it was natural for political leadership to rest with the community's traditional social leaders, the wealthy and well-born, and that the populace was to respectfully defer to those in authority. This logic was grounded on the assumption that leaders would subordinate their private interests to the public good. Given the sometimes life-and-death nature of the issues decided by the politicians, it is surprising at first glance that the elite dominated the political system for so long. In part, they succeeded in convincing the population that the mysteries of governance would be unfathomable to what Colonel Washington called "the grazing multitude" or to what John Adams referred to as the "common Herd of Mankind" and still others labeled the "unthinking mob" or the "ignorant vulgar." Such people had "no idea [of] Learning, Eloquence, and Genius," it was said, whereas the educated, and those of exalted rank with first-class temperaments, were endowed with the character and virtue to govern in a selfless, prudent, and wise manner.[43]

Guidebooks abounded that offered instruction in the proper deferential behavior when in the presence of one's social superior. But more than printed guides propped up the elite. Their wealth could be coercive. They could loan money, or oxen, or tools, or they could decline to do so. They could hire the sons of their neighbors, or they could choose not to do so. Through their near monopoly of the judiciary at the local level, they almost solely determined who received licenses to operate a multiplicity of small businesses. Through their monopoly of command positions in the militia, they could determine who got choice assignments and who was given undesirable duty when the trainband mustered. Lest anyone forget these realities, there were abundant reminders of social hierarchy. Those at the top were usually quite deliberate about displaying their riches, whether in their manner of dress, travel, or housing. Society, moreover, was suffused with inequality. Only the poor and middling sort were subjected to corporal punishment, and only those in society's upper echelons could expect to become field officers in the provincial military. Those who worked with their hands were not thought of as "gentlemen" and were not addressed as "sir." Seating at Sunday's worship service was arranged, as was nearly every other aspect of life, in a hierarchical manner, with the most affluent and influential occupying the most desired—and most expensive—pews. Even college classes were rigidly hierarchical. Lower classmen were expected to display proper respect to upper classmen, or be punished severely for their failure to do so. One additional factor that held together the system was that the members of the ruling elite took considerable pains to avoid bruising political battles. They understood that open, divisive factionalism could serve as the opening wedge for popular intrusion into the political process.

Like nothing before it, the French and Indian War opened the citizenry's eyes to the reality that governmental decisions touched their lives. In addition, many were made aware that the elite did not always act selflessly in wielding their considerable authority. Governments awarded military contracts, chose which merchants could trade in the Caribbean, selected the entrepreneurs who could be licensed as priva-

teers, levied troop quotas, appointed the highest ranking military officers, allocated lucrative military contracts, imposed taxes, and spent the
revenue they raised. The booty invariably went to the elite, making the
rich richer and the powerful yet stronger. Andrew Oliver, already one of
the most influential figures in Boston, stayed at home and gorged at the
public trough while more than 3,000 men from Massachusetts—about
one in every four males of military age—risked life and limb, and sometimes suffered unimaginable hardships in the service of the colony. Indeed, roughly three of every 10 soldiers raised by Massachusetts perished
between 1756 and 1758, roughly four times the mortality rate for civilians
of military age in Boston.[44] That the system served Oliver so much better than those who were not "gentlemen" did not go unnoticed.

The war only pulled back the camouflage from the reality that many
within the "selfless" elite were on the make and used political office, and
the public purse, to further enhance their wealth and authority. The widespread American dissent that followed the long, costly war further illuminated the disjunction between the rhetoric of the prevailing order
and unseemly reality. As perhaps never before, the disenfranchised and
politically apathetic understood that public affairs affected their daily
lives. Thereafter, as Samuel Adams explained, many were ready to take
politics into the streets when the traditional "wheels of government"
were "somewhere clogged."[45] In many places, moreover, popular involvement through the customary processes grew to unprecedented levels.
For instance, the turnout among qualified voters in Philadelphia County
elections had averaged about 20 percent between 1727 and 1760, but in
1765, during the Stamp Act crisis, it leapt above 50 percent. Furthermore,
active leaders began to learn that political success increasingly hinged
on advocating the interests of the constituency. A political transformation was beginning in which any leader who blithely ignored the voice
of the "common Herd" courted great peril, while those who listened,
understood, and acted on behalf of popular sentiment might flourish.[46]

In some provinces new political faces replaced the old. Dramatic
changes occurred in Virginia. Patrick Henry's astonishing triumph in
moving a sluggish assembly to act immediately catapulted him into a
position of political prominence. Astute and ambitious politicians immediately saw the opportunity that Henry's bold action had opened.
Richard Henry Lee was one such individual. Born ten months after
George Washington, and just five miles below the site of his birthplace
on the Potomac, Lee hailed from a socially prominent Northern Neck
family. After an extended formal education that included seven years in
an English academy, young Richard Henry returned to Stratford Hall at
age eighteen. By his twenty-fifth birthday he had been elected to the

House of Burgesses, but during the next seven years, until 1765, he remained a backbencher. Unlike Henry, he did not radiate charisma. Tall and thin, almost gaunt in fact, with narrow piercing eyes and unruly, receding hair, he resembled a pedantic schoolmaster more than an artful statesman. But his advance was primarily hampered because power in the Virginia assembly rested almost exclusively with the Tidewater gentry. Lee yearned for power and acclaim, and he appears to have sought to rise in influence by casting his lot with the reform-minded element in the legislature, mostly representatives from the Piedmont and Northern Neck. He advocated an end to the slave trade, expanding the suffrage, relief for insolvent debtors, and greater religious freedoms. He also was a candidate for every lucrative vacant office. Indeed, he tried for so many public offices in Virginia and England that his foes publicly scorned him as "Bob Booty," a man who relentlessly pleaded for a better post.

In 1764, when the newspapers first carried word of the pending Stamp Act, Lee applied to be a stamp agent, even though he had played a significant role in drafting the remonstrance against the proposed tax that the House of Burgesses adopted in December. He later explained, somewhat sheepishly, and not terribly convincingly, that he had failed to fully understand the nature of the bill. Once he became aware that the tax would "be in the highest degree pernicious to my Country," he claimed to have "exerted every faculty I possessed" to thwart its implementation. In reality, Lee's public campaign against the Stamp Act followed Henry's spectacular resistance speech and the adoption of the Virginia Resolves. Lee jealously watched the laurels go to Henry. He protested that he had been "the first to try this, but another received the honors." Denied the attention that he felt was rightly his, Lee at least climbed on the bandwagon, and soon emerged as one of the most open and outspoken enemies of the Stamp Act. He waged a vitriolic, if somewhat hypocritical, campaign against the colony's designated stamp agent and authored a pamphlet that attacked parliamentary taxation, asserting that "if the Stamp Act should go down here, the people of England will go on to tax us every year *because the more they tax us, the less necessity will there be to tax themselves.*" Lee also wrote a defiant denunciation of the Stamp Act that was adopted by Westmoreland County and organized street demonstrations in tiny, dusty Leedstown to intimidate merchants who contemplated paying the tax in order to obtain clearance for their vessels to sail. Following Henry's lead, Lee pursued open resistance to ministerial policies to greater prominence in the House of Burgesses. Lee and Henry not only emerged as powers in the assembly, but after 1766 they were perceived as leaders by those who longed to reform Virginia. Patrick Henry became their lodestar because he was a fresh, fearless personality, and Lee, riding in the slipstream, at last emerged as a leader both because he understood public opinion in Virginia and because he already enjoyed a reputation as a reformer.[47]

The Stamp Act altered the political landscape elsewhere as well. In Massachusetts, for instance, James Otis Jr., long an ambitious assemblyman, was elected Speaker of the House. He had been the most visible foe of the Sugar Act and of Britain's attempt to streamline its enforcement of the acts of trade. Otis also was the province's only delegate to the Stamp Act Congress who was not characterized by the governor as a supporter of the imperial government. Samuel Adams gained attention in the course of the protest and for the first time won election to the assembly. Meanwhile, nineteen assemblymen who were publicly identified as "friends" of the Stamp Act, or associated with attenuated responses to the mother country, were turned out of office by the voters.[48]

However, not all the colonies shared the political upheavals of Virginia and Massachusetts. Things were different in Pennsylvania. Prior to Britain's attempt to tax the colonists, the hottest political issue in that colony had been a campaign to persuade London to terminate the proprietary rule of the Penn family and establish royal government. In 1681 the Crown had given William Penn and his heirs much of the huge expanse of land lying between Maryland and New York, a region that comprised some 47,000,000 acres. Two years later, Penn and the initial colonists arrived in carefully planned Philadelphia. Following Penn's demise in 1718, the "True and Absolute Proprietaries," who lived in England, continued to send a Penn family member, or a surrogate, to Pennsylvania to serve as governor and in turn to appoint the colony's magistrates.

The antiproprietary initiative, which crystallized around the time of the French and Indian War, was the program of the Assembly Party, or Quaker Party, as its enemies dubbed it, a faction dominated by Franklin and his political partner, Joseph Galloway. Franklin and Galloway and their adherents fought the proprietors for several reasons. They sought more autonomy for those who lived in Pennsylvania. Many also despaired at what they believed had been the proprietary family's chronic mishandling of Indian relations. Still others were angry that the proprietors refused to permit taxation of their vast landed domain within the province, or to adequately open their lands for settlement. Rumors circulated as well that the Assembly Party's leaders had a personal stake in royalization. Franklin, according to the buzz, was in line to become the colony's first royal governor and Galloway its chief justice.

Franklin had acted soon after the Albany Conference to build the party, bringing together a rich array of Pennsylvanians who supported the military effort against the French. The antiproprietary program jelled simultaneously, and by the early 1760s it had become the heart of the party's program. Franklin was suited in many ways for building and leading a political faction. Warm, tireless, and blessed with a good sense of humor, he additionally was unsurpassed in his skill at the appropriate public persona to serve his ends. Furthermore, he was a former artisan who had retained close ties with Philadelphia's working class. The middling sort in Philadelphia respected him as a worldly, outgoing, intellectually curious, and civic-minded resident who had done much to improve the city and the quality of life of its inhabitants. Workers admired him for those qualities, but also venerated him as a shining example of one who had succeeded in rising above his origins through savvy and industry. They called him "the great Patriot."[49] A masterful writer, Franklin had no equal in his ability to communicate with a mass audience, and no one had a greater facility for easily engaging others, regardless of social position or intellect, in direct interpersonal relations. But he did have liabilities. He confessed that he was a "bad Speaker, never eloquent." Furthermore, he haphazardly divided his energies between a thousand and one activities, leaving too little time to devote to the daily, sometimes hourly, needs of managing a political faction. Worse, perhaps, Philadelphia's elite shut him out of their world, looking down on him as a parvenu.

In the mid-1750s Franklin tapped Galloway, a bright young assemblyman, to be his legislative assistant. Despite, or more likely because of, their

dissimilar backgrounds and temperaments, the two were gradually drawn together in a political partnership. Galloway, who was twenty-four years Franklin's junior, possessed the attributes that Franklin lacked. The son of a prosperous merchant, Galloway had become even wealthier through marriage. He chose the law as a career and opened a practice while only eighteen years of age. Unlike Franklin, Galloway was aloof, overbearing, even imperious, and sometimes hot-tempered, a man who was esteemed for his talents, but never loved. Yet his family and business ties gave him entree to the highest circles of social and economic power in the province, and he was such a distinguished orator that he

Joseph Galloway. Engraving (detail) by Max Rosenthal after anonymous artist.

was often called the "Demosthenes of Pennsylvania."[50] Furthermore, Galloway thrived on the day-to-day scut work necessary for success in a legislative chamber, appearing to enjoy the confrontational and arm-twisting aspects of legislative management that Franklin loathed. Franklin and Galloway pooled their talents into an effective one-two punch that was spectacularly successful.

Their Assembly Party captured control of the legislature in 1757 and for the next seven years never faced a serious challenge. However, in 1764 an opposition faction that called itself the New Ticket—and was variously labeled the Presbyterian, or Proprietary, Party by its foes—emerged to fight against royalization. Diversity characterized this faction. There were proprietary officeholders, of course, but the bulk of the party's following was derived from dissenting religious groups—chiefly Scotch-Irish Presbyterians and Germans, some of whom were Lutheran, but many of whom were adherents of small sects—who feared that royalization would result in the Anglican Church becoming the established church in the province. Residents of the backcountry, people who could not find a site too remote from royal authority, also gravitated toward this faction. The leader of this rival faction was John Dickinson, who like Galloway was the son of an affluent Maryland gentryman, a superlative penman, and a distinguished lawyer.

The Proprietary Party waged a brilliant, even modern, campaign in the assembly elections of 1764. It charged that the antiproprietary campaign was merely a ruse to avoid granting greater representation to the underrepresented western counties. John Dickinson, who had seen England at first hand, not only spoke of the corruption that stalked the mother country but charged that Franklin and Galloway were imprudent in wishing to swap proprietary rule for the threat of monarchical intrusiveness in Pennsylvania's affairs. Dickinson would have agreed with the foe of royalization who predicted that "the King's little Finger we should find heavier than the Proprietor's whole Loins."[51] What is more, in a sign that popular opinion counted more now than previously, the Proprietary Party revealed that Franklin had fathered an illegitimate child, charged that due to his "fumbling age"—he was now fifty-eight years old—he no longer was sufficiently alert to hold important office, and jabbed at Galloway's alleged deviousness. Although this was the sternest challenge yet faced by the Assembly Party, the Proprietary faction won only about one-third of the assembly seats that fall. Yet it won half the seats in Philadelphia and Philadelphia County, and for the first time ousted both Galloway and Franklin from the assembly.[52]

The next autumn, in the very midst of the tempest over the Stamp Act, Galloway was reelected to the Assembly. Franklin, who had been sent to London by the legislature to fight for terminating proprietary rule, did not stand for reelection. Upon retaking his seat, Galloway resumed the campaign for the royalization of Pennsylvania. He marshaled every ounce of his authority to curb open resistance to the Stamp Act, fearing that any display of defiance would anger the ministry in faraway London and thwart his campaign to oust the proprietors. He succeeded in preventing his assembly from remonstrating against the Stamp Act, unlike most of the other provincial legislatures. But outside the assembly hall, riots and demonstrations swept over Philadelphia, as they had in Boston. Furthermore, much to Galloway's chagrin, Philadelphia joined numerous other port cities in an embargo of British trade.

But Galloway's greatest battle was against the Proprietary Party, which now had a new issue. It castigated the Assembly Party for its servility toward London. It portrayed Galloway as a ministerial lackey and Franklin as a "dangerous enemy" of the province who had secretly helped author the Stamp Act. Its tactics did not succeed, in part because whatever goodwill it earned from opposing the Stamp Act was forfeited by its identification with the proprietors, a largely discredited element in Pennsylvania. Pennsylvania politics turned more on local matters than on imperial concerns, and the Assembly Party increased its hold on the legislature in the elections both in 1765 and 1766, winning control of twenty-eight of the thirty-six assembly seats. Furthermore, in both elections Galloway defeated Dickinson. In October 1765, at the apex of the crisis over British taxation, Galloway won 20 percent more votes than in the previous year's election. Soon, too, he was elected Speaker of the House.[53]

However, if Galloway emerged from the crisis in a stronger position, Franklin was nearly destroyed politically. Following his defeat in the election of 1764, Franklin had been dispatched to London by the Assembly Party to fight for Pennsylvania's royalization. When the ministry first brooded over imposing a stamp tax on the colonies, Franklin let those officials know that he was "not much alarm'd about your Schemes of raising Money on us. You will take care . . . not to lay greater Burthens on us than we can bear." Even after he saw the details of the ministry's proposed tax, Franklin predicted that the colonists would protest only if the duties were oppressive. He also divulged that he had no qualms about the British raising a revenue through the regulation of colonial trade. Franklin's intense personal ambition—including in all likelihood his hope of crowning his extraordinary career by becoming the governor of his adopted colony—and his burning hatred of the proprietors blinded him to other realities.[54]

Enough of Franklin's sentiments were made public to cause him grave trouble at home. He was pilloried in the Philadelphia press as a ministerial toady. One newspaper ran a cartoon that depicted him in terms strikingly akin to the way Boston's radicals portrayed Oliver. Franklin was shown selling himself to the devil, above these lines:

> All his designs concenter in himself,
> For building castles and amassing pelf.

When the riots erupted in Philadelphia, Franklin's friends feared that his house, like Oliver's, would be targeted. His wife, Deborah, implored friends to "fech a gun or two" and defend her home. Galloway helped to organize a vigilante party of 800 men, mostly workers who revered his partner and hated the proprietors, to stand guard at Franklin's residence until tempers cooled.[55]

When he learned of these rebukes, Franklin, always somewhat of a chameleon, changed colors. He realized it was time to denounce the Stamp Act. And good fortune smiled on him as well, for a new ministry bent on repealing the troublesome duties had come to power. It wanted to use Franklin as its centerpiece in a parliamentary inquiry in which he would testify about the colonies' grievances. This was a role he embraced, as it afforded him an opportunity to repair his tattered image at home. Indeed, he eventually disseminated a small pamphlet that contained his testimony, as did friends in Philadelphia who yet thought him a useful asset through which votes might be harvested. His last-minute conversion worked. Not only was his reputation saved, but astonishingly as Esmond Wright, his biographer, has written, Franklin emerged from the Stamp Act crisis as "the voice of colonial America."[56]

Franklin told the House of Commons that the Stamp Act alone had not caused the eruption in the colonies. The fury had been provoked as well by the restrictions on paper money and the establishment of the Admiralty Court. Parliament had been deeply wounded in the eyes of the colonists, he advised. The Americans had always looked on Parliament as their protector against arbitrary ministers, but now it was viewed as the author of unconstitutional acts and as a body that had turned a deaf ear to colonial entreaties.

Franklin also emphasized the revolutionary nature of the whirlwind that had been unleashed. Whereas the colonists' attitude toward the mother country once had been the "best in the world," it now was "very much altered." If Great Britain continued on its present course, he warned, not only would a "total loss of the respect and affection the people of America bear" toward Great Britain be the result, but "all the commerce that depends on that respect and affection" also would be lost.[57]

Nine days after Franklin's appearance, Parliament repealed the Stamp Act. It acted, in part, because of its apprehension over the damage to

Anglo-American ties. However, that was a minor consideration. Politicians as a rule are most insightful when it comes to finding the means of remaining in office, but few exhibit much ability to discern, and respond efficaciously to, extraordinary new trends and watershed events. In this instance, many merchants in England were howling over their losses in the American trade embargo. They told the Commons that commerce with America was down sharply, debts might not be recovered, and unemployment would soar. These powerful constituents, more than the distant colonists, swayed Parliament.

However, many politicians in London looked on the Stamp Act not as misbegotten but merely flawed. They did not question the thinking that had brought on the new colonial policies. They merely searched for an alternative means of raising a revenue and tightening control of colonial commerce. Many in fact were anxious to clamp down on the Americans, for they had been riled by the colonists' defiance. If many Americans had been set to rethinking their position within the empire, at the same time what Franklin called a "settled Malice against the Colonies" had congealed in some political circles in England.[58] When this point of view collided with the colonists' new perspective, the British empire faced a most pernicious future.

3

1766–1770

"To Crush the Spirit of the Colonies"

The Stamp Act crisis had caused numerous Americans, as never before, to contemplate their rights and liberties, the degree of autonomy they possessed within their empire, and the economic realities of their dependent status. John Adams was not alone in subsequently concluding that American independence was born during the Stamp Act episode. David Ramsay, a South Carolinian who in 1789 published one of the first histories of the American Revolution, wrote that the crisis, and especially London's capitulation, "was the first direct step to American independency." Peter Oliver, brother of the victimized Andrew Oliver, even earlier had written a history of the rebellion in which he reached the same conclusion. Each argued that the colonists "swelled with their own Importance" when Parliament backed down. Thereafter, they wrote, the provincials not only knew their own power, but discounted the prowess of the mother country.[1] Some in the colonies did not have to await the judgment of history to deduce that a watershed event had occurred. Three months after the riots in Boston, Governor Bernard concluded that many colonists, "much ... altered" by what had transpired, harbored "repugnant" notions about the imperial relationship. Henceforth, he predicted, they would respond with even greater defiance against anything that London sought to impose.[2] At almost the same moment, General Thomas Gage, the commander of the British army in America, told his superiors in London that at bottom the question raised by the colonists' actions was "the Independency of the Provinces." The issue, he added, was simple: Were the colonists "Subject to the Legislative Power of Great Britain?"[3]

Bernard and Gage notwithstanding, the future was unfathomable to those living in 1766. When the Stamp Act was repealed, many in fact believed the imperial crisis was at an end, at least in their lifetime. Although repeal had been accompanied by the Declaratory Act, a bold pronouncement declaring that capitulation on the Stamp Tax issue did not mean that London concurred with the constitutional stand of the American radicals, and indeed that Parliament had the authority to make laws for the colonies "in all cases whatsoever," most Americans dismissed the statement as simply the bravado of a defeated ministry. Many friends of America in London told the colonists to pay no attention to Parliament's assertion, and many in America believed them. John Adams "expected it would not be executed." He was convinced that "good humour" between the colonies and parent state had been restored.[4] Franklin, a witness to Parliament's act, wrote home dismissing the measure as a step taken "merely to save Appearances" and to "guard against ... the Clamour" that would ensue if it appeared that "the Rights of this Nation are sacrificed to America."[5]

Furthermore, those early histories were misleading in implying that all who became revolutionaries were transformed by the Stamp Act upheaval. The crisis had come on too abruptly, and ended too quickly, for a broad revolutionary outlook to take shape. Many were yet convinced that London had made a mistake. Revolutionaries do not spring from such a conviction. Many thought the ministry had learned its lesson, and perhaps most believed that some sort of accommodation would be worked out in the near future, some settlement that served the deeply entangled interests of both parties. Months after the American riots in 1765, for instance, Franklin remained convinced that the "Americans ... have not the least desire of independence" and that "wise and honest men" on both sides will "settle [matters] wisely and benevolently."[6]

This is not to suggest that the Stamp crisis was unimportant nor to maintain that some true radicals had not been active in the upheaval. While some activists must have harbored prior hatreds toward Great Britain, or already loathed America's linkage to the empire, many more— as John Adams and Bernard ruminated—were transformed and never again would see the mother country, or the colonists' relationship with London, in the same light. However, what was even more important in 1766 was whether London would proceed with its new colonial policy. The truth was that an American insurgency could continue, and grow, only in response to British actions. That, of course, was what occurred, and it was John Adams who got it most nearly correct. Many years later he reflected that it had been the cumulative weight of events between 1765 and 1775 that transformed the "minds and hearts of the people,"

and that the resulting "radical change in the Principles opinions, sentiments, and affection of the people, was the real American Revolution."[7]

The British ministry had made a fundamental mistake in bringing
on the crisis, but its greatest misstep was to have gone into the breach
with absolutely no idea what it would do if it met resistance. Had the
ministry in fact brought the crisis to a head in 1765, employing force to
face down the protest, it well might have solved its problems then and
there. The colonists in 1765–66 were disunited and probably would have
been fatally divided in a showdown. Though rioting had occurred, moderate forces predominated everywhere. Furthermore, few colonists were
yet sufficiently radicalized to cope with the stern demands of insurgency.
Britain's cataclysmic fecklessness was the most substantive factor in the
entire episode, for London's prospects for crushing colonial dissent would
never again be so favorable. Britain's government soon compounded its
errors. Having backed down, it would have been wise for the ministry to
have sought the accommodation that Franklin anticipated. Failing that,
it would have been prudent to have abandoned its new policies for a
time, perhaps until this generation passed away and another, with little
memory of what had transpired in 1765, emerged.

But either course would have faced mountainous hurdles in London. The Stamp crisis had changed minds within the parent state as
surely as in the colonies. A palpable rage toward America now was readily
apparent in some circles. Franklin, who had been so optimistic as 1765
drew to a close, soon expressed oppressive doubts, and by the spring of
1767, in a series of letters and essays, reported that "Every step is now
[taken by the government] to enrage [the populace] against *America*."
He added that opinion now was "strong against America in general,"
and that a "general Rage against America" burned throughout Britain.
Many hard-liners were anxious to test the mettle of the colonists, he
reported. The "wolf is determined on a quarrel with the lamb," was how
he put it.[8] Yet it was not merely fury that drove the ministry. Governor
Bernard thought it now or never if London was to "inforce their [the
colonists'] Obedience" to the principle that Parliament indeed was "the
Supreme Imperial Legislature, to which all Members of the Empire, whether
represented or not, were subject in all Matters & Things." He proposed
that the colonists be represented in the House of Commons, but simultaneously that the government of every province be restructured, limiting the authority of the assemblies until they became "perfect for a
dependent" status.[9] Others, such as Charles Townshend, who soon would
head the ministry, believed that "a set of factious men closely cemented
together" from within several provinces would, unless Britain acted, set
in motion a "fixed plan" to bring about "the ruin of the dependency of

the colonies upon Great Britain."[10] His was a wildly misleading view of what was occurring, and what was possible at that moment, in the colonies. However, such thinking prevailed. Great Britain's leadership acted as politicians, not as statesmen. Fearing dishonor, the ministry abandoned whatever chance might have existed to find a middle ground and proceeded with its new colonial policy.

First, Parliament passed the Revenue Act of 1766, a measure that lowered the tax on foreign molasses imported into the colonies, a big ticket item in New England, where molasses was distilled into rum. Lower duties would mean greater trade, the ministry believed, and the plethora of customs agents, who patrolled the docks in cities such as Boston and Newport, would ensure that considerable revenue would be collected. There was little pretense in London, as there once had been, that this legislation was part of a complex regulatory scheme designed to bring the greatest good to the greatest number. This was avowedly a revenue-raising measure, as its very name trumpeted.

So too were the Townshend Duties, new taxes enacted in 1767 on the sale of glass, paper, lead, paints, and tea. The stamp tax could not have been avoided by most colonists. Townshend's taxes, on the other hand, were to fall only on those who chose to consume the duted commodities. Some ministers deluded themselves that this would make the new taxes palatable. The legislation was to raise a revenue for the purpose of paying the salaries of royal governors in the provinces, as its preamble candidly acknowledged. The prime minister told Parliament that it had to be done, both because the revenue was needed and as it was essential to demonstrate the sovereignty of Parliament. Finally, to streamline the regulation of provincial commerce, the act created the American Board of Customs. It was to be headquartered in Boston.[11]

These revenue-raising measures reignited the fires that had been extinguished by the repeal of the Stamp Act, but they were not London's only provocative steps. In 1766 the ministry, with Parliament's concurrence, suspended the New York assembly for its refusal to comply with the Quartering Act. The ministry's action posed a clear threat to each colony's domestic autonomy and led many Americans to conclude that Parliament was out of control. Indeed, this latest measure encroached upon powers traditionally exercised by the Crown. Never before had any official other than a colonial governor, often acting on orders from the Crown, prorogued and dissolved a colonial assembly.

Many northern merchants soon had another bone to pick with Parliament. Although the Revenue Act had reduced duties on imported molasses, in 1766 and 1767 many merchants petitioned the House of Commons to permit American exports to the Caribbean sugar islands, whether they be French, Spanish, or Dutch colonies. Their argument was simple. Free trade meant more trade, which would result in greater American prosperity, and that in turn would augment colonial purchases of British manufactures. Everyone would benefit, save for the British sugar planters and slave traders, who already prospered to a degree that few could conceive. However, the pleas of the American businessmen fell on deaf ears. The Commons in fact responded in high dudgeon at the temerity of the Americans who had suggested free trade. That sort of commercial reform was not in the cards. Parliament was tightening, not loosening, its trade laws, and its policies appeared to many to be biased against Americans.[12]

The mystery was not that the Anglo-American crisis was renewed but that so much time was required for colonial resistance to take shape. Whereas the Virginia Resolves had been enacted within hours of the receipt of official word of the Stamp Act, and mobs had surged into the streets of Boston and New York months before the Stamp Act was to go into effect, eighteen months or more elapsed after news of the Townshend Duties reached some colonies before meaningful protest occurred.

Several factors inhibited an effective dissent. Fewer merchants were interested in a protest against the Townshend Duties than had been the case two years before. Pecuniary interests colored their outlook. The Stamp Act had been enacted while the colonists languished in a slough of despond caused by a postwar recession. Many merchants had welcomed an embargo on imports in 1765, for it afforded the opportunity to liquidate their large inventories.[13] However, as news of the Townshend Duties arrived in the midst of economic recovery, many merchants were unwilling to countenance another trade boycott that surely would threaten returning prosperity. Numerous workers, just now back at work, were just as wary of doing anything that might imperil precious jobs.

In Massachusetts, moreover, Governor Bernard fought tenaciously to defuse the popular movement. He had abundant weapons, as the political system favored entrenched interests. Wealth and power go hand in hand, and whatever elite predominates inevitably fashions a governmental system not only with an eye on ensuring its perpetuity but with a design on facilitating its further accumulation of wealth. The British system in Massachusetts conformed perfectly to this model. The Royal governor, a Crown appointee, exercised enormous patronage power and ordinarily appointed to office only those "most distinguished, for their wealth, understanding, and probity," as one of Bernard's predecessors observed.[14] Throughout the 200 or so farming communities within the colony, the leading men invariably were named as justices of the peace, judges of the inferior courts, even as sheriffs. Many of these same men were also designated as field officers in the provincial militia.

Having flourished from the system, these men were seldom inclined to disrupt it. Moreover, if they had not previously supported Royal policy, they usually made an about-face and utilized their standing and authority to keep the community in line with the policies of the governor. Samuel Adams called them "tools of power."[15] John Adams once remarked that merely the "distinction [of] a man among his neighbors" was a sufficient step by government "to purchase and corrupt him." He watched in dismay as his college chum and fellow attorney, Jonathan Sewall, was co-opted through an offer to accept appointment as a Judge of Admiralty.[16] Soon thereafter Adams was similarly tempted. After he wrote a remonstrance against the Stamp Act that was adopted by more than forty communities, Governor Bernard dangled the post of Advocate General of the Court of Admiralty before him. This was an extraordinary plum for a young man with merely seven years' experience as a lawyer. Adams knew that the position would be only the "first Step in the Ladder of Royal Favour and Promotion," and that someday he, like Hutchinson, might be the lieutenant governor, or even the chief executive, of Massachusetts. But he also knew that accepting the office would place him, like Sewall, "under the restraints, or Obligations of Gratitude to the Government." Adams disliked Hutchinson, in part because he regarded him as a traitor to his homeland, and he believed the populace hated both the lieutenant governor and Oliver for much the same reason. Adams declined the offer.[17]

Nor was patronage the end of the governor's power. The Royal governor of Massachusetts could act as a roadblock against the aspirations of dissenters. Following the publication of Otis's treatise questioning the constitutional limits of Parliament's power, Governor Bernard vetoed his election as Speaker of the House of the provincial assembly. The chief executive additionally held veto power over those selected by the lower house to the Council. This was of crucial importance. The Council, which exercised authority in each of the three branches of the Massachusetts government— it served as the colony's supreme court, upper house of the legislature, and the governor's cabinet—was rendered something of a satellite of the Crown's official. Governor Bernard, who vetoed the selection of approximately 25 percent of those chosen for the Council, succeeded in establishing—perpetuating, actually—a Council that one scholar correctly characterized as "unabashedly elitist."[18]

Governor Bernard, effectively utilizing the system designed for maintaining conservative prowess, and acting more resolutely than during the Stamp crisis, had erected barriers to resistance by the time word of

the Townshend Duties arrived in 1767. In Boston, for instance, the radical leaders failed on three occasions that year to induce town meetings
to endorse another nonimportation agreement. Furthermore, nearly
three months after the Townshend Duties went into effect, the Massachusetts assembly overwhelmingly rejected a proposal to embargo British goods. However, the situation changed drastically in 1768. Much of
the change resulted from the shrewd leadership of Samuel Adams.

Samuel Adams was the son of Boston Puritans. His father, often referred to as Deacon Adams for the lay position he held in his church, was
a brewer and merchant who married well, shrewdly invested his earnings, and lived comfortably, though not opulently. But politics, not beer,
was Deacon Adams's passion. For years he served Boston as a justice of
the peace and selectman, both elective posts, and late in life the city sent
him to the Massachusetts assembly. The Deacon was active in the Country Party, a faction, rather than a formal political party as exists today,
that was aligned not only against the royal governor—faraway London's
deputy who sought to advance the interests of the powerful in the mother
country—but also against the Massachusetts elite's nearly ironclad control over the province's currency. In the late 1730s, the Deacon took part
in the Country Party's push to establish a land bank that would issue
large sums of money backed by the property owned by the subscribers.
This was an unmistakably inflationary scheme to aid struggling workers
and farmers who were on the cusp of despair.

Creditors and Court Party stalwarts, such as Andrew Oliver and
Thomas Hutchinson, were arrayed against it. Instead, they favored—as
Hutchinson acknowledged—"drawing in the paper bills and depending
upon silver and gold currency." Their contractionist, or "tight money,"
policies, as contemporaries referred to their strategy, was aimed at keeping prices and wages stable and at ensuring that any money loaned out
would be repaid in like value. Hutchinson snorted that the land bank's
supporters were "generally of low condition . . . and of small estate, and
many of them perhaps insolvent."[19] From his elevated station, that was
doubtless true, although it was not an apt description of an industrious,
and rather successful, skilled artisan such as Deacon Adams. But
Hutchinson lost this fight, temporarily at least. In 1738 the assembly sanctioned the creation of the land bank, and Deacon Adams was not only
among its first subscribers but also appointed to its board of directors.
Throughout America's political history, however, conservatives have usually been the winners, particularly when the issues involve the economy.
That was true in Deacon Adams's case as well. The contractionists quickly
solicited the assistance of friends in England, and in 1741 Parliament—
seeking to protect British merchants who frequently advanced credit to

colonial merchants—dissolved the land bank. Parliament decreed that members of the bank's board of directors were to be personally responsible for returning the funds of the subscribers, with the interest that had accrued. Deacon Adams faced financial ruin.[20]

Samuel came along in more halcyon times. Born in 1722, he grew up in comfortable surroundings and received an excellent education. After several years at the Boston Latin School, he enrolled at Harvard College and earned a bachelor of arts diploma in 1740. Three years later, he was awarded a master of arts degree by Harvard, a rare occurrence in colonial days. Upon the completion of his studies, Samuel—through his father's influence—was taken on by one of Boston's largest mercantile firms. But, like his father, Samuel's overriding interest was politics. He devoted little attention to his work and lasted only a brief time in the countinghouse world before his employer dismissed him as temperamentally unsuited for such pursuits. Thereafter, he worked for his father, who for five years patiently tolerated Samuel's inattention to his responsibilities. He probably hoped Samuel would learn the business well enough to keep it going when it was someday passed on to him. If so, the Deacon's aspirations were in vain. Soon after Deacon Adams died in 1748, the brewery closed its doors, in all likelihood due more to Samuel's indifference than to ineptitude.

Samuel Adams. Oil on canvas by John Singleton Copley, about 1772.

Much of Samuel's life during the next fifteen or so years remains obscure. Indeed, the adult life of no other important Founder is as hidden from view for such a lengthy period. It is known that he married at age twenty-seven, a bit late by the habits of the time, and that he took for a wife the daughter of the pastor of what might have been Boston's largest church. She bore five children in six years, of whom only two lived more than a few days. Nineteen days after she delivered a stillborn child in 1757, she too perished, of complications from the pregnancy. Adams did not remarry for seven years, until 1764, when with his former father-in-law presiding, he wed the daughter of an English immigrant. Samuel was forty-two; his new wife was twenty-nine. He had inherited what remained of his father's estate, and some of his biographers feel that he received financial assistance from both his former and current father-in-law. In addition, he held a variety of public jobs. Some—like that of town scavenger—were not coveted, but he also served as a tax assessor and tax collector. In all likelihood, his moves from one municipal post to another were occasioned by his improvident manner. At best, these positions would have provided meager salaries and reduced Adams's standard of living to an unaccustomed level. For a time at least, that appears to have been the case. Acquaintances subsequently recalled one point at which Samuel Adams and his two children were so poor that the neighbors supplied them with food and clothing. By 1772, however, Samuel Adams was living more comfortably. After visiting him early in the year, John Adams portrayed Samuel as a person who feigned indifference to wealth but who, in fact, entertained lavishly and furnished his home with genteel elegance. As is true of so much regarding Samuel Adams, his material status cannot be determined. Typically, what little is known appears to be contradictory. For instance, he possessed the financial wherewithal to purchase a female slave, yet his second wife apparently worked to supplement the family income.[21]

What is known beyond the shadow of a doubt about Samuel Adams is that he was captivated by politics. He was immersed in politics as a youngster, listening as the Deacon talked endlessly about political affairs, and living in a home that was a frequent gathering site for politicians and political activists. His own political outlook took shape early on, much of it crystallizing in the course of the land bank affair that occurred as he completed his undergraduate studies. John Adams once remarked that the land bank episode provoked more agitation in Massachusetts than did the Stamp Act. While an exaggeration, there can be little doubt that Samuel Adams was substantively imprinted by the tempest. He grew furious with a political system that enabled the supporters of the land bank, whom Hutchinson had said were "very numerous," to be thwarted by an element that was "very small," in the words of the lieutenant governor.[22] Furthermore, Parliament's action against a bank sanctioned by the Massachusetts assembly was an object lesson in the plight of provincials who lacked autonomy and the ability to control their own destiny. In addition, for seventeen tortuous years after Parliament shut down the bank, Samuel Adams struggled against what must have appeared to him to be a succession of vengeful Royal officials in Boston who sought to seize and sell his late father's estate in order to settle land bank accounts. In the course of his battle, Adams discovered that he could use the press as a weapon against those officials, and he wrote numerous essays that sought to arouse the public against office-holders whom he portrayed as a menace to liberty and property. Implic-itly, the threat hung heavy that the confiscation of the Deacon's—now Samuel's—property might trigger damaging riots. Ultimately, Samuel Adams won his battle. In 1758 Boston's sheriff, apparently intimidated by the rant in the press, backed down on holding a publicized auction of the estate, and Samuel's ordeal ended.[23]

Years had been required for him to develop the political muscle to contest successfully with those who held power. Following graduation from Harvard, Samuel and friends formed a club to debate political issues, and soon he acquired a reputation for writing on current political matters in Boston's newspapers. One of his early squibs addressed the proposed Al-bany Plan of Union. He opposed it. Then, as later, he steadfastly resisted encroachments on Massachusetts's autonomy.[24] By the late 1750s, Adams belonged to every liberal political club in Boston, including the Boston Caucus, or "Junto" as its foes labeled it, a steering committee of sorts for the Country Party. Like his father, Samuel fought to expand the money supply and resisted the concentration of power in the hands of a few royal satraps, such as Hutchinson and Oliver. Already, it appears, Adams mani-fested the outlook that he would popularize in the 1770s, a return to a "Christian Sparta," a virtuous, egalitarian society.[25]

Thomas Jefferson has often been described by scholars as inscru-table, but next to Samuel Adams he was an amateur in the art of con-cealment. Yet through the testimony of acquaintances, as well as through a wonderful portrait by John Singleton Copley, we can get a sense of Adams's appearance and character. When in his midforties, at the time both of the Townshend Duty crisis and the Copley painting, he was stout and of medium height. Ruggedly handsome, with a sentient face, he had the appearance of what today is often called "a man's man," an indi-vidual with whom most men quickly feel at ease, a man whose company is prized by other males. However, nothing about his appearance sug-gests any charismatic qualities that would explain his success as a leader. Some of his accomplishments may have been due to his skill as a dis-sembler. He was so artful, in fact, that Abigail Adams, who had met just about every important figure in provincial Massachusetts by 1776, was led to believe that he was less given to pretense and dissimulation than any man she had ever met.[26] A recent biographer has written of how Samuel "carefully cultivated" and "crafted" an image of "an ordinary Bostonian."[27] He dressed simply, often in a threadbare coat, spoke freely of his middling status, and dwelled in a house that to outward appearances was in ram-shackle condition. Some adversaries even said that his persona of piety

was deceitful, adding that he donned the "religious Mask" to fool "an ignorant & deluded People."[28] That allegation, however, surely was incor-
rect, for throughout his life he remained a believer and churchgoer.

Effective politicians often are good actors, and Samuel Adams was
no exception. However, he could not have deceived everyone forever,
and it is unlikely that he bamboozled a sophisticate such as Jefferson,
who called him "truly the *Man of the Revolution*," or that he pulled the
wool over the eyes of John Adams, who was in daily contact with him for
years. Adams subsequently concluded that Samuel was the indispensable figure in orchestrating the American Revolution, and he pronounced
him the greatest man of his age. Adams thought Samuel a man of steel
who possessed the courage to confront dangerous and formidable adversaries. Samuel, he said, was "cool, abstemious, polished, refined," but
also "zealous, ardent and keen in the Cause." He was "staunch and stiff
and strict, and rigid and inflexible" in the defense of American rights,
and always prudent in his judgment.[29]

Hutchinson and Oliver thought Samuel Adams' success as a political leader occurred because he was a "great Demagogue" who would
resort to any "criminal" ploy, any "low art and cunning" deceit, to augment his power.[30] Others believed his hatred of the British was so deep
that he could not rest until America was free of the mother country.
Stories circulated, and were believed, that he taught his dog to attack
every person it saw wearing a red coat and that he instructed little children to despise British soldiers. Others suspected he sought revenge
against the likes of Oliver and Hutchinson for the ruination of his father. Excluding the hyperbolic stories about Queue, his dog, there is some
truth in these surmises, although sturdier explanations can be found for
his artful leadership. For one thing, politics was his life. From all accounts, Samuel was a good husband and father, but he appears to have
spent the better part of most days, and many nights, politicking. He attended meetings, socialized with other activists, and regularly entertained
politicos. Furthermore, he apparently possessed the rare ability to mingle
easily with people from every social and economic background. He had
grown up in Boston and knew city people. Years of working at his father's
brewery acquainted him with the conversation, as well as the cares and
interests, of artisans and laborers. He sought them out and was at ease in
their presence. According to one contemporary, Adams was "well acquainted with every shipwright, and substantial mechanick, and they
were his friends."[31] Samuel was such a consummate urbanite that he did
not learn to ride a horse until he was well past fifty, yet he also discovered how to converse effectively with farmers, a tribute as much to his
carefully cultivated social skills as to his desire to succeed in politics.

But Adams, who had earned two Harvard diplomas, was equally comfortable discoursing with the educated. Abigail Adams gushed at his "good breeding." Her husband, a Harvard graduate himself, thought Samuel a gentleman of "genteel Erudition [and] obliging, engaging Manners."[32] Unencumbered by a job that consumed much of his time, and at home in the company of men from all walks of life, Samuel divided portions of the daytime hours between the grog shops or eateries habituated by workers and the coffeehouses or watering holes frequented by artisans and professionals. He gave over some of the evening hours to socializing with the politically active in partisan, civic, and debating clubs. He spent a good portion of Sunday at church, where his rich, melodious voice was treasured in hymn singing.

Samuel Adams, as John Adams once observed, displayed the most remarkable sense of the character and temper of the people.[33] The Tory, Peter Oliver, subsequently characterized Samuel Adams as a man of "serpentine Cunning" who would "discharge [his] muddy Liquid, & darken the Water to such a Hue" that his followers were lost in his "Cloudy Vortex." But John Adams's assessment is more nearly accurate. Samuel Adams did not so much hoodwink the people as he understood what they desired. Instead of "turn[ing] the minds of the great Vulgar" populace, as Oliver remarked, he told them what they wanted to hear.[34] He talked with them. Better, he listened to them and came to understand that they yearned for something truly revolutionary: control over their lives and destinies. Not only had his generation been sucked into two of England's wars during the past twenty years, but their jobs and their incomes, the prices they paid for the commodities they purchased, and the very quality of their lives all too often were the result of decisions reached in a distant country and enforced by those who served that faraway land. This did not necessarily mean that Adams's countrymen sought independence. However, it meant that they yearned for greater autonomy. Earlier than most, Samuel Adams divined how thin was the line between enhanced self-control and independence, and how the quest for one led toward the other. Yet in another sense, as Samuel also knew, the people were deeply conservative. Like their ancestors who had fled England and Europe to escape the long, and often heavy, hand of government, they too remained ready to resist London's attempts to intrude further into their affairs. Nevertheless, few wanted to change what they and their forebears had instituted in the course of a century and a half of relative remoteness from London. Samuel Adams understood this because he personally embraced these beliefs. Tireless, understanding, intelligent, a good speaker and a better writer, persuasive, passionate, and utterly fearless, Samuel Adams possessed every quality needed to lead the popular protest in Boston.

Adams did not invent the mechanisms of protest—he exploited those already in place. An effective propagandist, he made skillful use of the press, a skill he honed a decade or more earlier while fighting against the seizure of his father's estate. He wrote tirelessly and with a clarity and vitality that informed and energized his readers. His invective could deeply wound his prey. Governor Bernard once remarked that Adams's pen "stung like an horned snake."[35] But it was his mastery at planning and organization that was truly unsurpassed. Boston teemed with societies and clubs, and Samuel Adams understood intuitively that they could be put to effective use. Some of these organizations and associations were social in nature, while others were intellectual, utilitarian (such as the Fire Club), or professional, and a few were political establishments. In addition, looser knit entities of workers existed, one in the North End of Boston, and one on the south side, and each created a steering committee to articulate its views. Still another group, the Loyal Nine, may have originated as a super committee designed to bridge the gap between workers from different, and what at times had been rival, neighborhoods. Finally, there was the Boston Caucus, whose origin stretched back about three generations and in which Deacon Adams had been active as early as the 1720s. From the outset, its primary purpose had been to protect Boston's workers and broad middle class, and on their behalf the Caucus worked to preserve the integrity of the city's traditional town meeting system of governance, ensure the election of fair and honest tax collectors, and champion programs that were popular with its constituency, including "soft money" initiatives. The Caucus was where various interest groups met to decide what would be brought before the Boston town meeting. John Adams left a description of a typical Caucus meeting. Those in attendance, he wrote, "smoke tobacco till you cannot see from one end of the garret to the other. There they drink flip, I suppose, and there they choose a moderator, who puts questions to the vote regularly; and selectmen, assessors, collectors, wardens, firewards, and representatives, are regularly chosen before they are chosen in the town." Revealingly, however, he added that once the caucus made its decisions, "They send committees to wait on the merchants' club."[36] His description makes the caucus sound like the smoke-filled rooms of a later era of American politics, the cloistered site at which competing interest groups sorted through differences and reached concerted decisions. But his description also makes it clear that the great merchants traditionally exerted sway, albeit after learning of the wishes of the Caucus and keeping in mind the street power this body could mobilize. Thus, if the various groups of artisans, laborers, neighborhoods, and professional groups achieved their goals, it was only with the consent of the principal businessmen in Boston.

This thicket of associations and committees had been around for some time. Samuel Adams, in fact, had been active in these clubs for twenty years or more before the Townshend Duties were enacted. After 1765, however, he turned the tangled system to his own ends, and drawing on his multifaceted talents, achieved more with it than any previous political leader. He was not an original thinker, and he was an effective orator only "when his deeper feelings were excited" and he was moved to speak with a "nervous eloquence," as John Adams said.[37] But he was unsurpassed as an organizer. He hosted dinners at which he brought together affluent merchants and working-class leaders. He wanted them to get to know one another so they could act cooperatively, and he sought to convince them that despite their differences they shared a common enemy in London. He formed singing clubs among artisans, a means of building liaisons. He knew something of crowd psychology as well. It was probably his idea to annually commemorate August 14, the day that Oliver's house and businesses had been pillaged, with festive celebrations that brought people together for food, drinks, patriotic singing, and plentiful speechifying on the dangers posed by the imperial government. He also knew how to use crowds. His disclaimers notwithstanding, he likely had a hand in unleashing the mob that tore down Oliver's property, and he was probably behind Oliver's abasement in December 1765, when the old man was made to stand before a large throng in the cold rain for a second time to resign his commission as stamp collector.

But Adams understood the dangers of mob action. He knew that violence could be counterproductive, that many—including the most influential Bostonians—would be repelled by it. Indeed, not only could mob actions sow disenchantment, but Adams knew that street violence could invite greater British intervention, which he sought to avoid in the early years of the protest. Thus, one of his master strokes was to create Boston's Sons of Liberty. It served several functions. It was a vehicle for building a mass base of protest. It could be a medium for unleashing rampages in Boston's cobblestone streets, if necessary. But it was also a vehicle for preventing disorder and possible violence, for the Sons of Liberty was an organization that Adams, and the other principal leaders in the protest movement, could carefully control and direct.[38] It served another purpose as well. Adams must have envisioned it as the instrument that could effectively supplant the caucus. It was his genius to fathom the resentment and rage of the workers, and above all else to discern the potential power of laborers and artisans in a mass movement. He realized that it could bring together workers and merchants more or less as coequals, as brethren in protest, and if he could be the broker that reconciled their interests to the broader ends of the popular protest, the movement could have the numbers, muscle, and unity to prevail.

Samuel Adams pursued interrelated goals in 1768. He longed to see the Americans act in concert, speaking to London with one voice. He also understood the value of confrontational politics. He knew that London, if pushed, was likely to overreact, and its exaggerated response would help drive the colonists into one another's arms to resist the common danger. Adams struck when the assembly convened in January. He prepared a resolution denouncing the Townshend Duties as unconstitutional, and asked the assembly to pass the resolves and send it to the other provinces for their approval. He desperately wanted Massachusetts to play the same role in the protest against the Townshend Duties that the Virginia Resolves had played in attacking the Stamp Act. The assembly was willing to speak out, but the more conservative members, mostly from small towns in rural western counties, refused to conspire with other provinces. Seemingly defeated, Adams bided his time. The propitious moment arrived about forty days later when many assemblymen from the outback, weary of expensive Boston, departed for home, even though the assembly had not adjourned. Adams seized the moment. He reintroduced his proposal, and it passed at once. The Massachusetts Circular Letter, as it came to be known, was carefully constructed, and if John Adams was correct, it was largely the handiwork of Samuel Adams and James Otis. It included the provocative statement that parliamentary taxation "overleap[s] the bounds" of the imperial constitution, which "limits both sovereignty and allegiance." However, Adams was careful not to get ahead of public opinion. The resolution made no attempt to delineate the powers that Parliament actually possessed. The Circular Letter also sought to institute a common front against the mother country, appealing to every American province to "harmonize with each other" in protesting these taxes.[39]

Adams got what he wanted. Not only did some assemblies endorse the Massachusetts Circular Letter, but London went too far in response. The judicious course for officials in the imperial capital would have been to disregard Massachusetts's pronouncement, as they had ignored colonial remonstrances during the Stamp Act furor. Instead, fatuity prevailed. Wills Hill, Lord Hillsborough, the new secretary of state for American affairs, which included the thirteen mainland colonies, ordered the royal governor of Massachusetts to dissolve the assembly should it refuse to rescind the Circular Letter. He also directed all other governors to refuse to allow their assemblies to meet if they endorsed the principles laid down by the Bay Colony radicals, resolves that he labeled "most dangerous and factious," and "calculated to inflame the minds of his [majesty's] good subjects."[40]

Franklin once described Hillsborough as a man of "wrong headed bustling Industry" who was "proud, supercilious, extreamly conceited" and "fond of everyone that can stoop to flatter him and inimical to all that dare tell him disagreeable Truths." In this instance, his lordship had displayed all the savvy of one who attempts to extinguish a blaze by dousing it with gasoline. The Hillsborough Letter, as the secretary's directive was known, was thought by most colonists to be arrogant and threatening. In the minds of many, it banished whatever lingering feelings existed that the mother country had merely blundered into its new policy. Some now glimpsed more vividly the outlines of the showdown that loomed between America and Great Britain. If Parliament adhered intransigently to its claim to unlimited authority over the colonies, and the colonies persisted in the belief that there were limits to Parliament's power, a collision could not be avoided. During the Massachusetts assembly debate on the question of repealing its Circular Letter, Otis thundered: "We are asked to rescind. Let Britain rescind her measures, or the colonies are lost to her forever."[41]

The Hillsborough Letter provoked a reaction exactly opposite to what its author intended. No assembly withdrew its endorsement of the Massachusetts Circular Letter. Some that previously had attempted to ignore the gathering storm denounced British taxation in ringing resolves. The Maryland assembly coldly told Hillsborough that "What we shall do . . . is not our present business to communicate to your excellency." Even Maryland's governor informed the secretary that to dissolve the assembly would only make the incumbents wildly popular with the voters.[42] Hillsborough accomplished something else as well. In the spring of 1768, Boston and New York had agreed to once again boycott trade with the mother country if Philadelphia joined in. Philadelphia's merchants demurred for eight long months, but they consented soon after the arrival of the Hillsborough Letter. The embargo commenced immediately in several colonies, and within a year had spread to the Chesapeake colonies and South Carolina.

In that crucial year the colonists' view of their rights and place within the empire took on greater clarity. No polemicist was more important than John Dickinson in bringing that outlook into focus among articulate colonists. The son of a slave-owning tobacco planter and land baron, who owned in excess of 16,000 acres, Dickinson was raised in opulence at Croisadore, a majestic estate on Maryland's eastern shore. When tobacco prices plummeted around 1740, his father simply moved to virgin land that he owned in Delaware, built still another mansion, Poplar Hall, and commenced raising grains. Year after year private tutors were brought to the plantation to teach John, until he was sent to London to study law at the Middle Temple, a practice among colonists even more rare than Samuel Adams's pursuit of an M.A. degree. Dickinson, who remained in England for three years, was one of the few political activists of his day to see the mother country at first hand. He liked some of what he saw, but also ruefully concluded that the English were an intemperate and immoral people, that the Anglican Church was doomed as an influential force, that the political system was hopelessly corrupted, and that the nation was in the hands of diabolical mediocrities.

Dickinson returned to the colonies ten full years before the Townshend Duty crisis erupted. He opened a law practice that flourished immediately, and soon thereafter was elected to the Delaware assembly. He rose rapidly to become speaker of the house. When his father died, and he inherited a vast domain in Pennsylvania, Dickinson won election to the assembly in that province. There, too, he quickly became a force to be reckoned with. Less than three years after his initial election, he led the Proprietary Party against Franklin's and Galloway's seemingly insurmountable hold on the assembly. The following year, in 1765, the Pennsylvania legislature selected him as a delegate to the Stamp Act Congress, where he was a key figure in drafting substantive sections of the resolution that assailed the proposed tax.

John Dickinson.
Painting by Charles Willson Peale.

Yet a young man—he was thirty-five in 1767—Dickinson had come a long way in the decade since he completed his schooling. His rise to prominence owed nothing to his mostly nondescript physical appearance. Slight, and of ordinary stature, Dickinson exhibited the soft and pallid features of an office worker and the genteel, somewhat stuffy air of a confident man at ease with himself. Although he would have been out of his element conversing with laborers and artisans in their haunts near the Delaware River docks in Philadelphia, Dickinson impressed the city's lawyers, merchants, and politicos with his keen intellect and rea-soned arguments. His polish and urbanity, as well as his unthreatening manner, won over many who would remain his warm and loyal friend. Furthermore, Dickinson possessed talents with a pen that few could match.

In 1765 he had published an essay attacking the Stamp Act in which he said little of American rights. He had preferred to argue instead that imperial taxes would result in economic adversity for the colonists, es-pecially for the very poor, and he sagely remarked that London was teach-ing America to think of its interests as different from those of the mother country. He also was one of the first to divine what lay behind British policy and to include the word "independence" in a published essay. Al-luding to the ministry's hope to prevent America's drift toward inde-pendence by tightening its control over the colonies, he had written: "Evils are frequently precipitated by imprudent attempts to prevent them. In short, we never can be made an independent people except by Great Britain herself; and the only way for her to do it is to make us frugal, ingenious, united, and discontented." He added that "many states and kingdoms have lost their dominions by severity [but] . . . I remember none that have been lost by kindness."[43]

In his writings against the Townshend Duties three years later, Dickinson—doubtless because of the Declaratory Act—grounded his arguments on a constitutional edifice as never before. He homed in on the limits of Parliament's power. His principal effort, *Letters from a Farmer in Pennsylvania*, which first appeared in a dozen installments in a Phila-delphia newspaper between December 1767 and February 1768, was ulti-mately printed in twenty-one of the twenty-five colonial newspapers. Finally, the separate essays were gathered and issued in a pamphlet that outsold every other political tract published in America before 1776. Letter after letter throbbed with the message that Parliament did not have the authority to tax America, as it was not—and could not be—represented in the distant House of Commons. During the Stamp crisis, some such as Dulany and Franklin had maintained that Parliament could levy cer-tain kinds of taxes on the colonies, including what today would be called a sales tax, as Townshend himself remarked in prefacing his legislation. Dickinson challenged that view, asserting a "total denial of the power of parliament to lay upon these colonies any 'tax' whatever." If, he added, Parliament succeeded in "tak[ing] money out of our pockets, without our consent, . . . our boasted liberty is but a sound and nothing else." In the wake of the "Farmer," the presumed distinction drawn between vari-ous kinds of taxes was no longer an issue.[44]

Dickinson said something else as well. A public official in a mercantile province with deep, salubrious commercial ties to the parent state, Dickinson emphasized America's trade connections with Great Britain and Parliament's legitimate authoritativeness in the governance of that traffic. Parliament, the "Farmer" wrote, unquestionably possessed a legal authority "to *regulate* the trade of Great Britain, and her colonies." Dickinson, for all his presumed radicalism, had staked out a moderate position in the popular protest. He believed, as did the powerful merchandising and mercantile forces within his home base, that Pennsylvania's growth and prosperity hinged on the benefits that Philadelphia's merchants derived from the imperial connection. London's regulation of American trade, he insisted, was "essential . . . and necessary for the common good of all," and above all the linkage to Great Britain afforded Philadelphia's traders with customary and sound markets and the protective shield of the world's mightiest navy.[45]

The year 1768, the season of Hillsborough's folly, was packed with other fractious events that changed the outlook of many colonists. The year had hardly begun before the imbecility of placing the Board of Customs in Boston became all too evident. The Board began to enforce the age-old imperial trade laws, a rare occurrence in this city. Before the first spring flowers bloomed, Governor Bernard reported that the inhabitants of the city were uttering bellicose comments about British trade policies, something that had not been an issue during the Stamp crisis, and in fact had barely been an issue in Massachusetts for seventy-five years. In June, at the very moment the governor complied with Hillsborough's order and dissolved the assembly, the Board seized the *Liberty*, a sloop owned by John Hancock, and charged the owner with smuggling wine from Madeira. Mobs emptied into the streets for the first time since the homes of Oliver and Hutchinson had been pillaged three years earlier. Some customs officials were chased through the streets by an angry mob and barely escaped with their lives. Their residences were not as fortunate in the face of angry crowds. The Boston town meeting, which had acted so pusillanimously when confronted with news of the Townshend Duties the year before, appeared to draw sustenance from the crowd actions. It denounced the Board of Customs as additional evidence of Parliament's wish to reduce the colonists to slavery.[46]

The mood in Boston was tense throughout that summer as rumors flew that the British army had been ordered to the city to enforce Britain's objectionable policies. This tattle was not new. Since the days of the Stamp Act, Boston's newspapers had reported that the troops were coming, but this time the stories were correct. In mid-September Governor Bernard revealed that two British regiments soon would be posted in Boston, although he denied that the redcoats were being sent to enforce the imperial laws. No one believed him.

Some radicals talked openly of resisting the landing of the regulars. Samuel Adams, who was beside himself with fury at what he regarded as an armed invasion of his homeland, talked wildly of raising an army of 30,000 militiamen to prevent the army's disembarkation. Some observers remembered hearing him say: "If you are Men behave like Men; let us take up arms immediately and be free and seize all the King's officers." Near the time the troops were scheduled to arrive, Adams published an essay in which he told his readers that the governor had lied. The army was sent to Boston to enforce an "unconstitutional act." First the provincial assembly had been dissolved, he wrote. Next "placemen and their underlings" on the Board of Customs had been unloosed to "swarm about them," wrecking the Massachusetts economy. Finally, the last of the colonists' liberties was "threatened with military troops." Resist the king's blackguard legion, he exhorted, "or become poor deluded miserable ductile Dupes, fitted to be made the slaves of dirty tools of arbitrary power."[47]

But Massachusetts was not ready to fight. Scores of towns sent delegates to a convention held at Faneuil Hall in Boston late in September to consider the province's options. The moderates were in control. They understood that armed resistance was folly in the absence of at least regional—and preferably national—unity. The convention merely passed the customary resolutions, and the redcoats landed unopposed on October 1.

Nevertheless, the entire affair played into the hands of Boston's radicals. The governor's dishonesty about the reason for the presence of troops not only undermined his credibility but contributed to the growing impression of habitual deceit among British officials. Furthermore, daily reminders of the ubiquity of British soldiers on the streets of Boston proved to be a propaganda bonanza for the foes of the British policies. Samuel Adams was in his element. He and his acolytes churned out a steady diet of newspaper essays that roused the citizenry to a fever pitch. The army had hardly disembarked before Adams published an essay cautioning that private property might be seized for use as quarters for the soldiery. Later he warned of the inherent danger of an army. Put arms in the hands of any man, he said, and that individual soon will see himself as master and the people as subjects. He thought it illegal for an army to exist in peacetime. He expressed outrage when soldiers looking for deserters stopped and searched the carriages of civilians. He claimed that soldiers sought to intimidate those who attended town meetings. The troops, he added, were causing disorder, rather than preventing it.[48]

Meanwhile, radical activists also published the *Journal of the Times*, accounts in newspaper form of Boston "under military rule." In pieces prepared by Samuel Adams and other adroit propagandists, the *Journal* characterized the arrival of the soldiery as an "invasion" and described the presence of troops as an "occupation" of Boston. It also provided a laconic compendium of real and fictitious—and almost daily—provocations committed by the regulars. One commonplace allegation was that the profligate behavior of the soldiers had a deleterious impact on the city's impressionable youth. One yarn after another purportedly documented instances of plunder committed by the truculent "lobsterbacks," as Bostonians referred to the soldiery, and it suggested that the British regulars had been sent for the express purpose of carrying out a massacre. Once blood was spilled, this theory ran, an insurrection would ensue, providing the pretext the ministry required for suppressing American dissent by force.[49]

Scribblers in Boston's newspapers simultaneously sought to demonstrate that evidence was growing of British despotism. Customs agents, they asserted, had been sent to pilfer the profits of what should have been the province's legitimate commerce. In a series of essays, Samuel Adams portrayed these royal officials as parasites sent by the "*whore of Babylon*" to gorge on the "*golden* Calf." But the radicals did not ignore the army. Adams, and others, wrote at length about the danger of a standing army, the tool of tyrants throughout history. Adams contended that the two British regiments had been sent by those who exercised "arbitrary power" to break the "spirits of people as yet unsubdued by tyranny."[50] The pieces of a jigsaw puzzle were coming together, the essayists seemed to say. It was a crucial turning point in the Anglo-American crisis, the moment when many, like a despairing Boston parson, came to believe that they never again would witness "harmony between Great Britain and her colonies." Adding that "all confidence is at an end," the pastor predicted that "the moment there is any blood shed all affection will cease."[51]

By early 1770 passions ran at a white hot pitch in Boston. Tempers were strained further by an imprudent decision on the part of the commander of the soldiery. He permitted his men to take part-time employment as laborers. As jobs were lost to the moonlighting redcoats, the atmosphere turned even uglier. Fistfights between soldiers and local toughs were commonplace, and on occasion unwary soldiers who strayed into the wrong neighborhood were mugged. At this very moment, moreover, Boston's nonimportation agreement sprang more leaks than a sieve.

Merchants, whose first loyalty was to earning profits, had begun to traffic in merchandise from the mother country. Every businessman who broke the boycott was an example, and a temptation, to others who contemplated following suit. The danger was great that Boston's embargo might come unraveled. The threat was very real, too, that if the protest fizzled after coming this far, it might never again be revived. The radical leadership, which had struggled in 1765 and 1767 to rouse and shape protests, now fought to keep alive the popular movement and was willing to use force to achieve its ends. It summoned protestors to the streets. Beginning late in February, mobs attacked homes designated by placards that read simply "IMPORTER," distinguishing the residence as the domicile of one who was busting the boycott. Demonstrators smeared the houses with filth, broke windows, and shouted threats at the terrified occupants.

In this boiling caldron, some tragic event was virtually inevitable. The sort of incident that many had long expected—and which some welcomed, and a few may have deliberately provoked—at last occurred on March 5, 1770. John Adams ever after called the incident "the murder in King Street." Most referred to it as the Boston Massacre. It did not come out of the blue. That bitterly cold Monday evening had been preceded by three especially tense days. On Friday, a bloody brawl between dozens of workers and up to forty off-duty soldiers, who were looking for work, had occurred at John Gray's ropewalk. The employer ultimately called off his workers, and British officers got control of their men. However, that night, and throughout Saturday and Sunday, rumors coursed through the city, and especially in working-class taverns and neighborhoods, as well as in the army's barracks, that the fight was to recommence. Soldiers, in clusters of ten or twelve, roamed the streets, as did little knots of workers, some carrying cudgels, even cutlasses. A few found what they were looking for. Fights were commonplace that weekend, and some combatants were severely beaten.

Monday was calm throughout the daylight hours. But a restless suspense and enmity gripped both sides, fueled in part by untrue rumors that a brawler or two had been killed in the weekend skirmishes. That evening, soon after dark, an incident occurred between a soldier and a young apprentice on a Boston sidewalk. The soldier cuffed a barber's apprentice who attempted to collect an overdue bill. The soldier, in turn, was harassed by a small crowd of outraged Bostonians.[52] Word of trouble spread quickly, and men on both sides took to the streets. An alarm bell in downtown Boston sounded just before 8:00 P.M. Would-be brawlers, who had been looking for action along the docks and in the Commons, hurried to the center of the city, but so too did many residents who believed the alert had been sounded as the summons to fight a fire. Along the way, some rowdies encountered soldiers and fell to fighting. Incidents appear to have occurred at several locations on the periphery of downtown. Some who were caught up in these free-for-alls likely never made it to King Street.

Others did, however. Within minutes of the sounding of the alarm, hundreds had descended on Brattle Square Church, the site of the pealing bell. Quickly discovering that there was no fire, the crowd pushed toward nearby King Street, where the Main Guard, Boston's military headquarters, stood. Many must have begun to suspect that the warning signal was somehow connected to the troubles of the previous seventy-two hours, a logical deduction as ugly reports swirled that some Bostonians had been attacked by soldiers earlier in the evening. But all was quiet at the Main Guard. Suddenly, more alarm bells rang. These were further down King Street, in the vicinity of the Custom House. The crowd surged in that direction. It was not clear, then or later, who was ringing the bells, but people were being lured inexorably to the Custom House.

The Boston Massacre. Engraving (detail) by Paul Revere, 1770.

By 8 o'clock or so, a crowd of at least 300, and perhaps as many as 400, had gathered on the hard packed snow before the Custom House. Through the feeble light, a small—very small—squad of regulars was visible, having been dispatched to guard the building. All the pent-up tension generated by the army's fifteen-months presence in Boston, the fiery rhetoric and hyperbole of the agitation against the Townshend Duties, and the brawling and head-breaking that had ensued during the past few days and nights, burst forth in this spectral setting. Amid the flickering shadows of torches, hotheads in the crowd, egged on by the festival exhilaration of the occasion, shouted imprecations at the soldiers and threw rocks, bricks, chunks of ice, and snowballs at them. Some shouted, "Fire, Fire"—not the most prudent thing to scream at badly shaken armed men. This seething mob scene had been under way for only about fifteen minutes when a soldier was knocked down by an object hurled by someone in the crowd. Angry and frightened, and out of control, he rose and immediately fired into the mob. At the startling sound of a musket discharged by a comrade, and perhaps convinced that in the din on this moonlit night they had failed to hear the command to open fire, other soldiers fired as well. None had been ordered to fire. The soldiery had acted spontaneously.

The crowd was momentarily stunned, but after a few seconds some began to push toward the soldiers. Some soldiers fired again, this time in sheer panic, as it must have appeared that otherwise they would be torn limb from limb. The crowd stopped again, and before it could recoup and advance once more on the red clad soldiery, the British captain in charge repeatedly shouted at the top of his lungs: "Do not fire! Do not fire!" That did it. No soldier fired again. Moreover, the crowd, now aware that some of its members had been shot, and seemingly realizing that someone at last was in charge, stopped in its tracks. The Boston Massacre was over, and sufficient order prevailed for the captain to march his men back to the Main Guard without further incident. Behind them, on the bloody, trodden slush, lay five dead, or dying, and several wounded.[53]

Many on the British side believed these events had not occurred by happenstance. General Gage sifted through the reports of the incident and concluded that the bloody engagement had been "contrived by one party," the radical leadership in Boston.[54] Hutchinson agreed that "wicked and designing men" among the radicals had plotted the tragedy.[55] Even some colonists who were sympathetic toward the popular movement concurred. John Adams privately reflected this had been "an explosion which had been intensively wrought up by designing men who knew what they were aiming at."[56] Some historians, mostly British scholars, yet believe that this was not "a spontaneous incident. The sequence of events on 5 March points to premeditation," the historian Peter D. G. Thomas has written. Few American historians have concurred, and most would probably agree with Robert Middlekauff, who concluded that the Boston Massacre was "not . . . the result of a plot or plan on either side, but rather the consequences of deep hatreds and bad luck."[57]

It would be ludicrous to suggest that the precise events of that cold March evening had been prearranged. No radical activist could have known beforehand how either a mob or a squad of British soldiers would behave. However, the circumstantial evidence suggests that much that ensued in the combustible atmosphere that existed after Friday's spontaneous melee at the ropewalk was not entirely without orchestration. The Boston Massacre was the latest in a series of violent occurrences that had begun thirty days earlier in the carefully planned assaults on those who transgressed the embargo. On the night of the shooting, the unprecedented ringing of alarm bells to summon a crowd into the presence of armed British troops is difficult to explain as an unpremeditated occurrence. So too was the revelation, brought out at the subsequent trials of the soldiery, that early on the evening of the shooting a mysterious individual in obvious disguise—he was wearing a white wig and a red cloak—hurried about the waterfront seeking to whip up passions against the army and exhorted off-duty workers to scurry downtown in search of redcoats. The radical press long had spoken of the likelihood of bloodshed, and at times it appeared anxious that it occur. When it did occur, eighteen months after the British army arrived, it came at a moment when the radical leadership, despairing at the threatened collapse of the boycott, was desperate to keep the resistance alive.[58]

While the culpability of the radicals is open to question, it is beyond doubt that they effectively utilized the bloodshed of that tragic evening. They now had another date to commemorate annually, this with solemn services and speeches that painted a vivid picture of British villainy. Furthermore, in the first weeks following the shooting, Samuel Adams and others produced a record number of newspaper essays about the incident that aimed to sustain the inflammatory mood within the city. Nor was the outrage confined to Boston, and the anger it provoked should have been especially troubling to London, for word of the bloodshed on Boston's soiled snow contributed to the slow and fatal erosion of good will toward the mother country. For many colonists, learning of the tragedy just about five years to the day after they had first heard of the Stamp Act, the Boston Massacre confirmed what the radicals had said repeatedly: The mother country was conspiring to destroy liberty in the colonies.[59]

Outside New England, New York came closest to experiencing substantive political change as a result of the events after the autumn of 1768. The conservative Livingston faction, which had slighted the Massachusetts Circular Letter and appropriated funds for sustaining the British army, was swept from power in the election of 1769. Telling change also occurred in Pennsylvania. Despite its indifference to the Stamp Act, the Assembly Party not only had maintained its control of the legislature in 1765, but soon after the tempest in Philadelphia, Galloway had been elected Speaker of the House. It was hardly surprisingly, therefore, that Galloway and his party failed to grasp the danger they faced when word of the Townshend Duties arrived. Continuing to adhere to the quest for royalization, the Assembly Party immediately took essentially the same stance it had taken two years before: Pennsylvanians should shoulder a portion of the empire's economic burden, Parliament's taxes would be slight, and if they proved to be onerous, London would happily accede to the province's "dutiful remonstrance" to reduce the level of taxation. Once again, too, Galloway and his party sought to block Philadelphia's participation in a trade embargo. In numerous published essays, Galloway maintained that a trade boycott was a deception perpetrated by New England to steal away Philadelphia's commerce.

For a time the ruling party's strategy worked. In the spring of 1768, the Pennsylvania assembly refused to assent to the Massachusetts Circular Letter, the only provincial legislature to ignore the pleas of its brethren to act in concert. As late as that autumn, moreover, Galloway, confident that his actions would win points in London and aid his antiproprietary campaign, boasted to Franklin of his success in thwarting those who sought a nonimportation agreement. Pennsylvania's "Dutiful Behaviour during these Times of American Confusion," he flattered himself, had won copious friends in London.[60] Through the first eighteen months of the Townshend Duty crisis, Galloway succeeded because Philadelphia's mercantile interests were powerful and conservative and heavily overrepresented in the assembly. Although Philadelphia and Pennsylvania's three eastern counties included only about half the province's population, they controlled nearly two-thirds of the seats in the assembly. This region, home to pacifist Quakers, affluent farmers who did not want the boat rocked, and merchants who were desperate to maintain economic ties with the mother country, sought a resolution of the imperial troubles with the least upheaval.

Pennsylvania might not have moved off this course during this episode had it not been for Lord Hillsborough's clumsy intrusion. His letter threatening dissolution of the Pennsylvania assembly was like a body blow to Galloway and his party's forlorn campaign to extirpate proprietary rule. Many who had believed that royal government would be benign, or had so viscerally hated proprietary rule that they were willing to see it replaced by a royal regime, now had second thoughts. The opposition party—the Dickinson-led Proprietary Party—saw its opening and seized the moment. It organized massive protests against the Townshend Duties and easily succeeded in branding their domestic adversaries as craven toadies of corrupted and dangerous royal officials. Galloway was painted into a corner, or to be more accurate, he had positioned himself in that corner. He no longer was capable of preventing the assembly from endorsing the Massachusetts Circular Letter, nor of sending a remonstrance to London, nor of stanching the boycott movement. Soon after Philadelphia learned of the Hillsborough Letter, it joined with Boston and New York in an embargo of British imports. In addition, in the aftermath of Hillsborough's misguided act, Pennsylvania experienced a political realignment, much as had Massachusetts and Virginia three years earlier. While the Proprietary Party won acclaim as the fervent defenders of American rights, the Assembly Party suffered heavy losses in its urban working-class base. Because of the misapportionment of representation in the assembly, Galloway's party retained control of the legislature, and he remained its Speaker. However, when Galloway stood for reelection after 1770, he was compelled to switch from his customary district in Philadelphia to a district north of the city that had always been rock-ribbed Assembly Party territory. Even there, he just scraped by in several elections in the early 1770s. In contrast, Dickinson was swept back into office for the first time in years.[61]

If Galloway's political future was clouded, his partner, Franklin, demonstrated far greater acumen, flexibility, and resiliency. Franklin had some advantages over Galloway. Living in London, he was much better informed about Britain's intentions and the prospects for success for the antiproprietary campaign. At the very outset of 1768, before any American protests had occurred, Franklin concluded that "a new kind of loyalty seems to be required of us, a loyalty to P[arliamen]t; a loyalty, that is to extend, it is said, to a surrender of all our properties, whenever a H[ouse] of C[ommons] . . . should think fit to grant them away without our consent." He added that "this unhappy new system of politics tends to dissolve those bands of union, and to sever us for ever." It would be years before many Americans, including Galloway, understood things so clearly. But then few were as savvy as Franklin. Indeed, even though he was in London, Franklin had a better grasp of American opinion than did Galloway. Franklin's brush with political disaster during the Stamp Act crisis, occasioned by being out of touch with viewpoints in his homeland, gave him an added incentive to keep his finger on the pulse of his fellow countrymen. He corresponded with numerous Philadelphians, probably a greater cross-section of influential residents of the city than Galloway ordinarily consulted. Franklin additionally heard from others throughout the colonies, including the Massachusetts assembly's Committee of Correspondence. What he had learned by 1770 from the radicals in Boston convinced him that Britain's enforcement of its imperial trade laws augured "a total disunion of the two countries."[62]

Galloway suffered one further disadvantage. Franklin did not divulge to him all that he knew. In mid-summer 1768 Hillsborough told Franklin straight out that the royalization of Pennsylvania was a dead letter. Franklin informed Galloway of the Secretary of State's comments, but misleadingly intimated that more favorable conditions would prevail when the existing ministry fell, which would occur shortly, he reported. Franklin continued to pass along unduly optimistic appraisals of the situation in London. He led Galloway to believe that a "Party is now growing in our Favour." Six months later he reported that "our Friends are evidently increasing." He reported to Galloway that a move was afoot in London to revise all trade laws that the colonists found objectionable, tattle that no informed observer in London should have taken seriously. Franklin also informed Galloway that Lord North, who became the prime minister in 1770, "had such a Regard for Pensilvania, which had behav'd so well in all the late Disturbances in America," that he would not "vote for rejecting any Petition from that Province." Franklin's disturbing behavior remains puzzling, but it is difficult to escape the conclusion that his enmity for the proprietors, coupled with his gnawing ambition, was such that he remained eager to keep alive the ailing antiproprietary movement, whatever the cost. What is clearer is that in 1769–70, and for years thereafter, Galloway believed that the breach between the colonies and parent state could be repaired and that his personal ambitions could yet be realized by overturning proprietary rule.[63]

While Galloway reached that conclusion, Franklin—convinced both by the unrest in the colonies in 1768 and the line laid down by Lord Hillsborough—gleaned that this was a deeper crisis than he had previously imagined. He renewed his earlier initiative of refashioning his image in America. Above all, he no longer wished to be seen as cozy with ministerial officials. Never a proponent of a trade boycott during the Stamp Act protest, Franklin by 1769 openly sympathized with the nonimportation movement, and he told everyone who would listen, including Galloway, of his support of the embargo. Aside from war, he said, nonimportation was the only available means for securing redress and the only way to convince Great Britain that the current ministry was unworthy "to hold the Reins in governing America." He also loudly denounced Britain's attempt to use new taxes to pay the salaries of the royal governors and judges in America. For one who had come into politics relatively late in life,

Franklin exhibited a deft feel for the game. Long before Galloway discerned that new political winds were blowing in Philadelphia, Franklin not only realized that the city's tradesmen were shifting allegiance, but that the rival Presbyterian Party had begun to attract the ambitious, enterprising, younger men who soon would be in the vanguard of the American Revolution in Pennsylvania. He sought to patch up his relationship with those political adversaries at home who appeared to be ascendant. He opened a correspondence with men such as Charles Thomson and Thomas Mifflin, who in a few short years would be the secretary of the Continental Congress and a general officer in the Continental army, respectively. Furthermore, he arranged for the publication in London of Dickinson's *Letters from a Farmer in Pennsylvania* and even wrote a preface for the edition.[64]

Franklin was not alone in being changed by these dramatic, vertiginous events. A significant alteration also occurred in the outlook of Colonel George Washington, who first emerged as an important political leader in the course of the Townshend Duty crisis. Washington had been revered as a soldier in Virginia since the French and Indian War. During the war, in fact, he had been elected for the first time to the House of Burgesses, and thereafter he was reelected annually. Yet before 1769 Washington had been a backbencher, an individual who truly was a fish out of water in a legislative chamber. With little formal education, Washington felt awkward in the presence of college graduates and especially uncomfortable with the numerous attorneys who were his colleagues in the Burgesses. Unpracticed in public speaking, he was reticent to declaim before an audience of men whose livelihoods depended on their rhetorical and debating prowess in Virginia's courtrooms. Jefferson, who sat in the Burgesses with him for nearly seven years, characterized Washington as one who learned to write in a ready, "easy and correct style," but who, as a conversationalist, or an orator, was "not above mediocrity, possessing neither copiousness of ideas, nor fluency of words." When "called on for a sudden opinion," Jefferson added, Washington was habitually "unready, short and embarrassed." He appeared to be a man of action, not contemplation, and during the initial decade or more that he sat in the Virginia assembly he neither introduced any significant legislation nor was given an important committee assignment.[65]

However, Washington seldom missed an assembly session. He made the long trek from Mount Vernon to Williamsburg each spring and fall, and quietly, but scrupulously, attended most of the daily meetings of the Burgesses. In his spare time, he shopped, dined in the company of other assemblymen, attended festive balls, and frequently relaxed at the country home of the royal governor. But he saw to it that his legislative responsibilities did not interfere with more serious business, and on occasion he did not remain in town for the entire session. In 1765 Washington had departed by the time Henry delivered his electrifying speech on the Stamp Act and, according to his diary, while the assembly passed the Virginia Resolves, he was at Mount Vernon where he "Sowed Turnips. . . . [P]ut some Hemp in the Rivr. to Rot. . . . Seperated my Ewes & Rams. . . . [and] Finish'd Sowing Wheat."⁶⁶ Three years later, when the assembly responded to the Hillsborough Letter, Washington once again was absent. However, his behavior changed in 1769.

Early that year Washington wrote a remarkable letter to his neighbor, George Mason, an influential assemblymen, that indicated he had undergone a political transformation. Two threads ran through Washington's missive. Like a growing number of disillusioned colonists, he had come to see British policy as a deliberate, concerted attack on American liberty. In addition, in strident language Washington expressed disgust with his second-class status as a provincial.

Rich and powerful as he was, Washington could exert no authority over many things that truly mattered to him. Too many crucial issues were decided in London, where the interests of residents of the mother country outweighed those of provincials. On substantive matters, the colonists too often were treated as dependents who were meant to serve the parent state, not compete with it. Colonel Washington, who had clawed his way to the top of Virginia's society through enormous sacrifice and risk, bridled at the thought of being considered second-rate by anyone. It had galled him during the late war that, although a colonel in a colonial army, he had been outranked by every officer who held a royal commission, even the most callow and lowly redcoat lieutenant. That outrage, however, was trifling in contrast to what he faced by the late 1760s.

George Washington. Oil on canvas by Charles Willson Peale, 1787.

During the war Virginia had promised bounty lands to those who soldiered, and following the peace there was considerable talk of setting aside approximately 200,000 acres near present-day Charleston, West

Virginia, for veterans. Washington knew that when that land was finally allocated, he stood to be virtually unrivaled within Virginia as a land baron. He already owned considerable land in the West through his investments in the Ohio Company and steady speculation in frontier lands, which he first had entered into during his days as an adolescent surveyor. The pending award of plentiful bounty lands enabled Washington to dream of the prospect of someday possessing clear title to perhaps as much as 60,000 acres in what is now Pennsylvania, Ohio, Kentucky, western Virginia, and West Virginia. However, toward the late 1760s, Colonel Washington had begun to wonder if he would ever turn a profit from his western domain. First, the Proclamation of 1763 had slowed the western advance of Virginia's land-hungry citizenry to a snail's pace. Washington had initially been unconcerned and treated the edict as a temporary inconvenience. But after five years it no longer appeared to be so temporary. He and other speculators had grown dismayed. One or two had sailed to London to plead for opening the West, and some, such as Richard Henry Lee and his brother, who together with Washington had invested in the Mississippi Land Company, had concluded that the ministry was driven by an anti-American bias.

Nor was that all. In 1768, royal officials negotiated a treaty with the Cherokee Indians that permitted the Native Americans to retain possession of lands in present-day Kentucky claimed by Washington, Jefferson, and scores of other speculators. At war's end, Washington had hoped and believed that the imperial authorities soon would create a new colony there. He believed that colonial rule would hasten the establishment of order within the bounds of the new colony, which in turn would attract settlers and result in a steady escalation in frontier land prices. A colony would serve his interests perfectly. By the late 1760s, however, it was clear that the creation of a colony would not serve the ministry's interests. Opening a new colony, London feared, would trigger a costly western war. Powerful figures in England, including Secretary Hillsborough, who owned vast tracts of rental property in Ireland, also feared that a new province in the Ohio Country would drain off their tenants. Virginia's land speculators were increasingly frustrated and bitter, and none more so than Washington. He looked upon the Ohio Country as a domain won by the blood and toil of the army he had commanded and by years of personal sacrifice on his part. Yet he and his countrymen were prevented by London from opening the area. Colonel Washington's frustration mounted during 1768, and to it was added a growing anxiety. Disturbing whispers circulated in Williamsburg that year about Virginia's authority to dispense the bounty lands. London, it was said, might void the dispensation. If that scuttlebutt proved true, Washington might never obtain the lands he had been promised for his military service. Every aspect of Washington's western dreams were in the hands of faraway royal officials, with whom he had no leverage, and his letter to George Mason early in 1769 dripped with malice: "At a time when our lordly Masters in Great Britain will be satisfied with nothing less than the deprication [*sic*] of American freedom, it seems highly necessary that some thing shou'd be done to avert the stroke and maintain the liberty we have derived from our Ancestors."[67]

Washington and many other Virginia planters and speculators were equally troubled by British trade laws. Their concerns antedated the ministry's new colonial policy by a quarter century. After tobacco prices plunged around 1740—the decline that induced Dickinson's father to take up grain production—the House of Burgesses petitioned Parliament to repeal its legislation that mandated the shipment of American tobacco only to English markets. A free trade policy would permit world markets to set the price of tobacco and could not but elevate the profits of Virginia's planters. At about the same moment that Washington wrote to Mason in 1769, Richard Henry Lee published an essay that predicted doom for Chesapeake tobacco planters unless London sanctioned free trade. London refused to budge. Nor was London's restriction on the American tobacco traffic its only restraint on the province's economy. The Currency Act, one of the first of the new colonial policies, restricted the emission of paper money. Earlier, Parliament had prohibited the manufacture of certain types of iron and forbidden the production of finished woolen products. The most powerful residents of the colony were, without a doubt, severely affected by one or more of these inhibiting acts. One caused a money shortage, exacerbating the dilemma of planters on the cusp of indebtedness, perhaps even insolvency. The others constituted a roadblock in the path of straitened planters who were searching for an alternative to growing tobacco. Some in Virginia had begun to carp, and the more farsighted, such as Mason, feared that "Some Bungler in politics" in London would further restrict American manufacturing. It was a concern shared by Washington, who had put many of his chattel to work making textiles.[68]

Washington spoke to Mason in 1769 of arming against British tyranny. He, like some other activists, had begun to contemplate moving from remonstrating to the use of force to achieve greater, provincial autonomy. He was coming to understood that his ends could be realized only by gaining independence from Great Britain. Talk of taking up arms was in the air. Six months before Washington broached the idea, Samuel Adams had spoken of armed resistance to prevent the landing of British troops in Boston. A few months later, Dickinson told his readers that

"English history affords examples of resistance by force."[69] He also wrote a "Liberty Song," which was belted out at Sons of Liberty conclaves and other gatherings:

> Our worthy Forefathers . . .
> For freedom they came,
> And dying bequeath'd us their Freedom and Fame.
> In freedom we're born and in freedom we'll live
> Come join hand in hand brave Americans all,
> And rouse your bold hearts at fair Liberty's call,
>
> No tyrannous act shall suppress your just claim.
> Or stain with dishonour America's name,
> In Freedom we're born and in Freedom we'll live,
> We'll keep what they gave, we will piously keep.[70]

Washington told Mason that he believed the time for remonstrances had passed, but added that the day for fighting had not yet arrived. Instead, he spoke of Virginia joining the other colonies that had already instituted nonimportation agreements. Washington, Mason, and Richard Henry Lee soon met and prepared a trade embargo measure for submission to the Virginia assembly. When it was adopted later that year, Washington—for the first time in a dozen years as an assemblyman—had played a crucial role in the enactment of seminal legislation.[71]

Barring an accident, the first shot in a war with Great Britain would have to be fired by the parent state. Most Americans understood, as Franklin soon put it, that "a premature struggle" would only mean that America would "be crippled and kept down another age." However, Great Britain was not ready to use force to bring the colonies to heel. Although by 1769 public opinion throughout England was "in full cry against America," as Franklin reported from London, the ministry shrank from coercion. Distracted by numerous problems, including the possibility of hostilities with Spain, the ministry was almost eager to back down by the end of 1769. Imperial officials wanted time to discover the correct formula for the peaceful preservation of British sovereignty. They were genuinely frightened by the "dangerous combinations" that their policies had spawned across the ocean. They were mortified, too, by the impact of the colonists' trade embargo. Exports to the colonies throughout 1769 were only about half those of the previous year, and total British exports sagged by an alarming 10 percent. In March 1770, the British government capitulated once again. All but the tax on tea was repealed—Franklin indicated to Galloway that the inside gossip suggested it, too, might be rescinded within six months—and the Quartering Act was modified to appease the protestors in America.[72]

The crisis was over. Indeed, many colonials believed the Anglo-American crisis was at an end for all time. Radicals struggled briefly to keep alive the crippled boycott in order to secure the repeal of the tea tax, but they swam upstream. The nonimportation agreements had always been tenuous. Virginia and Maryland, for instance, loudly brandished the effectiveness of their boycotts in 1770, but in actuality the value of imports to those colonies actually rose during the first year of their boycotts. Other colonies did a better job, good enough in fact that by mid-1770 many of their inhabitants were tired of doing without British commodities. As soon as word reached America of the partial repeal of the Townshend Duties, the boycott movement collapsed. Newport was the first large urban center to abandon the embargo. Its action was akin to pushing over a row of dominoes. Backcountry towns throughout New England immediately cut their ties to the nonimportation agreements, and Baltimore, New York, and Philadelphia soon joined the parade. However, Virginia and Massachusetts, and a few other provinces, continued to boycott British tea, the lone item still on any exclusion list.[73]

The Townshend Duty crisis had ended. Yet despite the wishful thinking that Anglo-American troubles were a thing of the past, imperial tensions could not be laid to rest until an accommodation was reached on the question of political sovereignty. Exasperation and bitterness prevailed in London. Taxation had failed to raise revenue. Neither the imposition of troops nor threats to dissolve colonial assemblies had proven efficacious in the quest to secure additional revenue from America. The imperial leaders shrank from widening the conflict, as would occur if they attempted constitutional reform or prosecuted the most visible ringleaders in the colonial protest. Yet at the same moment they feared that leniency would be construed as irresolution, and retreat as weakness, if not cowardice. Britain's leadership was in a box, afraid to go forward, unwilling to turn back. By 1770, after five years of agitation, majority opinion in the colonies rejected Parliament's claim to the right of taxation over America. Informed colonists knew, as Franklin remarked, that the day was certain to arrive when the issue would be drawn between whether "Parliament has a power to make *all laws* for us, or that it has a power to make *no laws* for us."[74] When that day arrived, there would be no easy and, in all likelihood, no peaceful answer to that disquieting query.

4

1770–1774

"The Cause of Boston Now Is the Cause of America"

With the repeal of the Townshend Duties, Franklin was optimistic, even though, as he remarked, the "Duty on Tea . . . remains to continue the Dispute." While the majority in the mother country was "zealous for maintaining" its "dignity and sovereignty over the colonies," he said, most also wished "to be on good Terms with us" and merely hoped to preserve "the Dignity of Parliament." As events soon demonstrated, Franklin's optimism was misplaced. The ministry formed in January 1770 under Sir Frederick North—Lord North—was committed to the proposition that there must be no retreat from the premise of Parliamentary sovereignty. Every official feared that if Great Britain lost its political and economic control of the colonies, it would cease to be a great power.[1] The great challenge that faced North's government was to find a means of maintaining British sovereignty without provoking another uprising and perhaps even a war.

Lord North failed. That much was predictable, as his government inherited a well-nigh unsolvable puzzle. He made a good start at accomplishing that which his predecessors had set in motion, although to many it appeared that he was doing next to nothing. A political foe, who ardently wished to see the colonists put in their place, charged that North dreamily hoped the American troubles somehow would "blow over [and] the evil would remove itself."[2] North did indeed hope to avoid a confrontation. Not only were no new taxes promulgated in the first three years of North's ministry, but his government early on rejected Hillsborough's recommendation that the Massachusetts charter be altered, a desperate, draconian gamble to silence the resistance movement. Once rebuffed, even Hillsborough acted with solicitude. When Rhode Island in 1770 set aside a judgment of the Privy Council—an act that today would be akin to a state court invalidating an executive order of the president of the United States—the colonial secretary looked the other way. William Legge, the earl of Dartmouth, who succeeded Hillsborough in 1772, was even more accommodating. He relaxed the restrictions on colonial currency.[3]

But North had not thrown in the towel. He was playing for time. After five tempestuous years, he wanted to let things cool down, to ease the suspicions that had surfaced in America and to unhinge the structure of radical protest that had come together in the two great protests. He knew that revenue was being gathered from the enforcement of the trade laws and the duty on tea. These funds were originally earmarked for paying the salaries of the Royal governors in America. North extended the coverage to include superior court judges. His objective was to transfer control of the executive and judicial branches in the provincial governments from the colonial assemblies to the imperial government. If successful, governors and the highest judges in America would be independent of the colonists in every sense. The power of the Royal government would be dramatically enhanced. Within two years of taking office North had made considerable headway. All the highest officials in Massachusetts were being paid by the Crown by 1772. So, too, were the attorney-general and chief justice in New York and the chief legal officer in New Jersey.[4]

Historians once portrayed these years between 1770 and 1773 as "the lull" or "the quiet period," a time between crises when little of significance happened.[5] This period might better be called the "time of peril," as these were years of optimum danger for the popular movement. Samuel Adams was among the first to see the danger. While the radicals slumbered, content that they had thwarted North's predecessors, Adams realized that the imperial government was quietly, stealthily securing a stranglehold on the provincial assemblies. When John Adams subsequently concluded that Samuel Adams was the most important figure in the American Revolution, his judgment was based in large measure on his cousin's unerring sense of the threat to colonial liberties that lurked within London's designs. In addition, John Adams lauded Samuel's adroitness not merely in keeping alive the somnolent radical spirit in these parlous years, but especially his success in deepening provincial radicalism while most were convinced that the crisis had passed.

Samuel Adams sounded the tocsin in 1771, portraying North's campaign as a covert operation aimed at imposing a "Torrent of Oppression & arbitrary Power" on the backs of the colonists. Because of the subtlety of the ministry's tactics, Adams depicted North's initiative as "more dangerous" than the naked policies that London had pursued before 1770. He argued that a conspiracy existed between those in London, who pursued an agenda of "arbitrary power," and a cabal in America that long had sought "to render ineffectual the Democratical part"—the lower houses of the assemblies—within the colonial governments. This last was a reference to the Hutchinsons and Olivers in the Court Party, who had battled for two generations to stanch objectionable policies, such as soft money expedients. Adams reminded readers of the incident six years earlier when the crowd had pillaged Oliver's home and business. The "People shouted; and their shout was heard to the distant end of the Continent . . . and every Stampman trembled," he reminisced. This crisis, though less easily discerned, was no less real than that posed by the Stamp Act, he insisted. "If . . . we are voluntarily silent," he cautioned, the "tools of administration" will interpret America's silence as acquiescence." In that instance "we are undone" and reduced to "a State of perfect Despotism."[6]

In some respects Adams's campaign to keep alive the flickering American protest was his finest hour. It was far easier to arouse opinion against a bold threat than a hidden danger. In the thirty months or so after the repeal of the Townshend Duties, Adams, together with other radicals in Massachusetts, labored tirelessly to unmask North's shrewd campaign, deftly staging commemorative ceremonies on the anniversaries of the attack on Oliver and the Boston Massacre. On March 5, bells pealed solemnly throughout the day in Boston, illustrations depicting the British soldiers firing into a peaceful crowd were prominently displayed, mock funerals of the victims were conducted, and the day was capped by a quasi-religious service in the Old South Church, in the course of which a speech was delivered by a carefully selected orator known for his eloquence. Each year a capacity crowd of 6,000 assembled to listen. Though a different silver-tongued speaker was chosen each year, the message never varied. The audience was reminded, often in the goriest detail, of what had occurred that awful night when King Street had been bathed in blood. Each speaker, moreover, emphasized Britain's alleged lawlessness and the need to resist ministerial malice.[7]

One of Adams's most brilliant strokes during these years was the creation of a network of committees of correspondence. When he took this step he was not on the offensive, but counterpunching. The idea appears to have germinated, at least in part, in response to how the public outside Boston reacted to the Boston Massacre. To Adams's chagrin, the farm communities in the hinterland beyond Boston had not been especially roiled by the violent occurrences in the capital. Adams was learning a lesson that a future Boston politico—Thomas P. "Tip" O'Neill, Speaker of the United States House of Representatives late in the twentieth century—would characterize as the first maxim of politics: "All politics is local."[8] The concerns of the farmers and artisans in these communities in 1770 were local. Not yet capitalistic in outlook, these yeomen engaged in subsistence, or semi-subsistence, farming, much as their ancestors had done on these same lands for more than a century. They marketed whatever modest excess they produced in order to acquire necessities, not luxury items, and they were largely indifferent to capital accumulation or the economic risk-taking concomitant with profit-seeking farm operations. They were attentive to what affected them directly, such as building bridges, schools, churches, fences, and controlling pests, including wildcats and wolves. So local was their focus, in fact, that throughout most of the colonial past few of these towns thought it worth the expense to send a representative to the annual meeting of the Massachusetts assembly.[9] The hinterland's voice had remained muted throughout the imperial crisis. It had opposed Boston's radicals who had wished to arm and resist the landing of British troops in 1768, and in the aftermath of the Boston Massacre many westerners appeared to be more alarmed by where Boston's radicals wished to lead them than by the actions of a standing army. In the spring of 1770, the view was widespread in the countryside that the Boston Massacre had not been a spontaneous event, and some suspected that Boston's radicals had engineered the bloody occurrence. After most of the soldiers accused in the Massacre were acquitted in jury trials, that sentiment grew so pronounced that at least one western town adopted a statement condemning Boston's radicals as "subversive of government and destructive of the peace and good order which is the cement of society."[10]

Forced onto the defensive, Samuel Adams, writing as "Vindex," churned out essay after essay late in 1770. In these pieces he attempted to convince the farm population that the army had behaved in a "very imprudent and fool-hardy" manner throughout the occupation of Boston. Their conduct presaged, indeed made inevitable, the tragic events of March 5, he argued. Utilizing the testimony of unnamed eyewitnesses, whom he characterized as individuals of "liberal education and an unspotted character," Adams sought to demonstrate that the soldiers were ordered by their commanding officer to fire. The farm folk were correct, he appeared to say, to discern that the Massacre was not an accidental event. The sequence of events that culminated in the shooting in King Street could be traced back to decisions made by Lord Hillsborough. The Massacre was part of a "malevolent and wicked" British plot to destroy "our *old fashioned* Charter." Those who were gunned down by the regulars had been "victims to [the ministry's] rage and cruelty." Without quite saying so, Adams appeared to say that London had carefully planned

the Massacre. More directly, he charged that the soldiers had been acquitted only because biased judges had made mockeries of the trials.[11]

His contrived essays, designed to exculpate the colonists from responsibility for the Massacre, were not terribly convincing. No one knew
that better than Adams himself. However, he was resilient. He quickly
shifted to a different approach. Adams altered his writing style somewhat in 1771, often incorporating an imagery familiar to Bible readers.
The king became Caesar, the royal officials in America his "adulating
priestlings," and the excisemen now were "Swarms of locusts." More sig-
nificantly, he portrayed the colonists' struggle as not unlike that waged
by the Puritan founders of New England. Whereas the Puritans had
fought despotism of Stuart monarchs who allegedly were the disciples
of the pope in Rome, he depicted the popular movement in Massachusetts as grappling with an American-born governor who served his lords
in London. Adams spoke of preserving the righteous and spartan ways
of New England's forebears. His message was an exhortation to virtuous
behavior, and ringing within it was the notion of protecting the esti-
mable character of New England society from the "luxury"—which to
most meant sloth and self-indulgence—that supposedly prevailed in
much of the outside world, including both mercantile Boston and the
corrupt imperial metropolis across the sea. But in talking the language
of those in the countryside, Adams's hope was to strengthen the tie between Boston, the epicenter of the protest in New England, and the wary
husbandmen. To those in the alleys and countinghouses of Boston, he
spoke of the long tentacles of faraway London. To those on remote
backcountry farms, he addressed the social and economic changes that
originated in the distant mother country and that threatened to eradicate the old ancestral values and traditions. It was a masterstroke. Samuel
Adams saw what others had not seen. Both those in the city and the
residents of the backcountry feared the changes with which they were
confronted. Urban merchants and artisans wished to avoid the tighter
commercial regulation sought by London, while rural yeomen feared
the transforming ways of the commercial world. Samuel Adams, the
cosmopolitan Bostonian who had never left his ancestral church, found
the emotional link through which to bind city and farm folk in a viable
protest against the dangers that both beheld emanating from London.[12]

More troubles surfaced for Adams in the midst of this campaign. A
Court Party newspaper in Boston broke the story that the ongoing boycott of British dutied tea was a leaky vessel. Virginia and Maryland had
imported 60 percent more tea in 1771–72 than during the two previous
years. In the two years since the other Townshend Duties had been repealed, nearly 800,000 pounds of tea had entered the colonies, about 40

percent of it imported and sold through Boston.[13] To backcountry farmers, it was evident that the embargo, which had originated in Boston, was not being as scrupulously adhered to in the city as in the countryside. Adams knew that the danger was real that the country folk would feel that they had been duped by city slickers. It was in the midst of this emergency that he moved to establish committees of correspondence that would link patriots in the urban and rural areas. The idea for such committees was not original with Adams; merchants in the largest cities had corresponded when fashioning the initial boycott in the Stamp Act crisis, Sons of Liberty chapters in various colonies had explored concerted action from 1765 onward, and New York's radicals had briefly utilized corresponding societies in 1769. Before 1772 closed Adams had committees of correspondence up and running within Massachusetts, and his confidence was growing that rural and urban inhabitants alike "directed their Views to [the same] great objects."[14] When the Boston committee was created, one of Samuel Adams's associates remarked: "We are brewing something here which will make some people's heads reel." Adams had twin motives. He sought not only to unite opinion in Massachusetts but also to convince London that all of America, not merely Boston, opposed its colonial policies.[15]

Long after the American Revolution, Thomas Jefferson recollected that Virginia had taken the initiative in establishing intercolonial committees of correspondence. He was not entirely accurate. Adams first broached the idea to leading radicals in Virginia in 1771, portraying his brainstorm not entirely candidly as "a sudden thought" that "drops undigested from my pen." To friends in Massachusetts, however, he confided that his was a well-conceived scheme that was designed to "arouse the Continent" and lead to concerted protests by the several colonies. The Virginians adopted the idea and in 1773 the House of Burgesses proposed that the assembly in each provincial assembly create a committee of correspondence. By February 1774 all but Pennsylvania and North Carolina had instituted committees of correspondence.[16]

They were of crucial importance. Like an intelligence gathering agency, the committees in the separate colonies collected and disseminated information on British designs and activities. They also acted as propaganda machines, tirelessly broadcasting the warning that the imperial government plotted to curtail liberty in America. However, because they were official agencies of the colonial assemblies, their messages took on the patina of legitimate instruction. Furthermore, their educational efforts were not entirely propagandistic. The Boston committee, for instance, drafted a statement—which soon thereafter was adopted by a town meeting—that stipulated the rights of the colonists. Composed in 1772, it foreshadowed the language of the Declaration of Independence, asserting that "Among the natural Rights of the Colonies are these: First, a Right to *Life*; Second to *Liberty*; thirdly to *Property*; together with the Right to support and defend them in the best manner they can." It added that the colonists possessed the "*absolute Rights* of Englishmen, and all freemen in or out of Civil Society."[17] To some degree, as the historian Merrill Jensen observed, the committees of correspondence also functioned as a political party, pressuring legislators everywhere to defy Britain's menacing plans.[18] Finally, the committees, as was Adams's original intent, helped overcome the formidable barriers to interaction, those provincial instincts and habits that prevented colonies from marching together against the common threat.

Those today who read the writings of Samuel Adams and Benjamin Franklin in 1771 and 1772 might conclude that the two inhabited different planets. While Adams waxed on at length about Britain's "iron Hand of Tyranny," Franklin portrayed North's ministry as genuinely interested in a peaceful resolution of its American problems. In 1771 Franklin reported that hardliners, such as Hillsborough, were disliked by the majority within North's cabinet. The ministry, he added, hoped "to recover . . . the Good Will of the Colonies." That same year he rejoiced that "the Cloud that threatened our Charter Liberties seems to be blown over," and he informed Galloway that North would not take another step until "Time should have worne off the Ill Humour that prevailed with regard to us" throughout England. Early in 1772 he declared that conditions would improve, as "no further Duties are intended" by North's ministry. Later in the year he portrayed Lord Dartmouth, the colonial secretary, as a friend and totally unlike his malicious predecessor. However, early in 1773 Franklin expressed alarm. Suddenly there was renewed talk of taxing America. He reported, too, that the mood in England had turned ugly, as if the officials were bracing for a colonial backlash. The "tone of publick Conversation . . . has been violently against us," Franklin wrote home. Soon he added that "the breach becomes greater and more alarming."[19]

North's government never planned a showdown in 1773. Its strategy remained, as Franklin correctly reported, to play for time. However, as sometimes happens in history, a peripheral matter brought things to a head. The North ministry knew far better than backcountry farmers that, despite the embargo, a great deal of tea was being consumed in the colonies. It was delighted to be gaining a modest revenue, but it was also troubled by the knowledge that a considerable amount of foreign tea had been smuggled into the provinces during 1771 and 1772. Some believed that as much as 2,500,000 pounds of contraband had annually found its way into the colonists' teapots, perhaps four times the amount of taxed tea that was vended. Officials in the imperial capital reasoned that if the illicit trade could be stopped, and the tea tax collected, Britain would double the amount of revenue it derived from America.[20]

Sooner or later the ministry likely would have found this teapot at the end of the imperial rainbow too tempting to ignore. What propelled it into action in 1773 was the economic adversity that suddenly confronted the mammoth East India Company. Mismanagement had pushed the company to the brink of collapse, a calamity that would imperil the entire English economy, not to mention the investments of numerous members of Parliament. North's government was eager to bail out the nearly bankrupt firm, and one way to do so was to give it a monopoly in the American tea market. Another way was to reduce the tax on tea, cutting the cost of the beverage to a level that no smuggler could match. North chose both courses in the Tea Act, which Parliament passed midway through 1773. North had twin goals. He hoped to save the East India Company and, simultaneously, to garner imperial revenue. By early autumn nearly 600,000 pounds of duties tea was en route to Boston, New York, Philadelphia, and Charleston.

At first glance it appears surprising that any protest could be generated against legislation reducing a tax that many Americans had become habituated to paying. None were more surprised by the colonial dissent than the members of North's government. The resistance arose, in part, because many Americans, especially merchants and retail shopkeepers, bore a vehement antipathy to awarding monopoly rights to any English company. Furthermore, although the tea tax was six years old in 1773, it seemed to many Americans as if Parliament was attempting to impose a new levy. This oddity occurred because Parliament, in order to heighten the sales of the East India Company, had earlier considered repealing the tax on tea altogether. In fact, colonial newspapers in 1772 and 1773 had so often predicted its repeal that many Americans, having come to believe that the demise of the tea tax was a foregone conclusion, were jolted to learn of the Tea Act. But what most accounted for the readiness of many to protest the Tea Act was that in recent years they had grown substantively more radical in their attitudes toward the mother country.

No one avenue led to this metamorphosis. The broadest thoroughfare was a growing conviction that Great Britain was bent on tyranny. No single putatively despotic act had altered the colonists' thinking. Instead, the belief grew from a combination of British acts over a period of several years: attempts to tax the unrepresented colonists, the imposition of what many saw as an army of occupation, the suspension of elected assemblies, London's unwillingness to open the trans-Appalachian frontier, and its sudden zeal for enforcing long neglected commercial regulations. Some were already coming to suspect that this "long train of abuses and usurpations" evinced "a design to reduce them under absolute despotism," as the Declaration of Independence later stated.

Great Britain's new policies also left many in America to contemplate as never before the differences between the interests of their colony and those of the mother country. More and more Americans now wondered whether the vital concerns of the provincials could be served adequately within the imperial framework. This was nowhere more true than in the Chesapeake, which in the troubled years after the French and Indian War faced the shock of twin financial crises. The first, an economic downturn in the 1760s, resulted from a postwar depression. The second, which followed the collapse of great banks in England and Scotland in 1772–73, saw tobacco prices plummet nearly 50 percent. Each trauma led to tightened credit for Virginia and Maryland planters and plunged many who raised tobacco into indebtedness. Debt suits doubled in some Virginia counties, and instances of foreclosure and imprisonment for debt rose dramatically.[21]

Not every Chesapeake planter faced ruin. The brightest, most farsighted, and perhaps the most daring, such as Colonel Washington, diversified their farming operations. As early as 1766, for instance, Washington was growing more wheat than tobacco at Mount Vernon. He escaped debt. But most planters were not as sagacious or as adventurous. For them, it was business as usual. As their debts mounted, increasing numbers of planters blamed their woes on Britain's commercial laws, which compelled them to market their tobacco within Great Britain. Denied a competitive market, they confronted a "powerful engine" that drove them into debt, as Jefferson remarked. The planter faced a downward spiral, he reflected, until

the British merchants . . . got him more immersed in debt than he could pay without selling his land or slaves. They then reduced the prices given for his tobacco so that let his shipments be ever so great, and his demand of necessaries ever so oeconomical, they never permitted him to clear off his debt. These debts had become hereditary from father to son for many generations, so that the planters were a species of property annexed to certain mercantile houses in London.[22]

Some, including Jefferson, believed that Virginia's salvation lay in free trade. If their tobacco could be sold in the world market, the price it would fetch would be higher than in the captive market in England. However, tobacco prices were but one part of their problem, as Jefferson and Washington and many others understood. For instance, planters meeting in Chesterfield County, Virginia, early in the 1770s grumbled about their "dependent commercial connexion" with the mother country. Where once they had basked in the benefits brought by imperial ties, many now felt trapped. Tobacco planting increasingly appeared to be a dead end street. But what alternative existed? Their investments in frontier lands beyond the mountains—which Virginia's army had helped to win—were worthless, because London refused to permit the opening of that domain. Investment in many industrial activities was foreclosed because London inhibited American manufacturing. If planters could sell their growing surplus of slave laborers at a sufficient price, they could at least escape their smothering financial liabilities. But London had disallowed Virginia's recent law aimed at stanching the importation of slaves, an attempt at jiggling supply and demand that would enable desperate planters to vend their chattel at lucrative prices. So long as they remained under British hegemony, many Chesapeake planters were coming to believe, they were left to ride the back of that tiger down a path to perdition. Bitter and frustrated, by 1773 they were coming to see with painful clarity what Jefferson meant when he exclaimed that the mother country preferred "the immediate advantages of a few British corsairs to the lasting interests of the American states."[23]

An awareness of America's second-class status burgeoned in urban America as well. Although some merchants flourished, others faced ruin brought on by currency restraints, the credit crisis of 1772, and Britain's decision to at last enforce its commercial policies. Numerous companies shut their doors. Some insolvent merchants were flung into debtors' prisons. Cycles of boom and bust were hardly unknown to merchants, but what was so troubling in this instance was that many of the recent woes had resulted from decisions made by faceless officials in faraway England, ministers to whom the interests of the colonies appeared to be of secondary importance.

Nor were merchants alone in facing desolation. Sailors, laborers, and many tradesmen also struggled to make ends meet, and often succeeded only when their wives and children worked. Workers were not unaccustomed to adversity. Throughout the colonial era, many laborers and some tradesmen eked by on the margins of crushing poverty. Their wretched state worsened in the 1760s and 1770s, a time of economic volatility that witnessed declining wages and increasing prices, and threatened some with indigence even as they toiled. Most workers were tied inextricably to the merchant elite. When merchants crashed, workers busted along with them. In their growing desperation, both merchants and workers ached for better times, and many had concluded that times would not improve under Britain's new colonial policies. In New England, where prosperity had always been linked to trade beyond the bounds of the empire, some no longer saw good reason for remaining yoked to Britain. When Sons of Liberty in Boston alleged that Britain's victimization of Ireland—long since bled white by "pensioners and placemen"—was now being reprised in America, the rhetoric struck a responsive chord both in paneled boardrooms and at the workbenches and warehouses in the poorer neighborhoods. The feeling grew that it now was America's turn to be plundered. Together with an awareness that London's new colonial policy evinced a design of political despotism, some grew more cognizant than ever before of Britain's economic exploitation of its American subjects.[24]

Radical politicians in New England aroused other concerns as well. When it appeared that Britain and Spain might go to war in 1770, agitators played on fears that America might once again be dragged into a remote British conflict. The age-old New England hostility toward the Church of England was dusted off from time to time with warnings about the likelihood of the appointment of an Anglican bishop for America. When the ministry in 1772 appointed a commission to investigate a mob's destruction of the customs vessel *Gaspee* in Rhode Island, the radical press alleged that the real charge to the commissioners was to strip that corporate colony of its ancient charter. In each instance, the underlying theme was that the colonists lacked sufficient control of their lives. Their rights and well-being could not be adequately safeguarded in the current scheme of things.

But the most effective campaign waged by Boston's radical leaders involved purloined letters. Late in 1772, someone passed on to Franklin— who for the past two years had served as the agent for Massachusetts in London—a bundle of letters that Hutchinson and Oliver had exchanged several years earlier with Thomas Whately, a member of Parliament and sometime subminister. Franklin happily passed them on to the Speaker of the provincial assembly. He said that he did so because of his "Resentment against this Country, for its arbitrary Measures in governing us." He additionally suggested that the missives not be made public, a request that the savvy Franklin had to know was futile. The radicals waited a bit before publishing the letters, but only so the groundwork could properly be laid. Over a period of several weeks they promised to unveil "letters of an extraordinary nature . . . greatly to the prejudice of the province." By the time they finally got around to publishing the correspondence, all of Boston was panting with excitement at the prospect of sensational news. In reality, the letters contained little that was extraordinary. Much of what Hutchinson and Oliver had written merely duplicated what they had said publicly for years. However, many readers were genuinely appalled to discover that Hutchinson in one letter had urged "an abridgement" of liberties in the colonies as the only way out of the impasse.[25] Today, it is astounding that so many were so shocked by the contents of the letters. It is even more surprising that a political sophisticate such as John Adams was one of the most powerfully affected by the release of the Hutchinson-Oliver letters. Indeed, as if by magic, this incident almost immediately transformed Adams from a cautious bystander into a radical activist.

When the Stamp Act was passed in 1765, John Adams had been angry. He thought the legislation unconstitutional, but Adams was perhaps more ill-humored because he feared that the crisis over British taxation would be detrimental to his burgeoning legal career. Born in 1735 in Braintree, just eight miles south of Boston, Adams was raised in a farming household. His parents saw to his formal education, the last step of which was four years at nearby Harvard College. Following graduation in 1755, Adams taught for two years in a Latin School in Worcester to earn money for a legal apprenticeship. He read law for two years before opening a practice in his hometown, after which he faced a long struggle to succeed in that competitive profession. He had only two clients during his initial year as an attorney—he survived by living with his parents—and did not win his first case in a jury trial until the end of his second year in practice. Three years elapsed before he grew confident that he could make a living as a lawyer. His practice was growing, though it still was quite modest, when word of the Stamp Act reached him. "This execrable Project was set on foot for *my* Ruin," he pouted when he heard the news.[26] He fretted that if the tax was not collected, the courts would be closed and he would be put out of work. In addition, he was anxious that if he lined up on the wrong side—and who knew what in a few years would be seen as the right side—his practice would be irredeemably ruined.

That fear, and others, lingered in Adams's mind through the first several years of the Anglo-American difficulties, preventing him from fully committing himself to an activist's role in the protest. Bright and increasingly successful as the 1760s unfolded, Adams was approached repeatedly by Samuel Adams, his cousin, and other radicals about assuming a more visible role. His response seldom varied. He consented to backstairs assignments only. He wrote unsigned newspaper essays blasting London's policies, drafted blatant propaganda pieces, composed instructions to legislators on behalf of Braintree and Boston town meetings, and at the behest of radical leaders penned numerous letters to known friends of America in England. However, he repeatedly rebuffed every entreaty to take on a more open role, such as speaking at the Boston Massacre commemorative service. In 1769 Samuel Adams persuaded him to attend a Sons of Liberty meeting only by convincing him that many in Boston had concluded that he must, like Hutchinson and Oliver, be a Tory.[27]

Even as his legal practice flourished, Adams continued to fear that it would be damaged should he openly embrace the popular protest. It should be kept in mind that he possessed no crystal ball. Neither he nor anyone else had any idea what lay in the future for the Anglo-American relationship. What he did know was that he did not wish to burn his bridges with either side. Adams believed London's current policies were wrong, but the day might come when the imperial troubles were resolved and—given his lusty ambition—he might wish a judgeship in a Royal court. Moreover, Adams was still young in the late 1760s. He had turned thirty in 1765, the year of the Stamp disturbances, and was newly married. By 1770 he and his wife, Abigail, had four children. Nor was that all that troubled him. While he never doubted that Parliament had overreached, Adams suspected that some radical leaders, including Samuel Adams, harbored hidden agendas. He privately blamed them for Boston's riots in 1765 and the cruel treatment of Oliver, and deep down he suspected that they were responsible for the Boston Massacre. As early as 1770, he appeared to presume that some radicals secretly yearned for American independence and would do anything to keep the anti-British fervor alive. He raged in his diary that many radical leaders were merely "pretended Zealots for the public good" who would not be satisfied until they provoked "Warrs, and Confusions and Carnage." Madness lay at the end of the path they wished America to take, he insisted. For a long time Adams refused to believe the rhetoric about wicked British ministers and plots to enslave the colonists, and like Franklin, he expected an accommodation between mother country and colonies.[28]

The period between the Boston Massacre trials in 1770 and the Tea Act crisis in 1773 was decisive for Adams. Entering his late thirties in these years, he fell into a mid-life crisis. Half his life was over, he realized, and he felt unfulfilled. He had become a successful lawyer—he believed, probably accurately, that he had the heaviest caseload of any attorney in Massachusetts—but that was no longer sufficient. When he commenced his legal studies, he had frankly acknowledged his hope of winning fame and acclaim as the province's best known lawyer. He reached that goal in 1770 when he was chosen to represent the British soldiers charged in the Boston Massacre, only to discover that political activists such as Samuel Adams were far better known, not just in Massachusetts but throughout America and even in the mother country. Indeed, activists such as Dickinson and Samuel Adams were revered in a manner that no lawyer would ever be. As Adams's melancholy grew, Samuel Adams—probably not coincidentally—commenced what appears to have been his last ditch effort to win over this distinguished barrister to the radical ranks. It began late in 1772 when John Hancock, long a client of John Adams, dropped him as his legal counsel, turning instead to a more committed activist. Soon thereafter Samuel Adams called on his cousin and artfully endeavored to convince him of his moderate inclinations. Thomas Cushing, the Speaker of the House, and Joseph Hawley, long a powerful figure in the assembly, followed in Samuel Adams's slipstream, likewise courting John. They wanted his assistance in preparing the legislature's response to a speech by Governor Hutchinson, they said. The chief executive had opened the legislative session in January 1773 with an address that stressed Parliament's sovereignty over the colonies. Adams, somewhat astonished, and not a little flattered by the solicitations of such powerful figures, agreed to assist. He helped prepare a defiant answer to the governor that left little doubt that if Massachusetts were pushed to choose between greater autonomy or greater parliamentary control, Great Britain would be the loser.[29]

Hard on the heels of this episode came the Hutchinson Letters incident, which led Adams to what he subsequently characterized as his "great discovery." In reality, he made two discoveries. The correspondence convinced him of the existence of a ministerial plot to restructure the Anglo-American union and to restrict liberty in every sector of American life. Furthermore, he came to believe that Samuel Adams had been right all along. He and the radical leadership were not destructive revolutionaries, but defenders—conservators—of American freedom. The mother country, Adams now said, must be resisted.[30]

Adams was especially vulnerable at the moment of the Hutchinson Letters incident, but he was hardly alone in being lured—at least subconsciously—toward a radical orientation. Upwardly mobile young men in the colonies had always known that they faced limitations on their ability to rise simply because they were colonists. American politicians would never sit in Parliament or hold a ministerial post. A colonist might be an Indian agent who conducted diplomacy in a borderland wigwam, but he would never be a diplomat posted in the fashionable courts of Europe. Similarly, every aspiring colonist knew that the doors were shut to him in the highest places in the British judiciary, church, and armed forces. John Adams was on the money when he remarked that the most an enterprising young man in Massachusetts could hope for was to someday own an expensive carriage, be a colonel in the militia, and sit in the upper house of the provincial assembly.[31]

By the time of the Tea Act crisis, the belief was widespread in America that generations of colonists, with virtually no help from the mother country, had subdued the American wilderness east of the mountains and conquered its hostile Indian inhabitants. Blessed by a new world environment, and well removed from the British homeland, the ancestors of the revolutionary generation were said to have refashioned British practices, making available greater rights, liberties, and opportunities than existed in the homeland. The colonists of the 1760s and 1770s were coming to understand what their antecedents had known: that in Great Britain and Europe one was either "the hammer or the anvil," as Jefferson subsequently remarked, either free or unfree, as John Adams later observed. The belief was pervasive by 1773 that America was different. The British who lived in the American colonies were up to ten times more likely to own land than their counterparts at home, and considerably more apt to exercise suffrage rights, hold elective office, or achieve an officer's rank in a military unit.[32]

This sense of fortuity within the provinces made the lack of opportunities for those faced with "colonial subservience," as Jefferson put it, all the more galling.[33] Like Adams, increasing numbers of Americans dreamt of a new world in which there would be "a more equal Liberty," a world—as Adams would remark in 1776—in which the "Dons, the Bashaws, the Grandees, the Patricians, the Sachems, the Nabobs, call them by what name you please," were stripped of their privileges, and the meritorious could rise as high as their industry and talent could take them.[34] But to escape the dominion of those "Bashaws," or the "lordly Masters" that Washington had lashed out at in 1769, required American autonomy.

Thus, as the tea ships bore down on America's eastern seaboard, the American protest had taken on dramatic new meanings. The earliest opposition to British policies had issued from the colonists' desire to maintain the autonomy they enjoyed in 1765. Nearly a decade of protest had filled them not only with the hope of becoming even more independent of London, but of longing to fashion a new Anglo-American relationship. The most farsighted already knew that their aspirations could never be realized so long as a subservient relationship with Great Britain existed. They understood, as Samuel Adams had written three years earlier, that it was "the Business of America to take care of itself."[35]

The business that America took care of in the autumn of 1773 concerned dutied tea. The events that occurred in Boston are the best remembered—and were the most crucial for contemporaries—but the ship that brought the tea to the hub of New England was one of the last to arrive, and by the time it docked, important crowd actions had already transpired elsewhere. The tea ship *London*, bound for Charleston, was the first to reach the colonies. It sailed peacefully into Charleston harbor, but the city's mechanics immediately organized and prevented its cargo from being landed. After the vessel idled at the wharf for three weeks, South Carolina's royal governor confiscated the tea for nonpayment of duties. But he dared not attempt to offer it for sale. It gathered dust in a dockside warehouse for the next twelve months with Charleston's Sons of Liberty standing guard.

While a tense calm prevailed in Charleston, New York was swept by street protests immediately after the *New York Mercury* broke the news of the passage of the Tea Act. During the next thirty days, while the *Nancy*, the tea ship bound for New York was yet in the mid-Atlantic, public meetings adopted statements attacking the tax, and in November representatives of mass meetings called on the tea agents and demanded that they resign their commissions. The newspapers were filled with agitation against the tax, and retaliation was promised against anyone who assisted in unloading the tea once the ship arrived. In response, the governor blustered that he would see to it that the tea was unloaded, stored in a military installation, then sold. The radical leaders called his bluff. More meetings, and still more street demonstrations, took place, until the governor capitulated. He wrote London that blood would run in New York's streets if an attempt was ever made to unload the duted tea. If, and when, the *Nancy* arrived with its cargo of tea, he now said, he would not permit it to enter New York harbor.[36]

Philadelphia was next to explode. Its principal merchants were angry that the monopolistic East India Company had bestowed dispersal rights on only four local firms, but they did not lead the protest that autumn. Artisans, with help from the Proprietary Party, organized the resistance to landing and selling taxed tea. Ten weeks before the *Polly* arrived with its cargo of tea, foes of the Tea Act had issued broadsides, conducted public meetings, and flooded the newspapers with essays that enumerated the evils of the Tea Act. Two themes stood out. Monopoly practices were unfair and dangerous. Furthermore, if duted tea was sold, assessments would be laid on other commodities, until slowly, inexorably, the public was lulled into the habit of paying Parliamentary taxes. One liberty after another would be taken from them, many writers insisted, until every freedom had vanished. Their strident assault succeeded. By early October all the tea agents—remembering all too well the fate of the Stamp agents eight years before—had resigned their commissions. Several weeks later, when the *Polly* finally arrived at the foot of the Delaware River, several miles below Philadelphia, it was manifestly clear that any attempt to unload the tea would provoke tumult and probably violence. The authorities in the provincial capital quickly dispatched an emissary downstream to Chester to warn the ship's captain that the security of the ship could not be guaranteed. Without having caught a glimpse of Philadelphia, the captain of the *Polly* prudently turned for England.[37]

Boston's experience was both similar and dissimilar to those of the three other cities earmarked to receive the East India Company's tea. As with the others, agitation commenced early in October with a campaign of invective in the press. During that month, moreover, a town meeting adopted resolutions, prepared by the Boston committee of correspondence, that excoriated the tax. Nevertheless, Boston's radicals faced a tougher go than their counterparts. In Philadelphia and New York, for instance, the merchants—who trafficked in illegal Dutch tea to an extent unknown in Boston—were far better organized against the Tea Act, which they saw more as a commercial threat than a constitutional challenge.[38] Furthermore, Governor Hutchinson—he had succeeded Bernard as the acting chief executive four years before—had a long list of scores to settle and thirsted for a showdown. Buoyed by these realities, Boston's tea agents, unlike those in New York and Philadelphia, refused to resign. They fled into Castle William in Boston harbor, but they did not surrender their commissions. Hutchinson, meanwhile, dug in his heels. Now sixty-two years of age, he was seeking a pension from the Crown, a nest egg for his golden years, and an income that would be beneficial for helping with his feckless son and unmarried daughter. Hutchinson knew that his hopes for the pension would be dashed if he did not make a good faith effort to enforce the Tea Act.[39] He moved his family to his country estate in Milton, where their safety was ensured. Free from worry over Boston's mobs, he could afford to be inflexible.

On a bitingly cold day toward the end of November, the *Dartmouth*, a buff-colored vessel with 114 chests of East India Company tea in its cargo hold, reached the outermost station beyond Boston harbor just as the sun sank in the bright red sky. Harbor employees boarded the ship, as was customary with all arrivals, to ascertain that the crew had not fallen prey to any contagious disease in the course of its nine-week Atlantic crossing and to peruse the captain's papers. Several hours later, once those formalities were completed, a pilot arrived to lead the vessel through the black waters of Boston harbor. Near noon on Sunday, November 28, while most residents of Boston were attending worship services, the *Dartmouth* docked.

By that afternoon all the city knew that duties tea was in its harbor. What occurred during the next twenty days was a culmination of the eight long years of struggle and agitation that had preceded this moment. However, it also was the first act of the turbulent and pivotal decade that was to follow, for the congresses, the war, and the diplomacy that would fill the breathtaking years between 1774 and 1783 grew from the events in Boston during that cold December of 1773.

The Sunday that the *Dartmouth* docked was quiet, as the city's strict Sabbatarian laws, passed nearly 150 years earlier by the first Puritan settlers, kept the residents indoors and idle. But on Monday, and again the next day, thousands attended mass meetings that adopted resolutions demanding that the tea ship, with its cargo, return to England. Meanwhile, five area committees of correspondence pledged to resist any attempt to unload the tea. The radical press carried essays urging armed resistance, and stormy applause in a Boston town meeting greeted speeches that called on the citizenry to arm itself. The town meeting never voted to arm its residents, but it did agree to post a watch of twenty-one men—each probably carrying a cudgel—at Griffin's Wharf as a safeguard against any attempt to unload the tea.[40] Throughout Massachusetts, meanwhile, numerous committees of correspondence denounced the Tea Act, many in constitutional terms, and some, such as those in the villages of Colrain and Pelham, portrayed the tea tax as part of a plan to enslave America so that the English aristocracy could "glut themselves on our spoil."[41]

On Tuesday all the *Dartmouth's* cargo save for the tea—it included whale oil and various winter supplies from the mother country—was unloaded. No one touched the tea chests. The stevedores and longshoremen were solidly arrayed against the vending of taxed tea. The customs officials understood that a bloody resistance would likely ensue if they moved. Hutchinson gave no orders. He played a waiting game. On December 17, by law—a century-old statute that mandated the landing of all cargoes within twenty days of any ship's docking—the tea would have to be unloaded, probably under the watchful eye of the army. Days went by. On December 2 the *Eleanor*, another tea ship, arrived; five days later the *Beaver*, the last scheduled vessel bearing tea to Boston, docked. All three tea ships were berthed at Griffin's Wharf.

As the deadline approached, it was clear that if the radicals did not act, they would lose this standoff. Come December 17 the tea would be unloaded—given the army's presence, there was no mistaking that—and once the tea was taken from the ships, it would be sold. From time to time in early December, leaders of the town meeting met with Hutchinson or other officials and requested that the tea ships be sent away from Boston. The owner of the *Dartmouth*, either at the behest of the radicals or simply in a desperate attempt to save his cargo, and perhaps his ship as well, beseeched Hutchinson to permit the vessel to sail from Boston. The governor remained intransigent. Less than seventy-two hours before the deadline, December 14, thousands attended a rally at the Old South Church. The meeting was held to frighten the authorities, but the radical leadership also wished to buck up the spirits of Boston's residents in preparation for the destruction of the tea, if it came to that. Once again Hutchinson refused to buckle. One final meeting was called for late in the morning on December 16, a rainy, wintry day. More than 7,000 packed into the Old South. Almost half had come in from the countryside, eager for the show, hoping to see Hutchinson humiliated once again, and in many instances perhaps longing for a piece of the action, if violence flared that day. After hours of florid oratory that whipped the assemblage into a carnival frenzy, Francis Rotch, the twenty-three-year-old son of the *Dartmouth's* owner, was hauled before the crowd. He was asked to order the ship out of the harbor. He refused to break the law. He was then directed to ride to Milton, seven miles away, and make one final appeal to the governor to permit the vessel to depart. The meeting adjourned, pending his return. Many in the audience retired to nearby grog shops to wait out what was likely to be a delay of several hours. Some doubtless sought to strengthen their resolve for what might be a dangerous evening on the streets of Boston.

Three hours passed, then three more, before Rotch at last returned from Milton. Just before 6 P.M., the proceedings in the Congregational meetinghouse resumed. The audience was smaller, but thousands yet were in attendance. The Old South, a cavernous structure, illuminated now by candles, was dark and gloomy and reeked of damp wool. It took a minute for the presiding officer to quiet the audience. Then, in the eerie silence, Rotch, wet and exhausted, and not a little frightened, was brought before the assemblage to reveal Hutchinson's answer. Two or three preliminary questions built the mood of expectancy. Then the moderator asked if Hutchinson had agreed to permit the tea ships to sail away. "No," Rotch replied in a low voice. "A mob! A mob!" someone shouted from the rear of the church. Others took up the chant. Pandemonium prevailed for a moment, until Dr. Thomas Young, a forty-two-year-old physician who had been active in the popular protest in Boston since 1766, got the floor. Young beseeched the audience not to harm Rotch or his father's vessel. With order restored, further questions were directed at Rotch regarding his intentions about unloading the tea. He pledged that he would not order the *Dartmouth* to be unloaded, unless compelled to do so by the governor or the Customs Service. He did not wish to break the law and go to jail, he said.[42]

With that last statement, Samuel Adams was on his feet. As if he were capitulating, he cried out that the Bostonians had done all they could do to protect their liberties. But far from surrendering, Adams's terse utterance was a prearranged, coded statement that at once was meant to exculpate the leaders of this meeting of responsibility and to set in motion those famous events that were about to unfold. No sooner had Adams spoken before someone in the balcony cried out: "Boston harbor a tea-pot tonight!" Then another in the audience shouted: "Hurrah for Griffin's Wharf!" Some other insider cried out: "The Mohawks are come! Every man to his tent!" The hall erupted in loud cheers and applause that could be heard three blocks away.[43]

There was an alternative to the Boston Tea Party that followed. The radicals might have permitted the tea to be landed and sold, then resisted Parliament's legislation with the existing boycott against dutied tea. But the embargo had been a weak vessel for years, and there was little reason to hope for better results now. In addition, some radicals appear to have concluded that the time was right to bring the contest with the mother country to a head. Never before had so many citizens of Massachusetts been so incensed. The time had arrived to goad London into violent retaliatory measures by destroying the East India Company's property.

The defiant act of the night of December 16 was not spontaneous. It had been carefully planned for days, perhaps weeks. As many as 2,000 noisily spilled from the Old South through the streets of Boston to Griffin's Wharf. But once the crowd reached the waterfront, the vast majority simply stood on the docks as spectators, while 150–200 men went into action, implementing a carefully orchestrated plan. Some served as lookouts or were part of guard units posted to resist the Customs Service or the local constabulary, if necessary. Approximately 30 men, disguised as Indians, boarded the three ships. They were joined by up to 100 others, whom Samuel Adams subsequently identified as residents of communities outside Boston and who consequently saw no need for any concealment beyond a blackened face. Some who boarded the tea vessels were probably activists from suburban committees of correspondence, but most were likely longshoremen who knew their way around the dark hold of a ship and who were accustomed to hard physical labor. But not everyone who boarded the three tea ships was expected to do heavy work. George Robert Twelves Hewes, a Boston cordwainer who was barely five foot tall, was assigned the task of getting the keys to the hatch from the ship's captain and supplying candles for those toiling below deck. The work went forward expeditiously and quietly, with an almost military precision. After merely four hours, 342 broken tea chests—according to Samuel Adams's tally—bobbed in the black waters of Boston harbor. Nearly 10,000 pounds of East India Company tea, worth approximately $1,000,000 in today' currency, had been destroyed.

As they came off the three ships, every participant probably knew that he had taken part in a pivotal event. So did the residents of Boston and the other colonies, when they learned of the Boston Tea Party during the next hours and days. Many must have responded as did John Adams, who wrote that the act had been "so bold, so daring, so firm, so intrepid and inflexible, [that] it must have so important Consequences, and so lasting, that I cant but consider it as an Epocha in History."[44]

The violence at Griffin's Wharf confronted London with a momentous choice. More than ever, the *London Evening Post* asserted, the "decisive question" was "whether the *right* of taxation be *here* or *there*." Among articulate Londoners the answer was crystal clear. Franklin wrote of the "torrent of clamour against us." There now was a "high and general" tendency to be tough on the colonists, he said. At its first meeting on the matter, the North ministry agreed to take "effectual steps . . . to secure the dependence of the colonies on the mother country." After one or two additional meetings it agreed to act only against Massachusetts, although it knew that the colonial defiance of the Tea Act had been universal. London was playing "divide and conquer," but was convinced as well that the heart and soul of the American protest was situated in Boston. North's government proceeded on the assumption that it could kill the serpent by severing its head. Suppress the popular movement in Boston, many believed, and it would die elsewhere.[45]

Draconian legislation soon followed. The Coercive Acts—labeled the "Intolerable Acts" by many colonists—closed the port of Boston until the province compensated the East India Company. The legislation also radically altered governance in Massachusetts. Town meetings were restricted, the elected upper house of the assembly was replaced with a chamber whose members were appointed by the royal governor, the assembly was forbidden to meet in Boston, and the executive was given more sweeping powers than those possessed by any other royal governor.

The line had been drawn. Parliament clearly meant what it had said in the Declaratory Act eight years before. The colonists understood that the crisis that had percolated for a decade had reached the reckoning point. Franklin looked toward "impending Calamities." Virginia's House of Burgesses prayed that "the evils of civil war" might be averted. John Adams predicted that London would turn a deaf ear toward every colonial petition for redress.[46]

Boston's radicals had begun to prepare for this eventuality immediately after the Tea Party. The city's committee of correspondence had carried out a carefully orchestrated campaign designed to convince the other provinces that Governor Hutchinson was to blame for the destruction of the East India Company's tea. Had he acted the statesman, in the

manner of the chief executives of Pennsylvania and New York, it was alleged, there would have been no crisis. According to Boston's committee,
Hutchinson had wanted violence. He had sought a "pretense" in order to
act with "unprecedented severity" against Massachusetts. In addition,
Boston's radicals endeavored to convince all Americans that the yoke of
slavery would descend upon them should they "tamely and without a
struggle submit" to the Coercive Acts. They spoke of the ecstacy that came
from successfully defying London. Samuel Adams wrote rhapsodically of
"the height of joy that sparkles in the eyes and animates the countenance
as well as the hearts of all" Bostonians with the courage to stand up to
North's government. The Boston committee tried one other tactic. To demonstrate that the popular protest had widespread support beyond Boston,
it had other committees of correspondence throughout Massachusetts
appeal to the twelve other provinces for assistance.[47]

Not every colonist had to be primed by Boston's radicals. The immediate response of Colonel Washington, for instance, had been that
"the cause of Boston . . . now is and ever will be considered as the cause
of America."[48] But some had to be persuaded that Boston's popular leaders
had harbored no designs beyond their opposition to the Tea Act. Furthermore, many outside New England, who had privately expressed displeasure at news that a Boston mob had destroyed private property, had
to be made to understand that if Parliamentary taxation was to be precluded, no satisfactory alternative had existed to the destruction of the
tea.[49] Throughout the spring a consensus appeared to build that all colonies must stand "in the common cause," as Silas Deane of Connecticut
told Adams.[50]

After the second week in May, when news of the Coercive Acts
reached the colonies, there was no doubt that America would resist both
the Tea Act and London's retaliatory measures against Boston. Closing
the port of Boston, in effect a British boycott of Massachusetts commerce, caused concern, but it was word that North's government sought
to arbitrarily alter the charter of Massachusetts that truly provoked palpable rage from one end of the land to the other. If London succeeded,
many said, no charter would be worth the paper it was written on. If the
charters were not safe, the security of provincial land titles, religious
freedoms, and myriad other matters long ago supposedly determined
by the residents of each colony would be an open question. As one Boston activist pointed out, Lord North had succeeded in precipitating "the
perfect crisis of American politics."[51]

What remained to be decided after May 1774 was the best course of
resistance. There was immediate talk of a national congress, but Samuel
Adams hoped to avoid such a meeting. He wished to stick with what had

worked in the past, a widespread American boycott brought about through an appeal by Massachusetts. Adams knew that Massachusetts could not stand alone. Only a boycott similar to the nearly unanimous trade embargo that had been achieved by 1769, and which had led to the repeal of the Townshend Duties, might compel London to rescind the Tea Act and the Coercive Acts it had levied against his city and province. Nevertheless, Adams feared what might occur at a congress of all the colonies. If the Stamp Act Congress offered any guidance, the radicals would not be in control. If Massachusetts's fate was left in the hands of more conservative men from other provinces, a boycott of British trade would be problematical. Worse, under such leadership a dangerously feeble—Adams would have thought it cowardly—statement on American constitutional rights might be adopted. Adams also worried that even if a congress sanctioned a national boycott of Great Britain, months might pass before a cumbersome assembly finally acted. He wanted immediate action. He knew that the longer Boston harbor was closed, the more difficult it would be to bolster morale and maintain resistance in Massachusetts. Adams preferred that Massachusetts act as it had in 1768, when it sent out the circular letter urging each American colony to participate in an immediate boycott of all commerce with Britain.

Adams won the battle on his home turf. On May 13, three days after word of the Coercive Acts arrived, a Boston town meeting, chaired by Adams and acting on a recommendation of the Boston Committee of Correspondence that he had helped draft, appealed to the other provinces to join in a boycott. Paul Revere immediately set out with his colony's entreaty. But then Adams's wishes went awry. Sentiment was strong that all the provinces should convene in a general congress. This was true even in New England. By the first week of June, Rhode Island and Connecticut let it be known that they would join a boycott only if sanctioned by a national gathering. Before taking a step fraught with dark uncertainty, they wanted to gauge the pluck of their countrymen. But numerous other reasons also existed for demanding such a conclave. Many in the popular protest were convinced that a trade embargo adopted by a national assembly not only would be more effective but would make a greater impression in London. Some provinces sought assurances that the pitfalls of the nonimportation experience in 1768–70 might be averted. Philadelphia's merchants, for instance, had joined in the boycott in 1769, but when their counterparts in nearby Baltimore declined to take part, the Philadelphians lost their commerce—which in some instances was never recovered—to their commercial rival on the Chesapeake. Thereafter, Philadelphia's merchants vowed to participate

only in a truly binding national boycott. In addition, many in the protest movement understood that another boycott might deepen, rather
than resolve, the Anglo-American crisis. Hostilities might ensue. Should
there be war, a congress could be essential for laying vital preparatory
groundwork for American unity.[52]

The more moderate colonists believed that a congress offered the
best hope for reaching an accommodation with Great Britain. Praying
for a peaceful resolution of the Anglo-American nightmare, many moderates and conservatives wanted an intercolonial conclave because they
did not fully trust Boston's radicals, whom they held responsible for the
destruction of Oliver's and Hutchinson's homes, the Boston Massacre,
and now the Boston Tea Party. These colonial leaders believed that a
national congress, under their direction, might protect America's interests while it simultaneously restrained the most dangerously zealous
activists. A gathering led by prudent and reasonable men, they felt, might
extend a placatory hand that would lead to reconciliation. The bonds of
loyalty to Great Britain remained deep even after years of agitation and
protest, and even within the hearts of many who had been active in the
American resistance to Parliamentary taxation. Many still looked on the
parent state as Europe's most politically enlightened and religiously tolerant nation, and the British people were yet thought to enjoy a degree
of liberty—including trials by jury, habeas corpus, and free speech—
unknown elsewhere. Many Americans worshiped weekly in the Church
of England. Others, especially in the mid-Atlantic provinces (Pennsylvania, New York, New Jersey, and Delaware) flourished through inextricable economic ties to the parent state, which remained a primary market
for their exports and virtually their sole supplier of manufactured commodities. Myriad cultural, educational, and scientific links existed between the colonies and the metropolis.[53] But beyond the filial ties and
the economic bonds, conservatives also trembled at the uncertainties
that would ensue if the Anglo-American crisis resulted in hostilities. War,
with its potential for producing unintended changes, was unthinkable.
The most conservative colonists were desperately anxious for reconciliation, if only it could be had on terms that did not vitiate their interests.

Only the most conservative of the provincial conservatives hoped to
prevent a national congress from convening. Implacably loyal to Great
Britain, they believed that everything had changed with the passage of
the Coercive Acts. After years of appeasement in the face of colonial protest, Great Britain had refused to back down when confronted with the
upheaval against the Tea Act. With crystal clarity the extreme conservatives foresaw that London would respond with force should America
defy the Coercive Acts, a step they believed that Congress was virtually

certain to take. In short, a congress would make war inevitable. As the chill of early spring gave way to the first warmth of the summer that lay ahead, the most conservative leaders in New York and Pennsylvania fought a desperate rear-guard action to prevent their colonies from participating in what they believed was fated to be a defiant national gathering. Their object was to prevent the emergence of a united front. The stakes were enormous, for if New York and Pennsylvania refused to attend a national conclave, it might break the back of defiant, concerted American action.

Ultimately, the reach of these conservatives exceeded their grasp. In Pennsylvania, for example, they were buried by an avalanche of public opinion and by better led and organized foes. On May 20, the day after Revere reached Philadelphia, the radical leadership convened a mass meeting in the City Tavern. The principal organizers exhibited a tactical skill that equaled anything yet undertaken by Samuel Adams. Radical orators, including Joseph Reed, Charles Thomson, and Thomas Mifflin, all leading lights in the Proprietary Party, kicked off the meeting with bombast designed to frighten the moderates. They demanded that Philadelphia immediately join Boston in a total embargo of British trade. A furious debate followed. At length, John Dickinson rose to play his preassigned role. Posturing as the voice of unruffled circumspection, he spoke calmly, reassuringly, suggesting that it would be more prudent to convene a deliberative congress, where the best statesmen in the colonies might discover some way to resolve America's differences with London. He asked this gathering to petition the governor to convene the assembly, which in turn could ponder Pennsylvania's best response. The meeting overwhelmingly endorsed Dickinson's proposition.

To no one's surprise, the governor demurred. Speaker Galloway also possessed the authority to summon the legislature into session, but he too acted precisely as the radicals imagined he would. A steadfast foe of boycotting the mother country, he refused to call a special session of the legislature that would meet for the purpose of sanctioning a congress to contemplate nonimportation. The radicals had guessed correctly, and they had maneuvered the Assembly Party into appearing foursquare against any resistance to the Coercive Acts. The odds seemed considerable that the Assembly Party would pay dearly for its folly in the October elections. But the radicals were not finished. They wanted Pennsylvania to be represented in the national congress. Once again, they turned to the people. An open-air meeting, attended by thousands of Philadelphians, was held on the balmy evening of June 18. After considerable speechifying, this gathering agreed to the creation of a colonial convention. The assembly, badly malapportioned and an intransigent obstacle to the popular protest, was to be bypassed altogether, perhaps even swept aside, by an extralegal body. Promising fair representation for the more radical western counties, the convention was certain not only to send a delegation to the national congress but to choose more radical delegates than the assembly would ever have chosen.

Speaker Galloway immediately capitulated. He summoned the assembly to a special session, which ultimately committed Pennsylvania to the national congress and elected seven conservative delegates. Galloway was one of those selected. He now was anxious to attend, hopeful that he might utilize his legislative and oratorical skills to persuade congress to choose a moderate. He and his allies used their clout to prevent Dickinson's inclusion in the Pennsylvania delegation. Although distressed by the composition of the delegation chosen by the assembly, the radicals acquiesced. It would have been counterproductive to have responded differently. Even so, as historian Richard Ryerson has demonstrated, Galloway and his followers emerged from this fight tainted as obstructionists who were too comfortable with the despised British measures. The radicals had not gotten all they sought, but they had laid the groundwork for the demise of the ultraconservative element that had dominated the assembly throughout the imperial crisis, and they were confident that Galloway, and his brethren, were destined to fail in an American congress that would speak for an aroused provincial populace.[54]

During September and October, fifty-six delegates met in Philadelphia, the centrally located site that had been agreed to for the First Continental Congress. Not all the congressmen were present at once, and Georgia, the newest and smallest province, declined even to send a delegation, as it was seeking help from London to pacify its smoldering Indian frontier. Only two congressmen, George Washington and Samuel Adams, were known beyond their colony's border, the former from his exploits in the French and Indian War, the latter from the fame he had won in leading the popular protest in Massachusetts. As the remainder were strangers to one another, the first order of business was for the congressmen to size up their colleagues. In some instances, the process commenced even before the congressmen reached Philadelphia. The Massachusetts delegation, for example, rendezvoused in Boston and traveled south together. It was Samuel Adams's first trip ever outside Massachusetts, and only the second for John Adams, who two years before had visited a health spa just across the neighboring Connecticut border. These congressmen stopped along the way in Connecticut and New York, where for the first time they met the delegates from those colonies who would attend Congress. They also picked up tattle here and there about various representatives from other provinces. While in Princeton, New Jersey, they heard of Patrick Henry and Richard Henry Lee, learning that both were stalwart patriots who would befriend Massachusetts. Once in Philadelphia, most delegates socialized extensively, dining together, relaxing in the evening over beer or wine, or joining with others as the dinner guests of affluent residents of the city.[55]

In less than a week John Adams knew that "a Tory here is the most despicable Animal in the Creation. Spiders, Toads, Snakes, are their only proper Emblems." He was also aware that Galloway was considered a Tory by the radicals in Pennsylvania. Within a few days, Adams concluded that Congress was divided into two factions, those who would support a boycott and those who feared that another embargo would mean war.[56] While two blocs did exist in this Congress, the truth had more shades of grey than Adams realized. One bloc consisted of congressmen who were unwilling to make any substantive concessions and wished to deny that Parliament possessed any authority over America. It is likely that some within this faction, including Samuel Adams and perhaps Washington, had been secretly committed to American independence for some time, although neither openly admitted such a radical view, for they were aware, as John Adams put it, that "Absolute Indepen[den]cy &c. are Ideas which Startle People here."[57] Others in this faction, with varying degrees of regret, believed that independence was being forced on the colonies. Doubting that the means to an accommodation any longer existed, these representatives—which likely included John Adams and Richard Henry Lee—had concluded that independence now was inevitable, and they looked on this Congress as the vehicle for preparing for the exigencies that lay ahead.

A moderate faction—strongest among delegates from the mid-Atlantic colonies and representative of mercantile interests who hoped to patch up the tattered empire—prepared to battle for reconciliation. Like their counterparts, these men were determined to secure the rights of the colonists, and most even were willing to go to war, if no other option existed. They held to the hope that a peaceful solution was yet possible, but differed over how to pursue that end. Some believed that London would cave in to America's demands if the colonists evinced a united and determined front. Others felt that the only hope of accommodation lay in preventing Congress from taking any provocative steps.[58]

Galloway, on the one side, and Samuel Adams, on the other, were the key figures in Congress. Each played a leading role in cobbling together a workable faction from the disparate outlooks that were represented. Galloway, working as tirelessly as his opposite number, found some who opposed a boycott and others who longed both for an embargo and some accompanying anodyne that might serve as the basis for an Anglo-American accord. Summoning the skills that he had honed as the speaker of the Pennsylvania's assembly over two decades, he found the means of bringing these diverse elements together around a plan of constitutional reform.

Samuel Adams kept his designs well hidden. Because the Massachusetts congressmen were under suspicion as radical firebrands, he thought it imperative that his delegation "act with great Delicacy and Caution." His plan, as a member of the Massachusetts delegation confided, was to "insinuate our Sentiments . . . by means of other Persons." Behind the scenes, Samuel Adams soon found that most Virginians, and certainly Lee and Henry, as he had been told during his journey to Philadelphia, were prepared not only to institute a tough embargo of British trade but also to stand firmly against the parent state, even if war ensued. His discovery was the birth of what some soon would call the "Adams-Lee junto," an alliance between Massachusetts, the dominant entity in New England, and Virginia, the most powerful Southern province, that would constitute the largest and most effective bloc in Congress during the next five years. At this Congress, the Virginians would be the "other persons" who would "insinuate [Massachusetts's] sentiments," while John and Samuel Adams, the most radical members within the Massachusetts delegation, remained behind the curtain. It was a clever strategy, and it worked so well that Joseph Reed, a sophisticated Pennsylvania lawyer and political activist who kept a close eye on Congress, early on concluded that "the Bostonians are mere Milksops" next to the Virginians. A Maryland congressman was even duped into believing that the Massachusetts delegates were among the most moderate in attendance.[59]

The outcome of this conclave was not foreordained, though that seemed to be the case to many historians. John Adams was more nearly correct when, some forty years later, he remembered that "all the great critical questions about men and measures from 1774 to 1778" were savagely contested; their outcomes, he added, were always uncertain, and indeed many were decided by the vote of a single colony and often by the vote of a single congressman.[60] Thus, the duel between Samuel Adams and Galloway was a desperate struggle, with the fate of the colonies, and the empire, hanging in the balance. Samuel Adams, who already had been active in the colonial protest for a decade, and who would sit in Congress until 1781, subsequently remarked that Galloway was his most dangerous and formidable foe throughout the entirety of the American Revolution. For his part, Galloway described Adams as a man who "eats little, drinks little, sleeps little, thinks much, and is most decisive and indefatigable in the pursuit of his objects." He also concluded that Adams was unequaled in "popular intrigue, and the management of a faction."[61] Although Galloway's power was eroding as American sentiments shifted, he had been sufficiently adept politically to dominate the Pennsylvania assembly for nearly twenty years and to take command of one of the factions at this gathering. Yet Adams was his superior in Congress. Adams deceived his colleagues with his charade of moderation, accurately read the pulse of Congress, and dexterously cultivated allies. He compromised on, or conceded, peripheral issues that a less clever politician would have contested. Adams's gambit was to win friends, and he succeeded through his conciliatory and restrained manner. He resisted every temptation to engage in radical rhetoric and bombastic pronouncements, often saying nothing, and joining in debates only when it was imperative that he do so. Patience was one of his greatest attributes. It was Adams's genius to take one step at a time, to gain what was possible, and to wait for events to further radicalize his more moderate comrades.

This congress, the opening chapter in America's history as a nation, convened on the cool, misty morning of September 5, 1774. The forty-eight delegates who were in town gathered in the City Tavern to select a permanent meeting site. They quickly accepted the invitation of popular leaders in Philadelphia to use Carpenter's Hall, a choice most believed would be "highly agreeable to the mechanics and citizens in general." The newly constructed building was owned by the Carpenters Company, a fifty-year-old guild of tradesmen. The brick Georgian building, built in the shape of a Greek cross, consisted of a ground floor with ample space for the congressional sessions, and a second story that had been rented to the Library Company, and which some delegates prized as a pleasant retreat for research and reflection. Situated well back from the street, it provided a sylvan retreat half hidden behind a small green sward and verdant trees, an excellent site—as several delegates observed—for private conversations and a bit of exercise.[62]

Once it organized, Congress's first substantive business was to determine the voting procedure, a thorny issue that immediately produced a wrangle. The larger colonies—including Massachusetts, Pennsylvania, Virginia, and New York—wished to allocate votes according to the number of inhabitants in each colony. The smaller provinces demanded that each colony have only one vote. Two days passed before the small states won out, in part because Massachusetts—as part of Samuel Adams's obliging tactics—relented.

Once the procedural hurdles were cleared, Congress was off and running. Anxious to complete their work and return home, the delegates

met in secret sessions—to hide divisions both from the American public and officials in London—six days each week from 10:00 until 4:30.
These sessions, John Adams noted, were tiresome ordeals of "nibbling
and quibbling," as the congressmen, who universally regarded themselves
as "great Witts, . . . subtle Criticks, . . . refined Genius's, . . . learned Lawyers, [and] . . . wise Statesman," were unable to resist the temptation to
speak forth on every issue and respond to every comment. This weary
life was accompanied by festive evenings, as the delegates were treated to
a nearly "perpetual Round of feasting." Indeed, much of the business
transpired in the dining rooms, coffee houses, and taverns of Philadelphia, where the congressmen felt free to speak candidly, and to exchange
information, plot strategy, and negotiate bargains. Like John Adams, most
of the delegates probably initially found this unique experience to be
energizing and exhilarating, but for all save the most consumed political
operatives the novelty soon enough wore off, leaving the congressmen
drained and eager to bring their stay in Philadelphia to a close.[63]

On its fifth day in session, after receiving a shocking—and untrue—
report that Boston had been shelled by the British army, Congress finally tackled Anglo-American differences. It created a Grand Committee,
consisting of one representative from each colony, to prepare a statement on American rights. While that panel deliberated—almost a month
passed before it completed its work—Virginia proposed a national nonimportation agreement. Congress divided immediately between those
who favored a boycott and those who were opposed, but in addition a
split soon was evident within the ranks of the proponents of a trade
embargo, the first North vs. South clash in American history. Massachusetts had come to Philadelphia to secure an immediate ban on all commerce—exports as well as imports—with Great Britain. The Chesapeake
and Carolina delegates objected. Tobacco and rice planters, who had set
out their crops before they learned of the Boston Tea Party, much less
the Coercive Acts, insisted on marketing the current year's crop prior to
the implementation of nonexportation. The question was resolved by
the submission of the northern congressmen, a pattern that was to become habitual during the next couple of decades. In this instance, New
England sought—had to have—unity. It settled for nonimportation only,
although the southern colonies agreed that nonexportation would commence in September 1775 if the imperial crisis had not been resolved.

Immediately after Virginia proposed the boycott, and before Congress acted, Galloway was on his feet to offer his faction's alternative. Tall
and spare, with a pinched face that endowed him with a permanent air
of biliousness, Galloway presented his ideas in a long, dramatic speech,
an effort that drew on the extraordinary oratorical skills that had helped

to catapult him to a position of political preeminence in Pennsylvania.[64] He asserted that the colonies had been well served by the imperial relationship. They had grown, their commerce had flourished, they enjoyed freedoms of which most Europeans could only dream, they were secure under British protection from foreign threats, and they could look forward to a happy and prosperous future that included a rapid expansion across North America and, someday, hegemony over South America.

However, Galloway continued, two great dangers loomed that threatened everything. First, Great Britain had reached a point beyond which it would not retreat. Beyond a doubt, this meant that the unhappy, but inevitable, result of an American embargo would be an Anglo-American war. This would be a war, he stressed, that was unlikely to turn out well for America. It was doubtful that the colonists could win a war against Great Britain. The colonists lacked a trained army and experienced military commanders, and they were unaccustomed to cooperating with one another. In the French and Indian War, before Great Britain saved them, the result had been repeated failures against motley collections of Indians and Canadian militiamen. Furthermore, the provincials had no means of supplying their soldiers, and with each colony marching to its own drummer, financial disaster was certain to be swift. America's only hope of victory, he added, would be to link itself with France and Spain, Roman Catholic countries with far more absolutist traditions than the mother country. Hostilities, therefore, would confront America with an unwinnable situation. If America, aided by France and Spain, defeated Great Britain, it would find itself at the mercy of despots in Versailles and Madrid who were far worse than the most arbitrary monarch who had ever sat on Britain's throne. What was more likely, however, was that even with foreign assistance America would be defeated. It then would be subjected to bitter retaliation by London, reprisals that would make the Stamp Act and Tea Act seem inconsequential.[65]

Even if the present crisis was somehow peacefully resolved, a second danger loomed—civil discord. Insurgency was in the air, Galloway said, fanned by radical bombast in the course of the opposition to London's new imperial policies and by the firebrands who took mobs into the streets to pillage the property of the affluent. London was too far away to help when such disorders erupted. Nor could help be anticipated from neighboring colonies. Each colony "by its own internal legislators . . . [could] regulate its own internal police, within its particular circle of territory. But here it is confined." The provinces, in essence, were "so many perfect and independent societies" in relationship to one another. In a worst case scenario in which a colony's government was unable to suppress radical dissidents, all hope was lost for the privileged, as the colonies were "destitute of any political connection, or supreme authority, to compel them to act in concert for common safety."[66]

Galloway's protracted speech led inexorably toward solutions that he proffered for both problems that he beheld. War could be averted through compromise, and the middle course that he envisioned also contained the mechanism for coping with popular disorder. Galloway depicted the imperial crisis in constitutional terms and asserted that much of what both sides desired was proper. The colonists were correct to assert that their rights as British subjects had been threatened when Parliament sought to impose taxes. Furthermore, the provincials were justified in their expectation of exercising autonomy in their domestic spheres. Nevertheless, it was equally valid for the parent state to insist that there must be a sovereign head in every polity. It was absurd to believe that both the colonies and the imperial government possessed sovereignty. Such an arrangement would be what he called an *imperio in imperium*, a government within a government. In every political system, he said, a sovereign executive authority and a sovereign legislative authority must be recognized, and all subordinate entities must yield obedience to those that possessed ultimate authority. Anything else would lead to ruination.

Following these remarks, Galloway proposed a plan to reconcile the conflicting constitutional differences. He drew on the scheme that his political partner, Franklin, had introduced at Albany twenty years earlier. But the Galloway Plan of Union, as it came to be called, was more than nostalgia. It was farsighted in that it proposed a federalist scheme of governance, an idea that lay in America's future. He urged the creation of an American national government that would consist of a unicameral assembly in which each colony was equally represented and a president-general who was to be appointed by the Crown. This new government was to become the "American Branch" of Parliament, a third house coexisting with the House of Commons and House of Lords. Imperial laws would take effect only when sanctioned by each house in the new tricameral Parliament. Under this plan, power was to be shared between colonies and mother country. The Crown would retain its authority. It would continue to appoint Royal governors and numerous judges, invalidate laws enacted by colonial assemblies, enforce Parliament's commercial and monetary acts, and select the chief executive of America. The existing Parliament would lose. Its two houses would have to share authority with the American house. Henceforth, taxes and other legislation could be imposed on the colonists only if the American Branch consented. In addition, the new national government that was the American Branch would possess the authority and might to preserve the "security of the colonies" by "acting for their general protection."[67]

What Galloway offered was a compromise, a desperate attempt to find a middle way that might avert hostilities and preserve the empire, and at the same time provide a national authority that could suppress lawless, destructive insurgents. Both sides would have gained something through his plan, but both also would have forfeited authority that it presently possessed. America would be given adequate representation in the Parliament, with which it henceforth would have the capability of protecting itself from the metropolis. Britain would obtain the colonists' assent to the sovereignty of Parliament. These gains, however, would be matched by major concessions. Each colony would have to surrender some of its autonomy to the new American Branch and to Parliament. British interests in the homeland, on the other hand, would have been compelled to surrender their monopoly control of the levers of imperial authority.

Galloway's plan provoked heated debate before it was tabled by a vote of six colonies to five, with Rhode Island's two congressmen dividing on the issue. Close to half the congressmen, perhaps even a majority, voted for the proposal, for nearly 45 percent of those in attendance were from the middle colonies, which overwhelmingly endorsed the scheme, and an occasional New England or Southern delegate viewed the plan as a suitable conciliatory measure to send to London alongside word of the boycott. But voting was by colonies, which doomed the measure.

The Galloway Plan failed for many reasons. It defined the dispute in constitutional terms, but for many colonists economic, social, and ideological issues, as well as concerns over individual opportunity and advancement, were at the heart of the matter. Furthermore, to have attempted to create a national government would have cluttered the table with divisive issues, which in fact was what Samuel Adams believed it was designed to do. An inordinate amount of time would have been required to complete work on the plan Galloway presented—years down the road, the Constitutional Convention would consume four months— and this at a moment when Massachusetts faced a compelling crisis that cried out for immediate action. Galloway was undone too by his record of habitual opposition to the popular resistance movement since 1765, and he was additionally stained in the eyes of many for having prevented the inclusion of Dickinson—for many, outside as well as inside Pennsylvania, the most widely admired, and trusted, provincial in the popular protest movement—in the Pennsylvania delegation. Galloway also was fatally, and unnecessarily, wounded when many in his faction opposed

nonimportation. Congressional passage of a trade embargo was a foregone conclusion. Not only had nine of the twelve delegations been instructed by their provinces to vote to boycott British trade until the Tea
Act and Coercive Acts were repealed, but the moment word of the Coercive Acts arrived, sagacious merchants, including many in Philadelphia,
stopped ordering British goods, suspecting that an embargo was inevitable. Finally, many at the Congress were unwilling to open the door to
any acknowledgment of Parliamentary jurisdiction over the colonies,
which of course was conceded in Galloway's Plan of Union.[68]

Once Galloway's plan was tabled, Congress at last received the report of the Grand Committee. Some of what the committee had hammered out had been easygoing. The bulk of their recommendations
hardly deviated from the resolves adopted by the Stamp Act Congress.
But questions over the colonists' rights had stirred a firefight. The radicals in the committee insisted that Americans had derived their rights
from nature; two years later this would become the now familiar "truth"
that "all men are . . . endowed by their Creator with certain inalienable
rights." Conservatives argued that the rights enjoyed by the colonists
had been bestowed by the English constitution and the colonial charters. The differences were resolved by a compromise. The eventual Statement of Rights and Grievances listed all three as sources of the rights of
the colonists.

An equally difficult issue confronting the committee had arisen over
defining the power of Parliament. The most radical congressmen wished
to declare that Parliament had no authority over the colonies. Others
believed that Parliament must possess the power to regulate colonial
trade. After more than thirty days of wrangling, the committee remained
evenly divided. This issue, too, was resolved by a compromise, with John
Adams asked to craft the final statement. The committee consented that
Parliament possessed the authority to regulate American trade, but only
because it was necessary to secure "the commercial advantages of the
whole empire to . . . its respective members." Congress squabbled for
days over the committee report, but ultimately accepted it virtually unchanged.[69] Its approval, and the adoption of the nonimportation agreement, swept Galloway's Plan of Union into oblivion. It never again came
to the floor for discussion or a formal vote, and ultimately Congress
struck it from the published record.

Having secured a resolute stand on American rights and defeated
Galloway's compromise scheme, the radicals mollified the more moderate delegates by agreeing to a temporizing Address to the King adopted
near the end of the eight-week meeting. Pledging fealty to the "royal
Authority and our subordinate Connection with Great Britain," Con-

gress said that it sought only "Peace, Liberty, and Safety" for the citizenry in the colonies.[70]

Declarations were important, but two steps taken by this Congress were more crucial. When it adopted the Continental Association, as the nonimportation agreement was called, Congress stipulated that the embargo was to be enforced by town, city, and county committees elected by those qualified to vote for assemblymen. Because of the colonists' experience with leaky embargoes in the past, Congress sought a means of ensuring the effective execution of this boycott. It achieved that goal with spectacular success. In its initial year the Continental Association slashed British imports by roughly three times as much as that achieved by the embargoes occasioned by the Townshend Duties. But the radicals achieved even more. The creation of the Association resulted in the election of 7,000 committeemen, some of whom had never before held office, and all of whom recognized that the moment Anglo-American differences were resolved they would cease to hold such a prestigious local position. In addition, these committees were usually the first government entity to identify Tories, or Loyalists, those who were unwavering in their continued support for the British government. During the winter of 1774–75, many committees asked the citizenry to take loyalty oaths pledging adherence to the embargo. Those who demurred came under suspicion, and many were disarmed the instant that war erupted.

Congress's second pivotal step was to urge each colony to put its militia "upon a proper footing."[71] Massachusetts had taken this step twelve months earlier, but for the other colonies the congressional request prompted their initial planning, organizing, and training for hostilities. Some congressmen had wanted more, as they were convinced that the boycott made war inevitable, but this was as far as Congress would go. John Adams lamented that Congress would neither create a national army nor assist the colonies in readying their militias. Congress, he said, was "fixed against Hostilities and Ruptures, except they should become absolutely necessary; and this Necessity they do not yet See." The majority, he went on, desperately hoped to avoid hostilities. War would "make a Wound which wold never be healed. It wold fix and establish a Rancour which would descend to the latest Generation. It would render all Hopes of a Reconciliation with Great Britain desperate." But Congress's fear of war went beyond the shattering of all hopes of reconciliation. According to Adams, every congressmen knew that war could not be confined to Massachusetts. It would "light up . . . flames . . . through the whole Continent," and it "might rage for twenty years, and End, in the Subduction of America as likely as in her Liberation.[72]

Galloway had warned that an embargo made war inevitable, and Patrick Henry had predicted that "Arms are a Resource to which We shall be forced."[73] If the conservative Galloway and the radical Henry agreed that war was unavoidable, most congressmen must have shared their thoughts. Yet whereas the more radical faction won on the issue of the boycott, the more conservative element prevented the creation of an American army or other steps leading to national military preparedness. Clearly, the majority at this Congress sought to leave London room to maneuver, even as it agreed that reconciliation had to be on America's terms. It also wished to avoid the appearance of provocation. It was imperative that if war came, the American public believe that London was solely responsible.

Congress stood its ground, but it sought reconciliation, and most congressmen appear to have believed that they had succeeded in keeping the door open for that possibility. Nevertheless, John Adams was correct when, many years later, he remarked that most Americans had experienced a transformation in their sentiments about Great Britain and the empire in the decade after the Stamp Act crisis. Less than a week after Galloway appealed to Congress to seek an alternative to war, Pennsylvania conducted its annual assembly elections. Twenty percent of the seats changed hands. The new assembly immediately deposed Galloway as speaker and added Dickinson to the congressional delegation. Congressional radicals instantly understood the metamorphosis in Pennsylvania. It was "a most compleat and decisive Victory in favour of the American Cause," John Adams told his wife. He added that the subjugation of Pennsylvania's conservatives would "change the Ballance" in subsequent congresses. Thereafter, the more radical delegates were likely to have a freer hand to act.[74]

5

1775–1776

"To Die Freemen Rather Than to Live Slaves"

By mid-summer 1774, London knew that an American congress was about to meet. It also knew that the Coercive Acts had provoked outrage across the length and breadth of the colonies and that yet another provincial boycott was virtually inevitable.

Some in the North government had suspected that war was unavoidable when the Coercive Acts were passed. Others, notably Lord Dartmouth, hoped against hope for peace. He expressed a willingness to negotiate with the American Congress if it "should chalk out any reasonable line of accommodation, or make any moderate or temperate proposal." Lord North expected nothing and called parliamentary elections in the autumn, hoping to solidify his base for the bold steps, whether for peace or war, that his government would face.[1]

The news that North received was uniformly bad. General Gage, now also the royal governor of Massachusetts, reported the collapse of British authority in New England and evidence of a widespread rebellion throughout America. The governor of South Carolina confirmed that the colonies pulsated with a "universal spirit of jealousy against Great Britain and of unanimity towards each other." The governor of Georgia sounded like Joseph Galloway. He warned that the only solution short of war was "a new imperial constitution."[2]

Weeks prior to receiving official word of what Congress had done, key officials in London moved steadily toward a decision to use force. In October, when it was learned that Gage had proposed that the Coercive Acts be suspended, several ministers privately rebuked him for quailing before the American rebels. In November, George III told North that "blows must decide whether they are to be subject to this country or independent." In December, at the ministry's behest, the attorney-general and solicitor-general reported their belief that rebel leaders in Massachusetts had committed treason. About a week later, the government learned of Congress's actions, including its rejection of Galloway's plan of reconciliation.[3]

By the beginning of the new year, North and most of his ministers were ready to issue war orders, but the king insisted that the government's plans be well "digested." That postponed the final decision for a month, but nothing came of the reprieve. The ministry rejected as pusillanimous a proposal by Dartmouth that a peace commission be sent to the colonies, and a move by William Pitt, Lord Chatham, to utilize Congress's temperate remonstrance to the king as a wedge for peace also came to naught. Instead, Parliament spent several weeks in February and March 1775 debating a new initiative hatched by North, which he grandly labeled a "conciliatory peace plan." The prime minister proposed that Britain would abandon American taxation if the provincials appropriated sufficient revenue to meet their defense and governmental responsibilities. The catch, of course, was that the ministry would determine what amount of revenue was necessary and might possibly assign quotas to each province. Furthermore, when Parliament considered the scheme, it did not know that the cabinet had already decided to employ force against Massachusetts. On January 27, Dartmouth, at the ministry's behest, directed General Gage to use "a vigorous Exertion of that Force" at his command, and to seize the "principal actors & abettors" in the Massachusetts resistance movement. The army's action would constitute "a signal for Hostilities," he added. Dartmouth was confident that Britain would prevail easily in the war that followed. Any resistance by the colonial militia against British regulars "cannot be very formidable," he predicted.[4] Had the ship bearing the government's order made a rapid crossing of the Atlantic, the Anglo-American war would have commenced in early March, while Parliament debated North's "peace" initiative.

Most colonials expected war, but hoped for peace. For Benjamin Franklin, however, all promise of peace had vanished. By early 1775, he knew that war was inevitable. Franklin had come to England nearly a decade before to beseech the authorities to make Pennsylvania a royal colony. He stayed on long after that hope had vanished. He was at home in cosmopolitan London and loath to trade its many amenities for a backwater provincial capital, even one such as Philadelphia, where his wife of forty years resided. Indeed, those at the apex of society in Philadelphia had always appeared to turn up their noses at Franklin, respecting his facility for getting things done, even grudgingly admiring his rise out of the artisan class, yet persisting in looking on him as a cunning, relentlessly driven upstart. In England, in contrast, Franklin had been made to feel welcome by the scientific community and many gentrymen and women from the moment he arrived in 1757. Long since elected to the Royal Society for his experimentation with electricity, he was awarded honorary degrees by St. Andrews and Oxford. He was welcomed as an equal into the homes of great merchants, was friendly with several members of Parliament (who encouraged him to run for election to the House of Commons), developed close ties with England's most famous scientists, was sought out by esteemed philosophers, writers, and historians, and even vacationed with the king's physician.[5]

Throughout these years Franklin, who turned sixty-five in 1771, appeared to be a man who hoped that the Anglo-American relationship could somehow be sustained for the few years that were likely left to him and that he might be permitted to live out his life in London where he was widely acclaimed. He seemed desperate to avoid ever having to face the choice between loyalty to Great Britain or to America, but should that terrible eventuality occur, he tried to hedge his bets by keeping one foot planted in each camp. After his misstep during the Stamp crisis, he took pains to keep the radicals at home happy by consistently attacking Britain's attempts to tax America. At the same time, he did what he could to constrain the militants in America. Franklin had much to lose in this high stakes contest. Not only had he been America's postmaster since 1753, a lucrative post that helped forestall his need for actual employment, but he owned property from Philadelphia to the prairies beyond the mountains. Furthermore, down to 1772—and perhaps even later— Franklin still believed that he had a chance of securing appointment as a subminister in the imperial government. Therefore, he chose not to comment on many inflammatory occurrences, such as the landing of British troops in Boston in 1768, and he often displayed excessive caution in his correspondence with activists at home, simultaneously hinting that Britain's objectionable policies might soon be abandoned and counseling restraint in the protest against Parliament's tax on tea. His letters to Boston's popular leaders between 1771 and 1773 often urged that agitation be shunned, and even sought to convey the delusive notion that if the Americans avoided provocation, they would win out "in Time, and that Time is at no great Distance."[6]

But Franklin's game came to a screeching halt in 1774 when his role in the Hutchinson Letters incident became public knowledge. Franklin, who appears to have looked on Hutchinson as a provocateur bent on bringing Anglo-American tensions to the flash point, may have put the correspondence into the hands of Samuel Adams in the hope of hastening the political demise of the royal governor and preventing a tumultuous crisis.

Instead, it was Franklin who was undone by the affair. On Christmas Day 1773, nine days after the Boston Tea Party, he admitted responsibility for having sent Hutchinson's and Oliver's letters to America. That sealed his fate with the imperial government. Not only was he hastily stripped of his postal position, but North's ministry publicly humiliated him. In a scene not unlike that of Oliver having been made to stand in the rain before the Liberty Tree, Franklin was compelled to remain on his feet throughout an hourlong hearing in the Cockpit, the Privy Council chamber, and listen as Britain's solicitor general poured a torrent of verbal abuse upon him.[7]

For years Franklin had procrastinated about returning home, often telling his wife that he would leave England within a few weeks, when in fact he had no intention of sailing. But immediately after his execrable treatment in the Cockpit, he informed Deborah that he would sail for Philadelphia within ninety days.[8] He meant it this time, although he ultimately reneged on that promise as well. News of the Boston Tea Party, then the Coercive Acts, and finally the calling of a Continental Congress, led him to stay on to see if "my Presence here may . . . be of Use."[9] He appears to have longed for one last roll of the dice to rehabilitate himself in London and to help prevent a war fraught with difficult personal choices. He could act, moreover, in the knowledge that he ran no particular political risk at home, as both the Galloway and Dickinson factions in Pennsylvania yearned for a peaceful solution to the imperial woes.

For a time, it appeared that Franklin's hopes might be fulfilled. Late in November, just after news of Congress's boycott reached London, Dartmouth's physician approached Franklin about drafting a plan of reconciliation. The intermediary shortly brought into the discussions a Quaker businessman, also an envoy of the colonial secretary, and ultimately Admiral Richard Howe as well. As another cold, damp winter settled over London, Franklin produced a seventeen-point proposal for fashioning what he called a "durable union" between the colonies and the parent state. He would have had Massachusetts compensate the East India Company, but he asked for the repeal of the Tea Act and Coercive Acts. While he proposed that the colonies signify their adherence to the imperial trade laws by reenacting those statutes, he recommended that all revenue raised in America from the duties on commerce go into the provincial treasuries. He conceded that the colonists would be obligated to provide revenue to the Crown during wartime, but he urged the repeal of all restraints on American manufacturing. He wished for an end to the Crown's right to invalidate colonial laws and insisted that all British troops be removed from the colonies. As if acknowledging that he was asking for enormous concessions, Franklin said that he wished not only to "put a stop to the mischief at present" but also to eradicate "every cause of jealousy and suspicion" that stood in the way of maintaining a "cordial union."

Just after Christmas, Admiral Howe confessed that "there was no likelihood of the admission of these propositions," and he urged Franklin to revise his proposals. He hinted, too, that for such a service Franklin could "with reason expect any reward in the power of government to bestow." Franklin saw immediately that he was being used, probably as a vehicle for dividing opinion in America. Had he proffered another proposal, London might have used it as an alternative to the demands of Congress. It was a game that Franklin was unwilling to play. Indeed, he characterized Howe's proposition as akin to "what the French call 'spitting in the soup.'" Although he submitted another paper, he refused to strike any of his original demands, and he even upped the ante by asking that London accept the legitimacy of the Continental Congress. His only concession was to endorse the notion bruited by the intermediaries that a peace commissioner be sent to America by North's government. Franklin's talks with Dartmouth's party spun on for six more weeks, until the third week in February, when Lord North introduced his peace plan, making further discussion pointless.[10]

In the waning days of the talks Franklin, who now plainly saw the hopelessness of the situation, wrote Galloway of the "impending Calamities," which he attributed to "Imprudencies on both Sides." At last, the time had arrived to choose between America and Great Britain. In many respects his decision had been made long before, at least from the day that he had been ridiculed in the Cockpit. That much was clear from the manner in which he responded to Dartmouth's intermediaries. Nevertheless, he seemed compelled to explain himself. To some, he contrasted Great Britain's "Corruption, Venality and Schemes of arbitrary Power" with the recent American Congress that had consisted "of Men [who were] the free, unbias'd, unsolicited Choice of the Freeholders of a great Country." To others, he spoke of the "iniquitous Acts" to which London had intransigently adhered since 1763.[11] But it was to Galloway that he offered the fullest explanation of his feelings, committing them to paper in all likelihood on the very evening that it became apparent that the search for peace was at an end:

When I consider the extreme corruption prevalent among all orders of men in this old rotten state, and the glorious public virtue so predominant in our rising country, I cannot but apprehend more mischief than benefit from a closer union. I fear they may drag us after them in all the plundering wars which their desperate circumstances, injustice, and rapacity may prompt them to undertake; and their wide-wasting prodigality and profusion is a gulf that will swallow up every aid we may distress ourselves to

afford them. Here numberless and needless places, enormous salaries, pensions, per-
quisites, bribes, groundless quarrels, foolish expeditions, false accounts or no accounts,
contracts and jobs devour all revenue and produce continual necessity in the midst of
natural plenty. I apprehend, therefore, that to unite us intimately will only be to corrupt and poison us also.[12]

A few days later Franklin sailed for America. He never again set foot on
English soil.

The war that Franklin knew was coming erupted before his letter reached
Galloway. Dartmouth's order directing the use of force, written in January, was slow in arriving, but when it reached Boston, Gage acted on it
promptly. On April 19 he put into operation a plan long in incubation.
Gage hoped to disarm the colonists, or at least reduce their available
artillery and powder, vitiating his adversary in the first moment of hostilities. Through his intelligence network, he was aware that in recent
months several arsenals—facilities for the stockpiling of weaponry—
had been established throughout Massachusetts. As his first step in the
employment of force, Gage ordered the destruction of the arsenal in
Concord, eighteen miles northwest of Boston. He did not select Concord by accident. Understanding that speed was essential to the success
of the operation, Gage chose the town housing an arsenal that was closest to Boston—where the regulars were posted—in the hope that his
troops could complete their destructive work and return to the relative
safety of the city before the Americans could adequately respond. For
months, Gage had known that village militia units were training weekly,
sometimes two or three times each week, in preparation for war. The
men were marching and drilling, loading and firing their muskets, and
generally learning to take orders; the officers were growing accustomed
to giving orders, a crash course for callow would-be leaders in the art of
commanding scores of men who had no military experience. Gage also
doubtless knew that one-third of the men in each militia company were
to be designated "minutemen"—they were to be ready to march on a
minute's notice when the alarm sounded. This made the element of surprise no less important than the speed with which the operation was
carried out, for Gage knew that, if alerted, these minutemen would descend on Concord. Gage chose Concord for one additional reason. His
intelligence network had informed him (correctly) that John Hancock
and Samuel Adams were lodged in that village, and Dartmouth's orders
had further directed him to arrest the leaders of the rebellion.

As twilight turned to sooty darkness on the damp Tuesday evening
of April 18, Gage put his army to bed without a word of what was in-

tended later that night. Only those on his staff who had been involved in the planning of the operation, and a handful of officers who would lead the incursion, knew what was pending. Those men who were earmarked for the mission got little sleep. Somewhere around 9 P.M., after perhaps ninety minutes slumber, they were rousted and ordered to ready themselves for marching. Unfortunately for Gage, the stirring in dimly lit barracks was known to activists in the popular protest. They, too, possessed a spy network. Indeed, they already were aware of Gage's intentions. Whether loose lips betrayed Gage, or the insurgent intelligence gatherers simply guessed correctly after compiling myriad loose ends of information, the Americans knew that the regulars were marching that night for Concord. The British soldiers were still gathering their arms and stuffing their cartouche boxes with balls and flints when Paul Revere and other dispatch riders left Boston to alert Concord and warn the countryside of the imminent danger.

On this night, the regulars did not move with haste, a forerunner of things to come in subsequent operations in the war that was about to begin. A formidable fighting force of nearly 900 regulars from twenty-one companies—some light infantry, some grenadiers, both the elite of the redcoat army—were selected for this mission. By 10 P.M. they were on the move. They marched to Boston's Back Bay, where the navy was to transport them across the Charles River, nearly a mile wide at the rendezvous point. Here things began to go awry. The navy had brought too few boats. What should have been a brief operation consumed several hours. At 2 A.M., now on the chilly moonlit morning of April 19, 1775, all the troops at last were across from Boston on Lechmere Point and the march toward Concord finally got under way. The trek was expected to take about five hours—a bit more than three miles per hour. They actually made considerably better time than that. However, what the cold, wet regulars did not know was that two hours earlier, near midnight, Paul Revere, riding Brown Beauty, the fastest mount that could be found for him, had reached Lexington, eleven miles away on the Concord Road. There, men with grim faces listened to the news that Revere brought. While the alarm bell in the tall, white meetinghouse tower pealed, Revere found Hancock and Samuel Adams and urged them to flee to safety. Unable to linger, he then set out to alert Concord. Behind him, Revere had left a beehive of activity. The tolling of the alarm bell, borne faintly on the wind across the silent landscape, summoned sleepy members of the Lexington militia from their homes, this time to muster for the emergency that so long had been anticipated. Soon, too, this small village sent out dispatch riders of its own to arouse trainbandsmen in nearby towns and start them toward Concord.

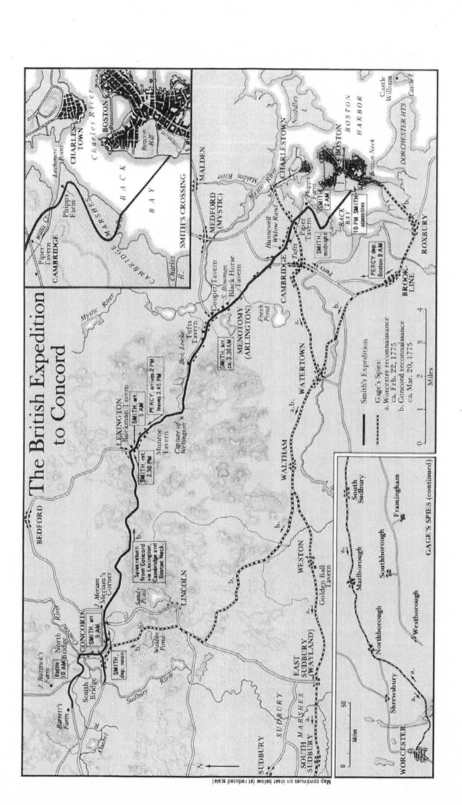

The British Expedition to Concord

Map continues on inset below (at reduced scale)

Smith's Expedition
Gage's Spies:
a. Worcester reconnaissance ca. Feb. 22, 1775
b. Concord reconnaissance ca. Mar. 20, 1775

0   1   2   3   4
Miles

GAGE'S SPIES (continued)

0   50
Miles

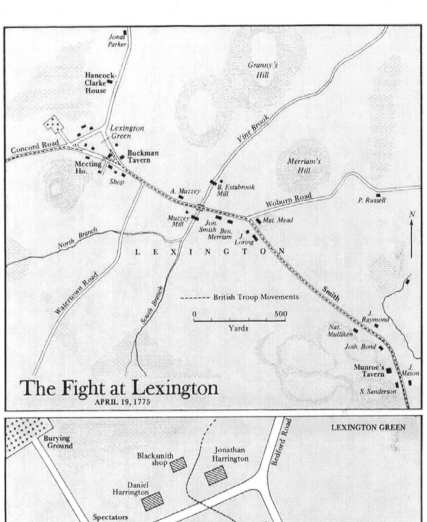

The Fight at Lexington
APRIL 19, 1775

Jonas Parker

Hancock-Clarke House

Granny's Hill

Lexington Green

Concord Road

Buckman Tavern

Meeting Ho.

Shop

A. Muzzey

B. Estabrook Mill

Vine Brook

Merriam's Hill

Woburn Road

P. Russell

Muzzey Mill

Jon. Smith Ben. Merriam

J. Loring

Mat. Meal

North Branch

L E X I N G T O N

Watertown Road

South Branch

------- British Troop Movements

0   500

Yards

Smith

J. Raymond

Nat. Mulliken

Josh. Bond

Munroc's Tavern

J. Mason

S. Sanderson

N

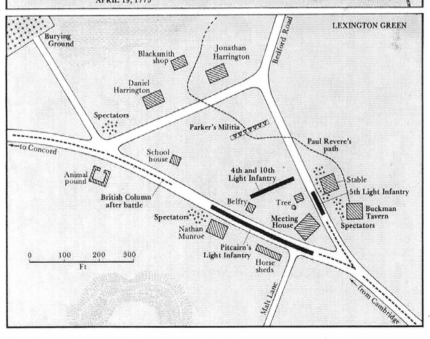

Burying Ground

Blacksmith shop

Jonathan Harrington

Bedford Road

LEXINGTON GREEN

Daniel Harrington

Spectators

Parker's Militia

Paul Revere's path

to Concord

School house

Animal pound

British Column after battle

4th and 10th Light Infantry

Belfry

Tree

Meeting House

Stable

5th Light Infantry

Buckman Tavern

Spectators

Spectators

Nathan Munroe

Pitcairn's Light Infantry

Horse sheds

Malt Lane

from Cambridge

0   100   200   300

Ft

Revere had thought the British regulars would not be far behind him and that they might reach Lexington within only an hour or so of the alert having been sounded. Instead, when he returned around 3:30 A.M., Revere discovered not only that the lobsterbacks had not yet arrived but that Hancock and Samuel Adams had not yet departed. Somehow on his second try Revere succeeded in getting them to leave, and the two patriot leaders rode for Woborn, a village north of Lexington, leaving just minutes before the British soldiery arrived.

Showers from the previous day blew out, and the skies in eastern Massachusetts cleared during that busy night. First light was visible at 4 A.M. Thirty minutes later, as the regulars approached Lexington, streaks of orange and purple in the eastern sky heralded the dawn of what was to be a historic day. An advance party—six companies of 238 red-clad regulars—reached Lexington Common at 4:30 A.M. They discovered a single company of sixty local militia, the Lexington trainband unit, drawn up on the Common. It was hardly a spit-and-polish unit. These Americans were citizen-soldiers, mostly dairy farmers and a sprinkling of artisans, who appeared to the regulars to be a ragtag collection of troublemakers. As the regulars deployed before the Common, amid the rattle of drum and fife, and the clatter of horses, Major John Pitcairn, who commanded the detachment, briskly rode forward to face his counterpart, Captain John Parker, a tall, weather-beaten forty-six-year-old farmer with some combat experience in the French and Indian War. Pitcairn did not exchange pleasantries. Brusquely, and with tangible contempt, he commanded: "Lay down your arms, you damned rebels!" Parker never hesitated. He wanted no part of leading a heavily outnumbered force in the treasonous act of killing the king's soldiers. Parker ordered his men to step aside, although he did not command them to surrender their weapons. Not one man laid down his arms. In this anxious moment in the half light of daybreak, someone fired a shot. No one ever knew who squeezed that trigger. It may have been a nervous militiaman or a zealous regular, or even someone sequestered behind a nearby stone wall, and the shot may have been fired by accident or by design. What is more apparent is that when this shot rang out in this moment of churning anxiety, several jittery regulars and white-faced militiamen instinctively fired, and some even got off more than one shot. Others never discharged their weapon. That was especially true of the militiamen, most of whom broke and ran within an instant of the first gunfire. A few got only a step or two before they were shot down, and some who were wounded were bayoneted by suddenly undisciplined regulars, moved now by a firestorm of passion. To most participants, the incident seemed to unfold over several minutes, but in fact this historic event likely consumed no more than thirty or forty seconds. By then, eight colonists lay dead and nine others wounded, almost one-third of those who had fallen out that bright morning with the Lexington trainband. One regular, a private, had been injured.

When order at last was restored and Lexington Common was secured, several British officers—who of course now knew that dispatch riders were alerting the countryside—sought to convince Lieutenant Colonel Francis Smith, whom Gage had placed in charge of the operation, to call off the march to Concord. He refused. He would comply with the orders he had been given, he said, although he sent a request for reinforcements back to headquarters in Boston. After nearly two hours in Lexington, the regulars set off once more for Concord, six miles to the west. It was about 9 A.M. when they arrived on what, otherwise, would have been a delightfully cool, sun-soft spring day. The regulars had met no resistance between Lexington and Concord, and they were unopposed when they marched into this little New England village. The Concord militia had long since mustered and had been joined by some minutemen from the surrounding area, but like their counterparts in Lexington, they too were heavily outnumbered. They took up a position on the field where for weeks they had been assembling for their training exercises, a site across the North Bridge that spanned the Concord River, and nearly a half mile from the heart of the village. They neither interfered with the grenadiers, who set to work destroying the arsenal in town, nor attempted to stop a party of redcoats who crossed the North Bridge, marching toward a suspected second magazine roughly a mile from the center of town.

The morning ebbed away. The British found little in either supply depot, as most of Concord's stores had been transferred elsewhere two weeks earlier following an alert by Boston's Whigs. However, they destroyed, or sought to demolish, all the ordnance they found. An hour passed. Then another. More militiamen from outlying communities arrived, farmers and artisans, for the most part, who had hurried to Concord, not in support of an American union—which in reality did not exist—but to defend their province, Massachusetts, against what they believed to be the malevolent intentions of a far off imperial government. By about 11:00 A.M., roughly 500 armed Americans gathered at Concord. All were under the command of Colonel James Barrett, a sixty-four-year-old miller from Concord, who on this day was attired in an old coat and leather apron, as if he planned to spend his morning grinding grains. By midmorning the torpid Barrett was under pressure from his men to do something. They had not descended on Concord to take in the sights, they said, and some added that while outnumbered, the odds were better than earlier. Barrett, who was no more anxious than

Captain Parker to order the shooting of British regulars, forestalled his men for the better part of an hour, until about 11:00, when distant smoke from the center of Concord was seen curling above the bare trees.

Colonel Barrett could wait no longer, for it appeared as if the regulars were torching the village (in fact, they were burning wooden gun carriages found in the arsenal). He ordered the men to load their weapons and marched them toward the North Bridge. There they found 115 regular infantry posted on the opposite side to secure the road into town. These British soldiers were in disarray, scattered and relaxing, and enjoying as best they could what until now had turned out to be a relatively pleasant morning. As the Americans were seen approaching, the regulars were ordered to hastily assemble. The Americans were tense and excited as they advanced; the regulars were no less anxious. As the Americans moved forward, a shot rang out, this time unmistakably fired by a regular, either in panic or by accident in the confusion of racing to regroup with his company. When the gunshot was heard, other shots— as at Lexington—instinctively were fired. Then a volley was discharged by the regulars. Incredibly, not a single shot had yet been fired by the allegedly undisciplined militiamen, who continued to advance on the bridge. Only when men began to fall with wounds was the order given to return the fire. The militiamen unloosed their own volley. Twelve regulars were hit, three fatally. The regulars, outnumbered perhaps five to one, broke and ran.

The carnage at the North Bridge presaged what was to come during the remainder of this fateful day. Colonel Smith secured his position, and no further casualties were taken by the regulars in Concord, but he prudently decided nevertheless that he would be courting trouble to prolong his stay. Precisely at noon, the beleaguered regulars, who on this long day already had marched eighteen miles, performed strenuous physical labor in destroying the arsenal, and been party to two firefights, started back toward Boston. They soon discovered that what they had experienced to this point was like child's play in contrast to what lay ahead.

All along the slender Concord Road (after this day it would be called Battle Road), steadily increasing numbers of militiamen gathered. By early afternoon more than 1,000 provincials were present to fight, giving the Americans a numerical superiority for the first time all day. Some had taken up position about a mile east of Concord at Meriam's Corner, but here and there all along the remainder of the route to Lexington, militiamen fired on the retreating regulars from behind barns, trees, haystacks, and stone walls. These ambushes were deadly, for the Americans repeatedly caught their prey in a crossfire. Among those who pitched in were Captain Parker and the Lexington militia, now 120 strong and no longer reluctant to kill the king's soldiers, perhaps even eager to do so as just retribution for the deaths of their comrades nearly eight hours before.

The regulars had sustained heavy casualties by the time they reached Lexington, where they found the reinforcements that Smith had called for, but worse was yet to come. At Lexington, what had until now been a largely disjointed, almost vigilante corps of colonial militia, was organized into a martial force with a plan. The men came under the command of General William Heath, an affluent Roxbury farmer, who conceived the idea of sending circles of skirmishers to attack the regulars who were seeking to muscle their way home by marching in a square formation. The heaviest fighting all day, and the greatest number of casualties, occurred at Menotomy, about halfway between Lexington and Boston, but the fighting raged throughout the afternoon. It ended only when the sun sank and the weary regulars, some of whom had marched nearly forty miles on this grim day, were at last able to stumble home safely in the starry darkness. Gage's most hellish nightmares had come true. Not only were 50 colonists dead and 44 others wounded or missing, but the regulars had suffered 65 dead and 207 wounded or missing. All knew, as people instantly know when an event of colossal magnitude occurs, that their world would never be the same. One who most assuredly knew that to be the case was Samuel Adams, who from Woburn heard the distant rattle of gunfire at daybreak in Lexington and immediately remarked to a companion, "It is a fine day."[13]

When Congress adjourned in October, it agreed to reassemble in Philadelphia on May 10, unless Anglo-American differences had been resolved in the interim. Instead, the crisis had reached the point of bloodshed. British troops had battled Americans, and the city of Boston was effectively under military occupation. Three weeks after blood was spilled at Lexington and Concord, Congress gathered again, this time in the Pennsylvania State House. Fifty of the sixty-five delegates had sat in the previous Congress. A few representatives, such as Galloway, refused to be part of a body that was waging war against the mother country. Thus, all who took seats in the Second Congress supported the war—but deep divisions nevertheless were readily apparent. Congress was split over war aims and divided on the issue of pursuing negotiations with Great Britain while hostilities raged. Furthermore, as was true of the previous Congress, those who attended were politicians, not the inhabitants of a philosophical ivory tower. They sought to protect the interests of the American provinces. Even more, in most instances, they came to defend the interests of the colony they represented, which in reality usually meant sustaining the interests of the most powerful elements at home. But unity was crucial if the American insurgency was to succeed, and the most savvy understood the necessity for give and take among rival American interests.

Dickinson soon emerged as the leader of a faction that drew its greatest support from the commercially dominated mid-Atlantic colonies. Many in this bloc were the very congressmen who had backed Galloway six months before. They sought reconciliation with the mother country on terms laid out by the earlier Congress, embraced the union of the colonies, and steadfastly supported the war effort. Dickinson told Congress that he wished to preserve America's "Dependence & Subordination" to the Crown and to a Parliament that regulated imperial commerce, a power that it had "been always in the possession & Exercise of."[14] Like his old foe Galloway, Dickinson now searched for some middle ground that might save the empire.

The members of this faction sought a reconciliation for several reasons. Change always frightens some, and uncertainty over where change will lead can have a paralyzing grip. Some in 1775 feared that the hegemony of the elite might be diminished, or terminated altogether, as popular revolutionary regimes emerged in the course of a long, desperate war. Remove the protective mantle of the empire, they believed, and what had been flourishing economic enterprises might wither and die. Throughout New England, for instance, the fishing industry had been big business for a century, and it in turn brought prosperity to ship construction yards along the coast from Newport to Portsmouth and employment to thousands of mariners. However, if New England left the British Empire, access to the fisheries off the North American coast—traditionally dominated by France and Great Britain, Europe's two great maritime powers—would be problematical. Far to the south, rice planters in the Carolina lowlands, unlike their counterparts in the Chesapeake, were not plagued by acute economic problems, and before the inauguration of London's new colonial policies a decade earlier, little evidence existed that they were unhappy subjects. Indeed, they not only continued to enjoy handsome profits from their staple, but many added to their wealth by growing indigo, a crop subsidized by Parliament. In addition, most had a continuous need for slave laborers, many of whom were acquired from the British sugar islands. Nor did wealthy South Carolinians speculate as heavily in the lands across the mountains as did Virginia's planters. They were more likely to invest in Charleston's ship construction industry or in the production of naval stores, much of which was sold to shipyards in the mother country. To sever ties with Great Britain was to endanger numerous lucrative pursuits.

As the middle colonies in the eighteenth century were drawn steadily deeper into the economic web of the Atlantic world, the merchant communities of New York and Philadelphia exerted ever greater sway in their colonies and to some degree even over neighboring New Jersey and Delaware. Although most urban merchants abhorred British encroachments on the rights of Americans, and even willingly made sacrifices in protesting London's policies after 1765, a break with the mother country raised the specter of austerity and perhaps ruination at a time when the economy was neither depressed nor disordered. Merchants, as the historian Thomas Doerflinger has written, had "no compelling financial reason to break with England."[15] Many had excellent motives for wishing to preserve their ties with Great Britain. Business was good. Among Philadelphia's merchants after 1760, an annual profit margin of 12 percent was a realistic expectation. Nevertheless, operating out of American provinces that were habitually deprived of capital, many merchants survived only as the result of extensions of credit supplied from the metropolis. Moreover, unlike most Americans, merchants were in constant contact with the mother country. They knew residents of the old country on a firsthand basis, relied on marine insurance acquired in England, the protection of the Royal Navy, and the diplomatic corps of the imperial government. Furthermore, the prosperity of these businessmen depended on monetary stability. Any shift in the supply or value of money could adversely affect their ledger books. To a degree unknown by other provincials, American merchants could neither forget that they were part of the British world nor that their prosperity in large measure was dependent on decisions made in the faraway mother country. To them the British Empire was very real. To separate from Great Britain raised the specter of real and fundamental threats to their business operations, to their easy existence, and ultimately to their social prominence. Most supported protest that aimed at reconciliation on terms that were favorable to America, but independence, as one Philadelphia merchant remarked in 1775, was "unnatural, and will assuredly prove unprofitable." The "advantages of security and stability," said another, "lie with America remaining in the empire."[16]

Still another factor led many activists to prefer reconciliation. Like Dickinson, many were convinced that America was too weak, and too divided, to stand against the empire. Only when it had grown "so strong & united, that . . . We should have nothing to fear from any other Power," Dickinson said, could America contemplate independence. Rather than leap into independence, he proposed that Congress take three steps: wage war, petition the king for redress, and send diplomats to London to negotiate the terms of reconciliation. Dickinson and his allies were playing for time.[17] If a congressional declaration of independence could be fore-stalled, the day might arrive when Great Britain, chastened by military reverses, was forced to offer acceptable terms for reuniting the empire, or when both the colonies and the mother country, mutually exhausted by the attrition of war, could find common ground on which reconcili-ation could be arranged.[18]

A more militant faction, drawn principally from New England and the South, coalesced in opposition to the reconciliationists. Some among these radicals, as Dickinson had fathomed, already secretly and ebul-liently favored American independence, but they dared not use the word *independence* in public through 1775. Others, with some disappointment, saw a break with Great Britain as unavoidable, or preferable to what they perceived as the servile and dependent status that Dickinson had outlined. Still others yet hoped for reconciliation, but feared that be-seeching London to negotiate, as Dickinson would have had them do, displayed weakness and might provoke fatal internal divisions. This fac-tion soon had a new leader in the Second Congress. Samuel Adams stepped from the shadows and played a more open role, and for a time Patrick Henry remained influential among the radicals. However, like a cake that is transformed between the mixing bowl and the oven, the nature of Congress changed dramatically as it evolved from a protest body to a government that waged war. As it metamorphosed, new lead-ers eclipsed the old. By midsummer, some had come to see John Adams as the "first man in the House" among the radicals.[19]

The emergence of Adams as a leader in the Second Congress was striking. A year earlier, when he ar-rived in Philadelphia, he had been a virtual novice in politics, having pre-viously held only inconsequential posts in Braintree and a seat in the Massachusetts assembly for one term. Adams had been virtually invisible in the initial congress. Not only had he been awed at the prospect of serving beside the "greatest Men upon this Continent," but Samuel Adams had kept him in check.[20] However, John Adams's confidence in his own abili-ties grew as he observed other con-gressmen, until he saw himself as their equal or, in most cases, their superior.

John Adams. Portrait by Charles Willson Peale, about 1791–1794.

Bright, tireless, and keenly ambitious, Adams returned to Congress in 1775 ready to play a more active role, especially now that Massachusetts was at war, and eager to win acclaim.

Adams feared that his quest for greatness would be thwarted by his physical limitations. "By my Physical Constitution I am but an ordinary Man," he said, a reference to his unprepossessing physique. He was about five feet seven and overweight. He also was balding, pale, ungainly, and as one observer noted, "careless of appearances." Other liabilities dogged him as well. His visage was usually grim and stern, his manner gruff and grumbling, and he was often brusquely impatient with those who differed with him. He conceded his inadequacy in the art of easy, meaningless patter, acknowledging his shortcomings in telling jokes and confessing discomfort at spinning off-color yarns. When the talk turned to what he thought were men's favorite subjects—horses, dogs, and women—he said that he was unable to add anything to the conversation. Furthermore, Adams not only was well aware that many found him to be vain and irascible but he readily admitted that he was captious and contrary.[21]

Nevertheless, Adams balanced his limitations with attributes that served him well in a legislative chamber. Many who were initially put off by his churlish demeanor eventually came to see him as honest, self-effacing, and even good-humored. He had formed numerous lifelong friendships from among his chums in college and fellow lawyers in Boston, and now did the same with colleagues in Congress. Furthermore, he came to Congress after years of experience in courtrooms, where he had honed his skills as a debater and grown to be a competent, though not dynamic, orator. He was bright and industrious, and soon acquired a reputation for mastering the details of the subjects for which he was assigned responsibility. His associates came to see him as Congress's most knowledgeable member on the subjects of diplomacy and political theory, and as the war went on he gained a specialist's understanding of weaponry, naval craft, and military organizational techniques, even though he had never served as a soldier. No one ever complained that he avoided work. He probably served on more committees than any other congressman between 1775 and 1777, more than sixty altogether, a regimen that often kept him at work from before sunrise until long after nightfall.[22]

Adams lacked Samuel Adams's talents as an artful schemer, organizer, and manipulator—indeed, he was put off by these practices—nor did he possess Patrick Henry's thespian flair for oratory. He may have been better off for his deficiencies. Samuel Adams's penchant for machination led others to distrust him, and in time Henry's histrionics not only wore thin but his associates found that behind the fire and thunder

lurked a rather ordinary mind. Faced with war and the most momentous choices, Congress sought leaders noted for prudence, honesty, fair-
ness, imagination, acumen, and dedication. When Thomas Jefferson
arrived in Congress in June 1775, he was immediately impressed that the
leaders were "sober reasoning . . . cool-headed, reflecting, judicious men."
Jefferson was especially struck by Adams, whom he characterized as "profound in his views . . . and accurate in his judgment" and "as disinterested as the being who made him." Samuel Adams's halcyon days of
political leadership were fading in this new milieu. So too were those of
Henry, who seemed aware that he was out of his element in the wartime
Congress. Midway though 1775 he left Philadelphia and returned to his
old seat in the Virginia assembly, and in Jefferson's estimation he was
"wonderfully relieved" to do so.[23]

Samuel Adams's master stroke at the First Congress had been to dis-
courage intemperate behavior by the Massachusetts delegates. It was John
Adams's genius in 1775 to grasp intuitively that it would be counterproductive for the radicals to get too far in front of popular opinion. He
quickly perceived that the "idea of independence was as unpopular . . . as
the Stamp Act itself," and that a policy of patience was the prudent course.
"We cannot force Events," he counseled. Adams believed that the battlefields of the Anglo-American war would determine America's future.
Not only would the war determine whether the insurgency lived or died,
but he was convinced that hostilities would inevitably radicalize his countrymen. In time, he sensed, the radicals would have their way, but until
then it was imperative that the radical faction propitiate the reconciliationists, so that the two factions moved together "like a large Fleet sailing under Convoy." That meant that the "fleetest Sailors must wait for
the dullest and slowest . . . that all may keep an even Pace." Otherwise,
the war would be lost due to divisions on the home front. Once, in fact,
in the course of a passionate dispute in the State House yard, an angrily
incandescent Dickinson had made clear to Adams that if the radicals
refused to "concur with us in our pacific system, I and a number of us
will break off from you in New England, and we will carry on the opposition by ourselves in our own way."[24]

Thus, Dickinson largely had his way throughout 1775. Congress not
only adopted a resolution in late May that proclaimed its desire to be
reconciled to the mother country, but two months later it agreed to send
yet another petition to the king. Dickinson saw the entreaty as a "Measure of Peace" that might spark negotiations. The radicals thought it a
"Measure of Imbecility," as Adams remarked in private. Franklin, who
arrived home on the eve of the Congress and was quickly added to the
Pennsylvania delegation, characterized the gesture as an act of futility.

He forecast that the Crown would have "neither Temper nor Wisdom enough to seize the Golden opportunity."[25]

These actions cleared the decks so that at last Congress could contemplate military necessities. Since April 19 the British army of about 4,000 had been besieged in Boston by a New England army of approximately 16,000 men. Regional newspapers called it the Grand American Army, but in fact it was a much less potent force than the name suggested. It consisted of militiamen, who would return home after a few weeks, and enlistees whose service would be up at year's end. Furthermore, the army faced conspicuous shortages. Only six cannon were fit for service. Gunpowder was lacking. A tent was available for only one soldier in twenty. The pantry was likely to be bare in a few weeks. The siege army's officers, and leading New England politicians, beseeched Congress to create a national army supplied by all the colonies.[26]

The issue was never in doubt. From the outset, the Second Congress was committed to creating an army under its centralized control. The fate of colonists who lived far from New England was now intertwined with the course of events on faraway battlefields, and they sought to exert influence over the army that marched to the battle sites of this war. At stake too was the shape and tenor of the army. New England was far more egalitarian than the mid-Atlantic and Southern colonies, and its army reflected the character of the region. More often than not, lower grade officers—lieutenants and captains—were farmers and artisans who often had been friends at home with the men they commanded. Their relationship in camp with the enlisted men frequently continued to be one of easy-going camaraderie and socializing. The officers at times gave their men haircuts or repaired their shoes, and sometimes they even consented to the pooling of all pay before it was divided equally. It was a citizens' army, and its presence in the fluid political and military atmosphere of 1775 held the potential for contributing to momentous domestic change.[27]

The protest movement had generated political and social tensions from its inception. When mobs tore down the residences of silk-stocking Bostonians during the Stamp Act riots in 1765, and when carefully managed protestors destroyed the East India Company's tea, many horrified colonists wondered where these attacks on private property would lead. Long before 1775 the customary deference of the lower sort to their social betters had begun to erode, prompting Thomas Hutchinson to lament that "a gentleman does not meet [any longer] with what used to be common civility." In Virginia, political candidates who inveighed against laws that compelled non–slave owners to ride night patrol to "keep . . . a

142   ✦   A LEAP IN THE DARK

rich man's slaves in order" were being elected to office. Such a turn of
events prompted John Randolph, the attorney-general of the colony, and
the brother of the president of the First Continental Congress, Peyton
Randolph, to grieve that the insurgency was handing over the "reins of
government" to the "ignorant vulgar" within society.[28] Some in Congress worried that the army under creation might wind up in the hands
of this very sort. Indeed, months before Galloway had anticipated that
possibility and, in a sulky pamphlet written on the eve of hostilities, had
warned of war waged by a marauding New England army composed of
"Companies of armed, but undisciplined men, headed by men
unprincipalled," save for their commitment to sowing democracy and
social leveling.[29]

More than one congressman shared Galloway's concern. The wrong
army in the wrong hands could lead matters in the wrong direction. The
army could become an "armed monster," they cautioned. Using language
almost identical to that of Galloway, some congressmen who supported
the war expressed fear in 1775 that "an Enterprising eastern New England Genll proving Successful, might with his Victorious Army give
law to the Southern & Western gentry." These congressmen believed the
officers in the national army must be drawn from throughout America,
and from among the elite that had traditionally provided leadership in
colonial America. Others looked with a jaundiced eye on New England's
army. Still others simply placed no confidence in a military force that
consisted mostly of militiamen. Like Samuel Adams, they distrusted
standing armies, but they also believed that only a regular army could
fight successfully against British professionals, and that only a trained
and disciplined force would have the staying power to see this war
through to victory.[30]

These myriad concerns integrated in the notion that the national
army should be comprised of a soldiery that enlisted for single year
hitches and served under leaders who were deemed socially responsible.
On June 14, more than a month after Congress assembled, John Adams
nominated his colleague, George Washington of Virginia, to command
the new army. Although Adams believed Washington possessed the qualities to lead the army to victory, he later confessed that he also acted to
allay fears of New England leveling and to further solidify the Virginia-
Massachusetts glue that helped hold together the radicals in Congress.[31]
In fact, Washington's selection would mean that Artemus Ward of Massachusetts, the commander of the siege army, would have to be removed.
For the second time in nine months New England's congressmen had
made a substantive concession to Southerners.

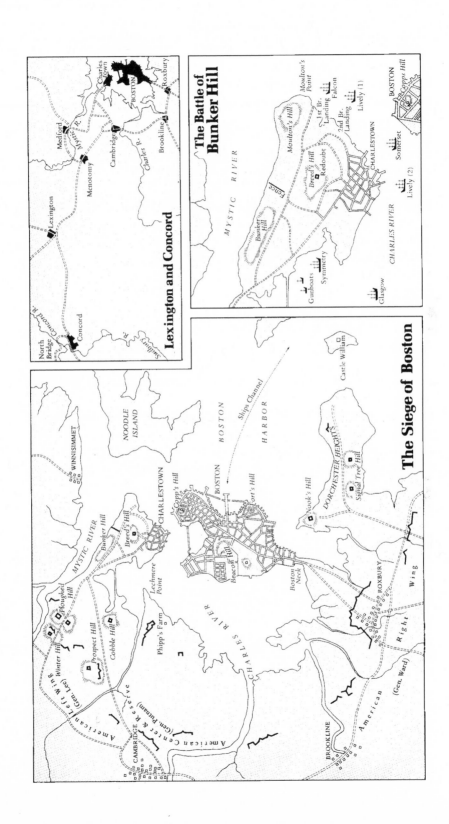

Lexington and Concord

Charles Town
BOSTON
Roxbury
MYSTIC R.
Medford
Cambridge
Brookline
Menotomy
Charles R.
Lexington
Concord
North Bridge
Concord R.
Sudbury R.

The Battle of Bunker Hill

MYSTIC RIVER
Moulton's Point
1st Br. Landing
2nd Br. Landing
Falcon
Lively (1)
BOSTON
Copps Hill
Moulton's Hill
Breed's Hill
Redoubt
CHARLESTOWN
Somerset
Fence
Bunker Hill
Lively (2)
CHARLES RIVER
Gunboats
Symmetry
Glasgow

The Siege of Boston

Castle William
Ships Channel
BOSTON HARBOR
NOODLE ISLAND
WINNISIMMET
BOSTON
Copp's Hill
Fort's Hill
Nook's Hill
DORCHESTER HEIGHTS
Signal Tree Hill
CHARLESTOWN
MYSTIC RIVER
Bunker Hill
Breed's Hill
Lechmere Point
Beacon Hill
Boston Neck
Ploughed Hill
Prospect Hill
Cobble Hill
Phipp's Farm
CHARLES RIVER
ROXBURY
Right Wing
American Left Wing (Gen. Lee)
Winter Hill
American Center & Reserve (Gen. Putnam)
CAMBRIDGE
BROOKLINE
American Right Wing (Gen. Ward)

Congress approved Washington after two days of secret deliberations. Much of the time likely was spent eliciting the opinions of
Washington's fellow delegates from Virginia, but some congressmen
apparently opposed his selection. Those who questioned Washington's
appointment did not doubt his abilities so much as they fretted that the
existing force might implode if General Ward was dumped, or that New
England soldiers might not follow a Southerner. In the end, Washington
was an overwhelmingly popular choice. He was in good health, had ample
leadership experience, and at age forty-three was young enough to command with vigor throughout what might be a protracted conflict. Finally, Washington had sat in both congresses. His colleagues had taken
his measure and thought he could be trusted with the responsibility they
were about to bestow.

Once appointed, Congress undertook what may have been America's
first public relations campaign. One New England congressman after
another wrote home extolling Washington's virtues, talents, and courage. A man of "great Modesty," Washington would be an exemplary role
model, a Connecticut congressman advised the home folk. "Our youth
[will] look up to this Man as a pattern to form themselves by." He "Unites
the bravery of the Soldier, with the most consummate Modesty and Virtue." He was described as "amiable, generous and brave," and as a
"Gent[elma]n highly Esteemed for his Military & other accomplishments." Another predicted that he was "Suited to the Temper & Genius
of our People." Those at home were urged to treat him "with all the
Confidence and Affection, that Politeness and Respect, which is due to
one of the most important Characters in the World."[32]

Congress next appointed the remaining general officers. This was
messy, and an augury of politics to come. Despite considerable talk in
recent years of the corruption in British public life that inhibited the
selection of men of talent, Congress's choices for military leadership resulted mostly from political factors. It intended to create eight such posts,
but to satisfy colonies that felt slighted, four major generals, eight briga-
dier generals, and an adjutant general were eventually appointed. Some
who were selected soon proved to be notoriously incompetent, although
Washington, a superb judge of men, succeeded for the most part in rapidly identifying those who were inadequate and posting them in less
vital assignments where they could do little harm. Congress set the size
of the army at 15,000 men, organized it, took steps to supply and fund it,
and adopted uniform standards for the thirteen provincial militias.[33]

These matters were quickly resolved. Settling on a statement that
explained the colonists' reasons for waging war proved to be more difficult. Congress rejected the report of the committee initially assigned the

responsibility and restructured the panel, adding Dickinson and Thomas Jefferson, who only two days earlier had alighted from his phaeton to take a seat in Congress. Seldom has a new member of Congress been so instantly acclaimed as was Jefferson. "Yesterday the famous Mr. Jefferson a Delegate from Virginia . . . arrived," a congressman from Rhode Island noted. Actually, Jefferson, who was yet a year away from drafting the Declaration of Independence, was not yet famous. He had served eight mostly inconspicuous years in the Virginia assembly, although a pamphlet he had published earlier that year had won for him a reputation as a writer. John Adams greeted Jefferson's arrival, remarking that he had a "happy talent for composition," and Congress immediately availed itself of his literary skills, assigning him to the committee that was preparing what amounted to an American declaration of war.[34] Not surprisingly, his colleagues on the committee asked him to draft the statement.

Jefferson's draft accused London of seeking to "erect a despotism of unlimited extent" over America. Dickinson immediately objected. Strident accusations, he said, would make it difficult for the Crown to mediate the differences, and he offered revisions that modulated the tone of the document. Dickinson's version was accepted as the radicals once again gave way. The final version of the Declaration of the Causes and Necessity for Taking Up Arms proclaimed that "we mean not to dissolve the union" and that "We have not raised Armies with ambitions of separating from Great Britain." Jefferson's allegations of British tyranny and rapacity were nowhere to be found, nor was his prior claim set forth in the *Summary View of the Rights of British America*, the pamphlet that had earned him a measure of acclaim, that Parliament had no authority whatsoever over the colonies. Nevertheless, even this toned down version, which Congress adopted, was a bold, confrontational document. "Our cause is just. Our union is perfect," it stated, and it went on to declare that the colonists would fight on, seeking foreign assistance if necessary, until the mother country acceded to their demands. Americans, it concluded, were "resolved to die Freemen rather than to live Slaves."[35]

With the army in existence, and General Washington off to the front, Congress on July 8 approved the "humble petition" to the king that in principle it had agreed to six weeks earlier. John Adams privately sneered at the naivete of such a step. Dickinson's faction, he said, held to the hope that Parliament would back down when it learned of the bloodshed at Lexington and Concord. Such expectations were chimerical, he believed, but those bent on reconciliation had to be accommodated lest "Discord and total Disunion" result.[36] The petition, written chiefly by Dickinson, made no mention of American rights and blamed the imperial woes on the monarch's irresponsible ministers. It also cautioned the king that the war would only radicalize growing numbers of colonists, making reconciliation even more tenuous. It beseeched George III to act while time remained. Congress adopted the entreaty, in part to assuage those who held the hope of reconciliation, but also as historian Jerrilyn Marston has demonstrated, from a desire to centralize control of America's external affairs in its own hands. In 1774 New York and New Jersey had petitioned the Crown even while Congress was in session. Congress had not been happy. Such conduct demonstrated—or at least hinted at—divisions among the colonists. Congress wished London to believe that wartime America was undivided. From this point forward, America's relationship with the mother country was solely in the hands of the Continental Congress. Soon thereafter, in fact, Congress rejected Lord North's so-called peace plan, although the ministry had pointedly sent it not to the Congress, but to the assemblies in each of the thirteen colonies. Even the most conservative congressmen had repudiated North's scheme, branding it "invidiously devised to wear the face of peace, and Embarrass us in the Choice of evils."[37]

While Congress contemplated these matters, word arrived of the Battle of Bunker Hill, fought in Charlestown, across the river from Boston. It was the first pitched battle of the war, an encounter brought on when the siege army took possession of the heights commanding Boston harbor, the first link in the umbilical that tied the British army to its supply depots at home. Faced with retaking the hill or surrendering the city, General Gage acted against the insurgents. He put General William Howe, newly arrived with reinforcements from the mother country, in charge of the operation. Howe could have taken Bunker Hill almost bloodlessly. Through adroit maneuver, and by utilizing the Royal Navy, the British might simply have cut off the siege army's lane of retreat. However, Howe shared Dartmouth's conviction that the American soldiers were not to be taken seriously. With ineffable recklessness, he marched his men up the heights against an entrenched adversary. Howe lost 1,054 of the 2,400 men who fought that day. Entire units were wiped out, and nearly one hundred officers were killed. Howe's twelve staff officers were on the battlefield. Each was a casualty.[38]

The fighting qualities and devastation wrought by the Americans both on April 19 and now in June at Bunker Hill, convinced the radicals that "we are able to cope with the whole force of Great Britain, if we are but willing to exert ourselves." Those who yearned for reconciliation reached a different conclusion. Upon learning that the British army had again suffered "so severe a drubbing" at Bunker Hill, they now more than ever believed that London would be compelled to reassess its policies. At the very least, officials in London would see that they "have Men to deal with, tho' unexperienced, and not yet well armed." Many believed that the ministry, aware at last "that this is a harder nut to crack than they imagined," as one congressman remarked, would seek an accommodation. Franklin did his part by attempting to convince friends in London that Great Britain could never accomplish its ends through military means. Not only would the cost of suppressing the rebellion be backbreaking—he claimed that the British army had "killed 150 Yankies this campaign, which is £20,000 a head"—but the day soon would come when London could not maintain the colonies through force, as the inhabitants of America would vastly outnumber those at home. Britain's long term interest, he appeared to say, cried out for reconciliation.[39]

Nevertheless, Dickinson and those in his faction also knew that the war was taking on a life of its own that could threaten their tenuous hold on Congress. Many Americans, like Jefferson, believed that once "blood was spilt," the demands made in 1774 by the first Congress were no longer sufficient. Had they been aware of his views, many colonists would have concurred with Jefferson, who in private remarked that America thus far had made only minimal demands in order "to convince the world they were not unreasonable."[40] If Britain rejected such modest demands, Americans likely would seek more radical ends.

Even the most myopic among the reconciliationists could doubtless see that the mood of much of the country was far ahead of that in Congress. As many might have expected, for instance, Boston greeted Samuel Adams as a hero when he returned from the initial Congress, but it must have surprised some in May 1775 when crowds of cheering Philadelphians thronged the streets to welcome the Massachusetts delegation back to Congress. No other delegation received such a greeting. Numerous signs of deep change abounded that crisp autumn. Some wealthy individuals in the Connecticut Valley, who long had controlled everything, and everyone, within their purview, suddenly faced contumacious challenges by their defiant neighbors. One or two were physically harassed. In rural New York, juries now consistently ruled against suspected Tories in land title controversies. When local officials in Albany refused to institute a "burghers' watch" to maintain security, Albanians took power and erected their own people's militia. Some men throughout America took up arms to soldier because they saw it as an opportunity for self-enhancement. Captain William Scott of Petersborough, New Hampshire, who was taken prisoner in the Battle of Bunker Hill, told his captors that he knew nothing of the imperial tempest, but that by soldiering he believed he could become an officer-hero, which would afford him the "Chance to rise higher" in his hometown.[41]

The tenor of the pamphlets written by the more conservative activists changed as well after hostilities commenced. The earlier polemics had focused almost entirely on issues of constitutionalism and the colonists' rights. However, in 1775 some scribes for the first time addressed the concern that the radical protest was eroding the bonds of society. To some extent, this was a response to the Tory outcry that followed the First Congress. Galloway, for instance, not only gave warning of New England armies spreading egalitarian notions, but he dilated on the "calamity" of "civil discord" that would result from lessening London's restraining hand. Other Tories cautioned that the libertarian rhetoric, symbols, and rituals employed by the radicals could lead to unsettling political and societal change. Some argued that humankind was naturally unequal and that chaos would ensue if the hierarchical order of society crumbled. Still others advised that in urging America to put its interests above those of the empire, the radicals were encouraging ambitious and avaricious colonists to place their self-interest above that of society.[42]

Many radicals responded by acknowledging the danger of anarchy, and even Samuel Adams admitted the peril risked by placing excessive power in the hands of the people. Some radical writers sought to counter fears by demonstrating that the people remained adequately checked, and John Adams took the position that even where provincial conventions had supplanted the charter assemblies, the new legislative bodies had acted "with as much order as ever, and conducted their opposition as much by the constitution as ever." Somewhat lamely Jefferson added that where mobs had arisen and violence occurred, the perpetrators "were amenable to the laws of the land" and the punishment society dictated.[43]

At the same time, some radical essays took on a new air. Homilies on the proper behavior of the good citizen appeared in 1775. The people were exhorted to place the good of the whole above personal ambition. "Sacrifice" and "virtue" were the words of the moment. The virtuous citizen, it was said, would unselfishly relinquish his own ends for those of the community. Patriotism and public virtue were said to be synonymous. Indeed, Congress had already sought to wrap its policies in a mantle of moral purity. The First Congress had proscribed horse racing, cockfighting, rolling dice and playing cards, the theater, and ostentatious dressing, and had even sought to regulate the mourning process. It was as if Congress wished to show the colonists, and the world at large, that resistance to Great Britain was moral and principled, and conducted by a virtuous people.[44]

Dickinson's thin hold on Congress began to unravel during the autumn. Word arrived early in November that the king had proclaimed

America to be in a state of rebellion. He branded all colonists who henceforth joined the American resistance as guilty of "traitorous designs." Soon thereafter Congress also learned that the monarch had contemptuously refused to accept its Olive Branch Petition. The news came as a surprise only to Dickinson and his comrades. The more radical congressmen exulted that their hands at last were untied. A Rhode Islander thought the king had been of "immense Service" in guaranteeing that Congress's "Resolutions will henceforth be spirited, clear, and decisive." Another representative thought all Americans would now see that the monarch was bent on "vengeance against all those in America who refuse absolute submission" to the wishes of the parent state. Jefferson proclaimed him "the bitterest enemy we have."[45]

The initial indication that Congress was changing came quickly. When the king's proclamation reached Philadelphia, Congress was deliberating an inquiry from New Hampshire about the wisdom of supplanting its provincial government, established generations earlier under the colony's charter, with one more suitable to the changed times. This was not the first time Congress had been approached about such an action. Massachusetts had sought similar counsel five months earlier. At that time, Congress recommended that the Massachusetts government conform in "spirit and substance" to the colonial government established under the Crown-issued Charter of 1691. But Congress was demonstrably more radical by late autumn. On the day after learning of the king's pronouncement, Congress advised New Hampshire to create a new government that would provide "a full and free representation of the people, and that . . . will best produce the happiness of the people." Congress also soon passed on similar advice to other colonies.[46]

The reconciliationists were stunned, but fought back. Dickinson hurried into the chambers of the Pennsylvania assembly, which met one floor above Congress in the State House, and secured passage of new instructions to the province's congressional delegation. The Pennsylvania congressmen were told to "utterly reject any propositions . . . that may cause or lead to a separation from our mother country." Pennsylvania acted on the same day that Congress instructed New Hampshire. Delaware and New Jersey soon rigidly bound their congressmen to reject radical steps as well. New Jersey even contemplated sending its own Olive Branch Petition to the king, reasoning that the monarch might respond to an entreaty from a legitimate assembly. However, even Dickinson thought such a step imprudent. He traveled to Burlington to address the assembly, and cautioned the legislators that the cause of reconciliation would not be well-served should diverse communications from several legislatures persuade London that America was disunited.[47]

The reconciliationists had shored up their damaged position, but events were overtaking them. In November word coursed through America that Lord Dunmore, the royal governor of Virginia, had promised to liberate slaves who joined his troops and helped suppress the rebellion. Virginia's radical congressmen railed at the "Diabolical Scheme" of "this Monster," while the remaining reconciliationists in the province, now faced with the prospect of having their throats cut in the course of a slave insurrection inspired by their governor, turned their backs on the Crown forever. Nor were the shockwaves released by Dunmore's act confined to Virginia. North Carolina, which had little history of assisting its neighbors, immediately dispatched 400 soldiers to Virginia to assist in its defense against the royal troops.[48]

A few weeks later the text of the king's truculent speech opening Parliament in October reached Philadelphia. The monarch had observed that the object of the "desperate conspiracy" in America was independence. He also announced that German mercenaries would be secured to help suppress the "rebellious war." Days later came word of a bill introduced by Lord North—it would result in the American Prohibitory Act—that would terminate commerce with all the colonies for the duration of the war. British policy "don't look like a Reconciliation," was the response of John Hancock.[49] It was in this milieu that Thomas Paine's *Common Sense* was published.

Paine, a skilled artisan, sometime bureaucrat, drifter, and lethargic visionary, had come to Philadelphia from England eighteen months earlier, hoping at age thirty-seven to begin life anew. Like Patrick Henry and Samuel Adams, he had failed in many endeavors. He washed out of school, twice was fired as a tax collector, and in his mid-thirties ran a small business into ruin. Little evidence existed before 1776 that he possessed any remarkable talents. Had normal times persisted, Paine in all likelihood would have remained undistinguished. But these were not normal times, and the war, which erupted six months after Paine's arrival in the colonies, had already begun to churn and sift society. "When the pot boils the scum will rise," remarked some Tories who were bewildered by the changes all about them. "The cream rises" in such circumstances, radicals countered.[50]

Paine had published a few short essays before leaving the old country, and without a job in his adopted city, he rapidly turned to writing to earn rent money. He churned out about one published essay every two weeks during his initial ten months in Pennsylvania. He wrote about the war, attacked slavery, and mused on science, mathematics, ancient history, dueling, and unhappy marriages. It soon was clear that Paine was no ordinary writer. He wrote with a blazing flair and energy that brought him to the attention of leading luminaries in the popular movement. Finding evidence that Paine's sentiments tallied with theirs, emissaries from the radical camp sounded him out in the autumn of 1775 about composing a pamphlet that openly urged independence. Benjamin Rush, the Philadelphia physician, even bluntly told Paine that he had little to lose by writing such a tract. What could the British authorities do to an impecunious, propertyless, jobless idler?

Paine consented, though he began timorously. In October he obliquely mentioned the inevitability of American independence in an essay on slavery. Next he began work on three separate essays on independence, but at Rush's suggestion combined them into a single pamphlet. Rush also induced Franklin and Samuel Adams, among others, to read and critique Paine's handiwork, and persuaded him to change the name of his tract from *Plain Truth* to the more pithy *Common Sense.*[51] It rolled off the press during the second week of January 1776.

America had never experienced such a pamphlet. Dickinson's *Letters from a Farmer in Pennsylvania*, published in 1767, had reached the largest audience of the approximately 250 political tracts issued since 1765.[52] Roughly one hundred times more copies of *Common Sense* were purchased in 1776 than the Dickinson's tract had sold in eight years. Countless others read *Common Sense* in their newspapers, copyright laws not being terribly stringent in those days. Furthermore, at Washington's orders, whole regiments of Continental soldiers listened as portions of it were read to them. Conservatively, between January and July probably a quarter million colonists read it or heard it, roughly every other free adult living in Anglo-America. Paine was a powerful writer who possessed an uncommon gift for presenting ideas

Thomas Paine. Oil on canvas by John Wesley Jarvis, about 1806/1807.

with clarity and turning a crisp phrase. Unlike most political pamphleteers, his literary style neither read like a legal brief nor groaned beneath Latin phrases. Indeed, his thoughts seemed to explode from the pages. At once, he exuded euphoria at the prospect of sweeping change and simmered with a palpable rage at England—a combination that captured the popular mood.

The pamphlet dilated on four themes. In the earliest section, and the least well remembered, Paine sought to demystify government for those who had been told all their lives that affairs of state were so abstruse that they must be left to the educated and social elite. In a few brief paragraphs he explained that as government existed to secure the safety and well-being of the citizenry, "common sense" dictated that the citizenry should share in the governing process. He denounced as an "aristocratical tyranny" every government that failed to represent the citizenry. He next proceeded to demythologize monarchical rule, painting it in ogreish hues. He stripped away every argument that had been used since time immemorial to legitimate hereditary monarchy. He additionally portrayed royalty as a system that habitually elevated idiots, incompetents, and rogues above the citizenry. All that America required for its government, he stated, was a unicameral assembly that was broadly representative of the inhabitants of the land.

Thereafter, Paine waded into the unspoken contest that had divided Congress for eight months: reconciliation or independence? Reconciliation was not in America's best interest, he cautioned. It would inhibit American commerce, lead to exorbitant taxation to rescue England's squalid ruling class, bequeath hegemony over the American continent to a "second hand government" 3,000 miles away, and drag the colonists into one unnecessary war after another, conflicts waged all over the globe for the benefit of the British social and economic elite. Independence, however, would gainsay the iniquities of the imperial union. Peace and prosperity, freedom and happiness, harkened down the road of independence. The felicity of generations yet unborn hinged on this generation's decision. "'Tis not the concern of a day, or year, or an age; posterity are virtually involved . . . and will be more or less affected even to the end of time, by the proceedings now," he forecast, seeking to transform a nine-month-old war over taxes and port closings into a sacred cause and endowing it with a millenarian spirit. Independence was merely the initial change. Indeed, independence and transformation were to go hand in hand. Paine daringly proclaimed that a "new era for politics is struck—a new method of thinking has arisen," and to those who dared to dream with him he added: "We have it in our power to begin the world over again. . . . The birthday of a new world is at hand." Although he did not elaborate on the sweeping changes that he had in mind, he made it apparent that liberty hung in the balance. Freedom had been destroyed in Europe, Asia, and Africa, he wrote, but if the American Revolution succeeded, liberty would be safe in the New World, where the new American nation would offer an "asylum for mankind."

One part of Paine's vision of the new world that would come with independence was evident in his sketch of the best government for the new United States. Believing that "government even in its best state [was] but a necessary evil; in its worst state an intolerable one," Paine proposed "something better" than Europe's monarchical systems. He urged weak and unintrusive governments with just enough authority to insure freedom and security, but with too little clout to become tyrannical. Paine recommended that the central government in the American union consist solely of an annually elected unicameral congress. Beneath it were to be similarly elected one-house assemblies in the states. He conspicuously shunned any hint of a balanced system—he omitted an upper chamber and an executive—a favorite contrivance of conservatives both for preventing hasty, passionate legislative action and to impose hurdles in the way of sweeping change. Paine wanted the government to represent the people, and he wanted the people to be able to act. Even so, in all these legislatures, Paine advocated that bills could be enacted into law only after three-fifths of the assemblymen assented.

Finally, *Common Sense* argued simply—in some instances simplistically and disingenuously—that America could win a protracted war to secure its independence. In part, this section was Paine's anodyne to those who anguished over the uncertainties of independence. "The *time hath found us*," he declared. In a mystical argument that swirled about this chosen generation's destiny for greatness, Paine maintained that the nimbus of youth, stamina, exalted energy, wisdom, and, above all, virtue would see the revolutionaries through to a satisfactory end. With assurance, he proclaimed that fate had conspired to insure that the American Revolution would be "a memorable era for posterity to glory in." America would be victorious. Britain's prowess was overrated, not least because its strength was sapped by a debilitating corruption that stalked the land. America, on the other hand, would be well served by its manpower, resources, unity, and limitless domain. Indeed, rather than a hazard, independence would actually "settle our affairs," for in the certain peace and prosperity of the postwar world, it was inevitable that the new nation would be sustained by its inhabitants' long "spirit of good order and obedience to continental government."[53]

Samuel Adams, in one of his more considerable understatements, reported that *Common Sense* "has fretted some folks here more than a little." Amazingly, however, those who favored reconciliation still saw a ray of hope. They believed the king's speech offered proof that he misunderstood the American protest. Thus, on the day that *Common Sense* was published, James Wilson, a Pennsylvania congressman, and Dickinson's man Friday, proposed that Congress address the people and state categorically that it was not seeking independence. Wilson's intended audience was as much the Crown as the provincial citizenry, and he and his brethren conceived of their ploy as yet another attempt to jumpstart negotiations with London. The radicals wanted no part of it. Not only would such a congressional declaration tie their hands, perhaps for years to come, but it held the potential for causing serious harm to the war effort. "How strangely will the Tools of a Tyrant pervert the plain Meaning of Words," Samuel Adams fulminated privately at Wilson's interpretation of the king's act. "What a pity it is," he added privately, that Wilson and his comrades were "so degenerate and servile." They called the monarch's address "*most gracious*," when in fact it revealed the king to be "a Man of a wicked Heart."[54]

Nevertheless, the radicals lacked the votes to prevent Congress from electing a five-member committee—and packing it with reconciliationists, including Wilson and Dickinson—to draft an "Address to the Inhabitants." However much their control may have slipped, and whatever people across America may now have believed, those who favored reconciliation, not independence, yet constituted a clear majority in Congress. Had a vote on independence been taken early in 1776, no more than five delegations in all likelihood would have supported separation. Even Massachusetts's congressional delegation remained deeply divided, as Hancock and Robert Treat Paine were committed to reconciliation. However, a majority of the delegation, the two Adamses and Elbridge Gerry, who had entered Congress in January, were ready to break from the mother country. Had Wilson's committee moved quickly to cobble together an address that repudiated independence as a war aim, and insisted that America sought only "Peace & Reconciliation"—as their eventual statement suggested—it might have been adopted by Congress.[55]

However, the drafting committee moved at a glacial pace. Dickinson squandered precious time by continuously wrangling over immaterial wording in the draft, as he had argued with Jefferson six months earlier over the language of the declaration on taking up arms. Whereas Jefferson soon would require but two or three days to draft the Declaration of Independence, Dickinson and Wilson consumed nearly three weeks in preparing their draft. By then bad news from the war front had dramatically altered matters.

That America's military woes proved fatal to Dickinson's faction was their just dessert. In June 1775 General Washington had proposed an invasion of Canada. Not only was the region lightly defended, but he anticipated that the French citizenry would welcome the invaders as liberators. Victory in Canada might end the war immediately, he believed, for it seemed inconceivable that North's ministry could survive such a crushing blow. At the very least, possession of Canada would give the colonies a bargaining chip. Congress might have offered it in return for London's repeal of the Coercive Acts and renunciation of parliamentary jurisdiction over the mainland colonies. Congress approved the invasion, though against the wishes of the mid-Atlantic colonies, the reconciliationists' stronghold. Not only was Canada a long way away from New Jersey and Pennsylvania, but some of Dickinson's persuasion feared that a failure north of the border might compel Congress to seek aid from Britain's European rivals, a course he feared almost as much as had Galloway at the First Congress. The invasion went forward, but from the outset many radicals grumped that the "Indecision" of the conservatives not only had delayed operations, but that their intransigence was detrimental to the "Support and Prosecution" of the campaign. Ultimately, the Continentals suffered heavy losses in a disastrous attack on Quebec on the last day of 1775, the first martial setback of the insurgency. News of the debacle reached Philadelphia while Wilson and Dickinson painstakingly labored with the terminology in their resolution, and just as many were coming to the conclusion that the initial opposition of Dickinson and his closest acolytes had made the Canadian venture a disaster that was waiting to happen.[56]

The Canadian disaster convinced every American that it was hopeless to expect a short war. Indeed, the ominous news from Canada brought home to many in Congress the reality of the dilemma it faced. "We have not yet got powder to effect any thing considerable," a Virginia congressman moaned. Others pointed out that no European power had any incentive to assist America so long as its aim was to reconcile with Great Britain in a vibrant empire. "Their politics plainly tend to drive us to extremity," one congressman remarked. *Common Sense*, whose appearance coincided with the bad news from Canada, addressed this very issue. Although nearly one-third of the tract explained how the colonists possessed the strength "to repel the force of all the world," Paine did not in fact believe his own propaganda. Toward the end of his tract he argued for the necessity of foreign assistance, succor that would never be provided if the colonists "mean only to make use of that assistance for the purpose of repairing the breach" with London.[57] By mid-February 1776 it was clear that to continue to fight for reconciliation meant that America would face a protracted war that it was ill equipped to wage.

The colonists' politics had long been driven by outside events. What London did after 1765, from the taxes it enacted to the congressional entreaties it rejected, shaped the contours of American politics. But with the question of independence, the engine that powered American politics was in considerable measure set in motion by what transpired on faraway battlefields.

Many in Congress understood the new reality by the time Dickinson and Wilson overcame their senseless hairsplitting and produced an address that attacked independence. These two reconciliationists were too late. The congressional majority they once possessed was gone forever. The new majority, a New Jersey congressman exclaimed, "did not relish [an] Address & Doctrine" that could hobble Congress while London divided wartime America by dangling ever new allurements of accommodation.[58]

Congress tabled Dickinson's address rather than rejecting it. The "fleetest sailors" might now constitute a majority, but they yet needed the slowest if they were to have an overwhelming majority when independence was declared. In the space of one hundred days, the period between the arrival of the king's intemperate remarks in November and word in February of the mortifying defeat of American arms in Canada, the hold of the reconciliationists had been broken. Only the date that independence would be proclaimed remained uncertain. That February John Adams told his wife that there was "no Prospect, no Probability, no Possibility" of reconciliation, but "Time must discover" when independence would be declared. "Perhaps," he added in April, "the Time is near, perhaps a great way off."[59]

Since the onset of war "one Event has brot another on," Samuel Adams reflected that spring. It was precisely the scenario John Adams envisioned when he had preached patience and restraint as the Second Congress assembled nearly a year earlier. Now, in the winter and spring of 1776, the demands of war drove Congress. While tangled grey clouds shrouded wintry Philadelphia, Congress created the Secret Committee and the Committee of Secret Correspondence. Each was to seek foreign assistance, as was Silas Deane, hitherto a Connecticut congressman who was sent to France on a secret mission to procure arms and arrange commercial ties. Several weeks later, as the first evidence of spring appeared, Congress threw American ports open to the trade of all nations. That act, John Adams exclaimed, was tantamount to a declaration of independence.[60]

Wartime necessity drove Great Britain as well. Lord George Germain, a hard-liner throughout the crisis, replaced Dartmouth, who was thought to be too friendly toward the colonies, as the colonial secretary and virtual war minister. Lord North also announced that more troops were being sent to America. In November 1775 Edmund Burke led the last great parliamentary fight for peace and reconciliation. When he failed,

Parliament passed the American Prohibitory Act, which cut off trade with all the colonies. The foes of the measure in London pronounced it a "declaration of war."[61] Most Americans saw it in the same light.

All that was left to those who yearned for reconciliation was to obstruct and temporize, hoping to delay independence. They clung to several shallow hopes, each of which would require time before it might be realized. In the event that the colonies scored a smashing military victory in 1776, the North government might collapse and Britain, as Dickinson dreamed, might abandon its "mad" course. At the least, therefore, their strategy was to forestall the decision on independence until the campaign of 1776 had terminated, probably deep into the autumn. Their second glimmer of hope was even less likely. Reversing course, many reconciliationists now suddenly prayed that France would assist the American rebels. This would confront London with the dreadful choice of fighting the French and Americans simultaneously or of acceding to the colonists' demands while it warred unilaterally with Versailles. Mostly, however, the reconciliationists took heart from ambiguous remarks by the king in his address that reached America in January. The monarch had vaguely alluded to "persons so commissioned" to negotiate who were en route to the colonies. Dickinson and his allies demanded that diplomacy be given one last chance. Wait, they insisted, until the terms brought by the peace commissioners—as North's government labeled them—were known. Once again, the radicals acquiesced. They were compelled to do so. "The Union is our Defence and must be tenderly cherished," one of them remarked.[62]

The radicals expected nothing from North's envoys. General Washington predicted that "no terms of accommodation will be offer'd . . . but such as cannot be accepted." John Adams cried out that the peace initiative "is a Bubble. Their real errand is an Insult." However, he sighed, "you may as well reason down a Gale of Wind" as attempt to persuade Dickinson that North's representatives would have nothing fruitful to offer. Although angry, several radicals glimpsed a silver lining, for some who yearned for reconciliation had confided that if the peace commissioners refused to "grant Us our Bill of Rights, in every Iota, they will hesitate no longer" to cut America's ties to the mother country. The scent of independence was growing stronger. The "day is not far distant when there will be such a Power, as the *free & Independent states of America,*" a New Hampshire congressman proclaimed in late April.[63]

Change was sweeping America with cyclonic speed. In a two-week stretch during March and April, South Carolina, North Carolina, and Georgia sent revised instructions to their congressional delegations authorizing votes for independence. In May, Virginia told its congressmen to "declare the United Colonies free and independent States; absolved from all allegiance to, or dependence upon, the Crown or Parliament of Great Britain." Most of New England had taken, or was about to take, similar action. Even Delaware relented, sanctioning whatever steps its congressmen thought necessary "for promoting the liberty, safety, and interests of America." By mid-May only the delegations from New York, New Jersey, Maryland, and Pennsylvania lacked authorization to vote for independence.[64]

Word of still more disasters in Canada added to the momentum for independence. Deep into the cold spring the tattered Continental soldiery remained poised a mile outside Quebec, awaiting help that might permit yet another assault. Three New England colonies dispatched men, and Washington sent soldiers that he could barely spare. At one point the Continentals were twice the size of the British garrison, but the Americans had no sooner gained numerical superiority than they were ravaged by smallpox and desertion. The Continentals never sallied out of their defenses. When the St. Lawrence River thawed, and British reinforcements arrived in early May, the siege of Quebec abruptly ended. Outnumbered, and outgunned, the fatally debilitated American army commenced a long, vexed retreat out of inhospitable Canada. One general, John Sullivan of New Hampshire, was outraged. He told Congress of his mortification "that an Army Should Live in Continual fear of & Even Retreat before an Enemy which no person among them has Seen." Washington's daily reports reflected the pessimism: the situation was "very Alarming;" it was "not in a very promising way;" only "ill consequences" could be expected. In June the Americans finally attacked at Trois-Rivières, midway between Montreal and Quebec. The results were disastrous for the Continentals. The retreat resumed. Congress told the colonies that "our Affairs in that Quarter wear a melancholy Aspect" and might worsen drastically if British regulars were joined by Indians and German mercenaries, who were expected to arrive in America shortly. Although no one factor could explain the debacle, many agreed with congressman Gerry that a want of adequate supplies had undermined the army's effectiveness. General Charles Lee laid the blame on a dearth of artillery, which all knew could never be overcome but through foreign assistance.[65]

In May and June 1776, most of the slowest sailors in Congress finally caught up with the fleetest. For many the final straw was official word that the Crown had hired German troops. The Hessians, as the Americans called all the German troops who crossed the Atlantic, not only were reputed to be among the most savage of Europe's soldiers, but devoid of past ties with the colonists, they were expected to fight "without

Remorse or Compunction," as John Hancock put it. That they would "butcher" American soldiers was widely expected, and everyone appears to have anticipated that they would spread "horror and devastations" among the civilian population. Capturing the popular outrage that greeted the news, Oliver Wolcott, a congressman from Connecticut, roared that it was the height of infamy for the king to have hired such brutes.[66]

In the end, the few remaining congressmen who had fought so tenaciously for reconciliation were simply swept aside. Their attenuated position was underscored when Congress acted without waiting to talk to North's long-promised peace commissioners. Like Jefferson, most congressmen by mid-May felt as if "the whole object of the present controversy" was to break away from Great Britain in order to erect new governments fashioned as Americans saw fit. The time had arrived to gather the fruit that had ripened, Samuel Adams remarked.[67] What had begun in 1765 as a struggle to retain the few autonomous powers that Americans long had cherished, had grown into a successful movement in quest of full American sovereignty.

Nothing was more crucial in convincing the hesitant to make the leap into independence than the publication that spring of John Adams's ideas on post-independence governance in America. Adams privately acknowledged that he spoke out publicly as "an Antidote to the popular Poison" of Thomas Paine, whose exhortations about sweeping out the old and starting the world anew frightened many potential separatists. Independence was one thing. A sweeping domestic revolution was quite another. Yet Paine was only one of many who expanded on the prospect of radical change. A plethora of publications appeared in the wake of *Common Sense* discoursing on the texture of an independent United States. The Tories were first off the mark. The desperate salvoes they fired that spring raised the specter of "democratic tyranny," including social leveling and property redistribution, once all ties with Great Britain were severed.[68] The radicals answered those charges, and in the wake of Paine's philippic against monarchy, many at last wrote openly of the virtues of republicanism. While few called for the destruction of the gradations of social hierarchy, many defined republicanism as a system in which office holders would be beholden to the will of the people, not to royal or aristocratic preferment, and one in which social standing was to be a function of merit, not birth. Furthermore, whereas none advocated the redistribution of wealth, some portrayed a republican America as a land in which power, and by implication the fruits of prosperity, would be more equitably apportioned. The more radical scribes, such as the anonymous Massachusetts pamphleteer responsible for *The People the Best Governors*, urged universal manhood suffrage, a unicameral assembly based on population, the elimination of property qualifications for office hold-ings, elected judges, and a weak executive.[69]

The more conservative proponents of resistance grew anxious. What was occurring in the spring of 1776, said one of Dickinson's political allies in Philadelphia, was "totally foreign to the original plan of Resis-tance." It was a case, he added, of the "Mobility triumphant."[70] That May a Chesapeake planter wrote General Washington that the buzz within Virginia was that when independence rendered the populace "independt of the rich men, eve[r]y man would then be able to do as he pleased." Already, he fretted, the Virginia assembly included men who had never previously held high legislative office and who were "too . . . inexperi-enced to navigate our bark on this dangerous coast." One assembly, he went on, had even questioned why "a poor man was made to pay for keep-ing a rich mans Slaves in order."[71] The conservatives not only trembled at the prospect of a social revolution, they expressed concern at the seem-ingly bleak prospects for survival that faced any republic.

There were no republican commonwealths in 1776, anywhere in the world. Indeed, virtually every republic, whether in antiquity or in mid-17th century England, had been short lived. The prevailing view among this generation—which was not terribly far removed from the calamities that had accompanied the English republic in Cromwellian days during the previous century—was that republics were terribly fragile. They were dependent on the people, and too often the people had failed them, caus-ing most to end badly in an inexorable slide from riotous democracy to chaos, and finally to tyranny.[72] At bottom, much of Galloway's prediction of an inescapably bad end for an independent America was based on the premise that the new nation would have a republican government, and this same fear had all along led many who abhorred British policy to cling steadfastly to the dream of reconciliation.

No one was more aware than John Adams that many who had come to loathe America's ties to Great Britain nevertheless trembled at the prospect of independence. Adams, who was conservative in outlook, but pushing hard for a quick decision on separating from Great Britain, made speech after speech in Congress in 1776 in which he not only scorned the vision of an independent America set forth in *Common Sense*, but dis-paraged Paine as a menace who was a "better Hand at pulling down than building" governments.[73] Adams counseled that reforms were inherently too divisive to be contemplated in wartime, and he beseeched his col-leagues to put every thought of substantive change on the back burner until the war was won. Nevertheless, one alteration could not be post-poned. There was no getting around the fact that once independence was declared, the colonial governments—which were based on Crown charters—had to go. New state governments would have to be instituted to supplant the old royal regimes.[74] Adams' objective that winter and spring, therefore, was to reassure his colleagues that a stable, enduring, and—from the conservative point of view—safe system of republican government could be instituted, one in which order, authority, and due subordination could be maintained. What he meant was that a republican government could be fashioned so that some portions of it would be dominated by the propertied class, and that it could be structured in such a manner as to make sweeping change difficult to effect, and impossible to realize unless a broad consensus existed across class lines. So convincing was Adams that several congressmen, including two Virginians, beseeched him to commit his ideas to paper. When he had done so, Richard Henry Lee paid to have the tract published in April 1776 under the simple title *Thoughts on Government.*

Adams offered a model of government that he said was based on "established modes, to which the people have been familiarized by habit." That was hardly true for most Americans, although his plan was strikingly similar to the colonial governments of Connecticut and Rhode Island. Furthermore, the heart of his plan was a variation of the system of balanced government that was customary throughout Anglo-America. Otherwise, what Adams envisioned was devoid of much that had been commonplace in most colonies. The chief executive that he sketched would hardly resemble the Crown officials of old, and the upper house of the assembly that he envisioned would be quite unlike the oligarchic upper legislative chambers which had existed in most colonies. Adams proposed a division of power between an executive branch and a bicameral legislative branch. He acknowledged that it was possible, as Paine posited, to represent all the interests in society in a single legislative chamber. However, Adams cautioned that popular assemblies were often swayed by the passion of the moment and might make "absurd judgments." Besides, he said, legislative bodies were ill equipped to deal with certain problems. For instance, a separate executive official would be better able to cope with diplomacy and waging war. A balanced system, he preached, not only reduced the likelihood of fickle behavior by legislators, but built a firewall against both an ambitious man bent on tyranny or a single well-knit faction that sought to act "arbitrarily for their own interest." In Adams's republic, the people were to be the sovereign source of power. Government's objective was the collective welfare of the people. Republican government, he advised, sought to provide "ease, comfort, security, or in one word happiness to the greatest number of persons, and in the greatest degree." Through balances and elections, the interests of the people and their rulers would be harmonized, prerogative powers checked, dangerous factions muted, liberty preserved, and the rule of law constitutionally contracted. With these safeguards, the republic had good prospects of survival.[75]

Not everyone's fears were assuaged by Adams's tract. Carter Braxton, a conservative Virginian who had entered Congress only a month earlier, thought it a plan for an unfettered democracy, and privately predicted that immediately upon independence the radicals would "embrace their darling democracy." He dashed off a pamphlet urging that the executive serve for life and that a council of state, insulated from popular control, be established.[76] Others questioned whether the people were sufficiently virtuous to be entrusted with governmental responsibilities. In Virginia, Lee and George Wythe, the most respected legal scholar in the province, labored to overcome the objections. Elsewhere, the naysayers were largely overridden by the prevailing mood of optimism.[77] As the historian Gordon Wood has demonstrated, the belief crystallized that spring that Americans, youthful, vigorous, and untainted by Old World luxury and decadence, were "meant to be republican."[78] It was as much the fulfillment of the view, expressed from the Stamp crisis onward, that a corrupted political system in the parent state was in large measure responsible for having driven Great Britain to the long train of abuses it had inflicted on the colonists, as it was the germination of the intuitive sense of American exceptionalism, that America was meant to be different from the Old World, and that indeed the Americans were untainted by Europe's corrosive iniquities. It was something else as well. In the spring of 1776 this revolutionary people embraced both Paine's radical vision and Adams's conservative ministrations. Paine gave them a vision of what they wished to do. Adams comforted them with the lesson that they could safely do as they pleased.

Not only did Adams help break down the last barrier to separation from Great Britain, he led the fight in Congress for independence, prompting Richard Stockton of New Jersey to call him the "Atlas of American Independence." Adams was the perfect man for the task. In addition to having sharpened his leadership skills during the past twelve months, he had never been viewed by the reconciliationists as dangerously irresponsible. One student of Adams characterized him as "a radical in spite of himself," and that appears to have been how many of his colleagues saw him.[79] They understood that he was deeply committed to the rule of law, having not only been the leading attorney in pre-war Boston, but the chief counsel for the British soldiers charged in the Boston Massacre in 1770. His colleagues were aware too that Adams had only belatedly become a zealot in the resistance, signing on only around

1773 when he concluded that the colonial protest was the only means by which to secure an honorable protection against British tyranny, and to conserve the colonists' long legacy of freedom. Honest and inviolable, Adams was both a radical and a conservator, a reassuring blend in the eyes of many who were poised for the fateful break with the mother country, but who feared the uncertainties that would follow.[80]

In mid-April Samuel Adams noted that the "Child Independence is now struggling for Birth," but he counseled patience. "It requires Time to convince the doubting and inspire the timid," he said. Time ran out thirty days later. The realities of war spurred Congress to act, as did word from Maryland that arrived during the first week of May. Radicals in that colony, hamstrung by the province's proprietary government, suggested that a change in the colony's government could free Maryland's congressional delegation to vote for independence. Similar word from Pennsylvania's radicals reached Congress almost simultaneously. Both were asking Congress to help change their provincial governments.[81]

John Adams had known when it was inexpedient to act. But a great leader must know when the time for action has arrived, and must seize the moment. In May 1776 Adams knew that it was time. The British monarch had rebuffed Congress's remonstrance, the North Peace Plan was a chimera, a long desperate war loomed, and the people, more radical now than ever, appeared ready to break with Great Britain. On May 10 Adams introduced a resolution that urged each colony to establish a government equal to the demands of the times. In their dying breath, the reconciliationists charged that this was "a Machine to fabricate Independence." They were correct. That was precisely Adams's intent. But this time Dickinson and his faction could not prevent Congress from acting. Not only did the resolution pass, but five days later, when Dickinson left Philadelphia to transact personal business in Delaware, Adams induced Congress to add a lengthy preamble that changed the meaning of the resolve. It charged that inasmuch as Britain's behavior had made reconciliation unlikely, that the American Prohibitory Act had removed the colonists from the Crown's protection, and that the imperial government had hired German troops to destroy the colonists, "the exercise of every kind of authority under the said Crown should be totally suppressed, and all sources of government exerted under the authority of the people."[82]

Adams rejoiced. This was "the last Step," he said, not foreseeing a formal Declaration of Independence. Congress "has passed the most important Resolution, that ever was taken in America," an action tantamount to "a total absolute Independence," he added. Congress's act was unmistakably definitive. Wolcott called it "a Revolution in Government."

Braxton unhappily reported that it fell "little short of Independence." A New York congressman said the measure had "occationed a great alarm" among those who continued to resist independence, although Gerry, who favored immediate separation, reported that former reconciliationists "are coming over to us." It was for the best that those who favored accommodation had for so long managed "to clog the affairs of the colonies," Gerry added. Congress was more united than ever, he added, for every congressman now knew in his heart of hearts that reconciliation could come only on Britain's unpalatable terms.[83] Adams concurred. The roadblocks built by the reconciliationists had given the people the opportunity to "maturely ... consider the great Question of Independence and to ripen their Judgments, dissipate their Fears, and allure their Hopes.... This will cement the Union, and avoid those Heats and Convulsions which might have been occasioned by such a Declaration Six Months ago." But it would have been uncharacteristic of Adams not to have complained a bit, and in the same breath he charged that had this step not been prevented for nine or ten months by Dickinson and his allies, the Americans would have been victorious in Canada and already in receipt of foreign assistance crucial for success in the pending military campaign.[84]

The resolution that Congress adopted in May set in motion the forces that broke down the last barriers to independence in Pennsylvania. Broadsides printed in English and German appeared immediately in Philadelphia urging that the Pennsylvania assembly be superseded by a provincial convention, the very ploy that Dickinson had used against Galloway two years before. Within the week over 4,000 Philadelphians, and a few congressmen, braved a cold rain to attend a meeting in the State House Yard that condemned the assembly's instructions to its congressmen and called a conference of county committees to plan a constitutional convention. A week later the assembly, in a futile effort to save itself, created a committee to reexamine its instructions to the Pennsylvania delegation. In early June, in one of its final acts, the assembly, dominated by Dickinson's followers since the autumn of 1774, released Pennsylvania's congressmen to act as they saw fit "for promoting the Liberty, Safety and Interests of America." The "Cloggs are falling off," John Adams rejoiced. Indeed, by the time the Pennsylvania assembly acted, Adams had been appointed to a committee to prepare a Declaration of Independence.[85]

In June 1776 Congress stood on the cusp of proclaiming American independence, a state that in reality already existed. In large measure, Anglo-America had been brought to this juncture by the unimaginative and maladroit policies pursued over the course of a decade by several governments in London. Ministries had come and gone, and at times the government had repealed unpopular measures. Yet London had never abandoned its commitment to tightening its control over the colonies, or to demonstrating Crown and parliamentary sovereignty. Its intransigence made war inevitable, and hostilities doomed the hopes of those who yearned for reconciliation.

Had London competently managed relations with its friends and allies in America, the imperial relationship might have taken a different turn. Had it thrown a lifeline to Galloway, or later to Dickinson, some compromise solution might have been fashioned. At the very least, London might have used individuals such as Galloway and Dickinson to more deftly exploit the divisions that existed within American opinion, or to find a way to bring together those who longed desperately for the maintenance of the Anglo-American union. Instead, throughout the decade long crisis London appeared to be blind to its opportunities. Ultimately, America's Tories were forced from public life and the reconciliationists were made to embrace the increasingly untenable position of making war with the very state with which it hoped to be reconciled. Dickinson and his allies, Britain's last real hope in the colonies, watched in despair during the twelve months prior to independence as their credibility was steadily eviscerated by London's increasingly draconian policies while, at the same moment, the radicals were made to appear ever more reasonable and farsighted.

Nor did those in the colonies who fervently hoped to preserve America's connection to the mother country act with consummate political dexterity. Galloway and Dickinson, for instance, shared many sentiments, including the belief that American rights were traduced by British policies and a yearning for reconciliation on terms that secured the rights of the colonists. Yet despite the monumentally high stakes, they were unable to rise above their old stormy differences. Their collaboration might have forestalled war. Had they united against the threat of independence after hostilities erupted, they might have built the alliances throughout the provinces that would have resulted in a network strong enough to ensure continued hegemony by those committed to reconciliation. But in the end, first Galloway, then Dickinson and his faction, were swept aside, "all fallen, like Grass before the Scythe, notwithstanding all their vast Advantages," as John Adams gleefully observed.[86]

Although the radicals did not always attain all their goals, they were victorious at each step from 1765 onward. They acted with sufficient acumen and mettle to induce the mother country to back down in 1766 and again in 1770. By 1774 the radicals had achieved a union of the colonies,

which they succeeded in maintaining through the boycott and the outbreak of hostilities. In the final showdowns they proved to be cleverer
than their adversaries. They acquiesced to their adversaries when necessary, compromised when timely, and kept the resistance movement intact. They were aware that quarrelsome, discordant, and coercive tactics
would be counterproductive, and that the war would do much of their
work for them. They divined their foes, both in London and within Congress. They knew when to yield, but they realized when the moment to
strike had arrived. They were patient, prudent, better led, and as the
warm days of June of 1776 settled over Philadelphia, victorious.

"America," wrote Pennsylvania's congressman Robert Morris that
month, "never set out with any View or desire of establishing an Independent Empire." He was correct. The commitment to independence
had come on gradually, as the hearts and minds of the colonists were
transformed by the events of the turbulent eleven years that began in 1765.
Many, perhaps most, had changed only reluctantly. In the summer of 1775,
John Adams had found that the notion of independence to be as unpopular in Congress as a parliamentary tax. At the beginning of 1776 it was
doubtful that a majority of colonies would have voted for independence.
But with Congress's resolution on May 15 the step for independence was
all but taken. Nevertheless, no one knew if independence could be maintained. The "Doggs of War are now fairly let loose upon us," as Congressman Morris also remarked.[87] The course of that war would determine
whether America survived as an independent nation.

6

1776–1777

"A Leap Into the Dark"

Since January, when momentum for independence had begun to build, the reconciliationists had cautioned repeatedly about the perils of breaking with Great Britain and the risks involved in a protracted war. None made the case better than "Civis," a Pennsylvanian who warned that to declare independence would be a "leap into the dark." What, he asked, will America derive from it?

Will it frighten Great-Britain into our terms? It will not. Will it secure us a foreign alliance? We know not that it will, but have every reason to think the contrary. Will it strengthen the hands of our friends in England, and our advocates in Parliament? Alas! it will have the direct contrary effect; it will unite the whole force of Great Britain and Ireland against us. . . . Will it lessen the influence, and weaken the hands of the ministry? No, but the reverse; it will confirm the unjust, the untrue reflections cast upon us by the ministerial hirelings, that we took up the sword to establish an independent empire, and will probably save them from destruction.

Suffer yourselves, therefore, to be either cajoled or frightened out of your charter liberties. Exert yourselves in the choice of men [to sit in Congress] whom you know to have the public good at heart, and . . . so shall ye be instrumental in preserving your country, and have the pleasure of enjoying liberty while you live, and transmitting it to the latest posterity.[1]

None who favored independence was blind to the uncertainty of the future. Without an ally, devoid of a navy, reliant on an untested and barely trained Continental army—which in turn was backed by even less adequately trained citizen-soldiers in the militia—and with no means of manufacturing the necessities for waging war, the new and untested union of states faced a prolonged war against one of Europe's richest, most powerful nations. Nor was that all. Many of the most committed revolutionaries, such as John Adams, shuddered at the "Rage for Innovation, which appears, in So many wild Shapes . . . encouraged by disaffected Persons." Adams and others knew that some among those who sought independence wished to destroy every vestige of British life and culture remaining in America. The more conservative revolutionaries feared that this Revolution, like so many throughout history, would "tend directly to Barbarism." No one could possibly know how much an independent America would change. Nor did any know whether the fragile union could withstand a push for sweeping alterations.[2]

The most fearful colonists, the Loyalists, had already refused to support the radical protest and the war against the mother country. Nothing aroused greater anxiety in their hearts than the prospect that independence would elevate to power a new class with a new social and economic perspective. All revolutionaries, on the other hand, were committed to some degree of change. All embraced republicanism, wished to substitute American officials for royal officers, sought home rule in place of imperial rule, looked forward to greater personal and economic freedoms and opportunities, and many yearned to escape the corrosive corruption that they believed was eating away at Britain. Probably most revolutionaries recognized that they were of the class that the Loyalists feared. Their ascent was merely one sign of how the Anglo-American upheaval was beginning to break down the hierarchical barriers of the old order. Most who supported the rebellion welcomed this change. Indeed, most were anxious to kick down doors that had been barred in order to prevent their ascent and to open doors to the meritorious.

However, those who sought independence were a diverse lot. While all were ready to escape London's political yoke, the more conservative activists envisioned an independent America that bore a striking similarity to the colonial society that supposedly was being left behind. Others wished to cultivate the political, social, economic, and cultural patterns they believed had germinated in the course of the long colonial past. Still others saw the break with London as a prelude toward truly radical domestic change that would make America a shining beacon to the powerless everywhere. Like Paine, they believed "the birthday of a new world [was] at hand" and the American Revolution was its midwife.[3] There were those who thought it imprudent to attempt any change before the war was won, lest reforms sow fatal divisions. And there were those who, from the beginning, had thought only of wrenching free of Great Britain, of escaping what the Declaration of Independence would refer to as London's "design of despotism." This last element may have been the largest. Since the Stamp Act crisis, many had focused exclusively on responding to British depredations. Only in the last flickering moments of Anglo-America, when *Common Sense* had brought the issue into the open, did public discussion commence about the meaning of independence.

On July 2, 1776, the United States leapt into the dark. During the next quarter century the new nation struggled toward daylight. It came close—closer than many in our time realize—to failing to establish itself as an independent nation. Furthermore, once independence was achieved, an almost equally desperate struggle followed to preserve the wartime union of states under an acceptable, popular national government.

On June 7, 1776, Richard Henry Lee introduced in Congress a resolution that called for a formal vote on the issue of independence:

Resolved, That these United Colonies are, and of right ought to be, free and independent States, that they are absolved from all allegiance to the British Crown, and that all political connection between them and the state of Great Britain is, and ought to be, totally dissolved.[4]

To those who for some time had been ready to sever all ties with the mother country, this moment had been a long time coming. They had chafed for nearly a year at the "silly Cast" imposed on "our whole Doings" by those who yet sought to be reconciled with Great Britain. The fatuous policies of the Dickinson faction, they believed, had put Americans "between Hawk and Buzzard," committing them to a war, but making them fight with one arm tied behind their back. Those who favored independence had drawn cold comfort from the knowledge that, as John Adams had sighed a year before, "We shall do something in Time."[5] Their time, at last, had arrived in the spring of 1776, brought on by military exigency.

After the military disasters in Canada, the question no longer was whether Congress would declare independence, but when it would act, and whether independence would have the support of all thirteen provinces. Most knew, as a Virginia congressman remarked, that America was confronted with a choice of "absolute submission, or foreign assistance." The war could not be waged successfully without French aid, and that succor could not be had until the colonists "break off all connection with G. B."[6] Independence reflected political, social, intellectual, and economic choices, but the timing of the final decision arose from military necessity.

Congress debated Lee's resolution for independence for two days. Though some delegations yet awaited authorization to act, it was reported that sentiment to break with Great Britain was "fast ripening" in the holdout provinces. By June 10 Congress knew that it would be only a matter of days, or weeks, "till the voice of the people drove us into it," as some congressmen curiously put it. Even so, the debate over declaring independence was furious. If Congress acted before their provinces instructed them to vote for independence, several mid-Atlantic congressmen threatened, they would "retire & possibly their colonies might secede from the Union." Their secession, they pointed out, would jeopardize foreign assistance, which they said was the only compelling reason for immediately announcing that all ties with Great Britain had been severed. New England and Southern congressmen fired back that immediate independence was essential for military operations in 1776. A vote for independence could induce France to join the war, and its navy could both tie down the Royal Navy and disrupt the flow of logistical support to Britain's armies in America. Some thought independence would buoy morale, as trade with France would ensure the availability of those necessities, including money, for which the civilians yearned.[7]

On June 11, after hours of vexatious debate, Congress agreed to table the issue for three weeks. Nevertheless, it appointed a five-member committee to prepare a statement on independence during the interim. The panel included Jefferson, who was respected for his literary abilities; Adams, who had led the pro-independence faction for the past twelve months; and Franklin, the best known American. The two other choices, Roger Sherman of Connecticut and Robert Livingston of New York, were less obvious. Sherman, who was pious and grave, may have been chosen simply because his comrades regarded him as industrious and reliable—they repeatedly named him to committees—and because he was a veteran congressman with seniority over many of his colleagues. Livingston was a conservative New Yorker who, as recently as 1768, had been turned out of the provincial assembly by outraged voters who thought him too supportive of British policy.[8] However, he did support independence—he opportunistically believed, he said, in "the propriety of swimming with a Stream which it is impossible to stem"—and Congress likely hoped his presence on the committee would induce other mid-Atlantic conservatives to vote for independence.[9]

The committee met immediately. It met again and again, in fact, if Adams's recollection was correct, to map out the broad outlines of the Declaration of Independence. It then unanimously "pressed on [Jefferson] alone to make the draught." He had come to Philadelphia a year before with a reputation as a gifted writer and had been chosen often to draft statements that Congress wished to promulgate. Only Franklin was his literary equal, but he lacked Jefferson's grounding in the law and

Thomas Jefferson. Painted by Rembrandt Peale in Philadelphia, 1800.

political theory, and in addition was suffering with the gout. Adams did not want the assignment. As a member of the newly created Board of War, as well as a committee that was wrestling with crucial issues of diplomacy, he was inordinately busy. In addition, because of New England's reputation for radicalism, Adams believed that national unity would be enhanced if the document were written by someone from another region. However, Adams also simply miscalculated. He never imagined that anyone would remember the Declaration of Independence. Who now remembers the Declaration and Resolves adopted by the First Congress or the 1775 Declaration on Taking Up Arms? By the summer of 1776, in fact, those statements were already largely forgotten, and Adams suspected that the Declaration of Independence would eddy into oblivion soon after it was written, approved, and published. Thus he did not resist Jefferson's selection and may even have nominated him for the assignment. No one would have given a moment's thought to naming Sherman or Livingston over Jefferson.[10]

Faced with a deadline, Jefferson drafted the initial version of the Declaration of Independence in just two or three days. He was ordinarily a rapid writer, and in this instance he had in his possession, and used as templates, both the draft preamble for Virginia's first state constitution and its Declaration of Rights. In addition, having taken copious notes during the debate on Lee's resolution on independence, he was well aware of the arguments that recently had been offered on behalf of an immediate break with Great Britain. His work was further expedited by the proposed outline prepared for him by the committee. Once his task was completed, Jefferson showed his draft first to Adams and Franklin and only later to Sherman and Livingston. His colleagues recommended modest changes, primarily stylistic in nature, which he appears to have made. On June 28, seventeen days after its creation, the committee presented the draft to Congress. Busy with other things, and still awaiting word that New York and Maryland would permit their delegates to vote for independence, Congress postponed the matter for three days.[11]

The Declaration of Independence, 4 July 1776.
Oil painting by John Trumbull, completed in 1820.

The Pennsylvania State House must have been stifling on the morning of July 1. Not only did the temperature top ninety degrees that day, but as on most summer mornings in Philadelphia the humidity was excessive. Furthermore, Congress habitually kept the several tall windows in its chamber shut, in order to preserve secrecy, as well as to muffle the cacophony of outside city sounds. The delegates were in an expectant and anxious mood that morning. They anticipated "the greatest Debate of all," as one put it, although the issue was not in doubt. Each was fully aware of the disquieting reality of what he was about to do. Each understood the stakes. May "Heaven prosper the new born Republic," John Adams exclaimed to a friend before he left his lodging.[12] He, too, knew that Congress at last was taking the leap. He did not know where—or how softly—the landing would be made.

At 10 a.m., as was customary, John Hancock, the president of Congress, pounded his gavel to call the session together. Conversations stopped, and the congressmen scurried to their hard wooden seats. Congress dealt with its routine business first, listening to reports from its generals at the front. While that transpired, word arrived from Annapolis instructing Maryland's congressmen to vote for independence. New York's delegates alone now lacked authorization to vote for Lee's motion. Near 10:30, the preliminary business was concluded. Lee's motion of June 7 was read again, Congress organized into a committee of the whole for the debate, and the floor was opened for discussion. John Dickinson was first on his feet. For the final time he spoke against independence, a wearying speech that consumed well over two hours. He rehearsed all the arguments that Congress had heard on innumerable occasions: It was too risky to declare independence before numerous thorny problems were addressed. The states should first adopt new constitutions. Agreements should be reached between the states on rival land claims. A United States constitution should be adopted prior to independence, and the new nation should not proclaim itself a sovereign entity until it enjoyed the security of a foreign alliance. It was better to know before independence was declared whether these matters could be resolved. He also maintained that a war waged for reconciliation on American terms would be shorter and less destructive and was virtually certain to lead to a "redress of all the Grievances complained of" by the First Congress nearly two years before.[13]

When Dickinson concluded, around 1 p.m., John Adams rose to answer. Adams subsequently wrote that Dickinson, his old nemesis, had spoken "not only with great Ingenuity and Eloquence, but with equal Politeness and Candour."[14] Adams thought it essential that he respond in a similarly disarming manner, and he summoned all the oratorical skills he had learned in sixteen years of addressing juries and in the course of two years service in Congress. His speech was eloquent and dramatic, and he impressed his listeners with his apparent guilelessness. So powerful was the oration that some may have responded in the manner of the Georgia congressman who, after hearing Adams speak on another occasion, remarked that he "fancied an angel was let down from heaven to illumine Congress." Of this speech, Jefferson later said that Adams had addressed his colleagues "with a power of thought and expression, that moved us from our seats." New Jersey's Stockton was mesmerized by the "force of his reasoning," and later remarked that Adams's oration left no doubt that there was but one choice, independence.[15]

The speech has not survived, but we can guess its contents, since Adams had been speaking of independence for months. No doubt he reiterated what he said were the seminal reasons for severing all ties with Great Britain: America must escape a corrupt and tyrannical parent; it must break free from the hegemony of distant nabobs; with separation, America no longer would be dragged into Britain's wars; independence would mean commercial freedom; autonomy would mean that Americans could control their destiny; morale on the home front, and among those bearing arms, would be boosted by transforming the aim of the war from reconciliation to independence, with all its attendant possibilities; finally, independence offered the only hope of procuring needed foreign assistance.[16]

It was late in the afternoon when Adams concluded. He too had spoken for hours, at one point continuing undeterred as a heavy thunderstorm raked Philadelphia with lightning and as wind-churned rains lashed at the windows of the State House. It grew so dark during his presentation that candles were lit, but the storm cooled the city and brought the temperature in Congress's chamber down to a tolerable level. Adams completed his declamation at around 4:00, Congress's customary time for adjournment. However, on this day, even though it had never recessed, and no one had eaten since breakfast, Congress remained in session. Others spoke, including many who were habitually silent. Each congressman wanted to weigh in. Each knew that this would be the greatest issue of his career in public service. None wished to let pass the opportunity to participate in this historic moment. One congressman after another spoke into the early evening. Their exhausted listeners endured. "[A]ll the powers of the soul had been distended with the magnitude of the object," Jefferson remarked later on the day's ordeal.[17]

Finally, the delegates were ready to vote. Parliamentary procedure required two ballots, a vote by the committee of the whole, followed by Congress's formal vote on independence. The first vote was 9–2 in favor of Lee's motion. To no one's great surprise, Pennsylvania cast a negative vote. To the amazement and consternation of many, South Carolina also voted against Lee's motion. Two colonies did not vote. New York abstained, and Delaware lost its vote when the two members of its three-member delegation who were present divided. Before the second vote was cast, South Carolina's Edward Rutledge, who had opposed independence, proposed postponing the second vote until the following day, hinting that his province might change its vote overnight "for the sake of unanimity." Congress quickly accepted his motion.

The congressmen viewed the next day's session as anticlimactic. "The affair of Independency has been this day determined," a New Hampshire delegate wrote home that night. Abraham Clark of New Jersey, who had only arrived and been seated that very afternoon, and whose initial vote as a congressman was in favor of American independence, rejoiced that the break had been made. However, his joy was tempered by his concerns at what lay ahead. The new nation, he said, had "embarked on a most Tempestuous Sea." The journey could end badly, he reflected, but added: "Let us prepare for the worst, we can Die but once."[18]

Two important changes were immediately evident when Congress reconvened on July 2. Dickinson and Robert Morris, members of the Pennsylvania delegation who had opposed independence on the preceding evening, were absent, but two of the three who attended on this warm morning were known to support separation from Great Britain.

Furthermore, Caesar Rodney of Delaware, who had been out due to illness the previous day, now was present; he was known to favor independence. If Rutledge had been correct about a switch in South Carolina's vote, Congress would vote unanimously—12 to 0—for independence.

The vote did not occur immediately. Following its routine chores, Congress once again debated the proposition at length, and the long shadows of afternoon had gathered outdoors before the roll call votes on independence at last began. Two full days of debate had been required to reach this point. Six months had elapsed since *Common Sense* brought the issue front and center. The war had been under way for fifteen months. Eleven years had come and gone since mobs had pillaged the properties of Oliver and Hutchinson. But at last Congress was ready to vote. After all the waiting, the voting was concluded within five minutes. Both votes were unanimous. With the first dark stains of night visible in the eastern sky, Congress on July 2, 1776, declared independence.

The news coursed through Philadelphia immediately. The "Facts are as well known at the Coffee House of the City as in Congress," a New Englander wrote home that evening.[19] The "greatest Question was decided" today, Adams wrote home that night. Despite his yearlong battle for independence, Adams confessed that he was "surprized at the Suddenness" of the break. What he meant was that a scant decade had been required to transform the colonists from loyal subjects into revolutionaries. Much affliction lay ahead, he predicted, and he worried that before peace was secured "America shall suffer Calamities still more wasting and Distresses yet more dreadfull." Nevertheless, he was confident that victory could be won and the "Greatness of this Revolution" secured. "[T]hrough all the Gloom," he wrote, "I can see the Rays of ravishing Light and Glory" that would accompany the military triumph. "Posterity will tryumph" as a result of American autonomy, he predicted, and he further prognosticated that future generations would exuberantly celebrate July 2 as "the most memorable Epocha, in the History of America," a day that would "be solemnized with Pomp and Parade, with Shews, Games, Sports, Guns, Bells, Bonfires and Illuminations from one End of this Continent to the other."[20]

Congress devoted its next two days to debating Jefferson's draft, before it finally adopted the Declaration of Independence on July 4. During those two sessions, as historian Pauline Maier demonstrated, Congress proved to be "an extraordinary editor." It trimmed Jefferson's draft by about one-fourth. It deleted unnecessary words and cumbersome sentences, excised baseless assertions and moderated other passages, cut statements that could antagonize potential allies in England, and at the insistence of Georgia and South Carolina expunged a lengthy and impassioned assault on slavery.[21]

What remained was a forceful, yet lyrical, statement on human rights, including the right to engage in revolutionary acts. In the best remembered portion, the earliest section (and that with which Congress tinkered the least), Jefferson's literary talents and ideology of human self-dignity and rights shone through. So did his commitment to republicanism. In ringing, euphonious passages he added a sheen to innumerable remonstrances of countless assemblies, but also articulated what many activists must have felt as they participated in trade embargoes, or acted outside the law in city streets, or now as they bore arms on bloodstained battlefields. The axioms that he enumerated were based on "truths," not theory, and established that this newborn nation embraced the precepts that "all men are created equal" and enjoyed God-given rights that included—but were not restricted to—"Life, Liberty and the pursuit of Happiness." His defense of revolution in general, and the American Revolution in particular, was brief and sure. Governments, "deriving their just Powers from the consent of the governed," existed to secure the natural rights of humanity. Should a government fail to protect the rights of its people, "it is the Right of the People to alter or abolish it, and to institute new Government." When a government, through "a long train of abuses and usurpations, pursuing invariably the same Object, evinces a design to reduce them under absolute Despotism, it is their right, it is their duty, to throw off such government, and to provide new guards for their future security." Great Britain had afflicted its loyal subjects in America with recurrent "injuries and usurpations" of its proper authority, "all having in direct object the establishment of an absolute tyranny over these states."

With simple uncontrived eloquence, Jefferson provided justification for those who hoped for more than a mere escape from London's tentacles. In mellifluent passages, he set forth a new meaning to the American Revolution. While the creation of the United States was the endgame of resistance to the designs of a faraway regime, its birth—at least in the mind of Jefferson—also was a celebration of human rights and opportunities. Through the Declaration of Independence, the goal the new nation set for itself was the salvation and spread of human rights. Here was vindication for those who wished a real American Revolution that swept out the worst of the old politics and society and ushered in a truly new day.

Lee's brief motion on independence on June 7 had also urged that "a plan of confederation" be prepared and "transmitted to the respective Colonies for their consideration and approbation."[22] Lee wished to legitimate the union of provinces spawned two years earlier by the Coercive Acts, but he additionally sought popular sanctification of an American national government. He desired something else as well. Although an extralegal body, the Continental Congress had wielded breathtaking power. Since 1774 it had implemented a national boycott, created and staffed an army, issued a currency, conducted secret diplomacy with France, authorized an invasion of Canada, defined both civil and military crimes, and declared independence. Lee and others wished now to set limits on the authority of the national government and protect the sovereignty of the states.

At the same moment that it impaneled Jefferson's committee to draft a Declaration of Independence, Congress responded to Lee's motion by creating a second committee, this to draft a constitution for the nascent United States. Each state was allotted one representative on the constitution committee. Curiously, nearly one-third of the committee members were foes of independence, at least at the moment of the panel's creation in June 1776. Indeed, at the very moment that Congress was poised to sever America's ties with the mother country, John Dickinson—Congress's leading advocate of reconciliation—was selected to draft the nation's first constitution. In part, this may have been a ploy to alleviate the reconciliationists' concerns about governance in the new nation and to win their support for independence. But this was also the first salvo fired by the most conservative revolutionaries, who placed on the panel as many congressmen as they could who were known to abhor the prospect of sweeping social and political change.

The draft that Dickinson wrote—he spent his final three weeks in Congress wrestling with the task—revealed that he was just as much out of touch with the feelings of most Americans on the issue of the authority to be vested in the national government as he had been on the question of breaking away from London. He proposed that the "colonies"—he refused to use the term "states"—retain their "present Laws, Rights & Customs," but in Article XIX he recommended a bestowal of sovereign authority on the central government in the most vital areas, including taxation, diplomacy, war and peace, boundary issues, monetary supply, and commercial matters. His scheme was not unlike that proposed by Galloway two years earlier, which Congress had rejected by a single vote, or the proposals Franklin had offered at the Albany Congress twenty-two years earlier. The three plans envisioned an American union under a central government that subsumed many provincial powers.

No one factor led Dickinson to this conviction. In part, it stemmed from his belief that only a strong national government could wage the war successfully and compel London to reconcile on America's terms.

Dickinson additionally dreamt of a strong national government that not only could manage the far-flung commercial interests of the Delaware Valley's merchants but which could superintend the opening of the West for provincial speculators and settlers. Dickinson also hoped to check the supremacy of state legislatures. Like other conservatives, he worried that as suffrage rights and more equitable representation were expanded in the course of a desperate war, those reconstituted, and unchecked, assemblies would have it within their power to institute sweeping change. Within only weeks, in fact, Dickinson would be in the forefront of the fight to defeat ratification of the extremely democratic first constitution of Pennsylvania, a document that he and other conservatives denounced as "ultraradical," "confused," and "dangerous."[23]

Many in Congress shared Dickinson's zeal for centralized governance. Some even desired that the Continental Congress draft a uniform constitution for each state.[24] That was out of the question. Most Americans in 1776 feared a stout and hearty national government. In the midst of a revolution to prevent the centralization of British authority over the colonies, they were in no mood to create a strong centralized national government of their own.

Nothing in the Declaration of Independence, or in the instructions and resolutions on independence adopted by numerous towns and counties, suggested that a large number of Americans in 1776 harbored any future designs that could not be fully realized by each state. Interests existed, of course, that would find a strong national government to be of use, but they chose not to make a desperate fight at this juncture. Winning the war was their first concern, an objective that would be imperiled should divisions abound. Besides, when the Tories, often an interconnected gentry that had acted as the glue in preserving old ways, were banished from the political process, the more conservative revolutionaries simply lacked the strength to have their way in the creation of the first government. Thus, the public discussion in 1776 revolved about the wish to escape Britain and the desire to create provincial governments based on popular choice. A national government was widely seen as essential only for shepherding the war through to victory, as it alone could implement a coherent military strategy, properly administer and supply the army, and conduct diplomacy. Otherwise, many throughout America doubtless would have agreed with the resolution adopted in the spring of 1776 by Buckingham County, Virginia, which declared that the central "Government erected among us is confessed on all hands to be only temporary, for the immediate purpose of opposing the arbitrary strides of *Great Britain*." Most citizens preferred that day-to-day government authority, the powers wielded in peacetime that truly touched peoples' lives, be left to each state. While a Patrick Henry might declaim that he was "not a Virginian, but an American," most of his countrymen in 1776 identified primarily with their state or region and believed that an authoritative government was safest when confined to the local and state levels.[25]

That the national government-in-the-making was foreordained to be weak was evident in the behavior of public officials with a keen sense of the locus of power. Although John Adams was widely regarded as the most knowledgeable member of Congress in the area of government theory, he did not seek a place on the committee that drafted the first national constitution. He preferred to devote his energies to more substantive matters, the army and diplomacy. Likewise, throughout the spring and summer of 1776, Jefferson bombarded powerful figures in Virginia with pleas to be replaced in Congress. He wanted to be in Williamsburg, where he could participate in writing Virginia's first constitution, a task that he saw as vastly more important than that facing Dickinson's committee. Adams and Jefferson were not untypical. Americans often spoke of their state as their "country" or, in the case of Maryland's congressmen, their "nation." Few in this era ever traveled far from their place of birth, and most Americans in 1776 had never been outside the colony in which they lived. Few had ties to, or affinity for, any other province. Traditionally, when Americans had looked beyond their colony's borders, their gaze extended across the Atlantic to the metropolis 3,000 miles away, not to their nearby neighbors. In some respects that was to be expected, as it was London that often gave shape to their world, determining with whom they could conduct commerce, choosing some of their governors, and deciding issues of war and peace. So accentuated were these patterns that even in wartime the colonists had found it nearly impossible to cooperate with one another.

Even the act of breaking with Great Britain was thought by many to have been undertaken separately by each state, not by Congress, a view encouraged by the Declaration of Independence, which stipulated that separation from the mother country was an act by "thirteen united States." Several congressmen, according to Samuel Chase of Maryland, did not even see "the Necessity of a Confederacy."[26] Nor was the populace aroused by the evolution of the first national constitution. Unlike the excitement and great debate aroused by the Constitution of 1787, or the furor that has accompanied the ratification of numerous constitutional amendments over the years, the Articles of Confederation generated little public interest.

Most congressmen had anticipated that writing a national constitution would be speedy work. Adams envisioned Congress spending no more than two weeks on the committee's draft, after which "Nothing . . . will remain but War."[27] He was wrong. Seventeen months elapsed before Congress completed its work, although it did not toil continuously on the constitution. Congress received the Dickinson draft on July 12 and debated it for nearly a month. These sessions were far more acrimonious than anyone had anticipated—so bitter, in fact, that on the eve of the British invasion of New York in August, Congress tabled the issue. Fearing that the attendant rancor and division would impair the war effort, it did not take up the proposed constitution again until the spring, by which time the military crisis of 1776 had passed. Even so, it did not send the document to the states for ratification until after the decisive American victory at Saratoga, when the populace brimmed with confidence that the war was as good as won.

The final version of the constitution recommended to the states by Congress divested the national government of strong powers. That decision had generated little friction, but stormy debates in July and August 1776 had arisen over two issues. An intense battle ensued over whether levies on the states were to be based on land or population, and if the latter, whether slaves were to be counted. In addition, high stakes were involved in the hodgepodge of rival claims among states that possessed lands beyond the mountains, as also was true of the division between so-called landed and landless states, those that possessed title to trans-Appalachian lands and those that did not. However, as historian Gordon Wood has pointed out, neither matter touched on the question of national-state sovereignty. Sovereignty was at issue, not only in a peripheral sense, in the debate over a third substantive matter. Large and small states squared off over whether the states were to be equally represented or whether representation would be based on population or wealth, or both.[28]

If the former, the confederation would be an alliance of equal and independent states. If the latter, a nation in the real sense of the word would be created. In its first substantive decision in 1774, the Continental Congress had awarded each state one vote. The Dickinson draft embodied that formula and the smaller states fought tenaciously for its retention, lest their influence fade as the populous states grew and cast a steadily wider shadow. Many small states genuinely believed they would remain truly autonomous only so long as Congress maintained parity between the states. With conservatives and radicals joining hands, the larger states sought to base representation either on population or on the amount of money contributed to the national treasury. During the debates Adams, who represented the third largest state, contended that congressmen represented economic interests—merchants, financiers, slave-owning planters—that overlapped state boundaries. Jefferson, a representative of the largest state, declared that the issue was a matter of whether the national government reflected the opinion of a majority of the population or a majority of the states. To no one's surprise, both proposed that representation should be based on population.[29] They did not have their way, and the issue was never in doubt. The Articles of Confederation, the first United States constitution, was adopted by a Congress which represented states, and which allotted a single vote to each state.

Two additional factors contributed to Congress's decision. First, it acted in the midst of its first serious war crisis. Not only was the battle for New York City about to begin, but further to the north, on the Canadian border, a British army that had "increased amazingly" to 6,000 men—as one startled congressman exclaimed—was about to strike at a tattered, illness-ravaged American army half its size. No one underestimated the urgency of the moment. Many believed that the campaign for New York would "in all probability," in the words of the state's provincial congress, "decide the fate of America."[30] At such a menacing time, prudence dictated that Congress quickly resolve all boggles that threatened domestic division.

Second, in the course of the debate over taxation, which also occurred during that anxious summer, more alarming talk of disunion was heard. The Dickinson draft recommended that each state allocate funds in proportion to the total number of its inhabitants, excepting Indians. Several Southern congressmen immediately objected to enumerating slaves. They argued instead for basing taxation on land values, which were greater in the more populous North. Congress quickly divided along sectional lines. In the debate that followed, Thomas Lynch Jr. of South Carolina minced no words when he told Congress that "there is an end to Confederation" should slaves be taxed. His threat settled the issue, as Congress understood that independence was a chimera in the absence of a union of all the states. Furthermore, in that very debate New Jersey's John Witherspoon asked "what would it signify to risk our possessions and shed our blood to set ourselves free," if independence was followed immediately by strife between North and South over constitutional fracases. As was becoming habitual, a majority of the Northern states capitulated to the South's demands. It was agreed that taxes were to be based on the estimated value of "all land within each State, granted to or surveyed for any person."[31]

State sovereignty would be tested repeatedly during the next dozen years by concerns that were not, and in many instances could not have been, foreseen during that fateful summer. The trials of war and diplomacy, as well as the gradual realization that state sovereignty imposed limitations on the ability of powerful elements to shape society and fulfill economic aspirations, caused the matter to be repeatedly revisited.

For instance, during the first winter of independence, signs of a swelling economic crisis became evident. The war devoured money almost with the speed that piranha on a feeding frenzy consume their prey. Congress adopted a Continental currency and issued $2,000,000 in June 1775. Within eighteen months it had put $25,000,000 into circulation and was printing new issues every fortnight. Not surprisingly, the value of the Continental currency began to collapse that autumn. Depreciation, resulting from overly generous emissions of paper money, as well as shortages occasioned both by the loss of British trade and the enemy's ever-tightening naval blockade, threatened economic collapse.[32] To forestall that occurrence, the New England states convened in Providence in December 1776 to seek agreement on price and wage regulations, and monetary policy.

Some in Congress, however, objected to any governmental tampering with the marketplace, while others were put off by the intrusiveness of the states. These congressmen insisted that the economy, like diplomacy, was a national concern that should be left to Congress. Benjamin Rush of Pennsylvania argued that the "Salvation of this continent" hinged on repeated demonstrations of the "sacred . . . Authority and character" of Congress to lead. Together with John Adams, he induced Congress to recommend that the states increase taxes. Furthermore, at Adams's behest, Congress raised from 4 to 6 percent the interest rate on loan certificates, which it had first issued only weeks earlier. Designed to be a source of investment, not a circulating medium, it was hoped that loan certificates would take money out of circulation and hence be a deflationary measure. But Congress went no further. The majority, which yet consisted of committed decentralists, preferred that the states find palliatives for their economic maladies. The alternative was for Congress to centralize its control of the economy, a move fraught with danger for a shaky union in the midst of a military crisis. Thus Congress not only approved the initiative of the New England states in seeking "to remedy the Evils occasioned by . . . exorbitant Prices" but also recommended that the middle and southern states convene in York, Pennsylvania, and Charleston, respectively, to consider solutions to their growing dilemma.[33]

Constitutions and economic woes notwithstanding, from the moment independence was declared until the spring of 1778 it was the war that "engross[ed] our chief attention," a congressman noted.[34] Aside from the debacle in Canada that had been so important in determining when independence was to be declared, the war had gone well throughout its first year. Washington had assumed command during the siege of Boston, just after New England's hastily created army of citizen-soldiers had performed so spectacularly on the bloody farmlands that rose above the Charles River to form Bunker Hill. He spent most of that year "new modeling" his army, as he put it, making soldiers of civilians, searching for competent junior-grade officers, and patiently seeking to infuse his men with elan, pride both in being soldiers and in being part of the Continental army. But Washington could not seize the initiative, which he was restlessly eager to do, until he laid his hands on ample ordnance. Early in 1776 he found the weaponry he desired, and at once moved to replicate his predecessor's success at Bunker Hill.

During the worst of that cold winter, Washington had dispatched Henry Knox—who only weeks earlier had been an ambitious twenty-five-year-old anxious to escape the maiming obscurity of his lot as a Boston bookseller—to Fort Ticonderoga, an old British installation on New York's northern frontier that had been seized, together with its store of weaponry, by New England soldiers immediately following the outbreak of war. Acting with dispatch, Knox and his party of rugged teamsters—equipped with eighty-two sleds, 160 oxen, and more than 125 horses—wrestled fifty-nine cannon that weighed in excess of 120,000 pounds down to Albany, across the Hudson, and through the snowbound Berkshires to the outskirts of Boston. The operation had required seventy-five days of intense labor, a feat of military engineering that made onlookers marvel.

Under cover of darkness on the sixth anniversary of the Boston Massacre, March 5, 1776, Washington got his new artillery atop Dorchester Heights. From that vantage point, the Continental artillerymen could sweep Boston harbor of British shipping, severing General William Howe's lifeline to supply depots throughout Great Britain. When Howe awakened and glimpsed the sun sparkling on the gun barrels of the American cannon atop the eminence south of the city, he knew instantly that the British armed forces in Boston were in an untenable position. Washington confidently dared him to attack. He believed that the losses the British had sustained at Bunker Hill would be as nothing compared to the carnage likely to result from an attempt to wrest this high ground from the entrenched American soldiery. Washington was convinced that during the past year he had transformed his Continentals from civilians into soldiers; in addition, he had twelve times the number of cannon that had been available to the defenders of Bunker Hill. Howe briefly considered an attack, but soon decided it was best to bargain. He proposed that in return for his safe departure from Boston, he would not raze the city. Washington faced a dilemma. He could in all likelihood capture the entire British army in America. Or he could spare Boston. He chose the latter. He was fully aware that Congress was moving toward independence, which might bring foreign aid to his army, and just as alert to the reality that the ruination of Boston would only strengthen the hand of reconciliationists in other cities, especially in New York and Philadelphia, delaying indefinitely the break with Great Britain. Thus, Washington accepted Howe's proffer and during April the last of the redcoats, who had come in the hot summer of 1768 to maintain order and enforce the Townshend Duties, sailed away. What Samuel Adams had always called the "occupation" of Boston had ended.

Washington guessed correctly that New York would be Howe's next target. Britain's strategy was to isolate, then to destroy, the insurgency in New England. Suppress the uprising in New England, many in London insisted, and the upheaval would wither away elsewhere. New York was crucial to the realization of Britain's objective. Once conquered, its excellent harbor would be the home base for a naval blockade of New England. Furthermore, the British expected to follow its conquest of New York City with the seizure of the Hudson River northward to Albany and beyond, a step that would sever New England's connection by land to every province to its south. Choked and detached, New England would barely be capable of defending itself against an invasion from New York, the final act in the destruction of the American rebellion.

Washington hardly took the time to enjoy the plaudits of Bostonians in April 1776 before he hurried south to oversee the preparation of defenses on Manhattan Island and Long Island. He had less than five months to complete the work before the British army and Hessian mercenaries debouched onto Long Island during the last hot days of August 1776. Washington expected "a very bloody Summer of it," but he was confident that the enemy would do most of the bleeding. General Charles Lee, who had supervised the planning of the fortifications, thought the "field of battle so advantageous" that it would "cost the enemy many thousands of men to get possession" of New York. Franklin and Jefferson were convinced that the Continental army could repulse the enemy or, at worst, make the British gain a Pyrrhic victory.[35] Events took quite a different turn.

In the first morning of fighting on Long Island, the British nearly succeeded in surrounding the Continentals. In a disorganized retreat, the Americans broke and ran for the hills, the redoubts in the high ground of Brooklyn that had been under construction throughout the spring and summer. But their presumed security in these defensive positions

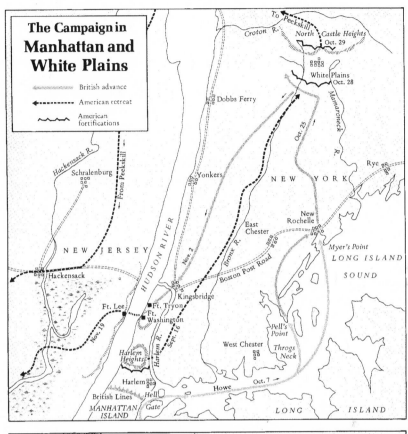

The Campaign in **Manhattan and White Plains**

British advance
American retreat
American fortifications

To Peekskill
Croton R.
North Castle Heights Oct. 29
White Plains Oct. 28
Mamaroneck R.
Dobbs Ferry
Rye
NEW YORK
New Rochelle
Myer's Point
LONG ISLAND SOUND
Oct. 25
From Peekskill
Hackensack R.
Schralenburg
Yonkers
East Chester
Bronx R.
Boston Post Road
NEW JERSEY
HUDSON RIVER
Nov. 2
Pell's Point
Hackensack
Nov. 19
Kingsbridge
Ft. Lee
Ft. Tryon
Ft. Washington
West Chester
Throgs Neck
Harlem R.
Sept. 16
Harlem Heights
Harlem
Howe Oct. 7
British Lines
Hell Gate
MANHATTAN ISLAND
LONG ISLAND

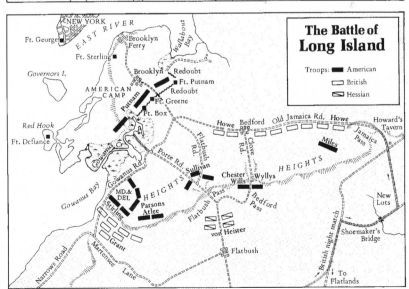

The Battle of **Long Island**

Troops: American
British
Hessian

NEW YORK
EAST RIVER
Ft. George
Brooklyn Ferry
Wallabout Bay
Ft. Sterling
Governors I.
Brooklyn
Redoubt
Ft. Putnam
Redoubt
AMERICAN CAMP
Putnam
Ft. Greene
Ft. Box
Howe Bedford Old Jamaica Rd. Howe
Howard's Tavern
Red Hook
Jamaica Pass
Ft. Defiance
Flatbush Rd.
Clove Rd.
Miles
Gowanus Cr.
Porte Rd.
Sullivan
Chester Wyllys
Wills
HEIGHTS
New Lots
Gowanus Bay
Gowanus Rd.
HEIGHTS
MD.& DEL
Stirling
Parsons
Arlee
Flatbush Pass
Bedford Pass
Shoemaker's Bridge
Grant
Narrows Road
Martensee Lane
von Heister
Flatbush
British night march
To Flatlands

was illusory, as they were very much trapped, pinioned against the East River. Washington, however, was fortunate and daring. When Howe paused before delivering the knockout punch, Washington took advantage of deteriorating weather—a dense fog rolled in and shrouded the river, reducing visibility to bare inches—to extricate his snared men. Nevertheless, it soon appeared that disaster had only been postponed, not averted. Washington brought the men he had rescued from Long Island to Manhattan Island, and posted half his force at the lower end of the island and the remainder in Harlem Heights, several miles to the north. When the British landed in mid-September at Kip's Bay, on the east side of Manhattan Island, they stormed ashore midway between the two halves of the Continental army. A cataclysmic defeat once again appeared to be inevitable. Had the British moved expeditiously to seal off every road, each half of the American army would have been enveloped and doomed. But Howe's army was incapable of rapid movement. His redcoats proceeded languidly—on reaching shore some paused to brew a pot of tea—allowing the Continentals in the south to escape along open roads and reunite with their comrades in Harlem Heights before nightfall. Thereafter, Washington at last got most of his army off these indefensible islands, although he did leave a large garrison at Fort Washington in the northeast sector of Manhattan.

Congress was rattled by what had occurred. Some expressed concern that these near disasters would strengthen the hand of those who favored reconciliation. Waiting impatiently for word from Silas Deane, who reached France on his mission in quest of foreign assistance just prior to the Battle of New York, some frightened congressmen even expressed a readiness to accept an alliance with Louis XVI on any terms that the French monarch dictated. Blame for the poor showing was heaped on the militia that had been sent by surrounding states to assist the Continental army. Inexperienced and poorly trained, many trainbandsmen—not unlike their counterparts in the Continental army—had fled in the face of the British regulars and the green-clad Hessian Yagers and their blue garbed brethren among the grenadiers. A Virginia congressman called them "ineffectual" and "expensive," and an exasperated New Englander labeled them "lifeless." The Continental regulars did not fare much better in the postmortem. In some engagements "not a single man faced his enemy or fired his Gun," a North Carolinian charged. When the enemy landed, he went on, the Continentals "made way for them as soon as their arrival was announced." Nor did Washington escape criticism. The "enemy out-generalled our people," more than one congressman asserted.[36]

Washington made stupendous blunders during the Battle of New York, but the most egregious error—to defend these islands against an adversary that possessed the world's finest navy and an army of regulars that outnumbered the American citizen-soldiers—was imposed on him by Congress. However, Washington had not balked at Congress' wishes. He believed his new-modeled army of patriots who fought for liberty could stand up to regulars who had no stake in the outcome of the Anglo-American quarrel. Soon enough, however, Washington's callow soldiers and equally inexperienced officers proved a bitter disappointment. Yet they were not entirely to blame. Washington made an incredible mistake at the very outset of the contest when he divided his army in the face of a superior foe. He posted half his men on Manhattan Island and the remainder in and around Brooklyn Heights on the western end of Long Island. After barely surviving that blunder, he repeated it on Manhattan. By the narrowest of margins he survived that misstep as well, but he foolishly remained on Manhattan long after Congress had authorized his flight to the greater safety of New Jersey or the mainland above New York. Good fortune alone appears to have saved him from himself. Late in September, as Washington at last was attempting to get his army off Manhattan Island, the British moved to cut off his every exit and almost brought it off. They were slowed by poor maps and inadequate knowledge of the terrain, and Washington's Continentals barely made their escape.

Throughout the debacle, Washington had commanded with the panache of an amateur. Indeed, he was not a professional soldier. He was a private citizen who had experienced a bit of war several years earlier and who after fifteen years as a planter-businessman had taken up arms once again. He had never led an army of more than 2,000 men, nor had he ever commanded against an army of European regulars, much less one that possessed total naval superiority. His own inexperience was exacerbated by that of the officers about him, men whom he had neither selected nor knew very well. Furthermore, even with the laurels that came from his victory in the siege of Boston, Washington remained unsure of himself. Throughout the campaign for New York, he appeared fearful of ignoring the advice of other general officers, which at times was improvident, or of disputing with Congress. Given the state of the Continental army in mid-1776, the most capable veteran officer would have faced insurmountable problems in New York, but that did not stop probing questions about Washington's capability from being quietly raised.[37]

Once Washington was off Manhattan, he divided his army into thirds. He posted one wing in Connecticut to guard against an invasion of New England, while a second was left in the Highlands above New York to defend the Hudson River. With the remainder, Washington crossed into New Jersey, hoping to protect that state and shield Philadelphia. Although no one knew it at the time, the low point of the war before 1780—both for the American cause and for General Washington—was about to be reached. In mid-November the British seized Fort Washington. The Americans lost 3,000 men killed, wounded, and captured. Washington had adequate warning of the peril, but was frozen by indecision. A few days later Fort Lee, directly across the river, fell with the loss of irreplaceable supplies and arms, especially artillery. Both losses were inexcusable, as it should have been readily apparent that neither installation could be held. For the moment, all that was left to Washington was to run for his life, which he did, with the implacable earl of Cornwallis in relentless pursuit.

Washington stayed one step ahead of his foe, sometimes exiting a glum New Jersey village while redcoated advance parties entered the other side. Ultimately, Washington got his men across the Delaware River at Trenton. There, with the wide, fast-flowing river between the pursuer and the pursued, the Continentals enjoyed a sunbeam of safety. Shortly, in fact, when the rains of late autumn increased, turning America's primitive roads into a gluey mud, the British called off the chase until spring. They went into winter quarters, posting detachments of their regulars and the Hessian mercenaries throughout New Jersey and New York.

"I think the game is pretty near up," Washington confided to his brother late that autumn. Not only did the rebellion appear to be ineluctably doomed, but the commander was aware that the nimbus attached to him following his success in Boston had faded. Washington correctly suspected that there were some in Congress and the army who doubted his fitness for his post. Various congressmen invidiously pointed in private to Washington's mistakes, saying that he had "again blundered" or acted "very injudiciously." A well-informed Virginian reported the existence of a "Dark design against him [Washington]" in October, and John Adams around this same time acknowledged disaffection within the ranks of New England's congressmen. There was talk as well of a soldiery that was "much disgusted" with its leaders and of officers who feared their commander was fatally indecisive.[38]

It was in this pernicious atmosphere that Washington struck back, attacking the Hessian cantonment at Trenton on Christmas night. It was an act of desperation. Even Washington conceded that nothing "but necessity, dire necessity" could justify the risks he ran. He was seeking to save himself and his army, for the one-year period of enlistment that had commenced during the siege of Boston was about to expire. No one knew better than Washington that men could not be recruited to an army that was perpetually on the run or that habitually faced defeat. If he was to have an army in 1777, he needed a victory. Yet Washington did not act recklessly. Intelligence gathered from local German-Americans led him to believe that the Hessians, distracted by their exuberant Christmas revelry, might be vulnerable to a surprise attack. Still, his operation would place him in great peril. In taking the army across the Delaware, he risked the possibility that his Continentals might be discovered with their backs to the river and with no hope of escape.

What resulted was one of the few instances in this war when Washington's battle plan worked almost exactly as envisioned. Acting with an ingrained instinct for exploiting another's folly, Washington caught his adversary by surprise in a cold dawn assault, inflicting a fearful toll. More than 1,000 of the enemy were killed, wounded, and captured. Audaciously, Washington crossed the Delaware River a second time a few days later and fought Cornwallis to a draw on the Assunpink Creek near Trenton, repulsing one assault after another by the regulars. In the unsparing darkness of the night that followed, Washington slipped away and pushed his army northward, deeper into the lion's den. That morning, January 3, he fought again, this time at Princeton, a few miles above Trenton. Washington was in the lead astride his powerful grey charger, splashing across shallow streams and riding hard across the rolling brown terrain. A ready target, he nevertheless escaped unscathed while men around him suffered horrible wounds. Meanwhile, his men, once again fighting robustly, as they had in each of these contests, inflicted additional losses. In the three battles fought over a ten-day period since Christmas, the Continentals had succeeded in killing or wounding over 1,500 of the enemy. These were the first dulcet tidings for the American public since the British evacuation of Boston ten months earlier, and it moved Congressman Robert Morris to exclaim that "Good News sets all the Animal Spirits to Work."[39]

Long after the war, John Adams revealed that Congress had shielded Washington from a public disclosure of his errors.[40] Congress had little choice if faith in the army and its commander was to be maintained. Thus, even had he not scored the victories at Trenton and Princeton, Washington doubtless would have continued as commander in 1777. Short of personal scandal, or egregious incompetence, any congressional move to dump him at this juncture would have resulted in a political nightmare. Furthermore, most in Congress understood that if Washington was an inexperienced citizen-soldier, so was every other American-born officer who might have supplanted him. Every congressman also was aware that the unpracticed Continentals had been compelled to fight against an army of numerically superior regulars.

Many were heartened, too, by Washington's willingness to abandon his original, misplaced strategy of direct confrontation with the enemy. After Long Island and Kip's Bay, he had come to see that his inexperienced men were no match for European regulars. He informed Congress that henceforth he would employ Fabian tactics, fighting a war of attrition, retreating and avoiding hostilities until every advantage for a strike was in his favor. What he termed a "war of posts" was designed to exhaust the British and convince them that a costly protracted war was not in their best interest. Most congressmen applauded his flexibility and insisted that the new policy "reflects no dishonour" on the United States. Some called it a "master stroke" that "reflects great Credit upon the Military Capabilities of our commanding officer." When it was crowned by the victories at Trenton and Princeton, some in Congress gushed at how "the face of affairs is greatly changed."[41]

Like Washington that autumn, Congress itself adopted bold new approaches. At the end of 1775, during the siege of Boston, Washington had watched with horror as his army of short-term enlistees went home. He implored Congress to mandate longer enlistments, even for the duration of the war. Congress refused and also rejected pleas for using bounties to induce men to reenlist. Its actions stemmed from an abiding fear of standing armies. Many in Congress considered a standing army an "armed monster" and an "infernal machine." Samuel Adams, in language reminiscent of that which he had used during the British occupation of Boston after 1768, declared that soldiers in a standing army "are apt to consider themselves in a Body distinct from the rest of the Citizens." To the end of the war he wished that the Continental army consisted of militiamen conscripted for brief tours of duty.[42]

John Adams shared his cousin's fears, and added that an army which served for the length of the war would consist only of "the meanest, idlest, most intemperate and worthless men." Yet, as another congressman observed, the fighting in New York demonstrated that if the army was not restructured, "Our inevitable destruction will be the Consequence." Even so, the battle in Congress over "new modeling" the army, as many put it, was furious. Despite his concerns, John Adams led this fight and, simultaneously, a move to revise the Articles of War, so that discipline might be improved in the Continental army. He won both campaigns. Congress agreed in the autumn of 1776 to raise eighty-eight battalions consisting of 75,000 men who "may be enlisted for three years, or during the War, as shall be most agreeable to them." The new Articles of War, modeled on those governing the British army, provided for more draconian punishments, including raising the legal limit on lashes from 39 to 100. "The Times call for the greatest . . . Vigour of Conduct," President Hancock reported to the people.[43]

Congress was on the run when Washington struck at Trenton and Princeton, roughly only twenty miles from Philadelphia. Ten days before Washington's Christmas assault, as the enemy closed in on Philadelphia, the congressmen fled. They were in a vexed and churlish mood as they ran for their lives. Samuel Adams, who railed at New Jersey's "shameful" performance in failing to adequately respond to Cornwallis's invasion, blamed the reconciliationists for the citizenry's poor showing. Dickinson and his allies, he charged, had "poisond the Minds of the People" with their incessant prattle about being reunited with Great Britain. Others attributed the emergency to "capital Errors" made by the army's leaders. However, many remained stoic. Congressman Wolcott, for instance, reflected that Athens and Rome, in their infancy, had been "reduced to the greatest Distress," but had survived. Although the "present Scene" was "somewhat Gloomy," he remarked on his last day in Philadelphia, Wolcott was confident that the new United States would yet bask in "Security, Opulence and Power."[44]

Congress reconvened in Baltimore in January, meeting in what had recently been an undistinguished three-story frame tavern. News of Washington's daring triumph elevated the congressmen's mood. "The Year 1776 is over. I am heartily glad of it," a Pennsylvanian sighed. Now he radiated hope. The "Success at Trentown [is] a presage of future fortunate Events" in 1777. Nevertheless, the congressmen suffered through their two-month residency in Baltimore, which one described as a "dirty infamous extravagant hole." Hancock complained that lodging could be found only in a neighborhood inhabited by "Whores & Thieves," and indeed on his second day in town a "Trunk with Linnen, Books, papers, some hard Money, &c" was stolen from his quarters. At the end of February, amid great rejoicing, Congress returned to the Pennsylvania State House. A veteran congressman from Virginia, who admitted to never having previously liked Philadelphia, confessed his joy at the move and his delight in abandoning "cursedly Vex'd" Baltimore.[45]

Congress beamed that spring as the campaign season neared. The quest for foreign assistance, undertaken a year earlier, at last was reaping dividends. France had provided sufficient secret aid to arm and equip 20,000 men.[46] France had been eager to covertly help the Americans, or at least to do what it could to weaken Great Britain, long its hated enemy. The moment that London suspended trade with its North American colonies, merchants in France and the rebellious colonies began to explore the possibilities of doing business. Long before the leaves fell in the first autumn of the war, in 1775, ships sent out by Willing, Morris & Company of Philadelphia and the MM. Penet and Pliarne Company of Nantes were crossing the Atlantic. The American entrepreneurs shipped tobacco, rice, naval stores, and fish to France. The French merchants ran saltpeter, necessary for making powder, and guns to America. Just before Christmas 1775 an agent of the French foreign ministry arrived in Philadelphia and chatted privately with several congressmen. He told them that the French government might be willing to provide assistance. The Americans replied at once that they would accept it, and in March 1776 Congress sent Silas Deane to Paris. Two months to the day before independence was declared, and before Deane reached France, Louis XVI decided to give the Americans 1,000,000 livres for the purchase of munitions in France. That was only the beginning. Deane soon acquired even more war materials. As 1777 dawned, a French fleet arrived with 200 cannon, hundreds of muskets, tons of powder, 3,000 tents, and enormous quantities of bullets and cannonballs. This aid, historian Richard Van Alstyne has written, was tantamount to a lend-lease program for America. Too little of it arrived to be of help during the struggle for New York, but by the spring of 1777 nearly 90 percent of the small arms carried by the Continental soldiery and virtually all the army's field artillery, tents, and uniforms had come from France.[47]

Not everyone in Congress was happy with America's role as a French suitor. Many remembered France as Anglo-America's archenemy, a bitter adversary in several wars, and the facilitator of numerous deadly Indian raids along the New England, New York, and Pennsylvania frontiers. Others, blinded by religious bigotry, vilified France as a Catholic state. But most who were concerned expressed apprehension at what they suspected were France's "vile motives." Many shared the fears of the long departed Galloway, who had warned the First Congress that aid provided by Versailles would inevitably result in America becoming a vassal of France. Until the eve of independence, Jefferson cautioned that "properly limited" ties to the mother country were preferable to the price of accepting French aid. Adams counseled against an alliance. The French "intend to make Use of Us," he warned, adding that after it got what it wanted—the separation of America from Britain—Versailles would "leave us in the Lurch," alone and defenseless against the great powers in Europe. However, Adams defended the establishment of commercial relations with France, and Congress wholeheartedly agreed. The congressmen were willing to trade with France, and they certainly wanted the French to enter the war. But they feared an alliance. Thus, while it adopted Lee's famous motion of June 7, 1776, which had also recommended that the United States take "the most effectual measures for forming foreign Alliances," Congress late that summer instructed the envoys it dispatched to Paris to agree only to a commercial accord.[48]

Events in the last half of 1776 forced Congress's hand. With Washington in flight in November and December, and the rumor circulating that London would dispatch 30,000 Russian mercenaries to America during the next campaign, the realization grew, as Congressman Robert Morris put it, that "Our Situation is critical & does not admit of Delay." A desperate Congress, redolent with the acrid smell of disaster in its nostrils, was prepared to accept almost any French demand if it would provoke Anglo-French hostilities. Congress was no less anxious to induce Spain to join the fray, and late in 1776 it offered West Florida to Madrid as an inducement. Such steps were distasteful, but as one congressman remarked, they were "important . . . to the security of American Independence."[49]

Reservations persisted. Some in New England feared that France would reclaim Canada. Some in the middle states were anxious that Versailles would demand concessions in the Ohio Country. Everywhere the worry persisted that close ties with the French king would make it more difficult "to purge away the monarchical impurity" that had tainted the American body politic or that French cultural excesses might corrupt America. Henry Laurens of South Carolina, who would become the president of Congress late in 1777, could not shake his apprehension that France would betray the United States.[50] But there was no alternative. The riptide of this war had drawn Congress where it did not wish to go.

Meanwhile, changes that were distasteful to some had begun to occur in the states. By the end of 1777 every state, save for Massachusetts, had written a constitution or adapted its royal charter. From today's perspective, the changes that resulted seem quite pallid. But it is our perspective that is skewed, and understandably so. As the basic constitutional structure created in the first moments of independence remains barely changed even today, it is tempting to take for granted the changes that occurred in the American Revolution.

Royalty disappeared from America.[51] Not only was the long arm of the British Crown removed, but no state seriously considered creating its own monarchy. Republican governments sprang up everywhere. It was commonly agreed that republicanism meant not only a government without a king but a system in which the people were sovereign, although what was meant by "the people" was yet to be decided. Nor was it clear how the governments would be constructed. Two widely read pamphlets published in 1776 offered models.

The "new era for politics" envisioned by Paine in *Common Sense* was one in which royal and aristocratic influence ceased to exist. Instead, all power was to be vested in a unicameral assembly that was annually elected by "the whole body" of the people. While scholars have never determined the exact percentage of freemen who possessed suffrage rights in the colonial era, there can be no doubt that Paine offered a radical alternative to the existing practice. One additional proposition that he made would also have involved a substantive change. Before independence, it was generally presumed throughout America that an elected official was to exercise his judgment, regardless of the popular will. But Paine argued that it was essential for republican officeholders to exhibit "fidelity to the public." Those who did not do so, he added, should be removed from office by the voters.[52]

Thoughts on Government was intended by John Adams to be a conservative alternative to Paine's rapturous illusions. Whereas Paine wished to fashion a system that liberated officials so that they might act, and act quickly, Adams expressed grave doubts about unfettered officials. Throughout history, he wrote, liberty had been traduced by those in authority. Time and again, freedom had been driven "skulking about in corners . . . hunted and persecuted in all countries by cruel power." Those who exercised power, Adams reflected, neither sought greater liberty for the ruled nor served the liberties that the citizenry already possessed. For "the good of the whole community," Adams asserted, he wished to restrain the officials that Paine hoped to unharness.

But it was not merely despots who threatened liberty. For a century, enlightened opinion in Great Britain had held that liberty must be restrained if it was to be preserved and especially that it must be safeguarded from self-destruction brought on by carnival license. The approach of Paine and Adams could hardly have been more antithetic. Paine accentuated the preservation and expansion of liberty, whereas Adams worried that when people were too free, licentiousness could reach the point of anarchy, which could devolve into tyranny, as entrenched interests sought to restore order. Substantive differences also separated these two on the question of balanced government. Liberal thought in the eighteenth century supposed that liberty's preservation was linked to the balancing, or sharing, of political power, an arrangement that prevented rulers from accumulating excessive power while at the same time it checked the citizenry's supposed penchant for heedless indulgence. Adams thought balanced government was the key to good government, but Paine's preoccupation was with the limits of authority. Paine's solution to the "pride and insolence" of rulers who victimized the citizenry was to give untrammeled power to the people. Adams believed Paine's notion was simplistic, as it was devoid of a satisfactory check on the people. Paine believed that a constitutional system of balances in which one powerful component checked another was a "mere absurdity." Such a government, he said, was good only for inhibiting the will of the people and for making change difficult, if not impossible, to effect. For that very reason, the more conservative elements in American politics were drawn to the system of balanced government.[53]

For the most part, the state constitutions adopted in 1776 and 1777 were written by the state legislatures. Most assemblies were yet dominated by the very men who had controlled the colonial assemblies on the eve of independence. Not surprisingly, Adams's conservative formula was more popular with them than was the vision of radical change propounded by Paine. Indirect elections and bicameralism were rules of thumb in the initial constitutions. In many states popular participation in government remained as effectively checked as had been the case under the colonial regimes. Almost everywhere, high property qualifications restricted suffrage and prevented most citizens from holding office. Furthermore, in most states the upper house remained a preserve in which the largest property owners protected their interests.

Nevertheless, when contrasted with the old colonial systems, the new constitutions introduced some striking changes. Many included a bill of rights which stipulated the sovereignty of the people, guaranteed their right to alter or abolish the government, and either provided for various liberties, including freedom of press, religion, speech, and trial by jury, or restricted governmental intrusiveness. Everywhere the executives were elected, either popularly or by the assembly. Nor were the governors vested with much power. Few had absolute veto power, and none could prorogue their assembly. In addition, three constitutions lowered property qualifications for voting, while four states extended suffrage rights to all adult white male taxpayers.[54]

The adoption of the new constitutions did not terminate the struggle over the shape of America. Democratic elements fought on in several states to broaden the suffrage, shorten terms of officeholders, and secure equal representation for the backcountry. Conservatives, meanwhile, were shocked by Pennsylvania's radical constitution, which they feared might shine like a beacon for reformers in their states.

Pennsylvania's constitution, alone among those adopted in 1776–77, was not drafted by the state assembly. A broadly representative Provincial Convention, consisting primarily of men of moderate economic status, wrote this charter, a document which, as historian Jackson Turner Main commented, "perpetuated the democratic aspects of the colonial government while moving far beyond it into the future." Indeed, two generations would elapse before any other state adopted the advanced ideas of the Pennsylvania framers. Pennsylvania came closer than any state during the American Revolution to truly embracing the egalitarian ideals of the Declaration of Independence, for here all taxpaying male citizens were eligible to vote and hold office. If the citizenry desired change, little could prevent it, as the people were proportionately represented in a unicameral assembly. To a degree unmatched at the time, Pennsylvania's constitution cast aside much of its colonial political heritage in a splendid attempt, in the words of a radical Philadelphia polemicist, to make "the interest of the legislator and the common interest perfectly coincide."[55]

Alarmed conservatives feared that Pennsylvania offered a preview of the political future in revolutionary America. One congressman charged that Pennsylvania had substituted mob rule for orderly government, unleashing an "execrable democracy." Adams denounced its "wretched Ideas of Government." In the licentious environment likely to arise, he predicted, the citizenry would come to feel that they were neither safe nor free. "It is an unhappy Truth," a conservative in Congress insisted, that "People in general do not know their own happiness." Less than 100 days after independence, another congressman lamented, "We have over-rated the public virtue of our country."[56]

Conservatives had championed the American Revolution and, as Gordon Wood has observed, never lost confidence in it, although within a year of independence several changes—in addition to those in Pennsylvania—had given them pause. The Loyalists often were replaced in office by popular leaders who were less educated, less sophisticated, and—at least in the eyes of some—ungentlemanly. In addition, by 1777 a couple of states, desperate for revenue, had imposed property taxes that fell most heavily on the wealthy. Several other states had moved toward taxation schemes that were consistent with one's ability to pay. Some states even had taken steps to reduce the privileges of the great property owners and to make land more readily available to the landless. Three states had introduced the secret ballot.[57]

Conservatives were wary during the first year of independence, but not panicky. Theirs was an "Age of political Experiments" in which many things would be tried, then discarded as failures, John Adams counseled.[58]

In the dark days of December 1776, Washington and his army had appeared to be beaten, and some doubted that independence would be achieved. A year later, most thought America was on the cusp of winning the war and gaining independence. An amazing military turnabout occurred in 1777, due in part to France's secret aid, but also because of Great Britain's muddled prosecution of the war.

General Howe drew up a plan of operation for 1777, discarded it in favor of another scheme, and eventually abandoned that one as well. His

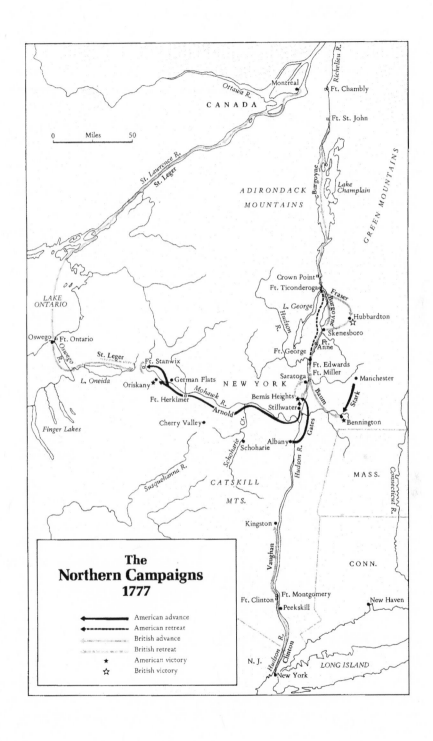

Ottawa R.
Montreal
Ft. Chambly
CANADA
Richelieu R.
Ft. St. John

0   Miles   50

St. Lawrence R.
St. Leger

Burgoyne
Lake Champlain

ADIRONDACK
MOUNTAINS

GREEN MOUNTAINS

LAKE
ONTARIO

Crown Point
Ft. Ticonderoga
Fraser
Burgoyne
Hubbardton

L. George
Hudson R.
Skenesboro
Ft. Anne

Oswego   Ft. Ontario
St. Leger
Ft. Stanwix
Oswego R.
L. Oneida

Ft. George
Ft. Edwards
Ft. Miller
Manchester

German Flats
Oriskany
Ft. Herkimer
Mohawk R.
Arnold
Cr.
NEW YORK
Saratoga
Bemis Heights
Stillwater
Baum
Stark
Bennington

Finger Lakes

Cherry Valley
Albany
Gates
Hudson R.

Schoharie R.
Schoharie

Susquehanna R.

CATSKILL
MTS.

MASS.
Connecticut R.

Kingston

CONN.

Vaughan
Hudson R.
Ft. Clinton
Ft. Montgomery
Peekskill
New Haven

N.J.
Clinton
LONG ISLAND
New York

The
Northern Campaigns
1777

→ American advance
•---• American retreat
British advance
British retreat
★ American victory
☆ British victory

final plan was to invade Pennsylvania. His primary objective was Philadelphia, to which he attributed great importance, as Congress had met
there for three years. However, he also hoped to compel Washington to
abandon his Fabian tactics, making him stand and fight in defense of
the capital. Meanwhile, General John Burgoyne, in London, had contrived a plan of his own, which had won the assent of the king and the
colonial secretary. Burgoyne was to invade New York from Canada. By
the time Howe learned of this, he was ready to move south, and thought
it too late to coordinate his campaign with that of Burgoyne. Such folly
arose from the administrative chaos that had been permitted in the imperial government. Lord North's cabinet included army, navy, and colonial ministers, but not a war minister. Incredibly, too, none of the
ministers perceived the awful danger that Burgoyne would confront
against a potentially huge army of Continentals and New England militiamen in the rugged northern wilderness.

London was confident that it could suppress the American rebellion
during 1777. It was aware of France's "secret" aid to the rebels, and it knew
that the American armies in 1777 would be far better supplied than those
which the redcoats had fought against the previous year. North's government had also learned of Congress's initiatives in lengthening enlistments
and hardening discipline in the Continental army. Nevertheless, the British government betrayed little consternation. It continued to believe—
indeed, the campaigns in Canada and New York in 1776 had confirmed
London's prewar convictions—that citizen armies, no matter how well
equipped, were no match for British and Hessian regulars.[59]

Like their adversaries, congressmen radiated enthusiasm as the campaign of 1777 drew near. Some believed that Washington and the general
officers had taken "extraordinary pains" to make their new troops "invincible." Some expected that the new-modeled American army would
give Howe "a very Severe Drubbing." Samuel Adams was confident that
Howe "will be cut off and [his] Design frustrated." Maryland's Chase
predicted that the British would be "totally ruined" by the combined
might of the continentals and militiamen, if the militia turned out. When
the continentals marched through Philadelphia in August on the eve of
the battle for the capital, the congressmen, together with thousands of
residents, lined the streets to see the spectacle. John Adams found the
soldiery to be "extreamly well armed, pretty well cloathed, and tolerably
disciplined," but he was a realist as well. After a close inspection, he concluded that "Our soldiers have not yet, quite the Air of Soldiers," and as
soon as the military parade concluded, he hurried to a church to pray.
He no longer expected a triumph on Pennsylvania's battlefields, yet he
drew solace from the knowledge that Britain's military successes in 1776

had "not done them much Good, nor the United States, as a Community, much harm." That, Adams thought, was about as much as could be hoped for in 1777.[60]

What ensued that autumn resulted in incredible harm for Great Britain. It began alarmingly for the revolutionaries. Howe came dangerously close to inflicting a decisive defeat on Washington, who displayed a brooding vacillation and indecision in the Battle of Brandywine, an engagement fought just west of Philadelphia in mid-September. Washington escaped intact, but the British soon marched unopposed on the city. In the catacomb silence in the wee hours of September 19, the congressmen were awakened by a messenger sent by Alexander Hamilton, an aide to Washington, and told to flee immediately for their safety. The redcoats had secured a ford across the Schuylkill River, a few miles west of the Pennsylvania State House, and advance units of the British army might shortly be in downtown Philadelphia. In boarding houses throughout the city, sleepy congressmen dressed quickly by candlelight and gathered a few cherished possessions. Then they scurried. Most rode on horseback, searching in the country blackness for the lonely roads that afforded an escape from imperiled eastern Pennsylvania, praying all the while that they would not encounter a party of British cavalry. Probably most, like John Adams, were ineffably shaken. "Ruin . . . seems to await" the American Revolution, he reflected as he rode in the inhospitable darkness. "We have as good a Cause, as was fought for. We have great Resources. The People are well tempered." But disaster followed disaster. Adams and all his colleagues reached safety and eventually were reunited in York, on Pennsylvania's western frontier, where Congress sat for nearly eight months.[61]

Once the congressmen unpacked in their safe new home, the emotional erosion of August and September largely vanished. They soon saw that Howe, the apparent victor, had accomplished little. He had taken Philadelphia, but as one congressman remarked, the city had actually captured him. His army was "cooped up" in the city, another jeered, for Howe was compelled to use all his resources to defend the prize he had won. His predicament was made clear a week later when Washington, in the still, deep frost of sunrise, struck suddenly at the British defenders posted at Germantown, a dusty, suburban village on the road that lead from Philadelphia to Reading. His daring attack failed to produce a victory akin to that at Trenton a year earlier. In fact, American losses were twice those of the British. Nevertheless, Washington's bold stroke captured the imagination of the French government, and the American public, which heard only Washington's and Congress's disingenuous accounts of the fray, looked upon the engagement as a moral, and even an actual, victory.[62]

Even better news from the military front swept across America three weeks later. Early in the summer Burgoyne had started south from Canada with 9,000 men, while a diversionary force of nearly 1,000 redcoats, Loyalists, and Iroquois advanced from the west. The two forces were to rendezvous at Albany, after which the combined armies and the Royal Navy would seize the Hudson River down to Manhattan, isolating New England. Burgoyne's campaign started so successfully that Congress for the first time in this war removed a high-ranking general, replacing him with one it believed to be more capable.

Congress was not unaccustomed to the politics of military command. When it appointed the first general officers in 1775, the process had immediately become politicized. Early in 1777, as a result of the death, or resignation, of three of the initial appointees, and because of the proposed expansion of the Continental army, Congress was compelled to appoint—promote, in fact—several new general officers. It wrangled for weeks over the rules of promotion, causing more than one congressman to speak of the distasteful process as "perplexed" and "irksome." Congress finally decided that promotion was to be determined on the basis of seniority and merit, as well as by the number of troops furnished by each candidate's state. The latter criterion rapidly became the most crucial. This "may possibly give Disgust," one congressman remarked. That was a considerable understatement. Resentment and rancor followed as deserving aspirants were ignored and some states were spurned entirely. Even the men whom General Washington had recommended were rebuffed. So acrimonious was the process that Congress shrank from removing two or three of the original general officers who, by early 1777, were universally viewed as inept. It also emphatically rejected an effort by some New England congressmen, led in all probability by Samuel Adams, to remove General Philip Schuyler, who from the beginning had been the commander of the Northern Department.[63]

The New England congressmen thought Schuyler, whom they labeled as dilatory, and even as America's counterpart to Howe, was to blame for the failed invasion of Canada in 1775 and the army's disastrous retreat back into New York in 1776. There was considerable merit to the allegations, at least with regard to Schuyler's culpability for the 1775 debacle at Quebec, as his reproachful indecision had resulted in delays that helped wreck the campaign. In many ways, Schuyler was similar to Washington. The scion of an illustrious family, he too had soldiered as a young man in the French and Indian War, acquired thousands of acres of frontier lands as a high-rolling speculator, and become prominent politically within his province. However, despite his cold and formal manner, Washington never exhibited the aristocratic hauteur that characterized Schuyler's demeanor and earned him countless enemies. Furthermore, Washington learned from his early mistakes as commander of the Virginia Regiment, and during the War of Independence he avoided habits that had earned him severe criticism twenty years earlier. In this war he remained with his army through thick and thin, and always at least sought to give the appearance of suffering along with his men. Schuyler, on the other hand, absented himself from his army for long stretches while he remained at his splendid estate near Albany.

From the outset in 1777 New England's congressmen were convinced that their militiamen would not serve under an imperious, landjobbing New York aristocrat, especially one whose military record included repeated failures. Recruiting did proceed slowly that summer, so languidly in fact that one congressman remarked that the trainbandsmen "Take the Field Tardily as if they were going to be Hanged." New Englanders increasingly put their faith in General Horatio Gates, who readily displayed a garrulous charm. Gates had been a successful officer in the British army before he resigned his commission and moved to Virginia on the eve of the final Anglo-American crisis. His experience and professionalism were only one reason for New England's enthusiasm. Gates had embraced radical reform politics while still in England. Years before Congress declared independence, he had broken with Great Britain because of its anti-republican and anti-egalitarian nature. His views tallied with those of Samuel Adams, who favored a republican war effort in which citizen generals commanded a people's militia. Gates, a Hessian officer reported, was the "darling" of the most radical Americans, whereas Schuyler, whose lineage went back to the Dutch aristocracy, was popular with the more conservative congressmen who favored social distinction, hierarchy, and a strong national government under conservative leadership.[64]

Schuyler's position was secure until things went awry in the summer of 1777. Once Burgoyne began his steady ascent up the Champlain Valley toward Albany, support for Schuyler eroded. It collapsed entirely in July when Fort Ticonderoga was surrendered without a fight. With Schuyler finished, delegates from the middle states sought to have Washington select his successor, confident that he would name Nathanael Greene, a New Englander thought to be a conservative nationalist. Washington declined, not only from a wish to remain aloof from congressional politics but because he knew that Greene had recently forfeited considerable support in New England by threatening to resign in a dispute over rank. In the end Congress made the decision. In August it put Gates in charge, although many of Schuyler's supporters loudly opposed the move and attributed the change to "unworthy suspicion and unprovoked malice" among the New Englanders.[65]

Soon thereafter Burgoyne reported to London that thousands of militia were assembling alongside Gates's continentals. In part, Schuyler's dismissal had opened the floodgates, but in addition Gates galvanized opinion in the background by issuing statements that ingeniously played on depredations wrought against the frontier settlers by Britain's Indian allies. Soon, over 5,000 militiamen were at the front, 80 percent more than Schuyler had commanded throughout July. In no time the British army was outnumbered and trapped, unable in two hard fought battles—at Freeman's Farm and Bemis Heights—to muscle its way through to Albany and without hope of retreating to faraway Canada. On October 17 Burgoyne surrendered what remained of his surrounded army—nearly 6,000 men—at Saratoga.[66]

Congress rejoiced. Many congressmen lauded Gates's "glorious Success." They lavished praise on his ability to induce the citizenry to "Step forth in the Sinking cause" and to "give New life and Vigor" to the war effort. A New Yorker who had been loath to remove Schuyler acknowledged that the triumph at Saratoga had "rescued this devoted Government, already almost ruined, from total Destruction." Many spoke of the "high spirits" in Congress that resulted from the "glorious close to this campaign." All prayed that Saratoga would induce France to enter the war. James Lovell, a Massachusetts congressman, thought France no longer had a choice. Saratoga, he conjectured, would compel Britain to seek peace based on generous terms of reconciliation, and France would be drawn into the conflict to prevent America from reuniting with its former parent.[67]

North's government did offer peace terms. Together with others, Alexander Wedderburn, the solicitor-general who had abused Franklin in the Cockpit in January 1774, drafted conciliatory legislation that Parliament enacted in the spring of 1778. Britain was willing to repeal the Declaratory Act, Tea Act, and Coercive Acts, and to acknowledge that it lacked the authority to tax the colonies, but America's commerce would be subject to imperial control. What Dickinson had predicted three years earlier had occurred. After a brief, savage war, Great Britain was willing to give its colonies everything the First Congress had demanded in 1774. Parliament authorized the North government to send commissioners to America who were to seek an armistice and negotiate the terms of the Anglo-American relationship. Typically, however, the British moved at a snail's pace. Parliament did not act until nearly 100 days after news of Saratoga reached London, and the commissioners did not reach America until another seventy-five days had elapsed.

The French government, on the other hand, acted with dispatch after learning of Saratoga. For the past eighteen months, the foreign minister, Comte de Vergennes, had done what he could short of entering the war to sustain the American rebellion. Volunteers had been permitted to cross to America to fight and smuggle shipments of arms and equipment dispatched to the Continental army. Indeed, the lion's share of the arms and munitions in the hands of Gates's men at Saratoga had been provided by France. In addition, some French ports had been opened to American privateers, and $3,000,000 had been loaned to the struggling new nation.[68] Nevertheless, Vergennes had been cautious, not wishing to back a losing cause. After the Continentals' debacles in New York and New Jersey in 1776, France's foreign minister wanted to see what the ensuing campaign would bring. Furthermore, down to the fall of 1777 he was unwilling for France to go to war with Great Britain without a European ally. In 1776, and again in 1777, he conducted talks with Spain about backing the Americans. When those discussions went nowhere, Vergennes watched and waited, all the while preparing France for war.

The news of Saratoga reached Paris and London almost simultaneously in December 1777. Vergennes, according to British intelligence reports to North, moved quickly. Washington's assault at Germantown, and Gates's victory at Saratoga, convinced him that Britain could not suppress the American rebellion. He was certain, as well, that American independence would seriously weaken Britain. The balance of power in Europe would be altered in France's favor, and grand commercial benefits would accrue to the French. The British government soon knew that Vergennes immediately opened talks with the "rebel agents" in France, a fact that was reported in a London newspaper shortly after New Year's Day. Four weeks later, on February 6, 1778, the Franco-American treaties were signed at the palace of Versailles. The American diplomats, Franklin, Deane, and Arthur Lee, had been instructed by Congress in 1776 to seek only a trade agreement, but they took what they could get. They agreed to both a commercial accord and to a military alliance that France wished. The pact stipulated that the alliance would prevail at least until Great Britain acknowledged the sovereign and independent status of the United States. Each party promised never to make a separate peace with the British. Its terms could also be interpreted to mean that the United States was obligated to provide unspecified assistance to France in the event that its Caribbean possessions were jeopardized.[69]

Congress learned on April 20 that Parliament was considering conciliatory measures. Ten days later it received the French treaties. At the outset of 1776 the reconciliationists in Congress might have mustered the votes to accept North's tender, but the votes were no longer there in the spring of 1778. Congress, and the American public, were thoroughly committed to independence, which now appeared certain with France's intervention and even more plentiful assistance on the way. Reconciliation or independence was not a debatable issue. Congress has seldom acted with such speed. It ratified the French treaties within forty-eight hours of their arrival, weeks before London's peace commissioners at last disembarked in Philadelphia. No one expressed the sentiment of the revolutionaries better than General Washington: "I believe no event was ever received with more heartfelt joy."[70]

Many in Congress, such as Richard Henry Lee, thought the French alliance meant that victory was imminent. They were certain that London "will not war with the house of Bourbon and N. America at the same time." Others believed the alliance guaranteed victory, but that "There is blood[,] much blood[,] in our Prospect," as one put it. Some even glimpsed a danger in the treaties. Like Henry Laurens, they feared that "we shall lull our selves into a fatal security in the mistaken weakness of Britain & Strength of our Ally."[71]

While the American envoys secured the treaties, Washington's army suffered through the winter in execrable conditions at Valley Forge, twenty-one miles west of Philadelphia. Illness and death stalked this cantonment. Ragged soldiers shivered in hastily constructed log huts and too often languished without adequate supplies of food and clothing. The army contained 11,000 men when it entered Valley Forge at Christmas 1777. By February 7,000 soldiers were too ill for duty. Altogether, 2,500 died that winter. Another 1,000 men deserted, some "Covered with Rags and Crawling with vermin." Many were assisted in their getaway by local Tories. Droves of officers simply quit during that desperate winter. Fifty resigned on one day in December. By mid-March more than 300 officers had gone home. Although most remained with the army, they simmered with anger at their wretchedness in a land of plenty. They were further embittered by the arrival that winter of French officers who possessed commissions—issued by Silas Deane—which stipulated that they outranked veteran continental officers. Some who had stayed on through the desperate days of January and February now threatened to quit. They exacted a high price for staying. As the first daffodils emerged in late winter, those officers still at Valley Forge collectively told visiting congressmen that they wanted a guarantee that following the war they would be given a lifetime pension equivalent to half their yearly salary, a long-standing tradition in the British army. Implicit in their request was a threat of resignation should Congress fail to act.[72]

Their pension proposal "meets with great opposition," a New York congressman laconically noted that winter. In fact, it aroused a firestorm. Congress was a hot mass of feelings at what many thought was the treachery of the officers. Its president bristled that it was "dangerous," "unjust," and a "*foul play.*" He privately excoriated the officers for threatening civilian leadership. Some skeptics even thought that the adoption of such a prize would cause the officers to embrace "any terms for encompassing Peace" so that they could immediately begin drawing their pension. Others thought it unfair and unrepublican to provide the officers with what was never contemplated for the men in the army.[73]

However, the officers had Congress by the throat, and the legislators ultimately approved a measure that promised a half-pay pension for life following the end of the war and demobilization. Although most congressmen found the legislation to be "exceedingly disagreeable," it was enacted by a majority of only one state. It passed because Congress feared that the army would collapse, or that the original officer corps, drawn largely from the elite sectors of American society, would be replaced by men from the lower social orders. Furthermore, Washington lobbied hard for his officers, telling Congress that he would personally never accept such a pension, "yet he did most religiously believe the Salvation of the Army depended upon it." Congress voted the men an $80 bonus as a mollifying gesture.[74]

The survival of the army was not Washington's only concern that winter. Fifteen months before, in the aftermath of the ongoing disasters of the summer and fall of 1776, he had become aware that some questioned his ability. Trenton and Princeton temporarily silenced the whispers, but Gates's sensational victory, which occurred at nearly the same moment that Howe occupied Philadelphia, was the signal for the doubters to emerge once again. In early November, Washington learned from a friendly source that General Thomas Conway, a French volunteer, had supposedly written Gates that "Heaven has been determined to save your Country; or a weak General and bad Councillors would have ruined it." Soon thereafter Patrick Henry informed Washington that Dr. Benjamin Rush, a prominent Philadelphia physician who served as the medical director of the army's Middle Department, was advocating Washington's dismissal and Gates's appointment as commander-in-chief. Washington, bitter, frustrated, and insecure, magnified these scattered instances of taletelling into a full-blown conspiracy. He was certain that many congressmen and high-ranking army officers wished to see him dismissed.[75]

It was true that some in Congress were unhappy with Washington's performance. The president of Congress confided that "there may be some ground" for the criticism. "We want a General," a bitter New Jersey congressman fumed, and added that he was weary of appropriating funds for an army that was habitually misused. A Massachusetts congressman advocated the annual appointment of all officers, a step that would immediately result in the replacement of several of the original officers, including perhaps the commander-in-chief. But others anguished that Washington, through his brilliant and daring successes at Trenton and Princeton, and as a result of congressional public relations efforts on his behalf, had grown to be a "Demi G[od]." That presaged doom for the republic, they despaired. Adams concurred that a danger would exist should the public ever come to believe that Washington alone was responsible for America's military success—he even privately rejoiced that it had been Gates, not Washington, who had scored the great victory at Saratoga—but he never supported those who wished to remove the commander. It was Adams's view that Washington should be thought "wise, virtuous, and good," but it was folly to see him as "a Deity or a saviour."[76]

Adams's outlook was probably typical, even among those who were most vocal in their criticism. To be sure, there were those who wished to remove Washington. Some had tired of a commander whose army seldom fought and who rarely won when it did fight. Some charged that Washington surrounded himself with incompetent advisors. Some were convinced that he was indecisive under fire. Some thought him a poor administrator, and fretted over the army's wastrel habits. But not all who criticized Washington sought his removal, and those who did wish to see him relieved of his duties were scant in numbers. Elbridge Gerry of Massachusetts, who had an excellent sense of the national legislature, thought Washington's standing remained "high in Congress." He believed the heart of the movement against Washington was in the army and was confined to a few jealous and ambitious officers. Furthermore, most congressmen realized that in 1777 Washington had fought the cream of the British army, while Gates had been blessed with favorable terrain and numerical superiority. Most in Congress knew that Washington's performance and virtuous habits had made him popular, and they strove throughout the war to enhance his popularity. They understood, as one congressman remarked, that Washington had become the great "prop" of the Revolution. To remove him would be "very injurious & disgusting" to the army and the cause.[77]

When the grim Valley Forge winter ended, all America was ebullient. Washington proclaimed a day of exultation for his army. It paraded and cheered amid the fresh spring greenery and flowering trees of the once forlorn camp, and its commander was confident that it was stronger than it had been upon entering Valley Forge. Congress shared that enthusiasm. The army "is amazingly advanced" in discipline and strength, the president of Congress rejoiced. The mood of the country was also upbeat. Trade with France was expected to become "very great & very lucrative," and by the second anniversary of independence many ships laden with American merchandise, especially Chesapeake tobacco and Carolina rice, were sailing for French ports. Not only did America appear to be insuperable, but some thought that the Continentals, with French help, would recapture New York during 1778. Many were confident that the end of war was within sight. America's prospects in May 1778 appeared as bright as the spring sun that radiated on the "United States of North America," as Congress officially titled the new nation.[78]

7

1778–1782

"This Wilderness of Darkness & Dangers"

Throughout 1778, many Americans thought peace was at hand. Congressman James Lovell predicted during the autumn that Britain, now at war with America's new ally, France, would redeploy its troops to Canada and the Caribbean. The Hessians would remain, he forecast, but only to guard New York. Samuel Adams concurred. He expected that Spain would enter the war as France's ally and that Britain would "be obligd to withdraw her Attention in a great Measure from America."[1]

During 1778, moreover, the remarkable unity persisted that had characterized congressional affairs since the Declaration of Independence twenty-four months earlier. Sharp divisions had occurred from time to time, brought on, in John Adams's estimation, by the "Diversity of Religions, Educations, Manners, Interests," as well as by clashes between gigantic egos. Nevertheless, during the unrelenting military crisis in 1776–77, most congressmen shrank from discord. Adams in fact was amazed by the extraordinary measure of "internal Concord" that persisted. He attributed it to his colleagues' "considerate Forbearance with one another and prudent Condescention on both sides." A measure of good fortune helped as well. Congress experienced extraordinary turnover and absentee rates in these years, which as historian Jack Rakove has demonstrated, reduced the festering rancor that ordinarily occurs when the same strong personalities clash day after day. The turnover rate exceeded 16 percent in 1776 and climbed above 40 percent in 1777 and 1778.[2]

However, plentiful French assistance, including the arrival of a Gallic fleet in July 1778, encouraged the belief that victory was imminent.

That heady optimism ushered in a new era in American politics that began in 1779, one that was characterized by sharp divisions. For fifteen years politics had revolved about resistance to British policies, and whether to declare independence, but the prospect of victory triggered struggles between the competing sections over the shape of postwar America. Politics in the United States would never again be the same.

The changing nature of politics could be seen during the very week that rumors reached Congress that a Franco-American alliance had been concluded in Paris. Mid-Atlantic delegates, who represented maritime states, not only immediately inaugurated a campaign to reopen American ports to British shipping the moment peace dawned, but to negotiate a commercial pact with Britain. Others were active as well. About this same time Virginia dispatched an army westward to defend the Ohio Country and beyond, which it claimed under its colonial charter. Many New England delegates fell in behind General Gates's proposal for an immediate campaign to seize Montreal and Quebec, arguing that their region's security could be assured only if Canada was wrested from foreign hands, and they spoke out on the importance of the northern fisheries. The fishing industry, said one New Englander, was no less "Valueable . . . to Old Massachusetts than the Tobacco Fields . . . or the Rice Swamps [to] the South."[3]

But it was France that first pried open the lid on the Pandora's box that had largely contained the competing sectional interests. Soon after the Franco-American treaties were signed, Vergennes's persistence with Madrid was rewarded. Early in 1779, Spain agreed to propose that an international conference be called at which it would mediate the four-year-old war. If Britain refused its offer, Spain would ally with France and enter hostilities. France paid a steep price for what seemed likely to be Madrid's certain entry into war. It secretly promised not only to remain at war until Spain gained Gibraltar and East and West Florida, but to protect its ally's interest in North America against the avaricious inclinations of the United States.

As a peace conference now was possible during 1779, Vergennes enjoined the French minister to the United States, Conrad Alexander Gérard, to ask Congress to determine its peace terms and appoint a minister plenipotentiary to participate in the negotiations. Gérard made his request to select members of Congress on February 15, 1779, a date that might serve as the birthday of modern American politics.[4]

At first blush it seems astonishing that Congress could have waged war for thirty months since declaring independence without having determined what it hoped to gain from hostilities. But there were good reasons to avoid the issue. As peace talks were out of the question, why risk opening wounds that not only might damage the war effort, but endanger the quest for a European ally? However, Gérard's petition made it impossible to delay the matter further. The United States had to be prepared for the eventuality of mediation. Moreover, Article 8 of the military pact with France stipulated that neither country would conclude a separate peace with Great Britain. Hence, the states had to agree on acceptable peace terms, and Congress had to arrive at an understanding with France.[5]

Congress quickly established two committees. A five-member panel was to make recommendations concerning America's peace demands. A second committee, composed of a congressman from each state, was to deal with the selection of America's envoys, including the peace negotiator, the minister to France, and a diplomat who would be sent to Madrid to beseech assistance. The peace terms committee reported first. Several of its proposals were widely, even unanimously, embraced by Congress. No one disagreed with its recommendation that British recognition of United States independence must be a precondition to any negotiations, and that, with peace, the British troops must be evacuated from American soil. Nor was there appreciable resistance to its proposals that called for cession of Nova Scotia to the United States, or independence for that domain, a western border on the Mississippi River, a northern boundary that extended westward along a line running from just below Montreal to the head of the Mississippi River—believed to be considerably north of present Minnesota—and a southern boundary at the thirty-first parallel, essentially today's Georgia-Florida border, but extending westward to the Mississippi River.

Two further recommendations also ran into trouble. One was a proposal that America have both the right to a "full and free Navigation of the Mississippi River" to the thirty-first parallel and access to a port on that river in Spanish Louisiana. The other recommended that Congress demand American fishing rights in and around Newfoundland.[6] Had Congress formulated its peace demands prior to the French alliance, and Spain's likely belligerence, it is probable that all the stipulations proposed by the committee would have been adopted. However, France's role in the congressional deliberations changed things. Vergennes wished to moderate America's demands. He was anxious to assure that what the United States sought would not one day inhibit the peace negotiations. He also wished to protect French fishing interests from American encroachment. Finally, he was committed to protecting Spain's interests in the Mississippi Valley, interests strongly at odds with those of the United States.[7]

Many Americans had a stake in the Mississippi River. Western land speculators understood that farmers would not move west if denied use of that artery to ship their produce to urban centers on the East Coast, or to European and Caribbean markets. Nationalists realized that the growing power of the postwar United States was linked to the growth of the Union. People everywhere were aware that western land sales might constitute the lion's share of the national government's postwar revenue, keeping taxation at a minimum. But none had so great an interest as Virginia, which possessed capacious western claims stemming from its seventeenth-century charter.

Unlike Spain, France had no stake in the Mississippi. Having lost the French and Indian War, France in 1763 ceded to London all territory that it had claimed east of the Mississippi River. Spain had relinquished its claims only to Florida. France had no interest in reclaiming the prizes it had lost, and pledged as much in its treaty of alliance with the United States. What it sought were Britain's valuable sugar islands in the Caribbean. Spain, on the other hand, wanted security for the vast domain it claimed west of the Mississippi River. It also wished to reacquire Florida. The northern boundary of Florida—and hence the southern boundary of the United States—was undetermined, but everyone conceded that Florida's western boundary had traditionally extended to the Mississippi River. Although Congress could only guess at the game Gérard was to play, the French minister set out to protect what Spain wanted.

Gérard expected to find Congress neatly and simply divided along North-South lines. That division did exist. New England's fishing industry was not vital to the South and the western ambitions of many Southerners aroused no sympathy in New England. Neither region wished to risk losing the war by prolonging hostilities to secure the interests of the other. But Gérard soon found the situation to be far more complex than he had imagined.

Congressmen from the middle states were often influenced by what one scholar has called the "mercantile combine," the integrated interests of merchant princes from New York and Philadelphia.[8] Their objectives were sometimes similar to those of New Englanders, sometimes tallied with those of Southerners, and sometimes were inimical to both. Gérard also found that the South was far from monolithic. Not only did some Southern states have no western claims, but in 1779 the war was just coming to the South, and the resulting terror and destruction were changing the views of many residents.

When France entered the war, Great Britain sent a considerable portion of its army in North America to the Caribbean, much as Samuel Adams and Lovell had predicted. However, what those two congressmen had not foreseen was that London would keep about half its army on the mainland for use in a new "Southern Strategy." Having failed to suppress the rebellion before France entered the conflict, London was aware that it was unrealistic to believe that it could any longer hope to secure its original war aims. But it had not lost the war. If it turned this conflict into a stalemate, peace might eventually be negotiated on the principle of *uti possidetis*, each belligerent retaining what it possessed at the moment of the armistice. Deadlocked wars in Europe often were terminated in such a manner. Thus, if Great Britain successfully defended its possessions in Canada, the trans-Appalachian West, and the Caribbean, while it pacified several rich Southern colonies, the postwar British empire in America would be formidable and lucrative indeed. British North America might yet sweep from the jewels of the West Indies to the plains of Canada, encompassing in a great arc the windswept frontier prairies beyond the Appalachian mountains and the fertile rice and tobacco lands in the humid South. And this mighty empire would surround the diminutive United States, a union of perhaps no more than nine or ten states.

The Southern Strategy commenced late in December 1778 when a British armada seized Savannah. It did not require the talents of a visionary to see that once tiny Georgia was subdued, South Carolina would be invaded. Then would come the turn of the Upper South. Suddenly, some in Virginia and the Carolinas were extremely anxious to secure an immediate victory. They were willing to make concessions that would keep France happy and lure Spain into the conflict, as Allied naval superiority hinged on Madrid's belligerence.[9]

Gérard looked upon the multiplicity of interests in Congress as manna from heaven. It opened the door for him to play one group against another to secure his ends, and soon enough he achieved every objective that he had been sent to secure. First, in the spring of 1779, Congress rejected the inclusion of the rights of navigation and deposit on the Mississippi River in its peace ultimata. A congressman from the middle states, who noted that he had voted against fighting on until those ends were won, said simply that he thought it imprudent to "continue the War for that."[10]

The fisheries proved to be tougher for Gérard, and in some respects more crucial, as France wanted them for itself. But they were also critical to New England, where thousands not only toiled as mariners or labored in peripheral industries, such as the ship construction business, but great fortunes were at stake. The four New England states fought tenaciously for months. They even drew some support from the mercantile states, which hoped for a role in the carrying trade that would stem from American access to the fisheries. However, it was New England's anticipation of steadfast support from Virginia, its ally in Congress since its inception in 1774, that kept alive the region's hope for success. Those expectations collapsed in the wake of a devastating British raid along the Virginia coast in the late spring of 1779. When a flotilla of twenty-eight Royal vessels destroyed towns, plantations, ships, shipyards, and thousands of hogsheads of tobacco, and also liberated numerous slaves, the zeal with which the Virginia delegation had stood by Massachusetts rapidly corroded.[11] Thereafter, virtually every Virginian concluded that the "exhausted and distressed" province was "not able to carry on the War for objects which are not absolutely necessary." Many doubtless agreed with Jefferson, who in June, upon becoming the governor of Virginia, advocated abandoning pursuit of the fisheries. Defeat the British now, he suggested either with considerable naiveté or disingenuousness, then fight another war against them sometime in the future to secure New England's fishing rights.[12]

Virginia was not Gérard's only ally. He hired numerous polemicists throughout America to write newspaper essays criticizing New England's pursuit of the fisheries. In what became the new nation's first public foreign policy debate, these scribes portrayed New England as myopic and selfish, and insisted that it was in America's interest to place no roadblocks in the way of securing peace and independence. New Englanders shot back that postwar prosperity, and American naval strength, hinged on the fishing industry. They painted their congressional foes as dupes of Versailles. Within Congress the debate produced deep strains. Many "unjust & impolitick" things were said, much "invective and abuse" was hurled, much "delusive stuff" was uttered, various congressmen confided. In the end, a New York congressman remarked, the question came down to whether it was "just or prudent to continue the present war, in order to compel Great Britain to acknowledge that we have as good a right to the fisheries as she does?" Ultimately, a majority of representatives from the middle and Southern states agreed that it was not. Like the representative from beleaguered Virginia, they were willing to abandon New England and "chearfully acquiesce" in Britain's monopoly of the fisheries if that step hastened London's recognition of American independence.[13] New England was beaten, and its alliance with the South, which had carried every substantive issue since the decision to embargo the mother country in 1774, was sundered.

Gérard was less successful with regard to the selection of America's envoys. The committee of thirteen learned that its diplomats in Paris— the original triumvirate of Arthur Lee, Franklin, and Deane, as well as John Adams, who resigned from Congress late in 1777 and accepted an appointment as Deane's successor on the American commission to secure French assistance—had all along been profoundly divided by "suspicions and animosities," even to the detriment of "the honor and interests of these United States." The committee recommended that the lot of them be recalled. Franklin, who had been appointed minister to France only five months earlier, easily survived this threat. Gérard campaigned for his continued presence in Paris, arguing that Franklin was exceedingly popular both with the French people and government, but neglecting to mention that Vergennes found him to be pliable, and therefore quite useful. Franklin was aided too by the letters to Congress sent by Adams, who throughout 1778 had unfailingly portrayed his colleague as honest and the best man to represent America at Versailles.[14]

The post of peace commissioner, an official whom the committee of thirteen hoped would also be vested with authority to seek to negotiate a postwar commercial accord with Great Britain, had to be filled as well. The middle states backed John Jay for the position. New England pushed for John Adams. The former sought a representative of the mercantile combine who would look after its commercial interests. New England understood that the right minister plenipotentiary might someday win for it an advantageous boundary with Canada and the fishing rights that Congress had neglected to pursue. Gérard waded into the controversy, backing Jay. The French government wanted a malleable peace commissioner. Although Jay was an unknown quantity, Vergennes was all too aware that Adams was unconquerably independent. He and Adams already had crossed swords on one issue. Late in 1778, Adams—with the backing of Lee—presented Vergennes with a statement that implicitly criticized France for not having made a greater naval commitment in North America. Furthermore, by 1779 Vergennes had come to suspect that Adams mistrusted his ally. The French Foreign Minister was correct. Adams's outlook had grown steadily more jaded throughout his first year in Paris until, by 1779, he cautioned Congress that the United States was caught up in a "dangerous Connection" that could result in its interests being subsumed by those of its mighty ally. Adams did not advocate severing ties to France, but he wanted Congress to be aware that France was pursuing its own ends, which included the wish to reduce its weak partner to the status of a client state.[15]

The battle over Adams's appointment occurred simultaneously with the struggle to name a minister plenipotentiary to Madrid, an envoy who would seek closer relations with Spain, including commercial ties and a much needed loan. Virginia fought to send Arthur Lee to Madrid, but from the outset he had two strikes against him. In 1777 he had presented Congress with charges concerning financial irregularities and misdeeds by Silas Deane, his fellow commissioner in Paris. Although Congress recalled Deane, numerous congressmen—principally Deane's Connecticut allies and the representatives of middle state merchants, with whom he had established close ties—thereafter sought revenge against Lee. Furthermore, Gérard labored behind the scenes to block Lee's appointment. Aware that Lee had joined Adams in questioning France's conduct of the war, he made it crystal clear that the French ministry had a low opinion of the Virginian.[16]

Clearly, Adams and Jay could not both be the peace commissioner, but a solution was found. Delegates from New England and the middle states, who had opposed one another on almost every major issue from 1774–76, came together. Adams was named peace commissioner and Jay was sent to Madrid.

The South was the great loser in the congressional struggle that had continued for eight long months. Frustrated in its western demands, it now was shut out of Europe as well. The bruising battle was of enduring importance. Not only was the New England-Virginia alliance wrecked, but the worst fears of what might result from close ties with a European power—as Galloway and Dickinson long ago had warned—had become a reality. Some in Congress now saw "Roguery" in the conduct of France, and described its ally as a "Vulture" that preyed on America's vital interests. Some discerned too great "Servility" on America's part. A heightened awareness crystallized that America must guard against "laying aside political Watchfulness." Increasingly, Congress understood that the United States' only safety would come from its own success on the battlefields of this war. The best hope of realizing its postwar objectives lay in "writing the Treaty of Peace with the Bayonett," as one congressman remarked.[17]

However, by the late summer of 1779, when the diplomats were selected and the peace ultimata approved, the optimistic mood ushered in by the victory at Saratoga was gone. Securing independence had become more problematical than at any time since the dark days in the autumn of 1776. The United States had entered its greatest crisis of the war.

No huge land battles had been fought since Brandywine and those near Saratoga nearly two years earlier. The Continental army had trailed the British army across New Jersey in the summer of 1778, when the British abandoned Philadelphia and retreated to New York, in preparation for its Southern Strategy. Late in June, Washington had struck the redcoats near Monmouth. But the battle, waged between only portions of the two forces, had been inconclusive, and thereafter the British continued their march to Manhattan unmolested. Monmouth was to be General Washington's last major engagement for more than three years.

Washington grew steadily more cautious after France entered the war, willing to act only in concert with his ally, and hesitant to risk what at the time had appeared to be Britain's inevitable recognition of American independence. With the first snows of late 1778, when Washington put his army into winter encampments, the war had shifted far from his northern headquarters. The French fleet, which had appeared off New Jersey in mid-summer, had long since sailed for the Caribbean. Much of the British army was in Georgia. When his Continentals emerged amid the lush green bounty of spring in 1779, Washington beheld a new problem. He believed his army was too poorly provisioned and manned to act alone.[18]

The size of the army had actually increased during the winter, although it was nowhere near the 75,000 men that Congress had voted in 1776 to raise. Washington had commanded 24,000 in May 1778. Twelve months later 28,000 men were enrolled in the army. He wanted more before he would act, but recruiting had grown especially difficult. Only 10 percent of the quota for the two eastern brigades in the Connecticut Line had been raised as that campaign season approached, and ultimately the state as a whole secured only one-third the manpower it set out to procure in 1779. Most states did better than that, but like Connecticut most also failed to meet their quotas. Sometimes states came up short because their men fled to other states that paid higher bounties for volunteers. For instance, Virginia and North Carolina lost heavily to South Carolina, and men from New Hampshire often were lured away by Massachusetts. Some states met their quota, only by furnishing men who were physically unfit or far too old for the rigors of army life.[19]

Far more often, however, shortfalls in the ranks of the soldiery occurred because men were reluctant to enter into the maw of despair that awaited those who served in the Continental army. Some of the desperation was due to the supply system. This was an army that consumed prodigious quantities of supplies. In two not untypical months in 1778 the Continentals went through 4,500,000 pounds of beef and flour, while their horses devoured 253,000 bushels of grain and 2,500,000 pounds of hay. Locating this amount of provisions month after month strained the capabilities of the Quartermaster Corps. What Washington called "Artificial scarcity"— shortages that arose because the farmers were reluctant to sell their produce for depreciated money—added to their woes. Once the supplies were found, they had to be delivered to the army, which given the shortage of wagons and teamsters, and dearth of good roads, was no easy task. In addition, the states sometimes shirked their responsibilities to the army, if they believed compliance would mean hardships for the citizenry at home.[20]

The condition of those who bore arms varied from time to time and place to place, but beyond a shadow of a doubt many soldiers in this long war experienced extreme deprivation. Food shortages were commonplace, especially in the winter months. At times, many men were shoeless and devoid of coats and blankets. Often, they were without socks and wore trousers that "put decency to blush," according to a visitor to one camp. A guest in a New England encampment discovered men who had never been issued tents sleeping under piles of leaves. It was little wonder that a bemused British officer remarked that "no nation ever saw such a set of tattermalions." Nor was it surprising that observers found men covered with lice and often suffering with the flux or fever.[21] War was a dangerous business, and in this war roughly one soldier in ten who served in the Continental army never came home. At least six of eight who died, and perhaps seven of eight, perished of disease rather than battlefield wounds. The prospect of a long, slow, inglorious death in a desolate and lonely cantonment presented recruiting sergeants with a nearly insurmountable obstacle.

A collapsing economy was the underlying cause of Washington's supply nightmare, and the tribulations that resulted from it. Runaway prices had begun to take their toll. By May 1779, a bushel of wheat sold for forty times what it had fetched two years earlier. The Quartermaster Corps that year spent in excess of $100,000,000 and derived less than it had for 10 percent that expenditure early in the war. Furthermore, quartermasters often lacked the funds to pay market value prices, which farmers demanded. Sometimes farmers sold their goods to the British, who paid in sound currency, and sometimes they stopped producing for the market altogether, feeling that their backbreaking work simply was not worth the return.[22]

By 1779 there could be little doubt that America's financial woes were the greatest impediment to an adequate military supply system and a vigorous prosecution of the war. General Washington was learning what soldiers and statesmen discovered since the days of Cicero, who had proclaimed that the "sinews of war [are] unlimited money."[23] The root of America's fiscal troubles was that too much paper money had been issued without adequate provision for its redemption. Inevitably, the currency declined and prices rose. But many attributed the affliction to another factor. " Tis a real Truth," a "Soldier" wrote in a Boston newspaper that winter, "that an insatiable thirst after gain . . . is the grand cause of that enormous height to which the price of things has risen."[24]

While General Washington did not entirely agree, he sympathized with that assessment. Summoned to Philadelphia to confer with Congress in the winter of 1778–79, he could hardly believe what he beheld.

Having watched helplessly for more than a year as his hungry, unpaid, ill-clad, and poorly housed soldiers suffered, and sometimes died of deprivation, he was aghast at the sumptuous lifestyles of the affluent in this city. The rich wore the finest clothing, rode in elegant carriages attended by servants in livery, and dined at tables laden with every conceivable delicacy. One Philadelphian reported attending a dinner at which 169 dishes were served. In this wartime society, many wealthy Philadelphians openly simulated French and British aristocrats, donning silk and embroidery, taking up dueling, wearing their hair after the fashion in elite circles in Paris and London, and eschewing the old familiar dances for the *minuet-de-la-cour*. They persisted in their consumption as if there was no war, purchasing and hoarding in a mad frenzy of conspicuous acquisitiveness. There was "little virtue and patriotism" to be found, the commander remarked sadly. Henry Laurens thought "luxury flourishes as it would among a people who had conquered the world." Joseph Reed, who had been an aide to the commander before he became the chief executive of Pennsylvania, found it unbelievable that only three years after the campaigns for Boston and New York he heard "public Frugality, Spirits, and Patriotism laugh'd at." To the Philadelphia elite, and those everywhere on the make in a mad scramble for the riches unleashed by the military conflict, the war was faraway and largely forgotten.[25]

A new tone crept into Washington's letters. He recognized that the sacrificial spirit of 1776 was gone, replaced by what he thought was a corrupting ethos of greed, a self-serving frenzy that undermined the war effort. But whereas Washington had earlier appeared to believe that the common people posed the weak link in the successful prosecution of the war, he now said that the unsurpassed rapacity among the most affluent constituted a greater threat to victory than all the legions that Great Britain could possibly transport to America's shores. The "Speculators, various tribes of money makers, and stock jobbers of all denominations," he railed, were attempting to turn the war to "their own private emolument, without considering that their avarice, and thirst for gain must plunge every thing (including themselves) into one common Ruin." To another correspondent he raged that the "speculators, forestallers and others . . . [were] preying upon the vitals of this great Country and putting every thing to the utmost hazard." A few weeks later he again lamented the "extinction of public spirit." To his brother, he stormed that "Speculators, with all their concomitants, have taken such deep root . . . that little else but money making is attended to, the great business [of winning the war] may get forward as it can." He added that these "infamous harpies, who to acquire a little pelf, would involve this great continent in inextricable ruin." To another, Washington fumed that "virtue and patriotism are almost kicked out of the United States." Those given to what he labeled foppery and vanity were unwilling to sacrifice. They "seem to think the contest is at an end." They demonstrated an enthusiasm only "to make money, and get places." They were indifferent to the plight of the army. They were "pests of society." Worse, they were "murderers of our cause."[26]

Likewise, many in Congress expressed a sense of malaise and apprehension at the pending "ruin . . . in our internal & domestic affairs." This "monstrous . . . depreciation of the paper Money" emasculated the new nation, a Virginian complained. Everyone understood the desperate need for still another foreign loan, but all knew too that France, now at war herself, was an unlikely benefactor. "We cannot . . . obtain a Sufficient Loan for the carrying on the War till Spain becomes a party in it," a Maryland delegate lamented, and no guarantee existed that the monarchy in Madrid would assist the insurgent republicans in America. Taxes could produce revenue, and perhaps arrest the inflationary spiral, but Congress had no authority to tax. "The disordered state of our Finances are truly distressing," one congressman cried. Another warned that "Congress are at their wits end. . . . We are now at the very pinch of the game," sinking under a worthless currency and facing the likelihood that the army could not be supplied much longer. Twelve months earlier the future of the United States had seemed bright. Now it had plummeted into a "Wilderness of darkness & of dangers," according to Congressman Jesse Root of Connecticut.[27]

In the summer of 1779 all could see how the crippled economy was affecting the war effort. The "Enemy are in motion," it was often reported, while the Continentals remained immobile. The British army proceeded with the pacification of Georgia during 1779, eventually restoring royal government in that province. Washington meanwhile authorized a foray against the Iroquois on the remote New York frontier, and undertook small raids against British posts above Manhattan on the lower Hudson, but the year passed without a major campaign by the Continental army. At years' end, worrisome evidence reached Congress that France was growing displeased with America's inactivity, and the Connecticut congressional delegation warned officials at home that unless a solution was found to the nation's financial woes, it might be "impractical to carry on the war another year."[28]

Others worried that the financial distress would breed a resurgence of those who longed to be reconciled with Great Britain. "We still have concealed enimies among us" who now more than ever would relinquish independence for peace, many said.[29] Most thought it unlikely that it would come to that. France, in fact, was beginning to be a greater concern than those Americans who yearned to be reunited with Great Britain. From the outset, realists had known that the French government, which clearly wished for American independence in order to weaken Great Britain, would remain at war only so long as it believed that the fruits of victory outweighed the costs of hostilities.

In the course of the black year of 1779 the realization dawned that the United States was caught in a stalemated war. The buoyant mood that had swept the country following France's entry into the war had long since vanished. Indeed, apprehension had increased over France's staying power. Should Versailles conclude that the United States could not carry its weight militarily, it might force its ally into peace talks, leaving America with a horrendous choice of accepting less than it wished—reconciliation with Britain, in a worst case scenario, or possibly independence only for those states that were not occupied by the British army—or of continuing to fight on alone. Even the best likely outcome seemed to many to be less than favorable. Independence might be achieved in name, but a tiny, enfeebled, postwar United States that was surrounded by a powerful British empire in North America would hardly be truly independent. It would be no more than a French satellite. For some, the warning that Galloway had voiced long before—America might exchange dependence on Great Britain for dependence on France—had come to have an eerily prophetic ring to it.[30]

Still others worried that the new financial straits might bring about popular convulsions, for alongside the luxurious habits of the elite, ordinary people were being driven to want by the runaway prices. Most congressmen understood the plight of the people, for they too were forced into austerity measures. Numerous delegates moved to less expensive lodgings, shared quarters with a colleague, or dined at common tables in boarding houses. Every congressman had a friend who had been compelled by financial necessity to quit public service. Yet most congressmen were considerably more affluent than the artisans and laborers in urban America. After nearly five years of war, ordinary workers were severely pinched. Prices in 1779 were eight times greater than when the war began. Wages had seldom kept pace. Widows, orphans, clergymen, and salaried officials were especially hard hit. Some in Congress, such as Gouverneur Morris of New York, anguished that the day would come when those citizens in reduced circumstances would rise up, acting on the principle "let us take our Neighbor's Property and convert it to our Use."[31] That day appeared to have come on October 4, 1779.

That afternoon Philadelphia militiamen engaged in a gun battle with several influential men who had taken refuge in the home of former congressman James Wilson. The incident, which came to be known as the "Battle of Fort Wilson," stemmed directly from the hardships caused by rising prices. Because of the presence of the British army in 1777–78, Philadelphia was one of the first cities to experience serious shortages accompanied by runaway prices. Soon after the redcoats abandoned the city, the state government sought to stabilize food prices by prohibiting exports of agricultural commodities. Nevertheless, prices continued to climb throughout 1778. Allegations soon swirled through the city that the richest merchants had colluded to make windfall profits by manipulating the food supply. Suspicion focused primarily on Robert Morris, the former congressman who had been lukewarm toward independence in 1776, and who had become perhaps the wealthiest man in America in the course of the war.

In the scarce winter and spring of 1779, Philadelphia's newspapers bulged with charges that wealthy businessmen were "indolent and depraved." Workers' committees, which last had functioned effectively in the struggle for independence three years earlier, were revived. The artisans declared that if the state would not, or could not, act decisively, their committees would serve as regulatory agencies to ensure that the residents of the city could purchase food and other necessities at affordable prices. Public meetings were held, attended by thousands of desperate and angry residents. At one such gathering in May, General Daniel Roberdeau, a militia commander and former congressman—John and Samuel Adams had briefly lodged in his house in 1777—told an excited crowd that unscrupulous businessmen, who were "getting rich by sucking the blood" of their countrymen, were "the greatest cause of our present calamities." He added that "the community, in their own defense, have a natural right to counteract" the dishonest practices of the unpatriotic and devious tycoons. That meeting elected two committees to regulate prices, and a week later those committees set prices for tea, coffee, sugar, molasses, flour, salt, rum, and whiskey. At another meeting the Philadelphia militia was asked to enforce the price edict.

Not everyone was happy with price controls. The greatest merchants opposed them, but so did some shopkeepers and artisans. One of their spokesmen, James Wilson, asserted that the "whole power of the Roman emperor could not add a single letter to the alphabet," and Pennsylvania could never successfully fix prices.[32] He and others argued that regulation only led to greater deficiencies, as farmers would not sell in Philadelphia's artificially rigged markets. On that score they were correct. Shortages of virtually every necessity existed throughout that summer, including salt, which before the war sold for a dollar a barrel but by 1779 was only available on the black market, and then for $36 a barrel. Regulatory committees or not, prices continued to rise. Passions rose alongside the escalating costs. Twice during that parched summer of 1779, the regulatory committees accused Morris of price-gouging. In midsummer, the militia adopted an address charging that "the disaffected, Inimical, or Self Interested; and, we might presume to say, the most Obnoxious part of the Community"— the city's biggest businessmen— had "advanced the prices on everything." In early autumn, on the eve of the annual harvest, the militia concluded that only a campaign of terror could forestall the rapacity of the merchants. A Committee of Privates formed and resolved to seize and exile some of the worst offenders to British-occupied Manhattan. The affluent responded by forming what militiamen termed the "silk-stocking brigade," a paramilitary defense unit that patrolled merchant neighborhoods. Even so, the militia struck on October 4, taking four captives, whom they labeled as no better than Tories. As word of the seizures spread through the city, alarmed merchants, and those who had been most vocal in defending the businessmen, banded together for protection. Up to forty heavily armed "gentlemen" crammed into Wilson's residence.

In midafternoon, several score of militiamen, their four captives in tow, set out for the docks, parading through the city streets before large crowds. However, instead of marching directly to the waterfront, the militiamen followed a circuitous route that, not by happenstance, took them before Wilson's home. Although an early advocate of resistance to parliamentary taxation, Wilson had never been a popular figure in Philadelphia. A native of Scotland, he had immigrated in the 1760s, studied law with Dickinson, and launched a practice that flourished in Carlisle, a community in western Pennsylvania that teemed with contentious Scotch-Irish denizens like himself. Those who served closely with Wilson in the popular protest found him to be quite bright and well read, but reserved and aloof. Others, who had a passing acquaintance with him, often were struck by his intense, saturnine manner, and many concluded that he was stern and supercilious. But it was his stance on numerous public issues that ruined him with most Philadelphians. Together with Dickinson, he had been in the forefront of the fight to prevent Congress from separating from Great Britain, although he ultimately voted for, and signed, the Declaration of Independence. Thereafter, he opposed Pennsylvania's democratic constitution of 1776 and steadfastly denounced price controls. By 1779 many in Philadelphia seem to have looked on him as Bostonians once had viewed Andrew Oliver. His image was that of a haughty, grasping aristocrat, a foe of political reform who radiated a cold indifference to the plight of those who suffered most from the economic calamities.[33]

The intent of the Committee of Privates in detouring by Wilson's residence will never be known, but Wilson and his comrades, who saw the militiamen as a mob, believed that unless they defended themselves they would be taken captive and run out of town. Given what ensued, their surmise was probably correct. As the soldiers drew up before Wilson's house, gunfire rang out. It was never proven which side fired first, but the shots set in motion a battle that lasted ten minutes. It ended only when Joseph Reed, Washington's former aide who now was the chief executive of Pennsylvania, arrived on horseback with a small force of cavalry. When order was restored, it was discovered that nearly two dozen men had been killed and wounded. There were casualties on both sides. More than a score of militiamen were arrested. Neither Wilson nor any of his comrades in the citadel-house were taken into custody.[34]

The foes of price regulation in Congress immediately railed at the "great tumult" provoked by a "Mobb of Militia," and charged the Philadelphia trainbandsmen with fomenting a "violent Insurrection." Gouverneur Morris lashed out at the "Tyrannous" practice of establishing public regulation and demanded that affairs be restored to their "proper Channels," in which the marketplace would regulate itself according to the laws of supply and demand. But the backlash against high living and presumed profiteering had cost this element whatever popularity it once had enjoyed. Moreover, many Americans had come to see Congress, which once had acted with vigor and acumen in leading the protest and war against Great Britain, as no longer equal to the task it faced. Increasingly, as one observer remarked, it was viewed as a body that had wasted its time in contentious "Debates upon Subjects beneath the Robin Hood Society," while victory, once at its fingertips, had been permitted to slip away.[35]

Likewise, Congress had lost confidence in itself. Never having had financial powers bestowed on it by the states, Congress in late 1779 relinquished to the states the economic controls it had nevertheless wielded during the past four years. It stopped printing Continental paper and revalued the currency. It turned over to the states the pay of the army and left to them the responsibility for regulating Continental officials, especially army supply officers. Its deference to the states came with advice. Congress encouraged the states to resort to "speedy, vigorous & repeated Taxation," as taking money from circulation was the best antidote against inflation. It additionally pressed them to confiscate and sell Loyalist properties, a revenue-raising measure that might generate funds with which to supply the army.

Congress manifested an air of desperation. "[W]e are Pretty near the End of the Tether," one congressman remarked near the beginning of 1780. The national government was powerless. The economy was in shambles. Victory was uncertain. The states alone appeared to have the power to save the American Revolution, yet few in Congress placed much hope in them. "We are now beginning to call on the several States" to provide the revenue to sustain the war effort, Henry Laurens told General Washington, but he "doubt[ed] the practicality, the possibility of a compliance." "I most feelingly dread the consequence" if they do not act, Laurens added. In "the mildest terms," he concluded, it would result in "much confusion & derangement of public affairs . . . & convulsions in the Army, in the Country, & in the Cities."[36]

Laurens's doubts were not misplaced. The states, which verged on bankruptcy, lacked the means and the will to cope effectively. This at the very moment that the war intensified, for early in 1780 the long expected invasion of South Carolina finally commenced. The Continental army not only required immediate funding, but it suddenly needed more of everything than had been the case in years. During the past two or three years the states had tried a variety of expedients to find revenue. Loan drives had been a favorite recourse, but they almost always failed. The states had additionally piled £85,000,000 in taxes on the citizenry in 1779–80, almost 100 times the duties assessed by the colonies in peacetime a few years earlier, but so rampant was inflation that the revenue actually collected was always inadequate.

By early 1780, just when the military crisis grew pronounced, most states began to shrink from instituting still higher taxation. If "too heavily pressed," Pennsylvania's chief executive remarked, the citizenry would "readily renew their connexion with Great Britain." Instead, most states began to seize and sell the property of the Loyalists, the expedient that Congress had encouraged. The Massachusetts General Court, for instance, passed legislation that permitted the seizure of property belonging to "Certain Notorious Conspirators," including Hutchinson and some survivors of Andrew Oliver, and another act that authorized the confiscation of property owned by "absconders," those refugees who were considered to be "open avowed enemies." Every other state followed with similar legislation, and in no time a considerable amount of property had been confiscated and seized. For example, Suffolk County, Massachusetts, which included Boston, seized and sold thirty-five parcels within ten months, whereas Dutchess County, New York, appropriated and sold 469 forfeited lots. Millions of dollars was garnered, but it was in depreciated currency. Often, too, the property sold for only about a quarter of its assessed value. As a result, most states quickly suspended all sales, although some used confiscated Tory properties as security for state loans.[37]

Furthermore, at the very moment that the confiscated properties were being sold, most states abandoned price regulation. They did so to meet another emergency: food shortages. The states capitulated on price controls in the hope of making agricultural staples more abundant, and many permitted farmers to pay taxes with their crops. Prices rose like a balloon released on a windy day. In the end the states had been no more successful than Congress in coping with the fiscal dilemma. Every effort had been unavailing, as they too were vanquished by runaway inflation and the endless expenses occasioned by the war.[38]

General Washington, who daily coped with a dearth of supplies, had been one of the first to understand the likely magnitude of the crisis as it blossomed in 1779. In the last days of winter in 1780, he had warned that the new nation now faced a more "eminent danger" than in the blackest days of 1776. The United States was "verging . . . fast to destruction" and a "common Ruin," he cautioned. The "goodly fabric" that had been fashioned in the popular protest and the early phase of hostilities had been rent by avarice. The evil machinations of speculators was sapping the nation's strength and strangling the people's will to endure. Two months later he said that the "cries of the distressed" were growing louder. Late that summer he characterized the collapsing economy as the "greatest evil" that could befall a people at war.[39] Some in Congress came to a similar conclusion. That autumn South Carolina's Henry Laurens, the president of Congress, railed that the "stock jobbers [and] Monopolizers," whom he labeled as "Enemies of our Peace," had brought the war effort to "the brink of a precipace" that led to national ruin.[40] As the mild days of spring nudged aside winter, every citizen at last knew what Washington and Laurens had long since known: the American Revolution was in great peril. When Arthur Lee, recalled by Congress, landed in his homeland midway through that year, he found that morale had nearly collapsed. Alarming numbers, he reported, were ready to end the war on any terms, even short of independence. Around this same time, the secretary of Congress concluded that Great Britain might lack the "power to subdue us by force," but it could yet win the war merely by protracting hostilities and awaiting America's collapse through the "derangement of our finances."[41]

In fact, it was not just the economy that crashed in 1780. In May, American resistance in Charleston collapsed as well. The British captured the city, together with 5,000 prisoners of war and irreplaceable military equipment. Ninety days later, General Gates suffered an egregious defeat at Camden, leaving much of South Carolina and all of Georgia in British hands. In September, General Benedict Arnold turned coat. One of America's most esteemed soldiers, Arnold tried to deliver West

Point—and control of the Hudson River—to the enemy, a treasonous act so monstrous that it may have provoked even more widespread despair than that aroused by the military defeats in the South. Worse followed. Mutinies in the Continental army, the first of any scope in this war, ushered in 1781. An aide at Washington's headquarters pronounced that the Continental army "is now a mob, rather than an army, without clothing, without pay, without provision, without morals, without discipline." On the second day of 1781, Congressman Lovell wrote an American envoy in Europe that the United States was "bankrupt with a mutinous army."[42]

Watching helplessly through this crisis, several influential men had come to believe that the national woes could be solved through better leadership. Once again, Washington was one of the first to raise the point. "[W]here are our Men of Abilities," he asked as early as March 1779. "Why do they not come forth to save their Country?" He was perplexed by the absence of former congressmen who had been active in the halcyon days of the struggle. He knew that in many instances, the states, in a game of keep-away with the national government, monopolized the talents of some who remained committed to public service. But he believed that some were absent because they had fallen into habits of "idleness and dissipation." Specifically, Washington inquired about the whereabouts of Thomas Jefferson.[43]

Jefferson's national service had been short-lived. He sat in Congress for fifteen months during 1775 and 1776, returning home soon after independence was declared. He had no more than reached Virginia when Congress urged him—actually John Hancock's letter said that Congress expected him—to accept appointment to the three-member diplomatic team it was sending to France. Several leading figures in Virginia implored him to undertake the assignment. Richard Henry Lee reminded Jefferson that "every thing depends on" France becoming belligerent in the increasingly desperate war. Jefferson demurred, implying that his wife's delicate health would not permit him to be away from home. Many were unconvinced by his excuse. Lee directly accused him of preferring his "private enjoyments" to making sacrifices. John Adams privately concluded that Jefferson lacked the courage to cross the Atlantic during wartime, a view that Lee shared.[44]

From time to time thereafter, members of Congress appealed to Jefferson to reassume his seat in Congress. "We want your Industry and Abilities here," Adams wrote about a year after Jefferson's departure. Similarly, General Washington sought to induce him to return to Philadelphia in 1778, but Jefferson was not swayed.[45] Not only did he never leave Virginia in the six years after he departed Philadelphia, but before 1779 he seldom came down from his hilltop mansion outside Charlottesville. Although a member of Virginia's legislature, he attended only about a quarter of its sessions during this period. He devoted his time and energy to his family, business operations at Monticello, and the never-ending construction of his mansion. He gave some attention to legislative assignments while at home, including seminal work on the codification of the state's laws, but on the whole, public service often appeared to be far from Jefferson's thoughts, especially the suffering that so many endured in the war.

By 1779, as concerns grew about the course of the war, Jefferson was subjected to unrelenting pressure to play a more active role. Lee, who never let up, beseeched him "to suffer every thing rather than injure the public cause." Edmund Pendleton advised Jefferson that he must make sacrifices for "the rising Generation." A friend candidly charged that he had "seen little, of patriotism and public virtue" from Jefferson, while a closer friend brutally advised him to "Deny yourself your darling Pleasures" and serve the public.[46] It was in this milieu that Washington for a second time inquired, joining the growing chorus of Virginians asking: "Where is Jefferson?"[47] That spring Jefferson at last bowed to the entreaties and stood for election as chief executive of Virginia. He won the post and served two one-year terms, beginning in June 1779.

Clearly, however, Jefferson was not alone among revolutionary activists in discovering an aversion to national political service. Only six of the fifty-six delegates who had gathered at Carpenter's Hall for the First Congress in 1774 remained in that body in 1779. Attrition among those who had signed the Declaration of Independence was even greater. Only five of the signers were yet congressmen on the fourth anniversary of independence.

Where had they gone? Some had accepted other offices. Many were more loyal to their state—the home of their ancestors for several generations, in many instances—than to the new national government. Some took state judicial posts or—like Henry and Jefferson—a legislative seat. Five who had sat in Congress in 1775–76 subsequently served as wartime state governors. Three left Congress to serve abroad as diplomats, and two, Washington and Schuyler, resigned to take up arms. Several, finding it difficult to cope with the travail brought on by service, left public life altogether. Congressional service exacted numerous sacrifices. Most delegates were separated from loved ones for ten or eleven months at a time. They usually got home only once a year, and then for just a few days. While in attendance, most lived in cramped quarters and subsisted on an unfamiliar diet. A few left Congress for pecuniary reasons, opportunistically returning home to seek a fortune in the wartime milieu. Far

more were compelled by financial necessity to resume their prewar avoca-
tion, managing an estate or reviving a moribund legal practice. A few resigned for reasons of health. Some were just utterly exhausted by their
responsibilities, which included the necessity to make life-and-death decisions. With considerable hyperbole, one delegate lamented that the lot
of soldiers was "a Bed of Roses, a Pillow of Down" compared with that of
members of Congress, but the health of some congressmen did deterio-
rate. John Adams was convinced that the cares of public service had broken his health, and Gouverneur Morris agreed, adding that his inability to
exercise and the "pestiferous Climate" of Philadelphia had resulted in a
decline in his physical well-being. Congressman Lovell, who for a time
was virtually a one-man Department of State, was so frequently ill with
chronic maladies that his colleagues attributed his woes to overwork.

Most congressmen faced an arduous schedule that included numerous committee assignments in addition to the lengthy daily session. Not
many complained about their heavy load, but grousing about the mo-
notony of the wearisome sessions was commonplace. Many wrote home
about the endless speeches and interminable debates that rendered these
"Consultations very tedious." One, who spoke of the "exquisite tedious-
ness" of the sessions, concluded that the problem arose because Congress was composed of too many attorneys. They "love to talk." Too often
there was too much talk and too little reflection, he added. Serving in
Congress, one delegate lamented, was as useful as spending a lifetime
"in dissecting a fly." The only time Congress acted quickly, said another
congressman dryly, was "when it was ignorant of the subject."[48]

As Congress moved from making a Revolution to managing a war,
the desultory and repetitive nature of its business undoubtedly drove
some men away. General Washington's query about those who were no
longer active, or at least not serving at the national level, was in large
measure prompted by his belief that Congress had come to consist largely
of second-raters. He was not alone in this conviction. Some in Congress
were also concerned with the diminution of talent within its ranks. It
took James Madison less than a week after joining Congress in March
1780 to conclude that the body was plagued by a dearth of "adequate
Statesmen." Given its lackluster composition, he remarked, Congress was
"likely to fall into wrong measures" or simply, from indecision, to pass
the buck to the states, where he believed even less talent was on view.[49]

While there was some truth in the views of Washington and Madison, there was much humbug as well. The demographics of Congress
had changed. By 1780 many men from what had been the elite social
strata in the colonial era were gone, replaced by congressmen drawn
from the "middling sort." However, this fulfilled what many had hoped

would be the case with the American Revolution: that independence would open opportunities to talented men from what had previously been the less privileged classes. These men were not necessarily inexperienced or devoid of talent. In fact, virtually every new member of Congress after 1778 had previously sat in a state legislature or on a revolutionary committee, often one that exercised considerable authority. It is true that Congress by 1779 was struggling unsuccessfully with its most pronounced problems, but its failure was due more to its want of power, and its lack of an executive arm and adequate staff, than to the deficiencies of its members.[50]

Indeed, the unrelenting calamities of 1780 led many to conclude that the states had also failed to meet the emergency. Many came to believe that the only solution was to vest Congress with greater powers. That autumn both the New York assembly and a convention of New England states adopted resolutions that urged the "investing [of] full power in Congress for an effectual prosecution of the War." The New England statement additionally recommended bestowing dictatorial powers on Washington for the purpose of prying needed supplies from the states.[51] Both proposals were too radical for Congress, but substantive changes gradually occurred.

By the time Charleston fell in May, nearly thirty months had elapsed since Congress had sent the Articles of Confederation to the states for ratification. All save Maryland had acted, but that state refused its assent until the four states with major western land claims surrendered their dominions to the United States. Many Marylanders, including Charles Carroll of Carrollton, who ultimately would be the last surviving signer of the Declaration of Independence, and for whom many towns and counties throughout the United States are now named, had invested in private land companies that purchased "titles" to western lands from the Indians. If these speculative interests could compel the "landed states" to relinquish their claims, the land companies faced the prospect of an economic bonanza.

As the years slipped by, three states with royal titles to western lands relinquished their claims, but through most of 1780 Virginia remained intransigent. At one point it even sent Congress a remonstrance asserting its western claims in the language of many a subsequent states-rights manifesto. However, the growing success of Britain's Southern strategy began to change minds in Virginia. With South Carolina seemingly nearly subdued, the British army appeared set to invade North Carolina in the autumn. Virginia, which already had suffered one devastating coastal raid, might be invaded within a year. However, it was not an invasion but a second raid that finally forced Virginia's hand. On New Year's Eve,

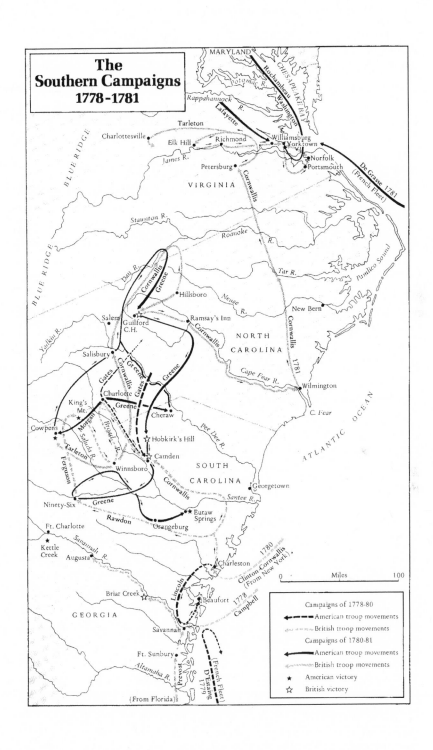

The
Southern Campaigns
1778-1781

MARYLAND

Rochambeau

Washington

CHESAPEAKE BAY

Potomac R.

Rappahannock R.

Lafayette

Tarleton

Charlottesville

Elk Hill

Richmond

Williamsburg

Yorktown

BLUE RIDGE

James R.

Norfolk

Petersburg

Portsmouth

De Grasse 1781 (French Fleet)

VIRGINIA

Cornwallis

Staunton R.

Roanoke R.

BLUE RIDGE

Dan R.

Cornwallis

Greene

Hillsboro

Tar R.

Neuse R.

Pamlico Sound

Salem

Guilford C.H.

Ramsay's Inn

Cornwallis

New Bern

NORTH CAROLINA

Cornwallis 1781

Yadkin R.

Salisbury

Cornwallis

Greene

Gates

Greene

Charlotte

Gates

Cape Fear R.

Wilmington

King's Mt.

Greene

Cheraw

Pee Dee R.

C. Fear

ATLANTIC OCEAN

Cowpens

Morgan

Tarleton

Saluda R.

Broad R.

Hobkirk's Hill

Camden

Winnsboro

SOUTH CAROLINA

Ferguson

Cornwallis

Georgetown

Santee R.

Ninety-Six

Greene

Rawdon

Orangeburg

Eutaw Springs

Ft. Charlotte

Kettle Creek

Savannah R.

Augusta

Charleston

1780

Clinton-Cornwallis (From New York)

Miles

0   100

Briar Creek

Lincoln

Beaufort

1778

Campbell

GEORGIA

Savannah

Campaigns of 1778-80
— — → American troop movements
········· British troop movements
Campaigns of 1780-81
———→ American troop movements
········· British troop movements
★ American victory
☆ British victory

Ft. Sunbury

Prevost

(French Fleet) D'Estaing 1779

Altamaha R.

(From Florida)

a British force, led by Benedict Arnold, was spotted in the Chesapeake. Governor Jefferson responded slowly, and Arnold's green-clad troops—he had 1,600 men and twenty-seven vessels, including five heavy warships, in his armada—penetrated to Richmond, laying waste along the James River and within the new capital to plantations, arsenals, shipyards, and warehouses, and liberating scores of slaves.[52] Thereafter, Virginia quickly yielded its western claims, but on one condition. It would cede its claims only if Congress rejected all private claims.

Maryland, the holdout on private claims, was also being squeezed. It was under intense pressure from the new French minister, le Chevalier de la Luzerne, to ratify the Articles. Luzerne told the authorities in Annapolis that the implementation of the Articles of Confederation would be seen in Europe as an impressive demonstration of American solidarity. Underlying his assertion was the implied threat that French perseverance might rest on what was decided in Annapolis. Further intransigence could only make Maryland appear to be both selfish and a roadblock to victory. Like Virginia, it too was beaten, and soon it caved in. In January 1781 Maryland ratified the proposed constitution and Congress set March 1, 1781, as the date that the Articles of Confederation were to take effect.[53]

When the Articles were written in 1776–77, no mood had existed for creating a national government that would subsume the powers wielded by the states. As a result, the new Congress, like its predecessor, was powerless to raise a revenue, regulate trade, or compel the states to comply with its regulations. However, at this darkest moment of the war, some congressmen now demanded that changes be made. With such a weak Congress, some said, "We can never manage the publick Interests with Success." America would never gain "a decided Superiority over our Enemies," others remonstrated. Congress needed authority to "enforce their Decisions," a New Yorker insisted. Madison thought the cries for greater congressional authority arose from the "shameful" behavior of the states, which all too often had failed to provide the army with adequate supplies. He labeled Delaware a singular culprit and told Jefferson that the American Revolution could be lost because of the obstruction of "the most inconsiderable State in the Union." James Varnum, who had resigned his commission as a general officer in the Continental army to sit in Congress, likewise thought that sustaining the war hinged on granting Congress greater authority. He understood his countrymen's fear of abusive government, but he warned that "when that Caution is carried too far," it "may be fatal."[54]

Fatal indeed. Deep into 1781 the military situation appeared hopeless. Although a French army of 8,000 men had arrived in America in

July 1780, it remained idle during its initial twelve months on American soil. Washington meanwhile fixated on a joint operation to retake New York City, to the exclusion of every alternative action. Even Governor Jefferson, who otherwise never questioned Washington's abilities, wondered at the breadth of the commander's strategic thinking. Moreover, Comte de Rochambeau, commander of the French troops, was cool to the idea of a campaign to liberate New York, and pointed out that the allies lacked sufficient manpower to conduct a siege of Manhattan. As the seasons passed, the allies did nothing, waiting in vain for the arrival of the French navy and additional French infantry units. Not even the British invasion of Virginia, which finally commenced in May 1781, stirred Washington. Rochambeau and Vergennes grew disillusioned. The former, startled by the paralysis of the Continentals, privately told the French government that the American army soon might disintegrate. The foreign minister let it be known that he was perplexed by Washington's behavior. How, he asked, could this general, who had been so daring in 1776 and 1777, have grown so cautious?[55]

Nor was it only the army that appeared to be paralyzed. The vibrancy that once had characterized the war effort was utterly gone. Congress, for instance, in June 1781 secretly instructed Adams to "govern yourself" by France's "advice and opinion" in making peace. Congress had reduced the United States to a client of France, and in the process had virtually surrendered whatever slim chance remained to secure a peace settlement that would protect America's myriad interests.[56]

Three years after the heady days that followed Saratoga, many concluded that the war had to be won in 1781, or victory and independence would be lost forever. Adams, for instance, informed Congress that the conviction was growing in France that it had become saddled with a costly and unwinnable war. He feared that America's ally was looking for an honorable way to make peace. Adams also reported that several neutral nations in Europe, weary of a war that harmed their commercial interests, were exploring the likelihood of mediating the conflict. If the war dragged beyond 1781, the likelihood was considerable that a general European peace conference would be convened and that Versailles and London would readily settle this war on the basis of *uti possidetis* at a time when Great Britain could lay claim to Canada, South Carolina, Georgia, and the trans-Appalachian West. Nor did any imagine that France would agree to American rights to the fisheries. In June 1781, as the Franco-American armies languidly watched yet another campaign season rapidly disappear, Joseph Reed predicted that Great Britain soon would make peace and simply await "a more favourable opportunity to recover the whole" of the United States.[57]

Pushed by this crisis, Congress in 1781 appointed several committees to find a solution. One, composed of Madison, Varnum, and New York's James Duane, proposed that Congress actually possessed the "implied power" to coerce the states into compliance with national laws. Congress did not wish to take this step. After all, the American protest had come into being nearly twenty years earlier to resist Parliament's coercion to comply with its implied authority to act "in all cases whatsoever" for the colonies. Congress was left with two other choices. A second committee proposed that Congress request that the states permit it to exercise greater powers for the duration of the wartime emergency. Still another committee prepared seven constitutional amendments for submission to the states. Each would have granted greater powers to Congress, including authority to seize property in the states that failed to furnish the money and soldiers demanded by the central government. Those opposed to centralization of authority defeated both committee reports.[58]

Although the three proposed alternatives went nowhere, they reflected the new directions taking shape in the minds of many in Congress. Sentiment for increasing the authority of the United States government was increasing. The most vocal advocates of a stronger national government were former Continental officers, who had firsthand experiences with a soldiery left to suffer and an army rendered inactive through inadequate resources. Varnum, a distinguished lawyer before the war, and Ezekiel Cornell, a self-educated artisan who also hailed from Rhode Island, had become general officers and served in the siege of Boston, as well as the campaigns for New York and Rhode Island. They joined with John Sullivan, who had fought in Canada, New York, Pennsylvania, and Rhode Island before joining New Hampshire's congressional delegation, and Philip Schuyler, who after being shown the door by Congress in 1778, was sent to the national legislature by New York.

These former soldiers were disgusted with what they discovered upon entering Congress. They found it to be little better than a languorous debating society. Congress dithered away valuable time "in disputes about diction, Commas, Colons, Consonants, vowels, etc.," Cornell charged. Varnum despaired that such a government could ever see the war to victory. These former soldiers were joined by members of the mercantile combine, which sought a national government that not only could bring order out of the chaos caused by thirteen states marching to thirteen different drummers, but which could restore a sound currency and implement an enlightened commercial policy. Numerous Southern congressmen, including Madison and Joseph Jones of Virginia, and John Mathews of South Carolina—who saw independence, the American West, and their slave properties slipping from their grasp in the face of Britain's Southern strategy—were also driven to support a stronger government. So too were numerous younger men in Congress, many of whom had first become politically active during the revolutionary struggle, and who had always exhibited what has been called a "Continentalist" outlook. Their vision had been shaped by their focus on attaining national goals: American independence, American victory, and the establishment of a powerful republican nation.[59]

The desperation of those who sought greater powers for the national government mounted as they were unable to sway Congress. Sullivan charged that "our Confederation is not in force." America's political system, he added, was "a Monster with Thirteen heads." A new congressional committee, the Committee at Headquarters, which was sent off to investigate conditions in the army, reported that the nation's military force was so enfeebled it probably could not successfully defend itself, much less wage offensive operations. Cornell ruminated that America required a dictator. Varnum proposed a constitutional convention that would lay "aside as Useless" the existing Articles of Confederation and create a "kind of Government sufficiently energetic to obtain the Objects of Peace." Congress endorsed neither notion, but it did act, stirred to do something, one representative privately acknowledged, in order to "prevent stupid plans of creating absolute Dictators to get supplies without paying for them." In the winter and spring of 1780–81, Congress created four executive departments, Foreign Affairs, Finance, War, and Marine, and it sent to the states a constitutional amendment proposing that it be given authority to impose a 5 percent duty on imports. The revenue that was derived, many thought, would "enable Congress, in some measure to fulfill their promises," but the great hope was that with its credit shored up, the United States could entice France or Spain, or both, to make still another loan. Congress also dispatched to France Colonel John Laurens, son of the former president of Congress, to be its "Beggar," as Gouverneur Morris labeled his position.[60] These actions by the nationalists, those who favored the augmentation of the national authority, launched a new era in American politics that stretched ahead to the Constitutional Convention six years later and the Federalist regimes of the 1790s.

While it took these steps, Congress also appointed Pennsylvania's Robert Morris, who had served in Congress from 1775 until 1778, as the first Superintendent of Finance. Forty-seven years of age, Morris was a pallid, jowly, heavyset man with a full head of graying hair, combed straight back, and stern features, punctuated by dark, furtive eyes. He could be congenial, if it served his purpose, but for the most part he was brisk and formal, not unfriendly, but neither genial nor gregarious. Few appear to have ever grown close to him, and it is revealing that none of the dozens of officials with whom he dealt during a span of a quarter century of public activity characterized him as an endearing man or remembered him for any displays of humor or generosity.

When he was thirteen, in 1747, Morris and his father had immigrated from England. They settled in Maryland, where his father worked as a tobacco agent. When his father was killed a year or so later in an accident, young Robert was sent by his guardian to Philadelphia to begin an apprenticeship with the mercantile firm of Charles Willing. Morris soon discovered his calling, displaying a zest for the countinghouse. When he was twenty-three, Morris and Willing's son, Charles, set up their own firm. Although three years younger than his partner, Morris was the one who made things click. The company came into being just as the French and Indian War erupted, and Morris quickly learned that a war could do wonders for the right business under the proper management. With lucrative defense contracts in hand, his firm flourished. It did just as well, if not better, when peace broke out. By the time war came again, this time with the mother country in 1775, Morris's company was one of the most prosperous in Philadelphia. In addition to his carrying trade in Europe, the Caribbean, and Africa, Morris had invested in land, mines, mills, and the companies of at least four other Philadelphia merchants.

He was active in the protest movement from the beginning. Morris thought London's new colonial policies were outrageous, though he never desired independence. Having made a fortune as a colonial businessman, he was apprehensive that the end of the empire would send him and other merchants down a blind alley fraught with potential cataclysm. When Morris came to Congress in 1775, he allied with the Dickinson-Wilson element that sought to block the colonists' separation from Great Britain, and when independence at last appeared inevitable in the spring of 1776 he despaired that "there are some amongst us who cannot bear the thought of reconciliation on any terms." Although he abstained on the vote for independence, Morris shortly signed the Declaration of Independence. A cynic might argue, with considerable merit, that he did so to prevent his mercantile company from drying up. Where other revolutionaries went on at length about natural rights, Morris spoke instead about the abundant opportunities for making money in this war, if one was on the right side. He knew that it was highly improbable that any American who sided with Great Britain would make money during the duration of what appeared likely to be a protracted war. However, making money from American war contracts, or from the trade with France, that as an insider he knew was about to commence, held great promise. Soon after independence was declared, Morris told a friend that the "present opportunity of improving our fortunes ought not to be lost." He also reflected that never in human history has there been "so fair an opportunity of making a large fortune."[61]

Morris discovered early on that sitting in Congress could be beneficial to his business operations. As a member of the Secret Committee, he was privy to confidential information that other businessmen and private citizens would have loved to possess. Before the end of 1776, for instance, he was profiting from the clandestine and lucrative trade with France, a commerce hidden from the world and from most Americans.

But Morris also rendered important services to the United States. When Congress fled Philadelphia late in the dark autumn of 1776, it left Morris in town to look after affairs. It was to him that General Washington turned for supplies, and Morris got arms and powder to the Continentals that proved essential in the eventual rout of the Hessians at Trenton and the army's splendid performance at Princeton. Moreover, his spadework in facilitating the secret trade with France resulted in the shipment of vast amounts of military hardware to the Continentals, weaponry that proved crucial in the pivotal campaign of 1777. These efforts catapulted him to what would be the pinnacle of his personal popularity. After Saratoga, one colleague told Morris that he was "the only man [in Congress] whom they all . . . think well of," while Hancock praised the "great good" that had resulted from his tireless work. Morris remained in Congress until 1778, sitting in the Pennsylvania assembly and continuing to operate his multifarious businesses all the while. He failed to discern any conflict of interest in controlling vast amounts of public money while making numerous private investments. In fact, he declared that his actions were "as disinterested and pure as ever were made by Mortal Man."[62]

Others, however, questioned his practices. He was criticized in 1779 by a Pennsylvania committee for hoarding scarce materials and running up prices, despite the widespread suffering that resulted. Some also knew that he had sold food aplenty to the French armed forces, which had cash, while he ignored the penniless Continentals. As early as 1777, Thomas Paine published a blistering attack on Morris's *low dirty Tricks*," including his allegedly habitual practice of selling well above a fair profit margin. Paine thought it unconscionable for Congressman Morris to have private business relationships with agents and merchants doing business with the United States, and he suspected that a considerable portion of the public monies that passed through the hands of Morris and the public officials and businessmen with whom he dealt wound up in their collective pockets. He thought Morris largely responsible for having introduced to American society a "degree of corruption" not present in the prewar era, and he charged that Morris's presumably shady practices posed a roadblock to military victory.[63]

Morris was never beloved by the public or other officeholders, and when Congress turned to him in 1781, it was an act of desperation. No step taken by Congress or the states during the past two years had worked. Morris, however, appeared to have the Midas touch when it came to his private financial transactions. Furthermore, he not only appeared to understand the causes of the economic tribulations, but the persona he manifested convinced most that he was fully capable of making the pitiless decisions that might be necessary to reverse the nation's economic woes. In this grave emergency, few in Congress appeared to be overly concerned about his personal ethics.

Congress approached Morris about becoming Superintendent of Finance in February 1781, but he did not take office until May. First he presented Congress with a set of demands. He would not take the post, he said, unless he was given the absolute power to hire and fire within his department. He also wanted permission to conduct his private businesses while holding public office. Congress consented. Most delegates in fact were ecstatic. "[N]o man in the united States is better qualified" for tackling the nation's financial woes, one gushed. The assent of "The Financier relieved my Solicitude," another remarked. Most believed that Morris would "give vigor to our military operations," and that his experience and contacts with businessmen in numerous countries would "give great advantages" to his chances of success. Almost everyone in Congress anticipated "the happyest consequences" from his service.[64]

Morris assumed office with a multifaceted plan in mind. First, the cost of waging war was to be divided among the states. Second, the national government was to assume some of each state's indebtedness, while the states set about retiring what remained of their debts. Third, Morris almost immediately quit paying the soldiery, and indeed most of the men who would continue to risk life and limb for their country drew no more pay until they were discharged, two years or more down the road. Morris reasoned that it was sufficient that those who bore arms were housed and fed. Fourth, Morris had a plan for reducing the wastrel practices of the commissary system that had been in place since the creation of the Continental army. His scheme was twofold: virtually remove the states from the logistical process and introduce the contract system of low bidding with the army's suppliers. Financing for Morris's elaborate plan was to come in part from a Bank of America. Once created, it could issue sound notes and provide loans, ensuring that speculators and businessmen—if not the soldiery—had access to adequate revenue. In addition, Congress would use its assumption of state debts as the carrot with which to induce the states to grant it revenue-raising powers and to pass the impost amendment. With ample resources, the national government could eventually provide a stable circulating currency. Morris's immediate object was to restore public credit, which he hoped might not only persuade France and Spain to remain in the war for another year but pry open the vaults in Paris and Madrid, leading to additional loans. Someday, too, Washington and Rochambeau, at last provided with ample resources, could act in concert and break the stalemate.[65]

Congress gave Morris what he wanted. Although numerous congressmen voted against some parts of his plan, his proposals were enacted with the support of mid-Atlantic and Southern delegates. Merchants in the middle states had long since equated the realization of their commercial and financial dreams with the existence of a strong central government, whether an imperial or a national polity. From Franklin to Galloway, from Dickinson to Morris, they yearned for a central government possessed of the means to regulate trade, build a navy capable of protecting American commerce, and field an army that could open the West, with its exquisite opportunities for speculation. Save for the West, few Southerners shared these concerns. The popularity of Morris's scheme in the South was due mostly to the wartime emergency. Southerners saw Morris's plan as the last opportunity to save their states from British occupation and to save the American Revolution.[66]

Virtually everyone in Congress now referred to Morris as "The Financier." Once he had been in office a few months, some privately also called him "The Dictator." He did as he pleased. He had "Congress at [his] mercy," Joseph Reed said, adding that Morris was a man "whose dictates none dare oppose, and from whose decisions lay no appeal." When Colonel Laurens came home from France with a loan in the amount of $500,000 in cash, Morris took it all, using half of it as startup capital for the Bank of North America. During the next twenty-four months, Morris the superintendent borrowed $1,250,000 from Morris the banker. There was a bright side to this turn of events, Reed sardonically remarked. Congress's job had been simplified. The once overworked congressmen were now "at leisure to read dispatches, return thanks, pay and receive compliments, &c." while Morris did all the work and made all the decisions. Arthur Lee, who now sat in Congress, was convinced of Morris's "excessive avarice" and worried that this all-powerful financier was "a most dangerous man to the Liberty of this Country."[67]

Gouverneur Morris and Robert Morris.
Oil on canvas by Charles Willson Peale, 1783.

Some historians have portrayed Morris as the savior of the Revolution. Nothing could be further from the truth. He took office only ten weeks before the siege of Yorktown began. The outcome of that pivotal engagement would have been the same had Morris never become Superintendent of Finance. Richard Buel, the scholar who has most recently studied Morris in depth, concluded that his performance was "uneven at best." Buel also decided that no one knew "the limits of his influence" more acutely than Morris himself. The Financier brought about some overdue reforms, especially the introduction of a creditable currency and a more efficient military supply system. He profited considerably from a booming trade in 1781 with Europe and the Caribbean, for which he was not responsible. The capstone of his program, the impost, might have raised sufficient revenue to change the history of the ensuing decade, but it never went into effect.[68]

At 2 A.M. on October 22, a messenger rapped on the door of Thomas McKean, the president of Congress. Unhappy at being awakened, he nevertheless must have smiled as he read the message sent by Governor

Thomas Sim Lee of Maryland. An hour later, slumbering congressmen came awake with a start when a Philadelphia city watchman, a German immigrant, shattered the breathless hush of night by belting out the substance of Governor Lee's tidings in every street in the capital: "Basht dree o'clock, und Gorn-wal-lis isht da-ken." This was the news that Congress had waited years to hear. The allies had scored a decisive military victory. "God be praised," New Jersey's Elias Boudinot scribbled when he arose. It was a "compleat success," said another. One congressman predicted that the date of the British surrender, October 17, would be forever celebrated throughout America. With the arrival of Washington's dispatches on October 24, which were taken to be the official word, every member of Congress, together with the French minister, assembled at Philadelphia's Lutheran Church for a Thanksgiving service.[69]

The long stalemated war had turned quickly, unexpectedly, in this pivotal year. Since the spring, Washington and Rochambeau had known that the French navy would come north from the Caribbean. Washington inveighed once again for a siege of New York. Rochambeau ostensibly agreed, although he appears to have surreptitiously requested that Admiral François Joseph Paul de Grasse instead bring his fleet to the Chesapeake, as Cornwallis's army was on the loose in Virginia. The French general saw what Washington only slowly glimpsed. Here was the possibility of trapping a British army between the French navy and the allied armies. What ensued was one of the few times in this maddening war that a general officer's plans went according to script.[70]

In mid-August, the allies learned that de Grasse was nearing the Chesapeake. The pincers had begun to close on Cornwallis. The men under Washington and Rochambeau immediately raced south. By the end of September, the British general knew that his situation was hopeless. His seaborne escape route was blocked by the French fleet. His land exit was sealed by the allied armies. Cornwallis put off capitulation for as long as possible, but with disease rampant in the ranks of his army, and his pantry nearly bare, time ran out for the British general in mid-October. He agreed to surrender terms, and under a cerulean sky on a mild autumn day more than 7,000 men under Cornwallis's command laid down their arms. In more than a dozen years of soldiering in two wars, this was the first time that Washington had ever presided over the formal surrender of a foe.

Some American officials thought more hard fighting lay ahead, but all knew instantly that the great fears with which they had lived daily during the past thirty months—the collapse of American will, abandonment by France, an adverse European mediation—had vanished the moment Cornwallis surrendered. By the spring of 1782, word from London arrived that the North ministry had collapsed, succeeded by a government committed to peace negotiations: Such tidings "put a period to the war," one congressman exalted.[71]

The transforming military situation produced additional changes. With the diminution of Britain's threat to the Southern states, many congressmen from the region lost interest in Morris's economic scheme. For instance, Virginia, which earlier had ratified the impost amendment, rescinded its action in the course of 1782. For the time being, the impost scheme had been dealt a fatal blow.[72] Morris knew too that once hostilities ceased—and peace talks opened in Paris in the late summer of 1782— little chance existed of reviving that taxation scheme or of strengthening the national government. After all, it had been the common threat posed by Great Britain that had produced the Union in 1774. With the removal of that menace, as Virginia had already demonstrated, some states were certain to see little further justification for a vibrant national government. Privately—very privately—Morris even prayed the war would go on a bit longer, serving as the lever for enacting his financial program.[73]

Morris made one final attempt at securing his objectives. He told the nation that it could not sustain itself by foreign loans and the sale of western lands. As an alternative, the only alternative, he proposed national head, land, and excise taxes. He and his allies broadcast their alleged belief that Great Britain was not yet ready to agree to peace terms that America could accept. No choice would exist but to continue the war, perhaps for a very long time. But The Financier's machinations were unsuccessful. After Yorktown, a new mood prevailed. Although they were endorsed by a grand committee of thirteen, Congress rejected each of Morris's proposed taxes. Those who sought a stronger national government had once again been foiled.[74]

It is "my warm Wish that you may find a Place in Congress," The Financier wrote to young Alexander Hamilton in August 1782. It is a "Line [of endeavor] more important, as it is more extensive than anything you have undertaken heretofore."[75] Hamilton had just been added to the New York congressional delegation. He arrived in Congress in November 1782 and served until the following July.

Hamilton, who had served in the Continental army from 1776 to 1781, much of the time acting as an aide to General Washington, shared the nationalistic perspective of the field officers who had come to Congress during the great crisis after 1779, and for some of the same reasons. But other factors also shaped his outlook. Hamilton had come to New York in 1772 from St. Croix, where he grew up, making the long voyage alone at age fifteen. As Richard Brookhiser has observed, Hamilton thereafter never "wrote a fond word about the Caribbean," nor did he ever seriously consider returning, even for a visit.[76] The reasons are not difficult to divine. Hamilton had spent his youth in humble circumstances. Worse, given the mores of the times, he was made to bear the stigma of an illegitimate birth. In the early 1750s his mother, Rachel Lavien, ensnared in an unhappy marriage, left her husband and took up with James Hamilton, something of an insouciant Scottish drifter who had temporarily dropped anchor in her neighborhood. He stayed long enough to sire two sons. Alexander, the second child, was born in 1757. Soon thereafter James Hamilton moved off to the Leeward Islands, and though he and Alexander sporadically corresponded during the next forty years, they never again saw one another.

Left alone with two small sons, Rachel operated a small store to make ends meet. She provided a decent living for herself and the boys. The family lived in a modest house and never faced destitution, in part because the boys worked as well. Young Alexander toiled in the store for a time, but in his early teenage years, he gained employment with a New York mercantile firm with an office in Christiansted. For a considerable time it appeared that this work would be his lot for the remainder of his life. He was disconsolate with his maiming obscurity. He wanted more. In one of his first letters, written when he was twelve, Alexander "contemn[ed] the grov'ling and condition of a Clerk or the like, to which my Fortune &c. condemns me." He told a friend that year that he wished a war would erupt. He would join the army and seek upward mobility through soldiering, as had Washington and countless other young men.[77] No war loomed, and when Rachel died later that year, Hamilton, orphaned at age thirteen, appeared to face an even bleaker future. But while his older brother labored as a carpenter and probably spent his life as an artisan in the Caribbean, Alexander came to the attention of benefactors on St. Croix. This facility for making himself known to—and winning the approbation of—powerful men was a skill that he employed on numerous occasions during the next two decades.

In this instance, Hamilton caught the eye of the local Presbyterian minister, the Reverend Hugh Knox, as well as that of his employer, Nicholas Cruger. Each found him to be formidably bright and incredibly industrious. Those traits, in combination with an ambition that knew no bounds, led them to surmise that Hamilton could go places if given half a chance. Knox's parishioners raised money for Hamilton's college education at Princeton, a Presbyterian college in New Jersey, and Cruger provided some additional needed funds. Hamilton sailed alone for the mainland colonies in 1772.

Princeton, it turned out, would not admit him without additional preparatory schooling. Unwilling to delay the start of his college education, Alexander successfully sought admission at Kings College, now Columbia, in Manhattan, and he breezed forward with his studies. During his junior year, at age seventeen, Hamilton engaged in the pamphlet war with the Tory Samuel Seabury, writing two influential tracts in defense of the First Continental Congress. Later in that eventful academic year, the war erupted. Not only was Hamilton committed to the popular cause, but he continued to realize, as he had at age twelve, that bearing arms might advance his career. He dropped out of school to soldier, joining an artillery company and seeing action in the Battle of New York in the late summer of 1776. That autumn he was part of Washington's bedraggled army that retreated across New Jersey. He came under fire once again at Trenton and Princeton.

A few days after those engagements, once the army had gone into winter quarters at Morristown, Washington advertised for an additional aide de camp. Someone recommended Hamilton, who was interviewed. Slight, wispy even, he appeared to be still an adolescent—which in fact he was—but he was glib and earnest, and his quick intelligence impressed those at headquarters, as it had captured the imagination of Knox and Cruger on St. Croix. Hamilton, not quite twenty, got the job and joined Washington's "family" in March 1777.

Hamilton dealt with Washington's correspondence, ran errands, and as he grew older and more experienced, sometimes acted as the commander's emissary in meeting with state and national officials. When he was at headquarters, which was most of the time during a stretch of nearly four years, Hamilton was in Washington's presence on a daily basis. At the end of many days, when the work at last was done, the aides relaxed with the commander, eating snacks, drinking a glass of wine, and talking. Hamilton found much to admire in Washington, but he also said later that he discovered some attributes that he disliked, character traits that he promised to someday divulge to the world, but never got around to, leaving posterity to guess at what he might have intended to reveal. If Hamilton was generally impressed by his commander, Washington was dazzled by his young aide. Hamilton was bright, polished, articulate, and appeared to be well informed about an incredible array of subjects. In many ways he must have resembled Lawrence Washington, the older half brother who had been a role model for young George. In those lively nocturnal discussions, in which Hamilton likely stood out among the aides, Washington listened thoughtfully as this glib young man expounded on numerous topics, especially on the tawdry morality of slavery, political theory, and the American economic malaise. Working as an aide did not mean that Hamilton was exempt from the dangers of the war. He saw action at Brandywine and Germantown in 1777, suffered through the dastardly winter at Valley Forge, and had a horse shot from beneath him at Monmouth in 1778. In 1781 he begged Washington for a field command. The commander obliged by giving him an infantry brigade, which he led in a nighttime assault at Yorktown. It captured an important British redoubt, and Washington subsequently lauded Hamilton for his "firmness and bravery" under fire.[78]

Hamilton was twenty-six when he left the army a few weeks after Yorktown to study law in New York City. Whereas Adams and Jefferson, whose experiences were rather typical, studied law for two years before they began to practice, Hamilton was admitted to the bar after only three months of study. He was a young man in a hurry. He had come a long way in the ten years since boarding the vessel in Christiansted that sailed for the mainland colonies. He had won the admiration of General Washington and was widely and justly acclaimed as a brave veteran and combat hero. He had married a daughter of General Schuyler, one of New York's most powerful figures. Schuyler was merely the latest in a long line of influential men who had come to admire Hamilton in the course of the war. While still a young aide at Washington's headquarters, Hamilton had met congressmen Gouverneur Morris and Robert Livingston. They were so impressed with this precocious young soldier that they invited him to regularly communicate his views about military and political affairs. They and others brought him to the attention of The Financier, who in 1782 beseeched Hamilton to come to Congress.[79]

Morris was intrigued with this young man not just because of his skills but because of his nationalist point of view. As he had not grown up in a mainland colony, Hamilton was not attached to any state. Jefferson's lifelong habit of referring to "my country, Virginia," would have made no sense to Hamilton. He had entered public affairs in 1775 as a proponent of American rights, not the liberties of New Yorkers. He had fought for American independence, dreaming all along of the day when a strong United States would exist. Like others who saw the American Revolution from the perspective of the front lines, he saw the fatal weaknesses of a decentralized polity. Early on he cried out for a strong national government that could win the war and secure the vital interests of the United States. While still with Washington, his reputation as a nationalist and economist grew, and although only twenty-four years of age when Congress created the Department of Finance, some congressmen contemplated nominating Hamilton to be its first Superintendent, though Morris was named instead.[80]

Hamilton's plans had matured by the desperate summer of 1781. He explained them to whomever would listen, and 100 days before the commencement of the siege of Yorktown he began to publish them in the first of six articles entitled *The Continentalist*. He stated his theme in the initial paragraphs. Unless the "WANT OF POWER IN CONGRESS" was corrected, the war could not be prosecuted with vigor, the economic ills could not be corrected, peace and security in the postwar world could not be achieved, and the Union could not be preserved. Reform the system now, he went on, or "the affairs of America MAY CEASE TO BE OF PRIMARY IMPORTANCE." Many solutions had been proffered, but only one was expedient, he wrote. The Articles of Confederation must be amended to "ENLARGE THE POWERS OF CONGRESS." At issue was whether the inhabitants of America would be a "CONQUERED PEOPLE" or a "HAPPY PEOPLE."[81]

In the final *Continentalist* essay, published on July 4, 1782, just as Morris's report advocating national taxes and greater congressional powers was submitted, Hamilton outlined his vision of "a great Federal Republic." He imagined a political system for America that bore a striking resemblance to parts of the scheme that Galloway had recommended to the First Continental Congress eight years earlier. The national government would "neither be independent nor too much dependent" on the states. Power would be shared. However, Congress would have specific powers, and they would be suitable for pursuing the "common interest" of the Northern and Southern states and ample for making the United States "tranquil and prosperous at home, respectable abroad." Once attained, "Happy America!" Hamilton closed, for then, and only then, could the "jarring, jealous and perverse" meanderings of thirteen states marching in thirteen directions be terminated.[82]

By the time he took his seat in Congress, Hamilton's dreams and Morris's schemes had been dashed by the promising military situation and the peace talks in Paris. Hamilton brooded over what he called "the fatal opposition to Continental views." Unless the national government was made sufficiently strong to override the "prejudices in the particular states," he feared that the Union would not long survive. Unless the national government possessed the strength to stabilize the national financial plight, he was anxious that chaos might ensue. Unless the national government had the ability to provide for national security, he believed that true independence would remain elusive. However, as 1782 wound down, and peace appeared to be at hand, Hamilton saw no prospect for augmenting national powers. The nationalists, he said, could achieve their ends only if some new national crisis erupted. "Necessity alone can work a reform," he told George Washington.[83]

8

1783–1787

"The Present Paroxysm of Our Affairs"

On August 9, 1782, in the dismaying swelter of a late summer afternoon, word reached Philadelphia that peace negotiations had begun in Paris between the United States and Great Britain.[1] One year had passed, almost to the day, since Washington and Rochambeau had set out with their armies for Yorktown.

Although hostilities yet raged on the high seas, no major military actions had occurred since Cornwallis's surrender, and none were anticipated, as London had not replaced the army it lost. Yet few in Congress believed that peace was imminent. Not only was America precluded by the terms of its alliance with France from signing a separate peace, but many feared that Great Britain's "thirst for war" had not been slaked. Many suspected that Britain hoped to "chicane and deceive" the United States into passivity, then launch another campaign. When word of a major British naval victory over France arrived late in September, virtually every congressman assumed that London would "now draw the negotiations into length with a hope of further advantages during the campaign as would enable her to rise in her demands."[2]

In November, Congress learned that the British had sent a full team of negotiators to Paris. Nevertheless, most congressmen, having experienced repeated disappointments in this long war, remained wary. "Bets run high & spirits low alternately," said one delegate. Anxious weeks passed with no word. Suddenly, early in February 1783, auspicious tidings abounded. First, unofficial news arrived from the West Indies that a peace accord had been signed. Next, toward the middle of the month, an express from New York brought a report that the Crown had informed Parliament that a peace treaty with the United States had been signed.

American Commissioners at the Preliminary Peace Negotiations with Great Britain.
Unfinished painting by Benjamin West, about 1783.

Hope quickened. The "appearances of peace are rather encouraging than otherways," a New Englander reported home. Some, like Pennsylvania's John Montgomery, gushed that "Amirrica will be free. . . . Poor torris [Tories] must now hang their heads. The day is now Come when the Sun will Raise on Amirrica never to set. I look forward to the happy days that our Children will see."[3]

That same day, Congressman Alexander Hamilton wrote a letter to General Washington. Curiously, this former soldier, who had risked everything for so long, betrayed no joy at the happy tidings reverberating through Philadelphia. After reiterating the details of the financial crisis, he observed that if a way was not found to "restore public credit and supply the future wants of [the national] government" before the end of the war, all hope of strengthening the United States government would be lost. What he next told General Washington was perplexing. But if "properly directed," the Continental army could yet assist in the realization of the hopes of all those who had come to appreciate the necessity for a powerful national government.[4]

Hamilton's puzzling missive grew out of a dark, impenetrable conspiracy that had been in motion since the demise of the impost amendment and the inception of the peace talks in Paris. With war's end and demobilization on the horizon, no group displayed a greater sense of urgency than the army's officers.[5] Neither they nor the enlisted men had been paid for months, and once the war ended it was problematical whether they ever would receive their back pay from bankrupt states or an impotent national government. It seemed equally unlikely that the officers would receive the lifetime half-pay pension that Congress had promised in 1780. In December 1782 the officers encamped at Newburgh, New York, agreed to petition Congress for their benefits. Just after Christmas, Major General Alexander McDougall, accompanied by two colonels, brought the remonstrance to Philadelphia.

Many officers, the petition correctly observed, had grown poor, or at least had missed out on the opportunity to grow rich, as a result of years of service. Some had lost their youth in America's cause. Many had forfeited their health. All were "worn down and exhausted" by the conditions they had endured. It was only "honorable and just," they asserted, that the commitments made to them by America's public officials be kept. But the petition also pulsated with a barely concealed threat. Should Congress fail to do justice to the army, it could result in "fatal effects."[6]

Some congressmen knew in advance that the officers' petition had been in gestation. General Henry Knox and Secretary of War Benjamin Lincoln, who were in on the secret, had been in consultation with friends in Congress for weeks. However, most congressmen were startled by the supplication, which arrived just hours after word reached Philadelphia that Virginia had repudiated its approval of the impost, an action that all knew meant the death of the amendment.

It is not too much to imagine that Hamilton, if not the leading conspirator in Congress, was deeply involved in a cabal to utilize a bitter army to leverage Congress into reenacting the impost and to frighten the states into ratifying the amendment. Hamilton wrote the report of the committee that Congress created to consider the petition, and on January 25, Congress agreed to seek adequate powers to "obtain . . . substantial funds" for "the object of funding the whole debt of the United States."[7]

By now, the most savvy congressmen had deduced what was afoot. On January 29 Arthur Lee told Samuel Adams that "Every Engine is at work here" to increase the power of the national government. The "terror of a mutinying Army is playd off with considerable efficacy," he wrote, adding that what the conspirators were doing was "neither wise nor safe." At the very least, he went on, it amounted to "subverting the Revolution" that had been waged against centralized authority.[8] A sufficient number agreed with Lee to defeat a bill that would have commuted the lifetime half-pay pension to a full-pay pension for five years following the war.

Stymied for the moment, the conspirators in Congress sent one of McDougall's colonels back to Newburgh to stir the pot. The cabal apparently wanted either another, more strongly worded petition or a mutinous act that aimed to wrest control of the army from Washington's more moderate hands. The latter seems to have been their most likely hope, although the plotters did not wish for a successful mutiny, and they certainly harbored no hope that Washington might be overthrown. Indeed, Hamilton's remarkable and cryptic letter to Washington was written to alert him to the danger.

Hamilton was circumspect, but he knew that Washington could decode the meaning of his message by talking with Knox and others. "Your Excellency's influence" must be employed to derail the mutineers and "bring order, perhaps even good, out of confusion," he wrote. The aim of the plotters, Hamilton all but said, was for Congress to be so frightened by the army's extremists that it would consent to the demands of the "confidential and prudent" officers, led by General Washington, who had thwarted the hotheads. Furthermore, by saving the "public tranquility," Washington would be applauded for having "preserve[d] the confidence of the army without losing that of the people." In other words, should Washington cooperate, his already legendary stature with the people would only grow.[9]

Washington responded with a letter of effusive gratitude at having gained the "foreknowledge" that he was "upon the brink of a precipice ... [without being] aware of his danger." He had spent "many contemplative hours" trying to sort out his conflicting responsibilities "as Citizen and Soldier," choosing how to balance his yearning to resolve the "sufferings of a complaining army" with his wistful longing to compel the states and national government to "promote the public weal." Now, he seemed to say, he had resolved his predicament by agreeing to play out the script that Hamilton had prepared for him. The success of the American Revolution was at stake, he concluded, "for it is clearly my opinion, unless Congress have powers competent to all *general* purposes, that the distresses we have encountered, the expences we have incurred, and the blood we have spilt in the course of an Eight years war, will avail us nothing."

Thereafter events moved quickly. In early March, the conspirators in Congress laid the groundwork by circulating dark rumors that Washington was losing control and that restless, menacing sorts in the army might attempt a coup d'état. Robert Morris, The Financier, simultaneously declared his intention to resign—he would not be a "minister of injustice," he vaingloriously declared—if Congress was not empowered to raise revenue. More vaguely, but no less ominously, he said that Congress might have to ignore the states and simply levy taxes, using its implied powers under the Articles of Confederation.[10] Forty-eight hours after Morris spoke, an unsigned declaration circulated through the army camp on the Hudson. It is too much to assume that the timing was coincidental. The Newburgh Address, as it would be called, reprised the complaints of the petition presented to Congress seventy-five days earlier. But it went much further. It denounced Washington, whose "moderation and ... forbearance" sentenced the officers to live out "the miserable remnant" of their lives in the "vile mire" of poverty. It was contemptuous of the citizenry for having betrayed the army that had won for them "the chair of independency." Finally, it proposed that if the commutation scheme was not funded, Congress would be confronted with an ultimatum: Should the war continue, the soldiery would disband; should there be peace, the soldiery would refuse to demobilize.[11]

The authors of the Newburgh Address summoned all officers to a meeting the next day. Washington promptly preempted this threat by issuing general orders for a meeting of all officers at noon, March 15, five days hence. General Gates was to preside. The commander implied that he would not be present.[12] Throughout the week menacing rumors spread through the camp, but no action was taken.

Late in the morning on that clear, cold Saturday in mid-March, the officers gathered in the Temple of Honor, a facility so recently constructed that the smell of freshly cut wood permeated the hall. Plays, social gatherings, and worship services were ordinarily conducted here, but this day was different. A supercharged tension permeated the atmosphere as Gates, precisely at noon, called the meeting to order. Conversations ceased. Men scurried to their seats. An anxious hush fell over the room. But just as Gates was ready to proceed, a side door opened and Washington entered. Startled, Gates stepped aside as Washington, looking "sensibly agitated," strode to a lectern mounted on a low stage.[13] Never comfortable as a public speaker, Washington nervously unfolded a sheath of papers, took a deep breath, and began to read a speech that he had drafted in recent days. He excoriated the Newburgh Address, calling it an "insidious" and "shocking" document that betrayed both the army and the nation. It would "open the flood-gates of civil discord" and "deluge our rising empire in blood," he cautioned. He reminded the officers that Congress had "a variety of different interests to reconcile," and like any legislative body it acted slowly. At the close of his prepared speech,

Washington pledged to lobby Congress "in the most unequivocal manner" on behalf of commutation.[14]

Having reached the end of his text, Washington intuitively sensed that his prepared text had been insufficient to sway his audience. Something else was needed. Many who had observed Washington over the years thought his talents as a thespian were unsurpassed, and he now marshaled every skill in his repertory.[15] Pausing, he slowly extracted a letter from his inside coat pocket, remarking that it was a missive from a Virginia congressman. He unfolded the letter carefully, deliberately, then began to read. He stumbled aimlessly through its opening sentences. Washington paused again. He fumbled in his pocket once more, this time producing a pair of spectacles. The officers were taken aback. Few had ever seen their robust leader wearing glasses. Apologizing, Washington explained: "Gentlemen, you will permit me to put on my spectacles, for I have not only grown gray but almost blind in the service of my country."[16] Washington's contrived gesture immediately altered the mood in the Temple of Honor. Many officers, flintlike men who had spent the last several years on the rough side of life, broke down and wept openly.

When Washington had read the meaningless letter, he left the hall. His magisterial performance had won numerous converts, who now joined with those who had never wished to "sully the glory" won by the Continental army by endorsing the address. An overwhelming majority rapidly adopted a resolution that expressed the army's "unshaken confidence" in Congress. Yet this portentous conspiracy had worked to perfection. Washington had played by the script. He had thwarted what appeared to be a mutinous cabal within the army, and for his trouble his prestige ascended to new heights. Congress immediately voted for the commutation plan it had rejected eight weeks earlier, agreed to compensate the soldiery for three unpaid months, and in April adopted a new impost amendment and sent it to the states for ratification.[17] And all this was achieved after March 12, the day that Congress received official word that the representatives of the United States and Great Britain had signed a peace treaty.

"They acknowledge the Independence of the States," a Delaware congressman sighed as he read the terms of the treaty. "Thus drops the Curtain upon this mighty Trajedy," reported John Adams, who had been sent to Paris more than three years earlier as America's sole peace commissioner.[18]

However, when the peace talks commenced, Adams no longer was Congress's only peace envoy. Five months before Yorktown, the French foreign minister, Vergennes, had launched a campaign to have Adams removed—he sought a more malleable individual, preferably Franklin—and to persuade Congress to place his successor under greater French control. In perhaps its most shameful act, Congress surrendered to its ally, as it had never done to its mother country. In June 1781, it stripped Adams of his sole responsibility by adding Franklin, Jefferson, John Jay, and Henry Laurens to the peace commission, and instructed its envoys "to govern yourselves by [France's] advice and opinion."[19]

Congress's timorous stance was of no consequence. America's three envoys—Jefferson never sailed and Laurens was captured while crossing the Atlantic—were made of sterner stuff than those in Congress. Adams and Jay in particular understood that France longed to keep its ally weak and dependent. They knew that Vergennes supported American independence, but they also suspected that he wanted little else for the new nation. If enfeebled, and surrounded by British-held Canada, Florida, and the trans-Appalachian West, the United States of necessity would be a French client state. America's envoys sought much more. They longed for true American independence, for the new nation to be permitted to pursue its destiny without foreign hindrance. The breakthrough in the talks, which had proceeded sporadically through the spring and summer, came in September 1782 when the Americans hinted that they were willing to conclude a separate peace. London, understanding that such a turn of events would compel France to accept less favorable terms, or fight on alone, moved resolutely to wrap up negotiations. On the last day of November, under leaden skies, the United States diplomats signed a separate preliminary peace treaty in the Hotel Muscovite in Paris.[20]

Congress was delighted with the accord. The pact "contain[s] everything we ought to wish," said one delegate, while another thought the terms "Equal to the most Sanguine Expectation." Actually, the treaty achieved far more than Congress had sought in its peace ultimata in 1779. American territory would stretch to the Mississippi River, access to the Newfoundland fisheries was won, and the northern boundary was set near the line that Congress had wanted. Moreover, British troops were to evacuate American soil and, by sleight of hand, neither the national government nor the states were obligated to compensate the Loyalists. America's envoys made concessions as well. Not only were debts incurred prior to 1775 to be paid, but America's southern boundary, though inexact, was unlikely to extend below the 31st parallel.[21]

When the peace preliminaries had been approved in the respective capitals, and accords had been worked out by all the belligerents, the emissaries gathered again in Paris to negotiate the definitive treaty. No substantive changes occurred. The Treaty of Paris was signed on September 3, 1783, two days short of the ninth anniversary of the convening of the First Continental Congress at Carpenter's Hall.

Peace did not break out a moment too soon. In May, Washington furloughed most of his troops, after giving them three-months pay in worthless "final settlement" certificates, or "Morris notes," as many enlisted men contemptuously called them. Washington hoped these men would scatter to their homes throughout America, never to reassemble. It was better this way, he explained, for if the soldiery remained together "enraged, complaining of injustice," they might "perpetuate enormities." But not all who had borne arms to win independence vanished quietly. In June, a large group of acrimonious and well-armed Pennsylvania veterans surrounded the State House in Philadelphia and demanded their back pay. They departed only when placated with promises that Congress would set things right.[22] A few weeks later, a company-sized contingent of Pennsylvania soldiers from Lancaster arrived and made similar demands. This time Congress fled. Chased from Philadelphia by British regulars in 1775, and again in 1777, Congress was run out of town by eighty anxious and tetchy Continentals from the Pennsylvania hinterland. As if to keep its whereabouts secret, Congress stayed on the move, meeting in Princeton, then Trenton, and finally Annapolis during the last six months of 1783.[23]

Meanwhile, most soldiers went home. Many were compelled to beg for handouts during their journey, and others stopped and worked at odd jobs to earn cash that might get them home. While these veterans, like mendicants, struggled to return to their families, Washington traveled to upstate New York in search of land to purchase, and the officers at Newburgh created the Society of Cincinnati, an elite organization for officers and their descendants, from which the enlisted men were barred. It was a shameful end to a war that had begun when leaders urged the citizenry "to arms, to arms," and exhorted them to sacrifice and fight like "Freemen contending for Liberty."[24]

In December, when the last British troops in New York boarded transports that would take them from the United States, Washington, with the diminutive army that remained, reentered the city that had been lost seven years earlier. He was toasted at one ceremony after another in Manhattan, and again in Philadelphia and Baltimore, which he passed through en route home. Late in the month he made one final stop, in Annapolis, where the peripatetic Congress was meeting. The legislators honored Washington at a dinner so stately that "not a soul got drunk," according to one congressman. In a brief ceremony at noon on December 23, Washington surrendered the power that Congress had bestowed on him. It was proper, the general said, that he step down now that the United States was a sovereign and "respectable Nation." Then: "I retire from the great theater of Action."[25]

It was a remarkable act, and together with his triumph at Yorktown and his action in squelching the Newburgh conspiracy, it solidified Washington's position. The surrender of power "excites the astonishment and admiration" of his countrymen, the painter John Trumbull soon thereafter remarked, for "'Tis a Conduct so novel." George III observed that Washington's novel forfeiture of power made him "the greatest man in the world."[26]

Only one congressman who witnessed the resignation ceremony had sat in Congress on that sunny June morning in 1775 when Washington had been chosen to command the Continental army. That congressman, Thomas Mifflin of Pennsylvania, left Congress for good in May 1784. With the end of the war it sometimes was difficult to get those who were elected to attend. The Treaty of Paris, for example, gathered dust for seven long weeks, until Congress at last mustered a quorum and ratified the accord just prior to the expiration of the time limit for its approval. Sparse attendance characterized every congressional session between 1784 and 1787. Only rarely were more than thirty delegates, about half the elected membership, in their seats. It was not uncommon for sessions to be scrapped for lack of a quorum or for votes on substantive matters— which required the approval of nine states—to be postponed until additional delegations were present. The problem worsened with each year, until by the autumn of 1786, when it met in New York, Congress was able to conduct business only about 15 percent of the time.[27]

Numerous factors contributed to this situation. Whereas most state assemblies met for no longer than six to eight weeks annually, Congress sat throughout the year, longer than most delegates wished to be separated from their families, and a practice that Washington and Jefferson, to no avail, criticized as early as 1784.[28] In addition, delegates from the larger states, who were frustrated by the ability of tiny provinces to stymie congressional action, often were reluctant to attend a body that they saw as only a useless debating society. For many, too, the pulsing sense of urgency that had prevailed since Congress's inception in 1774 waned quickly after Yorktown.[29] Political activists, a breed that craves influence, are lured to the fountains where power flows. No one imagined that the United States Congress fell into that category. It was no coincidence that during these years Hamilton, Madison, and Samuel Adams sat in state assemblies, Jefferson and John Adams served abroad as diplomats, Jay acted as Secretary of Foreign Affairs and Knox as Secretary of War,

Hancock, John Rutledge, and Benjamin Harrison were state governors, Gouverneur Morris and Robert Morris pursued business enterprises, and Washington eschewed public life altogether.

Many despaired that the United States had "but the shadow of a government." One disgusted congressman carped in the spring of 1786 that "Congress have done very little. . . . [I]ndeed with so few States [present], it is out of their power to do any thing of material consequence." The conviction grew in some circles that the "public business in consequence is suffering extreamly." The United States, a New Jersey congressman charged, was "supinely inattentive" to its "Dangerous Situation." Like "a flock of Sheep [on] their way to a slaughter Pen," he said, the nation was headed toward ruin.[30]

These dark and pessimistic views were heightened by the fate of the impost amendment that Congress had adopted and sent to the states immediately after the Newburgh alarm. Once again, the amendment came close to being ratified. Progress was slow, but after thirty-six months every state save for one had acted favorably. Even habitually recalcitrant Rhode Island approved the proposed amendment, as did Georgia, which had never acted in 1782. No one factor was responsible for these favorable votes. General Washington's public endorsement helped sway the Virginia assembly, but that state and others also longed for federal help in retiring their heavy burden of debt brought on by the war. So considerable was the debt in some states that it was a struggle even to retire the annual interest charges. In some states, approval was garnered after Congress disseminated the repeated reports of John Adams, the United States minister to Great Britain, that the establishment of public credit was crucial to opening commerce with the former parent state. All this nearly brought about the unanimous approval of the impost, but in 1785 New York rejected the amendment. At one time or another in the 1780s, every state ratified an impost agreement, but New York's rejection in the refulgent midst of peace was the final nail in the coffin of these initiatives. The impost was dead and, with remittances lagging from the states, the United States was unable to service its foreign debt.[31]

Some powerful interests suffered from an inefficacious national government, but not everyone was ill-served by the conditions that prevailed in the immediate postwar period. Newspapers rang out with poems and essays that held forth great expectations for the new nation, described by Joel Barlowe in his epic, *The Vision of Columbus* (1787), as a "blest land." To many, the future of the United States appeared bright and unclouded. It was a republican nation, independent of faraway Europe, with its monarchies and great armies and recurrent wars. It was unhindered by domestic princes or an entrenched aristocracy. Hardly a day passed that immigrants from the Old World did not debouch onto America's shores, eager to begin life anew in the new nation. Up to 20,000 entered Pennsylvania alone in the initial half dozen years of peace, and at least as many disembarked elsewhere.[32]

The United States possessed a vast new domain beyond the mountains. Settlers had not crossed the Appalachians at the time of the Boston Massacre in 1770, but twenty years later nearly 110,000 land-hungry immigrants were scratching out a living in those fertile regions. Nor was trans-Appalachia the only frontier magnet. Nearly 100,000 people moved from the four New England states in the 1780s, mostly to newly opened tracts in New York and Vermont. South Carolinians flooded into the Georgia backcountry, swelling that state's population by 50 percent in five years. Pennsylvanians and Virginians hurried beyond the head of the Ohio River, into the region that young Washington had fought to win thirty years earlier.[33] Although life in the hinterland was hard and often dangerous, thousands exuberantly moved in quest of land they otherwise could never hope to own, chasing the dream that life as a frontier property owner would be better than that which awaited a tenant or landless farmer, or a mechanic or unskilled laborer, in the crowded East, or in Europe.

Unprecedented opportunities also appeared within reach of the citizenry that remained in the East. Up to 100,000 Loyalists chose exile in the course of the Revolution, creating vacancies in the public and professional offices they vacated, and forfeiting the land and businesses they had owned. For many, life had never been better. New schools abounded. Not only did several states create public universities in the 1780s, but numerous private academies opened, including church-related institutions that sprang up like spring flowers. Every Southern state broke the perdurable hold of the established Anglican Church, and some passed laws providing for liberty of conscience. Philadelphia pioneered free smallpox inoculations for the needy. Several states reformed their criminal codes, reducing the number of capital crimes and eliminating most of the hideous medieval punishments that had been brought to America in the seventeenth century. New England states and Pennsylvania constructed roads that linked east and west, and elsewhere projects were begun to construct canals that were to tie the tidewater to the deep backcountry.[34]

A brief but serious commercial depression ushered in peace, provoking considerable hardship, especially in the Northern urban entrepots. However, the pinch was brief and few entrepreneurs were ruined. By 1786 prosperity was returning. Indeed, the average value of imports from

Great Britain in the half dozen years after the Treaty of Paris was almost identical to that of the last half dozen years before hostilities commenced. Although American exports to Britain suffered badly, these losses were at least partially supplanted by trade with France, Holland, and Portugal, as well as China, which some New England merchants were searching out. The tonnage that cleared the harbors of Boston, Philadelphia, and New York in 1788 exceeded the traffic in each of those ports in 1772, a time of prosperity prior to the Tea Act crisis.[35]

Many Americans testified to the happy conditions. Franklin returned home in 1785 to discover that the copious reports in British newspapers about America's woes were "all Fictions, more English Wishes, not American Realities. . . . I never saw greater and more indubitable marks of Public Prosperity in any Country," he rejoiced. Property values were climbing, farmers flourished, commerce boomed, and "Working people have plenty of employ and high pay for their labour," he added. Congress's secretary, Charles Thomson, not only testified about his countrymen's happiness but concluded that no other peoples on earth were "rising into consequence with more rapid strides." Although the merchants complained, he added, the common folk of New York, where Congress was meeting, were "well clad, well fed and well housed." Abigail Adams reported that all who sought employment in Boston found it. General Washington told Europeans that America was a bustling, energetic place. Roads and bridges were under construction, rivers were being improved, farms were back in operation, and governments were functioning smoothly. "In short," he said, "the foundation of a great Empire is laid."[36]

Yet however happy and optimistic the great majority of the people appear to have been, some powerful interests were deeply troubled. Major creditors who had provided wartime supplies anguished over the failure of state governments to meet their financial obligations. Entrepreneurs seethed as fortunes were lost because the states could not cope with British commercial discrimination. Merchants in smaller port cities, such as Providence, angrily charged that they suffered from high state duties imposed by large neighboring provinces. Some speculators railed at the economic chaos that resulted from interstate rivalries, especially when a smaller state, such as Connecticut, fell victim in a contest with a powerful neighbor, such as New York. By 1785 newspaper essays and petition campaigns in favor of national trade policies were commonplace. The end they sought was a vigorous, expanding, interdependent continental economy. To some, in fact, the primary purpose of a national union was to facilitate a continental marketplace that could operate free of obstruction by contrived, and unnecessary, provincial entities.[37]

Nor was the discontent limited to economic concerns. Despite the rosy picture he painted for European acquaintances, Washington spoke for many American nationalists when he expressed dismay at the national enervation and what he believed was the erosion of national pride. He knew that the war had nearly been lost, in large measure due to the impotence of the national government, and he feared that the nation might not be so fortunate during the next emergency. As early as June 1783, six months before he resigned as commander of the Continental army, Washington had spoken with deep sincerity of "the present Crisis." The Union could not long endure, he had said, under a central government that lacked the strength to compel foreign governments to acknowledge American independence. In time, he cautioned, steps would have to be taken "to give such a tone to our Federal Government, as will enable it to answer the ends of its institution." Otherwise, America once again would "become the sport of European politics." Following his retirement, Washington from time to time spoke privately of being "mortified" by what he called the "shameful & disgusting" "scurge" of national impotence. "No Morn ever dawned more favourable than ours did—and no day was ever more clouded than the present," he confided to friends.[38]

Many nationalists also looked with disgust on a Congress that not only was habitually itinerant and plagued by absenteeism but that, in their estimation, overflowed with mediocrities. Few "men of enlarged minds and conciliating Tempers" any longer sat in Congress, one critic alleged. Even had Congress been filled with distinguished men, another lamented, it did not possess the power to "coin a copper." It was shattering for those like Washington, who had sacrificed for years so that the United States might become "a respectable Nation," to know that for want of a reputable government the great powers in Europe scorned and ridiculed the enfeebled United States.[39]

Others, who often shared the dismay of the nationalists, were no less discomforted by the changes unleashed by the American Revolution. All had known that the break with Great Britain would be a leap in the dark, and all had known as well that the eventual landing might be made on treacherous ground. Nevertheless, all had leapt but those timorous souls who had chosen loyalty to Britain. Some who leapt—perhaps the overwhelming majority, for all we know—had yearned for radical change, wishing from the outset to make the world over, as Paine had dreamed. But some Revolutionaries never aspired to radical domestic change. They had sought to free America from foreign dependence, to become citizens, not subjects, and to throw open the window of opportunity for personal fulfillment, a casement which they knew could never be fully jimmied up so long as they remained colonials. They expected and welcomed some changes in America's political system, but there was much about life in pre-Revolutionary America that they liked and yearned to preserve.

These conservative revolutionaries had been startled by the unforeseen vicissitudes of the long struggle that ensued after 1775. When Congress adopted the Declaration on the Necessity of Taking Up Arms, no one had imagined the war would last for eight years. Nor did anyone expect that over 100,000 men—most from the lower social orders, including approximately 5,000 African Americans, and even many slaves—would serve in the Continental army. No one could have known that thousands more would bear arms, some repeatedly, in militia units, or that many would serve in America's nascent navy or ship out on risky privateering ventures. No one foresaw that countless women on the home front would spend incalculable hours making bullets and clothing for the soldiers.[40] No one imagined the staggering burden that would fall on America's taxpayers. No one anticipated the economic changes brought on by the war and the despair and disillusionment that would result as the public debt rose and states teetered on the edge of bankruptcy, making it impossible to redeem claims for goods and services rendered during hostilities.

Some were shocked to discover how substantively the war and Revolution transformed some citizens. Few in 1776 had fully understood how service in a citizen's army, or even nonmartial sacrifice to further the war effort, would cause many to expect greater rights in the new world they had helped to fashion. Not everyone foresaw that the florid rhetoric of natural rights and egalitarianism, and the grandiloquent declamations about resisting the British plot to "enslave" Americans, would lead some to rethink existing belief systems about their rights and their society. Few grasped that a social revolution would accompany political independence. Despite the warnings of Tories that "a people does not reform with moderation," or that excesses would go hand in hand with liberty, or that "the Demon of Anarchy" and "sons of Darkness" would stalk the land after America wrenched free of Britain's restraining hand, many revolutionaries were in midstream before they realized what was occurring.[41] Connecticut's Oliver Wolcott, who had signed the Declaration of Independence, was typical. It was deep in the war before he grasped that "the natural consequence of any great revolution in government is to produce a bold and independent manner of thinking." What is more, he added dolefully, it had come to pass that there was "hardly a peasant who does not arrogate to himself a right to be informed and decide the most important secrets of government."[42]

At war's end some conservatives were uneasy—more troubled by the future, they said, than they ever had been by the prospect of defeat by the British. In due course many began to recite the mantra that theirs was a "critical period," a chant they uttered with such wearying frequency that for some it grew into a self-fulfilling prophecy.[43] For those who had wished for independence with little social upheaval, the American Revolution had bewilderingly "turned the world upside down," as one distraught former rebel remarked. Another ruefully meditated that the "people have turned against their teachers the doctrines which were inculcated in order to effect the late revolution." The more conservative former Revolutionaries were horrified when some states relaxed their suffrage qualifications, but it was the emergence of new men in politics after 1776 that aroused the greatest concern, even fear. Men who once would never have been elected to a local office now held seats in their state legislature, and others who earlier might have been a backbencher in a colonial assembly now sat in Congress. The reaction of Thomas Mann Randolph of Tuckahoe, the scion of an old and powerful family in colonial Virginia, was typical of many conservatives. He was mortified that "the spirit of independency was converted into equality, and everyone who bore arms esteemed themselves upon a footing with his neighbor." Worse, Randolph lamented, "each of these men conceives himself, in every respect, my equal."[44]

Abraham Yates of New York typified those who seized the opportunities opened by the American Revolution. Born in 1724 to a middling farm family, Yates was apprenticed in adolescence as a cordwainer. When he came of age, and when he was not making shoes, the ambitious and industrious Yates became a self-taught surveyor and lawyer. At age thirty, and at almost the same moment in 1754 that Franklin alighted from his Hudson River ship for the Albany Conference on colonial defense, Yates became both the sheriff of Albany and a member of its city council. Seven years later he was elected to the New York assembly. During all these years before independence, Yates primarily served the powerful and aristocratic Livingston clan, evicting tenants from their vast landed empire in the Hudson Valley and defending their interests on assembly roll calls. But Yates was transmogrified by the American Revolution. A member of the colony's provincial congress in 1776, he chaired the committee that wrote the state's first constitution and pushed for the democratization of New York. He urged annual elections, the popular election of traditionally appointed offices, and the secret ballot. He sought to weaken executive authority, stripping the governor of a veto and truncating his customary appointive powers. He pushed for an uncultivated land tax that would fall most heavily on the greatest landowning families, fought the conservatives to confiscate Loyalist properties, and advocated that the land taken from the Tories be redistributed on the basis of need.

Before the Revolution, Yates had risen by grasping the coattails of powerful elite figures. His ceiling had been the lower house of the assembly. The war changed things, opening the doors to greater mobility. Sycophancy was no longer essential for an ambitious and talented man. Yates catapulted into the upper house of the New York legislature. In 1787 he was elected to Congress, where he served with James Madison, among others. In the 1780s he resisted the nationalists' calls to augment national powers. He opposed the impost, stressed that Congress had no power under the Articles to collect taxes in the states, and denied that national treaties were the law of the land. Steadfastly, Yates advocated a policy of loose money and warned of the nationalist plans to overturn the Articles of Confederation and strip the states of sovereignty.[45]

In some ways Yates resembled the most esteemed Founders of the nation. Like John Adams, he hailed from a humble farm family. Like Washington, he was a self-educated surveyor who sought prominence and material comforts through land speculation. Like Hamilton, he turned to the law, opening a practice after minimal study. But Yates was different. Not only was he uneducated and devoid of the gentlemanly sheen—his spelling reflected his lack of schooling, as "suspicious" was rendered "suspitious," "weight" became "waith," and "whether" was spelled "wether"—but he embraced a more radical politics.[46] To be an arriviste was not uncommon, but his advocacy of democratization ruined him in the eyes of many conservative revolutionaries. Yates was vilified as belonging to the "antifederal Peasants" who resisted the nationalists' objectives, lumped among those disdained as "little folks," branded a demagogue, called an "old booby" by the Livingstons, and limned by Philip Schuyler as the "late cobbler of laws and old shoes." Hamilton sarcastically claimed that Yates's "pertinacity" was exceeded only by his "ignorance and perverseness."[47] To many he was pertinacious, the very type that caused Colonel Randolph to squirm at the thought that such a man would deem himself the equal of old-line wealth and authority. And, indeed, after 1776 Yates unequivocally believed himself the equal of every man. With relish, he left instructions that his tombstone was to be inscribed that he was a friend to "the equal Rights of Man / And the essential interests of his country."[48]

However, it was neither new men such as Abraham Yates nor a pending social revolution that brought to a head the great crisis of the Union in 1786–87. It was a gathering unwillingness among powerful forces to remain any longer under a national government that was incapable of fulfilling their interests. In the Northern states the emergency exploded out of repeated frustration over commercial woes and a simmering resentment that potential fortunes were being lost. Simultaneously, in the heat and stillness of summer below the Potomac, fear and anger abounded that the Articles of Confederation unmistakably, and unfairly, relegated the South into a sectional minority without adequate safeguards for the protection of its vital interests.

The North's commercial problems were not new. They had become apparent in the final days of the war. Shortly before the definitive peace treaty was signed in September 1783, the Privy Council in London promulgated Orders in Council which signaled that the United States would be treated as a foreign nation. Britain's colonial ports in the West Indies were closed to any vessel flying the American flag. Imports of tobacco and naval stores, chiefly Southern commodities, were permitted through English ports, but only in ships owned by British subjects. Although New England and Middle Atlantic merchants found other markets, the loss of Caribbean customers, together with the demise of the carrying trade to England, was a heavy blow in the maritime states. It was as if London had erected an invisible shield that foiled merchants in quest of vast fortunes. As trade languished, collateral industries, among them fishing, whaling, and shipbuilding, suffered egregiously. Many urban mechanics faced austerity, and throngs of unskilled workers were confronted with frightening want and uncertainty. It must have seemed to many embittered Northerners that London remained capable of wreaking havoc in their lives, as had been true before independence.

With peace, Congress dispatched Jefferson to Europe to act in concert with Franklin and John Adams in seeking to conclude a reciprocal commercial treaty with London. The three envoys made no headway. Nor did Adams, following his appointment as United States minister to the Court of St. James in 1785. Public opinion in the former mother country was "high against America," Minister Adams quickly discovered. The only hope, he told Congress, was for the United States to adopt retaliatory measures that might function as a lever to compel Britain to open its ports to American vessels. But such a course was impossible because Congress lacked the power to regulate foreign commerce.[49]

Commerce was primarily a Northern concern. Opening the West was a front-burner issue for the South. It desperately wished to keep this area tied to the Union, and it looked on the eventual Western states—which, like those in the South, were likely to be agrarian economies—as potential political allies. It also wanted the area opened expeditiously. Two wars now had been fought to win, and open, the West. For thirty years settlers had been eager to cross the mountains and carve out a living on this virgin soil. For thirty years, too, speculators who had gained incredible chunks of this domain had been no less anxious for settlement to commence.

Prior to 1776, British intransigence had prevented the opening of the area. Following the War of Independence, Great Britain still blocked the path of many who longed to move west. Despite London's pledge to withdraw its troops from United States soil, three years after the Treaty of Paris the British army yet occupied several strategic forts where the various Great Lakes intersected, controlled the principal route from Lake Erie to the Ohio River, and funneled arms to the Indians in the Northwest.[50] London declared that it would honor the peace accord when America complied with the stipulation mandating that prewar debts be paid. Neither the states nor most individual debtors had the means with which to retire the debts, and Congress was incapable of raising the revenue with which to field an army capable of dealing with either the redcoats or the Native Americans. Only a fraction of those who yearned to move to the trans-Appalachian frontier had migrated by 1786. Most would-be immigrants shrank from the risks involved in settling in a war zone, and with good reason. By the mid-1780s nearly 1,000 of those who had settled beyond the mountains since 1783 had paid with their lives in an undeclared war with the Indians.

Settlement of the Old Southwest lagged as well, for immediately after regaining Florida in the Treaty of Paris, Spain closed the Mississippi River to United States traffic. The United States claimed that its southern boundary terminated at the 31 NL. Spain insisted that the northern boundary of its colony of Florida extended to 32 NL. This left roughly the southern half of present Mississippi and Alabama in dispute. However, even an immediate resolution of the territorial question in favor of the United States would not have solved the quandary faced by would-be settlers in the Southwest, as both sides acknowledged that Spanish Florida extended to the Mississippi River. This meant that under even the most generous settlement the coveted port of New Orleans, and over 100 miles of the wide and rushing Mississippi River, would lay within Spain's jurisdiction. Settlers muscled into Kentucky and Tennessee in the 1780s, but their numbers were minimal in comparison to what might have occurred had the Mississippi remained open. Denied access to the sea, and unable to reach distant markets in the Caribbean, or Europe, or the urban enclaves along the East Coast of the United States, settlers in the Southwest faced an unsavory future as dirt poor subsistence farmers. No help was to be had for these settlers. The United States lacked the strength to pry open the Mississippi River, or to prevent Spain from encouraging separatist movements among the settlers.

These festering sores suddenly turned infectious in 1786. It was a failed diplomatic initiative with Spain that brought matters to a head and ushered in what appeared to some to be the death knell of the Union. In 1785 Madrid had sent Don Diego de Gardoqui to parley. Boundary issues, navigation of the Mississippi, and a pact to inaugurate commerce were on the table. In May 1786, after almost twelve months of discussion, John Jay, the Secretary of Foreign Affairs, realized he could obtain some, but not all, that Congress sought. He told Congress that Madrid was ready to sign a treaty that opened Spanish ports to American trade, but on the condition that the United States renounced navigation of the Mississippi for twenty years. It was that or nothing. Jay requested guidance. With swiftly mounting emotions, Congress debated the matter for days. These were by far the most rancorous sessions that Congress had experienced since it coped with the peace ultimata seven years previously. The Southern states, which got nothing from Madrid's offer, were opposed to the Spaniard's tender. The Northern states, desperate to partially offset its trade losses with the former parent state, were favorable. In the end, Congress voted strictly along sectional lines—seven northern states to five southern states—to make the agreement. However, as nine states were required to ratify a treaty, it was apparent that such a pact would never pass. The Jay-Gardoqui negotiations were terminated, but the damage had been done.[51]

Many Southerners and Westerners seethed at the North's willingness to scuttle their interests. Fear also abounded. Southerners, who had been shut out in the determination of the peace ultimata, once again saw themselves as a lonely minority in a Union in which "the balance of Power is now in the Eastern States." It was a circumstance, according to many Southerners, that arose because each state was accorded equal representation in Congress. Under the Articles of Confederation, New Hampshire, New Jersey, Rhode Island, and Delaware, whose combined populations did not equal that of the free population of Virginia, and barely exceeded the number of free inhabitants of North Carolina, each enjoyed one vote in Congress. Some Southerners were apprehensive that neither their personal interest, nor that of their region, any longer was safe. To some, it appeared that their interests were no better served by the American Union than they had been in the empire. Young Colonel Washington, and many other Southerners, had turned away from Great Britain in the 1760s, in part, because of London's unwillingness to open the trans-Appalachian West. Twenty years later, and a decade or more since independence had been declared, the West remained largely closed, partially because of the inadequacies of the Articles of Confederation, but also because opening the frontier was of less concern to most Northern states than prying open Atlantic commercial opportunities.

If the South was frustrated and angry over the North's willingness to approve a Jay-Gardoqui Treaty, many Northerners were no less bitter that the South had blocked the commercial possibilities offered by Madrid. Nationalists in the North fought back with the same tactics Southern states had used on at least two prior occasions. Many suddenly spoke of leaving the Union if their interests could not be satisfied. James Monroe told Jefferson that talk of "dismembering the confederacy" was rampant, and he informed Madison that the Northern provinces were conspiring to "break the Union" and form their own nation. Such dangerous talk "to me is very alarming," he confessed.[52] None was more energized by these threats than Madison, who according to historian Jack Rakove was plunged by the crisis of the Union into "the grip of a deep-seated intellectual passion."[53] Madison's concern with the state of affairs had been building to a crescendo over a period of some time. He acted in 1786 not only from fear for the Union, but also from the realization that the time was ripe for achieving long cherished objectives.

Madison hailed from the preeminent family in Orange County, Virginia, in the green rolling hills west of Fredericksburg. He sparkled as a student both in his preparatory school and at Princeton. However, when he left college in 1772—after taking only two years to complete his degree, then staying on for one year of postgraduate study—Madison appeared to be confused and adrift. With little notion of a career, his life was without direction or purpose for three years. For much of this time he was in the thrall of a troubling emotional crisis that wracked him with hysterical fears of a fatal disease and left him obsessed with the probability of an early demise. Meanwhile, he brooded over whether to preach or practice law, or simply run Montpelier, his family's estate. He finally chose the law, mostly because it seemed less disagreeable than the alternatives, though he also was haunted by oppressive doubts that he could ever deliver persuasive arguments before a jury. The American Revolution saved him from attempting to earn a living as an attorney. Through his father's influence, young Madison won election to his county's Committee of Public Safety, a board charged with enforcing Congress's boycott of Great Britain, and was appointed colonel of the county militia. The feel of power, and the esteem that it carried, resonated with him, but there can be no question that he also was committed to the colonial rebellion. A disciple of the Enlightenment, he was intrigued with the prospect of initiating reforms in Virginia, and in 1776 won election to the state assembly. A year later he moved to the Council of State, which advised the governor. He sat on that board for three years, including a portion of Governor Jefferson's first administration.

Although almost thirty years old when he was first elected to Congress in 1780, Madison struck most observers as a mere boy. The first portrait for which he sat, painted after he had been a congressman for three years, captured a man who appeared to be as young and fragile, as delicate and soft, as a very young adolescent that one might find today in a high school yearbook. Indeed, when Madison arrived in Philadelphia to assume his congressional seat, some members mistook him for a student who had gained employment as a congressional clerk. Few politicians ever faced so many personal liabilities to their ascendancy. Small and frail, he was painfully shy, devoid of skills as an orator, and without the remotest talents of persiflage. He was not just without panache, but in the memorable phrase of the historian Joseph Ellis, "His style was not to have one."[54] Of all the leading Founders, Madison stands out for not standing out. Washington struck observers with his stature and majestic presence. Franklin was charming, witty, clever, and erudite. Jefferson was a gifted conversationalist who seemed able to talk learnedly on scores of subjects. Hamilton was glib, facile, and dashing. Incandescent John Adams never tired of displaying his profundity. But Madison at first glance appeared not to merit a second glance.

Nevertheless, Madison rapidly gained stature in Congress and during his third year emerged as an important figure. The diminished quality of the personnel in Congress had something to do with his emergence, but so too did the attributes that Madison possessed. He was well served by his formidable intellect, as well as by his ability to convince others of his apparent guilelessness. If his manner did not have an electrifying effect on everyone, it put off almost no one. No one thought him unctuous or supercilious. No one thought him wan or irresponsible. He could be remote and distant toward strangers, but never acerbic or threatening. Much of his success came through diligent, patient, unremitting work. Politics became his all-consuming passion, and he quietly, but intensely, struggled to achieve prominence. Madison never went home during his three years as a congressman. He stood out in this regard. States sent multi-member delegations to Congress, a practice that enabled representatives to return home for long stretches a couple times each year. But month in and month out, year in and year out, Madison—who was unmarried—remained in Philadelphia. He dwelled in a modest boardinghouse, living in quarters not much larger than a room in a typical college dormitory. Politics had become his life. He had no other interests, a colleague from New England remarked, adding that politics "is rather a science than a business, with him."[55]

When he entered Congress, shortly before Britain launched its campaign to take Charleston, South Carolina, Madison conceded that the national government was too weak. However, he did not at first favor greater centralization of authority. While he thought Congress should have slightly greater powers, he did not wish to grant it an independent power to tax, and in 1781 he voted against both the impost and the amendment that would have augmented Congress's authority to coerce delinquent states. Then came the success of British arms in the South prior to Yorktown, victories that occurred in some measure because of the ineptitude of the national government. It changed Madison's thinking. So too did the Newburgh affair in 1783, which lead him to fear that neither the Union nor republicanism could long survive unless strong measures were taken to correct the flawed Articles of Confederation. One way or another, the wealthiest and most powerful elements in the land would have their way, with or without the national Union, with or without a republican system. Knowing full well that if the United States dissolved, the achievements of the American Revolution would vanish, Madison rallied behind the notion of vesting the national government with an independent taxing power. However, until the mid-1780s he remained a foe of extending Congress's authority over commerce, fearing that the Chesapeake tobacco trade would be monopolized by Northern merchants, who would make Southern planters their vassals. Throughout 1784 and 1785, moreover, he was lukewarm to the importuning of those who advocated a constitutional convention, apparently doubtful that Virginia could emerge from such a meeting with "our power and importance" intact. It was the crisis brought on by the Jay-Gardoqui negotiations that finally changed Madison, convincing him that little time remained to find solutions and prevent the dissolution of the Union. In addition, he had come to believe that it would be productive for Northern and Southern politicians to sit at the same table and open a constructive dialogue. In this frame of mind, Madison abandoned his previous strategy of working for gradual reform and embraced the notion of a constitutional convention called for "making the Union respectable by [awarding] new powers to Congress."[56]

While Madison is often portrayed—and properly so—as among the leading thinkers of his day, his intellectual ferment in this period was not the activity of a dispassionate ivory tower philosopher. Committed, like all nationalists, to the belief that increasing the powers of the national government was the elixir that could cure the ills of the day, Madison additionally was an anxious conservative dismayed by signs of emerging democracy and fiscal unorthodoxy in the states. Indeed, in the year after the war ended he and a circle of friends put together what historian Norman Risjord termed "Virginia's first political party," a coalition committed to a tight money policy and a comprehensive creditor program.[57] It successfully opposed a small farmer supported debtor-relief movement led by Patrick Henry, resisted the paper money advocates, advocated payment of British debts, and fought to create special courts for the collection of debts.

Madison was searching, he said of his lucubration, for a means through which to balance "stability and energy in government." The national government must have the energy to safeguard national security, provide "protection against domestic violence," and realize the seminal interests both of the North and South. However, it must also ensure stability, by which Madison appears to have meant, among other things, that he wished for a national government that might shore up protection for the Southern minority and provide the means within a republican framework to construct adequate defenses against popular majorities, injustice, faction, confusion, and—he mentioned this only in private—the "leveling spirit."[58] Madison thus set for himself to solve a conundrum: was it possible to establish a national republican government with the strength to satisfy the cravings of the most powerful elements within the land, yet somehow ensure that this government not only would remain in "safe" hands, but that those who wielded authority would be properly restrained? In short, was it possible to bring into being a government capable of saving the Union that would not ultimately result in the destruction of the Union?

Madison began by identifying what he thought were several throbbing problems, but each in some way flowed from the system of state sovereignty embodied in the Articles of Confederation. He specifically mentioned that festering vexations went unsolved because each state pursued its parochial interests at the expense of the national well being; that the states acted independently, often pursuing measures that were adverse to one another's interests and resulted in rancorous and dangerous disputes; and that the states repeatedly "invade[d] the national jurisdiction," and never more egregiously than in the realm of foreign policy. America's attenuated national government was "utterly irreconcilable with . . . [national] sovereignty," he charged, but what is more its continued presence assured a climate of peril for the existence of the Union, for the wishes of powerful interests were thwarted.

Nor was Madison concerned only by the enervation of the national government. He also denounced the "viscious" character of the states, which resulted, he said, from the abundance of new men in the state legislatures. As with many conservative New Yorkers who had pillaged Abraham Yates, Madison turned up his nose at the "sphere of life from which most of [state assemblies] members are taken," and bemoaned the lack of "*wisdom* and *steadiness*" these men introduced into politics. These artless lawmakers, he went on, were easily seduced by dexterous rhetoric or made "the dupe of a favorite leader."[59] On some level he must have understood that had the new world that was in the offing been in place in 1774, it would have been unlikely that such a reticent, meek young man as himself—no matter that he hailed from colonial America's traditional leadership, and despite his fine education—would have secured even such a modest position as a seat on the Orange County Committee of Public Safety, not to mention appointment as a militia colonel. Madison clearly was disturbed that many of these new assemblymen were revolutionaries who sought more change than had been secured by 1786. He expressed chagrin at the broadening of suffrage rights—many of these new voters were "more likely to join the standard of sedition than that of the established Government," he blustered privately—and at the "general rage for paper money" among many of the newcomers. When he read of state assemblies inflating their currency, or enacting stay laws, legislation passed to protect debtors from creditors, he was apoplectic over the "folly" and "tyranny" of the "popular torrent," a condition that he labeled a "disease." Madison was uneasy for he knew that successful debtor-relief measures, as Gordon Wood has written, were measures that "struck directly at the kind of stable and static proprietary wealth that was the principal source of the gentry's authority and independence."[60]

What Madison thought of as fiscally irresponsible legislation was rare in America before 1776, as the successes of the likes of Hutchinson and Oliver attest. When debtor relief, or loose money laws, occurred episodically after the war, the most conservative Americans concluded that the "plain republican style" of the early period of the American Revolution had been replaced by "savage and wild" politics that, in the words of Fisher Ames of Massachusetts, sent the new nation "sliding down into the mire of a democracy."[61] Madison concurred, and told Washington of the "dark and menacing . . . evils" that the new men were introducing "under the name of relief to the people." "[M]en without reading, experience, or principle," he railed, were producing state laws that were "a nuisance of the most pestilent kind." These same men blocked amendments to strengthen the national government. Madison warned of an imminent backlash that could spell doom for the Union, or for republicanism, or both. Even now, he told Washington and others, "Many individuals of weight"—the conservative elite—"are suspected of leaning towards Monarchy" as a corrective. Nor might this be the worst that was to come. In 1786 he penned a tract that he knew he could never publish. In "Vices of the Political System of the United States," he fretted at the possibility that the propertyless majority might link up with some faction among the enfranchised to gain dominion. Who knew what changes such a coalition might produce?[62]

Madison's rigorous reflection bore fruit before the first torrid days of summer arrived in 1786. In fact, he blazed new territory. Madison now insisted that unless the national government was "arm[ed] ... with a negative *in all cases whatsoever* on the local Legislatures," it "will be easily and continually baffled by the Legislative sovereignties of the States." Not only was this precisely the jurisdiction that Parliament, in the Declaratory Act of 1766, had claimed over the colonies, but it was tantamount to the "Kingly prerogative"—Madison's term—that America had spurned in July 1776. But he declared that such a step could not be avoided. It had to be taken to safeguard "national rights and interests," and to "restrain States from thwarting and molesting each other." It was necessary too to prevent the "aggression of interested majorities on the rights of minorities and individuals." Once done, the states would be rendered "subordinately useful." He did not propose that all authority be stripped from the states. With such power vested in the central government there was no need to do so. Instead, he spoke of the national government operating within its sphere and the states within their arena. He could be confident that through his system the states not only would be prevented from traducing the federal sphere, but that the national government would be enabled to check changes that blossomed in the more democratic provinces and to protect entrenched interests in the states from popular governments.[63]

There was another matter. Madison and the "most considerate and virtuous citizens"—as he described those who shared his class and outlook—were troubled by the prospect that a popular faction built on democratic impulses might capture a newly structured national government, sowing the very "instability" that he believed presently haunted the states. The new nation, after all, not only was divided between a powerful Northern "manufacturing ... mercantile ... [and] moneyed interest" and a Southern "landed interest," but various other social and economic factions were certain to arise as a result of America's "unequal distribution of wealth." One could easily imagine factions of small yeomen, landless farmers, urban artisans, city workers, and frontiersmen, among other interested parties. Was it not possible that a combination of these interests might fashion a popular national movement? Was it not conceivable that such a coalition could become an "overbearing majority" that would ride roughshod over the "rights of the minor party," whether the South or the social and economic elite? What, he asked, was to arrest a popular movement guided by a "rage for paper money, for an abolition of debts, for an equal distribution of property, or for any other improper or wicked project?" What "adequate control" could be instituted to check popular majorities? Was there not some way, short of destroying liberty, with which to make it formidably difficult to effect substantive change?[64]

Madison discovered a way. His most original thought, and most substantive discovery, was to discern that with the proper structuring of balanced government, popular majorities that sought profound change could be effectively thwarted even in a republican government. The key, he reasoned, was the enormous size of the United States, a nation whose territory was so vast that the settled region east of the mountains—which constituted only about one-third the national land mass—was four or five times larger than France or Great Britain. Madison deduced that the spatial dimensions of the United States could be enlisted to "lessen the insecurity" of the various component parts of the whole. At the state level, where only two or three powerful interests existed, one was almost certain to predominate. In the South, it had been the slaveocracy. In the mid-Atlantic region, it had been the mercantile combine. But in the nation that he envisioned, where a plethora of interest groups competed, no one faction could predominate. Two results were likely. One was that stalemate might occur, frustrating every effort to govern effectively. Or, secondly, various factions might bond together to gain power, but each would have to moderate its most intemperate demands as it sought to build a coalition. This would reduce the probability that any one faction would ever be able to secure its extreme ends. Thus, wrote Madison, a faction that harbored a "rage for paper money, for an abolition of debts, for an equal division of property" would likely exist, but it was "less apt to pervade the whole body of the Union."[65]

What Madison had proposed was a system in which even modest change was to be made difficult. Substantive change could be had only when an overriding consensus existed for a protracted period. For change to occur numerous factions from throughout the polyglot United States would first have to coalesce, gain power within a majority of the states, and then endure for a sufficient period to secure hegemony within all branches of the new government.[66] And Madison envisioned more branches in his new government than existed in the Articles of Confederation, with its unicameral national legislature. Madison's government would have a bicameral assembly, an executive, and a judiciary, each chosen in a different manner, each with terms of varying length. To effect change, a faction composed of diverse interests would have to gain control of four separate entities within the new national government, and maintain its control of each for a very long time.

This was not a plan for rolling back the American Revolution. However, Madison was resolute about protecting the propertied class from what he believed were the democratic excesses of the American Revolution and, at the same time, guarding Southern interests, which to a considerable degree meant preserving the well being of slave owners against a Northern majority. Stability, of which Madison spoke so much, in reality meant making change difficult to effect, both to protect the salient republican reform already effected by the American Revolution and to defend his class and section. In the blueprint that he constructed, change would be possible, but not easy to effect. It would be next to impossible to secure enactment of sweeping reforms that were popular in one section only, or that resonated with only one element within society. Madison had hit upon the means through which the American Revolution could be realized. Here was the formula through which to save the Union, preserve independence, and achieve the dreams of republicanism implicit in the American Revolution. But it would come at a steep price: henceforth, the fulfillment of other, more radical, sentiments that sprang from Whig ideology and the logic of the Revolution, or of which future generations might dream, would come only slowly, if they came at all.

Madison was not alone in 1786 in broadcasting the warning that a great crisis of the Union had arrived, or in searching for the opening that would permit the strengthening of the powers of national government. The nationalist mantra now was that change was essential, or the Union "must decline." For instance, Hamilton, who had left public life to pursue a legal career soon after the Newburgh Affair, reentered politics in 1786 and was elected to the New York assembly, where he spread the word that the United States now faced the "mischiefs of . . . bankrupt[cy] and ruined public credit." His principal aim, according to his biographer Forrest McDonald, was to lay the groundwork for his state's support for enhanced Congressional authority over commerce. All nationalists concurred that the power of the states had to be reduced. Like Madison, they insisted that the states "pursued their own whimsical Schemes," indifferent to the national interest. "The Mischievous Consequences of our Folly are now pressing upon us," one nationalist said, and another remarked that the flawed national government "cannot fail to bring on a Crisis of some kind ere long."[67]

Rumors of likely secessionist movements were unleashed. There was buzz as well that some states planned to abandon the American Union and form a regional confederacy. America, it was said, would go the way of Europe, and ultimately three or four, or more, confederacies would spring up. Speculation focused on the likelihood of the emergence of a New England confederation, a union of the middle Atlantic states, a Southern confederacy, and still another union involving the entities in the trans-Appalachian West. Not only would these confederations be capable of taking steps that were beyond the ability of Congress under the Articles, but in private some portrayed such a step in a positive light, in as much as the regional union could adopt constitutions that secured property rights and maintained order. Alongside these unsettling reports, there were whispers of the need to revive monarchical government. "[M]any, very many wish to see an emperor at the head of our nation," one magazine reported.[68]

In the midst of this growing frenzy, some nationalists gently sought to prod Washington to use his voice to "divert the evils which menace our existence." Washington, who had been retired from public life since Christmas Eve, 1783, listened as Jay told him that the "Errors in our national Government . . . threaten to blast the Fruit we expected from our "Tree of Liberty." In the very week that Madison endorsed a national convention, Jay informed Washington that "an opinion begins to prevail that a general convention for revising the Articles of Confederation would be expedient." Henry Lee, who had served under Washington during the war, stressed the contempt with which America was held in Europe. Its flag was insulted and its ambassadors despised as "the shadow of a shade," he said. The United States soon might face real peril if it was unable to overcome its "degrading supiness," he predicted. Of more immediate urgency, he added, was the reality that "foederal distresses gather fast to a point" and threaten the very existence of the Union.[69] But Washington made no public pronouncements in 1786.

By then time was running out—may in fact have already expired—for those who wished to preserve the essential character of the decentralized system of governance established by the Articles of Confederation. For five years or more they had known that powerful forces ardently wished to strengthen the national government. They had responded by blocking their adversaries at every turn. What is more, they had made no effort to initiate even modest reforms to correct obvious flaws. Confident that a widespread sentiment for change was lacking, they foolishly underestimated their foes. But their misjudgments do not adequately explain their failings. For one thing, some decentralists appear to have welcomed future reform of the Articles, but preferred to postpone reformation until after their state's war debts were retired, lest they be shouldered with an even more formidable national indebtedness. Others were ready to act, but were without national leaders. Many of their earlier champions had abandoned the national stage and returned to provincial politics. Samuel Adams, for instance, had departed Congress in 1781, a few months before the siege of Yorktown, and spent the next five years in the Massachusetts senate struggling to restore what once had been thought of as virtue in a Boston now rife with acquisitiveness and consumerism. The focus of those who remained in Congress was suffocatingly parochial. Not only did they often seem insensible to national issues, but they neglected to form the alliances and construct the interstate organization that could would enable them to respond adequately in the time of need.[70]

Their last chance came in the spring of 1786 when Charles Pinckney of South Carolina told Congress that either a national convention should be called to consider constitutional changes or that Congress must address the matter. He gave Congress the first crack by moving that it create a grand committee—one representative from each state—to recommend amendments for consideration by the states. Congress created the committee, which in turn proposed seven amendments to make "the federal government adequate to the ends for which it was instituted." Congress was to be given powers to regulate commerce and secure revenues, including the authority both to fine recalcitrant states and to collect taxes in provinces that refused to make requisitions or gather up the funds. In addition, the authority of the federal judiciary was to be expanded and the problem of non-attendance in Congress was addressed.[71] The alarm of 1786 notwithstanding, Congress leisurely discussed the proposed amendments, but failed to act.[72]

Pinckney's call for a national gathering was neither the first nor the last such plea, and the road that lead ultimately to the Constitutional Convention was dark and rocky. A successful four-day conference between commissioners from Virginia and Maryland, held at Mount Vernon in March 1785, provided the initial ray of hope for nationalists. That meeting culminated in the signing of a compact that opened the Potomac River to the commerce of all states; the two states additionally agreed to share the expense of erecting lighthouses, beacons, and buoys. Encouraged by the cordial atmosphere, the commissioners subsequently explored similar talks with Delaware and Pennsylvania. Furthermore, the indefatigable Madison, who shepherded the Mount Vernon agreement through the Virginia legislature, may have been the author of a resolution—which the assembly adopted at the outset of 1786—that urged every state to send delegates to an interstate commercial convention to be held at Annapolis in September.[73]

Privately, Madison told James Monroe that "Something . . . is necessary to be done, towards the commerce at least of the U.S." If "anything can be done," he added, the achievement would likely result "f[rom] the present crisis." Reiterating his belief that "a correction thro' the medium of Congress" was hopeless, Madison looked on a "Continental Convention"—as he referred to the Annapolis conclave—as a crucial first step. It was imperative that delegates from the several states be brought together. An experienced politician, Madison knew that when political activists talked and reached a "full discovery of one another," common ground might be found. The footing might be treacherous, but he was confident that sufficient commonality of interest could be found, and the necessary compromises effected, to solve what troubled the national government. Although each meeting had its own dynamic, he was confident that the delegates at Annapolis might discover a way "to defeat the designs of [ignorance] by humouring the prejudice of [iniquity]." Nevertheless, he clearly saw the Annapolis meeting as only a "first instance" that, if successful, might be repeated with regard to "other defects" until "the present paroxysm of our affairs" was finally resolved.[74]

Madison's reach exceeded his grasp, as the Annapolis Convention fizzled when only five states sent delegates. Madison had been warned. Some nationalists had thought the time had not yet come for a constitutional convention. For instance, William Grayson, a Virginia nationalist and foe of paper money who was Madison's eyes and ears in Congress, had cautioned his friend in May that "affairs are not arrived at such a crisis as to assume success to a reformation." To meet at this juncture and "probe . . . to the bottom"—that is, to recommend sweeping constitutional reforms—was to risk a popular rejection that would set back the movement.[75] If Grayson was correct, Madison and his compatriots were fortunate that the Annapolis Convention never got off the ground. Nevertheless, not all was lost. The delegates, as Madison had envisioned, engaged in frank discussions as they awaited the never-to-be-realized quorum. They discovered that within the states they represented—New York, New Jersey, Delaware, Pennsylvania, and Virginia—strong sentiment existed both for discussing commercial arrangements and for seeking an "adjustment of other parts of the Foederal System." Encouraged, they not only laid plans for another convention with a more comprehensive agenda, but for taking steps in the interim to assure its success. Deciding too that observers such as congressman Grayson were correct, they decided to scuttle the meeting rather than to wait longer for lag-gards to reach Annapolis. In fact, when word arrived that two additional delegations were en route to Annapolis—which would bring to seven the number of states in attendance, and achieve a quorum—the del-egates hastily packed their bags, adopted an "Address," and went home. The "Address" urged another try at a continental convention, this one to gather on the second Monday in May 1787 in Philadelphia for the pur-pose of investigating the "important defects in the [constitutional] sys-tem," and for "digesting a plan" that would "render the constitution of the Foederal Government adequate to the exigencies of the Union." Hamilton, the author of statement, and the delegates who unanimously approved it, clearly envisioned that the Philadelphia Convention would not limit itself merely to amending the Articles.[76]

Nationalist reformers took several steps during the intervening eight months to assure that the Philadelphia Convention would at least get off the ground. With some difficulty they secured Congress's blessing for the meeting. Suspicious of what might occur in Philadelphia, Congress let nearly five months pass before it endorsed the Convention, and then sought to limit its scope by decreeing that the meeting was lawful solely for the "express purpose of revising the Articles of Confederation." The nationalists also realized that they had erred in not inviting General Washington to attend the Annapolis meeting. They vowed not to repeat their mistake. Washington was so revered that knowledge of his intent to participate might lure others to Philadelphia. His presence would add luster to the proceedings and conceivably aid in the adoption of what-ever was recommended, for as an Englishman who was touring the United States that year remarked, the American "people have no confidence in any other man." Madison had hardly returned from Annapolis before he launched a campaign to persuade Washington to be part of the Vir-ginia delegation. He not only averaged a letter to the general every three weeks that autumn, but paid a visit to Mount Vernon for good measure. Henry Lee and Edmund Randolph, the governor of Virginia, also en-couraged Washington to attend.

Washington shared their concerns and most of their views. Since 1783, in public and in private, he had repeatedly proclaimed that he had "ever been a friend to adequate powers of Congress, without which it is evident to me we never shall establish a national character, or be consid-ered as on a respectable footing by the powers of Europe." Like Madison, he believed there was "more wickedness than ignorance in the conduct of the States," given their propensity to peruse "private views and selfish privileges."[77] He also agreed with Madison that the Union was doomed unless the state and national debts were retired, commerce was properly regulated, and private property rigorously protected.[78] Washington had never minced words. "We are either a United people, or we are not. If the former, let us, in all matters of general concern act as a nation, which have national objects to promote, and a national character to support." But before 1786 Washington had remained confident that in good time the citizenry would see the folly of the Articles of Confederation and, in a groundswell of public opinion, demand the correction of its flawed sections. At the outset of peace, he had characterized the age as a time of America's "political probation." He also equated the first years of independence with that of a youngster who, having "come a little prematurely to a large inheritance," lived irresponsibly until age and maturity pointed him in the proper direction.[79]

But in the autumn of 1786 Washington knew that the citizenry had not yet demanded changes in the national charter. Those plumping for the Philadelphia Convention were a small minority within the political spectrum. No evidence existed of widespread popular sentiment on behalf of altering the Articles of Confederation and strengthening the national government. Washington did not wish to squander his exalted reputation on a meeting that turned into a fiasco, or that produced a document that would be distasteful to the great majority of Americans. Nor did he have any appetite for being part of an improper, and perhaps illegal, meeting. But he was politically savvy. He sensed the "verging" crisis, and "tremble[d]" that the Union "must soon fall" if reforms were not made to assuage the most powerful elements in the land.[80] Cautiously, indecisively, he waited and watched as months passed. Only after he ascertained that a sufficient number of states were sending delegates to achieve a quorum, and he learned that Congress had sanctioned the conclave, did Washington agree to go to Philadelphia.[81]

No one factor was responsible for the willingness of the twelve states that ultimately agreed to participate in the Philadelphia Convention. It requires little imagination to conceive of the backroom activities that must have occurred following the abortive meeting in Annapolis to induce state assemblies to commit delegates. Furthermore, knowledge of General Washington's consent to attend must have swayed some, as many likely interpreted his willingness to emerge from retirement, and to make the arduous eight-day journey from Mount Vernon, as a signal of the gravity of the crisis. The Northern nationalists' alarming rhetoric about the dismemberment of the Union doubtless propelled still others to Philadelphia. For many, however, the outbreak of a bloody rebellion in central and western Massachusetts in the autumn of 1786 clinched their decision to act.

Disorder flared in Massachusetts as farm prices, and the wages of farm laborers, shrank during the postwar depression, yet taxes rose. Many who worked the land lacked the money to pay taxes and mortgages. The number of frontier towns listed as delinquent on the tax rolls steadily increased. Nearly 3,000 cases of debt were prosecuted in Hampshire County alone in the twenty-four months before July 1786, a 262 percent increase over similar court proceedings in the immediate prewar years. By late summer 1786 the jails were filled with debtors. Foreclosures skyrocketed. So too did resentment among the yeomen, especially after the creditor-dominated state legislature turned a deaf ear to their pleas for stay laws and an inflated currency. To many yeomen a familiar scent hung heavy in the air. Scant years after the overthrow of the British lackeys in charge of colonial Massachusetts, the state government had acted in a manner reminiscent of the days of Hutchinson and Oliver. The anger of western farmers simmered when countless Revolutionary War veterans spent the tenth anniversary of independence in debtors' prison, yet businessmen and financiers, most of whom had never gone near an army encampment, lived sumptuously in eastern Massachusetts. As New England's fiery autumn burst forth, western protest turned to insurrection. Led by Daniel Shays, a Pelham farmer who had fought at Bunker Hill, Saratoga, and Stony Point, and suffered battlefield wounds, the insurgents armed and mobilized in several counties. Their immediate objective was to prevent county courts from sitting, and authorizing, foreclosures. The state responded by sending an army of 4,400 troops armed with cannon to the west. The desperate farmers were easily routed.[82]

"Good God!" Washington exclaimed when he learned of the disorder. Washington was apoplectic, and not just about lawless farmers. "There are combustibles in every State, which a spark may set fire to," he told a correspondent, doubtless thinking of restless slaves or disillusioned settlers in the trans-Appalachian West who might take matters in their own hands if the clouded frontier questions were not soon resolved. Spain might be enticed to bargain with the dissatisfied western settlers, Washington ruminated, adding that Great Britain could be expected to pounce on "every opportunity to foment the spirit of turbulence within the bowels of the United States." Thank God, he said, Shays' Rebellion had "terminate[d] entirely in favor of Government by the suppression of the insurgents." His worst fear had been that the insurrection might swell beyond its original limited objectives, or that the conflagration might spread to neighboring states. He knew that the national government was powerless to aid Massachusetts. He knew too that it could never do the least thing to aid any state threatened with serious disorder.

That realization quickened his apprehension at the enfeebled Congress. It was imperative, he concluded, that the national constitution must be changed to give "energy & respectability to the Government." While in Philadelphia, he said, he would seek to "correct the defects of the federal System." In all likelihood, he closed, the meeting in Philadelphia would be the final opportunity to save the American Revolution and the Union it had spawned.[83]

The Philadelphia Convention would have met even if the western farmland of Massachusetts had not been bathed in blood in the autumn of 1786. But Shays' Rebellion changed the environment in which the delegates would gather.

9

"So Much Unanimity and Good Will"

F ifty-five men from twelve states came to Philadelphia in May 1787 to consider alterations to the Articles of Confederation. Only the delegations of host Pennsylvania and Virginia were in place on May 14, the starting date set at the abortive meeting in Annapolis, but late starts remained as commonplace as they had been in 1754, when Franklin and others had come to Albany to plan for a likely war with France. Travel conditions had not improved appreciably over the years, and in 1787, after one of the wettest springs in memory, many delegates had to negotiate roads that had been rendered quagmires.

Madison had been one of the first delegates to arrive. When all his Virginia colleagues were in town, the delegation caucused daily for discussions. Madison likely dominated the sessions, turning them into tutorials, as he outlined the sweeping changes he had conceived during his brainstorming over the past year. The Virginians soon sought out members of the Pennsylvania delegation for informal talks and thereafter conversed with arriving delegates from the other states. To their delight, they discovered that sentiment for making sweeping changes was widespread. By the time the initial session was gaveled to order on May 25, Madison was confident that instead of deliberating over a few amendments, the Philadelphia Convention would draft a new constitution.

Most delegates were members of America's social, economic, and political elite, leading Franklin to pronounce it "une assemblee des notables" and George Mason to remark that those in attendance were the "first characters" in the land.[1] Three had sat in the Stamp Act Congress and three-fourths had been members of Congress. Nine had been congressmen in July 1776, of whom one-third—John Dickinson, Robert

Morris, and George Reed of Delaware—had voted against independence. Edmund Randolph was the governor of Virginia, and Dickinson and Alexander Martin of North Carolina had earlier served in that capacity in their respective states. More than half had military experience, and fifteen had soldiered for several years during the late war. Several were lawyers, and some had sat on the bench or acted as the attorney-general of their state. These were not disinterested men. More than half, including several delegates from northern states, were slave owners. Nearly one-third were actively involved in foreign or interstate commerce, or they were lawyers whose principal clients were powerful merchants. The overwhelming majority speculated in land, and several owned thousands of acres in the trans-Appalachian West. More than half owned certificates of public debt, the market value of which would appreciate if a strong, stable national government could be realized.[2] Each not only represented a state but fully understood the necessity of serving the interests of that state. In his private cogitation, Madison had noted that "the various and unequal distribution of wealth" had "divided mankind into parties." At the bottom were those who owned no property; skilled workers and yeomen formed a middle strata, and above them were the "creditors . . . a landed interest, a manufacturing interest, a moneyed interest."[3] The men in the Philadelphia Convention were overwhelmingly from the top rung.

This convention was characterized as much by who was not present as by those who attended. Jefferson and John Adams were yet in Europe on diplomatic missions. Patrick Henry had refused to serve because, as

A northwest view of the Statehouse in Philadelphia. Engraving, 1778.

he allegedly remarked, he "smelt a rat," sensing that his fellow Virginian, Madison, and others of his persuasion, harbored plans that they had not divulged to the public.[4] Samuel Adams would have liked to attend, but as a decentralist with democratic leanings, there had been less likelihood that the Massachusetts assembly would add him to the state's delegation than there was that Boston would be struck by a July snowstorm. No delegate resembled the activists who had comprised the Loyal Nine twenty years before. No urban artisans or laborers, who once had been useful to the popular movement for their willingness to act as dispatch riders, or for dumping tea into a harbor, were in attendance. Nor had any small farmers, whose service once had been solicited, or coerced, at places such as Bunker Hill or Saratoga, been appointed as delegates. Southern yeomen who possessed small farms, but no slaves, were noticeably absent as well, as were the inhabitants of rustic backcountry villages throughout the land.

The overwhelming majority of those in attendance embraced two core ideas. First, said Dickinson, "All agree that the confederation is defective" and that the powers of the national government must be increased. Many roads led to this view. The Georgia delegation wanted a national government with suitable power to provide its residents with protection against their neighbors in the Creek Confederation. Delegates from New Jersey and Connecticut believed the existence of a strong national government would liberate their states from economic thralldom to New York.[5] The Massachusetts and New Hampshire delegations wished for a government with sufficient power to protect the region's fishing interests against European competitors. Many delegates believed that only a potent national government could serve as the lever to reestablish commercial ties with Great Britain. Some wished for a vigorous national government capable of preventing France from becoming America's new "lordly master." Most wished to restore—or assert—national pride. All wanted a government capable of protecting national security. There were those who hoped to prevent the states from violating treaties or trespassing on one another. Some sought to attain uniformity in the currency that circulated. Many longed for national immigration and copyright laws. Virtually every delegate was exasperated by the seeming impossibility of amending the Articles of Confederation. Some sought a national government with the muscle to pry open trans-Appalachian farmlands for sale and settlement. Many, alarmed by what one delegate described as the "symptoms of a leveling spirit" coursing the land, hoped to find the means to inhibit democratic excesses.[6]

Yet, while every delegate wished to augment the power of the national government at the expense of the states, none was willing to vitiate the vital interests of his own province. That was the second essential idea that drove these men. In general, Southerners would not countenance threats to their slave properties and Northerners would have no truck with reforms that might imperil their commercial endeavors. Most wanted a government that would expand opportunities for the "distinct interests" and "classes"— Madison's terms—that they represented. However, the delegates differed over whether to absolutely eviscerate state authority or to contrive a system in which power was divided between, or shared by, the states and the central government. Furthermore, the traditional sectional divisions, evident since the debate over the embargo at the First Continental Congress, existed in Philadelphia.

Success, therefore, was uncertain, but failure was unlikely. These men desperately wanted to succeed. All knew that if the national government was not strengthened at this juncture, years might pass before another opportunity for reform presented itself. Some, in fact, thought this convention represented the last chance for saving the Union. Returning home empty-handed might portend disunion, the eradication of real and potential Revolutionary reforms, domestic insecurity, and foreign threats. Most preferred the unpredictability of where a new constitution might take them to the unquestioned perplexities posed by doing nothing. Most had been willing in 1776 to make the leap into the dark required by independence, and once again, most were prepared to make decisions that would usher in an ambiguous future. They were seasoned in politics, skilled in the practice of debate, artful in bluff, bluster, and impudent deception, practiced in what John Adams once referred to as the customary "deep Intrigues of Politicians," and with a sixth sense derived from ample experience most knew when the moment had arrived to yield and make an arrangement.[7] Nothing was foreordained, but it was probable that these delegates would find sufficient common ground on which to complete a document whose ratification, as Madison put it weeks earlier, "would not be attended with much difficulty."[8]

The Convention made two crucial decisions in its initial hours. It selected Washington as its president, thus inextricably tying his name to the product it would ultimately send out for ratification. It also agreed to meet in secret, only partly in the hope of ensuring free and candid discussion. Secrecy was also imperative if the delegates, contrary to Congress's mandate, were to consider drafting a new constitution. Had the public known what was occurring behind closed doors, the popular clamor would have immediately stopped the proceedings.

The broad shape of the new federal system that ultimately emerged was agreed on during the first days of this four-month conclave. On

May 29, after the delegates took their seats in the same paneled room in the Pennsylvania State House in which Congress had declared independence eleven years earlier, Governor Randolph spoke to the convention, reading a speech that was tantamount to a keynote address. He told his colleagues that the young nation faced a crisis of fatal proportions. Many here and abroad, he said, were predicting "the American downfall." The national government was too weak to prevent war and powerless to adequately wage hostilities. But, he insisted, "our chief danger arises" from state constitutions that lack "sufficient checks against . . . democracy." He then laid before the Convention the Virginia delegation's proposal for radical reform, confessing that it was posited on "the idea that the states should be nearly annihilated."[9]

The Virginia Plan, which Madison had crafted, called for a national government in which power was balanced between legislative, executive, and judicial branches. The national legislature was to be bicameral and—a proposal not unexpected from a large state—both houses were to be apportioned on the basis of population. The plan also called for emasculating the states, as Congress was to possess the authority to pass laws "in all cases to which the separate states are incompetent, or in which the harmony of the United States may be interrupted by the exercise of individual legislation." The national government would further have the authority to negate state laws and to use force against any state "failing to fulfill its duty." Nor was that all. Madison had confided to Jefferson that his proposed system of representation would cause congressmen to represent people, not states, and by recommending that constitutional amendments required the assent of specially chosen assemblies, he was confident that the state legislatures would gradually lose still more influence.[10] In short, Madison had conceived the means of making states obsolete. Most delegates liked at least some of what they heard, and by June 20 enough of the plan had been adopted that the superstructure of the eventual constitution was readily apparent. But much remained to be done. During the next dozen weeks, the Convention struggled over the degree of state subordination and debated the nuts and bolts of the new central government.

Several troublesome obstacles confronted the drafters, but in reality only two matters posed a genuine threat to wreck the Convention, and neither issue came as close to laying waste to the aspirations of the nationalists as many scholars have imagined. Contention between large states and small over representation in Congress was stormy and protracted, and so too were the clashes over slavery. Some historians have portrayed the convention as hopelessly deadlocked on both problems until nearly miraculous compromises saved the day. However, resolution came somewhat less dramatically. The solution to the representation issue was virtually foreordained, and every delegate knew it. The quandary over slavery was ultimately resolved as much by the indifference of many delegates as by statesmanship.

Having been thwarted repeatedly since 1774 by the small states, the large states were eager that their greater weight be evident at the national level. In Madison's view, this was an issue of nearly equal import with that of the supremacy of the central government. Representation based on population must be "the first step to be taken" by the Convention, he had remarked beforehand, as it would protect Southern interests in the immediate future and ensure "their expected superiority" in a generation or two when the agrarian Southern states and new farming provinces in the West forged an indomitable alliance.[11] But this was a fight they could not win, and they knew it. Dickinson, in fact, told the delegates at the very outset that it was "politic" and "unavoidable" that they would have to make "mutual concessions" on matters of representation. He specifically told the big states that they would have to relinquish control of one house of Congress to the small states. Dickinson even privately explained to Madison that "Some of the members from the small States are friends to a good National Government; but . . . would sooner submit to a foreign power, than submit to [large state domination] in both branches of the legislature." Indeed, some immediately perceived Madison's scheme as a ploy, in the words of Gunning Bedford of tiny Delaware, "to provide a system" that was designed to furnish "Va . . . an enormous & monstrous" influence at the national level.[12]

If the logic and insight of the likes of Dickinson and Bedford were not sufficient, the Convention rules, adopted at the very outset, predestined the failure of the big states. The rules decreed that voting would be by states, as had been the case in Congress since 1774. In a convention of twelve states, the six smaller provinces—New Hampshire, New Jersey, Delaware, Georgia, North Carolina, and Maryland—enjoyed parity with the half dozen larger entities. Seemingly stymied, the large state delegates, with considerable resilience, floated a variety of proposals that were couched as concessions but which clearly were aimed at securing greater representation in the upper house for the more populous states. Madison at one point urged that the free population only be represented in the upper house and that the total population, free and slave, be counted for representation in the lower chamber. Another proposal was to limit the largest states to a maximum of five senators. Still another was to make Congress tricameral, with the states given equal representation only in a third house. Although they postured and blustered for several weeks in June and July, delegates from large states were always aware that their inflexibility would wreck the convention. They were too close to getting enough of what they wanted to permit that to occur. From the outset, they knew that compromises would have to be made. Even before he packed his bags for the trek to Philadelphia, Madison privately spoke of the need for seeking some "middle ground" that would nevertheless "support a due supremacy of the national authority," his overriding objective. The issue was resolved in mid-July by what has often been called the Great Compromise, an accommodation whose time came after six weeks of rancorous debate. The delegates agreed to what Oliver Ellsworth of Connecticut characterized as a "partly national" and "partly federal" system. Inasmuch as the House of Representatives was apportioned according to population, and the states were given equal representation in the Senate, what Ellsworth meant was that the two chambers were balanced between people and states. In theory, the House would act on the popular will, while the Senate was constituted as a bulwark for minority states and regions.[13]

Slavery and issues attendant to it also generated heat. Whether because of the Enlightenment or the natural rights ideology of the American Revolution, increasing numbers of citizens by 1787 had begun to question the institution of slavery. In 1780 Pennsylvania became the first state to provide for its gradual end, followed soon thereafter by Connecticut and Rhode Island, which enacted abolition laws. In 1781 courts in Massachusetts interpreted the state constitution as outlawing slavery, something that Vermont had explicitly done in the constitution it adopted in 1777. In 1784 Congress failed by one vote to ban slavery from the western territories, but three years later it passed the Northwest Ordinance, which prohibited slavery in a vast territory that would ultimately include the states of Ohio, Indiana, Illinois, Michigan, and Wisconsin.[14] Antislavery societies had begun to spring up in the North, and as early as 1785 Southerners understood that if they took chattel with them into Pennsylvania, they ran the risk that their slaves might be liberated during their residency in that state.[15] Yet, despite the inroads made by the foes of slavery above the Potomac, abolitionism was hardly a burning issue for most white residents in the Northern states. While Northerners appeared to be increasingly eager to stop the expansion of slavery, it was an inescapable fact that many—probably most—Northern whites were simply disinterested in the plight of slaves. There were those, of course, who genuinely loathed slavery, and within the decade emancipationist legislation would win out in every Northern state. But when the choice was between saving the Union or eradicating slavery, the peculiar institution took a backseat, and the Northern representatives in Philadelphia happily embraced the notion that the Southern states should be left to deal with slavery within their respective jurisdictions as they saw fit.

Slavery was a substantive matter for the class of Southerners who attended the Philadelphia Convention. They wanted protection for their institution and were not in the least embarrassed to act in its defense. "The security the Southn. States want is that their negroes may not be taken from them," a delegate from South Carolina explained to his Northern colleagues early on. Later, another South Carolinian told the convention that his delegation, and that from Georgia as well, would vote against any constitution that "fail[ed] to insert some security to the Southern States agst. an emancipation of slaves." The slaveholding interests had a full agenda. They wanted constitutional guarantees that the federal government would be forbidden to banish slavery in the states and that Congress would have no power to tax slave imports. Furthermore, they wanted no restrictions on their ability to move slaves from one slave province to another, and they sought assistance from the national government in returning runaway slaves and suppressing slave insurrections. South Carolina, the most militant of the Southern states, even desired a clause defining slaves as property and guaranteeing that slave owners could take their chattel into free states at least temporarily.[16]

Although the word *slavery* did not appear in the constitution that this convention produced—slaves were designated as "other persons" or as a "person held to Service or Labour"— slavery was immediately part of the ongoing debate, surfacing on the very day that discussion commenced on the Virginia Plan. Ultimately, the Northern delegates made several substantive concessions to the slave interests. In the three-fifths clause, slave states were permitted to include 60 percent of their chattel in the population count that would determine the apportionment of representation in the lower house and the electoral college. Congress could terminate the African slave trade, but not before 1808, and in the meantime it was prohibited from imposing excessive duties on slave imports. The fugitive slave clause allowed slave owners to recover slave runaways. Congress was prohibited from taxing exports, a move that prevented slavery from being taxed indirectly through the imposition of duties on the cash crops produced by chattel. Finally, the central government could protect states from "domestic Violence" by "suppress[ing] Insurrections," which would include slave revolts.[17]

Not every Northern delegate was happy with what was conceded to the South, especially as the South gave up little in return. Indeed, the South, the section that had lost the most in the battle over the peace ultima in 1779, appeared to many to have won the most at the Constitutional Convention eight years later. For instance, the Northern concessions on counting slaves in determining representation dramatically augmented Southern power at the national level. With approximately 40 percent of the nation's free population, the South controlled 47 percent of the seats in the House of Representatives throughout the 1790s, and an equal percentage of the votes in the electoral college in the bitterly contested elections of 1796 and 1800. By 1820 only about 30 percent of the nation's free population lived in slave states, but the states below the Potomac possessed 36 percent of the nation's congressmen and presidential electors. Gouverneur Morris of Pennsylvania, who was the most outspoken of those rankled by the concessions to the slave states, remarked that it was hypocritical of the Convention to create a national government for the "protection of the rights of mankind," while it allowed Southerners additional representation based on counting those subjected to the "most cruel bondages." Morris found it a piercing irony that while free Southerners were to be overrepresented in the halls of power, Northern men inevitably would be overrepresented on the nation's battlefields, as slaves would not be expected to bear arms. What is more, in the event of Southern slave insurrections, Northern men might be compelled "to march their militia for the defence of the S[outhern] States."[18]

Others from the North thought that too much had been conceded, but most appeared to believe that what had occurred was defensible. They were convinced that they had little choice but to make concessions. When it came to slavery, the South—and South Carolina and Georgia in particular—were not bluffing. Furthermore, the Northern delegates understood that the slave South consisted of only five states, leaving the states above the Potomac to enjoy a certain and considerable majority in Congress and the electoral college during the first crucial decade under the new Constitution. Although far from pretty, Northern interests won some prizes by agreeing to concessions that were part of bargains in which the South also yielded. For instance, the South not only relinquished its demand that commercial regulations would require a two-thirds vote of Congress but agreed to the prohibition of the African slave trade after 1808 in return for the capitulation by Northern delegates who wished to vest in Congress the power to establish export duties.[19] Through these bargains, and more, the commercial North preserved the Union and obtained a system of governance that could further its economic interests, gains that it believed were of infinitely greater importance than the welfare of African-American slaves.

The South was delighted with its victory. Near the end of the convention, Charles Cotesworth Pinckney of South Carolina gushed that he "had himself prejudices agst the [Northern] States before he came here, but would acknowledge that he had found them as liberal and candid as any men whatever." The slave states had gotten all they sought. "We have a security that the general government can never emancipate them [slaves], for no such authority is granted," Pinckney subsequently told the South Carolina ratification convention, and whatever authority was not explicitly given the national government was "reserved by the several states."[20]

The battle between big and small states and the clashes over slavery have dominated the recent scholarship concerning the Constitutional Convention. However, two other substantive matters occupied the delegates. For instance, while some, such as Gouverneur Morris, claimed to have come to the meeting solely as a "Representative of America," the overwhelming majority of delegates attended with the scarcely hidden expectation of defending the interests of their states. The lofty rhetoric in the daily debates almost obscured the "state prejudices," in Madison's words, that lay in the underbrush as virtually every issue was hammered out. When the Convention debated Congress's power to regulate commerce, for example, at least five separate local interests sparred: the New England fishing industry, which sent most of its catch to the West Indies; New York mercantilists who urged free trade practices; delegates from Pennsylvania and New Jersey, provinces anxious to protect their exports of wheat and flour; Chesapeake planters who shipped tobacco to European markets; and South Carolina and Georgia rice planters who traditionally had sold much of their produce to Southern Europe. It is difficult to imagine any issue that failed to produce similar labyrinthian conflicts.[21]

How best to arrest the democratization of America was another matter that was never far from the minds of many delegates. Randolph had addressed the issue in the Convention's first major speech, but Alexander Hamilton delivered the most candid remarks on this score. In a remarkable six-hour speech on June 18, he contended that because the people are "turbulent" and "seldom judge or determine right," the national government should be fashioned in such a manner that it could serve as a shield against the "imprudence of democracy." He advocated a government in which the lower house of Congress, whose members unavoidably would be regularly elected by popular vote, would be balanced by an upper chamber consisting of members elected for life and an executive, whom he styled an "elective monarch," that also would serve a life term. Hamilton further urged that his monarchical-like executive not only be given absolute veto powers but that he and Congress be vested with authority to appoint state governors. He additionally recommended that the national government be permitted to invalidate state laws.[22] Finally, Hamilton proposed a national government that replicated that of

Great Britain and a federal-state relationship that would bear a striking resemblance to what London had fancied for the colonies' relationship with the imperial government. Soon thereafter a delegate confessed that Hamilton's recommendations "had been praised by everybody," though he added that they were too radical to be accepted.[23]

Knowing that would be the case, Hamilton had prefaced his comments by saying that his proposals were not "a thing attainable by us, but . . . a model which we ought to approach as near as possible." For its duration, the convention struggled with pragmatic means through which to limit state power and "check . . . changeableness, and excess," as Gouverneur Morris put it. Some delegates were so zealous to eradicate state independence, in some instances even to have the states wither and die, that the more moderate and more pragmatic came to see that if the radicals had their way the constitution would never be approved. Thus, the manner in which the federal relationship was constructed—the degree of sovereignty bestowed on the national government and the consequent forfeiture of authority by the states—became the utmost challenge that faced the convention, greater even than the divisions between large and small states, free and slave. Ultimately, the hard-liners were kept in check, and schemes to negate all state laws, such as that outlined in the Virginia Plan, were never explicitly incorporated in the Constitution.

Yet the proposed national government was to be vastly more powerful than its predecessor. The national law was to be the "supreme law of the land," and the proposed constitution moved the nation from the voluntary compliance of the states to a system in which the national government could enforce its laws through coercive means if necessary. To the limits on state powers imposed by the Articles of Confederation—prohibitions on making treaties and declaring war—the new constitution forbade the states to tax or restrain interstate commerce, coin money, impair contracts, or permit the payment of debts with anything but gold or silver legal tender.[24] Yet a degree of state authority was to survive. The states were to decide who was eligible to vote, and state legislatures were empowered to select United States senators. By recommending the election of the chief executive by the electoral college, rather than by a simple majority vote of those who were enfranchised, state authority was augmented. Some believed too that by enumerating the powers of Congress, the proposed constitution implied that all other powers were reserved to the states.[25]

The convention also eventually created a republican system through which democracy was to be inhibited. Like Hamilton, many delegates were eager to limit democratic impulses. James McHenry of Maryland declared that "Our chief danger arises from the democratic parts of our constitutions."[26] Roger Sherman advocated that the "people . . . should have as little to do as may be about the Government."[27] Elbridge Gerry of Massachusetts believed that the "evils we experience flow from the excess of democracy."[28] On three separate occasions Randolph urged checks against "the turbulence and follies of democracy" and maintained that ways must be found to restrain "the fury of democracy."[29]

In the end the Convention embraced what Madison subsequently called the "republican remedy" against radical change. Madison explained that it was unlikely that any one faction could control the central government and that the plethora of interests represented at the national level would be able to quash the "sinister views" of any single interest group. The compromises and trade-offs necessary for building a workable majority, he later explained, would mean that the greater "public good and private rights" would be secured, while "at the same time . . . the spirit and the form of popular government" could be preserved. In the unlikely event that one narrow faction gained control of the House of Representatives, the only national branch whose members were directly elected, it was improbable that the same interest could also predominate both in the Senate, which represented states, and the executive branch, which was a national office filled by a vote of the electoral college. Indeed, Madison boasted proudly that this system would "refine and enlarge the public views," resulting in national policies "more consonant to the public good than if pronounced by the people themselves."

Madison's subsequent remarks were meant to convince a wary public, haunted by an abiding fear of centralized government, that the proposed central government could not fall into the clutches of a tyrannical element. But somewhat cryptically he also explained why this new national government would not be susceptible to the sort of substantive changes that had occurred in several states. Few of the "new men" so visible in state politics, Madison said, were likely to rise to this higher level. The "vicious arts by which elections are too often carried" in the states would be unavailing in the national electoral systems designed by this convention. These state politicians of "Factious tempers, of local prejudices, or of sinister designs," who so often allegedly "betray[ed] the interests of the people," would be filtered out and confined to the emasculated states where they could do little harm. Conversely, those who held national office were likely to be men of "attractive merit and the most diffuse and established characters." National officials would be "a better class of leaders" drawn from "a better class" of society, as Jack Rakove has fairly summarized Madison's argument.[30] Madison's communication, first to the majority that attended the convention, then to like-minded nationalists throughout the country, was that the way had been found by which to make radical change difficult, if not impossible. Change at the state level would be impeded by the national government. At the national level, the separation of powers and numerous checks and balances erected within the proposed new constitutional system were to constitute purposeful barriers to change. In addition, the "republican remedy" would impede what he called "a majority of the whole" from acting in "concert and execut[ing] their plans."[31] Future change at the national level could be effected only with considerable difficulty and never impetuously. If this Constitution went into effect, the "change-ableness" that had been set afoot by the American Revolution would henceforth be unlikely or, at best, would occur at a glacial pace. Future change might be possible when willed by an overwhelming national mood, but even then reformers would face poor prospects.

It had been a remarkable performance by politicians whose skills have never been surpassed. Only the most adroit leaders could have con-vened the Philadelphia Convention in the first place. Not only had the nationalist movement appeared to be beyond hope when the war ended in 1783, but in the four years of peace that followed, prosperity was wide-spread and growing, and the United States had faced no immediate for-eign threats. Save for the nationalists themselves, the American people had betrayed no sense of suffering through a "Critical Period."

The Framers' greatest triumph came in getting twelve state delega-tions to Philadelphia. Once discussion commenced at the Constitutional Convention, success in agreeing upon a draft document was likely. Too much has been made of the divisions that separated the delegates, for in reality this was remarkably homogenous assembly. By and large, the del-egates desperately wanted to achieve their ends, and they possessed the political skills to see their way through the shoals that abounded. They did what artful politicians have always done to succeed in a free and open process. They bullied and hectored, ranted and threatened, con-ceded and compromised, ignored some things that were too thorny to touch (the qualifications for voting, for instance), cleverly glided past other potential impediments with a wink and a nod, such as with the matter of judicial review, and headed off trouble here and there by uti-lizing what a political scientist once called "definitional pluralism"— composing some clauses in such a manner that its meaning was left to the courts, or to succeeding generations, for future interpretation.[32]

The Philadelphia Convention had been the easy part. Securing the rati-fication of the Constitution would be more exacting. Nevertheless, the Framers had taken a crucial first step in holding in check the likes of

Hamilton and Madison. The watchword of the pragmatists had been to draft a constitution that resonated with what one called the "genius of the people." Pierce Butler, a delegate from South Carolina, said it best: The Convention "must follow the example of Solomon, who gave the Athenians not the best government he could devise but the best they would receive."[33] Even so, at the Convention itself the delegates foresaw unmistakable signs that ratification would be a grueling battle. Some dismayed delegates had quit the Convention and returned home, while Edmund Randolph and George Mason of Virginia, as well as Elbridge Gerry, stayed on until adjournment but refused to sign the finished product.[34]

The first substantive hurdle was to get the Constitution safely past Congress. Nothing in the Constitution, or in Congress's sanction of the Convention, stipulated that congressional approval must be attained. However, political realities made such a step impossible to avoid, especially as the Philadelphia Convention had gone far beyond the limits that Congress had authorized. Furthermore, a congressional sanction would start the ratification process on a high note. The Framers, moreover, were confident that Congress would endorse the proposed document, as fully one-third of its members had been delegates to the Philadelphia Convention, and many other Framers hurried to New York to lobby the undecided in Congress. In addition, a massive effort was launched in the press to sell the proposed new charter and to preempt possible objections that might be raised.[35]

For a time it must have appeared to many Framers that they had miscalculated. The Constitution ignited a firestorm of dissent in Congress. In three days of furious debate, attempts were made to add amendments prior to sending the document to the states, and some congressmen even urged another convention to reconsider the constitution. Richard Henry Lee, among others, proposed the inclusion of a Bill of Rights, as well as amendments that would have eliminated the vice presidency and created a privy council to "advise and assist" the president. Ultimately, the opposition was not so much beaten back as it simply conceded that it was prudent to send the Constitution to the states. Lee, for example, who opposed the Constitution, concluded that as twelve states had sent delegates to the Philadelphia Convention, and as "Men of respected characters have agreed upon" the document, it "would be indecent not to send it to the states." On September 29, without formal approval or disapproval, Congress referred the Constitution to the states.[36]

Securing the approval of three-fourths of the states was the next obstacle. The elimination of the requirement of unanimous consent, the factor that had inhibited the ratification of the Articles of Confederation for four years and repeatedly frustrated the enactment of an impost amendment, made the approval of this document a distinct possibility. So too did the fact that the framers had wisely agreed to bypass the state legislatures, which faced a loss of power and prestige if the Constitution went into effect. Instead, the proposed document was to be considered by ratification conventions "chosen in each state by the people thereof." Hence, the state assemblies were even prohibited from electing the members of these conventions. Nevertheless, the framers expected a tough fight to obtain the sanction of nine states and especially to secure ratification by each of the crucial large states, Pennsylvania, Massachusetts, New York, and Virginia.

Persistently localist Rhode Island had looked with such disfavor on the prospect of vesting a national government with extensive powers of taxation, and the sole authority over the money supply, that it had not even sent a delegation to Philadelphia.[37] As no one expected a favorable vote from that state, the contest was to win approval of nine of the remaining twelve. It soon was readily apparent that the Federalists were strongest in the urban centers and eastern counties in most states, while the Anti-Federalists usually predominated in the backcountry and particularly so in western New England, Pennsylvania, New York, South Carolina, and Virginia. Moreover, opposition to ratification was especially strong throughout North Carolina, a state with neither a large planter class nor a dominant commercial metropolis and in which power resided with the soft-money agrarian sector.

There, and in the rural sectors generally, small farmers echoed the Anglo-American Whig tradition of caution and jealousy toward governmental authority and were kindred spirits with Paine, who in *Common Sense* had asserted that "government . . . is but a necessary evil" whose only purpose was to provide "freedom and security." Season after season these people worked the land, and many sent scant harvests to market. They had little need for government assistance, except at the local level, where it could provide order and keep the roads and bridges in tolerable shape. They looked on centralized governments as dangerous. Centralization—what they repeatedly called "consolidation"— almost always resulted in faraway governments under the sway of those who harbored different ambitions and dissimilar interests. Frequently, too, power reposed in the hands of corrupt officials. Living in the umbra of despotism, the ancestors of these yeomen long ago had sought to escape the heavy hand of monarchical and aristocratically controlled central governments in England and Europe by fleeing to America. In recent years, they had been confronted with what they believed was the "same tyranny which drove the first emigrants from home." They had forcefully resisted what Paine had called a cruel British "King and his parasites" and "enterprising ruffians."[38] In the eyes of many, the proposed constitution once again raised the specter of encroaching government. While the nationalists had been absorbed with the dangers that arose from a powerless central government, many among those who lived unadorned lives in the green American countryside were, and always had been, preoccupied with troubling visions of officials armed with excessive power. Thus, beginning in the autumn of 1787, the Anti-Federalists fought back with fervor and intensity, waging a battle that grew from such a popular groundswell of opposition to the Constitution that historian Saul Cornell, the scholar who most recently has studied in depth those who were hostile to ratification, was prompted to write of the "democratic character" of their campaign against ratification.[39]

Most Anti-Federalists conceded that the Articles of Confederation was flawed and required remodeling to meet the nation's defense and security needs. Many Northern Anti-Federalists also appear to have welcomed the greater authority over commerce bestowed on the proposed national government. Yet, as Samuel Adams remarked, most of those who opposed the Constitution never wished for anything other than a system in which the "distinct sovereign States confederated for the purpose of mutual Safety and Happiness." Adams added that he was willing only that the states should contribute "to the federal Head such a Part of its Sovereignty as would render the Government fully adequate to those Purposes, and *no more*."[40] The overarching theme of the Anti-Federalists was that the proposed national government would be dangerously powerful. More implicitly than explicitly, they conveyed the notion that the shape of the proposed national government and that of the British government against which they had recently struggled were remarkably similar. Some feared that the president would have vast appointive powers not unlike those of the king of England. Furthermore, like the British monarch, who used his prerogative powers to exert a profound influence over Parliament, the American president soon might strip the national legislature of its independence. Numerous Anti-Federalists predicted that a president who was so detached from the people, in control of the army, and with a long term and the capability of repeatedly being reelected, would simply be too powerful, too independent, and too likely to evolve into a monarchy. Some insisted that Congress's powers of taxation would resemble that which Parliament had sought to establish over the colonial provinces. Others observed that the Senate, with only statewide representatives, would be too removed from the people and too likely to devolve into an overbearing aristocratic body, like the House of Lords. The Anti-Federalists devoted less space to the judiciary, but Elbridge Gerry, in perhaps the most influential tract written against ratification, predicted that the "judicial department will be oppressive," and others argued that its broad jurisdiction would destroy the integrity of state tribunals. Not only did the Anti-Federalists question the Founders' commitment to republicanism. They also doubted that republicanism could endure in a framework with a remote consolidated government that stretched over the vast spatial dimensions of the new United States. Should the new constitution be ratified, they cautioned, the "absolute ruin" of the Revolutionary experiment in republicanism would ensue. A nation state would evolve that was the mirror image of the former mother country "which you heretofore reprobated as odious." Indeed, liberty in America would be less safe than in Great Britain, for the latter had a Bill of Rights, yet the Framers had chosen to omit from their constitution a similar guarantee of the "unalienable rights of men."[41]

For many Anti-Federalists, the fundamental issue in this struggle was whether America was to be dominated by a well-born elite that looked on holding power as its birthright, or whether leaders were to emerge through a popular, even democratic process. For some Anti-Federalists the question took on class overtones. Many foes of the constitution presumed that the new national government, as was true of its counterpart in the former mother country, inevitably would be the tool through which the rich exploited the less fortunate. Were ordinary Americans, they wondered, to "become prey to [their] avarice, insolence, and oppression" until those in authority had "engross[ed] all property"? Were the common people, asked Patrick Henry, to groan under "dreadful oppression" at the hands of "unfeeling blood-suckers" bent on "totally . . . ruining the people" with "cruel extortions"?[42]

Nothing caused the Anti-Federalists greater concern than the belief that the states would be doomed to powerlessness, maybe even extinction, under the proposed central government. When Samuel Adams glimpsed the proposed constitution, he sighed: "I meet with a national government instead of a federal union of sovereign states." He added that "the Idea of sovereignty in these states must be lost."[43] Similarly, Henry argued that only "the constant vigilance of the [state] legislature[s]" had prevented the "most horrid and barbarous ravages" by a central government. He warned Virginians that when state supremacy was vanquished, "You will find all the strength of this country in the hands of your enemies."[44]

Lurking behind the specific arguments of many Anti-Federalists was the sense that the Constitution repudiated the American Revolution. They believed that a consolidated government, whose officials were removed from the people, yet given sweeping powers, was the very antithesis of what the American people had set out in 1776 to achieve. The

American Revolution, remarked an Anti-Federalist in the Massachusetts convention, "freed us from a *foreign subjugation,* and there is much to apprehend, that the [proposed constitution] will reduce us to a *federal domination.*" Samuel Adams warned, "The Seeds of Aristocracy began to spring even before the Conclusion of our Struggle for the Natural Rights of Man, Seeds which like the Canker Worm lie at the Root of free Governments" and can be expected to flourish, and to reseed, under the proposed constitution.[45]

But the Anti-Federalists failed to stop the nationalists. Within ten months they had been swept aside. Four states ratified the Constitution by the end of 1787, and a fifth approved it on the second day of the new year. Three of these states acted unanimously, giving the Federalists considerable momentum on the eve of the battles in the tougher states, especially in Massachusetts, where the ratification convention was gaveled to order in Boston on January 9. The showdown battle in Massachusetts was "the decisive conflict," according to the historian Jackson Turner Main, for if the Constitution failed there, it was a good bet that the Federalist juggernaut would go awry in some of the other closely contested states. Furthermore, the Federalists in Massachusetts nearly failed. Not only did two important leaders, Samuel Adams and John Hancock, at least initially withhold their endorsement, but the Anti-Federalists possessed roughly a twenty-seat majority in the ratification convention.[46]

Samuel Adams was deeply conflicted by the proposed constitution. On the one hand, he had long favored vesting the national government with greater control over commerce, both to aid the merchants and workers in Boston and to enable the United States to retaliate against London for the postwar restrictions it imposed on America's trade. Furthermore, he knew that most Bostonians favored ratification, and he feared that to reject the constitution was to risk disunion, a step that could jeopardize New England's security. However, he remained as much a decentralist as he had been when he resisted the imperial government's attempts to expand its authority over the colonies after 1765. Consolidation, he said, was a formula for giving faraway peoples, whose "Habits & particular Interests are and probably always will be so different" from those of New Englanders, sway over the denizens of Massachusetts.[47] One can only wonder, too, whether Adams, faced with a constitution that was designed in part to stymie soft money advocates, believed that a Federalist victory would mean that the soulmates of Thomas Hutchinson and Andrew Oliver had ultimately emerged triumphant.

On the eve of the ratification convention, Adams anonymously denounced the proposed constitution in the Boston press. He denied that the nation or its inhabitants were endangered by the decentralized system that existed. Warnings of imminent disaster, he said, were "a bug-bear" to deceive the populace. In reality, the nationalists' desire to strengthen the central government could in large part be attributed to their wish for economic self-aggrandizement. In "plain truth," he went on, the Constitution was the product of interest groups that wished for government help in regulating their commerce, promoting their manu-factures, and advancing their agriculture. In particular, he insisted, the Constitution was a ploy by Northern merchants to secure the carrying trade of Southern planters. He blasted the constitution for failing to in-clude a Bill of Rights, and insisted that the executive would be too power-ful, the states would be "annihilated," Congress would be too independent of its constituents, the scope of the federal judiciary was frighteningly wide, and the electoral college would be a swamp of bribery and corrup-tion.[48] Other oblique statements suggest that he shared the outlook of his old friend, Samuel Osgood, treasurer of the United States, who had recently written him cautioning that the proposed constitution was filled with legal abstractions whose meaning would ultimately be determined by appointed federal judges—" Scribes & Pharisees," Osgood called them—who served for life and were insulated from public control. Adams acknowledged that problems existed, but characteristically he charged that "we have brought [many of them] upon ourselves by dissipation and extravagance," not by a flawed government. Many ills of the day could be remedied "by industry and frugality," he said, and by abandon-ing "the luxurious living of all ranks and degrees." Yet Adams conceded the necessity to "give energy to the [national] government," and ulti-mately recommended amending the Articles to give Congress greater control over commerce. This, he said, would create "one Federal System of commerce" that would cut through "all local attachment, and estab-lish our navigation upon a most extensive basis."[49]

For all that he said, Adams never openly disavowed the Constitu-tion, and when he remained silent during the first several sessions of the ratification convention, many thought him indecisive. Perhaps he was, although as a savvy and influential public official, his taciturnity may have been designed to elicit concessions from the Federalists in return for his support. That appears to have been the tack that Hancock took, as he also refused to commit to either side during the first couple weeks of the meeting. Ultimately, Hancock was first to break his silence and announce his support for the Constitution. According to a story that was often repeated, Adams and Hancock, anguished over the prudent course to take, met at the latter's residence ten days or so into the con-vention in an attempt to reach a decision. Supposedly they talked deep into that cold winter's night, arguing the merits of the Constitution and exploring the dangers that would accompany rejection. At length, so went the story, hours of agonizing deliberation and careful reasoning brought both around to support ratification. The truth was less pretty. Each man was lobbied by both sides, the "rats" and "antirats," as Gerry labeled the contending factions. At least as far as Hancock was concerned, the Federalists had more to offer. Should he commit for the constitution, they pledged to support him for the vice presidency, and for the presidency in the event that Virginia failed to ratify, which would preclude Washington from the top post. They also agreed to support amendments to the Constitution that he wished.

The Federalists handled Adams differently, presumably because they knew that he was not for sale. Indeed, they appear to have concluded that the prudent course was to have their working-class adherents solicit his support. Convinced that the new constitution alone offered a prospect of opening trade with Great Britain and for pumping fresh life into the province's languorous economy, Boston's mechanics strongly supported ratification. Late in January, after the ratification convention had been in session for three weeks, they held a mass meeting at the Green Dragon Tavern and endorsed the Constitution. The resolution they adopted made clear that they acted from economic interest. "It is our opinion," their statement began, "that if said constitution should be adopted by the United States of America, trade and navigation will revive and increase, employ and subsistence will be afforded to many of our townsmen, who are now suffering from want of necessities of life." However, if ratification failed, "commerce . . . will be annihilated . . . [and] various trades and handicrafts dependent thereon must decay; our poor will be increased," and many workers will leave Massachusetts in search of greener pastures.[50] The workers nominated Paul Revere to deliver their resolution to Adams, and several hundred spilled out of the tavern to escort the patriot silversmith along Boston's snow-covered streets to their paladin's residence. Although details of the lengthy meeting that ensued between Revere and Adams are murky, it appears that Adams, who was genuinely anxious that his old friends and acolytes flourish, agreed to support the Constitution. However, like Hancock, he must have made clear that his support was conditional on the attachment of amendments to the Constitution.

Hancock was first to reveal his support for the constitution. Two weeks into the Massachusetts Convention, he took the floor and dramatically announced that he would support the ratification of an amended constitution. He then read a proposed set of amendments—they had actually been written for him by his new Federalist friends—that were designed to harness the new national government and expressly reserve to the states all powers not categorically delegated to Congress. Hancock had no more than completed his electrifying statement when Adams spoke for the first time, announcing his support for an amended Constitution. The amendments, he said, would provide a reasonable guarantee that "each state retains its sovereignty, freedom, and independence." Furthermore, the amendments gave him confidence that the "strongest guard against the encroachments of power" were to be part of the Constitution.[51] The events of that day, January 31, 1788, in all likelihood sealed the fate of the Anti-Federalists in Massachusetts. What is more, if Massachusetts's vote was truly as crucial as some historians believe, this perhaps was the moment that ensured that the requisite nine states would ratify the proposed constitution.

The Federalists had waged an adroit campaign in Massachusetts. They benefited from a cadre of savvy leaders who drew on their experiences in the popular protest and from years of public service, as well as from the support of the most important merchants, preachers, and lawyers in the state. Nor did it hurt that every single newspaper in Boston urged ratification, or that it was difficult to find a journal anywhere in the state that would print an Anti-Federalist squib. They also utilized tactics—including the unsavory variety—that were to become commonplace democratic practices in the nineteenth and twentieth centuries. The Federalists published misleading reports claiming that popular local figures favored the Constitution, when they knew the opposite to be true. They secured the election of one of their own as secretary of the ratification convention, and he saw to it that much of the Anti-Federalist critique of the Constitution was omitted in the published journal of the proceedings. Furthermore, there is credible evidence that some Anti-Federalists were bribed into switching sides. Oliver Phelps of Berkshire County, for instance, appears to have joined the Federalist camp immediately after he was released from a private debt obligation. Luck also played a role in the Federalist victory. Nearly three score towns in the solidly Anti-Federalist west, where the Shaysites had sought succor only a year earlier, were so economically hard-pressed that they could not afford to send a delegate to the convention. Had even a fraction of those delegates attended, it seems inconceivable that the Anti-Federalists could have lost.[52]

Just days after their spectacular success in Massachusetts, the Federalists suffered their initial setback. Friends of ratification in New Hampshire were compelled to push through an adjournment in that state's convention rather than risk almost certain defeat. Hard on the heels of that disappointment, North Carolina rejected the proposed constitution, but Maryland and South Carolina approved by comfortable margins during the next thirty days. With summer coming on, the Federalists were just one state short of ratifying the Constitution, with New Hampshire, Virginia, and New York yet to act.

The votes for ratification in New Hampshire and Virginia came just four days apart during the first warm days of summer in 1788. New Hampshire acted first, pushing the Constitution over the top, but everyone understood that the approval of Virginia, the largest and oldest of the thirteen states, was of infinitely greater importance. Federalists everywhere also understood that the issue was in doubt in Virginia and that as never before the defenders of the Constitution would face a formidable array of talent. Patrick Henry, Richard Henry Lee, former governor Thomas Nelson, Benjamin Harrison, James Monroe, and George Mason opposed ratification.

Nevertheless, Virginia's Federalists ultimately triumphed by a ten-vote margin in a convention that consisted of 168 delegates. The talent in their stable matched that of their adversaries. The war hero, Colonel Henry Lee (Light-Horse Harry as he was popularly known), was a Federalist, as were George Wythe, who had signed the Declaration of Independence, Governor Randolph, who bounced from side to side before landing in the "rats" court, up and coming John Marshall, the veteran Edmund Pendleton, under whose guidance the Virginia legislature had drafted the state's Declaration of Rights in 1776, and of course Madison, who easily could anticipate every Anti-Federalist argument, having heard every one at the Philadelphia Convention. Like their counterparts in Massachusetts, Virginia's Federalists won converts by pledging to work for a bill of rights. They reaped benefits as well from the towering influence of Washington, who though not a delegate was identified with the Constitution. Furthermore, during the deliberations in steamy July news arrived of New Hampshire's ratification. It now was a stark fact that the Constitution would be put into effect in a United States of at least nine states. If it rejected the proposed charter, Virginia would forfeit the opportunity—and the benefits that might accrue from it—of having Washington, its native son, occupy the new executive branch, and the state would have no voice in the shape given the national government.[53]

It was midsummer before New York's delegates gathered in Poughkeepsie, on the east bank of the softly flowing green waters of the Hudson River. New York's Federalists faced what appeared to be an insuperable challenge. As the ratification convention was elected so late, the foes of the Constitution had ample time to organize. The Anti-Federalists elected forty-six of the sixty-five delegates, but they failed here as well. Some undecided delegates eventually voted with the Federalists because they believed the foes of ratification failed to present a viable alternative to the proposed constitution. Others tipped to the Federalists from fear that the long list of amendments presented by the Anti-Federalists would have had a paralyzing impact on the new national government. Furthermore, what played out in Poughkeepsie bore a striking resemblance to the events six months earlier in Boston. As in the contest in Massachusetts, the New York press was heavily committed to ratification and hammered away at the virtues of the Constitution throughout the spring and summer. There is circumstantial evidence that bribery may have made turncoats of a couple Anti-Federalists, and others were stampeded into supporting ratification by the threat that New York City, together with four southern counties, would secede from the state and join the Union if the convention failed to ratify the Constitution. Finally, many delegates were swayed by the realization that the Constitution had been ratified—now by ten states—and without question would be implemented. Indeed, once word of Virginia's vote reached Poughkeepsie— Madison wrote Hamilton immediately upon the victorious outcome in Richmond—the issue ceased to be the Constitution and instead became whether New York should be in or out of the Union. The stakes were high. As with Virginia, New Yorkers feared losing their voice in the new government. In addition, to fail to ratify the Constitution meant beyond the shadow of a doubt that New York City would lose its chance of becoming the national capital.[54]

The ratification battle was over. Eleven states, including the four largest and most powerful, had approved the Constitution. While it is not surprising that the opponents of the proposed constitution failed, it is amazing that they came so close to repudiating the handiwork of the Philadelphia Convention. Despite having elected a majority of delegates in several states, the deck was stacked against them. Near the end of the Philadelphia Convention, Washington remarked that whichever side succeeded in shaping the public debate would win the battle over ratification. The Anti-Federalists never came close on this score. The Federalists burst out of Philadelphia with a defense of the proposed charter intact. Not only did they enjoy almost a free hand in the nation's newspapers but they were also better financed and better organized. In some measure, this resulted from their persistent campaign for reform from 1781 to 1787, as well as from the concerted planning for the ratification struggle that must have taken place during the final fruitful weeks of the Philadelphia Convention. What is more, the Federalists were led by shrewd and modern political tacticians. They often set an early date for the election of the ratification convention, scheduling the polling before their foes could adequately organize. In Massachusetts, they succeeded in infiltrating the Anti-Federalist caucuses, where they learned the plans

of their adversaries, and in New Hampshire they appear to have conspired to prevent the circulation of their foe's literature through the mail.
In state after state, and city after city, they held carefully planned proces-
sions, modeled after the enthusiastic rallies that rejoiced at the Declaration of Independence in 1776, to celebrate each ratification victory. Often
the site of the ceremony was renamed as Federal Hill or Federal Tavern.
Always, ratification was tied to nationalism and unity, which was observed symbolically by the firing of thirteen cannon or the drinking of
thirteen toasts.[55] However, perhaps the Federalists' most striking and most
surprising accomplishment was their success in somehow convincing so
many that the nation faced a grave crisis that could only be resolved by a
stronger national government.

The Federalists reaped the harvest of the trouble they had taken in
getting Franklin and Washington to the Constitutional Convention. The
knowledge that Washington endorsed the constitution proved to be a
magical asset throughout America. The General was especially useful in
Maryland, where he "meddled"— his term—and persuaded some undecided delegates of the wisdom of ratification. Nor did Washington
object when Federalists published accounts of phantom speeches in support of the Constitution that he allegedly had delivered during the Philadelphia Convention or when they leaked to Federalist newspapers some
of his recent nationalist-tinged correspondence. Perhaps the most savvy
of the Federalist strategies was not only to portray the Constitution as a
moderate document that had been produced by a convention characterized by repeated compromises but also to present it as having been
fashioned by statesmen dedicated to "sacrificing private opinions and
partial interests to the public good," as Madison claimed. With considerable cunning, the nationalists even scored a political coup by appropriating the name Federalist, though in fact to this point the term *federalist*
had designated those who, like Samuel Adams, had urged a union of
sovereign states in a national confederation. They were extraordinarily
skilled in winning converts, whether through influence or persuasion.
Moreover, from April onward, as the realization grew that ratification
was ensured, would-be office seekers climbed aboard the Federalist bandwagon. Indeed, whereas virtually no Federalists converted to the opposition, in many states numerous Anti-Federalists defected.[56]

Unlike the process of ratifying the Articles of Confederation after
1777, when little public heat had been generated, this was a furious battle,
especially in press and pamphlets. The quality of the Anti-Federalists'
literary effort largely equaled that of their adversaries, but the nationalists published far more essays. They also accounted for the single best
effort, eighty-five newspaper essays written by Madison, Hamilton, and

Jay that were eventually published collectively as *The Federalist.* Written under the pseudonym Publius, these essays appeared in New York newspapers and may have helped sway just enough delegates in that state, and Virginia as well, to secure victory. It was a sophisticated effort, an intermingling of artful popular politics with a reasoned and erudite defense of the Constitution. Although the three authors explored numerous issues, it goes without saying that they especially succeeded in reassuring many readers that republican federalism could act with energy, yet personal liberties would be safe and sufficient authority would be left to the states.[57]

The authors of the *Federalist* accomplished something else that has often been overlooked. For a people who knew warfare at first hand—America had spent roughly half of the thirty years between 1754 and 1783 at war—and who remembered all too well how close they had come to losing the War of Independence, the *Federalist* masterfully argued the need for a strong national government that could meet the national security needs of the young nation. Hamilton stressed that a national government armed with far-reaching powers was essential for coping with the inevitable territorial disputes and commercial rivalries, but he additionally emphasized that peace must always be considered problematical, for like humankind, nations—and the thirteen states—were driven by avarice, rage, resentment, jealousy, and "other irregular and violent propensities." A powerful national government would safeguard the new nation from foreign powers that inevitably would seek to cultivate tensions between the sections in the United States or to exploit the differences that already existed. Vulnerable and held in contempt by Europe, America was destined to be "a prey to every nation." Given these realities, it would be "the extreme of folly" to continue with a government with an "absolute incapacity to provide for the protection of the community." In contrast, a strong national government not only could deter the bellicose hand of Europe, but it could retaliate when a "*just* cause of war" existed. Hamilton told readers that America had won the War of Independence principally because the citizenry had been driven by "the enthusiasm of liberty." That was not sufficient for the future. Such a spirit would not always exist. Without remedial steps, America in its next war might be undone by the very ills that had nearly proved ruinous after 1776: obstructionist provinces, exiguous manpower levies, a lack of revenue, and a discontented army that was undone more by the foolery of its national political system than by European armed might. It was Hamilton, too, who offered the most breathtaking nationalist vision. Under a strong American government, he wrote, the United States could

take advantage of Europe's woes and perhaps even manipulate "the balance of European competitors in this part of the world as our interests
may dictate." There was a good chance, he insisted, that an energetic
government under the new Constitution soon would be "able to dictate
the terms of the connection between the old and new world." But there
was more. The great achievements of civil society could never be realized in a weak, distracted nation. Thus, above all else, Hamilton stressed
that the arts and sciences, literature, and the economy could truly flourish only in a United States that was powerful and secure.[58]

The Anti-Federalists had mounted a determined resistance, and when
time permitted they successfully galvanized effective local resistance movements. They succeeded, for instance, in electing majorities in almost every
ratification convention that met after January 1788. However, of those conventions, only North Carolina repudiated the Constitution. The Anti-
Federalists were injured almost everywhere by their inability to orchestrate a truly national campaign in opposition to the Constitution. They
failed even to establish interstate committees of correspondence, a staple
of the popular protest against Great Britain before 1776. Although in many
states the Anti-Federalists advocated the inclusion of a bill of rights in the
Constitution, they might also have coalesced around a core of essential
amendments that would have limited the authority of the proposed national government. Instead, through a scattergun approach they sought to
raise doubts about several portions of the constitution, but failed to project
a viable substitute for the flawed Articles of Confederation.[59]

In some respects, too, the behavior throughout the 1780s of those who
ultimately opposed the Constitution contributed to the slow and fatal erosion of their credibility. That they had previously disapproved much they
now recommended—including the seven proposed amendments that
Congress considered, and rejected, in 1787—must have struck some as
hypocrisy. Worse perhaps was the belief—as Madison charged—that the
foes of the Constitution "had no plan whatever." Madison overstated the
matter, but to many citizens it appeared as if the Anti-Federalists failed to
present a convincing alternative to the proposed constitution, ultimately
rendering the issue as one of choosing, with misgivings, the new constitution or of remaining with a patently flawed document whose continued existence imperiled the fragile Union. To many, the Anti-Federalists
were the "disorganizers," as the Federalists cleverly labeled those who
wished to prevent the dismantling of the existing national government.[60]

At the outset of the contest, the Anti-Federalists enjoyed widespread
support from a public that distrusted consolidation, but in time they
were overwhelmed as many Americans came to believe that fatal conse-

quences would ensue if the national government were not changed. In particular, the Anti-Federalists failed to answer the nationalists' claim that an energetic government was essential for providing for the national security. They countered with arguments that the president would become "a military king" who might lead America into foreign wars, that an American aristocracy would dominate the armed forces, and that liberty would be extinguished by a standing army. They insisted too that the real objective of the Federalists was not protection but the conversion of America into "a powerful and mighty empire." But they never adequately demonstrated that the existing national government could protect the peace or save the nation from a foreign peril.[61] Furthermore, by 1788 America was gripped with the sense that the handiwork of the Philadelphia Convention was the last hope to save the dreams of the American Revolution. No one imagined that adopting a new constitution was without risks, but balanced against the seemingly obvious hazards of rejecting the Constitution, its adoption seemed a necessary gamble. And one thing more. This generation had gambled once before, in 1776. Few believed that the Revolutionary leadership had betrayed the public trust. Faith in those leaders persisted, and many were certain that the trust vested in Washington had always been justified and would not be misplaced.[62]

The Federalist triumph, in some respects, signified that an elite not unlike that of the colonial era had recaptured authority. One need only read in tandem the frantic, eve-of-independence outpourings of an established colonial leader such as Joseph Galloway, who saw his world slipping away, and the hand-wringing in the "critical period" by those who disdained the new world that had been taking shape since 1776, to be struck by the numerous similarities in their viewpoints. Galloway, a Tory whose outlook mirrored that of numerous Loyalists, dreaded disorder and had been scared when desperate frontier farmers, the Paxton Boys, had threatened Pennsylvania with havoc in 1763. His mantra had been the imperative need for a strong central government characterized by checks and balances and vested with unquestioned sovereignty. Such a step was necessary to avert the ruin of America, he said. He had not cared much for the direct election of officials, and in a series of proposed plans of Anglo-American government he recommended that such a practice be limited to one house of the legislature. He feared and hated democracy and thought humankind so selfish, avaricious, ambitious, and aspiring that adequate controls could best be achieved through a somewhat remote national-imperial government capable of maintaining order, thwarting demagoguery, and harnessing blind, ruinous, selfish partisanship. He,

too, wished for an energetic government, one with the power and authority to safeguard America against corrupt Europe's predation, suppress civil discord, rein in states whose rapacity and rivalries threatened
the peace, and fulfill the colonists' expansionist dreams. All this could be
achieved, he believed, through the preservation of the Union, the Anglo-
American Union. John and Samuel Adams had opposed Galloway in
1774, seeing him as a master of "Machiavellian Dissimulation" whose
real agenda was the preservation of the existing ruling order. In 1788
many Anti-Federalists, in the hour of the Federalist triumph, suspected
that the motive of those responsible for the Constitution was to turn
back the clock and refashion a political order that Galloway—had he
not been forced into exile—could have relished.[63]

Ratification was an end and a beginning. While it closed the initial phase
of the nationalists' campaign that had begun to come together in the
aftermath of Yorktown, it inaugurated their campaign to dominate the
new national government. If the nationalists were to truly succeed, it
was essential that they persuade Washington to serve as chief executive
and prevent the Anti-Federalists from winning control of Congress.

Two years before the Philadelphia Convention, Washington had begun to speak of the need for a national government with an executive
branch. Thereafter, he could not have failed to notice that the nationalists longed to make him the chief executive in a reconfigured national
government, and from the moment he returned home from Philadelphia in September 1787 he must have pondered abandoning retirement
to undertake such a trust. As momentum built toward ratification, Washington knew that he soon would have to decide.

He was genuinely conflicted. Life at Mount Vernon was placid and
filled with seraphic luxuries, a mellow change after eight years of wartime danger and the daily cares of command. His greatest problems arose
from wasting droughts, destructive early freezes, runaway slaves, and
damage wrought by his neighbor's straying cattle. After nearly five years
at home, he was not convinced that he wished to abandon the rural stillness or exchange his insouciant lifestyle for the cares of public life. He
was nagged, too, by the knowledge that many males in the Washington
family had died at any early age, including his father and three half-
brothers who had perished before their fiftieth birthdays. At age fifty-six
in 1788, Washington feared that he had precious little time remaining,
and he wished to enjoy that which was left. Furthermore, he was reluctant to renege on his solemn pledge to retire forever from public life. To
do so might lead the public to conclude that he grasped after power.
Washington also feared the loss of his reputation should he once again

roll the dice on public service. If his presidency failed egregiously, either from events beyond his control or because of his lack of experience as a civil magistrate, the exalted reputation he had gained through his military service would be irretrievably lost.

However, other forces simultaneously pulled Washington back to public office. Deeply committed to the Union, he was aware that his presence might be crucial for helping the new national government through its first dangerous trials. What is more, while life was blissful at Mount Vernon, it was not exciting, and Washington appears to have missed the swirl of action and the rush that came from being at the center of great events. Yet he did not wish to pursue the office, lest he give the appearance of lusting after power. He wished to be coaxed to serve, and many who believed that the nimbus attached to Washington would ensure a reasonable chance that the new government would survive, did just that, beseeching him to quit retirement.

None who entreated his service was more persuasive—or more perceptive—than Alexander Hamilton. He told Washington that no ill will would result from breaking his pledge to never again hold office. Indeed, Hamilton tellingly remarked that it would be "inglorious" of Washington to fail to answer the call of his countrymen. His reputation, said Hamilton, who perfectly understood Washington, would suffer a far greater hazard from declining to serve than from assuming office. Late in 1788, Washington assented, telling all who listened that he did so "with more diffidence and reluctance than ever I experienced before in my life."[64]

Washington's decision determined the outcome of the first presidential election. Under the original Constitution, each member of the electoral college was to cast two ballots in the presidential contest, only one of which could be for a resident of the elector's state. If a winner was determined, the recipient of the second largest number of votes, whether or not a majority, was to be the vice president. If no one received a majority of the votes cast, the issue was to be decided by the House of Representatives. In February 1789 each elector cast one of his two votes for Washington, making him the unanimous choice for the new office. John Adams, the runner-up, was elected vice president. The nationalists, as it turned out, also had no cause for concern about the composition of the initial Congress. Only about 15 percent of the first House of Representatives and 10 percent of the Senate consisted of Anti-Federalists. Fully one in four of those who took their seats in the First Congress had been delegates to the Constitutional Convention.

A full year elapsed before Congress acted for the first time on the lingering postwar economic problems. But during those twelve months Washington carefully shaped the presidency. Many contemporaries, and some scholars, concluded that Washington was manipulated by more able men. Historian Forrest McDonald, for instance, has written that Washington was "beyond his ken" and that "his talents were not up to the tasks before him." Vice President Adams, who had finished second in the electoral college tally, subsequently portrayed the president as the "puppet" of Hamilton.[65] In fact, Washington assumed the presidency in April 1789 with a good notion not only of how to comport himself but how he wished to design his office.

Washington had learned through painful experience that improper behavior could rob an official of the public's affection. While a callow young commander of Virginia's army in the French and Indian War, Washington's conduct often had been unbecoming. Colonel Washington frequently had abandoned his army for weeks at a time to look after land purchases, visit friends at home, and lobby royal officials for a commission in the British army. At headquarters he sometimes enjoyed sumptuous pleasures while his men were in the clutch of privation. His self-centered habits nearly proved ruinous. Virginia's governor and some British generals judged him harshly, and he was savagely criticized in the colony's only newspaper.[66]

Washington learned from his early mistakes. While in command of the Continental army he lived simply, usually selecting modest farmhouses for his headquarters, eschewing pastimes, such as hunting, that had absorbed his attention at Mount Vernon, and before Yorktown he left his soldiers only when Congress summoned him for consultation. He worked long hours each day and exhibited a public demeanor that could best be described as Olympian. At times some questioned his military judgment, but no one took issue with the manner with which he comported himself. Washington had discovered, a French officer once noted, "the art of making himself beloved."[67]

Washington brought this seasoned outlook to the presidency, but as this was a civil office, and popular opinion was already rent over the structure of the new government, he sought the advice of Hamilton and others about how to comport himself. He was primarily concerned with what he called the "etiquette" of the office. He already knew how "to maintain the dignity of Office," he said, and was well aware of the line between "superciliousness" and "unnecessary reserve."[68]

Washington listened, but ultimately made choices that gave the presidency "a pretty high tone," as Hamilton put it. In actuality, Washington tried to blend republican practices, as he understood them, with royal formality. He eschewed the trappings of a royal court, dressing like a successful merchant or planter and throwing open the doors of the President's House for weekly levees, occasions when he greeted citizens in a receiving line, bowing stiffly and making a bit of small talk. He often was misunderstood. For example, Washington saw the levees as an attempt to make the chief executive available to the public, but many doubtless agreed with William Maclay, the senator from Pennsylvania, who remarked that it "escapes Nobody" that these ceremonies were "a feature of Royalty" and that as they were "certainly Anti-republican . . . cannot be much good."[69] Ironically, what the public perceived as his most egalitarian habit was misconstrued. A fitness proponent, Washington took a walk about the capital precisely at 2 P.M. daily, a ritual that won praise as a deliberate gesture to make himself appear to be a common citizen who shared the city's grimy sidewalks with ordinary Philadelphians. Much that Washington did was designed to fashion a courtly atmosphere. He traveled in a stately manner, riding in a handsome cream-colored carriage drawn by a team of six prancing horses and attended by numerous coachmen attired in livery. He hired the best chef in the capital, a man widely known as Black Sam Frances, and hosted stuffy dinners each Thursday, affairs that some congressmen privately excoriated as absurdly pompous occasions. Ultimately, the habitually imposing air that Washington long had exhibited, combined with the deliberately stilted and ritualistic manner with which he sought to vest the executive office, led none other than the secretary of the British legation to characterize the tenor of Washington's presidency as akin to that of a "very kingly style."[70]

Washington understood the psychology of power. As an unpolished and uneducated adolescent who had hungered to impress sophisticated men and women, Washington had begun to learn the art of influencing others. While still a teenager, he had discovered the secret of presenting himself in such a way as to play on his strongest attributes, his size, strength, and graceful athleticism. He had learned that the right clothing and the proper demeanor could accentuate those characteristics. Conversely, he grew adept at hiding his weaknesses. Early on, he found that if he said little in public, scarce likelihood existed that others would discern what he presumed were his inadequacies. He had worked assiduously to educate himself, reading what those whom he admired read, and he worked tirelessly to improve his writing style, so that he would not be embarrassed in his correspondence with formally educated officials and acquaintances. Later, when he soldiered, Washington took pains to teach his officers how to dress and comport themselves, and he carefully constructed a regimen both within the Virginia Regiment and the Continental army that underlined the authority of those in command.

As he had habitually made statements about himself through his habits and demeanor, Washington now fashioned a persona for the presidency. Although a committed republican, he sought to make the office suitably august and pulsating with energy and authority. Washington proceeded more deftly than Vice President Adams, who in attempting to vest his office with the dignity accorded a ministerial office in England or France, only aroused "ferment and disquietude" and even caused the president to snicker privately at his "high toned" manner. Washington found a prudent balance between ostentation and "too much reserve," between "respectability" and "too much familiarity." Moreover, during his first autumn in office, he took the presidency to the people. Accompanied by numerous local and state officials, and attended by carefully attired retainers, Washington journeyed through New England. For thousands it was their first, and for many their only, look at a federal official, a glimpse of the president of the United States, who exuded supremacy. Eighteen months later, he toured the South. During the two trips he appeared in countless towns and innumerable festive parades, nearly always riding behind the local militia, which marched and saluted smartly. He frequently uttered a few carefully rehearsed words in a brief ceremony in the town square or village green. Washington succeeded in making the presidency available to a republican citizenry, and he simultaneously conveyed to his countrymen a sense of the prowess and legitimacy of the new national government. Of no less significance, Washington carefully, calculatingly, exuded that same aura of unmistakable power before the Congress.[71]

The new national government came together slowly in 1789. Congress had been meeting for weeks before New York even elected its delegates, for instance, and it was late that cold spring before all the congressmen from the eleven states that had ratified the Constitution arrived in New York City, which remained the national capital. Summer passed and the first hints of coming autumn were in the air before Congress authorized the Treasury Department, the last of the various executive departments that the president desired. It was only then that Washington nominated, and Congress approved, Hamilton as secretary of treasury.

In the meantime, however, the government needed money to operate. Five months before Hamilton was nominated, Madison introduced revenue-raising measures in Congress. He proposed an impost of 5 percent on imports, the very measure that nationalists had sought to adopt at the time of the Newburgh affair, and a bill for slightly higher import duties on certain enumerated articles. Both passed, but his third measure foundered. Madison advocated that foreign ships pay higher tonnage duties than vessels flying the American flag, and that merchant craft from nations that had no commercial treaties with the United States pay still steeper taxes. Even many Southern congressmen deserted Madison on this bill. They opposed discriminatory duties out of fear that foreign shippers would be driven away, giving Northern merchants a monopoly over the Southern imports and exports. They joined with Northern representatives, who knew that merchants at home had no appetite for a ruinous commercial war with Great Britain, and the bill died in the Senate.[72]

Madison had better luck answering the Anti-Federalists' demand for the inclusion of a Bill of Rights in the Constitution. Speed was imperative, he thought, lest congressional inaction play into the hands of those who had demanded a second constitutional convention or that delay trigger movements in state legislatures for the passage of myriad emasculating amendments. By September, Madison's nationalist brethren, who wished to control this process, had passed and sent twelve amendments to the states for ratification. Although more than two years elapsed before the ten amendments that form the Bill of Rights were ratified, the rapid congressional action defused the movement in the states for additional changes to the Constitution. In addition, it helped secure ratification of the new national charter by Rhode Island and North Carolina, which thereafter reentered the Union.[73]

On almost the same day that Congress voted favorably on these amendments, it also directed Secretary Hamilton to prepare a plan for coping with the new nation's burdensome indebtedness. He was to report in January 1790. A good feeling existed. The Constitution and the new national government were up and running, and the first session of the First Congress had proceeded without searing fissures. President Washington captured the prevailing spirit when he rejoiced at the "Miracle that there should have been so much unanimity . . . and encreasing good will."[74]

Few realized, however, that time was running out on this era of good feelings. The bitter political battles of the early American Republic were about to begin.

10

1790–1793

"Prosperous at Home, Respectable Abroad"

reasury Secretary Alexander Hamilton, who had just turned thirty-two, worked tirelessly each day in the autumn of 1789 to complete his Report on Public Credit by the January deadline set by Congress. The First Congress thought its principal objective was to solve the national debt problems. It had lavished money on the Treasury Department, providing Hamilton with funds to hire a comptroller and an assistant secretary, as well as thirty clerks, eight times the number that either the State or War Department employed. The Treasury clerks conducted research for their boss, but Hamilton alone shaped his recommendations, often working deep into the chilly fall nights in his tiny, sparsely furnished office, seated at a plain pine table covered with a green cloth.[1]

The data unearthed by the clerks revealed that the United States had accumulated a foreign debt of $11,600,000, the result of wartime loans by France, Holland, and Spain, and the subsequent arrears in interest. A national debt also existed. Congress had tried to pay for the war by issuing unsecured paper money, loan office certificates—which were essentially bonds—and promissory notes. Although it seldom had the money to adequately provide for its soldiers, Congress nevertheless had rung up a staggering debt. Continental debts, including accumulating interest, were about four times greater than the foreign indebtedness, and that was only a portion of the domestic indebtedness. Prodigious state debts also existed. The states had attempted to meet their financial responsibilities between 1775 and 1783 through taxation, confiscation, and expropriation. None of these expedients raised sufficient revenue, especially in the last inflation-plagued years of hostilities. At war's end every state was in debt, although in the years since 1783 some provinces had made considerable strides toward reducing their indebtedness. Nevertheless, by 1789 the combined state indebtedness stood at approximately $25,000,000. Therefore, according to Treasury's data, the total war debt—foreign, national, and state—exceeded $76,000,000. As Hamilton hunched over his paperwork that fall, he discovered that the annual interest on these debts approached $5,000,000.

Every nationalist agreed—had agreed for nearly a decade, in fact—that the foreign and national debt must be dealt with. By 1789 most nationalists also had come around to the view that the new United States government should assume the state debts as well. Given Congress's revenue-raising capabilities, they believed that the national government, and it alone, would possess the resources for coping with the multilayered problems of indebtedness. That said, numerous alternatives existed for coping with the problem. Devaluation and redemption of interest-bearing certificates had been tried previously, but could be given another go. Revenue could also be had through an impost, the sale of western lands, or federal taxes. In addition, Madison's penchant (and, for that matter, Jefferson's and John Adams's hope) was for commercial coercion, which if it succeeded in prying open British ports to American ships, held the promise of ample sources of revenue and a windfall prosperity. Indeed, it was conceivable that any one of these expedients might have produced the returns with which to retire the debt, so long as the federal budget remained tiny.

Secretary Hamilton had other ideas, many of which should have come as no surprise to those who, like Madison, had been his colleagues in Congress in the early 1780s and his compatriots in the protracted nationalist movement. Hamilton had published many of his financial nostrums, including his sympathy for a national bank, nearly ten years earlier. Furthermore, his support of the plans of The Financier in 1783, including his assent to Superintendent Robert Morris's aim of having Congress assume the state debts, was hardly a secret.[2]

Not everything on Hamilton's mind could be known, of course,

Alexander Hamilton. Pastel on paper by James Sharples the Elder, about 1796.

but those—again like Madison—who ultimately would become the treasury secretary's most implacable foes, must have believed they could cope with any unpleasant surprises that he might spring. While Hamilton's proposal, whatever it contained, was likely to have strong support in the Northern mercantile centers, it would have to secure the assent of diverse factions in a bicameral Congress before running the gauntlet of the executive branch. This was the system of balances that the Federalists had touted during ratification, a firewall against any action that lacked a national consensus. Southerners were confident that their region was secure. The president was a Virginian.

During the next couple years, the South learned differently. Although a Virginian by birth, Washington habitually placed the national interest above provincial desires. As a young man, Washington's American Dream not only had been to open the trans-Appalachian West and link it to the settled eastern seaboard, but to liberate his countrymen from the political, social, and economic fetters of colonialism. He was driven by American nationalism years before independence was declared, and for eight long years after 1775 he sacrificed as a soldier to bring the American nation into being. He emerged from retirement to search for a means of safeguarding a national Union imperiled by sectionalists and localists, and with considerable misgivings he agreed to take on the presidency in an attempt to establish an energetic national government and a robust and truly independent United States. During his first autumn in the presidency, while Hamilton prepared his report, Washington toured New England. It was an eye-opening experience. He visited a textile mill or two, toured shipbuilding sites, and looked on as artisans worked in their shops. Washington was surprised by how well these workers and shopkeepers fared, at least by contrast with the rural South, where he believed "few good Houses" existed and only "small appearances of wealth" were visible. He was bewitched by the promise that manufacturing could improve the quality of life in America, even as it made the new nation more powerful and secure.[3] It was an idea he shared with the secretary of the treasury.

Hamilton long since had imparted his convictions to the world. In *The Farmer Refuted*, published between the First Continental Congress and the bloody incidents at Lexington and Concord in 1775, he first had written on America's bright future. He predicted that by 1830 America would have the manpower, natural resources, and "youthful vigour and strength" to be fully secure from Europe. "[T]he scale will then begin to turn in her favour," and its ascendancy to world power status would begin in earnest. By then, too, the United States would have the muscle to "extend her conquests" throughout the New World and enrich itself by commercial means. Hamilton returned to the theme of the golden future once again in "The Continentalist," published in the dark war year of 1781. He looked forward to better days when a "Happy America" would flourish in a "great Foederal Republic" that was "tranquil and prosperous at home, respectable abroad."[4]

However, Hamilton understood—and told the Constitutional Convention—that "happiness at home" depended on having the "strength to make us respectable abroad." He dilated on the theme in *The Federalist*. "Safety from external danger is the most powerful director of national conduct," he wrote. Nations that were insecure tended to be "less free," as they were compelled to adopt "institutions" that destroyed civil and political rights. Conversely, nations that were powerful achieved security and maintained their freedoms. What made nations powerful? Hamilton answered that national strength grew from the "prosperity of commerce." Trade generated wealth. Wealth engendered power. Power resulted in security. Security led to national greatness. But his argument was circular in nature. He also told readers of *The Federalist* that in order "to be a commercial people," Americans must possess the means "to defend that commerce" against rapacious adversaries. Thus, America would eventually grow strong through its far-flung trade, but it must first take steps to augment its power so that it could expand its commerce. This paradox formed the bedrock of Hamilton's outlook. With ratification, he knew that the moment had arrived to fulfill his dreams. The Revolutionary struggle against Great Britain was won. The localists had been vanquished. A Constitution that permitted a vastly strengthened national government was in place. Everything was ready for the "next great work to be accomplished," the creation of a powerful United States that would be truly independent of Europe. All that remained for its realization, and for the consummation of a strong maritime empire, was the industrialization of the United States, the embryo of which President Washington had glimpsed on his New England tour.[5]

Meeting Congress's deadline, Hamilton unveiled the first stage of his plan in January 1790. He proposed a means of coping with America's mounting indebtedness. But far more than that was involved in his 40,000-word Report Relative to a Provision for the Support of Public Credit. Hamilton urged that the national debt be refinanced. New securities were to be issued in exchange for the old, and instead of liquidating the debt as quickly as possible, it was to be "funded" through regular interest payments. Hamilton additionally recommended that the national government assume the states' wartime debts, in which case the current creditors would exchange their state securities for new federal securities. It goes without saying that he also wished to discharge the foreign debt.

In all cases, creditors could opt to hold onto their original securities, but incentives were built into his plan that encouraged their exchange for new national securities. The new public debt—for that is what it would be, inasmuch as the issuance of new securities was tantamount to opening subscriptions for a new loan—was to be funded at 4 percent, a rate that was made more attractive by the pledge that the government would guarantee the securities throughout their existence. Revenue, of course, would have to be found with which to discharge the new debt. The impost had been approved by Congress several months earlier. Hamilton now proposed an increase in the duties on certain items and the creation of a "sinking fund" built from the surplus revenues of the Post Office.[6]

Hamilton knew that the bulk of the new securities would be held by the most affluent denizens of the northern cities, merchants, professionals, and men of old wealth who possessed the specie with which to speculate.[7] Otherwise, they would be owned principally by investors from capital-rich Europe, especially by Dutch bankers and, to a lesser extent, French and English speculators. Foreign investment was crucial, as there was insufficient capital within the United States to finance the scheme. Hamilton, in large measure, had deliberately ruled out alternative solutions. He was especially anxious to incorporate in his mix the wealthy Northern merchants. Not only would those who propelled this system derive substantive, likely decisive, power in the new federal system, but they would be wedded to its survival, for if this government evaporated, as had the Articles of Confederation, and if the Union dissolved, their new securities would be worthless.

Hamilton had several additional objectives in mind. Using England's system as the model, he sought to turn the U.S. economy into a cash economy, fashioning an expanding money supply, but one that was more stable and certainly less inflationary than that of the Continental Congress and state legislatures, which during the late war had intemperately printed enormous sums of fiat currency. Furthermore, not only would retiring the state debts aid in attracting investors, but the states would be eliminated as competitors for tax dollars. Indeed, Hamilton may have quietly believed that the states would be placed on the road to extinction, for when the national government engrossed the strength of the states, they would be rendered harmless—and useless—anachronisms. There can be no doubt that as Hamilton also understood that as the impost would provide the lion's share of the revenue with which the government could meet its new loan obligations, and that as approximately 90 percent of the funds generated by the tariff would be paid by British shippers, it would behoove the United States to maintain good relations with Great Britain. Hamilton did not then, or later, seek to make the United States dependent on London. It should be America's policy, he wrote to President Washington that year, "to steer as clear as possible of all foreign connection, other than commercial and in this respect to cultivate intercourse with all the world on the broadest basis of reciprocal privilege." But he saw British trade as the fuel that would drive his economic engine, and he believed that Anglo-American commerce would be the salve that could eventually heal the dangerous wounds that had opened between America and its former parent state during the past quarter century. Finally, as the United States discharged its foreign debts and in the future met its obligations to the new foreign bondholders, its credit would be established and Europeans would feel no reticence about investing in the manufacturing plants that Hamilton longed to see spring up. Indeed, the Report opened with the remark that those nations "who observe their engagements are respected and trusted."

If it is true, as the historian Paul Gilje has suggested, that capitalism was "locked in the holds of the *Santa Maria*, the *Susan Constant*, the *Mayflower*, and the *Arabella*," and that throughout the colonial period it had been "germinating, spreading, and transforming the western world," it also is true, as Richard Brookhiser has written, that Hamilton's system, if approved, would transform America's yet primitive economy by "lift[ing] it into capitalism."[8] Hamilton's plan was to usher in a cash economy, providing abundant capital for entrepreneurs who soon would be known as capitalists. It is true as well that it was Hamilton's genius to comprehend that conditions were ripe for the sweeping changes he envisioned. The American Revolution had brought about a society more committed to equality and individualism, subsuming the colonial way of hierarchy and communal values, but also clearing the way for the rapidly approaching day when, as Gordon Wood put it, the "whole society should be taken over by moneymaking and the pursuit of individual interest."[9] Hamilton saw that the United States could experience a financial revolution akin to that which over the past century had caused the British economy to grow by leaps and bounds and its tax revenues to sextuple. But there was more. Hamiltonianism not only would be the crowning achievement of the nationalists' ten-year campaign to attain political centralization through economic reform, but at its base this system constituted a calibrated formula for speeding the day when the new nation would be strong, secure, and truly independent. His object was nothing less than the creation of a modern nation-state, one that was erected on a superstructure that would equip it to play as an equal on the world stage.[10]

Much that Hamilton recommended was unopposed, but his proposal to fund the domestic debt at face value and to assume the state debts provoked dissent, and it was Madison who took the lead in attacking the plan. No one was more startled by Madison's behavior than Hamilton, as the Virginian had been his nationalist ally from 1782 through the ratification of the Constitution. Hamilton soon came to see his old friend as honest and incorruptible, but jealous of his sway over Washington as well as unsophisticated, narrow-minded, and provincial. In fact, he soon saw Madison much as he had seen the new state leaders, such as Abraham Yates. Hamilton was a discerning judge of character, but in this instance it is a better bet that Madison simply was attempting to mend political fences in Virginia, where the state legislature in 1789 had refused to elect him to the United States Senate, leaving him with irrefutable evidence that his brand of nationalism was out of touch with his Virginia constituents. It is equally likely that Madison was playing a cunning game.[11]

He postured as the defender of the original holders of the Continental securities—those soldiers, farmers, and suppliers who had been paid with securities ten or more years earlier, but who in desperation had sold their certificates to speculators for desperately needed cash at some point before 1790. Helping those who had helped win the war, Madison said, was the "only honorable alternative." He proposed that 6 percent interest be paid on the entire debt, with the current holders to receive only the market value of the securities they subscribed and the balance to be paid to the original holders. In lachrymose terms he described to Congress how former soldiers, whose "sufferings can never be forgotten, while sympathy is an American virtue," had been compelled to sell their securities for a pittance. These "original sufferers," as he called them, would at least "receive, from their country, a tribute due to their merits, which if it does not entirely heal their wounds, will assuage the pain of them." Curiously, Madison had never previously supported discrimination between the original and current holders of securities. Actually, he had opposed discrimination while a congressman in 1783, and he remained silent when the question surfaced in the Philadelphia Convention. Nor did he comment on the issue when Hamilton asked his advice the previous autumn. Funding was not an issue of paramount importance to Madison, save that in 1790 he sincerely believed that the new national government would find itself in treacherous waters if Congress rejected what the northern mercantile interest had sought for nearly a decade. Madison was too good a politician to expect that his ploy to discriminate between the current and original security holders could win approval. That suited him. He had found the means to act against funding—yet not to mount a fatal opposition—and to simultaneously protect himself in Virginia. He could hardly have been surprised or terribly disappointed when discrimination was defeated in the House of Representatives by a three to one vote."[12]

Madison also opposed the assumption of state debts by the national government. During the final weeks of this battle he was joined by his friend Jefferson, who entered Washington's cabinet in the spring of 1790, at a time when the funding imbroglio had all but ended. Madison and Jefferson first met in the autumn of 1776 while serving in the Virginia assembly, but their friendship developed slowly. Not only was Jefferson nearly ten years older, but Madison initially had been overawed, awkwardly hanging back from his older colleague, whom he regarded as "one of the most learned men of the age." They grew closer after 1779, when Jefferson commenced his two terms as Virginia's governor and Madison sat on the Council of State, which met almost daily with the chief executive. In 1783, when both served in Congress, they lived in the same boardinghouse and spent end-

James Madison. Painting by Charles Willson Peale.

less hours in conversation, and in the five years after 1784, while Jefferson was abroad on diplomatic assignments, the two conducted a lively correspondence. Madison kept his friend abreast of domestic political developments, and Jefferson reported on conditions in Europe, but each used the other as a sounding board for ideas. They did not always agree. Jefferson took a more charitable view toward Shays's Rebellion, criticized Madison's Virginia Plan, which he believed would take too much power from the states, and captiously remarked that the Constitution went too far in its revision of the Articles of Confederation. However, their differences did not harm their relationship, and Jefferson had hardly returned to Monticello from France in December 1789 before Madison alighted at his door for a warm reunion and to beseech his friend to accept Washington's offer to become secretary of state. Jefferson brooded over the decision for weeks, but finally consented. By the time he arrived in New York, the fight over debt assumption had been under way for nearly sixty days. It is probable that Jefferson was more intransigently opposed to assumption than his friend Madison, but he demurred. He did not wish to question the opposition tactics that Madison had charted at such a late date in the battle, and having been abroad for years, Jefferson admitted to feeling ill at ease with the issues and opinion at home.[13]

From the outset Madison had believed that he had a better chance of winning the battle on assumption. However, once again his yearning to actually thwart Hamilton's scheme may be questioned. Madison knew that assumption was nearly universally unpopular among Virginians. Not only did they believe—mistakenly, it turned out—that they had already largely liquidated their state's internal debt, but they loudly insisted that they were unwilling to pay taxes that would retire the debts of those recalcitrant states that had done little or nothing to meet their financial obligations. Madison was concerned as well that if assumption passed, Patrick Henry might round up the Anti-Federalists for a renewed campaign against the new Constitution. But Madison was torn. While he could not ignore opinion at home and the consequences of assumption, he felt obliged to honor promises that he had made at the Constitutional Convention.[14] What is more, he continued to fear, as he had from the mid-1780s onward, that the Union might be sundered if Northern creditors were not assuaged. While a deft hand would be required, Madison gradually sensed that assumption was of such vital importance in the Northern urban entrepots that Virginia might reap a harvest of concessions if it played its cards properly. Indeed, there is good reason to suspect that his goal was not the defeat of assumption so much as it was secure adequate compensation to Virginia for the debt it had already retired. Thus, Madison cagily attacked assumption as he baited his hook, cast it into the water, and waited to see what he might catch.

Such a ploy was feasible, he believed, because assumption aroused considerably more opposition than funding. Three states—Massachusetts, South Carolina, and Connecticut, whose war debts were almost entirely unpaid—supported assumption. Three states—Maryland, Georgia, and Virginia, who believed that their debts had largely been retired—opposed Hamilton. The remaining states might go either way, but Madison assumed that North Carolina, which had just approved the Constitution and reentered the Union, would oppose Hamilton. Thus, his first task was to spin out the debates in the House from February to April, until North Carolina's congressmen at last reached New York and took their seats. He waged an artful campaign, one that the historians

Stanley Elkins and Eric McKitrick characterized as a "model in technique." Furthermore, as Madison hoped, North Carolina voted against the Assumption Bill, confronting Hamilton with a two-vote defeat in the House of Representatives. The vote was largely along sectional lines.[15]

Yet for someone who had triumphed, Madison did not appear to be happy. On the day after the House vote, he sounded like the loser, telling a friend that assumption "has some good aspects, and under some modifications would be favorable to the pecuniary interests of Virginia." He also knew that the fight was not over. The nationalists in the Northern states "are too zealous to be arrested in their pursuit" of assumption, he remarked.[16] Madison's varied comments that spring suggest that from the outset he knew he could live with assumption if it came with the right price.

As spring edged toward summer, he told friends that assumption might yet become law as a result of "circumstances not at present fully in view." It was as close as he came to revealing that political machinations had begun immediately after the House rejected assumption. The first salvo came from the Pennsylvania Society for Promoting the Abolition of Slavery, whose president was Benjamin Franklin. It chose this moment to petition Congress "to promote mercy and justice towards this distressed race" by immediately ending the African slave trade and by devoting "serious attention to the subject of slavery" in general. Franklin, in what was to be the last public gambit of his long career, was sincere, as he had recently liberated the slaves he had owned during most of his adult life.[17] But others, as Madison appears to have concluded, likely dangled this issue in the hope of finding a way to compromise on assumption. Willing to play, Madison immediately countered with his own ploy. He moved to impose discriminatory duties on British shipping and to prohibit ships flying the Union Jack from carrying American products. It is unimaginable that he could have believed that such legislation would pass the Senate, where the Northern states predominated. He acted instead to increase the logjam in the House. A compromise, or set of compromises, would be the only way out of the labyrinth, and it was possible—even probable—that by surrendering on assumption Virginia might profit handsomely. Not only might the state have its debt recalibrated, but it might win on the slave trade issue. After all, terminating the foreign slave traffic had been a goal of Virginians for thirty years, and Jefferson had even sought to denounce the African trade in the Declaration of Independence. Another matter was up for grabs as well. At this precise moment Madison informed his father that the permanent location of "the seat of Govt. has been again on the carpet."[18]

The residence question had been bruited about in Congress since 1779, with the rival factions continuously shifting like beach sand before rising and ebbing tides. Nevertheless, the debate over the location of the national capital had consistently focused on five primary sites: New York, Philadelphia, Baltimore, somewhere along the Susquehanna River in the backcountry of Pennsylvania, and at some undetermined point on the Potomac River. For a time the Virginians had believed that Philadelphia was the best location they could secure, but by early 1790 there were signs that some members of the Pennsylvania delegation were willing to agree to a Potomac River site in return for other bargains, including locating the capital temporarily in Philadelphia, perhaps for a decade or so. Not only would entrepreneurs in Philadelphia enjoy a bonanza during the interim, but once the capital was in their grip, the possibility existed that it might never be transferred. No one will ever know all the swaps that were proposed in the hope of landing a plum such as the national capital, but some time in the spring of 1790 Madison glimpsed the possibility of a bargain involving the approval of assumption and a decision to locate the Federal City on the Potomac. Hamilton, as ever, was eager to deal as well and had no misgivings about scuttling his city—New York—if that was required to enact assumption.[19]

Many players suited up for this game. Jefferson was one of the last on the playing field. By early June he had been in New York for only about six weeks, and for a portion of that time he had been incapacitated by a lingering migraine that he referred to as "a periodical headach."[20] He later claimed, with some justification, that he was too new to the capital to fully understand either the intrigues that were playing out or all the implications of Hamilton's assumption scheme. He also said that he was coaxed to participate—doubtless by Madison—in the search for a way to make assumption palatable; otherwise, "its denial [would be] so palpably injurious" that the "continuance of the Union" would be unlikely.[21] Jefferson trusted Madison's instincts. His friend not only had been the ally of the Northern nationalists and appeared to understand their thinking, but Madison was confident that securing a Potomac site for the permanent capital would be a windfall for Virginia. However, Jefferson was not led blindly by his friend. He worried that if assumption was rejected, "our credit . . . on the exchange at Amsterdam . . . will burst and vanish," a disaster that would usher in "the greatest of all calamities, the total extinction of our credit in Europe."[22] In addition, the congressional debate reached its crescendo at the very moment that information reached the administration, and especially Secretary of State Jefferson, that hostilities between Spain and Great Britain might be imminent. Jefferson, who feared for the safety of the United States in such an event, was convinced that it was imperative that the United States demonstrate to Europe "that we are in a condition for war." He added: "Whatever enables us to go to war, secures our peace."[23]

On June 14 Jefferson met with Pennsylvania's Robert Morris, a session that advanced the bargaining already under way. Discussions that likely involved Jefferson, Madison, and Hamilton, directly or through intermediaries, continued through the week and were concluded at a dinner party hosted by Jefferson—to which Madison and Hamilton were invited—on June 20. Often called the Compromise of 1790, it was agreed that Congress would award Philadelphia the capital for ten years, after which the seat of government would be moved to a site on the Potomac River to be selected by President Washington. To consummate the deal, Hamilton was to persuade some recalcitrant Pennsylvania congressmen to accept the southern capital, while Jefferson and Madison promised to persuade two foes of assumption in Virginia's delegation to switch their votes on Hamilton's proposed legislation. And there was more. Although the state debts to be assumed were scaled back by approximately 20 percent—totaling nearly $4,000,000—almost $500,000 was added to the share of Virginia's indebtedness that the national government would take over. As the middle states and Upper South were satisfied by the compact, the slave trade issue sank out of sight. The bargain agreed to at Jefferson's dinner was carried through in July when Congress enacted the separate Assumption and Residence bills. Madison, still mending fences at home, had the luxury of publicly opposing assumption to the end, as his vote was not needed to pass the legislation that he had worked covertly to secure.[24]

When Congress adjourned in mid-August, Jefferson and Madison appeared to be comfortable with what they had accomplished. Madison confessed that he was pleased that the public credit issue at last was resolved and in a fashion that "will very little affect the interest of Virginia." Furthermore, he rejoiced that the "spirit of accommodation" that resulted in the Compromise of 1790 was a promising augury for the well-being of the Union. However, both knew that more was to come from Hamilton. In his State of the Union message eight months earlier, Washington had urged Congress "to promote such manufactories" necessary for national security and true independence, and Congress in turn directed Hamilton to prepare "a proper plan or plans" to effect the president's wishes. The treasury secretary was expected to present his proposed plan when Congress reassembled in December. Rumors buzzed about Philadelphia that summer that Hamilton would recommend a national bank.[25]

Times were hectic during Congress's sixteen-week recess. The capital was transferred to its temporary site, and officials and staff scurried to

Philadelphia to find housing. The President's House, perhaps the grandest two-story Georgian mansion in the city, had been the former residence of The Financier, and before that of General William Howe—during the British occupation of Philadelphia—and John Penn, the last proprietary governor of the colony of Pennsylvania. Washington had dined there while a delegate to the First Continental Congress sixteen years earlier and had lodged there, as Morris's guest, throughout the Constitutional Convention. Treasury leased the home of its assistant secretary, Tench Coxe, while Hamilton rented for his residence the home of Dr. Benjamin Rush, situated about three blocks south of the President's House. Jefferson leased a comfortable house three blocks west of Washington's habitation and, together with a lone clerk, simultaneously moved into the State Department, located a stone's throw from the presidential mansion. Madison returned to the boarding house in which he had dwelled throughout his tenure in Congress a decade earlier. The four lived within a five-minute walk of one another and of Congress Hall, formerly the County Court House, which sat next door to Independence Hall.[26]

Once situated, Hamilton set to work on his next report while Madison and Jefferson hurried to Virginia for a three-month holiday. When the Virginians returned in November, sharing a carriage that inched along roads turned into a fetid ooze by autumnal rains, Jefferson's outlook, and perhaps that of Madison as well, had begun to sour. While at home, Jefferson discovered that assumption was met with "disgust" in Virginia, and that his compromise with Hamilton had been, as James Monroe remarked, "in every point of view impolitik."[27] Moreover, contrary to what Madison had apparently been telling him, few in Virginia appeared to care that the capital would be situated on the Potomac. Even before he started back to Philadelphia, Jefferson had come to regret his bargain with Hamilton, a deal that he soon would call the worst blunder of his political career. What is more, he believed that he had permitted himself to be "made a tool for forwarding" the schemes of others.[28]

In recent years the notion has grown that Madison was the idea man who shaped the course of opposition to the treasury secretary.[29] Hamilton saw things differently. He looked upon Jefferson as the leader and Madison as the follower, the "Generalissimo" and the "General," as some around Hamilton referred to the Virginians. There is truth in both views. Jefferson's breadth of knowledge surpassed that of most contemporaries, including Madison, but he was something of a learned dilettante who hopscotched from subject to subject. Madison was more focused, especially in political theory, and clearly the more original thinker of the two. Madison, moreover, was the more experienced in the often tawdry day-to-day politics of a legislative environment, and by temperament he was much better suited to a lifestyle that included hours each day devoted to parliamentary planning, maneuvering, scheming, and bargaining. Jefferson was put off by such things. He loathed contention and preferred to spend as much time as possible with solitary intellectual endeavors or in varied pursuits of self-gratification. Nevertheless, Jefferson was more insightful in fathoming others and infinitely better at grasping the big picture. Madison, immersed in legislative machinations, tended to let himself be swamped by the minutiae of his daily parliamentary endeavors. Jefferson, often mistakenly dismissed by his contemporary enemies, as well as by scholars, as a hopeless visionary, in fact was adroit at grasping the panorama of his time. Before most, he discerned trends and fathomed the pole star that lay hidden in the intent of others. Above all, he quickly was attuned to the implications of Hamilton's vista. Whereas Madison's outlook was clouded by years of incessant battling over nationalist-localist issues and by his mind-numbing immersion in the mechanics of lawmaking, Jefferson's views were fresher, less cluttered, and filtered through the prism of his recent experiences. Jefferson had spent the previous five years in Europe and was a changed man for it.[30]

As a youth Jefferson had struggled with the loneliness and hurt that resulted from his sense of having been abandoned. Although not literally rejected, while in early adolescence he suffered the death of a father that he revered and a relationship with his mother that appears to have been inadequate for his needs. Furthermore, at age six he had been shipped by his parents to a remote boarding school, and during the remainder of his youth he visited home only briefly each year. His subsequent behavior suggests that he felt deprived of the satisfactions, protection, and security of a family. Like many other "abandoned" children, young Jefferson withdrew from an outside world that he distrusted. He exhibited self-centered and reclusive habits, and often manifested a corrosive emptiness that he attempted to fill with grandiose fantasies. This long, unhappy period ended for Jefferson in 1770 when, at age twenty-seven, he met the recently widowed Martha Skelton. He courted and won her. The couple married on New Year's Day 1772.

During the five years preceding his wedding, Jefferson had occupied his father's old seat in Virginia's House of Burgesses, where he had wielded little influence. Not only was he young, shy, and inexperienced, but temperamentally Jefferson recoiled from the passionate battles on the legislative floor. Furthermore, he quite obviously was more committed to his private world than to his public responsibilities. Jefferson exerted even less influence in the two years that followed his marriage. Indeed, he rarely attended the assembly meetings in 1772 and 1773, and for all practical purposes he dropped entirely off the political radar screen. Deeply in love, and truly happy for perhaps the first time, he had found the emotional security and fulfillment that he had never known. Had Anglo-American relations not reached a flash point, it is unlikely that Jefferson would soon, if ever, have emerged from his insular experience. However, during the crisis over the Coercive Acts, in 1774, he wrote *A Summary View of the Rights of British America*, a radical polemic denying that Parliament possessed any power over the colonies, a more extreme position than the Continental Congress adopted that autumn. Thereafter, he emerged as a leading figure in the Virginia legislature, and when a member of the colony's congressional delegation died early the following year, Jefferson was chosen as his successor.

Jefferson took his seat in Congress in June 1775, though he found it difficult to tear himself from his haven at Monticello during the fifteen months of his appointment. He spent only about six of those months in Philadelphia, and soon after independence was declared Jefferson returned to Virginia for good. He reclaimed his old assembly seat and spent a few weeks in Williamsburg each year when the legislature was in session. Otherwise, while Congress, the army, and America's diplomats coped with one convulsive crisis after another between 1776 and 1779, Jefferson remained sequestered on his mountaintop, unable—or unwilling—to extricate himself from the loving family that was his bulwark. He turned a deaf ear to repeated entreaties that he serve abroad as a diplomat, or that he return to Congress, or that he simply play a greater role in the affairs of Virginia. In reality, he never was totally inactive. Like Paine, he had hoped that America's separation from Great Britain would result in more than escaping British restraints. He longed for changes in the fabric of life in Virginia, and between 1777 and 1779 Jefferson, from his desk at Monticello, acted on his reform impulses. He sought to reshape Virginia's first constitution, especially to check executive prerogatives and judicial sway, vesting virtually total authority in a legislative branch beholden to property-owning farmers. He additionally played a paramount role in the review and revision of Virginia's legal code. The separation of church and state was the greatest innovation that ultimately materialized from his initiative, but he also proposed reforms that would have made land available to the propertyless and extended free education to gifted children. On the whole, Jefferson was a conservative reformer, quite unlike Paine, the supercharged radical who thought in terms of starting the world anew. Nevertheless, Jefferson who was guided by an abiding loathing for Great Britain, wished for American autonomy, longed to terminate monarchic and aristocratic domination, and sought to ameliorate the social and economic inequalities that colored life in his Virginia.

Stung by General Washington's implicit criticism of his low key role, Jefferson reluctantly left Monticello in 1779 to serve two one-year terms as the chief executive of Virginia. It was a disastrous episode that nearly brought a permanent end to his political career. He was a diligent governor, working daily in his office and returning home only twice, and then only for brief vacations. However, it was his misfortune to be governor at the time of Virginia's greatest wartime peril. British forces invaded the state on three occasions during his stint in office, each time causing widespread destruction. Governor Jefferson was largely blameless for these military disasters, but he was not totally devoid of responsibility.

Patrick Henry, his predecessor, had seized and exercised emergency powers. Jefferson declined to follow his example, although with the additional authority he might have better readied the state for the British incursions. In addition, he was wretchedly slow in responding to the invasion led by Benedict Arnold in 1781, permitting more than a full day to elapse before notifying his Council and summoning the militia. Furthermore, he had earlier reacted indifferently to the pleadings of Continental army officers that redoubts be constructed at strategic points on the James River. Although these defenses would not have stopped Arnold, they might impeded his advance until the militia was in place to more adequately defend Richmond. As it was, Arnold pillaged Virginia's new capital, destroying property and military equipment, and liberating scores of slaves. Later in 1781 Governor Jefferson blocked the implementation of a daring plan endorsed by General Nathanael Greene that, with luck, might have trapped the British army under Cornwallis in North Carolina. Instead, the British regulars marched into Virginia in the spring of 1781. Jefferson's gubernatorial service ended calamitously in June when British raiders dispatched by Cornwallis descended on Monticello. Jefferson fled for his life, barely staying beyond the reach of the white-coated dragoons on his heels.

Jefferson escaped, but appeared to be politically ruined. Generals Greene and Frederich von Steuben, as well as George Weedon, the commander of the Virginia militia, criticized him as ruinously provincial and temperamentally ill-equipped for executive leadership. Even Madison quietly questioned his judgment. Henry went further. He called for a legislative inquiry leading to a vote to censure Jefferson's conduct as governor. The assembly's investigation, set for December 1781, never occurred. Three months after Jefferson's flight from Monticello, the siege of Yorktown commenced. Cornwallis surrendered just weeks before the assembly was to meet. With victory on the horizon, the mood to punish Jefferson vanished.[31]

When it was safe, Jefferson returned to Monticello, vowing never again to be active in politics. He had "retired to my farm, my family and books from which I think nothing will ever separate me," he declared. Later, he acknowledged that he had "folded myself in the arms of retirement," placing "all prospects of future happiness on domestic and literary objects." He doubtless meant it, and odds are that had his blissful family buttress not disintegrated, Jefferson would have remained at home from 1781 onward, planting and writing, and thankful to be spared public cares. However, in September 1782 Martha died of complications from childbirth. Jefferson's life was shattered and without meaning. For months, friends feared that he was suicidal. He characterized himself as in a "stupor of mind which had rendered me as dead to the world as she was whose loss occasioned it."[32] Many of those same friends urged him to leave Monticello, hoping that by escaping the haunting scenes of grief he could overcome his despair. Madison, in particular, labored to secure his election to Congress. When the Virginia assembly obliged by appointing him to Congress, Jefferson accepted immediately. During the next seven years, he was rarely at home, and not at all between mid-1784 and late 1789, when he served as a diplomat in Paris, chiefly as the American minister to France.

Jefferson's years abroad helped him cope more successfully with the tormenting demons in his private life, but they were crucial as well for giving form and substance to his political outlook. The catharsis came first. It had to come before he could get on with his public life. During his second year in Paris, and almost three years to the day since the death of his wife, he met Maria Cosway, an unhappily married English woman who was visiting France with her husband. Bright, attractive, and accomplished, and almost certainly the most cosmopolitan woman that Jefferson had ever encountered, Maria awakened a "sense of happiness" within him, as he put it, causing "Every moment [to be] filled with something agreeable." For six weeks, before her husband took her back to London, Maria and Jefferson saw one another daily. Although crushed by her departure, Jefferson acknowledged that she had restored gaiety to his life.

When Maria and her husband returned to Paris a year later, she and Jefferson picked up where they had left off. Their second affair lasted for three months, and while her affections liberated him from the grief he had suffered from the loss of his wife, it appears that Jefferson was the one who ultimately broke off the relationship. Having been abandoned

by every person with whom he had previously enjoyed a loving relationship, Jefferson was fearful of the inescapable pain that would result from
giving his heart to another. In all likelihood, in fact, his liaison with
Cosway flourished only because at some level he understood from the
outset that the relationship would never proceed beyond a brief, quiet,
adulterous affair. Perhaps when pressed by her to make a commitment,
or more likely when he began to fear his own feelings, he terminated
matters. The "pains which are to follow" from establishing a permanent
relationship were too great, he told her. "The art of life is to avoid pain,"
and the "most effectual means of being secure against pain is to retire
within ourselves," he added, as he walled himself from further contact
with her, resuming the reclusive manner of his early years.[33] Yet, while
their relationship ended late in 1787, the haunting melancholy that had
daily dominated Jefferson's thoughts since his wife's death ended, too,
liberating him so that once again he was able to turn his attention to
public matters. Indeed, during the ensuing half dozen years Jefferson
immersed himself in political matters to a degree beyond anything in
his previous experience.

Faced with only light ambassadorial duties, Jefferson spent considerable time at Parisian salons, the haunts of philosophes and cosmopolitan reformers, and in sightseeing throughout France, England,
Holland, Germany, and Italy. His travels and hours of discussion with
many of the finest intellects in Paris brought his views into focus. Never
a systematic thinker, he nevertheless had long since come to believe—
and a few years earlier had put his thoughts on paper in *Notes on the
State of Virginia*, his only book—that America would be a happy land if
it remained the habitation mostly of independent yeomen farmers. Indeed, he thought property-owning farmers were the model citizens for
America's experiment in republicanism. Virtuous and industrious and
with a stake in society, yeomen would take their responsibilities as citizens seriously. Furthermore, farmers had no need for a strong government, and the preservation of limited government had been Jefferson's
goal since before 1776. He never wavered in his commitment to a yeomen republic, although after seeing firsthand the oppressed lives of
Europe's peasants, he realized that the free inhabitants of America were
less downtrodden than he had previously imagined.

What particularly struck Jefferson during his stay abroad was the
utter powerlessness of most inhabitants of Europe. In America, he said,
"the will of every one has a just influence," resulting in "a great deal of
good" in the sense that the "mass of mankind . . . enjoys a precious degree of liberty and happiness." However, on the continent "every man . . .
must be either the hammer or the anvil." Nothing troubled him more

than the total dependency that characterized the lives of most Europeans. Once independence was lost, Jefferson had written earlier, all hope was gone, for "dependence begets subservience and venality, suffocates the germ of virtue, and prepares fit tools for the designs of ambition." He attributed Europe's sad state to its long experience with monarchy. Never a friend to royalty, his residence in France confirmed his belief that monarchical governments were "the curse of existence that must be guarded against at all costs." Monarchies, he said, were "governments of force" committed principally to serving the most powerful in society, those accustomed to wielding the hammer. Such regimes, he added, were akin to the rule of "wolves over sheep." Centuries of monarchical rule had been ruinous for the European peasantry, he reflected, reducing them to poverty and idleness while much of the countryside, almost wholly owned by a small class of landed aristocrats, lay uncultivated. Like Paine in *Common Sense*, who had written that kings had nothing to do but make wars and give away sinecures, Jefferson observed Louis XVI for a while and concluded that "he hunts one half the day, is drunk the other, and signs whatever he is bid." Kings, he added, are anything but "good conservators of the public happiness."[34]

But monarchy was not the only danger he perceived during his stay abroad. Jefferson beheld a Europe in the early throes of a financial transformation, the prelude to the Industrial Revolution. England especially, but France and other nations as well, were awash with new financial institutions, including stock markets, great banks endowed with unimaginably huge charters, monopolistic companies that undertook what once had been the province of small-scale household manufacturers, and a vast increase in patents awarded for an astonishing array of new inventions. Although he never fleshed out his reaction to what he saw, Jefferson appeared to blanch at the rampant commercial avarice, and beyond the shadow of a doubt he was aghast at the sight of growing numbers of destitute workers who lived and labored in Europe's squalid cities. Throughout its long, sad history, Europe's peasants, sequestered in the thrall of the landed aristocracy, had been "loaded with misery by kings, nobles, and priests." Now countless numbers in the cities would groan under the despair spread by the commercial elite, forced to live in dolorous conditions and to suffer beneath the whip hand of the new tyrants of finance, wealth, and power. In England in particular, Jefferson learned to his dismay, these powerful new forces already exerted steadily greater influence with the national government. They had begun to influence foreign policy and largely controlled fiscal policy, imposing land taxes that redistributed wealth in their favor and threatened to ruin many yeomen and landed gentry.[35]

Before he returned to America, however, Jefferson grasped at the hope that France might be liberated from monarchical tyranny and that the French people might gain sufficient power to protect themselves from other dark forces. The French, he wrote Washington in 1788, "have been awakened by our revolution."[36] This commenced his unwaveringly rosy appraisal of events in France between 1787 and 1789. Before the end of 1787 he reported that "the spirit of this country is advancing towards a revolution."[37] The revolutionary drama in France truly blossomed during the very week that Washington was inaugurated, as the French monarch was obliged to summon the national legislature to meet for the first time in well over a century. After a whirlwind of legislative activity, Jefferson rejoiced that the royal authority had lost much of its previous power. The National Assembly, he gushed that summer, had "prostrated the old government" and was in "complete and undisputed possession of the sovereignty."[38] Convinced that France was headed down the very road that America had taken, Jefferson celebrated that a "revolution in their constitution seems inevitable." Shortly before he departed France in the fall of 1789, Jefferson observed that the French revolutionaries were "trying their hands at forming declarations of rights" that contained "the essential principles of ours" from 1776.[39] He was confident that the dramatic changes unfolding in France would occur with little violence and still less bloodshed. As he sailed for Virginia that autumn, Jefferson pulsated with hope that republicanism could take root in France, then spread to England and across Europe, and that the citizenry, empowered at last, could protect itself from political and financial despots.

When Jefferson came to New York in March 1790 to join Washington's cabinet, he had been largely absent from the national political scene since 1776 and out of the country during the past five years. He was only dimly aware of how the last desperate war years, and the frustrations that had accumulated in some quarters during the era of the Articles of Confederation, had altered the outlook of many Americans. What first struck Jefferson on his arrival in the capital was that royalist sentiment had blossomed in certain circles, particularly among elite Northerners. "I cannot describe the wonder and mortification with which the table conversation filled me," he later recollected. "Politics was the chief topic, and a preference for kingly over republican government was evidently the favorite sentiment. . . . I found myself, for the most part, the only advocate of the republican side of the question."[40]

Shocked, Jefferson delved more deeply. A network of friendly congressmen, carefully cultivated by the secretary of state, passed on gossip and recounted conversations with Hamilton or his friends. Jefferson himself hosted regular dinners that many were deceived into believing were purely social occasions, but which in reality he also utilized for gaining insights into the mind-set and intentions of Hamilton and those about him. As the wine flowed and the guests lowered their guard, Jefferson heard excited reports of putative attempts within Washington's circle "to ape the corruption of the British court" and to establish the "foundation for an aristocracy or a detestable monarchy." Nor was deception and subterfuge always necessary for collecting information. A few newspapers, including some that had been Federalist organs two years earlier, now occasionally ran essays that warned of a conspiracy to vastly expand the powers of the national government or expressed dismay at President Washington's regal formality and the social style of those around him. Vice President Adams made it even easier. Already tainted in the eyes of some for having campaigned to bestow a princely title— something like "His Highness" or "His High Mightiness"— on the president back in 1789, Adams in 1790 published "Discourses on Davila," a series of turgid newspaper essays that appeared to many to extol monarchical government. A stunned Jefferson drew that conclusion. "Can any one read Mr. Adams ... without seeing he was a monarchist?" he asked. Alarmed at what he concluded was the apostasy of many former revolutionaries, Jefferson, in his private notes, began to label some around the president as "monarchist," "money-man," or "corruptor."[41] For the first time in the course of the American Revolution, Jefferson found himself worrying that the threat to repudiate the republican ideals of 1776 was very real indeed. By the time he took up residence in Philadelphia in the autumn of 1790, he was coming to believe that his generation was faced with the necessity of waging a second resistance movement to fully secure the American Revolution.

The foreign policy implications of Hamiltonianism completed the crystallization of Jefferson's outlook. Jefferson, like Madison, was outraged at Great Britain not only for having barred American ships from its West Indian ports but also for its refusal to adhere to the Treaty of Paris, especially with regard to the trans-Appalachian West. Like Madison, Jefferson hoped to use commercial coercion—the very leverage that had compelled London to repeal the Stamp Act and Townshend Duties—to open British markets to American merchants and impel London to remove its troops from American soil. Convinced that negotiations would never be fruitful, Jefferson was persuaded that coercive measures alone could pry open British ports. But, as he quickly discovered, Hamiltonianism, which tied the United States to the cash cow of British commerce, threatened to take the backbone out of America's policy toward London. Indeed, for the moment at least, Hamiltonian economics had all but rendered discrimination against British commerce a moot point. That was bad enough, as far as Jefferson was concerned, but he was especially concerned lest it have ruinous implications for American interests in the West. Ohio, Kentucky, and Tennessee, as President Washington once had remarked, stood "as it were upon a pivot: the touch of a feather would turn them any way," including toward separation from the United States. London, Jefferson feared, might wield that feather, offering frontiersmen a tantalizing swap: Britain's abandonment of the Indians in return for the settlers' secession from the American Union.[42]

Jefferson was no less troubled by the possibility that the "anglocrats" who espoused Hamiltonianism might bring the United States into Great Britain's orbit, jeopardizing the alliance with France and threatening republicanism. Jefferson saw the United States and France as formal allies as well as ideological comrades. The shining example furnished by these two republican nations, he believed, might foster the spread of the antimonarchical ideal. However, he was convinced that the survival of republicanism in each country was, to some degree, dependant on its survival in the other, and he believed that the crowned heads of Europe knew this as well. Even before he departed Paris, Jefferson expressed fears that the conservative powers, including Great Britain, would unite to destroy France. If only republicanism could last in France, he said, the "success of their government [would] ... stay up our own and ... prevent it from falling back to that kind of Half-way-house, the English constitution."[43]

This was Jefferson's mind-set when the next installment of Hamilton's program was divulged in December 1790. On consecutive days, Hamilton recommended an excise tax on distilled spirits and a Bank of the United States. Neither Jefferson nor Madison had been unduly alarmed by Hamilton's funding and assumption proposals, but the prospect of a bank caused them considerable concern. Madison feared that the bank's presence in Philadelphia might create interests that would be difficult to overcome in transferring the national capital from that city. He and Jefferson also knew that little sentiment for a bank existed in the South. Many Southerners were "against it but were not entirely sure why," according to the historians Elkins and McKitrick. That was not entirely true. Southerners, like a great many others, were indeed suspicious of things that were newfangled and unproven, but in addition they did not cotton to government-created institutions that were of no assistance to them, and a bank would be of little or no use to those who grew tobacco and rice. In addition, a few understood that the bank constituted further evidence that the national government was coming under the thumb of what Jefferson called the "stockjobbers." Wealthy men in the northern states, already the owners of the lion's share of the government's securities, would as well now be the principal stockholders in the Bank of the United States. Given their investment in a bank capitalized at $10,000,000, which was what Hamilton had proposed, Jefferson immediately recognized the incentive they would have, and the clout they would possess, to influence public officials. Congressman Michael Jenifer Stone of Maryland, who concurred with Jefferson on the potential dangers of the bank, indelicately stated the threat. The stockjobbers, he declared, would have the leverage to "bribe both States and individuals" to secure their every whim. There were those, too, who believed that throughout the eighteenth century the Bank of England had served as a prop for monarchy and an impediment to progressive reform, and feared that its counterpart in America would sustain those that were the least committed to republicanism. What was crystal clear in early February 1791, when Hamilton's tax and bank proposals sailed through Congress, was that the commercial North was "all powerful, and fails in nothing" that the treasury secretary sought for it, as a Pennsylvania congressman observed. It was evident to Jefferson and Madison that the Hamiltonians would attain even more unless a "more agricultural representation" was achieved in Congress.[44]

In the meantime, one ray of hope remained that the bank never would come into being. Confident that "the President is an anchor of safety to us," Jefferson and Madison mounted a last ditch fight in the only way that remained to them. They resisted the bank on constitutional grounds, hopeful that Washington would agree that Congress had exceeded its authority and veto the measure. Passage of the Bank bill, Jefferson told the president, had been a "step beyond the boundaries . . . specifically drawn around the powers of Congress," and its creation "is unauthorized by the Constitution." Privately, Jefferson likely also warned Washington, who was about to select a site near Mount Vernon for the new capital, that the bank might thwart their hopes of seeing the Federal City situated on the Potomac, as powerful forces would hope to see the Bank and the seat of the national government in the same city—Philadelphia. Hamilton, meanwhile, countered with a defense of Congress's powers for creating a bank. He constructed it on the doctrine of implied powers, a favorite concept of Madison ten years earlier when he had first wished to increase national powers. Congress, said Hamilton, had done what was "necessary and proper." To curtail its scope, as Jefferson had suggested, would eviscerate the government. A portion of Hamilton's argument recapitulated that of Galloway at the First Continental Congress. There must be a sovereign government that possessed ultimate authority. Under the Constitution, the national government was sovereign, and it was "vested [with] a right to employ all the means requisite, and fairly applicable to the attainment of the ends of power." Washington not only agreed on the need for a central government with the freedom to act when necessary, but he was one with his treasury secretary in understanding that the bank would become the driving force in the transformation of America into a modern, powerful manufacturing nation. The president signed the bill into law within thirty-six hours of reading Hamilton's defense.[45]

Although neither Jefferson nor Madison turned against Washington, both were rocked by his commitment to Hamiltonianism. A tincture of vanity perhaps colored their startled response. Madison, who had been closer to Washington than any other advisor between 1786 and 1789, knew that he had been eclipsed by Hamilton. Jefferson, esteemed in Virginia and venerated in France both as the author of the Declaration of Independence and as one of America's most enlightened sons, had expected to be the dominant force within Washington's cabinet. Instead, Hamilton, fourteen years his junior, had the ear of the president. But jealousy was the least of the motives that drove their reaction.

Jefferson and Madison now knew that neither they nor the South could count on the president in the battle against Hamiltonianism. After all, Washington had spurned not only their advice but also that of Virginia's Edmund Randolph, his attorney-general. It appeared to both that Washington would faithfully endorse every wish of his treasury secretary. Each also was certain that many in Congress, and probably a majority throughout the country, would always acquiesce in whatever Washington endorsed. Jefferson, in particular, reassessed his thinking. In the ten months since he joined Washington's cabinet, Hamilton had won on funding, assumption, taxes, and the Bank. Before that, he had been a colossal force in the nationalists' campaign against decentralization. Now fully aware of Hamilton's political talents, Jefferson alluded to his "cunning" in transforming "the republicans chosen by the people into anti-republicans." What was most amazing, Jefferson believed, was that in 1790 and 1791 Hamilton had succeeded despite the fact most Americans supported neither Hamiltonianism nor the higher taxes and bigger government that went with his economic measures.[46] Even more frightening to Jefferson was the knowledge that Hamilton's strength was growing. Whereas the Assumption Bill barely squeaked into law in 1790, requiring the compromise that Madison had so wanted in order to muster the requisite vote, the Bank Bill was enacted with majorities of two to one in the House and three to one in the Senate.

Congress, Jefferson believed, had fallen under the sway of a "corrupt squadron of paper dealers." Hamiltonianism, he said, had provided the commercial elite, and a profligate train of speculators, the "effectual means of corrupting . . . a portion of the legislature." In part, Jefferson was referring to the open secret that some congressmen who held government and state securities had backed Hamilton's program to secure direct personal gains. However, his concern ran deeper. He feared that commercial-induced avarice, once unleashed in the United States, would seep into every crevice in American society, transforming his country into a tenebrous mirror image of the Europe he had recently observed. As the American tableau came to resemble a "gaming table," he said, the frugality and industry endemic to yeomanry inevitably would corrode, to be replaced by a society that was not committed to the common good, that turned its back on the surging egalitarianism of the Revolutionary age, and in which the "habits of vice and idleness" that characterized the urban elite would corrupt everything that it touched.[47] What is more, Jefferson now was convinced that the inordinate concentration of wealth that inevitably would follow in the wake of Hamiltonian economics went hand in hand with the Federalists' master plan of "consolidation." The pieces of the puzzle had fallen into place. Unless stopped, Jefferson was convinced, the Hamiltonians would succeed in their plot to establish a government of exorbitant powers that was controlled by Northern commercial and financial interests.[48]

Something else gnawed at Jefferson. After a year at home, he had come to believe that the "ultimate object" of the Northern merchant elite, many of whom had resisted independence in 1776, was a counterrevolution. Many, he believed, sought to roll back the heart and soul of the American Revolution and fashion an American economy, society, and political system constructed on the template of British royal and aristocratic supremacy. The Northern states were already in their grasp, he believed. Through the power of their wealth, the debtor South soon would be their captive as well.

To this point, Jefferson had largely deferred to Madison. In 1790 he had been the outsider, unfamiliar with Hamilton and those about him, unseasoned in the labyrinthian politics of the turbulent 1780s, uncertain of sentiment in Congress, too recently returned to put his hand on the pulse of Virginia, and unquestionably incapable of divining opinion throughout the new republic. He had listened to Madison, who had fought the battles of the 1780s and who, despite extraordinary odds, had succeeded in his uphill quest for a new national constitution. Madison never confessed to having been duped by more savvy politicians in the framing of the Constitution, and Jefferson never said that had been the case. However, by the late spring of 1791, Jefferson, drawing on his European experience, had come to believe that he understood the urgency of the moment with greater clarity than his friend. At the very least, he now believed that Madison's tactics in coping with Hamilton in 1790 had been flawed and that the Compromise of 1790, which had awarded the treasury secretary all he wanted, had been an egregious blunder. It also seems to have become clear to Jefferson that Madison's grand scheme—his axiom that the presence of multiple factions would make it unlikely that any one faction could gain hegemony at the national level—worked far better in putting workers and yeomen into straitjackets than in restraining powerful, well-organized financial and commercial interests. For Jefferson, the enactment of the Hamilton program had been a primer— and a foretaste—of how an elite faction could make use of the national government, much as the most perceptive of the Founders at the Philadelphia Convention must have intended.

Jefferson had come to believe that the best hope for those who abhorred Hamiltonianism was to mobilize—at this stage it was more a matter of activating than organizing the foes of the treasury secretary— for the 1792 congressional elections, still more than a year away. Jefferson was convinced that in large measure Hamilton had succeeded because he had acted quickly and skillfully before public opinion coalesced against his program. Those days were gone, Jefferson believed. Most of the South, he knew, would join in against the Northern threat, and he suspected that there were strong pockets of opposition to America's commercialization in the Northern backcountry, much of it in the very Anti-Federalist bastions that had resisted consolidation. Indeed, much of the entrenched opposition to the urban commercial centers came from among the very progressive decentralists that Madison had been so anxious to crush. To Jefferson, it now seemed clear that these people whom Madison had so vilified had been dead on target, especially in "their predictions" about "Monarchical federalists." Their "prophecy . . . [had] now become true history," he sadly concluded.[49]

Madison concurred with Jefferson's appraisal. Indeed, he now jettisoned much that he had held dear during the nationalist campaign for constitutional reform to follow Jefferson, his guiding light in the emerging battle against Hamiltonianism. For the first time, Madison warned of an "antirepublican party" whose members, as long as ten years ago, were "openly or secretly attached to monarchy and aristocracy." No doubt remembering Hamilton's remarkable speech in the Philadelphia Convention, Madison at last cautioned the public about the powerful force in American politics that had never believed that humankind was capable of self-government. People of that persuasion, he now confided, believed they could maintain public quiescence through the "pageantry of rank, the influence of money and emoluments, and the terror of military force." They were enchanted with the English system, and from the outset had "aimed at a gradual approximation of ours to a mixed monarchy," first and foremost seeking to serve the "opulent." For the first time, moreover, he divulged that the plan of many who had been his allies in the nationalist movement had been to "convert the government from one limited as hitherto supposed . . . into a government without any limits at all."[50]

Despite what most contemporaries believed, Jefferson was the driving force behind the early efforts to organize those alarmed by the administration's economic vista and to shape the movement to stop the treasury secretary. Three days after Washington signed the Bank Bill into law, Jefferson took the first step toward luring Philip Freneau to Philadelphia. A chum of Madison at Princeton, Freneau had pursued a career as an on-again, off-again journalist, in the course of which he had exhibited an outlook resembling that of Thomas Paine as well as noteworthy literary skills. Jefferson wanted him to publish a newspaper to counter John Fenno's *Gazette of the United States*, which the secretary of state disdained as a Hamiltonian organ. Jefferson subsequently told Washington that it was solely Freneau's idea to publish a newspaper. That was poppycock. Jefferson negotiated with him for weeks and finally gave him a job as a clerk in the State Department, with a promise of public printing contracts, to sustain him. Madison pitched in as well, among other things lining up subscribers for Freneau's newspaper. It was enough to snare Freneau, whose *National Gazette*, conceived from the outset as an instrument of anti-Hamiltonianism, commenced publication in October 1791.[51]

Furthermore, once the Bank Bill became law, Jefferson tested the waters by sending out exploratory letters to activists in several states. He inquired of one correspondent whether a widespread abhorrence existed to what he called the "scrip-pomany" unleashed by Hamiltonianism, the frenzy of gambling in securities in the "rage of getting rich in a day." He wondered too at the likely reaction should a leader "come forward and help" galvanize those who were distressed by the treasury secretary's policies. What he learned was encouraging. Dismay existed, both with the Hamiltonian economic initiatives and the sudden expansion of congressional powers.[52]

That spring, in the midst of the negotiations with Freneau, Jefferson and Madison took a vacation in New York and New England. Madison had undertaken similar sojourns in the mid-1780s, when his object had been to build alliances among nationalists who might join together to overturn the Articles of Confederation. In those days he had vacationed in and around New York City, a hub of the nationalist movement. On this occasion, however, he and Jefferson mostly stuck to the backcountry, for what they publicly described as a "botanizing tour." Each man in fact was passionately interested in scientific inquiry, and for an entire month the two spent days slogging through the dense green wilderness studying flora and fauna or touring cultivated fields to inspect the Hessian fly, a wheat blight that was devastating the North and moving inexorably toward the Chesapeake. Yet more than scientific curiosity led them to make this trip. As Madison acknowledged many years later, he and Jefferson from time to time eschewed plants and insects in order to talk with backcountry leaders about other matters. They tried to be coy, and Jefferson probably pulled it off, as in the course of seven years of diplomacy he had learned valuable lessons in discretion, as well as in judging others and inconspicuously building connections. Whether the locals knew or not, they were being courted by Jefferson and Madison, who were laying the groundwork for the next round of elections.[53]

Jefferson was the most important public official active in the effort to galvanize the opposition to Hamiltonianism, but he hardly acted alone. For instance, some alarmed congressmen wrote circular letters to their constituents urging the mobilization of unorganized voters. Furthermore, some who were disenchanted had no need for Jefferson's guidance. They already had begun to organize. This was particularly true among some urbanites who, at their core, exhibited an outlook that in striking ways departed from Jefferson's anxiety at the incompatibility of the commercial economy with public virtue. The hardscrabble experiences of many within the emerging urban middle class of small merchants and skilled artisans had stirred a hunger to be treated with respect and dignity. They looked more to Paine, who had remained in their social strata, than to Jefferson, the well-born aristocrat, and they found guidance for their egalitarian yearnings in Paine's answer to critics of the French Revolution, *The Rights of Man*, published in Paris early in 1791. Paine exulted in industrialization, saw it as a force that could sweep aside tradition, and envisioned the possibility of realizing a world in which, as he proclaimed near the outset of his great pamphlet, "all men are born equal, and with equal natural rights." "Every age and generation must be free to act for itself," he went on, for "it is the living, and not the dead, that are to be accommodated." No truth was greater, Paine had added, than that "Every generation is equal in rights to the generations which preceded it, by the same rule that every individual is born equal in rights with his contemporary."[54] With no help from Jefferson, these urban adherents of Paine's republican vision established corresponding committees to spread their concerns, and at least in Pennsylvania and New York a rudimentary machinery gradually came together that permitted the framing and circulation of party tickets featuring candidates opposed to the Bank and other facets of Hamilton's program, and even led to considerable interstate consultation among those who wished to organize to prevent Vice President Adams's reelection.[55]

Meanwhile, as Philadelphia's heat and humidity gave way to the first chilly nights of autumn in 1791, the first truly anti-Hamilton newspaper, Freneau's semiweekly *National Gazette*, made its appearance. With Jefferson providing inside information on affairs in Europe, the editor spent the next few months attempting to establish his paper as a credible organ. However, in February, Freneau took off the gloves, sometimes utilizing information that Jefferson passed along, including tidbits gathered at his dinners or intelligence assembled by the clerk of the House of Representatives, John Beckley, a fellow Virginian who kept his eyes and ears open. Although his annual salary of $250 from the State Department kept the wolf from the door, Freneau showed no reluctance in savaging the administration that sustained him. The earliest invective in his paper poured from his own pen. Not everything that he wrote was true. But not all of it was untrue. He began with a series of essays that excoriated funding and the Bank as clever schemes to transfer taxpayer dollars to a cabal of well-placed "high fliers." Some congressmen were among those who profited from Hamilton's machinations, he said, and he named Elias Boudinot and Jonathan Dayton of New Jersey as two of the culprits. Unless the Hamiltonians were stopped, he predicted, the result would be unlimited government, soaring prices as monopolies were fashioned by favored manufacturers, and rising taxes. While the plutocrats reveled in wealth, he added, many Americans would sink in an "abiss of *discredit* and *poverty!*"[56] Jefferson subsequently claimed that he never wrote essays for the *National Gazette*. No evidence exists that he did. Throughout his life, Jefferson's style was to find others to do unpleasant things for him, and in this instance he appears to have recruited writers for Freneau's newspaper, including Madison. Nevertheless, he covertly assisted Freneau in framing certain arguments, including those to be used in attacks on the president that he served. If his behavior had a malodorous quality about it, there was nothing dishonorable about an opposition press or about Madison writing for an anti-administration organ. Nor was it untoward for Hamilton to have written anonymously for Fenno's paper. The treasury secretary, as well as Jefferson and Madison, were pioneers in the art of modern politics. They were searching for ways to influence public opinion, and their strategy, which included what today would be called negative campaigning, would become habitual in the nation's party wars.[57]

Madison, who never was able to say no to Jefferson, was persuaded to write for Freneau, and he contributed at least nineteen unsigned essays to the *National Gazette* before the fall elections. While he, too, occasionally employed a poison pen, his were the most thoughtful pieces that Freneau ran. Some of his essays presaged Karl Marx by half a century, in that he portrayed the partisan struggle in American politics as a class conflict. He limned the antirepublican element as "from particular interest, from natural temper, or from habits of life," the representatives of the wealthy, an element whose motivation was pitched "less to the interest of the many than of a few," and who cherished the belief that "the government itself may by degrees be narrowed into fewer hands, and approximated to an hereditary form." In contrast, he insisted that the foes of Hamiltonianism consisted of

those who believing in the doctrine that mankind are capable of governing themselves, and hating hereditary power as an insult to the reason and an outrage to the rights of man, are naturally offended at every public measure that does not appeal to the understanding and to the general interest of the community, or that is not strictly conformable to the principles, and conducive to the preservation of republican government.[58]

Some of Madison's essays reflected on the Constitution that he had done so much to bring into being. He covered the same ground that Jefferson had explored in discussing the unconstitutionality of the Bank, but then went much further. *Mea culpa*, he appeared to say, as he implicitly acknowledged that he had been misguided in several respects. He seemed to say that he had not realized how remote from the government the citizenry would be in such a vast republic as the United States. As a result, he had failed to foresee that the central government would inevitably respond mostly to special interests. Nor had he anticipated that the executive branch would so easily accumulate so much authority.

Madison proposed a twofold solution to these ills. First, clear limits must be maintained on the authority exercised by the national government and greater latitude must exist for each state to act as it wished. This was yet another amazing turnaround for Madison, who only five years earlier wished for a central government that could invalidate state actions "in all cases whatsoever." His second solution was no less astounding. Because the people must be better informed and more alert to the dangers to their liberties that existed, it was necessary, he said, to create a political "party"— Madison was one of the first to use the word *party*—to resist the entrenched power of the commercial sector and maintain a free state. Political parties were not new, he pointed out. Whigs and Tories had reflected the deep divisions in America in 1776, while

Federalists and Anti-Federalists had represented the bitter differences over consolidation in 1787. A new party now was needed to resist the "debauched" and "opulent" who had seized the government for the benefit of the few, perverting what had been foreseen as "the limited government of the Union into a government of unlimited discretion, contrary to the will . . . of the people." The opposition party—the "Republican party, it may be termed," he wrote—was coming into being to save republican government and to preserve the dream of the American Revolution, the dream that hereditary power had no place in this land.[59]

With the elections looming, Jefferson in May 1792 attempted one final tactic to undercut Hamilton. He wrote a remarkable letter to Washington in which he not only appealed to him to agree to a second term but implored him to drop Hamilton from the cabinet. Jefferson began by taking issue with Hamilton's economic schemes. He charged that the treasury secretary had exaggerated the public debt, creating an indebtedness greater than could be "paid off before . . . adding new debt to it," and established an exorbitant interest rate on the new federal securities. He predicted that because so many Europeans had acquired those securities, hard money would be sucked from the United States, leaving many of its citizens faced with penury. Hamiltonianism, he went on, was responsible for deep divisions that might ultimately prove fatal to the Union. Not only had the treasury secretary deepened the divisions between North and South, but by attempting to erect a system modeled on that in Great Britain, he had separated the supporters of the new government into the "Republican federalists" and the "Monarchical federalists."[60]

Washington was not impressed with Jefferson's arguments and never considered acting on them. If anything, Jefferson's letter was counterproductive. Washington appeared shocked at the secretary of state's presumption in approaching him on the matter, and his support for Hamilton only deepened. Convinced that Hamilton's economic intuition had rescued the United States from the desperate economic straits of the 1780s, the president now resolutely believed that Hamilton's achievements had vindicated his judgment in making him the treasury secretary. Washington immediately told Hamilton of his delight that the "Country is prosperous & happy" and then informed him of the allegations that had been levied against him. Washington meanwhile asked Jefferson to restrain Freneau—he probably had not deduced the connection between the two until he read the secretary of state's letter—and warned his fellow Virginian about embarking on a course that could result in fatal national divisions.[61]

When Washington transmitted Jefferson's allegations to Hamilton, he did not divulge the identity of the accuser. He told his treasury secretary that these were the sentiments of "sensible & moderate men" who were "known friends to the Government," and that he had heard them in the course of his recent journeys to and from Mount Vernon. Hamilton logically construed that the dissent came from the South, and he assumed that much of what he read could be attributed to Jefferson. He had known something of Jefferson's opposition to his program since the Bank Bill imbroglio. Furthermore, however much Jefferson and Madison had tried to make their New York vacation appear to be solely a botanizing venture, Hamilton had been informed immediately by his own network of informants that the Virginians were in fact engaged in "a passionate courtship" of his provincial enemies, including Robert Livingston and Aaron Burr. Two weeks before hearing from the president, in fact, Hamilton had told a friend that "Mr. Madison cooperating with Mr. Jefferson is the head of a faction decidedly hostile to me and my administration."[62]

Hamilton responded at once by attempting to persuade the president to dismiss Jefferson. Telling Washington that continued divisions within the administration "must destroy the energy of Government," he advised the president that his best course of action would be to remove the source of the trouble before it wrecked his presidency. Hamilton also answered Jefferson's allegations with a 14,000-word rebuttal. His defense of his economic scheme, and of the limits of the authority of the national government, were by now old hat and certainly not newsworthy to the president. However, he offered an ingenious repudiation of the charges that he was "prepar[ing] the way for a change, from the present republican form of Government, to that of a monarchy." It was folly, Hamilton said, to imagine that a monarchy could spring up in a government in which the offices were "continually changing hands." Yet suppose it could be done. As several generations would be required to effect the transformation, and as people in public life were motivated to act chiefly to realize "interest or ambition," he could see no reason why anyone would become involved in such an unpopular, and probably politically suicidal, undertaking that could only be realized following their lifetime. Hamilton told Washington that the populace was "so enlightened" that it did not want a king, and "so diversified" that monarchy could never be achieved while prosperity and order prevailed. At present, he concluded, "I believe nobody dreams of it."[63]

Was Jefferson correct? Or Hamilton? Jefferson was correct in charging that many Federalists had conspired to create a national government armed with far greater powers than they divulged to the public during ratification. Were Hamilton and the nationalists in his orbit closet monarchists? Jefferson painted his adversaries with a broad brush, drawing no distinctions among those who adhered to Hamilton's vision, but the reality was more complex. Some nationalists doubtless saw royal government as the best hope for forestalling social change and as the only adhesive that could bind together the unstable new United States. Hamilton, who at the Philadelphia Convention had dreamily extolled monarchy as the best weapon for thwarting democracy and preserving stability, was at least a fellow traveler with this crowd, although his primary agenda was to put in place a powerful central government that could exert an influence on all sorts of matters, including markets.[64] Many whom Jefferson suspected as monarchists—including those who wished to celebrate Washington's birthday, stamp his image on coins, and shroud his office in majesty and ceremony—were not royalists. While they embraced the trappings of royalty and would have made the presidential office resemble a European monarchy, their aim was not to make Washington a king but to enhance the dignity of the new government. Most nationalists of this sort were committed to a balanced government, and they believed passionately that a strong executive was essential as a check against a too passionate legislative branch. This included Vice President Adams, who believed that the chief executive—the sole national official in the new government—was in the best position to make the dispassionate and disinterested decisions that could truly protect the security interests of the United States. Congressmen, Adams feared, were so likely to be in the thrall of influential local interests that they could not always be trusted to act wisely with regard to issues of paramount national concern. Adams additionally saw the president as the guardian of the neglected in America, intuitively envisioning what subsequently came to pass when strong presidents, with a national constituency, acted as enlightened statesmen during the abolitionist and civil rights crises and in the blight of the Great Depression.[65]

Jefferson saw Hamiltonian economics with greater clarity. Hamilton's program did indeed portend drastic change for American society. Change frightens many, and in every age the uncertainty provoked by radical change has led alarmed observers to equate innovation and transformation with corruption and decay. Jefferson was cut from this cloth. Like many others, he had interpreted social and economic changes in eighteenth-century England as signs of debasement and decline that helped justify the American Revolution. In the 1790s the word *corruption* studded his hyperbolic rhetoric. Jefferson foresaw, correctly, that the world Hamilton wished to create would consist of considerable pain, including widespread

exploitation of white workers, among them very young children, un-
speakable urban squalor, and the emergence of a commercial and industrial plutocracy that would ravage the promise of individual liberty
that had been the cornerstone of the republican ideology of the American Revolution. However, the world that Jefferson hoped to sustain was
not without pain. It included abused slaves, who lived without hope under
the most abominable circumstances, and many free persons who eked
out a living from timeworn lands while paying homage to a squirearchy
that monopolized political power. Jefferson ignored some of this, and in
particular he was silent on the plague of African-American bondage.
What he held forth instead was a yeoman republic for the free white
population that was in stark contrast to what he imagined was on the
horizon in Hamilton's world. In Jefferson's rural utopia, virtuous and
largely autonomous property-owning farmers pursued their happiness,
uninhibited by government and uncorrupted by the snares of capital.

To the marrow of his being, Jefferson believed that the Hamiltonians hoped to destroy the great promise of the American Revolution.
For Jefferson, the essence of the American rebellion had been compelling those who possessed political power to reflect the popular will. He
once remarked "that the ground of liberty is to be gained by inches, that
we must be contented to rescue what we can get from time to time, and
eternally press forward for what is yet to get."[66] He rejoiced that several
additional inches of liberty had been gained by the eradication of monarchy in America and the subsequent erection of a decentralized political system, but he feared that the gains made since 1776 were under siege.
Unless the American people could be organized to protect themselves,
they were in danger of becoming the anvil upon which the elite beat out
their aspirations for self-aggrandizement. Jefferson chose to fight
Hamilton by drawing on his friendships with influential men in several
states who possessed the means to cobble together local networks consisting of those who, for disparate reasons, were opposed to the direction that Hamilton and his followers appeared to be taking the nascent
Republic. Jefferson did not envision the formation of a political party,
much less a national party, through which to contest his adversaries. But
he did seek to mobilize popular opinion, as Samuel Adams had galvanized a popular movement in Massachusetts against Great Britain before 1776 out of a growing sense of disaffection. Indeed, it was Jefferson's
genius to understand that Hamiltonian finance was leading the country
in a direction that most people did not wish to go, and to realize that it
was possible in time to stop the treasury secretary by informing the populace of the peril and by arousing the citizenry against his vision.[67]

In taking these steps, Jefferson did not create a new politics. He drew on what had been taking shape since those days when an interested and aroused populace was organized to pillage Oliver's estate, battle an occupation army in the dark streets of Boston, destroy dutied tea, adhere to boycotts, and wage war. In the 1780s, the most conservative Americans had expressed alarm at the swelling democracy unleashed by the American Revolution, and they had struggled to preserve the deference and passivity that had characterized Anglo-American political practices. In the lead up to the ratification of the new Constitution, many nationalists had written lovingly, albeit often in an encrypted fashion, of an older system in which those who held the most powerful offices were drawn almost exclusively from among the traditional elite, of a political process defined by a genteel decorum and in which strident partisanship was nowhere to be found, and of the virtues of government in which decision makers were scarcely troubled by popular influence. But the steps that Jefferson took to organize the opposition to Hamilton dealt yet another blow to the dying political practices of pre-Revolutionary America. Not that every nook and cranny in the new political system was immediately perceptible. Nevertheless, the lid on democracy had been laid aside, and by the end of the decade it was apparent to the most astute, as it was to Jefferson in 1792, that any faction which hoped to control the federal government must march to a drumbeat of popular sovereignty, recognizing that the intrusion of the electorate was inevitable in public affairs.[68]

Hamilton made one final report to Congress prior to the congressional elections. Nine months after the creation of the Bank, in December 1791, he urged Congress to promote manufacturing. With each step toward self-sufficiency, he wrote in his Report on the Subject of Manufactures, America would grow stronger and more truly independent. Many benefits would accrue. Agriculture would be stimulated, for farmers not only would have access to cheaper tools, but the manufacturing towns—inhabited by workers who were paid in cash—would consume what the yeomanry produced. Interstate trade, at the moment negligible in a new nation of former colonies that had focused on imperial markets, would be enhanced. America's chronic trade imbalance would vanish, for Europe would find American markets more attractive as the new nation's economy diversified. Hamilton predicted that some existing enterprises, such as the fishing industry, would enjoy growing markets as a greater percentage of the population worked in manufacturing. He acknowledged that "Northern and middle states should be the principal scenes" of manufacturing, but the South's indigo and hemp production and its forest industries would be aided by the changes in the economy. Hamilton saw a growing middle class and a more productive and affluent working class, though some of the latter's growing income would be earned by wives and children who were pressed into becoming mill hands. The treasury secretary recommended the creation of state-owned manufacturing facilities for the production of powder and weaponry. He implied, but did not specifically urge, that Congress should strengthen the young American navy and launch road construction and river improvement projects as aids to commerce. Enormous capital was required to start up manufacturing, Hamilton said, but America's excellent public credit would attract European investors. As always was his intent, the Bank would also nourish worthy entrepreneurs. Yet those sources would be insufficient. It was his recommendation, therefore, that Congress provide assistance, including a protective tariff and subsidies for the infant industries. It was a breathtaking vision of the machine-age America that was to flower in the nineteenth century, nothing less than "the embryo of modern America," as Hamilton's biographer John C. Miller observed."[69]

The prospect of mills and smokestacks on the landscape was unappealing to Jefferson and Madison, but what especially alarmed them was Hamilton's suggestion that the "general welfare" clause of the Constitution enabled Congress to aid the industrial process. The Founders, Hamilton had written, believed it essential to grant Congress authority to "provide for the Common defense and general welfare." Without such a clause, he added, "numerous exigencies incident to the affairs of a Nation would have been left without a provision." But this, Jefferson told Washington in a private meeting early in 1792, would vest Congress with unlimited powers. If Hamilton succeeded in establishing such a precedent, Congress thereafter might "take every thing under their management which *they* should deem for the *public welfare*, and which is susceptible of the application of money." If this is permitted, he warned Washington, there will be "no limits of their authority."[70]

Jefferson prepared notes and memoranda on the matter, doubtless in preparation for a campaign in the press. That proved to be unnecessary, for Hamilton's reach at last had exceeded his grasp. Not only was there little support in the South for his plan, but on this occasion his Northern supporters fragmented. Hamilton's call for protectionist legislation frightened some merchants, who feared European retaliation in the event that tariffs were imposed on European goods entering American ports.[71] His plan, which was at least a quarter century ahead of its time, died quickly in Congress without coming to a vote.

Partisanship did not die, however. The two sides fired away at one another in the newspapers throughout the summer and fall. Typically,

Jefferson, who like Washington always wished to be seen as above the fray, wrote nothing for publication, but Hamilton and Madison were active. To this point, Hamilton had merely defended his recommendations. Now he went on the attack, lashing out at Jefferson in essays in Fenno's newspaper. The public, he said, had been taken in by Jefferson's dissimulation, thinking him a "quiet, modest, retiring philosopher . . . [and a] simple, unambitious republican." In reality, he insisted, Jefferson was "a man of profound ambition and violent passions," a dedicated revolutionary whom he called an "intriguing incendiary." He revealed to the public that Jefferson had played a role in setting up Freneau's paper, equating his act with the treachery of "a cowardly assassin" given to "striking in the dark." Jefferson's connivance with Freneau, he continued, was a betrayal of President Washington. From the moment of his return from France, Hamilton alleged, Jefferson had plotted to become "the head of a party, whose politics have constantly aimed at elevating State-power, upon the ruins of National Authority." Indeed, Hamilton alleged incorrectly, Jefferson had secretly encouraged his friends to oppose the ratification of the Constitution. Jefferson, he concluded, was the "promoter of national disunion, national insignificance, public disorder and discredit." A war hero himself, Hamilton even needled Jefferson about his lack of military service, referring to him as the "Warrior" of "Monticelli."[72]

Both sides were active in the fall elections of 1792. They agreed on only one thing: that it was imperative that Washington serve a second term. However, the president was quite serious about retirement. When he had agreed to serve in 1789, Washington had considered retiring after only a few months, just as soon as the new federal government was running smoothly. The bitter wars over Hamilton's program, and perhaps the exhilaration he felt at once again being part of a supercharged atmosphere, soon persuaded Washington to complete his term. However, by early in 1792 the novelty of being president long since had worn off. Furthermore, Washington turned sixty that February, and he more than felt his age. Felled in 1789 by what his physician diagnosed as cutaneous anthrax, but which is now thought to have been a rapidly growing carbuncle that was surgically removed, and by what may have been pneumonia the following year, Washington had never fully recovered his strength. What is more, he complained of slight memory loss and failing hearing, and many observers noted that he looked old and tired. Anxious to be done with public service and to enjoy the tranquility of home during what he suspected would be the brief time left him, Washington asked Madison to draft a farewell address for presentation to the nation early in 1792.[73]

Insiders, such as Robert Morris and Henry Knox, who were aware of the president's intention, beseeched him to endure a second term. So did Jefferson, although he doubted that Washington could be dissuaded. He knew Washington was weary of the cares of public life and concerned for Mount Vernon, where the estate manager, who long had kept operations in motion during the president's protracted absences, was dying of tuberculosis. Nevertheless, Jefferson tried, taking the tack that the emerging partisanship posed a serious threat, and adding that "North and South will hang together, if they have you to hang on." Hamilton also pleaded with Washington to remain at the helm. Internal dissensions were growing, he cautioned, sounding very much like his counterpart in the State Department. Like Jefferson, he too warned that the Union might not survive if Washington were not available to provide the adhesive. But Hamilton knew better than Jefferson how Washington thought. He closed his appeal by warning—as he had when he implored Washington to accept the presidency in 1789—that the president's retirement would constitute the "greatest evil that could befall the country." Should the Union fail, the fickle public might blame Washington for its woes. To resign, he added as his clincher, might prove to be "critically hazardous to your own reputation."[74]

Washington kept his own counsel. While the president pondered his decision, he made two trips to Mount Vernon, the first time during his presidency that he had returned home twice in the same year. Late in his second vacation, he agreed to a second term. No one thing accounted for his decision. He was troubled by the manifold problems brought on by the profit-hungry landowners at the Potomac site designated for the Federal City, and fretted that the capital would never leave Philadelphia unless he stayed on the job and used his leverage to ensure that the snags were resolved. He had also grown increasingly concerned by twin dangers to the Union. For one thing, he suspected that a confrontation was inevitable between the national government and western farmers, who had begun to defy the excise tax on whiskey. By September he also knew that his attempts to calm the partisan waters had failed. Jefferson had refused to restrain Freneau, and the president learned that Hamilton was contributing vitriolic essays to Fenno's newspaper. Washington gradually had come to believe what everyone was telling him. Only his presence during the next four years could keep the Union intact.[75]

Those opposed to the treasury secretary's programs—some, like Senator Fisher Ames of Massachusetts, simply called them the "Antis," after their habit of opposing everything that Hamilton recommended—hoped to achieve three ends that autumn. One was to elect to the vice presidency New York's longtime governor and recently a foe of ratification, George Clinton, thus dumping John Adams, whom they feared would be Washington's successor, either as his heir-apparent in 1797 or due to the death, or incapacity, of the chief executive. Jefferson was conflicted. He regarded Adams as an old friend who in many ways was a capable, honest man, but who unfortunately had turned "Monocrat," or royalist, during his residence in London. Jefferson ultimately remained on the sidelines, permitting others, including Madison—who despised the vice president—to do the dirty work in concert with a few Pennsylvania and New York politicos who disliked Adams or admired Clinton, or both. Hamilton, meanwhile, worked to save Adams, though he barely knew the vice president and was hardly enamored with him. His object was to prevent the elevation of Clinton. Governor Clinton ultimately carried New York's electoral vote, but Hamilton succeeded in holding Pennsylvania and the remainder of the Northern states in line for Adams, who was easily reelected in a purely sectional vote. Nearly four-fifths of Clinton's vote came from the South. Excluding New York, Adams won fifty-eight of the sixty-three Northern votes.[76]

The second objective of the Republicans, as some in the crystallizing network of anti-Hamiltonians had taken to calling themselves, was to elect more of their own to Congress and the state legislatures, which chose United States senators. They were especially successful in state contests, where it was easier to quickly fashion a measure of cohesiveness. In Virginia, for instance, where the two factions in the ratification fight had equally divided the vote, sixteen of nineteen congressional seats were won in 1792 by candidates who campaigned against Hamilton's programs. The outcome in Virginia was replicated in many southern states. Jefferson was ecstatic. Those opposed to Hamilton had scored victories "every where South of Connecticut," he boasted, and for the first time had even elected a congressman in merchant-dominated Massachusetts. Jefferson believed that "the republican interest," the faction that he had labored to activate during this campaign, had won a majority of the seats in Congress. Henceforth, he rejoiced, the strength of the Hamiltonians would "retire and subside."[77]

When Congress gathered in December—it was the Congress elected in 1790, for under the quaint rules that existed well into the twentieth century, the newly elected Congress would not assemble for thirteen months, until December 1793—Jefferson and Madison pushed for their third objective. They sought to drive Hamilton from office. William Branch Giles, a young Virginian who was blindly loyal to Jefferson, introduced a set of five resolutions designed to launch an investigation into Hamilton's conduct as treasury secretary. It was a fishing expedition. The Virginians hoped to discover proof of financial improprieties, outright misconduct, or questionable judgment within the Treasury Department. In his startling letter to the president in May, Jefferson had alleged wrongdoings by Hamilton, but he had offered no evidence of improper or illegal activities. He now hoped for substantiation.

Hamilton promptly answered the charges with five lengthy rejoinders, and Giles followed by introducing nine new resolutions. He got nowhere. The House rejected Giles's resolutions by at least a two to one majority, a repudiation that Jefferson peevishly attributed to "the composition of the house 1. of bank directors. 2. holders of bank stock. 3. stock jobbers. 4. blind devotees [of Hamilton]. 5. ignorant persons. . . . 6. lazy and good humoured persons, who . . . acknoledged [the truth of Giles's assertions] yet were too lazy to examine, or unwilling to pronounce censure." Privately, however, Jefferson acknowledged that the Giles Resolutions were doomed to fail. He saw them, he said, merely as a vehicle for educating the public and building an organization opposed to the Hamiltonians.[78]

Although the Giles Resolutions had failed, Jefferson by March 1793 believed the threat posed by Hamilton had ended. An opposition press was in place and a Congress with a far greater number of members opposed to Hamilton's outlook would take office later in the year. His work, he now thought, was complete. Upon his return from France, Jefferson once remarked, he had observed such ominous threats to republicanism that he had felt it necessary to sacrifice every private pleasure in order to help fight the revived spirit of aristocracy and monarchy. Now, he said, the "duty no longer exists. . . . The difficulty is no longer to find [republican] candidates for the offices, but offices for the candidates" who had emerged in 1792 to stop Hamiltonianism. Hamilton saw matters differently. The work of building the national government had just begun, he told the president, and he anticipated further changes. Washington knew full well that the partisanship that had characterized 1792 was far from over, but he was hopeful that the greatest crises were behind him. The "great body of the people now feel the advantages of the General Government," he sighed, "and would not . . . do any thing that should destroy it."[79]

11

1793–1796

"A Colossus to the Antirepublican Party"

Dressed in a black silk suit, his usual attire for state occasions, President Washington climbed into his handsome carriage just before noon on March 4, 1793, Inauguration Day, for the short ride to Congress Hall. The cabinet, which at Washington's behest had planned the day, closed the ceremonies to the public. Thus, unescorted by floats or militia companies, Washington rode to the Senate chamber through Philadelphia's quiet streets. Upon alighting at his destination, however, he was greeted by a small but friendly crowd. The president hurried inside, where he delivered a three-paragraph Inaugural Address, the shortest ever given, took the oath of office, and departed. He was at home again within an hour of his departure.[1]

How different from earlier fêtes that Washington had enjoyed. A festive throng had welcomed him to New York when he took office four years earlier, and in Philadelphia tolling bells and effusive crowds had greeted him both on the eve of the Battle of Brandywine in 1777 and when he arrived to attend the Constitutional Convention in 1787. The striking difference on Inauguration Day 1793 perhaps reminded the president that he no longer enjoyed an immunity from public criticism. Only two weeks earlier, in fact, following the formal "birthnight ball" to celebrate his sixty-second birthday, the *National Gazette* had blasted the proceedings as a "monarchical farce."[2] This was merely the most recent attack. Criticism of the royal tone of his presidency had become a staple of Freneau's newspaper, and disparaging articles were beginning to appear in other newspapers that opposed Hamiltonianism. Mortified, Washington disingenuously told Jefferson that he had been misled "by persons he consulted at New York" into instituting the pomp and formality that surrounded his office.

They had "taken me in," he claimed.[3] His assertions were shockingly untrue and unconvincing. Furthermore, they ignored the harsh reality that many who hurled barbs at him acted from a heightened sense that America's Revolutionary republicanism was under a state of siege and that Washington was providing aid and comfort to those who preferred a formal—some said regal—system patterned on the British model.

Whatever he may have hoped for during the next four years, it is unlikely that on Inauguration Day Washington expected a tranquil second term. He had to have foreseen that foreign policy issues, which heretofore had not been a major concern, might become paramount. Much of Europe now was at war. Hostilities had erupted in April 1792 when France sought to spread its revolution, and Austria and Prussia fought back. At first, Washington had not been unduly alarmed, but when word arrived later that year that Louis XVI would be put on trial, the president began to fear the worst. Should the monarch be executed, and most Americans appear to have believed that would be his fate, it was widely suspected that Great Britain would—as America's minister to France, Gouverneur Morris, put it "— be wound up to a pitch of enthusiastic Horror against France" and join the allied coalition. The implications of Britain's belligerency were not lost on Washington. If Great Britain entered the war, America could expect the Royal Navy to blockade French ports, including those in the Caribbean. Havoc would be wreaked on American commerce.[4]

On the eve of his second term, anxious over what likely lay ahead, Washington confessed his misgivings at "the prospect of *commencing* another tour of duty." Soon after his Inauguration, he left the capital for Mount Vernon, his third trip home in ten months. If fortune smiled, he thought, he might escape Philadelphia until the autumn, when Congress reassembled. But luck deserted him. He had been at home less than a week when word arrived by express that Louis XVI had been guillotined in Paris and that Great Britain had gone to war with France. At once, President Washington rode for Philadelphia.[5]

In the late, drab days of winter, most Americans still saw the French Revolution in a positive light. After all, in 1776 they too had engaged in revolution and many, perhaps most, had considered themselves to be reformers, making the world anew, after the fashion of Thomas Paine. In 1793 many fervently and proudly believed that the American Revolution had inspired the reformers in France. Indeed, numerous old friends of America, such as the Marquis de Lafayette, were in the vanguard of the earliest revolutionary activities in France. The July 1789 liberation of the Bastille, the symbol of monarchical oppression, had been cheered throughout the United States, including at Mount Vernon, where Washington proudly displayed a key to the royal dungeon—a gift from Lafayette—in the main hall. The Declaration of the Rights of Man and Citizen, which echoed the spirit of the Declaration of Independence, was likewise applauded in America, as were the National Assembly's abolition of hereditary titles in 1790 and its attempts to establish a constitutional monarchy. Hamilton typified the buoyant mood, later confessing that the electrifying events in Paris between 1789 and 1791 had moved him as had nothing else since Lexington and Concord. John Adams, who had lived in France for nearly three years during the war, was one of the few American naysayers. Initially, he spoke out privately, cautioning that revolutions often spiraled out of control, leading to unintended excesses. From the start, Adams feared that "nothing but calamities" would come from the events in France, as the aristocratic reformers, in his judgment, were bumbling amateurs who were playing with fire. Once they let the genie out of the bottle, he predicted, nothing could stand in the way of "Vanity . . . Pride . . . Resentment or Revenge . . . Avarice or Ambition." Bedlam would prevail. In 1790 Adams went public. In his "Discourses on Davila," which Jefferson had found so reprehensible, Adams warned that the annihilation of the monarchy and nobility would lead to the destruction of discipline and subordination in society. Few listened. When word reached America in December 1792 that France had repulsed the Prussian and Austrian invaders in the Battle of Valmy, spontaneous rejoicing swept over the United States at the salvation of the Revolution. The greatest celebration occurred in conservative Boston, where despite the piercing winter cold, the city rejoiced with fireworks and a parade. Likewise in Philadelphia, Jefferson joyously reported, many residents were happily "taking to themselves the name of Jacobins," after a radical faction among the French revolutionaries.[6]

But by the spring of 1793, iterative reports of growing revolutionary terror and bloodshed in France crossed the Atlantic. First came tidings of the "September Massacres"— well over 1,000 executions in Paris alone during that violent month—followed by word of the slaying of the king and queen in January and forced de-Christianization throughout France. For the first time, numerous Americans grew uneasy with the French Revolution. The more conservative expressed concern over the "democratical hurricane" blowing in France, as Vice President Adams referred to it. Denunciations of the French excesses appeared regularly in the Federalist press, as the nationalists increasingly called themselves, and expressed concern that the upheaval not only might sweep through Europe but inspire similar radicalism in America. Nothing caused conservatives more anguish than the revolutionary egalitarianism in France.

They scoffed at the titles "Citizen" and "Citess" for all humankind, now fashionable in Paris, and recoiled from the new French taste in *sansculottes*. They were appalled when the formal bow gave way to men shaking hands or embracing one another, a practice that some conservative Americans denounced as "hugging and rugging . . . addressing and caressing." No one was more horrified than Chauncey Goodrich, scion of an old, elite family in Hartford, who worried that America's "noisy set of demagogues" would try to import the Parisian "contagion of levelism," and make him and his countrymen "all equal to French barbers." The French Revolution, Hamilton now cried out, had become like "one volcano succeeding another, the last still more dreadful than the former, spreading ruin and devastation," and spewing "Vice Anarchy Despotism and Impiety." These extreme conservatives did not represent the majority viewpoint. With some fervor, most Americans yet hoped that the French Revolution would succeed. Nevertheless, attitudes had begun to change in the northern cities. By summer the exultant mood inspired by Valmy had vanished almost everywhere, leading Congressman Fisher Ames to breathe a sigh of relief that Boston was "less frenchified than it was."[7]

Even so, many Americans continued to applaud the frenzied revolutionary activities abroad. While many expressed sorrow at the fate of Louis XVI, remembering him for having recognized and aided the United States during the darkest days of the War of Independence, a significant number doubtless would have agreed with James Monroe, who suggested that the king's execution and other violent revolutionary actions were merely "incidents to a much greater [cause] . . . which they wish to see accomplished."[8] Jefferson concurred, shrugging off what he called the "expunging of that officer" as necessary to prevent "the reestablishment of despotism." He lamented that innocent victims had died on the guillotine, but he compared their lot to that of civilians who perished in a just war. At least, he remarked, "their posterity will be enjoying that very liberty for which they would never have hesitated to offer up their lives." What ultimately made the horrors defensible, he said, not only was that the "liberty of the whole earth" hung in the balance but that "the form our own government was to take depended much more on events of France than any body had before imagined." Like Lenin a century later, who allegedly defended the carnage of the Bolshevik Revolution by remarking that "some eggs must be broken to make an omelet," Jefferson concluded that "rather than it [the French Revolution] should have failed, I would have seen half the earth desolated. Were there but an Adam and Eve left in every country, and left free, it would be better" than to have remained under the hammer of regal absolutism and privileged noblemen.[9]

As deep fissures appeared in the attitude of Americans toward the French Revolution and over how America might have to respond to European hostilities, the nation was fortunate to have as its first president a man who felt no need to prove his manhood. Washington had demonstrated his courage many times over in two wars. Yet another war had no allure for him, either personally or politically. Nor was Washington smitten with any European nation. Not only had he never traveled to Europe, but his family had inhabited Virginia for nearly a century and a half. He was thoroughly American. He looked with a jaundiced eye on all foreign powers and saw his principal objective as safeguarding the national security of the United States. He had no desire to hazard the interests of his country in an attempt to ensure the survival of any foreign nation. A month before he learned of Great Britain's belligerency, President Washington told his advisors that he hoped they had "too just a sense of our own interest" to wish to enter—or to permit the United States to be drawn into—Europe's war, in which America could contribute little but lose much. Even before he slipped off to Mount Vernon for his aborted vacation, the president was committed to American neutrality, and with his cabinet's approbation he issued such a proclamation in May.[10]

Nevertheless, the United States had only one ally, France, and Washington wished, within limits, to keep it happy. Thus, in February when financially pressed France requested that the United States make advance installments on its debt payments, Washington consented against Hamilton's wishes. The next month, when the president learned that the government of the French Republic was sending its first minister to Philadelphia, he decided to receive the envoy, although Hamilton thought it "a very unfortunate thing." But Washington never lost sight of his dictum regarding "a sense of our own interest." For instance, late in the winter he learned that France, which planned a naval attack on Spanish New Orleans, hoped the United States might help by simultaneously invading—and seizing for itself—Spanish Florida. Washington rejected any thought of American participation. Nevertheless, he understood that the United States might profit from the exigencies of the European belligerents. He directed Jefferson to be prepared to demand concessions from Madrid as the price of U.S. neutrality. Nor was that all. The Franco-American treaties of 1778 compelled the United States to aid France should that nation be at war. However, to do so would be to risk war with Great Britain. Washington's cabinet divided on the wisdom of adhering to the accords. Hamilton and Knox advised the president to suspend the treaties; Jefferson and Randolph urged that the pacts not be annulled. Washington resolved the matter by leaving the treaties intact and ignoring their disagreeable stipulations.[11]

The new French minister, Edmond-Charles-Edouard Genêt, disembarked in Charleston early in April and reached the capital five weeks later. He did not, as Hamilton had feared, invoke the treaties and request U.S. assistance for France, which was defending its West Indian sugar islands against British attack. Jefferson, who had not expected Genêt to make such a demand, believed that Paris would think the United States more valuable as a neutral than as a belligerent. He was correct.[12] Nevertheless, other difficulties quickly arose, for if ever an imprudent individual was vested with crucial diplomatic responsibilities, it was Genêt, and his rash behavior ultimately threatened American neutrality.

The thirty-year-old Genêt glowed with an intemperance that had already ruined his initial diplomatic assignment. Posted earlier in St. Petersburg, he had been sent packing by an autocratic Russian government that was offended by his unbridled revolutionary zeal. The French revolutionaries brushed aside the rebuke and quickly sent their envoy across the Atlantic, certain that it would be impossible for Citizen Genêt to offend the republican government in Philadelphia. They were wrong. Perhaps no diplomat in history ever wore out his welcome more quickly. Indeed, even before he reached the capital, President Washington learned that while in South Carolina, Genêt had commissioned privateers to prey on British vessels, erected a French court to condemn captured British prizes, purchased ammunition to be shipped to France, and set to work on finding volunteers to enlist in an expedition against Spanish Florida. Washington was horrified. Unless restrained, Genêt threatened to precipitate a crisis with Britain and Spain.[13]

Aside from having carefully crafted a presidential style, to this point Washington had not been a hands-on chief executive, at least with regard to the most substantive program of his administration. Hamilton had independently structured an economic policy, which Washington quietly endorsed. However, the president was less passive concerning foreign policy. In the cabinet debate on neutrality, for instance, Jefferson had argued against the executive's constitutional authority to issue such a proclamation. He contended that only Congress, which possessed the sole power to declare war, had the authority to decide the question of neutrality. The secretary of state also proposed that the declaration of neutrality be postponed and used subsequently as a bargaining chip. Washington rejected both arguments. Nor did Washington require coaching on how to cope with Genêt. When he received the French minister on May 18, 1793, Washington not only took pains to convey his displeasure at what the emissary had attempted in Charleston, but he sought to rein in Genêt before further difficulties occurred. Jefferson described Washington's manner as one of "cold caution," for the president not only bowed in the most icily formal manner he could muster; he even stood before paintings of the late Louis XVI and Marie Antoinette while greeting Genêt.[14]

Genêt responded by disregarding Washington in every possible way. He knew, as Jefferson acknowledged, that the Anglo-French war had regenerated "all the old spirit of 1776," and he opted to appeal over the chief executive to the American citizenry, hoping to stoke the lingering good will toward France and bond the world's two revolutionary peoples and republican nations.[15] Washington was outraged. He was not about to have American foreign policy made by an upstart French diplomat.

Through Jefferson, Washington immediately informed Genêt that the United States would not permit him to recruit its inhabitants to serve on privateers. Nor would it allow him to arm such vessels in its ports. Furthermore, the administration advised Genêt that it was suspending its advance payments on its debt. Unless the administration could be persuaded to reconsider, or Genêt changed step, his mission was doomed. Genêt showed no signs of relenting. Provocatively, he insisted that the treaties permitted him to arm privateers in American waters, as France had authorized the arming of American privateers in its waters during the final five years of the War of Independence. Genêt also maintained that the booming American economy was capable of sustaining the liquidation of the French debt, which would enable him to purchase war materials for his beleaguered nation. Jefferson, in the "hope of getting him right," counseled Genêt, urging him to act with restraint and patience. It was unavailing. Still more intemperate acts followed. In a letter to Jefferson, Genêt accused Washington of hostility to the French cause and rattled on about his intention of raising filibusters in Kentucky to march on Spanish Florida. In July he outfitted the privateer *Little Democrat* at the Philadelphia docks. Washington was furious. What "must the world think" if the United States submitted to Genêt's behavior, he wondered. By then, Jefferson was ready to wash his hands of this "absolutely incorrigible" envoy—"I saw the necessity of quitting a wreck," he privately told Madison—and well before the end of summer the administration demanded Genêt's recall.[16]

Genêt flamed out within eight weeks, but his turbulent behavior had helped inject foreign affairs into the political arena for the first time since the Jay-Gardoqui imbroglio seven years earlier. However, Genêt was hardly the only reason that European affairs intruded on domestic politics. Six months before the French minister's arrival, Jefferson had

concluded that the French Revolution might stop American conservatives in their tracks. The American political spectrum, he acknowledged,
had taken "a violent course" to the right after the War of Independence,
but the secretary of state was convinced that the radical events in France
in 1792, and especially the birth of the French Republic, had reawakened
the American citizenry's commitment to republicanism. He rejoiced that
just as the Hamiltonians "seemed ready to hang every thing round with
the tassils and baubles of monarchy," the resurgence of republican fever
within the United States had stayed their hand. Hamilton and his adherents, he said, had suddenly realized that further royalist behavior would
be politically suicidal. Before Madison, before most of his countrymen,
Jefferson glimpsed the political hay that could be made from the new
popular mood, especially from painting the Hamiltonians as Tories. With
"99 in an hundred of our citizens" yearning for the success of the French
Revolution, he said, the sentiments of "Hamilton himself and the
monocrats of his cabal" had become "extremely grating" to most Americans. Their "Anglomany," he predicted, would prove to be politically ruinous. In the long run, Jefferson was dead on target.[17]

Nothing better reflected the pulsating popular mood that Jefferson
noted than the Democratic Societies that began to spring up after Great
Britain entered the war. The Hamiltonians subsequently alleged that
Genêt or secret French agents in America were responsible for creating
these Democratic-Republican Societies, as most called themselves. Actually, they sprang from a spontaneous, populist mushrooming of democratic sentiment, and the first was organized among German Americans
in Philadelphia even before Genêt crossed the Atlantic. The public posturing by the French envoy was, at best, only a tangential factor in the
creation of the fifty or so additional societies in 1793–94. To some extent
these societies stemmed from hostility toward the conservative nationalists that had lingered since the bruising ratification struggle. Prominent former Anti-Federalists played leading roles in the creation of many
societies, and some clubs, such as the Vermont Society, even openly defended the foes of ratification as the real "friends and supporters of government [based] upon true republican principles."[18] Yet most members
of the Democratic Societies had supported ratification. Some had come
to believe that the policies of the Washington administration—first
Hamiltonian economics, now a neutrality that they perceived to be anti-
French and pro-British—threatened their dreams for Revolutionary
America. They expressed the traditional anxieties of zealous republicans. They were alarmed by encroaching executive powers and worried
that Hamiltonian economics would unduly aggrandize the national government. In addition, they opposed federal taxes, bridled at what they

beheld as the contamination of monarchy within the executive branch, and feared that the "rich and well-born," whom Hamilton and his followers appeared to serve, would destroy egalitarianism, meritocracy, and the democratic promise unleashed in 1776.[19]

There can be no question, however, that the French Revolution galvanized the disparate elements that comprised the membership of the Democratic Societies. Deep affection for France permeated the country. A member of the Baltimore Society, who doubtless captured the feelings of many of his countrymen, expressed his gratitude for French aid during the War of Independence in biblical terms:

We were strangers and ye took us in; we were naked and ye clothed us; we were pursued by robbers and ye put arms into our hands for defence; we wanted money, and we found thee a benefactress; by thy assistance were our right[s] defended; and by thy assistance . . . do we enjoy all our present blessings.[20]

In addition, many linked the fate of the American Revolution, which they believed was yet to be determined, to the survival of the French Revolution. The two great republican Revolutions, they said, faced the same enemies: aristocrats, monarchists, and Great Britain. Members of the societies believed that England's ruling caste, which distrusted humankind as dangerously irrational and wicked, had constructed a system that limited personal freedoms. The Democratic Societies saw the ideology of the French Revolutionaries, like that of their revolutionary brethren in America, as the diametrical opposite of such antiquated dogma. They additionally feared that if Great Britain destroyed the Revolution in France—in the process severing the Franco-American attachment—it would next turn its full fury on America. It was thus imperative that the Americans, who had first "kindled the Spark of Liberty," act to see that its "bright flame" continued to burn in France. Members of the Wythe County, Virginia, society also declared: "If all tyrants unite against free people, should not all free people unite against tyrants? Yes! Let us unite with France and stand or fall together."[21]

In reality, the societies constituted the first example of what would become a staple of American politics, a pressure group to shape public opinion. Their object, like that of the Jeffersonians, was to defend the American Revolution from internal threats and influence the foreign policy of the Washington administration.[22] They aroused great anxiety among the most conservative citizens—and not for their ideology alone. For one thing, the members of these societies believed fervently that the American Revolution had opened the possibility for every white male to be a political participant in a way that would have been impossible in the colonial era. For another, here were "butchers, tinkers, broken hucksters, and trans-Atlantic traitors," as one critic sarcastically limned the membership of the New York Democratic Society, and their very activism constituted a challenge to the older ideals of hierarchy, deference, and corporatism.[23] When these societies erected "liberty poles" and established mechanisms for communicating with like-minded individuals elsewhere, Hamilton and the most conservative Americans immediately understood that in style and technique they were akin to the Sons of Liberty and Committees of Correspondence, earlier organs of popular protest that had acted in concert in overturning a political system that had been the preserve of America's elite.[24] Hamilton knew, too, that here was the first evidence of grassroots discontent with the direction that he and his adherents were taking the new nation. What is more, the leadership of the societies often was quite unlike that of the opposition with which Hamilton thus far had vied. In fact, Jefferson and Madison also treated the societies as if they were venomous creatures best kept at arm's length. Like Hamilton, the Virginians remained attached to the idea that the traditional elite should guide the citizenry, furnish the leaders, choose the issues, and manage the battles. Neither Jefferson nor Madison, any more than Hamilton, was prepared for the advent of a populist groundswell. Unlike Hamilton, however, they did not denounce the Democratic Societies. The Hamiltonians were beside themselves. A Vermont assemblyman told Hamilton, in a letter that soon was published, that the Democratic Societies was a movement of "self-created societies and clubs"—*self-created* was a buzzword of the day that denoted populism or democracy—and he added that the societies had been formed for the purpose "of influencing, or dictating to, constitutional bodies." The "people ... are impatient of discussion, and incapable of reasoning," the Vermonter went on, and their influence would have "a very pernicious effect." Once the people were truly sovereign, he appeared to say, elite rule was imperiled. Hamilton soon also attacked the Democratic Societies, but his tack was more sophisticated. He argued that it was historically unprecedented, even madness, to conduct diplomacy through majority opinion.[25]

The American Revolution had brought to the surface democratic impulses that remained hidden, or carefully constrained, in the colonial era, and after 1786 the nationalist movement had gathered steam in some circles in part from its desire to check democracy in the states. The Democratic Societies were significant primarily because for the first time a citizens' movement, acting on its own initiative, had sought to influence the public policy of the national government. Here was an instinctive, voluntary movement that addressed critical national issues and sought to bend the federal leadership to its wishes. Some members of the societies were quite candid, in fact, in acknowledging that their credo would stand American political practice on its head, for they challenged both the dogma that the people's representatives were to act as they saw fit without consulting their constituents, and the notion that the people were to submit without petitioning their representatives.[26] Ultimately, they failed to shape the foreign policy of Washington's administration, but their potential to be a force in American politics did not go unnoticed.

Though unplanned, the one thing for which the Democratic Societies may have been responsible in 1793 was the timing of Jefferson's retirement. The secretary of state, who had spent little time at Monticello during the previous ten years, had long since grown eager to escape public service and have time for his own pursuits. He first spoke to Washington about his "excessive repugnance to public life" in October 1792, and confessed to the president his uneasiness with having to deal on an almost daily basis with merchants, speculators, financiers, and other public officials "which I know to bear me peculiar hatred." Immediately after that autumn's elections, when it appeared that his efforts to organize an opposition to Hamilton had succeeded, Jefferson informed Washington of his intention to surrender his office in March. He was confident that Hamilton's forces now lacked the power in Congress to truly injure American interests, and he remained convinced that Washington was too wise, and too resolute, ever to be stampeded into imprudent measures. Furthermore, Jefferson was confident that the vocal popular support for the French Revolution, manifested unambiguously by the Democratic Societies, had forestalled his adversaries' cherished hope of turning "the public feelings against France, and thence, in favor of England."[27] The president consented to Jefferson's wish to retire, although when Britain entered the European war, he prevailed on his secretary of state to remain at his post throughout the anxious year of 1793.

Several weeks before he left office, Jefferson and the president learned of British actions that "must bring on a crisis with us." In August 1793, word arrived that London had issued orders-in-council that banned neutral shipments of wheat, corn, and flour to France. Eight weeks later, the administration gained knowledge of additional orders-in-council that prohibited commerce between neutral nations and the French West Indies. The twin pronouncements led Jefferson toward his final steps as secretary of state. Against Hamilton's wishes, Washington agreed to Jefferson's entreaties to lay before Congress all correspondence between the State Department and the British minister. This made public the record of London's intransigence on the issues of removing British troops from the western posts, its discriminatory commercial policy toward the United States, and its embargo of neutral trade in French ports. Jefferson also at last complied with a three-year-old request by Congress that he suggest remedies that might open American commerce with Great Britain. Diplomatic considerations had earlier persuaded him to sit on his response. So, too, had the realization that before December 1793 there was no possibility that Congress would have acted on his recommendations. The success of the anti-Hamiltonians in the elections of 1792 changed matters. Jefferson now proposed what he had first urged nine years before and the cherished end that Madison had foreseen years earlier from empowering Congress to regulate commerce. Congress, Jefferson reported, must consider commercial retaliation against Great Britain. "[F]riendly Arrangements are preferable," he said, but the British "have not, as yet, discovered any disposition" toward reciprocity. In private, Jefferson admitted that there were political overtones to his statecraft, and indeed his actions had been determined in the course of a conference at Monticello between himself, Madison, and Monroe. By taking a tough stance with London, Jefferson believed that in pro-French America his actions would help "keep the people on our side." His admission would not have surprised Hamilton; he characterized the secretary of state as a "FIREBRAND of discord" who hurled an inflammatory recommendation at Congress "and instantly *decamped* to Monticello."[28]

Soon after submitting his report, Jefferson, as Hamilton had remarked, returned to Virginia to begin yet another "permanent" retirement from public life. Madison, however, remained in the House of Representatives, where he took over the day-to-day opposition to the Hamiltonians. He began by introducing a series of resolutions that embodied Jefferson's recommendations on trade. Madison told his fellow legislators that discriminatory duties on British manufactures and commerce were essential if America was to be truly independent. Otherwise, the United States would be the prisoner of "the caprice, the passions, the mistaken calculations of interest, the bankruptcies, and the wars of a single foreign country."[29] Hamilton fought back, writing newspaper essays and assisting friends in Congress who agreed to take on Madison. Hamilton pointed out that the United States sent some exports to Great Britain, received about 75 percent of its imports from the British empire, and found that British credit was essential for economic growth and prosperity. Furthermore, discrimination by the United States would be but a pinprick to mighty Britain. It would avail the United States little and might cause great harm. A disastrous commercial war, or actual hostilities, almost certainly would be the result of such a policy, either of which rend American society and politics.[30]

While the issue simmered, Hamilton's foes in Congress—acting in what soon would become the customary practice of opposition political parties—launched a second crusade to force their nemesis from office. Congressman Giles once again opened a probe into the treasury secretary's conduct. Giles, like Madison a graduate of Princeton, and like Jefferson a former law student of George Wythe, was utterly fearless, having in the course of his legal career represented over 100 British creditors with claims against his fellow Virginians. Loud, brash, combative, and known to drink too much, Giles was Madison's point man in the House, taking on the treasury secretary for a second time in what clearly was another wistful search for evidence of malfeasance.[31] Meanwhile, Albert Gallatin of Pennsylvania sought to conduct a similar inquiry in the Senate. Although the Senate probe never sparked to life, the House inquiry proved to be more vigorous than that of the previous winter. An investigating committee consisting of one representative from each state met three times a week for three months. Scrutiny focused on possible misuse of funds borrowed from Holland in 1790, the misappropriation of monies earmarked for reducing the foreign debt, illegal stock speculation, and Hamilton's private accounts with bankers. The committee compelled Hamilton to testify on numerous occasions, and doubtless caused him considerable anxiety, as he was convinced the panel was packed with "my decided political enemies" and lacked even "a single man . . . known to be friendly to me."[32] Nevertheless, despite considerable probing and ample zeal, Hamilton's accusers ultimately acknowledged that all charges of misbehavior were unsubstantiated.[33]

The Republicans, as the faction that Jefferson and Madison had taken steps to organize now called itself, also failed in its campaign to obtain discriminatory duties against Great Britain. The Federalist counterattack was brilliant. That Madison was painted as a "tool of France" was the least of it. What clicked was their argument that discrimination would ruin the British trade, a commerce that could not be replaced with business from other countries. Farmers who envisioned uncultivated fields and city workers who feared barren docks lost their taste for discrimination. Even the New York City Democratic Society declined to pass a resolution of support for discrimination against the former parent state. With hope eroding, Madison's only chance was to play for time. The Republicans postponed a vote, praying—as Madison told Jefferson—that London would take some further provocative step that "would strengthen the arguments for retaliation."[34]

News of British affronts did arrive. During the previous year the British had dispatched a sizeable army, and as much of the British navy as could be spared, to conquer the Lesser Antilles and St. Domingue,

French possessions in the Caribbean. The fleet was still in the Caribbean when the second orders-in-council kicked in early in 1794. By March every issue of the Philadelphia newspapers listed American ships and cargoes that had been seized. In no time, nearly 400 American vessels fell victim to the British navy. American trade in the West Indies ceased.

War fever swept the country at the news of the British depredations. Commercial discrimination, which had fallen out of favor and now suddenly seemed to many to be too mild anyway, died a quiet death. But what was to be done? Madison conceded the necessity of a "more active medicine," but had no plan of action ready in this emergency. Jefferson's presence was sorely missed, as had been true during the early stages of the battle over funding in 1790, for he was more adroit than Madison both at recognizing the broad contours of an issue and at sensing the vulnerabilities of an adversary. Indeed, with Jefferson gone, Hamilton and his followers seized the initiative for the first time since the Bank fight and waged one of the masterful campaigns in American political history. Despite their reputation as Anglophiles, the Federalists avoided being cast on the defense and ran circles around the forces led by Madison. Through "old tricks," they proceeded, as Madison himself ruefully acknowledged, "to acquire merit with the people" by posturing as anti-British.[35]

Theodore Sedgwick of Massachusetts, a spokesman for the Federalists in Congress, launched Hamilton's counterattack, but not until he had been thoroughly coached by the treasury secretary. Sedgwick urged a posture of military readiness, calling on Congress to respond to Britain's actions by creating a provisional army of 15,000. He also requested a thirty-day embargo of British commerce. At almost the moment that Sedgwick spoke, other northern congressmen, who were close to Hamilton, met with Washington "behind the curtain," as one put it. They beseeched the president to appoint an envoy extraordinary to travel to London to negotiate a settlement of differences with the former parent state. Washington quickly consented, although he vacillated for nearly a month over whom to dispatch across the Atlantic. Hamilton's name came up, but the president never seriously considered his appointment. Hamilton, he remarked, did not have the confidence of the American people. Hamilton himself advised Washington that the envoy must be an experienced diplomat and "friendly to the object." He was doubtless thinking of Jay, his fellow New Yorker, and secondarily of his friend Gouverneur Morris, the U.S. minister to France. Washington considered both, and he even contemplated asking Jefferson to undertake the mission. Five weeks after the idea germinated, Washington nominated Jay, declaring that the mission "will announce to the world" America's desire for "a friendly adjustment of our complaints and a reluctance to hostility."[36]

Meanwhile, gridlock prevailed in Congress. While the Republicans stymied the proposed army, the northern mercantile bloc rejected their proposal, conceived midway through the debates, to institute and maintain an embargo of British trade until London made restitution for the American property confiscated on the high seas. The Republican alternative, Madison told Jefferson, failed when the president dropped his bombshell about a diplomatic mission to London. It "had the effect of impeding all legislative measures for extorting redress from G.B.," he said. Congress eventually took two steps. The Senate confirmed Jay's appointment, and Congress adopted a thirty-day embargo of British trade. The northern merchant faction had gotten most of what it recommended and all that it really wanted. The Republicans had achieved nothing.[37]

Yet the episode left the Republicans with the illusory hope that the Federalists had burned their bridges. When Jay sailed for London on May 12, with instructions written by Hamilton stuffed in his pocket, every Southerner and Westerner realized that "the Mission," as Madison referred to Jay's assignment, was vested in a representative of New York merchants who, eight years earlier, had been willing to betray the South and West in his negotiations with Gardoqui. It was enough to provoke Kentuckians into hanging Jay in effigy, with a copy of one of Adams's "Davila" essays tied round his neck. Others looked on Jay as a member of the "British party." Jay had openly criticized Genêt. He also had loudly proclaimed that America's prewar debts to British creditors must be paid with interest, even though London's commercial policies long had inhibited repayment. Still others looked askance at Jay's selection because he was the chief justice of the Supreme Court. This amounted to plural officeholding, they raged, a commonplace of the rich and powerful in the colonial era—it had been one of the sorest of Samuel Adams's sore points with Hutchinson and Oliver thirty years earlier—but a practice supposedly terminated by the American Revolution. For that matter, the Democratic Society of Pennsylvania charged, Jay's selection was "contrary to the spirit and meaning of the constitution: as it unites in the same person judicial and legislative functions, [and] tends to make [the chief justice] dependent upon the President." A Democratic Society in western Pennsylvania wondered if Washington believed that there was a paucity of men with the virtue and talent necessary for the undertaking. The French Revolution, it went on, had successfully demonstrated that good generals could be elevated from the ranks and able officeholders could be found in small provincial villages. "Is our president, like the grand sultan of Constantinople, shut up in his apartment and unacquainted with all the talents or capacities but those of the seraskier or mufti that just happen to be about him?"[38]

The simmering fury over Jay's appointment was merely the tip of the iceberg of Western resentment toward the policies of the Washington administration. The president's actions, and the intemperate remarks of Hamilton and several of his persuasion, gave the administration a pro-British taint in the eyes of many Westerners. To put it mildly, little affection existed on the trans-Appalachian frontier for the former parent state. Many backcountry settlers harbored attitudes honed by bitter wartime experiences. Others had long lived in fear of Native Americans, who were armed by the British. The outbreak of Anglo-French hostilities in 1793 fueled the ever-present Anglophobia in the West, prompting calls for the United States to seize British-held Detroit and Niagara and to openly aid beleaguered France. A Pittsburgh newspaper captured the sentiments of many in the region when it asserted that France's friendship was "of the utmost importance to our security, and should be carefully cultivated. . . . A breach between us and France would infallibly bring the English again on our backs." To many, Washington's treatment of Genêt threatened the close relationship with Paris, and his appointment of Jay was tantamount to a commitment to bind the United States to Great Britain.[39]

Other issues troubled westerners as well. For example, many residents of the four westernmost counties in Pennsylvania uneasily noted a decline in their standard of living by 1794. The best lands now were often monopolized by wealthy absentee landlords, among them President Washington, who owned nearly 4,700 acres in western Pennsylvania. Moreover, while the wealthiest property owners steadily accumulated more land—and slaves, livestock, and local political offices—many hard-pressed yeomen had to make ends meet by selling off portions of what once had been their 100-acre farmsteads. If the Mississippi River were open to commerce and exports were multiplied to Europe, the Caribbean, and the urban entrepots on the Atlantic coast, prosperity would beckon. However, a dozen years after the preliminary peace, the river remained closed to the United States. Indeed, the Washington administration not only had constrained Genêt, who had sought to organize an expedition to open the Mississippi, but it had sent Jay to London, the diplomat who once had been willing to surrender his country's claims to the river. In addition, the British still occupied the western posts and still supplied the Indians. Washington had sent two armies to the Ohio Country to suppress the Indians, but both had suffered mortifying de-

feats, amid western charges that the soldiery had been doomed by eastern corruption that vitiated the army's supply system. To the West's per-
ception that the Washington administration was driven by Anglophilia,
the notion also had grown by 1794 that the remote national government
was in the hands of wealthy northeastern speculators who were indifferent to the plight of those on the frontier.[40]

When the West exploded in 1794, as Jay was crossing the Atlantic,
the catalyst was the excise on whiskey that Hamilton had proposed and
Congress had enacted three years earlier. The fury in the West should
have come as no surprise. As Hamilton's program unfolded in the early
years of Washington's administration, Jefferson advised the president
that a national government committed to an "accumulation of debt"
and to taxation to procure the revenue to meet the long-term obligations of indebtedness would be "of odious character with the people." It
would arouse "murmurings against taxes and tax-gatherers," he predicted,
and ultimately it could only be "enforced by arbitrary and vexatious
means."[41]

Washington and Hamilton knew in advance that the excise would
produce "clamor . . . evasion, and war on our own citizens to collect it."
Not only had Jefferson predicted as much, but the Pennsylvania assembly had condemned the measure before it was enacted by Congress. Tur-
moil occurred immediately after its passage. In the autumn of 1791, tax
collectors in western Pennsylvania were violently attacked. Protests,
mostly peaceful, continued episodically during the next two years. Passionate denunciations of the tax, including calls for evasion, were passed
by noisy public gatherings in Pittsburgh and nearby counties. Occasional
incidents occurred, and disobedience and evasion were commonplace.
Eighteen months after the tax went into effect, not a cent in revenue had
been garnered in western Pennsylvania. During 1793, almost two years
after the initial protests, the Democratic Societies opened fire on both
the tax and the president. The Democratic Society in Washington County,
Pennsylvania, south of Pittsburgh, told Washington that the western
farmers were the recipients of all the encumbrances and none of the
benefits bestowed by the new U.S. government. The farmers' woes
stemmed from the adverse "interest of . . . eastern America," it declared.
"[W]e can never be taught to submit" to this tax, it warned. Nevertheless, while the rhetoric was inflamed, no evidence existed that the protest in Pennsylvania was a separatist movement. This was strictly a
resistance movement against a hated tax.[42]

Nor were Pennsylvanians the only ones to protest. Resistance to the
whiskey tax bubbled in Kentucky and on the frontier in every state south
of the Potomac. However, Washington turned his gaze almost exclusively

on the dissenters in Pennsylvania. For one thing, Pennsylvania's violence against the tax collectors was nearly unique, for excisemen could not even be found to go into the backcountry elsewhere. In addition, Washington, like Lord North in the Coercive Acts crisis, sought to play divide and conquer, singling out only one dissident state rather than taking on every province that resisted the national law. The president also bided his time, praying that the tumult would eventually die down. Washington, who back in 1786 had cautioned that the mere "touch of a feather" might drive westerners from the Union, was not anxious to test his caveat. But he was boxed in, as his unwillingness to jettison Hamilton's economic program left him with few alternatives. The administration did successfully address flaws in the original law, lowered the duty, and sent emissaries into the West to appeal for obedience and peace. Washington displayed a tough side, too. In September 1792 he issued a strident proclamation denouncing the lawbreakers and promising that the statutes would be enforced. Pennsylvania cooled down somewhat thereafter, but the fury resumed in 1794, energized by the Anglo-French war and the Jay mission. Accounts of angry protests regularly reached Washington's desk that summer. Some of the most lurid were filed by federal officials on the scene, who often magnified minor incidents and depicted the protest as a vast conspiracy of Anti-Federalist sympathizers bent on destroying the new national government. But some accounts were accurate, and none troubled Washington more than word that the excise inspector in western Pennsylvania—John Neville, like himself, the product of a planter family in Virginia, a western land speculator, and soldier who had served with the Continental army at Trenton, Germantown, Princeton, Monmouth, and Valley Forge—had been violently attacked by a large mob.[43]

Pennsylvania officials met with Washington early in August. They advised him that many of the reports he had received were exaggerated. The state judiciary, they also told him, was capable of dealing with the dissidents. Federalist essayists painted a different picture, censuring the protestors in language remarkably similar to that employed by Royal authorities and Tories during the protests against British taxation after 1765. The insurgents were castigated as "levelers," an "ignorant herd," "the rabble," poor, provincial, irrational, disorderly, idle wretches, and as "restless sons of anarchy" who espoused "worn out ideas" such as localism and decentralization. Hamilton, who had been mortified when the Articles of Confederation Congress had been forced from Philadelphia by mutinous soldiers in 1783—the legislators' flight had been "to the last degree weak and disgusting," he had angrily charged—had long been anxious to demonstrate the power of the new national government. He wrote privately to Washington urging action. Sounding remarkably like the British prime minister on the eve of hostilities in 1775, the treasury secretary asserted that demagogues in western Pennsylvania were in fact the head of an anti-tax serpent. They had managed to "confirm, inflame, and systematize the spirit" of rebellion. The object of their "steady and Violent" protest was "to embarrass the Government" and "render [its] laws odious." He implied that the insurrection in Pennsylvania would spread if it were not quickly stamped out. The "very existence of Government demands" that an "imposing" force be sent to western Pennsylvania to crush the insurgents, he advised Washington. The president pondered the recommendation and, as was almost always the case, acted on Hamilton's advice. Using language strikingly similar to that employed by George III when he sanctioned his prime minister's wish to use force in 1775, Washington proclaimed that an "open rebellion" existed, brought into being largely by those few who sought "to sow the seeds of jealousy and distrust" in the national government until they succeeded in "destroying all confidence" in it.[44] In September the president authorized the use of force to suppress the disorders in Pennsylvania. He summoned nearly 13,000 militia and, together with Hamilton, rode west at the head of his army.

Washington's soldiery encountered an abundance of alienated citizens, but no army of "whiskey men." Most of the disaffected had availed themselves of an amnesty offered by the president or had simply run away into the vast wilderness. About 150 alleged rebels were rounded up—many were dragged from their beds in the dead of night—and confined in wretched circumstances until they could be interrogated. All but twenty were eventually released. Those who were to be prosecuted were sent on a forced march to Philadelphia in severe winter conditions. Just before Christmas, while a band played and merchant vessels in the harbor fired salutes celebrating the army's triumph, these shackled prisoners, dressed in rags, were paraded through the streets of the national capital. Only two Western men were ever convicted, one an imbecile, the other a mad man. Washington pardoned both.[45]

Just before the army's victorious return, Washington defended his use of force. In the State of the Union address, he laid the blame for the insurrection at the feet of the Democratic Societies, whose disaffection, he implied, stretched far beyond opposition to the excise. He had acted not only to prevent the spread of disorder but so that "an opinion of impotency or irresolution in the government" did not arise. Privately, Washington added that action had been necessary because the Democratic Societies were the product of a cabal of "insurgents" who hoped to "effect some revolution in government" and destroy the Union.[46]

Republicans in the House of Representative were furious. Not only was evidence lacking that the Democratic Societies bore responsibility for the violence in Pennsylvania, but most believed that Washington was unjustified in branding the members of the societies as dangerous insurrectionaries. Furthermore, the president had used the inflammatory term "self-created societies," which to many in that day carried the same combustible sound that coinage such as "red" or "pinko" connoted at the height of cold war passions. In the House's official response, Washington was applauded for having acted to crush an isolated insurgency. However, the House pointedly refused to censure the Democratic Societies. It was as close as either chamber ever came to rebuking Washington. In the course of the debate over its answer to the president's address, some Federalists attempted to link the Democratic Societies and the Republican Party. The ultraconservative Fisher Ames suggested that the public stability was compromised when a popular movement questioned governmental policy. The Federalist rhetoric in Congress prompted Madison and Jefferson to draw the conclusion that their adversaries had carried their campaign to a new level. By attacking the Democratic Societies, Madison charged, they now sought to extirpate a free speech and free press. He also reminded Congress that in a republican system "the censorial power is in the people over the government, and not in the government over the people." Jefferson concurred. He was aghast to learn that Washington, and those around him, had engaged in "an attack on the freedom of discussion, the freedom of writing, printing and publishing." Madison and Jefferson reached another conclusion. Washington's performance had transformed them. Where once he had been "the head of a nation," Jefferson lamented, Washington had become "the head of a party," the Federalist Party.[47]

Washington's improvident remarks offended some who had never sympathized with the whiskey rebels. Many hardworking, property-owning farmers, who understood the plight of their brethren in western Pennsylvania and were themselves the descendants of immigrants drawn to America by the expectation that government's yoke would be light, now saw the administration in a different light. Many merchants who traded with France, and who now took what Washington said and did as evidence of his Francophobia, were equally outraged. In addition, those who had come to see the Democratic Societies as vehicles for the egalitarianism supposedly won in the late war were appalled.[48] Madison noted privately that Washington's philippic had been "the greatest error of his political life." Like the president, Madison had believed that the Pennsylvania insurrection had to be suppressed, but he thought Washington had crossed the line to play "a most dangerous game" when he, like many

Federalists in Congress, implied that dissent was wrong. Madison appeared to suggest that the president had squandered his nonpartisan, statesmanlike stature. Furthermore, Madison implied, Washington's remarks after the fact were certain to cause many to question whether western Pennsylvania had teemed with revolutionaries or—as Jefferson had put it—merely with citizens engaged in "riotous" actions against the "infernal" excise. Thus, the administration's actions in suppressing the uprising became a watershed in America's political history, for the conclusion that increasing numbers reached by late 1794 was that the traditional deferential system of politics would no longer do. A party that represented the popular will was absolutely essential, lest the wishes of the citizenry be forever ignored, or overridden, by an elite bent on pursuing its own ends.[49]

A couple of days after returning to the capital with the army, Hamilton notified the president that he intended to resign within a month, on January 31, 1795. Hamilton was thirty-seven, thirteen years younger than Jefferson had been at the time of his retirement. Washington, who was deeply moved, wrote Hamilton an uncharacteristically heartfelt letter in which he confessed that his "confidence in your talents, actions, and integrity" had never been misplaced.[50] There can be no question of the impact of Hamilton on the new national government. Not only had he played a Herculean role in its creation, but during its first half dozen years he had done more than anyone to shape the substantive measures of the Washington administration. But if his influence cannot be questioned, his judgment and political acumen are open to scrutiny.

There was an alternative to Hamiltonian economics: commercial coercion against Great Britain, a policy advocated by Madison, Jefferson, and John Adams, among others. These leaders not only believed that discrimination could compel Great Britain to open its ports to American ships, but they were convinced that the revitalized commerce would provide sufficient revenue for quickly retiring the national and state war debts. In time, they insisted, commercial ties would foster a normalization of relations, resulting in the peaceful opening of the trans-Appalachian West. Their idea might have worked. As it was never attempted, even today no one can know whether it would have been fruitful. It was not tried because Hamilton, who had Washington's backing, favored utilizing the principles of British public finance to jump-start the transformation of the United States into a powerful modern state. The Hamilton-Washington design committed the United States to trade with Great Britain at all costs. In addition, as the impost on that British commerce produced inadequate revenue for meeting the requirements of funding and assumption, it soon forced the administration into internal taxation to make up the shortfall in gross receipts. Hamilton likely foresaw the need for taxation well in advance. After all, creating a national government with the authority to tax had been one of the imperatives behind the nationalist movement. But everyone knew that the American citizenry did not want to pay taxes. The Revolutionary generation, which already had paid in blood and money in a long struggle against a government bent on centralization, most especially did not wish to be heavily taxed, least of all by what many looked on as a faraway central government.

Had political parties that reflected public opinion existed in 1790–91, it is unlikely that all of Hamilton's economic program would have been enacted or that any of it would have passed Congress in the form that he proposed. But in 1790 the way was clear, and Hamilton, bold and visionary, seized the opportunity. Characteristically, as the historian Herbert Sloan has observed, Hamilton made a conscious choice to pursue "what might be possible" rather than "what was practicable," opting for a course that was too "bold, too ambitious, too much at odds with American realities, whether political or economic," and which required that Americans "subject themselves to a European system of discipline and taxation."[51] Hamilton was too sagacious not to anticipate opposition to his plan, but neither he nor Washington could have readily imagined what did occur. Between 1791 and 1794, a political party, in itself an unprecedented development, crystallized in response to what many perceived as Hamilton's "grand designs." There were those, such as Jefferson, who abhorred Hamiltonianism from a belief that it would eviscerate the traditional values of a republican, agrarian society. But many who opposed Hamilton had no qualms about his funding, assumption, and Bank; in fact, some in the opposition party applauded and profited from those endeavors. What united those disparate elements was the conviction that Hamilton and his Federalist Party wished to inhibit the liberating promise of the American Revolution, in its place fashioning an America that politically and socially resembled not only Great Britain from which the United States had escaped, but the colonial past from which most Americans were most anxious to flee. And what to many seemingly brought Hamiltonianism and the Federalist vista into sharper focus was its hyperbolic response to the French Revolution, its muted reaction to Britain's depredations on the high seas, and its visceral hostility to those who dared question constituted authority.

Hamilton, who saw the economic future with phenomenal clarity, was unable—or, more likely, unwilling—to grasp the new political forces taking shape. Where Jefferson was pre-democratic, Hamilton was anti-democratic. There was a world of difference. Jefferson's outlook cracked open the door that led to steadily more progressive political changes. Hamilton wished to bolt that door, lest the world of elitist supremacy vanish into the mists of time. Jefferson, within limits, was committed to the realization of the popular will; Hamilton was committed to the service of a preferred class and, even more, to what the elite—and it alone—judged to be the national interest. The accomplishments of Hamilton's side were remarkable. It not only overturned the decentralized system of governance for which most Americans had waged the American Revolution, but it put in its place a system designed to stymie reform. What is most remarkable, however, is how long it took for a truly effective opposition to emerge.

If Hamilton and his party one day would be undone by their belief systems, that is not to say that the long-term national interest would have been advanced by the repudiation of his economic program. Better than most—better than almost anyone, in fact—Hamilton understood how to stabilize the fragile Union through bold economic measures. He knew the way to unleash a fluid and voluminous money supply, with the result that he, more than any other single person, was responsible for making his age the essential transitory period between the capitalist seedtime in the colonial years and the muscular industrial state that was on the horizon. Few contemporaries grasped as well as Hamilton the forces that would prevail in the erection of modern states in the looming nineteenth century. He realized the necessity of superintending and managing the economy at the national level in order to begin the transformation of the new United States from a premodern to a modern state, a journey that would not be complete until the New Deal finished the work a century and a half later. The superstructure that he built enabled the inevitable industrialization to come more quickly, and more comprehensively, and the industrial might that resulted was a substantive factor in the salvation of the Union during the Civil War.

By the time he left office, Hamilton had realized almost everything he had sought to achieve. What he could not have known fully in January 1795, when he returned home to New York, was that he had reached the apex of his stunning public career and that the mounting popular resentment of the Federalist exercise of power would be his undoing.

Vice President John Adams, whose principal job was to preside over the Senate, was startled by the tranquility of the congressional session that began in November 1794. The senators "have no feelings this session; no passions, no animation in debate," he said.[52] Washington was no less surprised. Delighted, but fearing that this might be the calm before the

storm, the president proclaimed February 19 a day of national thanksgiving to celebrate both the return of peace in western Pennsylvania and
a recent United States military victory in the Ohio Country. The third
army sent by Washington to pacify the region above the Ohio River, a
legion commanded by General Anthony Wayne, had decimated the Indians in the Battle of Fallen Timbers, fought in the desolate northern
reaches of present-day Ohio. True peace had not arrived in this corner
of trans-Appalachia, as British troops remained in the region. Whether
more blood would be spilled in the Northwest Territory would in large
measure be determined by Jay's success or failure in London. Nevertheless, expectations in the capital ran high that Wayne's victory was a long
step toward disentangling a perplexing problem that had persisted since
Washington's youth and that had helped to shape the politics of the 1780s.
That winter Washington acted in the hope of capitalizing on Wayne's
triumph and of resolving still another western problem that had lingered since the days of the Articles of Confederation. He announced
that he was sending Thomas Pinckney to Madrid as an envoy extraordinary to negotiate a solution to the Mississippi quandary.[53]

Meanwhile Washington waited throughout that unhurried winter
for news from Jay. Unofficial communiqués from London suggested that
a treaty had been signed in November, but when January and February
passed without word, the president presumed that the rumors were false.
However, the rumors had been correct, and as luck would have it the
contents of the Jay Treaty reached the capital three days after Congress
adjourned in early March. As many of the legislators had already begun
their trek home, Washington could only summon them back to a special
session three months in the future. In the interim, he sequestered the
contents of Jay's Treaty.[54]

Washington had hoped for a very good treaty. Throughout the negotiations, which dragged on from June into November 1794, Jay appraised him of auspicious signs, and once in the early going even
predicted a favorable commercial accord. All signs were promising, for
Britain negotiated with its back to the wall. On the eve of Jay's discussions with the British foreign minister, French armies had inflicted mortifying defeats on allied forces in Flanders and the Netherlands. The last
thing that London needed was a new adversary. While hardly a military
power, the United Stares would confront Great Britain with a longer,
more treacherous war. Furthermore, members of the British laboring
classes, longing for many of the same reforms won by the French revolutionaries, moiled with sympathy for the republican storm across the
Channel. Evidence exists that Britain would have relinquished more had

Jay pushed harder, although London was not about to capitulate entirely to America's most extreme demands. Great Britain never saw the need to do so. It was confident that limited concessions would temper the war fever within the fragile United States. Furthermore, information that Hamilton covertly passed along to the British minister in Philadelphia had convinced London that Washington was so desperate for peace that he would accept half a loaf.[55]

Disappointment is the best description for what Washington felt when he first read the terms of the Jay Treaty on that dreary day in early March. He found that it contained no "mischiefs," as he put it, but London's only substantive concession was a willingness to pay compensation for spoliations that resulted from the actions taken under the orders-in-council. It pledged once again to withdraw its troops from United States soil, but this was a quid pro quo for Jay having reaffirmed the validity of the pre-Revolutionary War debts owed British creditors, something both sides had first agreed to in the Treaty of Paris. London refused to budge on questions of impressment or neutral rights, it would not liberalize its restrictive contraband list, and it declined to provide restitution to slave owners whose property had been carried from American soil by the British during the final months of the war. What most troubled the president, however, was that Great Britain had remained unyielding with regard to its commercial restrictions. Although the pact granted Britain most-favored-nation status in United States harbors, London neither reduced its tariffs nor threw open its ports to the American commodities that it had spurned since the enactment of the American Prohibitory Act almost twenty years earlier. In Article XII, Britain consented to open its West Indian ports only to American ships under seventy tons—disconcertingly small vessels, as most merchant ships were five or six times that size—and even then it stipulated that the bulk of the Caribbean products acquired in this trade could not be reexported by the United States.[56]

Washington had to decide whether to submit the treaty to the Senate. He knew it would provoke a firestorm. Not only had Jay been vilified in the press for the past ten months, but even as Washington wrestled with his decision—and while no one else but the secretary of state was aware of the terms of the accord—the first essay assailing the treaty appeared in a Philadelphia newspaper. The essayist, unable to scorn the particulars of the pact, argued simply that any treaty with Britain violated the spirit of the French treaties and jeopardized America's ties with its only ally.[57]

Washington returned to Mount Vernon in April, where according to many scholars, he found the solitude to think the matter through.

After months of careful deliberation, the story goes, he ultimately decided to submit the treaty for ratification. Truth be told, it was Washington's intention all along to submit the treaty, as he subsequently all but acknowledged. Although a bad treaty, it offered virtually the only hope of preventing a war with Great Britain. In many respects, it would have been easier for Washington to have rejected the accord. To be sure, by doing so he would have spared himself an avalanche of recriminations in the Republican press. But Washington neither wished for war nor believed that sufficient justification existed to start killing. It was clear that the national security was not threatened by British intransigence on the commercial issues. Indeed, Britain's trade restrictions notwithstanding, many in the United States had flourished since the end of the postwar depression. In addition, no one knew better than Washington how uncertain war could be. Going to war with Great Britain might turn into a simultaneous conflict with London's ally, Spain. Hostilities would be a scramble from which little might be achieved and much might be lost, including the vulnerable Union itself. In contrast, the treaty, flawed though it may have been, had three virtues as Washington saw it. It held the keys to pacifying the Ohio Country, the frontier that he had sought to pry open as a young warrior in command of the Virginia Regiment forty years earlier. It would lead to such a flow of population beyond the mountains that mounting pressure might build in Madrid to reach an accommodation with the United States on the Mississippi question. Finally, London's agreement to pay compensation for the spoliations would, for the time being, silence most who cried for war. In short, the accord might be a first step toward the peaceful resolution of a multitude of long-standing problems. Thus, early on President Washington decided to submit the treaty, and he prayed for its ratification.

Washington sent the treaty to a Senate that was composed of ten Republicans and twenty Federalists. The Federalists thus had a two-thirds majority, precisely what was required for ratification, but given the penchant of politicians for backroom deals, no one could know whether a bargain might be struck that would lead to vote switching. It is known that at least one such attempt was made. In a blatant move to charm Southern Federalists into breaking ranks with their party, Republicans sought to link ratification to the addition of a clause stipulating that Britain would provide compensation to slave owners for their wartime losses. The ploy failed. After three weeks of secret deliberations, the Senate ratified the treaty by a vote of 20–10, although it rejected Article XII. The vote was along party and sectional lines. Every Federalist voted for ratification, every Republican against. Eighteen who voted for ratification represented northern states. Seven who voted against the treaty were from the South or West.[58]

Washington thereafter waited several weeks before signing the treaty into law. At the time, some believed—and some historians have concurred—that he was vacillating indecisively. Washington encouraged that view by creating the impression that he would act on the advice of "dispassionate" men whose counsel he had sought. In fact, he never wavered from his desire to sign the accord. Washington dawdled because he was playing for time. The only "dispassionate" counselor that he approached was Hamilton, and he asked him not for instruction but to publish essays defending the treaty. He even coached Hamilton on how best to justify the treaty. There was nothing untoward in Washington's behavior. He was a leader who had set about to mold public opinion to support a decision he had made and soon would announce. Confident that "a plain and simple statement of facts" by the Federalist essayists would cause the overwhelming majority of the citizenry to "advocate the measure," Washington waited patiently throughout the summer as Hamilton, and a few of his compatriots, rushed essays into print to dash what the president called the "poison" and "odious points of view" of the Republicans. While these Federalist scribes straightforwardly maintained that peace and prosperity were intertwined with the treaty, many argued that it had been improper for the opposition even to question the accord. They challenged the right of Republican-dominated town meetings to petition against the treaty, and Fenno's *Gazette of the United States* even contended that it was dangerous for the public to debate the actions of public officials. In mid-August, about a month after the first of Hamilton's essays appeared, and nearly six months after he first learned of the contents of the accord, Washington at last signed the Jay Treaty, telling his secretary of state that while he was "not favorable to it," the accord had to go into effect in order to prevent war with Great Britain.[59]

President Washington was not alone in seeking to shape public opinion. Once the terms of the treaty were finally made public—just after the Senate acted—the public debate began in earnest. To an unprecedented degree, both Republicans and Federalists sought to enlist the support of the public. Both parties understood that the Jay Treaty resonated with choices of war or peace, trade or embargo, and possibly even the success or failure of the French Revolution. It also was big with possibilities for shaping the character of the post-Revolutionary United States. Once again, as often had been true in the past, a question of foreign affairs proved to be more crucial than domestic issues in shaping American politics. The colonists' relationship with a distant parent state had refashioned provincial politics in the years after 1765. The imbroglio over the peace ultimata realigned factions in 1779, and the Jay-Gardoqui embroilment in 1786 hastened the march toward a constitutional convention. In 1795 the Jay Treaty, in concert with the Anglo-French war, resulted in further divisions that led Republicans and Federalists to construct what one historian has called "national party machinery."[60] The reason for the impact of foreign affairs is not difficult to discover. As the historian Richard Buel observed, given "the national economy's lack of integration and the general provincialism of people's lives, it is hard to conceive of a domestic issue which could have affected the nation" as did such a substantive matter of foreign policy.[61]

Millions of words on the treaty, much of it invective, were uttered that summer and fall. No Federalist was immune, but Washington and Jay were the most reviled of those who supported the accord. It was alleged, untruthfully, that jubilant residents in London danced in the streets at the outfoxing of the unwary Jay, and the envoy was tarred, unfairly, as an Anglophile who only indifferently had sought to wring concessions from his British counterpart. Many critics assaulted the president for his "superciliousness and arrogance," which for six years, they charged, had caused him to habitually neglect public opinion. Washington thought himself the "*grand lama*" of the United States, said one foe. His objective, according to another, had always been to advance "the greatest good of the least number possessing the greatest wealth." Several writers characterized him as dishonest, others as in the grip of dementia. Whichever, he should be impeached, more than one critic demanded. Simultaneously, a campaign simmered to have Jay removed from his seat on the Supreme Court. It was alleged that he was a weakling and scoundrel who had negotiated with "his tail between his legs," and his effigy was burned at innumerable sites across the land, but especially in backcountry hamlets.[62]

However, more than personal vilification colored the attacks in the Republican press. The building blocks from which the Republican Party took shape can be traced to the meaning that some of its adherents attached to the American Revolution, as well as to their fears over consolidation. Funding, Assumption, and the Bank added additional brush strokes to the canvas on which the Hamiltonians were painting. But the French Revolution and Jay's Treaty made a discernable picture of what previously had been an indistinct swirl of colors. The year 1795 was the point at which this faction linked the various strands of the Federalist schema into a coherent whole, seeing a grand pattern in their adversary's domestic and foreign policies, their character and intentions. Many Republicans now believed that the Federalists were the literal descendants of the Tories. In the tableau painted by the Republicans, the Federalists existed expressly to arrest the changes promised by the American Revolution. Increasingly, the Republicans depicted their adversaries as a faction of well-born nabobs who, like their English counterparts, were comfortable with the stuffy etiquette of levees and reassured by a hierarchical social structure. The Federalists were also accused of having advanced an economic program whose intent included the establishment of an oppressive aristocracy. It was charged that they had corrupted Congress by filling it with speculators beholden to great merchants and financiers. The Federalists had seized the opportunity provided by dissidence on the Pennsylvania frontier, some now said, to intimidate their political foes everywhere. The Federalists were sketched as cherishing a systematic plan of erecting the United States on a blueprint of the British model, one that would maintain the genteel tradition and reduce the citizenry to deference. The Jay Treaty, they charged, was the first step on the Federalists' journey to bond Great Britain and the United States, so that ultimately the essence of the English social and political system would permeate America. But, the Republicans alleged, everything the Federalists held dear was threatened by the French Revolution, for if successful, its radical ideology would sweep across Europe and Britain, snuffing out every vestige of the Ancient Regime. Hence, the Republicans had come to believe, the Federalists had turned on America's only friend, transforming the United States into a Judas nation willing to suffer any humiliation so that London could destroy international Jacobinism, roll back the American Revolution, and safeguard the venal few whose primary loyalty was to their own self aggrandizement.[63]

The Republicans were political partisans, not unbiased scholars seeking the truth, and they painted the Federalists in exaggerated hues. Nevertheless, much in the Federalist litany lent authenticity to the Republican depiction. The Federalists never tired of asserting that those who had led the American Revolution had not sought radical change. Employing pseudonyms such as "No Revolutionist," they published essays insisting that the colonists protested not from a "spirit to subvert," but rather "to preserve old rights," to maintain existing *constitutional* rights and privileges."[64] Many Federalists had steadfastly looked askance at every sign of democratization. They had never hidden their desire—as Gouverneur Morris had urged in the Philadelphia Convention—to find "the proper security agst" the popular will. Repeatedly, they had pronounced it demagoguery to suggest that the "will of the people ought to prevail."[65] Many remembered those among the Federalists who had fretted over popular licentiousness from the moment that independence was on the horizon. Many recalled those, such as John Jay, who in 1776 had anguished that with independence "reformation may run mad."[66] Federalists were heard to declaim that the "people are without virtue," that the people were "vicious," or that the people were a "herd" that walks on "their hind legs." There were those who recollected Federalists who earlier had proclaimed that "our Countrymen [are] incapable of a free Government."[67] Memories endured of those who now were Federalists having denounced the most progressive of the original state constitutions, claiming that broadening the suffrage or relaxing political restraints would insure that a "mediocrity would gain possession of nearly all power" and implement a "mob equality."[68] Their chant had been that "the people must be *taught* to . . . reverence their rulers" and that leadership must be restricted to the "wise and good," a euphemism for those in the elite strata. Legions of Federalists had defended Washington's administration by maintaining that the infant republic benefited from a stabilizing regime composed of the "rich, the able, and the well-born."[69] Similarly, most Federalists appeared to be committed to rigidly maintaining the traditional hierarchical structure of society, and to wishfully dreaming of every American "learning his proper place and keeping to it."[70] What is more, to many Republicans it was fitting that in defending the Jay Treaty, many Federalist espoused the older, deferential notion that it was wrong for constituents to question the behavior of their representatives.[71]

Perhaps nothing aroused the Republicans to such fury as the Federalist contention that public offices should be limited to the gentility. To most Republicans, the essence of the Revolution had been about loosening the traditional restraints and opening opportunities to those with merit. What is more, a whiff of hypocrisy characterized the chant of the Federalists who were politically dominant in the 1790s, in as much as they in fact often were new men who emerged in the 1770s and 1780s. Senator George Cabot was the son of a middling ship captain who, through wartime privateering, built perhaps the greatest family fortune in his region. Senator Rufus King of New York first prospered politically after having successfully represented the legal interests of several powerful merchant-shipbuilders. Congressman Harrison Gray Otis, the nephew of James and Mercy Otis Warren, grew fabulously wealthy when he used his political influence to persuade Massachusetts to select a Beacon Hill site, where he owned considerable property, for the construction of a new state house. Other Federalists were the sons of ministers, small farmers, artisans, and in the case of Christopher Gore of Massachusetts, a Tory mechanic.[72] Many, like Robert Morris and George Clymer of Pennsylvania, Benjamin Lincoln in Maine, and Robert Troup in New York, had profited—literally so—from the American Revolution, becoming prosperous men as a result of speculation in war contracts, lands, and public securities. Henry Knox, for instance, was the son of a mariner who, after an apprenticeship, initially earned a living as a bookbinder. However, in 1771 he married into Boston's social elite—his wife's father was Andrew Oliver's successor as provincial secretary—and with the financial assistance of his in-laws opened a stationary and bookstore. He served as General Washington's head of artillery during the war, and as secretary of war for nearly a decade following hostilities. From 1776–1794 Knox cultivated friends among the war contractors with whom he dealt, bonhomie that paved the way to numerous lucrative speculative endeavors. He additionally used his political influence to regain much of the property that Massachusetts had confiscated from his Tory in-laws. At the time of the Boston Massacre, Knox had been a twenty-year-old small fry with little prospect of upward mobility. A quarter century later, midway through Washington's presidency, he built Montpelier, a nineteen-room mansion in Thomaston, Massachusetts, the largest and grandest private residence north of Philadelphia. By then, too, Knox exemplified those Federalists who hoped to perpetuate rule by the gentility and the preservation of the social distinctions that had prevailed in pre-Revolutionary America.[73]

No Federalist was more influential in Congress through the tempestuous 1790s than Theodore Sedgwick of Massachusetts, who served in the House from 1789–1796, and thereafter in the Senate. A resident of Stockbridge, in frontier Berkshire County in Massachusetts, Sedgwick was an uncommon Federalist in that he did not represent an eastern commercial district. In other respects, he typified the leadership in his party. Born in 1746 to a middling family—his father was a pioneer farmer who also operated a sawmill—he shone as a student, leading his parents, and an older brother, to sacrifice to find the means to send him to Yale. By 1771, when Knox was marrying into affluence, Sedgwick had a five-year-old law practice, a working farm of forty-six acres, and one slave. In Boston he would have gone unnoticed, but on the frontier his achievements elevated him to the status of a leading citizen. Like Jefferson, Sedgwick spent these years in private pursuits, marrying, then remarrying following the death of his wife, and beginning a family. He grew politically active only after the Boston Tea Party, and was supportive of the popular protest, but until the eve of independence Sedgwick quietly longed for the preservation of Anglo-American ties. He backed the war effort from the outset, served briefly in 1776 as a military secretary during the failed campaign in Canada, and for nearly three years was the Commissioner of Supply for America's army in the Northern Department. The paucity of records leave it unclear whether Sedgwick reaped a financial windfall from his latter service, but as he was quite well set financially by war's end, it is likely that, as was true of so many others involved in logistical operations, he too profiteered.

As he grew more successful, Sedgwick distanced himself from those in lower social orders. Despite his humble origins, Sedgwick expected obeisance from those beneath him. His daughter subsequently remembered that he demanded that middling farmers and artisans remove their hats in his presence and took umbrage when a social inferior dared appear at the front door, rather than the rear entrance, of his estate.[74] Meanwhile, he appeared to crave the respect of exalted figures in Boston and the eastern counties, even at the cost of his own popularity at home.[75] Throughout the American Revolution his rhetoric matched that of the most conservative activists in Massachusetts. The United States had barely separated from Great Britain before he published essays that warned of disorder, equating the unruly with those who took most seriously the egalitarian implications of the Declaration of Independence. Even before the war officially ended, Sedgwick led a campaign in the Massachusetts assembly—to which he had first been elected four years earlier—to permit Tory exiles to return to the state. When old friends among the Tories came home in the mid-1780s, no one labored more tirelessly, or successfully, to secure the restoration of their confiscated property. However, Sedgwick did little, or nothing, to aid his debt-encrusted neighbors who faced the loss of their farms after 1785, and when they acted illegally in Shays's Rebellion, he roared that for their "excesses [they] are the proper objects of gibbets, & racks."[76]

The Massachusetts assembly sent him to Congress in 1785, and again in 1787. Living in New York, the last home of Congress under the Articles of Confederation, he first met Hamilton, and like so many others fell under his spell. Until then Sedgwick, who was one with the nationalist movement, had opposed a convention to redraft the national charter, fearing that it would ultimately lead to a dominant national aristocracy. By 1787 his outlook had changed. He championed the Philadelphia Convention.[77] Hamilton had influenced him, but Shays' Rebellion had a more profound impact on his thinking. While he privately admitted that those in the backcountry were overtaxed and "greatly to be pitied," he could not condone their violence and lawlessness, and would have executed the ringleaders of the protest.[78] Shays' Rebellion was the determinative event in his life, an occurrence that he "never outgrew," according to his biographer, as he thereafter lived in fear of mob rule and anarchy.[79] In some ways, however, Sedgwick, a product of the frontier, appears never to have overcome a desire to win favor with fashionable Easterners. On issue after issue he ignored sentiment in the western districts, allying with powerful men in the East. He advocated commutation of pay for the Continental army officers, leniency for returning Loyalist refugees, a tight money policy, new national taxes, renunciation of the right of the United States to navigate the Mississippi River, and the Constitution produced in Philadelphia in 1787. While frequently posturing as distressed by his protracted absences from his family and frontier home, Sedgwick succeeded in spending a remarkable percentage of his life after 1776 in the East, in Boston, New York City, Philadelphia, or Washington, where he was "always engaged in something of Consequence," as his wife put it.[80]

Not surprisingly, Sedgwick was a leader among the Federalists at the Massachusetts Ratification Convention, nor was it particularly astounding that what he said publicly and privately was difficult to reconcile. On the floor of the Convention, for instance, he maintained that the new national government would exert little sway over the states, but privately he predicted that the federal government possessed the clout to "check, circumscribe and finally . . . annihilate all state power."[81] Almost from the moment that Sedgwick entered Congress, he acted as one of Hamilton's chief lieutenants. He played such a crucial role in shepherding funding and assumption into law in 1790 that a New York City newspaper christened him the "priest [who] baptized the infant" Hamiltonian economic program. He won the plaudits both of Federalist newspapers in Massachusetts and of President Washington. The chief executive "took me by the hand, and expressed much satisfaction to see me," he gushed after a levee, and acknowledged that the attention that Washington lavished on him "excite[s] a pleasing sensation of gratitude difficult to describe."[82] Soon, too, he was beginning to privately castigate his foes in a manner that the Federalist press later would adopt publicly. He thought Jefferson and Madison "Demagogues" and bridled at the latter's "scholastic ingenuity" in countering Hamiltonianism. He branded his Northern adversaries as "pittiful, low and malignant" apostates, and called them a "desperate faction" whose adherents were "seduced" by "insidious," "profligate," and "incorrigible" malcontents. He bloviated that Republican congressmen were "unprincipled rascals, madmen," and Madison's "mad associates." Some were no better than "an illiterate booby." He ridiculed Madison as "the Patriot," and charged that the Republican leaders were "cunning, artful & selfish" men of "intrigues" who wished to lead the United States into a ruinous war with Great Britain, principally in the hope of avoiding the payment of prewar debts owed to British creditors.[83]

Like Sedgwick, other Federalists countered the Republican attack. They staged public rallies at which they charged their adversaries with sophistry and a shameless knavery for making a political issue of a beneficial treaty negotiated by a true American patriot. They also flooded the President's House and Congress with petitions that championed the Jay Treaty, a campaign they deftly organized in the Northern port cities. Businessmen, for pragmatic reasons, were eager to have the pact ratified. At stake was compensation for spoliations in the amount of approximately $5,000,000. So too were underwriters, who feared that war with Britain would follow the rejection of the treaty, and had stopped insuring outbound cargoes, causing commodity prices to plummet. The Federalist argument on behalf of the treaty was a variant on a theme that had succeeded admirably during the battle to ratify the Constitution: catastrophe would follow the repudiation of the accord, but its approval, while a leap in the dark, at least held the prospect of maintaining America's fruitful peace.[84]

Even after Washington signed the treaty, the Federalists pursued a newspaper campaign in its support. They were compelled to do so as the result of a backdoor Republican effort in the House of Representatives to emasculate the implementation of the accord. In addition, the Federalists were both constructing the trenches they would occupy in the coming presidential election, now only a year away, and insulating President Washington by creating the impression that he had signed a treaty that had more widespread support than was actually the case. Their principal essayist was Hamilton. Typically, he more than merely responded to Washington's entreaties to help. Writing as "Camillus," Hamilton produced thirty-eight essays that appeared in New York newspapers during the six months after July 1795. His prodigious effort, which he entitled "The Defence," eventually totaled nearly 100,000 words. Hamilton employed the same technique he had utilized in *The Federalist*. He analyzed the accord article by article. The themes he played on were simple: the United States got the best deal possible; while the Jay Treaty did not resolve every problem, many vexations were laid to rest; whereas the United States had faced a stark choice between war or negotiation, the fruits of Jay's diplomacy meant that the prospects for peace were excellent.[85] This monumental effort led even Jefferson to praise Hamilton's extraordinary abilities. "Hamilton is really a colossus to the antirepublican party. Without numbers, he is an host within himself," Jefferson sighed. In fact, whereas Jefferson had once believed that Federalist support for Jay's mission, and his flawed treaty, had led the party "into a defile, where they might be finished," he now told Madison that he feared that Hamilton's "talents & indefatigableness" might save, and even strengthen, their adversaries.[86]

Some of Jefferson's remarks were exaggerated, as he was attempting, without success, to persuade Madison to answer Hamilton. One thing, however, was apparent. His prediction that the Federalists would recover from the initial damage caused by the Jay Treaty was accurate. As the fall proceeded, popular sentiment shifted in favor of the pact. Hamilton's essays probably played only a small role in the mood swing, although he and his party brethren displayed considerable ability as molders of public opinion, having honed their skills over the long haul from the imperial crisis through the campaign to secure the Constitution. In addition, as roughly three-fourths of all newspapers were Federalist, or Federalist leaning, organs, it was difficult for the literate public to escape the party's media saturation.[87] The Hamiltonians also drew on an inter-related, if not well-knit, mercantile community for help in shaping the public's point of view, and they were aided as well by Washington's support of the treaty. What is more, rancor toward Great Britain ebbed as incidents on the high seas declined throughout 1795, if for no other reason than American vessels had long since been swept out of the Caribbean.

Two additional factors were especially important in shaping public opinion. Westerners understood that the British army would quit their posts in the Ohio Country only if the pact took effect. Furthermore, news arrived on Washington's sixty-fourth birthday, February 22, 1796, that Pinckney's mission to Madrid had succeeded beyond the president's wildest dreams. In the Treaty of San Lorenzo, or Pinckney Treaty, as most referred to it, Spain granted free navigation of the Mississippi River, the right of deposit in New Orleans for three years, and recognized the 31st parallel as the southern boundary of the United States. Anxious that a stupendous American migration into the trans-Appalachian frontier would follow Wayne's victory at Fallen Timbers, and fearing that the Jay Treaty was but the first step in an Anglo-American *rapprochement* that pulsated with danger for Spain's New World possessions, Madrid caved in. It gave the United States what it had sought for the past fifteen years, vindicating both Washington's sagacity in seeking to exploit Spanish woes arising from the Europe's revolutionary warfare and the nationalists' 1780s claims that a strong central government would possess the means of resolving the western dilemma.[88] General Wayne's victory, which occurred as Jay was negotiating in London, and the news from Madrid, which reached Philadelphia after the Jay Treaty had been ratified and signed, placated the West, ending the furor over the Jay Treaty.

In light of the altered public opinion, the congressional Republicans would have been wise to abandon their attacks on the Jay Treaty. Instead, House Republicans launched an effort early in 1796 to block appropriations to fund the arbitration commission that was to settle all spoliation questions. Madison was the party leader in the House, but his role throughout his faction's campaign was muddled. Jefferson was not present to provide guidance, and Madison was left to wring his hands at a situation that he described as "truly perplexing." From start to finish, he was uncertain about what course to pursue.[89]

On the one hand, Madison was eager to do something. He loathed the Jay Treaty and was convinced that the House had the constitutional right to withhold appropriations to implement a treaty that had been ratified. Moreover, the Republicans appeared to have the votes to scuttle the treaty, as there were three Republicans for every two Federalists in the House. Madison additionally sensed partisan opportunities from prolonging the contest. By keeping alive the drumbeat of criticism against the accord, the Republicans might consolidate their support as the autumn elections neared. Furthermore, recent events in the Virginia legislature convinced Madison of the likelihood of still other gains. The assembly had adopted and sent to the other states a series of proposed constitutional amendments that Madison had helped conceive. One stipulated that treaties containing provisions that fell within Congress's purview—commercial matters, for instance—must be ratified both by the Senate and the House. Another would have reduced the terms of senators from six to three years. The last would have prohibited federal judges from simultaneously holding any other appointment. Madison believed that a highly publicized—and successful—battle over the Jay Treaty would serve as a wedge for raising support for some, if not all, of the proposed amendments.[90]

Madison's dilemma, however, was that he knew full well that if the House fought on against Jay's Treaty, Washington would be brought "personally into the question." If the battle came down to a "rub agst. the P[resident]," Madison acknowledged, the "policy of hazarding it is . . . questionable." Once the public perceived the contest as one of Washington versus the House, Madison understood that the "cautious opponents" of the treaty would defect and the battle would be lost. By early March, Madison still had not determined the best course of action. It is "truly difficult to decide on the course most acceptable," he confessed to Jefferson, who—given the time required to get letters to and from Monticello—was unable to provide counsel to his friend.[91]

Madison was still trying to decide what to do when zealous House Republicans seized the initiative and acted. A motion was introduced that requested the president to make public all documents that related to Jay's mission. Madison had not even been consulted. He succeeded in watering down the resolution, but even so Washington declined the House request, citing executive privilege. Madison probably would have terminated matters at this point, but the Republicans caucused for the first time and agreed to continue the battle, hoping to wreck the treaty. They hated Jay, were eager to thwart Hamilton and his brethren, and were especially bitter that London had persevered in its policy of impressing American seamen, even after Jay sent the treaty home. Madison had lost control of the House that he supposedly managed, and just as he had feared, the Republican majority gradually melted away.[92]

As late as April 18 Madison thought the Republicans had a twenty vote majority. Five days later, and less than a week before the House would vote, he conceded that his majority had been cut to only eight or nine votes.[93] The northern states, and especially their great cities, had rallied in favor of the Jay Treaty, once again flooding Congress with petitions expressing the fear of merchants, and those who toiled for them, that the rejection of the Jay Treaty would result in an end to prosperity and maybe even in war. In addition, Madison must have sensed that some previously undecided congressmen had been influenced by two stirring orations. Sedgwick, whom a visitor to Philadelphia included in a list of the four best speakers in Congress, gave what many regarded as his greatest performance in a speech that spring.[94] His long, erudite address, which focused on the framers' intent in limiting the scrutiny of treaties to the Senate, won the plaudits of his own party and converted some who were uncommitted to reject Madison's ploy—or so Sedgwick believed.[95]

A few days later, Sedgwick was overshadowed by Fisher Ames, whom Jefferson once called "a colossus of the monocrats and paper men."[96] Ames, who had entered Harvard at age twelve and graduated at sixteen, less than a year before the war erupted, was not much for soldiering. He served seventeen days on active duty as a militiaman, none in a combat zone. For the most part, he lived at home, teaching occasionally, but mostly reading and luxuriating in a life of self-indulgence until at age twenty-one he undertook legal studies with one of John Adams's former law students. In 1781 he opened a law practice, tending to it with little enthusiasm and serving in local public offices. Ames emerged as a political force in Massachusetts in the course of Shays' Rebellion, when he published several withering attacks on the insurgents. Thereafter, he was a Federalist leader in his state's ratification convention, won election to the state assembly in 1788, and, in perhaps the most stunning political upset of the age, defeated Samuel Adams in December 1788 in a contest for a seat in Congress.

The speech that Ames gave on April 28 in defense of the Jay Treaty was worthy of a superlative thespian. It immediately was hailed as the best speech among the hundreds given during the lengthy furor over

Jay's mission and his treaty, and had Washington not later presented a Farewell Address, Ames's oration likely would have been the best remembered declamation of this passionate decade. Even so, it was thought to be such a classic that Daniel Webster memorized whole portions of it in his quest to learn the tricks of oratory, and a half century later Abraham Lincoln purportedly often recited parts of it, telling listeners that it was among his favorite examples of political rhetoric.[97] Today Ames's oratory sounds exaggerated and mawkish, but he delivered the speech at a time when sentiment and sensibility were predominant forces.[98] While a few Republican "jackasses" laughed at his theatrics (or so Vice President Adams grumbled), most in the chamber sat spellbound, and some were misty eyed.[99]

Though only in his late thirties, Ames was pale and gaunt, the victim of a pulmonary disease that would take his life within a few years. Yet he found the strength to speak for nearly three hours, slowly building to a crescendo. At the outset, he offered a conventional defense of Jay Treaty, portraying it as but a first step toward a commercial accord with London. Only near the end, as he descanted on how the treaty would preserve the peace, especially in the Ohio Country, did Ames become theatrical. Observing that the pact obliged the British to withdraw from U.S. soil, he speculated that only this step could ensure peace in Kentucky and above the Ohio River. He also unmistakably implied that if the Jay Treaty were repudiated, every congressman who spurned the accord would have blood on his hands. The choices were stark, Ames added. Choose peace, and the West soon would be filled with settlers who owned affordable land. Choose the sword, and the Indians would answer with the tomahawk and other weapons furnished by the British army. Thus, to reject the Jay Treaty was to "light the savage's fires" and ensure that many innocent frontier inhabitants would be "roasted at the stake."

On this theme, my emotions are unutterable. If I could find words for them, if my powers bore any proportion to my zeal, I would swell my voice to such a note of remonstrance, it should reach every log-house beyond the mountains. I would say to the inhabitants, wake from your false security; your cruel dangers, your more cruel apprehensions are soon to be renewed; the wounds, yet unhealed, are to be torn open again; in the daytime, your path through the woods will be ambushed; the darkness of midnight will glitter with the blaze of your dwellings. You are a father—the blood of your sons shall fatten your corn-field. You are a mother—the war whoop shall wake the sleep of the cradle. Reject the treaty, he closed, and you will hear "the yells of savage vengeance, and the shrieks of torture. Already they seem to sigh in the West wind; already they mingle with every echo from the mountains."[100]

Ames's melodramatic oratory helped drive the last stake into the heart of the Republican's dying campaign, but in reality it was not Ames so much as the West that proved fatal to their effort. After all, Ames's fevered *coup de théâtre* resonated with the inhabitants of the frontier because he said what they already had come to believe. Following word of the Pinckney Treaty, Western support for the Republicans' battle against the Jay Treaty crumbled, and it died altogether once several Northern senators pledged to block ratification of the pact with Spain if Jay's accord failed.

The Republican campaign was doomed. On April 29 the House balloted and by a one-vote margin agreed to provide the funds needed to implement the Jay Treaty. Although only peripherally responsible for its inception, many heaped blame for the Republican disaster on Madison. For instance, Edward Livingston, a New Yorker, concluded that Madison "as a politician appears to [exhibit] . . . a want of decision and disposition to magnify his adversaries' Strength."[101] Even Madison had to admit that the battle had been a debacle for his faction. He confessed to Jefferson that the House endeavor had been a "wrong turn" that "left it [the Republican Party] in a very crippled condition." The party, he confided, now was likely to lose some elections that it might otherwise have won.[102] His misreading of the public temper demonstrated anew how badly he missed Jefferson's deft feel of the popular pulse.

The salvation of the Jay Treaty, Washington remarked soon after the failure of what he labeled Madison's "pernicious measures," was "one of those great occasions" in the history of his administration.[103] This first presidency was to be one of the great presidencies in American history. There were mistakes—the excessive response to the Whiskey Rebellion was the most egregious—but there were mostly accomplishments that served the nation and its people. Washington's presence had been crucial for the solidification of the new national government. Hamilton was his economic architect, but without the support of a leader of Washington's stature, it is not likely that the treasury secretary could have secured more than fragments of his program. But the Washington-Hamilton dream did become law, and at a crucial juncture it not only maintained the prosperity that had returned following the brief postwar depression, but it provided the superstructure upon which a modern economy and a modern state could arise. What is more, the United States in reality was an undeveloped country, plagued, as are all such nations, by a chronic shortage of capital. The Washington-Hamilton program put the nation on the road that led to the eradication of that crippling problem. Yet Washington's greatest successes came in the realm of foreign affairs, and no achievement was more spectacular than the preservation of peace. He was sufficiently strong and independent to resist the adventurers and those who demanded policies that might have culminated in hostilities with Great Britain. Once again, he marshaled the daring and resolve that had served him well in two wars, and it resulted in treaties that ensured that American settlers soon would penetrate to the nation's westernmost boundary, the Mississippi River. As he began his eighth year in office, Washington knew that he had achieved every major goal that he had set for himself in 1789.

Once the Jay and Pinckney treaties were safe, he told confidants that he intended to step down in March 1797 at the culmination of his second term. Many factors influenced his decision. He was disgruntled by the vilification to which he was almost daily subjected. Even a public official more accustomed to defamation, and with a thicker hide than the notoriously thin-skinned Washington, would have bridled at the steady drumbeat of contumely that he faced. Republican essayists encouraged him to retire, cruelly advising him not to permit himself to be dissuaded by the horde of "flatterers" with which he had surrounded himself. Benjamin Franklin Bache, Franklin's grandson—foes labeled him "Lightning Rod Junior"— ran a piece in his paper, the *Philadelphia Aurora,* instructing Washington that he should not feel that he was irreplaceable. There "are thousands among [us] who equal you in capacity, and who excel you in knowledge," Bache told him. The president was accused of hypocrisy for claiming to be nonpartisan and blasted for selecting only Federalists as his principal appointees. In fact, said one essayist, the executive branch was no better than the right arm of "British agents, old tories, . . . the Banks, and a long list of unprincipled speculators, who like leeches, stick to" Washington. He was criticized for owning slaves and accused of pro-British bias. One Republican editor savagely likened him to Benedict Arnold. Another allowed that while he had been a good soldier, he was a failure as a statesman. Some scribes even took issue with his generalship, charging that as a military leader he had been "ignorant of war both in theory and useful practice." A Virginia journalist proposed a toast: "A speedy death to General Washington." Still another commentator claimed that Louis XVI had "never treated his subjects with as much insult" as had Washington. The American people were the worse for having endured his presidency, said one writer, who added that "the American nation has been debauched by WASHINGTON." Yet another concluded that "the name of Washington has lost its magic."[104]

To some degree, Washington simply wanted to quit because he was weary of his public responsibilities and, if not obsessed with his health, he was at least concerned about how many good years might be left to him. During his second term he had a scare over what he erroneously suspected was a skin cancer and, following an equestrian accident, he suffered for a time with acute back pain. During these years he spoke of his awareness of "a gradual decline" in his physical endurance, and he frequently mentioned being on the "downhill slope" or of "hastening to an end" of life. Although he remained lithe and trim—he carried only 210 pounds on his 6' 3 1/2" frame—some of the artists for whom he sat rendered a subject whose eyes had lost the sparkle of youth, and many observers remarked that he looked old and tired, something that Jefferson had noted as early as 1792. Washington was ready to go home, where he hoped he might enjoy a few serene years in reasonably good health.[105]

However, Washington did not wish to go quietly. He had delivered a valedictory to the citizenry when he left the army in 1783, and he wanted to do the same before leaving the presidency, explaining why he had chosen to retire and advising his countrymen on the potential hazards that lay ahead. Not surprisingly, the president turned to Hamilton to prepare his remarks. The two not only shared a similar outlook but Hamilton had been writing public pronouncements for Washington for so long—since 1777—that whatever he wrote would have a Washingtonian ring to it.[106]

In September 1796, less than three months before the electoral college would choose his successor, Washington divulged his intention of retiring. His Farewell Address was not delivered as a speech; it was published simultaneously in two Philadelphia newspapers. After explaining that he had longed to leave office in 1793, but had remained at the helm because of the emerging foreign crisis, Washington broke the news that he soon would step down, adding that he now believed that the "perplexed & critical posture of our Affairs with foreign nations" had eased considerably. He expanded on the importance of the Union, reflected briefly on good citizenship, which he defined as obedience to authority, and—in a section that must have made him appear to be an anachronism, if not a hypocrite, to an increasing number of his countrymen—he admonished the citizenry on the evils of political parties. The longest section dealt with foreign policy. True independence, he advised, must always be America's goal. He warned of the imprudence of "passionate attachments" to France and "habitual hatred" of England. It was "folly in one Nation to look for disinterested favors from another," and should the United States draw too close to a foreign power, "it must pay with a portion of its Independence for whatever it may accept under that character." The "attachment of a small or weak [country], towards a great and powerful Nation, dooms the former to be the satellite of the latter," he cautioned. While an emergency might necessitate a temporary alliance with a European power, it was imperative that the United States "steer clear of permanent alliances." Otherwise, he warned—as had Franklin and Paine twenty years earlier—America would forever be sucked into Europe's interminable and meaningless wars.[107]

What Washington said was heartfelt and reflected the wisdom he had garnered in the course of nearly a score of years of public service. He especially hoped his admonitions might temper the partisanship of the times, and help the new nation through the dangerous shoals it faced in its early years. But there was another side to the Farewell Address, one that some contemporaries understood better than have later historians. Its benign qualities notwithstanding, the Farewell Address was also a partisan statement carefully crafted to advance the Federalist Party, and to ensure its hegemony for the next four years. A cryptographer was not required to see that when he elaborated on "the jealousies and heart burnings" of factious men who questioned authority and tampered with the "spirit of acquiescence in the measures" decided in the capital, he was alluding to the Jeffersonians. Nor was there much mystery to what he meant when he advised the citizenry that power and responsibility "belongs to your Representatives," stressed that "public opinion should cooperate" with their judgment, and denounced those who sought to "impair the energy of the system" by raising spurious constitutional issues that could only lead to the evisceration of national powers and the ruination of the "efficient management of your common interests."[108]

Such comments prompted Madison and numerous contemporaries to conclude that the Farewell Address "shews that [Washington is] compleatly in the snares" of the Federalists who surround him. Many Republicans treated the Farewell Address as a campaign document, and the Philadelphia *Aurora* characterized it as merely Washington's most recent attempt to deceive the nation.[109] Ultimately, the Address had little, if any, impact on the Election of 1796, or anything else in the near term, although during the next century and a half, Washington's admonitions about steering clear of European involvement served as an aegis for American isolationism and was made obligatory reading for generations of schoolchildren.

The Farewell Address, Congressman Ames remarked, was "a signal, like the dropping of a hat, for party racers to start" the campaign of 1796, the new nation's first contested presidential election. At Christmas in 1795 Martha Washington had confided to the vice president that her husband would decline a third term. Three months later, Washington finally informed Adams of his decision.[110] But Washington's intentions became official only with his public pronouncement in September.

Adams had been waiting a long time for this moment. After nearly ten years service in Europe, he had resigned his diplomatic post in 1788 to return home and seek a high national post under the new Constitution. Somewhat ruefully acknowledging that the presidency belonged to Washington, Adams issued an arch pronouncement: All other posts, save the vice presidency, were beneath him.[111] He was chosen as vice president, of course, and throughout his eight years in that lonely office looked on himself as Washington's natural heir. Most Federalists concurred, and Adams easily obtained the party's nomination in 1796, together with the somewhat obscure Thomas Pinckney of South Carolina, who had negotiated the popular treaty with Spain the previous year. They were selected by a caucus of the party members in Congress. Two candidates were chosen because under the original constitution each presidential elector was to cast two ballots for president.

Adams was not beloved by the members of his party. His vain, cantankerous, and acerbic manner alienated many who dealt with him, and moved some, such as Sedgwick, to wail that the "malignity of the man is . . . boundless." Sedgwick privately acknowledged that many Federalists hoped that Pinckney would outpace Adams in the electoral college, although he added that should the vice president prevail, most expected him to chart a wise course. More than one Federalist wondered if Adams was not a liability as a candidate, inasmuch as his published ruminations on government—his *Defence of the Constitutions . . . of the United States*, published in 1788–89, and the "Davila" essays—had led many to suspect that he was a monarchist. His reputation for being fiercely independent also caused some to fear that he might not always serve the best interests of the party, although as vice president he had cast thirty-one tie-breaking votes in the Senate and had never voted against his fellow Federalists.[112] Doubts aside, all agreed that Adams possessed strengths. It was axiomatic that New England, which possessed one-third of the electoral college votes, would cast all its ballots for Adams. Furthermore, although not revered like Washington, Adams was widely respected. He had won the public's approval for his truly heroic Revolutionary sacrifices, which included two hazardous Atlantic crossings in wartime and entailed a separation from his wife that spanned nearly six years. For a spell after the War of Independence, moreover, Washington, Adams, and Franklin were viewed as the great triumvirate of the American Revolution, eclipsing other luminaries such as Jefferson or Samuel Adams. Thus the Federalist Party honored Adams with the nomination, but it also chose him because it believed he could win the election.

There was never the slightest doubt that Republicans favored Jefferson, and he was nominated by the party's congressional caucus, together with New York's Aaron Burr. Jefferson's national reputation was of more recent origin than that of Adams, as he had served at the national level for only about twelve months during the American Revolution. It was not even widely known that Jefferson had been the principal author of the Declaration of Independence until more than a decade after 1776.[113] In the 1790s he and Hamilton emerged as the best-known members of the Washington administration, but even then only insiders realized Jefferson's role in shaping the fight against Hamiltonianism. It was a blessing for Jefferson that most of the public thought of the opposition faction as "Madison's Party," for it meant that he yet retained an aura as a nonpartisan public servant. Then again, that was the very persona that Jefferson, like Washington, had hoped to effect. Whatever the public thought, Jefferson had a large and devoted following among Republican activists. Seen as pleasant and agreeable, rather than as warm and engaging, and looked upon as exceptionally bright, without coming across as an egotistical know-it-all or an ivory-tower intellectual, Jefferson inspired loyalty. He won credit among the politically active both for being in the vanguard of opposition to Hamiltonianism and for fashioning an ideological defense against the Federalists' program, and among Republicans everywhere he was lauded for the pulsating and liberating rhetoric of his Revolutionary manifesto, the Declaration of Independence.

But while the Republicans wanted Jefferson to run, the trick was to somehow lure him from retirement. Eighteen months before the Farewell Address, Madison told his friend that the Republicans would wish to nominate him in 1796. You must begin "preparing yourself" to take on the presidency, he advised. Jefferson immediately responded that he would have none of it. Pleading old age and poor health—he was fifty-two, seven years younger than Washington had been at his inauguration in 1789, and quite fit—Jefferson said that he would never abandon retirement. "The question is for ever closed with me," he declared. His disclaimer notwithstanding, Jefferson's interest in public affairs had never disappeared, and by 1796 it had quickened. His zeal was aroused in large measure by his growing apprehension at the Federalists' action in violently suppressing the dissidents in Pennsylvania in 1794 and securing the Jay Treaty the following year, which left Jefferson alarmed that his adversaries aimed to conclude a formal Anglo-American treaty of alliance and sever all ties with France. Even so, as the election drew near, Jefferson continued to tell all who would listen that the Republicans must nominate Madison. In turn, Madison told friends that the Republican caucus must select Jefferson and "push him" to accept, for he "alone can be started with hope of success." In the end, Jefferson did not have to be pushed. Once nominated, he simply accepted.[114]

Jefferson was not as reluctant to reenter public life as he postured. Like other activists, he did not wish to appear to be pursuing power. He wanted the party to seek him, after which he could honestly say that he had been chosen "without concert . . . on my part." Furthermore, he once explained that "happiness requires that we should continue to mix with the world," and he admitted that living at isolated Monticello between 1794–1796 had an "ill effect . . . upon my own mind" that included "an antisocial and misanthropic" outlook. In addition, Jefferson knew that these were extraordinary times and that the decisions made during this pivotal decade could shape American life for generations to come. He had been blessed with the opportunity to be part of the American Revolution, and he had witnessed the early drama of the French Revolution. To play a further role after 1797, the major role in fact, in structuring the new nation, must have been irresistible. It is possible too that he had come to question the political acumen of his friend Madison. Not only is it unimaginable that Jefferson would have shared Madison's hostility for the states in the 1780s, but in 1790 he had deferred to his friend's judgment in the funding and assumption battles, a decision that he soon enough came to rue. Soon, too, Jefferson adopted a line on Hamiltonianism that was unlike anything that Madison had conceived. Finally, when he came home to Virginia early in 1794, Jefferson had left Madison at the helm of the new Republican majority in Congress, confident that the faction he had labored to constitute was capable of checking any new Federalist initiatives. After three years at Monticello, Jefferson sadly acknowledged that the Federalists were stronger than ever. As the presidential election approached, Jefferson more than anyone knew how badly the Republicans missed him.[115]

The campaign of 1796 bore marked similarities to today's presidential contests. Each party sought a sectional balance in its ticket, nominating a Northerner and a Southerner. In addition, many qualified voters stayed home on election day, as in Philadelphia, where only a quarter of the eligible voters took the trouble to cast a ballot. But this contest also differed substantially from modern contests. It was refreshingly brief, ending about six weeks after it commenced. Not one candidate delivered a speech. That was left to lesser figures in each party. Burr came closest to mounting the stump when he visited New England and courted some electors, but he took care to hobnob only with his social peers and ignored the general populace. Adams went home when Congress adjourned in the spring and remained there until deep in November.

Jefferson, who had not strayed more than seven miles from Monticello during his retirement, never left home during the contest. Both Adams and Jefferson were products of the eighteenth century, and both expected the voters to come to them, rather than the reverse. Neither party adopted a platform, and none of the candidates issued campaign statements. In fact, no one even used the word *campaign* to describe what was occurring. The election also differed from those today in that most presidential electors were selected by state legislatures. In some states the electorate could choose electors, but property qualifications prevented many adult white males from voting. Females and African Americans were disenfranchised everywhere, and all under age twenty-one were denied the vote. Furthermore, those with suffrage rights often voted orally rather than by secret ballot. In addition, as some electoral districts held their own elections separately, the modern winner-take-all process did not apply universally.

However, the greatest difference, as historian Joanne Freeman has demonstrated, was that partisan discipline was virtually nonexistent. The "parties" designated themselves as Federalists and Republicans, but partisan ties were fissile. These were core alliances that loosely coalesced around partisan figures, but at times individual ambitions and longstanding friendships, or enduring hatreds, often overwhelmed loyalty to the national ticket. So, too, did the tug of myriad local interests, which in 1796 remained as strong as a quarter century earlier when Samuel Adams had discovered to his chagrin that the backcountry viewed the Boston Massacre in an entirely different manner than did the residents of Boston. Indeed, in this presidential contest local and regional concerns sometimes overrode the vibrant appeal of national partisan figures and the polemics of party organs. In addition, the mode of electioneering—outside the cities, campaigning by letter predominated—also contributed to the fragility of partisan networks, as information about national affairs frequently was so sketchy, or so dated, that politicos often were hesitant to commit fully to the national candidates.[116]

Yet while local interests at times subsumed the national, this was a contest in which many, probably most, who participated were deeply committed to principles. An intense fever—ignited in some by the French Revolution and Jay's Treaty, and in others by democratization and the recent western disorders—burned in the hearts of many Americans. To these people, their party stood for something, and they stood for their party. This passion made many Federalists, who perhaps were not ecstatic about Adams, ardent about keeping "the Virginia Philosopher from the chair," as Sedgwick remarked. Conversely, for many Republicans this election was the culmination of steps first taken four years earlier to oust the "Anglomen" and "monocrats" from office. The nasty personal attacks that characterize today's campaigns were plentiful even then. Newspapers were loaded with vitriolic essays. The "Jeffs," as Ames called the Republicans, portrayed their adversaries as Anglophiles and monarchists, and lampooned Adams as the "Duke of Braintree," after his birth site in Massachusetts. The Republicans additionally caricatured the short, stout vice president as "His Rotundity." The Federalists fought back by portraying Jefferson as an indecisive visionary, atheist, Jacobin, and puppet of France who would plunge the United States into war with Great Britain, and one whose ardor for the people's interest was an affectation. One Federalist observed that, rhetoric aside, the only "real and truly dangerous aristocrats of our country" dwell in Virginia, and that by owning slaves they demonstrated that they "hate equality." Finally, this election, as has been true of most that followed, was also replete with behind-the-scenes machinations. Most occurred within the Federalist Party. Some Southern Federalists appeared to be more anxious to elect a Southerner than a Federalist, and there was abundant talk among them of voting for Pinckney and Jefferson. Other Federalists schemed to withhold a couple of electoral votes from Adams, giving Pinckney the majority and burying Adams once again in the vice presidency.[117]

In the end, most of the plotting fizzled. Not only were the risks great that the intrigue would backfire and result in Jefferson's election, but the prevailing culture of honor, which virtually defined genteel status, was for most men more binding than partisan feelings.[118] Yet everyone heard the rumors of skullduggery, including Adams, who was told by friends that Hamilton had "insidiously opposed his election."[119] Adams later denied that he believed these stories. However, having heard similar tattle of Hamilton's machinations against him in 1788 and 1792, Adams would have been uncommonly magnanimous had he not grown somewhat suspicious of the former treasury secretary.[120]

One aspect of the canvass that was decidedly unlike today's races was that the results were not immediately known. For nearly three weeks after the electoral college balloting, Adams believed he had lost the election. His correspondence during this period was gloomy and pulsated with anger at those whom he believed had deserted him, notably Samuel Adams, who at seventy-five retired that year from public life, delivering farewell remarks in Boston that lavished praise on Washington but ignored the vice president. A melancholy Vice President Adams said that he would be mortified if he lost to Jefferson, whom he viewed as his junior, or to Pinckney, whom he reckoned to be a nobody.[121]

Nor was it merely Adams who fretted. Throughout the election, other Federalists gloomily suspected that defeat was certain. Perhaps never again would a party in power enter a presidential election in a time of peace and prosperity with such oppressive doubts. The Federalists knew that much of their strength had come both from their ties to Washington's commanding presence and their identity as the party that had resolved the postwar crisis and saved the Union. Washington, however, was about to depart, and the helpful emergency mentality of earlier years had been laid to rest. Furthermore, although neither faction had built a solid organization, the Republicans had outpaced their adversaries in structuring rudimentary party machinery. Finally, at a time when American politics was in transition from the deferential practices of an earlier day to modern democracy, the Republican Party was more in touch with an American public that feared large and faraway governments, despised direct taxation by a national government, loathed Great Britain, and looked with suspicion on many of those who had served in the Federalist administration, notably Hamilton and Jay and to a lesser extent Adams.

Near Christmas Eve, definitive word of the outcome reached Philadelphia. Many thought it an upset. Adams, with seventy-one votes, had won a narrow victory. Jefferson, who obtained sixty-eight votes, finished second and would be the next vice president. The electors from only half the states had voted straight party tickets. Indeed, 52 of the 136 electors had cast a ballot for someone not nominated by their party's congressional caucus.[122] The results were largely sectional, as so many congressional votes had been over the past fifteen years. Jefferson failed to win a single electoral vote in New York, New Jersey, and the five New England states, but captured 51 of the 60 electoral votes south of Pennsylvania and Delaware. In the North only Pennsylvania—which grew more Republican in the aftermath of Washington's strident remarks about the democratic societies—was receptive to Jefferson, and in the South only Maryland, a Federalist bastion throughout the decade, went for Adams. A change of only two electoral votes would have made Jefferson the president. In a sense, therefore, the election turned on two electoral votes in the South. Adams received one electoral vote in North Carolina, from a coastal mercantile district where support was deep for the Hamiltonian economic program. He also won one vote in Virginia. It came from the anti-planter Loudoun-Fauquier district and was in reality more a case of the inhabitants spurning Jefferson than embracing Adams.[123]

While Adams was delighted with his victory, Jefferson may have been the happiest man ever to lose a presidential election. He was confident that the fiercely independent Adams would be more successful than his predecessor in keeping Hamilton and his followers at bay, and he knew full well that the incoming president shared his desire to avoid an alliance with Great Britain. He even thought Adams more deserving of the post. "I am his junior in life, was his junior in Congress, his junior in the diplomatic line, his junior lately in our civil government," Jefferson graciously remarked just after the contest. Jefferson knew too that the office he was about to enter would not be filled with onerous responsibilities. Vice President Adams had spent more than half of each year at home in Quincy, and Jefferson expected to spend at least that much time at Monticello. In fact, initially he did not even plan to travel to Philadelphia for the Inaugural ceremony, although he ultimately decided to go "as a mark of respect to the public."[124]

But neither Adams nor Jefferson appeared to be as happy as was Washington as March 4, 1797, drew near. Despite continuing Republican attacks in the papers—they "misrepresent my motives [and] reprobate my politics," he said in disbelief—Washington quite correctly felt that after eight toilsome years as president he was still blessed with the "approving voice of my Country." Above all, he was delighted that "the Curtain of my Political life is about to drop," and it showed. One congressman noted that Washington was unusually cheerful and seemed able to converse more easily than ever before. The president's only regret was the prospect of perhaps never again seeing trusted acquaintances with whom he had worked closely for so long, but he put his feelings in writing to only two men. One was Secretary of War Knox, his loyal and intimate advisor for sixteen years in war and peace. The other was Jonathan Trumbull of Connecticut, his former aide during the war and later the Federalist Speaker of the House and United States senator, who had returned home to serve as deputy governor of his state. Washington invited him to visit Mount Vernon. On his final full day in office he hosted a midafternoon dinner for department heads and diplomats. At its conclusion, Washington offered a toast in which he acknowledged that "this is the last time I shall drink your health as a public man." A mournful silence fell over the room, and the wife of the British minister wept openly.[125]

The next day—Inauguration Day—Adams, who said that he wished to keep things simple and thoroughly republican, dressed in a plain gray suit, eschewed elegant buttons and knee buckles, and rode to Congress Hall in a handsome new carriage drawn by only two horses. President Washington, wishing now to be seen as a private citizen, walked the three blocks from his residence. They entered a chamber packed with spectators who were "respectable, and behaved with the decent gravity, which the solemn occasion demanded," a Federalist observer noted. Many in the audience wept, disconsolate and a bit fearful of the future now that Washington was leaving the public stage for all time. When the incoming president took his seat on the elevated dais next to the outgoing president, he was struck by Washington's serenity and joy. Said Adams: "He seemed to me to enjoy a triumph over me. Methought I heard him say, 'Ay! I am fairly out and you fairly in! See which of us will be happiest!'"[126]

12

1797–1799

"A Game Where Principles Are the Stake"

Adams took Washington's exhilaration at leaving office as a foretokening of difficult days ahead, and after only a week on the job his suspicions were confirmed. He told a friend that the presidency was tantamount to a sentence of hard labor.[1] Nevertheless, Adams was optimistic as he embarked on his new job and encouraged by the realization that he started with considerable public support. Even Bache's *Aurora*, which so often had impugned Washington during the past couple years, lauded the new president as a "man of incorruptible integrity," honor, and patriotism, and predicted that his considerable intelligence rendered him "equal to the duties of his station."[2]

Adams's entire presidency and much of the politics in the remaining years of this passionate decade were shaped by two developments that occurred before he took office. One was beyond his control. The other was of his own making. Before Adams's election, Franco-American relations had begun to cool. The estrangement began with Washington's icy response to Citizen Genêt in 1793, but it was the ratification of the Jay Treaty two years later that caused America's ties to Paris to unravel. As early as 1795 Jefferson, in retirement at Monticello, had foreseen trouble, sensing that France would view the accord with London as an abrogation of the treaties of 1778. He wrote Pierre Adet, Genêt's successor, to remind him of the friendship that most Americans felt for the French. The two peoples had bonded through a "fellowship in war and mutual kindnesses," he said, and they enjoyed "so many points of union" that their ties could not be severed. Perhaps—but the next year, on the twentieth anniversary of the day the Continental Congress had voted independence, the Directory, the latest French government, issued a decree threatening to seize neutral vessels carrying British goods. Adet publicly promulgated the decree that autumn. Simultaneously, he announced that "as a mark of just discontent," France had suspended the activities of its minister to the United States. Paris would not restore its links with the United States until America abided by the terms of the alliance. In December, about 100 days before Adams took the oath of office, word of French spoliations on the high seas reached the capital.[3] As winter settled in, everyone in Philadelphia—and not least president-elect Adams— knew that the next chief executive would face problems with France that were every bit as dangerous as those with Great Britain with which Washington had struggled after 1794.

As Adams awaited Inauguration Day, he reflected on how to respond to France. Well before he took the oath of office, Adams decided to send a team of commissioners to Paris to seek a negotiated settlement of Franco-American differences. Utilizing multi-member commissions of diplomats once had been standard practice. Congress had dispatched three commissioners to France in 1776 in search of recognition and trade. Adams himself had been a member of the commission that negotiated the peace treaty with Great Britain, and he subsequently concluded that the team approach worked well, as he, Franklin, and Jay had brought their individual talents to the bargaining table.[4] Furthermore, the employment of a commission was likely to mute the kind of bitterness toward an individual diplomat that the South and West had displayed when Jay's appointment was announced.

Adams made one additional set of decisions before taking office. He selected his cabinet, blundering egregiously in his choices, a fateful act that would encumber his presidency. Adams chose to retain Washington's cabinet. His secretary of state was to be Timothy Pickering, a dour, acerbic, and querulous New Englander. Pickering had held innumerable posts in twenty years and had risen steadily both in the Continental army and the new national government, yet he had few successes to show for his efforts. General Washington had named him to his staff in 1777, only to conclude that Pickering was not up to the position. He wound up running the quartermaster corps, but his administration was misguided to say the least, and Washington more or less told him so. Despite these failures, and a lack of success in postwar business and farming enterprises, President Washington brought Pickering back into public service as postmaster general. Later, he served as an envoy to the Seneca Indians and performed adequately, though not spectacularly. Washington named him as Knox's successor as secretary of war in 1795, and a few months later, when an unexpected vacancy occurred, Pickering became the secretary of state. Washington settled on Pickering with great reluctance, turning to him only after his initial six choices had declined the offer and after being warned by Hamilton that all who knew Pickering had concluded that he was passionate and given to ill-considered judgments. He "will require . . . a vigilant moderating eye," Hamilton cautioned. That the president lacked faith in Pickering was apparent when he turned repeatedly to Hamilton, who was in New York practicing law, for counsel during the crisis over the Jay Treaty.[5]

Oliver Wolcott, who had served under Hamilton in a variety of posts in the Treasury Department, and eventually succeeded him in 1795, remained the treasury secretary. Twenty-five years younger than Adams, Wolcott was the son and grandson of governors of Connecticut. He had graduated from Yale around the midpoint of the War of Independence, but found soldiering to be inconvenient. He studied and practiced law during what was left of hostilities, then held various state posts throughout the Confederation years. He had many positive qualities, including an affable and courteous manner. Although terribly ambitious, Wolcott was smart enough to understand that he possessed only mediocre talents, for which he compensated with hard work and a penchant for devoting meticulous attention to detail. Unfortunately, he also concluded early on that scheming sometimes afforded the best means of getting ahead.[6]

James McHenry, who joined the cabinet in 1795 as head of the War Department after Washington's first four choices declined appointment, also agreed to remain at his post. McHenry was an American success story. Born in 1753 in Ireland, he immigrated with his parents when he was nineteen and almost immediately began to study medicine. Three years later, the war broke out. McHenry enlisted and served as an army surgeon before he joined Washington's staff in 1778. Whereas almost everyone seemed to loathe or fear Pickering, McHenry had an uncommon facility for making friends, and he grew close to Hamilton and several others who served Washington. Following hostilities, he entered Maryland politics and ultimately was part of the state's delegation at the Philadelphia Convention. Thereafter he served in the state legislature and the United States Senate before Washington asked him to succeed Pickering as secretary of war. Washington soon found that Hamilton, who had advised that McHenry "would give no strength to the administration, but would not disgrace the office," had accurately gauged the Marylander.[7]

Some realized immediately that Adams had erred in not choosing his own men. Jefferson, with his deft feel for politics and politicians, saw quickly that the loyalty of Adams's cabinet was to Hamilton, and he told others that the "Hamiltons by whom [the president] is surrounded are only a little less hostile to him than to me." Jefferson even wrote Adams to warn him of Hamilton's "spies & sycophants" who would seek to make a tool of him in order to serve their real master, but Madison, who saw the missive before it was sent, convinced his friend that it was imprudent to offer counsel to the leader of another party.[8] The incoming president never read Jefferson's letter, and he discovered his mistake only belatedly. Subsequently, in the dark afterglow of his time in office, Adams acknowledged that his myopic decision had ruined his presidency. He never claimed to have kept Washington's cabinet because those officials were indispensable. Indeed, he believed that after a while President Washington had been unable to attract first-rate talents to his administration; gifted men, Adams said, had no wish to serve a chief executive who listened only to Hamilton, and after 1794 his predecessor had been "compelled to take such as he did not like." Adams attributed his error in keeping Washington's secretaries to two factors. Had he dismissed the current secretaries, he said, a fatal political conflagration would have erupted, consuming and destroying his administration before it began. What is more, he confessed his own shortcomings as a politician. He was "unpracticed in intrigues for power," he said.[9]

There was considerable truth in both explanations. While the Federalists had nominated Adams, who had a reputation for independent behavior that bordered on nonpartisanship, even the party's most moderate forces expected him to advance the faction's agenda, if that meant only that he was to be a bulwark against Jeffersonianism. The more radical element within the party, the "High Federalists" or "Ultra Federalists," as scholars have labeled the faction that included Hamilton, and those in orbit about him, sought more. In particular, they believed that conditions were verging that might facilitate their long cherished aspirations of destroying the French Revolution, demobilizing its adherents within the United States, saving Great Britain—the last hope of civilization, according to Sedgwick, who expressed the feelings of many in the party—and aggressively exploiting the woes of Spain in order to expand America's frontiers and further ensure the nation's security. The president was crucial to the achievement of these ends, and from the outset the Ultras knew that their voice must predominate among Adams's counselors, though "without its being perceived," as Sedgwick remarkably acknowledged. Furthermore, now that Washington and Hamilton were gone, the Ultras wanted the Federalist-dominated Congress to play an enhanced role in the making of foreign policy.[10]

While president-elect Adams never guessed his advisors' sycophancy toward Hamilton, his antennae pulled in signals not only that many Federalists were suspicious of his fiercely independent bent but that it might prove ruinous to jettison Washington's cabinet. He understood his predicament with considerable acumen, but underestimated the powers he would possess as president. Part of his problem was that he was a stranger to executive authority. During eighteen of his twenty-two years of national service, Adams had occupied solitary diplomatic posts or the vice presidency. In neither instance had he possessed patronage or advisors. Even so, he should have known better. He had long before observed how Governor Hutchinson and other royal governors in Massachusetts had utilized patronage to strengthen their hand. President Washington, who had discovered the wonders of patronage while he commanded the army, furnished still another example for Adams. Furthermore, Washington had bestowed an exalted aura on the presidency. Had Adams been more self-assured, canny, and audacious, he would have surrounded himself with his own men, faced down the dissidents in his party, and compelled those who wanted offices and power—which were his to distribute—to serve him loyally.

This problem, and others as well, arose in part from how Adams understood both himself and the presidency. Unless an issue somehow was related to military or foreign policy, Adams viewed it as lying within the exclusive purview of Congress. His primary responsibility, he believed, was to safeguard national security. He referred to the chief executive as the national guardian, the lone national official under the new constitution and the only officeholder who was obligated to serve the nation as a whole. The president was not to advance the fortunes of one section, not to represent a single social and economic class, and not to be the advocate for any narrow factional interest. His objective must be to protect the nation against avarice, ambition, and passion, and in the pursuit of those ends, Adams wrote, he must be "more wise, more learn'd, more just, more every thing."[11]

In addition, in the area of foreign affairs Adams explicitly trusted his own judgment and looked askance on that of others. Not only was he without equal in years of diplomatic service, but as an envoy in Paris and Amsterdam during the war he had often been compelled to act alone, devoting lonely hours to the scrutiny of intractable issues and unilaterally making momentous decisions. He had borne the sole responsibility for providing America's answer to the challenge of European mediation of the war. He had struggled alone for two bleak years in quest of Dutch aid and recognition, ultimately attaining both. In 1780, while Franklin demurred, he had stood up to the French government, demanding that it send its fleet to cooperate with Washington and Rochambeau. When France did just that the following year, ordering Admiral de Grasse to bring his navy north to act in concert with the Franco-American armies, it set in motion the chain of events that culminated in the allies' victorious siege at Yorktown. During the peace negotiations with Great Britain in 1782, Adams had secured favorable northern boundaries and fishing rights for the United States virtually without assistance. President-elect Adams was accustomed to making epochal national security decisions, and confident that his diplomatic record of success vindicated his judgment and talent. Indeed, at the conclusion of the War of Independence, Foreign Minister Vergennes had hosted a dinner for Adams at Versailles at which he lauded him as the "Washington of diplomacy," an accolade that he bestowed on no other American envoy. Thus, Adams entered the presidency anticipating that the officials who served him were managers who were to administer what he or Congress decided. Given that point of view, it made little difference who served in his cabinet. It was an ingenuous notion and a thoroughly unrealistic one. His naive and flawed conception of leadership and power would haunt him at every step of his presidency.

Two days before the Inaugural ceremony, Jefferson visited Adams in the president-elect's room in the Francis Hotel. It was their first meeting in four years, and it was cordial, even friendly. Adams called on Jefferson the next day and disclosed that he planned to name a three-member commission to sail for Paris. He asked Jefferson to approach Madison about serving on the team, hopeful that the presence of a key Republican would vest his diplomatic initiative with a nonpartisan aura and ultimately lessen domestic disapproval. By the time the two spoke again, two days later, Madison's decision—which was negative—was a moot point. Later on the day that he spoke with Jefferson, Adams had divulged his plans to Treasury Secretary Wolcott. The secretary had erupted, furious that Adams had been so impolitic as to consult the leader of the opposition party before sharing his thoughts with his own advisors, and appalled at the thought that he would even consider the appointment of a Republican. The entire cabinet would resign if Adams made such a decision, Wolcott threatened.[12] Thirty-six hours into his presidency, Adams had his first inkling of what it would be like to work with a highly partisan, not to mention insubordinate, cabinet.

Before he could deal further with the commission, ominous news arrived. Adams learned that the Directory not only had refused to accept Charles Cotesworth Pinckney, the new American minister whom President Washington had appointed a few months earlier, but it had ordered him out of the country. In addition, word soon arrived that French ships had resumed their attacks on American commerce in the

Caribbean. These twin occurrences pushed America's troubled relationship with France into a full-blown crisis.

Adams responded by summoning Congress to a special session in May.
In the sixty-day interim, while he waited for the congressmen to return to
Philadelphia, the president contemplated his options and held his first
cabinet meeting. He told his advisors that he preferred war to national
humiliation, but mostly, he said, he hoped for an honorable settlement
reached through negotiation. He added that he remained committed to
sending a commission to France, but wanted his cabinet's counsel. Would
such a step, he asked, risk national disgrace? Pickering, Wolcott, and
McHenry not only expressed doubts about "the propriety" of attempting
to negotiate, but were stubbornly hostile to the notion of appointing a
commission. If anyone attempted to speak to the French government, they
said, it should be Pinckney alone. After a lengthy discussion, no resolution
had been reached, and the president asked his cabinet to submit their ideas
in writing prior to the convening of Congress.[13]

Adams never suspected that Pickering and Wolcott would inform
Hamilton of what had transpired in the privacy of the cabinet meeting.
"What is to be done?" Pickering cried out to Hamilton immediately after meeting with the president. Within the week he and his colleagues
had their answer. Hamilton advised that a team of commissioners should
be sent to Paris, as peace was crucial for maintaining prosperity and preserving the Union. He had no wish to further alienate France, he said,
which he feared was close to victory in Europe's war. That could "leave
us alone to receive the law from France," he warned. However, as the
American commissioners would be sent "to *explain demand negotiate*,"
they must be backed by a show of American willpower and military readiness. Dusting off the plan that he had prepared for Sedgwick to introduce during the Anglo-American crisis twelve months earlier, Hamilton
now urged Pickering and McHenry to recommend that Congress be asked
to upgrade the navy, cavalry, and artillery and to create a provisional
army of 25,000 men.[14] Although Hamilton sought more comprehensive
military preparations than Adams ever desired, his views otherwise were
strikingly similar to those of the president.

Much of the written advice that Pickering and McHenry ultimately
gave the president was copied verbatim from Hamilton's instructions.
Adams embraced those recommendations that tallied with the conclu-
sions he long since had reached. He ignored the rest. His object was twofold. He wished to make it clear to Paris that the United States would
stand firm, and he hoped to prepare the public for ominous times ahead.
In a truculent speech that opened the special session of Congress on

May 16, Adams warned that the United States must never exhibit "a colonial spirit of fear and sense of inferiority," and he pledged that during
his presidency the nation would never be "the instrument of foreign
influence." He did not recommend a provisional army. Always a navy
man—it had been his proposals in Congress in 1776 that led to the creation of the United States Navy—Adams requested that the fleet be up-
graded, just as his cabinet, and Hamilton, had urged. The president
additionally called for the reformation of the militia. Finally, he announced his plan to send a three-member commission to Paris, though
he did not name the envoys.[15]

While the Federalists applauded the president's message, the Republicans' response was the reverse of the position they had taken during
the British menace in Washington's presidency. After 1793, when Great
Britain entered the war against France, the Republicans had demanded
a pugnacious policy toward London. Now they expressed horror at what
they called Adams's chauvinism. Vice President Jefferson, almost all scholars agree, quietly took charge of the Republican opposition to the president. Jefferson thought it prudent to send envoys to Paris, but he was
"much disappointed" by the tone of Adams's speech. He was anxious
lest America's defensive preparations appear to the Directory to be "measures leading directly to war." Caviling about military preparedness was
strangely shortsighted for someone with Jefferson's diplomatic experience. Otherwise, his response was characteristic. He portrayed administration policy as the result of a cabal of Ultra Federalists, who "are English
in their relations & sentiments," and who wished to provoke hostilities
as the means by which to solidify the Anglo-American alliance.[16]

Soon after delivering his speech, Adams convened the cabinet and
announced that he would name Pinckney, John Marshall, and Elbridge
Gerry to the commission. Once again, the cabinet exploded. This time it
was Gerry that they did not want. One of three members of the Philadelphia Convention who had refused to sign the Constitution, an Anti-
Federalist during ratification, and now a Republican, Gerry was anathema
to most Federalists. For a second time, Adams relented. He substituted
Francis Dana, a Massachusetts Federalist. However, when health concerns led Dana to decline the appointment, Adams—without consulting his cabinet—named Gerry. Adams subsequently explained his
behavior by claiming that Gerry was one of only two nonpartisan public
officials in America (he regarded himself as the other) and that he wished
to demonstrate his independence to the cabinet. Actually, not every Federalist was unhappy with the inclusion of a Republican among the commissioners. Hamilton and Knox thought the presence of a member of

the opposition might increase support for the administration's foreign policy, and at the very least it would militate against an hysterical response, as had occurred when the result of Jay's negotiations were made public.[17]

In June, William Laughton Smith, a South Carolinian and ally of Hamilton, introduced in the House of Representatives the substance of the military preparedness recommendations that the former treasury secretary had furtively sent to his disciples in the cabinet. The Republicans blocked or modified much of the Federalist program. For example, while authorization was voted for calling up 80,000 militiamen if necessary, the Provisional Army bill died quietly. Moreover, the only naval funding that Congress approved was for the purpose of hastening the completion of war vessels that it had previously sanctioned.[18] In mid-July, the special session ended and virtually every public official fled the capital, fearing the onset of yet another summertime invasion of deadly yellow fever, a disease that had been visited on Philadelphia episodically since 1699 and in each of the previous four summers. Adams returned to Peacefield, his home in Quincy, outside Boston, where he remained for four months, a longer stretch than President Washington had ever been away from the capital, save for when he toured the Southern states in 1791.

While vice president, Adams had routinely spent up to eight months at home each year, coming to the capital only when Congress was in session. Little changed during his presidency. In 1797 he got away late because of the special session of Congress, but thereafter he customarily left the capital in March or early April, soon after Congress's adjournment, and started his journey back to Philadelphia early in November. As the round trip consumed a month—the carriage ride between Massachusetts and southeast Pennsylvania required about sixteen days—Adams ordinarily divided each year almost equally between Quincy and Philadelphia.

Adams saw nothing to criticize in his conduct. His behavior was not unlike that of virtually every member of Congress. In fact, he usually remained in the capital for a month or two longer than most congressmen. Nor did Adams believe that his habits adversely affected his work. He left the day-to-day administration in the hands of the cabinet officers, who generally remained in the capital for most of each year, but his correspondence was delivered to Quincy. There, the president—as had been his custom while in Europe—read and reflected and reached his preliminary decisions without consulting anyone, though he did not act on substantive matters until he finally met with his cabinet weeks later.

Adams's strained relationship with his cabinet doubtless contributed to his eagerness to escape their presence, but two additional factors likely also shaped his behavior. While a diplomat, Adams had rebuffed his wife's repeated pleas to join him in Paris or Amsterdam, fearing the hazards she would face in making a wartime Atlantic crossing. The two did not see one another between November 1779 and August 1784. She turned the tables on him after 1789. Finding public life distasteful, and suffering from rheumatoid arthritis, a malady that made traveling an agonizing ordeal, she rarely accompanied him to the capital during his vice presidency and likely refused to live in Philadelphia year round during his presidency. Whereas he had stoically borne the wartime separations, Vice President Adams had cried out now about the misery of lonely nights, sent Abigail more letters than she wrote to him, told her that living alone was ruining his health, exhibited signs of sexual desire that had not been present during their earlier separations, and confessed, a bit awkwardly, that he was melancholy when away, missing—as he put it—his home, horse, and mate. Sixty-one when he took the oath of office, and knowing that he faced an inordinately stressful job, Adams as never before craved his wife's companionship, but what he coveted could only be had in Quincy.[19]

Health considerations also may have contributed to Adams's wish to escape the capital. In 1771, at age thirty-six, he had fallen ill with a malady so severe that he was unable to work for months. The illness returned in 1775, again in 1781, and for the final time in 1783. His complaints—heart palpitations, visual impairment, skin eruptions, memory loss, insomnia, night sweats, acute anxiety, and possibly a goiter—were the classic symptoms of Graves' disease, a malady that results from an overproduction of hormones by the thyroid. Hyperthyroidism is an autoimmune disorder that may be triggered by stress. It may also lapse into remission. Medical science did not understand the purpose of the thyroid in Adams's lifetime, and thyrotoxicosis was not diagnosed until long after his death. Yet, while Adams was unaware of the likely cause of his affliction, he understood that it occurred in moments of great stress in his life. His initial illness commenced just after the Boston Massacre trials and the death of a daughter and during the first year that he held an important elective office, a seat in the Massachusetts assembly. He relapsed immediately after the outbreak of war at Lexington and Concord, again when he was summoned to Paris by Vergennes to respond to the European neutral powers' proposal to mediate the War of Independence, and yet again soon after negotiating the Treaty of Paris. After 1783, with the arrival of peace, a more leisurely pace was possible, and Adams adjusted his habits in the hope of preventing a further recurrence of whatever ailed him. He at last summoned his wife to Europe, altered his diet, and instituted a daily regimen of exercise that included walking several miles. Moreover, between 1784 and 1797—when he served as minister to Great Britain and as vice president—he held relatively low-stress posts that left him considerable amounts of free time, and the illness did not recur. However, on the eve of becoming chief executive, Adams expressed grave concerns about the likely pressures of his new job, and he appears to have consciously plotted his habits so as to minimize adversity. This included his annual flight to tranquil Peacefield, a strategy that may have contributed to the overall good health he enjoyed throughout his presidency.[20]

Adams left Peacefield only once during his four months residency in 1797, to attend a dinner in his honor in Boston. As was his custom, he took long walks each day, occasionally hiked in the Blue Hills near Quincy—an invigorating pastime that he had relished since boyhood— and even worked a bit alongside the hired hands on his little farm.

Adams did not expect to hear from the commissioners until after Christmas. What they would report about their reception in Paris was anyone's guess, but the messages that Adams received that fall from John Quincy, his eldest son, the first American minister posted in Berlin, were not encouraging. The Directory had been reconstituted following the failed coup d'état of 18 Fructidor (September 4, 1797), the young envoy reported, and now consisted of men with no kindred feelings for republican America. Minister Adams predicted that the diplomats sent to Paris by President Adams would fail.[21]

While the president awaited definitive word from abroad, he wrote his cabinet requesting their thoughts about the best course of action should the diplomatic initiative founder. Only McHenry touched base with his leader in New York, but he must have shared Hamilton's thoughts with Pickering and Wolcott, as all three cabinet officers ultimately offered recommendations that tallied with that of the former treasury secretary. Much of what they proposed involved a renewed request for military preparations. Hamilton had urged the expansion of the regular army to 20,000 men and the creation of a provisional army of 30,000, but he counseled against a declaration of war. Nothing was to be gained from hostilities, he had written, as France had neither territory nor trade in the vicinity. As a consequence, only Attorney-General Charles Lee, a Virginian who was not in Hamilton's thrall, urged war. Hamilton had additionally recommended that the president prepare the public for the worst. Adams, he said, should pursue a "vigorous defensive plan," and as a signal of America's continued willingness to negotiate, leave an envoy on standby in Europe. Ever mindful of the link between theatrics and political leadership, Hamilton even advised that the president make these recommendations to Congress "with *manly* but *calm* and sedate firmness & without strut." Hamilton's three satraps in the cabinet merely advised the president to be "cautious, solemn, grave."[22]

Meanwhile, with "nothing of real importance before us," as Senator Gallatin told the home folks, there was little for Congress and the president to do but await word from Paris. December passed, then interminable January and February. Finally, on March 4, the first anniversary of his Inauguration, Adams's expectant days ended abruptly. Late in the day, as the long shadows of twilight enveloped Philadelphia, the first message from Pinckney, Marshall, and Gerry at last arrived. It was sent to Pickering, who decoded just enough of the dispatch to understand its sense before he scurried into the gloaming to appraise the president. What Pickering had read caused him to bristle with anger and even to remark to an acquaintance that this should lead "*real Americans*" to go for their guns. Adams, reading the communiqué by the light of a flickering candle, at first was inclined to agree.[23]

What the president discovered was not just that the French foreign minister had refused to receive the commissioners, but that secret agents who greeted the envoys had demanded both bribes and an apology from the president of the United States as a condition for instituting negotiations. The apology was to be made for the anti-French remarks that Adams allegedly had made in his speech to the special session of Congress. Why France adopted such an extraordinary stance remains mysterious. The puzzle deepens when it is understood that the foreign minister, Charles-Maurice de Talleyrand-Périgord, was not offended by the Jay Treaty. He thought it a bad commercial bargain for the United States, but not an accord that violated America's trade agreement with France. The advice that Talleyrand had received throughout 1797 from his consul-general in Philadelphia—much of which was based on frequent and exceptionally candid conversations with Jefferson—was to take no provocative steps, as Adams and the Federalists were likely to be turned out of office in 1800, after which Franco-American relations would be normalized.[24]

Why then did France deliberately insult the United States? Paris's actions suggest that the French leadership felt hurt and betrayed. France had been the first and, for a very long time, the only friend of the United States. France's dazzling munificence had made possible the great triumph of arms at Saratoga in October 1777, and after 1778 its supplies and repeated loans—in the course of which Versailles spent itself to the cusp of bankruptcy—had been almost all that kept the United States afloat. Without the naval arm that France had provided, the British surrender at Yorktown in 1781 would never have occurred. Yet, despite

France's friendship and largesse, the United States had repaid its ally with a series of acts that struck many in France as the very soul of infamy. In 1782 it had violated the Treaty of Alliance, concluding a separate peace with Great Britain that might have left France to fight alone against a formidable foe. It had rebuffed Citizen Genêt and refused to aid France in its hour of peril after 1793. Finally, its actions after 1794 seemed to many to have provided succor to Great Britain through a weak-kneed acquiescence in London's repeated depredations. Viewed in this light, the insolent treatment of the three commissioners in the fall of 1797 was payback for what many perceived to have been America's repeatedly ignoble acts, a step that Paris could take, and enjoy, because it viewed the United States as a mere triviality.

President Adams was no less outraged than Pickering when he read the envoys' accounts of their despicable treatment. Adams had a tendency toward impulsive behavior, and that evening in his dimly lit office he stormed that he would ask Congress to declare war on France. However, Adams not only was fully aware of his proclivity for speaking in haste; as a skilled diplomat, he knew the value of carefully measuring his words. Thus, after his rant before the secretary of state, Adams gathered himself and thereafter exhibited greater restraint. Adams chose not to make an immediate pronouncement. Two weeks passed before he spoke in public, a period when he consulted with his cabinet and reflected quietly on the proper action. During that period, too, his bellicose mood moderated, as did that of Pickering and his fellow Ultras in the cabinet, who were counseled by Hamilton—they had immediately informed him of the broad outlines of France's conduct—to pursue "a *temperate*, but *solemn* and *firm*" course of military preparedness, but not to ask Congress to declare war. An "attitude of *calm* defiance suits us" better than hostilities, one of the secretaries advised the president, much as Hamilton had instructed. The final decision was for Adams to make. He had to know that there was no guarantee that the country would support what might be a protracted war against France, and he knew full well—as did everyone old enough to remember the last years of the War of Independence—that hostilities might have a devastating impact on the economy. Principally, however, Adams—like Washington earlier—feared that war might prove ruinous for the unstable Union. In the end, President Adams shredded the first speech that he had written in response to France's reception of America's envoys, a militant, rage-filled address, and crafted a more moderate, though still tenacious, message. He had been "liberal and pacific" in dispatching the commissioners, he declared, but France's behavior had convinced him that "no ground of expectation" existed that a settlement could be reached that was within the "essential inter-ests of the nation." Therefore, he urged Congress to take steps to protect the United States and its commerce, although the only specific measure that he recommended was the arming of merchant vessels. He had done everything that Hamilton and the cabinet had desired, save to ask Con-gress to create a provisional army or to reveal the reports of the commis-sioners. He thought a French invasion unlikely, and he feared that a revelation of the details of the French effrontery would provoke an irre-sistible war hysteria.[25]

Adams had acted cautiously, wishing to temper the public response and preserve his freedom of action in dealing with Paris. Therefore, he was surprised by the passionate Republican reaction to his speech. Be-hind closed doors Jefferson referred to Adams's message as "insane." He charged that the Federalists were a "war party" inhabited by "war gentle-men," who pushed a defense program that amounted to "war measures." Jefferson also portrayed President Adams as "the stalking horse" of "the Hamilton party," which, he alleged, aimed for war with France in the belief that hostilities would permit—virtually compel—the United States to conclude a treaty of alliance with Great Britain. Madison went even further. He refused to believe that the president was merely Hamilton's pawn, and claimed that the pugnacity of "our hot-headed Executive" was characteristic of the "violent passions . . . which have been long pri-vately known to govern him." He thought that Adams, who had never soldiered, was driven by inner demons to secure a reputation as a tough and manly individual. The president, he thought, was "a perfect Quixote as a statesman," a flawed leader who was "taking as much pains to get into war" as Washington had taken to keep America from hostilities. Soon the Republican press launched an assault on the president. It matched the contumely that Madison and Jefferson had expressed in private. Nevertheless, the opposition's efforts to stanch the gathering Francophobia were fruitless. Indeed, as they flailed about to discover the best way to oppose their Federalist adversaries, the Republicans succeeded in making a bad situation worse. First, they tried to win House approval of a resolution that branded war as "inexpedient," only to abandon that approach for lack of support within their own ranks. Next, Jefferson, who was pulling the strings, played for time, hoping to stymie Congress from acting before it reassembled in December. By year's end, he rea-soned, one of two things would have happened. Either France would have triumphed or would be so near victory that the Hamiltonians would shrink from bellicose policies that could leave the United States alone at war with a European superpower, or the French would face such dark clouds of uncertainty that the Directory would eagerly pursue an amicable settlement with the United States. To his dismay, however, Jefferson discovered that he lacked the votes for a prompt adjournment. The third Republican strategy was the brainchild of Madison. He demanded that Adams release both his instructions to the commissioners and their reports to him. Madison assumed that because the president had sequestered word out of Paris, the French must have received Pickering, Marshall, and Gerry in a less provocative manner than the administration had intimated. The release of the documents, Madison presumed, would muffle the popular reaction and disarm the congressional hawks.[26]

But Madison's scheme unwittingly led the Republicans into a snare. Congressman Giles of Virginia, who took charge of the Republicans' latest tactic, opened the campaign with a House speech studded with allegations that Adams deceitfully had cast French behavior in a bad light. He demanded that the commissioners' instructions and communiqués be made public. Adams complied, blacking out only the names of the French agents who had demanded bribes and identifying them merely as "X, Y, and Z." Thereafter the episode would be known as the XYZ affair. Seldom, if ever, has a major American political faction taken a stance that proved to be so destructive to the ends it sought, for the release of the envoys' dispatches "electrified all classes," Ames remarked, laying out for the public the details of France's offensive behavior. Not only did the documents immediately exculpate the administration of charges of treachery, but their release triggered a national fury. It is too much to believe that Adams cannily baited the hook and reeled in his unsuspecting adversaries, although that was precisely what some Republicans thought. Adams, in fact, had foreseen the public response and hoped it could be avoided, not from benevolence toward his political foes but because above all else he wished to prevent having his diplomatic maneuverability restricted by a firestorm of popular militancy.[27]

Jefferson soon understood Madison's blunder. The XYZ documents "excite disgust & indignation in Americans generally," he acknowledged, so that suddenly it became politically inexpedient to effectively oppose the Federalists' preparedness campaign. The heat was so great, he soon reported to Madison, that numerous Republicans now supported "the war measures so furiously pushed by the other party." A week later he told a friend that the Federalists could not be prevented from enacting any defensive measure they desired. As United States policy no longer was "neutral & pacific," Jefferson sadly concluded, the Federalists might take intemperate steps that would inevitably result in war with France.[28]

That did not stop the Republican press from flailing away at the Federalists. Their polemicists skirted the popular defensive measures that

Congress was considering, choosing to attack the burdensome taxes that would be occasioned by military preparations rather than to dwell on the measures themselves. Some Republican writers shaded their stories to caution that a French victory in the European war was imminent or to warn of the economic maladies that would ensue from Franco-American hostilities, as United States exports to France were vastly greater than those to Great Britain. It also remained politically safe to assail England, which was often portrayed as "*the great evil of the world.*" President Adams was alternately exhorted to send another envoy to Paris and assailed for creating an atmosphere that would "make war unavoidable." He was subjected to scurrilous assaults that were every bit as cruel as those hurled against his predecessor, including one that especially raised the First Lady's ire, as it characterized her husband as "old, querulous, Bald, blind, crippled, [and] Toothless." The *Aurora,* which earlier had predicted great things from Adams, joined in, portraying him as vain, jealous, and arrogant, deriding him as a coward for having quickly left Philadelphia when yellow fever recurred, and foolishly suggesting that he had appointed his son, John Quincy, to a European ministerial post in the hope that both would reap financial rewards from his diplomacy.[29]

Having blundered into the XYZ revelations, many Republican journalists saw national security matters as a minefield that was best left untouched. They stayed with the theme that the liberties secured by the American Revolution were not safe in the care of the Federalists. Under a "Lost & Found" heading, one Republican purportedly advertised: "Lost. The Declaration of the Rights of the Citizens of the United States." Others contended that rights of freemen promised in the Declaration of Independence soon would be a distant memory in wartime America. Another observed that Federalists spoke of the American populace as "subjects," whereas Republicans called them "citizens." For the first time, too, an occasional opposition essayist answered the Federalist denigration of democracy. A "*democrat* is one who advocates the people's rights, and a government *of* the people, or arising *out of the* people," wrote a New England Republican.[30]

One part of the Republican attack had a decidedly modern ring to it. Hamilton, long since targeted for his public policies, was maligned for his personal indiscretions. Seven years earlier, while treasury secretary, Hamilton had been visited one balmy summer evening by Maria Reynolds, an attractive young woman in apparent distress. Portraying herself as related to the Dutchess County, New York, squirearchy, she claimed to have been deserted by her husband. Penniless, Maria asked Hamilton for a loan. "[H]er situation was an interesting one," Hamilton later said. "It required a harder heart than mine to refuse it to Beauty in distress," he added, perhaps seeing similarities in Maria's plight and that of his mother, who had also been abandoned by the man she loved. He provided her with money, and more. That night, with his wife back in New York, Hamilton had slept with Maria. Thereafter, their trysts occurred frequently, until just before Christmas 1791, in roughly the sixth month of the affair, Maria's husband, James Reynolds, knocked on Hamilton's door. He knew of Hamilton's indiscretions and wanted hush money. During the next year, the treasury secretary paid $1,415 in blackmail, a stupendous sum, roughly equal to ten times the annual income of most skilled artisans in that day. Late in 1792, Reynolds, who appeared to have several nefarious irons in the fire, and a confederate, Jacob Clingman, were jailed in Philadelphia on numerous charges, including an attempt to defraud the government. None of the charges concerned Hamilton, but Clingman, hoping to cop a plea, accused Reynolds of colluding with the treasury secretary in illegal speculative endeavors involving federal monies. An explosive accusation such as this could not be kept secret. Word of Clingman's allegations reached some members of Congress, who quietly visited Hamilton to hear his side of the story. The secretary immediately revealed all, admitting to his amorous affair and providing the congressmen with numerous letters that had passed between himself and Reynolds. The congressmen were convinced that Clingman's story was bogus, a desperate attempt to secure a lighter sentence by ratting on his partner. The congressmen pledged to Hamilton that the sordid story would never pass from their lips.

For five years their lips remained sealed. But they possessed copies of the Hamilton-Reynolds correspondence, given to them by Hamilton— whether from trust, compulsion, or desperation is not clear—and eventually those missives fell into the hands of the Republican clerk of the House of Representatives. In 1797, soon after the Quasi-War Crisis erupted, someone leaked the letters to James Callender, a writer more interested in making money from a sensational story than in peddling ideology. He published the scoop. Hamilton responded in a manner that should have proven instructive to every philanderer who subsequently held office. He immediately rushed into print a fifty-page confession. He contritely acknowledged the affair with Maria Reynolds, but once again, this time publicly, demonstrated that no evidence existed of financial peculation on his part. The Republican press had a field day with the story. What, their essayists asked, did Hamilton's scurrilous behavior reveal of Federalist morality? Could anyone, they wondered, trust the motives of a Federalist who spoke of French degeneracy? In the end, however, little came of the dirt they dished. Hamilton had not held public office for two years. He appeared to be remorseful. His wife forgave him. Although titillated, the public was largely indifferent or sparing.

Indeed, nothing the Republicans tried appeared to work during that passionate summer of 1798. They were stymied, as Jefferson put it, while the "public mind appears still in a state of astonishment."[31] The Federalists had their way. Congress adopted the defensive measures that Adams had advocated and much more. By July, it had established a Department of the Navy and authorized construction, purchase, or refitting of thirty-seven warships, a course that the president had first urged a year earlier. But it also went further than Adams desired. Congress additionally created a Provisional Army, embargoed all trade with France, and terminated the two Franco-American treaties that the United States had so joyfully received twenty years earlier during the winter of Valley Forge. These measures had to be paid for, and as Jefferson ruefully observed, Congress appropriated more funds for this preparedness program than it had spent in any year during the War of Independence. New direct taxes were levied on land, houses, and slaves.[32]

The creation of the Provisional Army fulfilled a goal that Hamilton, and those around him, had sought for fifteen years. Its birth came without Adams's support. The president, like most of his Republican adversaries, was too much the Whig not to fear a standing army. He privately referred to it as "proper only for Bedlam," a "many bellied Monster" that was good chiefly for endangering liberty. He also viewed the army as a costly, mischievous liability that could provoke a political backlash. Mostly, however, the president thought the army unnecessary, for as Adams told his secretary of war, "there is no more prospect of seeing a french Army here, than there is in Heaven."[33] Most nationalists, however, had wanted a large army since the end of the War of Independence. As hostilities were winding down in 1783, before the demobilization of the Continental army, Washington and Hamilton had launched a campaign for a peacetime army of 3,000 men, although the economic realities of the Confederation era frustrated their hopes. At the Philadelphia Convention the nationalists secured a clause in the Constitution that authorized the creation of a regular peacetime army, but Congress did nothing until two armies sent into the Ohio Country by President Washington were decimated. Thereafter, Congress listened to the president's entreaties and expanded the army to 5,000 men. However, as soon as General Wayne scored his decisive victory at Fallen Timbers in the summer of 1794, Congress cut the army nearly in half. Until the genesis of the Franco-American crisis, and the onset of the combative mood that followed the revelation of the XYZ affair, the American public evinced no desire to have a large standing army.[34] Hence Pickering's glee at the opportunity to publish the XYZ documents, for he knew immediately that when the Directory's action was divulged it would bring to an end "opposition by Democrats in the House, and French worship ... outside."[35] The secretary of state was correct. The Federalists quickly passed legislation that increased the regular army to 15,000 and authorized a Provisional Army of 12,500 that was to be mobilized at once.[36]

The national mood, however, was for military preparation, not war. That disappointed some Ultras, including a few New Englanders who were so steeped in their region's age-old Francophobia that they would have welcomed hostilities with what one called the "factious, cutthroat, frog-eating, treaty-breaking, grace-fallen God-defying devils" in Paris.[37] Other extreme Federalists longed for a war they believed would result in the destruction here and abroad of "the Monster Jacobinism, the foe of property, morality and religion."[38] Hostilities, they believed, would forge closer Anglo-American ties, redounding ultimately to the commercial advantage of the eastern port cities. Congressman Ames, whose rhapsodic speech against war with Great Britain in 1796 had helped save the Jay Treaty, pounded the drums for hostilities with France early in 1798. It was "Cowardice" to "cry peace," he now said. "It is too late to preach peace.... [A] defensive war must be waged. ... That, or submission, is before us." He predicted that if America did not act, the day would arrive when "the French tiger comes to devour them." War would have another advantage, he added privately. It would immediately silence the Republicans as the off year elections approached in the autumn.[39]

However, more powerful Federalists counseled against hostilities. Although Hamilton had urged the army as a show of force to bring the Directory to the bargaining table, he opposed going to war in 1798. In a three-week period immediately after the XYZ disclosures, he rushed into publication seven lengthy essays entitled "The Stand." His rhetoric was reminiscent of that of Samuel Adams or Thomas Paine—and not totally unlike that of young Jefferson—twenty-five years earlier, except that they had directed their ire at Great Britain. The "FIVE TYRANTS of France, after binding in chains their own countrymen, after prostrating surrounding nations, and vanquishing all external resistance to the revolutionary despotism at home ... seem resolved ... upon the pretension to universal empire ... [and have] in fact tho not in name, decreed war against all nations not in league with themselves." The United States, he went on, was the victim of "a long train of unprovoked aggressions and affronts" that have insulted and humiliated the citizenry of the new nation. But Paris could not make the United States its puppet unless the American people were willing accomplices. " Tis only in our power to

do this by an abject submission to their will." Did this mean war? "No—
there are still chances for avoiding a general rupture," he wrote. Military
preparation by the United States was designed to "bring the present despots to reason." He urged "calm defiance," the same prescription he had
advocated privately a year earlier. Hamilton had achieved what he wanted.
He had the army that he had struggled for years to attain, the prospect
of a Federalist victory in the autumn elections, and the possibility that
the Republicans could be blackened to ruination by a growing public
conviction that these alleged Francophiles had formed an "unnatural
league . . . with the oppressors of their country."[40]

Nor did President Adams desire war, although at times during the
summer of 1798 he appears to have thought hostilities were likely.
Through his son in Berlin, he learned of alleged French plans to invade
the trans-Appalachian West—in the vicinity of present-day Mississippi
and Alabama—and detach the region from the United States. At one
point the president told the British minister that he expected war with
France, and the First Lady remarked that an undeclared war had raged
for months. Furthermore, presumably on the advice of her husband,
she began hoarding household supplies for the day when war came and
goods grew scarce.[41] But Adams never stopped hoping that hostilities
might be avoided. Like Hamilton, he believed that military preparations
offered the best hope of bringing France to its senses. Peace might be
preserved, he believed, if Paris understood that an American population
that yet harbored deep affection for the French people would nonetheless fight in self-defense. To foster that impression, and to prepare the
citizenry for the worst, Adams publicly answered seventy-one patriotic
messages that had been sent him by militia companies and various and
sundry other clubs and organizations. His responses, most of which were
brief statements that did not exceed a few paragraphs, were published in
local newspapers or distributed as handbills. They bristled with com-
bativeness. National dishonor was a greater evil than a just war! It was
cowardice to shrink from war! The national character would be ruined
if the populace failed to resist tyranny! This generation would betray its
colonial forefathers if it proved to be spineless! On occasion, an address
exuded a partisan tone. In a reply to the citizenry of Wells, Massachusetts, for instance, Adams not only warned of intrigues by French agents
with the United States but cautioned everyone to be on guard against
the "party in this country [that is] devoted to [the French] interest." Yet,
despite the president's bluster, he never called for war and never believed
that hostilities were inevitable. Nevertheless, it was Adams's fate to preside over the nation's first cold war, an undeclared war that witnessed

occasional bellicose incidents at sea. Scholars have come to call it the Quasi-War.[42]

Despite the wishes of Hamilton, and those of their president, some Federalists pushed for a declaration of war, even after a party caucus held early in the summer demonstrated that the votes for it were not there. A resolution in the House calling for the creation of a committee to prepare the declaration of war was voted down on July 5. Not a single republican voted in favor of the measure, and serious talk of immediately declaring hostilities was never again heard in Congress during the Quasi-War.[43]

Five years earlier, Jefferson had believed that the strength of the Hamiltonians had crested and begun to erode, but by the summer of 1798 the Federalists had never been stronger. President Adams, who throughout his public career had been respected, but not revered, was a case in point. As the Quasi-War heated up, he was esteemed by the public as never before. By mid-1798 he was proclaimed for his "manly fortitude," "manly spirited" actions, and "manly independence," and lauded for the "noble part" he had played in arousing public sentiment, including his vigorous popular pronouncements which had given "a tone to the national spirit."[44] When Adams journeyed to New York that summer, some observers believed that he received a more boisterous and affectionate welcome than had ever been lavished on any public official, including Washington. Some even thought that he now equaled Washington in the eyes of his countrymen, and one Federalist writer predicted that no leader of his era, including Washington, would be held in higher esteem by posterity than Adams. When he traveled, Adams was greeted by large, adoring crowds. When he attended the theater in Philadelphia, audiences cheered and sang "Hail Columbia," "Yankee Doodle," "The President's March," and "Adams and Liberty," newly composed in his honor. The First Lady told friends that the "Common People" were delighted with Adams and thankful that Jefferson—under whom "all would have been sold to the French"— had not been elected.[45]

Not only was Adams extraordinarily popular, but the Federalist Party was positioned for further electoral successes, which it indeed secured that autumn and in the spring of 1799, guaranteeing that it would remain in command in Congress at least into 1801. The Republicans could only despair at the strength of their adversaries. First in the Anglo-American crisis, and now in the Quasi-War hysteria, two Federalist administrations had discovered that their nearly unilateral control of American foreign policy afforded a means of tightening their grip on power. Half a dozen years after Jefferson had envisaged mobilizing popular opinion to stymie Hamiltonian economics, the Federalists were beating their adversaries at their own game. President Adams's addresses, Jefferson ruefully acknowledged, had roused the "multitude" behind the "war party." In the "spirit kindled up" across the country, the Federalists "will carry what they please," he added.[46]

Yet, despite the Federalists' remarkable popularity in the spring and summer, Jefferson clung to the belief that their ascendancy would be short-lived. Either events in Europe would cause the foreign crisis to run its course, extinguishing the war fever, or popular antipathy would mount once the public understood what the Federalist military measures entailed, especially in the way of taxation. What is more, from the beginning Jefferson had believed that the Federalists would overreach. Madison shared his outlook and in fact was the first to predict that the Federalists would accompany their preparedness campaign with an attempt to snuff out "liberty at home" under the guise of protecting "against danger, real or pretended, from abroad." Jefferson concurred. He expected "a fit of unguarded passion" on the part of his adversaries and trusted that it would prove to be self-destructive.[47]

The Republicans did not have long to wait. In April 1798, Ultra Federalists began to push the ill-judged and unnecessary Alien and Sedition Acts through Congress. Neither Adams nor Hamilton had urged the legislation. The president, however, made no attempt to prevent their passage, and indeed he appears to have welcomed the acts, in part because they demonstrated to France the drastic steps the United States was willing to take to ready itself for war, and partly because he was convinced that "French spies" and "intolerably, turbulent, impudent, and seditious" aliens "swarmed our Cities." Many years later, he said the legislation was "salutary, if not necessary," the closest he came to a criticism of the measures. Hamilton, on the other hand, found the acts so repugnant that he interceded in an attempt to moderate what the congressional Federalists were about. "Let us not establish a tyranny," he warned. "Let us not be cruel or violent." Hamilton never shared the anti–civil libertarian sentiments of many Ultra Federalists, and he was sufficiently prescient to see that repressive legislation would undermine unity in the midst of a national crisis. In addition, like Jefferson and Madison, Hamilton understood that these intemperate measures might be politically counterproductive. In fact, he was no less critical of Adams' strident rhetoric, calling it "indiscreet" and "violent" and potentially divisive. He even implored Washington to tour the South in an endeavor to calm the waters that Adams had moiled and to scotch the last lingering opposition in that region to administrative policies. Hamilton told his former boss that if "we make no false steps we shall be essentially united, but if we push things to an extreme we shall then give to faction *body* & solidarity."[48]

Hamilton's warnings about the Alien and Sedition Acts went unheeded. The more extreme Federalists pushed the legislation into law, acting primarily from a dread and hatred of the radical social and political world that they feared was taking shape. They saw the Quasi-War as a heaven-sent means to promulgate this supposed antidote to what they saw as the mushrooming democratic despotism and licentiousness. Sedgwick, who had opposed draconian legislation aimed at Massachusetts' Loyalists during the war, candidly embraced these Alien and Sedition Acts as "a glorious opportunity to destroy [the Republican] faction." According to his biographer, Sedgwick was so mortified by the ridicule to which he was subjected in the Republican press that he grew obsessed with extirpating those foes whom he regarded as atheistic Jacobins. Ames, bitter over how the Republican Party had allegedly "paralyzed" the national government since 1792, was similarly euphoric at the chance to silence his old political enemies. He thought his party faced a stark choice. Either the "mass of opposition . . . must fall, or the government will." What he appeared to mean was that the Union would buckle should the national government ever fall into the hands of democrats and egalitarians. This was the golden moment in which to destroy the Jeffersonians. If the proponents of democracy survived, said Ames, they "will soon rise from the mire, where they now lie," and spread their radical tenets. The summer of 1798, when both anti-French opinion and the mood of bellicosity were at a fever pitch, was the moment to strike. It was now or never. If the Federalists missed this marvelous opening, pernicious democracy soon would "paralyze and distract our measures and our counsels, and the public . . . will not again give the tone to government it has lately given."[49]

Ironically, the Federalists ultimately damaged themselves more than the opposition through these extreme measures. However, the greater irony is that they suffered this self-inflicted wound just as some in the party were beginning to understand and cope with the burgeoning democracy that was shaping the American political system. Jefferson's sense, evident as early as 1792, that the Federalists were doomed because they were out of touch with the sentiments of most Americans, had not been borne out. Through their foreign policy successes, they had grown steadily stronger, winning laurels for pacifying the Ohio Country, opening the southwestern frontier, and boldly standing up to France. Even Jefferson marveled at the Federalists' extraordinary ability to "excite . . . a general & high indignation among the people" who so recently had adored the French.[50]

But could they be sustained by foreign policy? What would the Federalists do once peace was restored in Europe? Would the party face a bleak future if no threat to national security existed? Years earlier, Jefferson had concluded that the Federalists' vision for domestic America was decidedly unlike that of most citizens, and indeed by 1798 increasing numbers of Americans looked on the party as a voice from an unhappy bygone time. The Federalists had come to be seen by many as the party of urban merchants and financiers, the defenders of social hierarchy, and the implacable adversaries of what Paine had called the "new world" of better opportunities promised by the American Revolution. Even in their manners and lifestyle, the Federalists exemplified a remote past that most Americans longed to escape. It was not just that Washington had hosted levees with a royal pomp, or that Adams, who once suggested a monarchical title for the chief executive, traveled now in a gaudy coach and six, attended by a legion of liveried servants. To many, the Federalists seemed set apart by their fancy clothes, grand balls in their great mansions, and elegant salons patterned after the court fashion of Europe's ancient regime. A reverence for old habits also shined through the Federalists' political practices. Their celebrations were more comely and their meetings more sedate than those of their rivals, a fact that the Federalist press proudly trumpeted, boasting that their assemblages were conducted with the "greatest decency and decorum," and without "riot and confusion" or the "noisy bustle of a promiscuous crowd." Many noted that when Jefferson left the State Department, which then supervised the United States Mint, Federalists removed depictions of the liberty cap—associated with the figure of Libertas in the Temple of Liberty in the Roman Republic—from all coins. They spoke often of liberty, but invariably hedged their rhetoric with admonitions about licentiousness and the virtue of order. Sometimes, however, it was not what they did so much as what they would not do that stamped the Federalists as remnants from a receding era. One never heard Federalists address one another as "Citizen," and while one might see them wearing the black "American Cockade," with metal eagle pins, they never were observed in a tricolor revolutionary cockade. Unlike Republican scribes, Federalist writers did not take pen names such as "Liberty," "Equality," "Fraternity," "Democraticus," or "Reformatist," and they never wrote under the name of a French Revolutionary, such as "Mirabeau." or "Marat." Federalists neither celebrated the triumphs of French arms during the European war nor the political and social transformations achieved by the French revolutionaries. They did not toast Thomas Paine. Nor did they sing the "Ç a Ira" or the "Marseillaise." Their Independence Day celebrations, which tended to be held in posh hotels and inns, were devoid of

Anglophobic exhibitions, and their oratory on these occasions skirted the egalitarian implications of the Declaration of Independence. Instead, their speakers tended to urge reverence of constituted authorities. They eschewed liberty trees and liberty poles—sites for gatherings and rallies, that in some instances could be traced back to the Stamp Act protests, and which were vested with symbolic meaning as representing freedom against tyranny—which came into vogue in some Republican and émigré circles after 1793. In Federalist territory one was unlikely to find, as was true in Republican Baltimore, militia units bearing names such as the "Republican Company," the "Sansculottes," or the "Democratic Greens." To many, the Federalists had become an old guard committed to exalting the dead hand of the past. Furthermore, while growing numbers of their countrymen had come to believe that the earth belonged to the living and that free persons had the capacity to grow and develop into productive citizens, the Federalists yet insisted that proper order could only be maintained by leaving authority in the hands of a traditional elite.[51]

Nor was that all. Hamilton, among others, sometimes spoke of Jeffersonianism as if it were a Southern phenomenon, but the sagacious knew that the Republican Party was gathering strength in the North as well. Backcountry farmers, the backbone of Anti-Federalism, had moved easily into the party, but it also was becoming apparent that the Republican movement was growing in the prosperous Northern centers where grains were grown and marketed. These regions were inhabited by people anxious for commercial growth—and who had not been especially adverse to Hamilton's economic package—but who saw the Republican Party, with its implicit pledge to loosen the bonds of society, as the embodiment of the promise of expanded opportunities. To growing numbers of commercial farmers and prospering tradesmen, the Republican message translated into equal access to political power and an equal opportunity to grow rich. It meant freedom from the traditional privileges enjoyed by the elite and liberation from government intrusiveness in the economy for the benefit of the few and the detriment of the many. It meant friendlier relations with France than the Federalists were inclined to offer, together with the economic benefits that would accrue from mounting trade with the French sugar islands. It meant a smaller national government than the Federalists desired and consequently lower taxes for the Lilliputian army and navy that the Republicans favored. Above all, whereas the message of the Hamiltonians appeared to mean reaction and repression, if need be, to maintain the hegemony of the elite, the Republican Party offered the prospect of pursuing one's happiness—that is to say, self-interest—unhindered by either ancient custom or the heavy hand of a government reserved for the benighted gentry.[52]

No one understood the party's dilemma better than the Federalists themselves. In times of crisis, Ames acknowledged, the public exhibited a "state of passive obedience" that contributed to the Federalist mastery. However, the moment the emergency ended, the Republican opposition "will sprout again, as unconquerable as the weeds" to once again "best us in industry, audacity, and perseverance."[53] Thus, it was not by happenstance that the Ultras pushed the Alien and Sedition Acts into law at this moment, nor was it coincidental that they simultaneously ushered into being the Provisional Army. The two were to assist in the final destruction of the despised French Revolution and the perpetuation of Federalist hegemony. Adams and Hamilton understood the imprudence of the repressive measures with which the Federalist Party thereafter would be identified, but the one did not lift a finger to prevent the bills from becoming laws and the other, for all his influence, was powerless to restrain the zealots.

By early June, Congress had enacted the Alien and Sedition Acts. Some Federalists, such as Harrison Gray Otis, who wished to prevent further immigration altogether, would have gone even further, but most were content with the four measures that were enacted. The Naturalization Act nearly tripled the wait to fourteen long years before immigrants—most of whom gravitated toward the Jeffersonians—could obtain citizenship and the right to vote. The Alien Friends Act authorized the president to deport dangerous aliens. The Alien Enemies Act, the only one of the four measures that enjoyed bipartisan support, permitted the deportation of aliens who hailed from a nation with whom the United States was at war. The Sedition Act, which became law one day after the twenty-second anniversary of American independence, set heavy punishments—fines of up to $5,000 and incarceration for up to five years—for those who conspired to thwart federal law or who made "false, scandalous, and malicious" statements about federal officials. Forty of the forty-four votes for the bill in the House of Representatives were cast by representatives from districts north of the Potomac River. Adams signed the measure into law on the ninth anniversary of the storming of the Bastille. Soon thereafter Jefferson responded that the Federalists could succeed in "warring against" the "real principles" of the "great body of the American people" only so long as the citizenry was persuaded to acquiesce from a belief that an unresolvable crisis with France existed.[54]

Adams largely ignored the clamor of Secretary of State Pickering to run aliens out of the country. He signed warrants for the deportation of only three aliens, but all three had fled abroad by the time the president acted. However, the Sedition Act was zealously enforced. During the thirty months that the law was in effect, the administration indicted seventeen

Republican editors and secured fourteen convictions. Some editors paid fines. Others went to jail. Some who were never prosecuted ceased publication rather than risk punishment. However, not everyone was cowed. The number of Republican newspapers more than doubled in the next two years.[55]

The passage of this repressive legislation was an egregious blunder. Any success that the Federalists realized—and it is debatable that they accomplished anything of a substantive nature through the Alien and Sedition Acts—was quite brief. The long-term implications were adverse, perhaps catastrophic, for the party. The measures resulted in renewed consideration of the meaning of freedom of the press, and ultimately helped in the formulation of a growing consensus not only that a free press was vital to popular enlightenment but that public opinion was paramount in a republican society. Some also were prompted to reconsider Anti-Federalist warnings about the scope of the authority of the national judiciary.[56] However, the most immediate result of "the reign of witches," as Jefferson characterized the Federalist measures, was that the opposition took concerted steps to organize. Already convinced that the Federalist Party was a war party, many Republicans now found in the Alien and Sedition Acts confirmation of every suspicion since 1787 about the black designs of the supporters of consolidation. In 1792, Jefferson had cautioned Washington that Hamiltonianism sprang "from principles adverse to liberty, and was calculated to undermine and demolish the republic." Now, he said, "this was a game where principles are the stake." Like nothing heretofore, the Alien and Sedition Acts led many Americans to see things in the same light as Jefferson.[57]

Before the summer of 1798, Jefferson had remained confident that the Federalist sway would be short-lived. When he retired to Monticello in 1794, he had been convinced that his labors to organize an opposition faction had succeeded in erecting a formidable firewall against further Federalist achievements. At that time, and for a while thereafter, he had explained Federalist hegemony as due largely to happenstance. The party, unfairly, had garnered the lion's share of the credit for the new Constitution and the survival of the Union. By fortuity, moreover, Washington, with his "irresistible influence and popularity," had been on their side. However, Jefferson also acknowledged that it was Hamilton's genius to exploit the opportunities that appeared, and through "cunning" and "great artifice" to make the most of the moment. All along, Jefferson had insisted that the political history of the decade had not accurately reflected "the natural state." The Federalists had flourished as a result of an unusual combination of circumstances, but in time the fates would catch up with them and "bring round an order of things more correspondent to the sentiments" of the majority of Americans.[58]

Jefferson's optimism drained away that summer. In August, with their military preparations going forward, and the Alien and Sedition Acts on the books, Jefferson confessed for the first time that he feared the Federalists might be invincible. The civil liberties that he had thought safe so long as entrusted to the states might now be gone. Without a free press, there was little hope of stopping the Federalists. Jefferson charged that they had already made the national government "more arbitrary, and [have] swallowed more of our public liberty" than monarchical England ever contemplated before 1776. What next? The Federalists held the hammer. Jefferson could "see there is no length to which [their authority] may not be pushed," no step "however atrocious, which may not be expected." He appeared to believe that they would strike against middling democracy, and in his worst nightmares he may have feared that the Federalists would use their Provisional Army to invade Virginia and snuff out dissent. What is more, Jefferson had come to believe that resistance along the lines that the Republican Party had pursued during the past half dozen years—the mobilization of public opinion through press attacks on their adversaries—would henceforth be unavailing. Resistance to the Federalist counterrevolution must take a new shape.[59]

Jefferson spoke of the need for the public to "rejudge" the limits of national authority. Like some Anti-Federalists in 1788, who had charged that the proposed Constitution was "made like A Fiddle, with but few Strings" so that those in power could "play any tune upon it that they pleased," Jefferson too was coming to the view that the Federalist "system" was to exploit clearly delineated national powers and "to seize all doubtful ground." The authority of the central government had swelled beyond all expectations, until it had become a "foreign jurisdiction . . . so pregnant of abuse" that civil liberties no longer were safe.[60] He wished to preserve the Constitution, he said, but according to "the true sense in which it was adopted by the States." A reassessment of federalism was necessary. It must be launched by an astounding act, much as the nationalists had staged high drama in the Newburgh Affair. And, similarly, safety was required. As Hamilton in 1783 had built safeguards by informing General Washington of what was occurring within the cadre of officers at Newburgh during that bleak winter fifteen years earlier, Jefferson took precautions in the parched summer of 1798 before he unveiled his audacious plan. In private, the vice president told some that his tact was "an experiment on the American mind, to see how far it will bear the Federalist abuse." He also confided that his was a ploy, that it might not be necessary to "be committed absolutely to push the matter to extremities," and that he wished only "to push as far as events will render prudent." However, Jefferson was deadly serious. He never wavered from the belief that the American Revolution had been undertaken to decentralize authority. He believed in a federal balance, a sharing of authority between the national and state governments, but he was convinced that the Federalists were shredding that equilibrium. In desperation, he took this step to restore the system of balances that appeared to be rapidly fading, and he gambled that the threat to the Union implicit in his action would so mobilize opinion that the Federalists could be stopped.[61]

In the last muggy days of summer, Jefferson sat at his desk at Monticello and prepared a statement that, if ever implemented, would at the least dramatically redistribute power between the federal government and the states. It might even portend disunion. Jefferson began with the notion that the states had gathered at the Philadelphia Convention to form a "compact" in which some explicit powers were granted to the national government, while the remaining authority—what he categorized as "the residuary mass" of the people's "rights to their own self-government"—was reserved to the states. But in the absence of a "common judge," he asked, who was to decide when questions arose about the legitimate exercise of powers by the national government? Certainly, he said, the federal authorities could not be the "final judge of the extent of powers delegated to itself." Jefferson's answer was that each state must decide for itself whether the national government had exercised undelegated powers. Each state must have the authority to declare illegitimate acts "void, and of no force" within its domain.[62] Vice President Jefferson had drafted a doctrine of state nullification.

Once written, Jefferson quietly turned over his draft to John Breckenridge, a member of the Kentucky House of Representatives, who agreed to protect the identity of the author and introduce the statement in his state assembly. Deep into that autumn the legislature approved, in a slightly altered form, what came to be known as the Kentucky Resolutions. While the Kentucky legislature deliberated, Jefferson for the first time appraised Madison of his course. Madison must have been aghast. Jefferson's statement savaged the philosophy of the Virginia Plan, as well as that of numerous *Federalist* essays that Madison had written. Nevertheless, when Jefferson encouraged his friend to draft a similar statement that would be introduced in the Virginia assembly, Madison complied. He was under Jefferson's sway, but he also shared his friend's anger and alarm at the recent repressive acts of the Federalist Congress. Madison additionally may have consented to act in the belief that he would prepare a somewhat more moderate statement than otherwise would be forthcoming should Jefferson turn to another author. Furthermore, Jefferson must have made clear to Madison that the promulgation of these nullification pronouncements was a tactic. By contriving an extreme states' rights response to meet the extremism of the Ultra Federalists, Jefferson not only hoped to rally moderates everywhere, but in this game of bluff he sought to persuade Congress to repeal the Alien and Sedition Acts.

Although he shunned some of Jefferson's combustible rhetoric, Madison's draft shared the heart and soul of the Kentucky Resolutions. He too declared that the states could annul federal laws. Madison's friends introduced his statement, and it quickly was adopted by the state assembly. It was popularly known as the Virginia Resolutions. Soon after its approval, Madison confided in Jefferson that he was just as uneasy with the prospect of a state legislature serving as the final umpire as he was with a branch of the federal government acting in that capacity. State assemblies, he advised, were no less likely to usurp power than the Congress. Madison was hardly the first, or last, politician to take a stand on terrain with which he was uncomfortable, but he saw the necessity of doing so in the hope of forestalling a growing crisis for the Union as great as that of 1787, and one that was less likely to result in such a salubrious outcome. His sense of the Federalist betrayal of the American Revolution, and of their repeated and unwarranted arrogation of state authority, led Madison to predict that at some point a dangerous "revolution" by their foes was inevitable, unless the Federalists could be ousted from power in the election of 1800. He thus acted out an unsavory role in the hope of preventing a dangerous collision that would threaten the survival of the Constitution, republicanism, and the Union. It was an act of some desperation that was designed, in Jefferson's words, to give rebirth to the day when the "unquestionable republicanism of the American mind will break through the mist under which it has been clouded."[63]

Jefferson had a dexterous feel for politics, for knowing when the time to act had arrived, for understanding and capturing the essence of popular thought, and for doing so in a manner that advanced the limits of public consciousness. In 1798, not for the first time, he engaged in a high risk adventure. At considerable risk, his *Summary View* in 1774 had outpaced many popular radicals in questioning the limits of Parliamentary authority. His draft of the Declaration of Independence defined the American Revolution in a manner that resonated with most Americans, but at the same time it opened a window that permitted succeeding generations to give it new meaning. At great hazard in 1789, Jefferson—behaving more audaciously than Citizen Genêt ever considered—had secretly conspired with Lafayette and other members of the French National Assembly soon after the Bastille was stormed to plot revolutionary strategy and write a French constitution. But nullification was different. While he was deadly serious about the circumscription of federal powers, the rest was tactical, an artful conjure that was never meant to be put into play unless the Hamiltonians—evincing a long train of abuses—furnished additional provocations. For that reason, it probably came as no surprise to him that his recommendations mostly fell on deaf ears. Other than Virginia and Kentucky, no state immediately embraced the radical prescription he had outlined. Nevertheless, the gauntlet had been thrown.

The passage of the Alien and Sedition Acts was not the only watershed event that occurred during the summer of 1798. At the very moment that Jefferson, in the heat and languor of a Monticello summer, drafted what became the Kentucky Resolutions, a behind-the-scenes drama was unfolding in torrid Philadelphia that ultimately would also have a seminal impact on events. It was brought on by the need to appoint the general officers in the new Provisional Army. Three weeks before Congress formally created the army, President Adams appealed to Washington to emerge from retirement and assume command of the new military force. Confident that Washington would accept, Adams appointed his predecessor and Congress approved his choice before word was received from Mount Vernon. Adams's conduct was not as clumsy as it might appear. Hamilton and some among his followers had sounded out Washington in the spring—after having largely ignored him during the initial year of his retirement—and he appeared willing to once again don his old uniform. The substance of those private communiqués must have been transmitted to Adams, who wanted Washington in the post. General Washington was trustworthy, and his presence would unify public opinion in the face of the crisis.[64]

On roughly the same day that Congress created the army, Washington's response to Adams's supplication reached the president's desk. To Adams's amazement, Washington was ambivalent. He might serve. Then again, he might not. It depended on circumstances, which Washington outlined in vague terms. Much of his letter dealt with the subordinate general officers. They should not necessarily be drawn from among those who had held the highest rank in the late war, as most of those men were now old, said Washington. The Provisional Army should be led by men of "sufficient activity, energy and health," especially as the French would be more mobile and daring than the British had been. Washington appeared to offer these thoughts as advice, and that was how Adams chose to read the missive. However, given what soon transpired, it is clear that

Washington was saying he would serve only if allowed to chose the principal officers.[65]

Faced with more questions than answers, Adams quickly dispatched Secretary of War McHenry to Mount Vernon. There, for three days in the breathless July heat, the two men talked. Washington immediately consented to serve, but on the condition that he "not be called into the field" until a French invasion appeared imminent. That was acceptable, but it made the selection of the other general officers—and especially the inspector general, the officer who would serve immediately below Washington, and who would command the army in his absence—all the more important. Much of the remaining discussion was devoted to assessing the possible choices. Washington said the post of inspector general must be offered to either General Charles Cotesworth Pinckney or Colonel Hamilton. No one else was qualified. McHenry—as Washington suspected would be the case—campaigned for Hamilton. Washington assented and prepared a list of men whom he thought acceptable for appointment as general officers. Hamilton's name topped the list.[66]

President Adams was appalled by Washington's unexpected behavior. Throughout the War of Independence, Washington had steadfastly refused to become involved in the process of ranking general officers. He had left such matters to the civilian leadership. No one knew this better than Adams, who as chair of Congress's Board of War in 1776 and 1777, had worked closely with the commander of the Continental army. Adams not only had expected Washington to behave as he had during the late war, but he never suspected that the former chief executive might presume to dictate to the president of the United States. But there was more to Adams's reaction. He anticipated that the lion's share of the soldiery in the Provisional Army would come from New England, as had been the case in the eighteenth-century colonial wars and the Revolutionary conflict. The president remembered how difficult it had been to recruit New England men to serve under the New Yorker, General Schuyler, and how Congress, in the face of Burgoyne's invasion in 1777, had removed Schuyler, replacing him with Gates. The president now feared that recruiting and morale problems would be endemic in an army commanded by Hamilton, who not only was highly partisan and a New Yorker but also Schuyler's son-in-law. Adams leaned toward the appointment of General Knox, who after Washington was the highest ranking surviving general officer from the late war. Adams's second choice was General Pinckney, four years older, but considered to be more physically fit than Knox. Furthermore, Pinckney, a South Carolinian, hailed from the very region widely believed to be the most likely site for a French invasion.

But Washington's behavior—which the former president would have found intolerable in any other man—presented Adams with a hideous problem. The president could ill afford the problems that would ensue should the public conclude that his intransigence had caused Washington to refuse to serve. No one, not even the president of the United States, could appear to think that his judgment was superior to that of Washington, least of all on martial matters. But Adams was just stubborn enough to make one attempt to call the Virginian's bluff. He proposed to Washington that the prospective candidates be ranked according to the date of their commissions in the Continental army. Under that formula Knox would head the list, followed by Pinckney, Henry Lee, Edward Hand, and Colonel Hamilton. Washington would not budge. Once again, he insisted that Hamilton be appointed inspector general. Adams folded.[67]

How can Washington's behavior be explained? He believed deeply in Hamilton, and never doubted his ability to mold the army into an effective fighting force or to lead it ably in battle. He unquestionably felt that the infant United States would be well served should Hamilton remain in command of the army for some considerable period. But there also may have been political overtones to Washington's behavior. His action may have been designed to advance Hamilton's political fortunes. While Washington's conduct entails speculation, no doubt exists with regard to the motives of McHenry, Pickering, and Wolcott, who sided with the former president against their own chief. To be sure, like Washington they were mesmerized by Hamilton's blinding energy, industry, zeal, and intelligence. In addition, they sought personal and party windfalls through Hamilton's elevation. Through his abundant appointment powers—hundreds of junior officers were expected to be named—General Hamilton could build and solidify a powerful Federalist political base in each state. What is more, whoever exercised military command in this crisis could dream of becoming the next Washington. George Washington was thought of as the sword of the American Revolution. The leader of the Provisional Army might emerge from the coming war with France as the savior of the infant nation. In 1798, Hamilton was two years younger than Washington had been at the time of his appointment to command the Continental army. Should he emerge from retirement to accept the public trust (as Washington had so often done), and should he also be crowned with laurels for his service in the French crisis, Hamilton's long shadow might stretch across America's political history for another generation, as had Washington's since peace came in 1783. Hamilton's votaries in the cabinet hoped that he might be the aegis through which they not only retained power but ascended to greater heights.

Some scholars have portrayed the Hamilton of the Quasi-War crisis in benign terms. He has been cast somewhat as a precursor of General Winfield Scott, the career soldier who presided over the American army with professional dedication from the aftermath of the War of 1812 until the onset of the Civil War nearly a half century later. Hamilton, according to this view, was a selfless patriot committed to preparing the nation for a fiery trial, and who otherwise merely wished "to become the permanent chief of a lasting American army," basking in the warm esteem that an adoring public lavished on a dedicated soldier. One historian has even maintained that Hamilton did not conspire to secure the appointment as inspector general, arguing that it was unwittingly foisted on him by Washington and Adams's cabinet.[68] Many of Hamilton's contemporaries, who in 1798 harbored dark suspicions about his intentions, would have scoffed at such an appraisal. Some believed the Ultra Federalists had manufactured this crisis with France—or at least gleefully seized on it—in the hope of advancing their party, striking a blow for an Anglo-American alliance, and reaping the political benefits that accrued from the war hysteria. Some skeptics suspected that the Federalists never anticipated a French invasion, but wanted the army for sinister ends. Abigail Adams, for instance, soon discovered striking similarities between Hamilton and Napoleon Bonaparte, including the desire to have an army for personal ends. Some thought Hamilton wanted the army in order to pursue adventures in the West, either to realize his expansionist dreams or to enhance the Federalist Party in a region where, after the Whiskey Rebellion, it had virtually no adherents. Others feared that he wanted an army to suppress American democracy or to stage a coup d'état. Even some of Hamilton's friends questioned what he was about. Robert Goodloe Harper, South Carolina's Federalist stalwart who admired Hamilton, thought him capable of nefarious acts. His inveterate enemies imagined that there were no limits to what he might attempt. Jefferson spoke of Hamilton as "our Buonaparte" and feared that his goal was to use the army "to give us political salvation in his own way." Their suspicions arose from what they saw and heard from Hamilton himself. They knew him as an individual who had spent his life chasing after power and fame, and lusting for the opportunity to soldier as the means of gaining adulation and renown. It was widely known that he had begged Washington for a shot at glory at Yorktown—Adams even credulously believed the yarn that Hamilton had gotten the opportunity to command an assault on the British lines by blackmailing Washington with threats to expose aspects of his private behavior—and later pleaded for the chance to lead the army against the Whiskey rebels in 1794. Jefferson also remembered, and often repeated the story, that at a dinner party at his home in 1791 Hamilton had confessed his belief that Julius Caesar was the greatest man who ever lived.[69]

There is no way to know with assurance which view is correct. Perhaps there is truth on both sides. Hamilton had to know that there were limits on his authority. He could hardly have imagined that Washington—who had labored tirelessly to build a virtuous reputation and who also was the titular commander of the army—would have permitted him to use that army in an illegal manner, and it went without saying that Adams would be a considerable obstacle to malfeasance. That said, Hamilton also was aware that during the previous twenty years Washington had always listened to him and usually followed his counsel. In addition, because he controlled three members of Adams's cabinet, he personally had influence with the chief executive. What is more, his reputation for independence notwithstanding, Adams appeared to be malleable. The president had accepted an army, and officers in that military force, that he did not want. Hamilton had to know, too, that control of the army would give him power. Having served on General Washington's staff for nearly five years, Hamilton surely would have been aware that with the army at his command, he would possess myriad means of shaping public opinion and exerting pressure on his civilian superiors. Furthermore, Hamilton was an opportunist and a master of intrigue, orchestration, and manipulation. His fingerprints were all over the Newburgh Affair, the calling of the Philadelphia Convention, the uphill victory achieved by the New York Federalists during ratification, and the decision to suppress the Whiskey Rebellion with force. He was the most influential voice within the Federalist Party, bigger in some ways than the chief executive. But if Hamilton wanted war, or hoped to use his army in military adventures, or contemplated employing his army against domestic political foes, or simply wished to utilize the army to shore up his political base, his plans hinged on one simple truth: the Quasi-War must continue.

The Federalists answered their opponents' press attacks that summer, and they gave as good as they got. The newspapers broadcast stories that Southerners and Westerners—perhaps even entire Southern and Western states—would openly embrace French invaders as liberators and make common cause against the United States. They reported—correctly, as a matter of fact—that George Rogers Clark, a Virginia hero during the late war, still held a commission in the French army, and that an esteemed Virginia lawyer, St. George Tucker, had been overheard in May remarking that he and 100,000 other Southerners might join with the French if an invasion occurred. Some press reports were scurrilous. William Cobbett, an English immigrant and Federalist polemicist who wrote under the pen name "Peter Porcupine," broadcast tales of Irish immigrants who were prepared to give aid to the French, and many newspapers carried lurid stories of French agents who allegedly had crept into the country and established contact with pro-French networks within the United States.[70]

In this supercharged atmosphere, street brawls broke out in the capital between pro-British and pro-French crowds. In addition, the Philadelphia police learned of threats to assassinate American leaders who defied the French. One purported plot, committed to paper by doltish conspirators who subsequently lost the incriminating evidence in the streets of the capital, was to murder President Adams. That alleged conspiracy stretches credulity, but Adams took it seriously and installed a small arsenal in the President's House so that he could, if necessary, defend himself. This tempestuous episode, from the creation of the army and appointment of Hamilton to the ghastly assassination qualms, changed President Adams.[71]

His attitude toward Hamilton was transformed. Adams and Hamilton appear not to have met until 1789, as the Washington administration was taking shape in New York City. Their relationship during the next five years, before Hamilton resigned in 1795, appears to have been cordial, but not close, which is hardly surprising of two men who were separated in age by twenty-two years. Nothing in the papers of either man suggests an estrangement prior to 1798. Adams not only repeatedly said that he placed no credence in the persistent rumors that the former treasury secretary had intrigued to prevent his elections in 1788, 1792, and 1796, but in 1795 he secured a position for one of his sons in Hamilton's law firm. Throughout the first eighteen months of his presidency, moreover, Adams was blithely unaware that Hamilton exerted great influence over his cabinet. When in the spring of 1798 a few congressional Federalists quietly approached Adams about bringing Hamilton into his cabinet at the expense of McHenry, he consented, although nothing came of the idea. Hamilton, meanwhile, betrayed no hostility toward Adams, and in fact lauded his "excellent disposition" and "general character."[72]

But Adams saw Hamilton differently after the tempest over the office of Inspector General. He felt humiliated at the way he had been treated by Washington, and he was angry that his cabinet officials had not backed him during the dispute, but mostly he trembled with enmity toward Hamilton, whom he blamed for the episode. The experience was something of an epiphany for him. "There has been too much intrigue in this business," the president said, and he knew that he had been made "the dupe of it." Adams once described himself as the "most ... unsuspicious man alive." Throughout his public service he was chary of rumors and innuendo, demanding unequivocal proof of execrable conduct before he judged others harshly. He had given the British Ministry the benefit of the doubt before 1773, until the Hutchinson Letters episode converted him into an American activist. Until he discovered that Franklin had covertly criticized him in Congress in 1780, Adams had discounted the tattle about his colleague's alleged penchant for treachery. Similarly, until the events of July 1798 aroused in Adams's mind the belief that Hamilton had labored "underground and in darkness" to manipulate others for his own ends, the president had brushed aside suspicions about the former treasury secretary. But after the events of that charged summer, Adams had come to see Hamilton as a sinister figure. He now knew beyond the shadow of a doubt that Hamilton was—as he put it—the puppeteer who pulled the strings of the false-hearted men within his cabinet. Adams gave Wolcott the benefit of the doubt, but he was convinced that Pickering and McHenry had betrayed him. He questioned whether they placed partisanship and their loyalty to Hamilton above the national interest. That, in turn, caused him to wonder at their motives in advocating a militant stand toward France. The conclusion that Adams reached by summer's end was that Hamilton aspired to be an American Bonaparte.[73]

Adams now privately alluded to Hamilton as "Caesar." He was persuaded that Hamilton had spent his public career seeking "to get rid of" every rival in order to "monopolize all power to himself." This episode concerning command in the army fitted together the last pieces of the puzzle for President Adams. The archconservative Anglophiles, he now believed, had tolerated Washington as the means of installing Hamilton in power. Many in this crowd had engaged in "hypocritical adulation" of Washington, he said, while in private they "spoke of him . . . in the strongest terms of contempt." To them "Hamilton was everything and Washington but a name." He believed that Hamilton had been the real power during Washington's presidency, yet he was merely the point man for "that class of people" which had resisted the most substantive change in the fabric of Anglo-America since 1776. "Washington . . . was only viceroy under Hamilton, and Hamilton was viceroy under the tories," Adams privately charged. He was convinced that Hamilton and the Ultras had sought to prevent him from ever becoming president, as they had known he could never be dominated. Characteristically, Adams now privately denigrated Hamilton's character, portraying it much as he had limned that of the earlier great adversaries in his public life: Hutchinson, the British Ministry, Dickinson, and Franklin. He blasted Hamilton's allegedly "libertine" makeup. This "bastard brat of a Scottish peddler" was "devoid of moral principle," and he had corrupted his age by serving those whose only end was the accumulation of wealth. Hamilton was so driven by ambition and vanity, Adams now firmly believed, that there was nothing he would not do to gain power and fame.[74]

Adams returned home in July, and for the next four months he had virtually no contact with the members of his cabinet. When he reappeared in the capital in late November, drawn and thinner than anyone could remember him ever having been, he met briefly with his advisors, telling them that dispatches he had read from Europe during the summer and early autumn provided hope that France might be ready to normalize relations. He quizzed them about the best course of action for the United States. The cabinet counseled against both a declaration of war and the dispatch of another diplomatic mission. The latter course would be an "act of humiliation," several of the secretaries said. Let France send a negotiator, or wait for definitive word that Paris was ready to talk.[75]

Adams was disturbed by this intransigent mood, and in the aftermath of the events of the previous summer, he was suspicious as well. Furthermore, he harbored fresh doubts over whether the public would indefinitely support a tough stance toward France. During his return trip to Philadelphia, in November 1798, the president discerned a change in the popular temperament, a shift that Jefferson likewise noted. The bellicosity of the spring and summer was flagging. Passions inevitably cooled with time, but both Adams and Jefferson believed that the Alien and Sedition Acts, and the new taxes levied to pay for the army, had tempered the firm and belligerent mood. In fact, riots against the increased taxation had already occurred in two Pennsylvania counties.[76]

As winter crept over the capital, Adams received additional information indicating that France had moderated its truculent stance. Dr. George Logan, a Philadelphia Quaker who had sailed for France earlier in the year, returned with encouraging tidings. William Vans Murray, America's representative at The Hague, and Elbridge Gerry, who had remained in Paris despite the XYZ affair, independently reported that France sought some way to extricate itself from the limb it had climbed onto. More importantly, John Quincy sent similar assessments, as well as hopeful messages from the French foreign ministry.[77]

Perhaps the most crucial packet reached Adams's desk early in February. It was from Mount Vernon. Washington enclosed a letter from Joel Barlowe, a one-time Connecticut Federalist who had resided in Paris for some time, and he included a missive of his own. Barlowe offered further confirmation that the Directory was ready to negotiate, but what was especially significant to Adams was that Washington, in his letter, advised that he now thought a settlement on "terms honorable" to the United States could be negotiated. The former president added that he believed peace was crucial for "this rising empire." The general's comments appeared to liberate Adams from misgivings that had dogged him from the outset that somehow the pursuit of peace was unmanly. What is more, Adams knew that he would have Washington's backing should he choose to pursue a diplomatic initiative.[78]

From November into February, Adams inched toward a decision to dispatch another mission to Paris. He not only abruptly terminated his practice of issuing truculent addresses, but against his cabinet's wishes he made public Gerry's notes and reports, which showed "that France is *sincerely anxious* for reconciliation," as Jefferson remarked. He also inserted a passage in his State of the Union message that indicated his willingness to negotiate should France provide unmistakable evidence that it too sought an accommodation.[79] Ultimately, however, after 100 days of restless indecision, Adams was not led to act by communiqués from Europe or by the realization that Washington longed for peace as much as he did. Instead, the timing of his action arose from what he believed were fresh signs of the sinister intent of the Hamiltonians. Fearing their menace to the new republic, Adams concluded that he must act as the nation's "father and protector," the term he had used nearly a decade earlier to describe the role that the nation's executive must play. As the sole official who represented the entire nation, Adams believed that he must defend the national interest, and he reasoned that the best antidote against the peril threatened by these zealots was to end the cold war through which they had thrived.

Matters came to a head soon after Congress convened in late November. Convinced that a French invasion was unlikely, Adams told the cabinet that he wished to ask Congress to reduce the Provisional Army. The Ultras would hear nothing of it. In fact, they introduced legislation—which had been drafted by Hamilton, as Adams must have learned—to increase the size of the regular army and triple that of the Provisional Army, expanding it to nearly 45,000 men. As this occurred, word swirled about the capital—based, as it turned out, on some very real comments that Hamilton had made in private—that the inspector general wished to use the army to seize Spanish Florida or to cooperate with British armed forces in liberating Spanish colonies in Central and South America.[80] But that was the half of it. At this moment, a party insider revealed to Adams private letters that Hamilton had written in recent days and weeks. In these missives, Hamilton had alternately fulminated about Virginia's "insidious plan to disunite the people of America[,] to break down their constitution," and to aid the French in every possible way. Chillingly, Hamilton also reflected on utilizing the army to suppress "internal disorders." For months, dark rumors had gathered in the capital that the Hamiltonians planned to use the army to invade Virginia, as western Pennsylvania had been invaded in the course of the Whiskey Rebellion, although now Hamilton's intent, it was said, was to snuff out the Republican Party and republicanism. It was in this exaggerated context that Adams perused these letters.[81]

Hamilton's letters had an electrifying impact on the president, much as the purloined Hutchinson Letters had shaped his thought twenty-six years earlier. Adams was aghast at what appeared to be a High Federalist conspiracy to lay waste to Virginia and engage in military adventurism. Aware that the extremists in his party had created an army and plotted to make Hamilton its commander, sensible that they had long talked of using that army to invade Florida and Louisiana in order "to obviate the mischief of their falling into the hands" of European powers, and mindful that Hamilton's minions in the cabinet had been implacably opposed to any initiative that might result in a rapprochement with France, the final outlines of what Adams concluded was a Hamiltonian conspiracy took shape in the president's mind. The Hutchinson Letters had made clear to him a despotic British plot to eradicate American liberties. The Hamilton Letters convinced him of the existence of a wicked plot within his own party and cabinet to prevent a peaceful settlement of Franco-American differences and to use the army for the personal and partisan advancement of Hamilton and his confederates. Adams now labeled Hamilton "the most restless, impatient, artful, indefatigable, and unprincipled Intriguer" in the United States. He and his minions, the president had concluded, had conspired "to close the avenues to peace, and to ensure a war with France."[82] Adams believed that he had no choice but to act.

In his *Defence*, composed nearly a decade earlier, Adams had written that in every society throughout history wealthy oligarchies had ruled. His antidote for at least muting the power of entrenched wealth was a balanced government that included a strong executive, a republican official who nonetheless possessed some of the powers customarily wielded by monarchs. If the executive remained above partisanship, he had written, and if he was rendered capable of "a free and independent Exercise of his Judgment," he could serve as the caretaker of the national security, the common good, and the guardian of the people from the rapacious moneyed class. Now Adams, like Jefferson long before him, concluded that the Hamiltonians posed the greatest threat since 1776 to the dreams of most American revolutionaries. Indeed, by 1799 the gap that separated the thinking of Adams and Jefferson had narrowed. "You are apprehensive of Monarchy; I of Aristocracy," Adams once told Jefferson, but both in fact now discerned the prospect of a counterrevolution carried out by the Ultra Federalists, a campaign that Jefferson feared would lead to fashioning America in the image of royal England and that Adams believed would make the United States a satellite of Britain, robbing the new nation of its independence from the European powers. Since 1791, Jefferson's answer to the threat of the monocrats had been the construction of a faction that could thwart the Hamiltonians. Adams's choice was different. In his tracts on government, he had portrayed the executive as the "essence of government," the patriarchal official who must be "Always ready, always able, and always interested to assist the weakest," to battle for the "simplemen" against the "gentlemen," to protect the nation and its citizenry from those driven by avarice, ambition, passion, and an insatiable love of glory.[83] As the national steward, President Adams concluded, it was his duty to act, and that action could not be delayed. The news from abroad suggested that a peace initiative might succeed, although there was no guarantee of success. He would have preferred to await more definitive word before he launched his peace initiative, but he believed that he no longer had the luxury of waiting. To protect the national interest, to sustain republicanism, to save the Union from the wild machinations of the Hamiltonians, Adams believed he had to take action immediately. The president acted on February 18, and he did so without consulting his cabinet.

Harrison Gray Otis was excoriating French behavior on the House floor when he was interrupted by the presiding officer to read the message sent by President Adams. The members listened in stunned silence. "Always disposed and ready to embrace every plausible appearance of probability of restoring tranquility," Adams had written, he was naming William Vans Murray as minister plenipotentiary to France.[84]

The Federalists were "thunderstruck," one observer noted, and another described the congressional Ultras as "outrageously angry." Many railed that sending an envoy to Paris made the United States appear weak and irresolute. No talks should take place until Paris sent a plenipotentiary to Philadelphia, they said. Some feared that settling with France would strengthen Paris's hand in dealing with Great Britain.[85] More than one Federalist called his president "wrong-headed" or alluded to his "half frantic mind." In private, some even charged that Adams was insane. Sedgwick, who earlier had derided Madison as a *great man*, now referred sarcastically to Adams in the same manner. He did not think Adams mad, but he believed the president was "influenced by caprice alone," and he characterized Adams as "an evil."[86] Adams was not a madman, but it had been decidedly impolitic for him to have acted without consulting his advisors and to have sprung a surprise on his party. However, an impolitic act was not the same as an unstatesmanlike act. Adams was painted into a corner. Had he first gone to the cabinet, it would never have consented to yet another diplomatic initiative, and some might have threatened to resign if he went forward. That would have prevented him from acting, for a divided government could not pursue a diplomatic initiative of such magnitude. As it was, his surprise step confronted his cabinet with an accomplished fact and with the unsettling realization that to resign might ruin the president's diplomacy and lead to war. None wished to hazard being saddled with responsibility for such an outcome. None quit. Adams also maneuvered the Federalists into focusing their opposition on the selection of Murray rather than in waging a public battle against a diplomatic initiative. His foes cried out for a multi-member commission, which in all likelihood Adams secretly desired from the outset. Appearing to make a concession, Adams immediately consented to their demands, and eventually Chief Justice Oliver Ellsworth and William Davie, the governor of North Carolina, were appointed to serve with Murray.[87]

Although President Adams had acted boldly, in the heated meetings that followed he made a concession that proved to be a costly personal blunder. He agreed that the envoys would not sail to join Murray until further assurances were received from Paris. Such a step was unnecessary and so angered the French foreign minister that it jeopardized the mission.[88] Moreover, it delayed the start of negotiations, so that from the outset it was clear that the Quasi-War crisis was unlikely to be resolved before the election of 1800. Adams had backed down in a desperate attempt to maintain a united front, lest America's partisan divisions emasculate the envoys in the forthcoming negotiations, and also to hold together his party as the elections approached.

Additional French reassurances eventually arrived in midsummer, and on August 6 Adams, who was vacationing in Quincy, directed his secretary of state to prepare the commissioners' instructions. The president expected the envoys to sail by the end of the month. However, Pickering stonewalled, preventing their departure for nearly two additional months. When Adams learned what was occurring—his loyal secretary of the navy, Benjamin Stoddert, wrote that "artful, designing men" were plotting to wreck the negotiations with France—he cut short his vacation and hurried south to see to the embarkation of Davie and Ellsworth.[89]

Adams's destination was Trenton, to which the government had moved when Philadelphia was yet again struck by an outbreak of yellow fever. The president had hardly unpacked before he summoned the cabinet, the first of several sessions over the next few days. Some meetings were probably rancorous, as Pickering, Wolcott, and McHenry sought a further postponement in the dispatch of the envoys. Adams refused. At some point Hamilton arrived from Newark, two days away by horseback. Despite his subsequent denials, Hamilton almost certainly came at the behest of those in the cabinet who wished him to make one last, desperate attempt to dissuade the president.[90]

The president's two accounts of the meeting, each written years later, are his only surviving record of what transpired, but as they closely resembled how the First Lady described the episode at the time, it is likely that Adams's subsequent recollection was reasonably accurate. Of course, had Hamilton left an account of the interview, it almost certainly would have differed in substantive ways. Adams remembered that Hamilton opened the meeting with a lengthy discourse on the European situation. The president thought it was presented as a professor might condescendingly lecture a class of callow freshmen. Adams also recalled that he sat quietly smoking a cigar, and enjoying the spectacle, as Hamilton worked himself into a passion. The thrust of Hamilton's argument was that Louis XVIII would be on the throne in France by Christmas, only a month and a half away. Given the monarch's certain outrage that the United States had attempted to deal with the Directory, Hamilton allegedly declared, Louis would refuse to receive the commissioners. The United States would appear to the world to be a weak-kneed and sniveling nation that had prostrated itself before France. Adams was bemused. "[N]ever in my life did I hear a man talk more like a fool," he said later. Adams recounted that he had rebuffed "with perfect good humour" every argument offered by this "[over]wrought ... little man." Hamilton allegedly switched tactics thereafter and asserted that an accord with France would initiate a war with Great Britain. Adams claimed to have demolished that red herring as well by demonstrating that the last thing beleaguered London would wish was to acquire yet another adversary.[91] Adams's portrayal of the proceedings was doubtless skewed by his visceral hatred of Hamilton, but one thing is clear. Hamilton, who had largely had his way with Washington, and who seemed always to win, had met his match in John Adams.

All that was left was for Hamilton, by subterfuge, to make one final attempt to frustrate Adams's peace initiative. He sought to persuade Judge Ellsworth not to sail. As the Senate would have to confirm the nominee who would serve as his replacement, that would postpone the departure of the commissioners until early in 1800. But Hamilton lost on this score as well. Ellsworth refused to play along, and the matter at long last was resolved. Ellsworth and Davie sailed from Newport, Rhode Island, on

November 3. Eight months—258 days—had elapsed since Adams first had announced his intention of pursuing negotiations with France, and three months had passed since the president had ordered his envoys to sail.[92]

The Ultra Federalists were furious with Adams for his every move since February. The president, whose sense of leadership was surely flawed, had brought many problems upon himself, first by retaining Washington's cabinet and then by failing to make changes among his advisors when he discovered their disloyalty. At the height of the Quasi-War Crisis, in mid-1798, Adams might have pleaded the need for a coalition government in an hour of emergency, dumping Pickering or McHenry, or both. To have acted then would have been to move against his foes at the time that his popularity was at its apex. His successors in the presidency would take such steps during subsequent crises, including the Civil War and World War II. In fact, Southern Republicans had made overtures to Adams to act in precisely this manner in the spring of 1798, but he demurred from the fear "it would turn the world upside down if I removed any one of them." Belatedly, Adams sought to enhance his strength through a judicious exercise of his patronage powers, and he tried to broaden his base of support by appointing influential Republicans, such as Aaron Burr and Frederick Muhlenburg, as general officers in the Provisional Army. The president's latter initiative failed when Washington, who had spoken so eloquently of the danger of partisanship in his Farewell Address, blocked his commander-in-chief. Thus, as his moment of decision approached early in 1799, Adams had found himself in an untenable position. "With all my ministers against me," the president said later, he was "no more at liberty than a man in prison, chained to the floor and bound hand and foot."[93]

Actually, Adams did have the liberty to act, and he exercised his authority throughout 1799, but the Federalist Party was fatally rent in the process. It had been a divided party for two years or more. Now, less than a year before the election of 1800, the Federalists were ruinously cloven, in part because of Adams's shortcomings, but also because the Hamiltonian wing, shackled with an unpopular program of its own making, had to chase after success—survival, in fact—through the perpetuation of a crisis that appeared to steadily growing numbers to be readily resolvable. Adams's peace campaign laid waste to their strategy, ruining their adventurous plans and casting a shadow over their chances of retaining power.

Many scholars have concluded that the outcome of the Election of 1800 was foreordained from the moment the Federalist Party began to split apart in February 1799. Jefferson, however, had a more accurate take. What doomed the Federalists, he later remarked, was not the disharmony within the party that followed Adams's unilateral peace initiative. It was the fact that the Ultras's intransigent opposition to the president's quest for peace exposed many Federalists as "seducers [who] wished for war." Jefferson was correct, too, in seeing in the course of 1799 that the "tide is evidently turning." He rejoiced that the dawning mood of the country showed that "the spirit of 1776 is not dead. It has only been slumbering. The body of the American people is substantially republican."[94]

13

1799–1801

"The Gigg Is Up"

dams was in low spirits when he returned to the capital in November
1799. He had delighted in quashing
Hamilton in their recent confrontation in Trenton, but he had to believe
that the vengeful inspector general would come after him with the unbridled fury of a wounded animal. Personal sorrow also clouded Adams's
mood. During that star-crossed autumn the president had learned that
his middle son—Charles, who was only twenty-nine—was ruined and
ill from alcoholism.[1] Nor had the president's own future ever been more
uncertain. He knew that his chances of winning reelection in 1800 were
uncertain, and probably unlikely, and that defeat would confront him
with troubling personal choices, the likes of which he had not been forced
to deal with for years. In addition, Adams had celebrated his sixty-fourth
birthday as he traveled south from Quincy. He had lived what for most
of humanity in eighteenth-century America was a normal life span. Indeed, only a few days after he returned to the President's House in Philadelphia, thoughts of his own mortality must have become paramount,
for he received the startling news that Washington had died recently at
Mount Vernon.

Washington, who had grappled in his latter years with the realization that many males in his family had been denied a long life, had left
the presidency in 1797 hoping to find serenity in the time left to him. His
hope had been realized. He tended to repairs on his mansion and at last
succeeded in selling lands in Pennsylvania, Ohio, and present West Virginia that he had been trying to unload for a quarter century. Most days
were spent in managing his planting and business operations, a routine
that he easily and happily slipped back into the moment he reached home.

Washington left Mount Vernon for a protracted period only once during his final retirement. He came to the capital in the autumn of 1798 to meet with Adams, Hamilton, McHenry, and the principal general officers in the Provisional Army. He was back home before Christmas. Soon thereafter he learned of the death of his brother Charles, leaving him the only male child yet living from his father's two marriages. However, Washington's health remained excellent throughout the year, and in fact he was planning another arduous business trip in the spring of 1800 to what in his youth had been called the Ohio Country. But on the morning of December 13, Washington awoke with a sore throat. He was concerned, but not alarmed, and went about his routine managerial chores throughout the day. During the ensuing night his condition worsened drastically, and the first of three physicians was summoned at daybreak. Their ministrations were unavailing. Washington declined throughout the day, and by late afternoon he sensed that he would not survive. As darkness engulfed Mount Vernon, Washington slipped in and out of consciousness. Near midnight on December 14, 1799, he died at age sixty-seven. Today it is believed that he perished from acute epiglottitis, which is caused by a virulent bacteria.[2]

On the day after Christmas, the capital grieved for Washington, thought by most in his generation to have been the indispensable man who had saved the Union both in war and peace. Walking behind a black-draped, empty coffin (Washington had been interred at Mount Vernon) and a riderless horse wearing Washington's saddle, President Adams, the members of Congress and the judiciary, and Alexander Hamilton led a vast procession from Congress Hall to the German Lutheran Church. Behind the dignitaries came hundreds of veterans and numerous militia companies, marching to muffled drums. More than 10,000 onlookers were estimated to have lined the streets to pay homage. Another 4,000 mourners crowded into the capacious church. They heard the best remembered of the hundreds, perhaps thousands, of eulogies that were delivered across the grief-stricken nation: Henry Lee, a cavalry colonel under Washington in the late war, pronounced him to have been "first in war, first in peace, and first in the hearts of his countrymen."[3]

Politics had taken a holiday after word arrived in Philadelphia of Washington's passing, but shortly thereafter the new year—1800, the presidential election year—dawned. Adams had returned from Quincy to the capital that fall harboring oppressive doubts about his chances of winning reelection. Not only had the war hysteria abated, but signs were abundant that the Federalists' electoral magic was waning. In a recent election the party, for the first time, had lost control of the New Jersey legislature. In the North, once an unassailable bastion of Federalist strength, the Republicans now held a majority of seats in three congressional delegations and that autumn they won the gubernatorial election in Pennsylvania. Disquieting cracks had appeared even in New England. In Vermont, Matthew Lyon, a former congressman who had been jailed under the Sedition Act, had just been reelected, despite having to campaign from an unheated jail cell in rural Vergennes.[4]

Nevertheless, the Federalists were not without hope. They had done well overall in the congressional elections both in 1798 and 1799 and remained in control of Congress. In fact, the party's six-seat edge in the House of Representatives on the eve of the XYZ affair had swelled to a twenty-seat majority by that autumn. In part, this resulted from striking gains in the South, which prompted Jefferson to moan that there was "a great deal of federalism" within his state. As the presidential election approached, the Federalists held eight of nineteen seats in the Virginia delegation, half of North Carolina's, all but one of South Carolina's, and both seats allotted to Georgia.[5] Hamilton, meanwhile, rejoiced that his party still enjoyed the "Good Will" of the people. The president's peace initiative had been well received in the South while the Virginia and Kentucky Resolutions had been scorned everywhere, save for the two states that adopted the threat of nullification. If word of a favorable accord with France arrived before Election Day, or if the Federalists in Congress demobilized the army, as Adams wished, or if the party united behind the president's peace initiative, claiming that its military preparedness campaign had brought France to the bargaining table, a Federalist election triumph in 1800 was entirely possible.[6]

However, among Federalists antipathy toward Adams ran deep. Hamilton railed in private at Adams's "Vanity and Jealousy," his "Passion," and his proclivity for acting on a "momentary impulse." He called the president "wicked" and "mad." When John Marshall, newly elected to a House seat from Virginia, arrived in Philadelphia late in 1799, he immediately found evidence of conspiracies within the party to dump the president and send him home forever. Early in 1800, moreover, some Ultras even quietly confessed that they preferred Jefferson's election to four more years with Adams, and a few appear to have believed that the party would be in a better position to rehabilitate itself were it to become an opposition party.[7]

Dogged by such rancor, it is hardly surprising that the party imploded that spring. The catalyst was a crushing defeat in the election of the New York legislature in April. Adams had captured all twelve of New York's electoral votes in 1796 and had won the presidency by three votes. But now he was certain to lose New York in 1800, for in that state, as in ten others, the assembly—now the Republican assembly—chose the state's presidential electors. No one could doubt that every New York elector would be a Republican, and as early as May some—including Abigail Adams—predicted this development would result in the failure of the president's bid for reelection.[8] Many factors contributed to the Federalist debacle. For one thing, the Federalists were resented for the higher taxes and the Alien and Sedition Acts that they had brought into existence. In addition, as Abigail Adams perceptively noted, many had come to see the party as an unpopular bastion of Francophobia and Anglophilia. Furthermore, New York's Republicans were better organized and led, and they had a surer feel for the modern style of political practices. While General Hamilton, the state's preeminent Federalist, was distracted by his military responsibilities, Aaron Burr guided the Republicans with the art of a thaumaturge. He was at least partially responsible for constructing a communications network that flowed downward from a central panel to district and ward committees. One observer noted that Burr "kept open house" for nearly two months, providing beverages and sleeping quarters for party workers who toiled around the clock. He also arranged, and often presided over, regular committee meetings at Martling's Tavern, a favorite Republican watering hole that they called the "wigwam." (Federalists labeled it the "pig sty.") Furthermore, Burr fielded a slate of candidates with name recognition, including a former governor, a Revolutionary War general, and the postmaster of the United States. The Federalists, in contrast, nominated lawyers, bankers, and prosperous Manhattan businessmen, supercilious sorts in "kid gloves [who] cannot shake hands with an honest man who is poor," according to one Republican. Burr also worked hard at turning out the vote. On election day he sent German-speaking party workers into the ward inhabited by numerous German immigrants to encourage them to vote, ran a caravan of "carriages, chairs, and waggons" to the polls, and personally worked for ten hours in the key Seventh Ward in New York City, micromanaging every phase of the proceedings. Later, one observer attributed the Republican victory to "Col. Burr's management and perseverance."[9] The First Lady said it all when she noted that the Republicans "laid their plans with more skill than their opponents."[10] Both might have added that Burr was an early and successful practitioner of the art of democratic politics.

However, the Federalists were undone by more than organizational shortcomings. Capturing control of the state assembly hinged largely on winning in New York City, where by the late 1790s there were twice as many propertyless as propertied voters. This sector of the electorate, which had supported ratification and the Federalist Party throughout

Washington's first term, had been shifting toward the Republican Party during recent years. Hamilton attributed their voting habits to class bias, and he appears to have been correct. Every "election in the view of the common people [is] a question between the Rich & the Poor," he sighed in 1796, and indeed in the city's elections that year two-thirds of those who possessed no property voted Republican.[11] That meant trouble for the Federalists. They had once been seen as a forward-looking faction that could, with some justification, claim to have saved the Union, and with it the American Revolution, and they were widely credited for the prosperity in the 1790s. But the Federalist Party now appeared to increasing numbers of workers to advance a reactionary agenda. To many who earned a living through manual labor, the Federalists seemed to be home to the gentry that had always scorned those who worked with their hands. To growing numbers, the Federalist Party represented the interests of stock-jobbers, speculators, great merchants, and the leisured gentility, those whose wealth—like that of Andrew Oliver before the American Revolution—was derived, as one worker put it, from "money at interest, rents . . . and fees that are fixed on the nominal value of money." Like the Olivers of yesteryear, New York's elite abhorred a loose money policy with its inherent inflationary effects, measures that often were beneficial to poor and middling workers. A writer in 1799, who styled himself "A Laborer," explained to workers that "the advantages the Few receive from the scarcity of money" were legion, but such a money policy "brings the Many into wants and necessities and obliges them to come to them [the elite] for justice, mercy, and forbearance." Mechanics, together with the propertyless, were crucial in pushing the Republican Party over the top in New York in the spring of 1800.[12]

Immediately after the setback in New York, Adams took the step that he had long wished to take. He dismissed Pickering and McHenry, the latter in a stormy session in the president's office. On the face of it, Adams appears to have acted spontaneously, flying into a rage when the secretary of war disagreed with him over a trivial matter. Many contemporaries, and some scholars, have held to this view, contending either that Adams was habitually at the mercy of his emotions or that all of his pent-up fury toward his untrustworthy and reproachful cabinet suddenly burst forth. There can be little question that the scene in the president's office was not pretty. Adams heaped one recrimination atop another, telling McHenry that he was no better than a simpering sycophant of Hamilton, and charging that he had repeatedly betrayed the president's trust. Working himself into a lather, Adams railed that Hamilton was deceiving and manipulative. Hamilton, he went on, was "devoid of any moral principle—a Bastard, and . . . a foreigner." Perhaps thinking that he could say nothing more shocking to a lickspittle of Hamilton, Adams told McHenry that "Mr. Jefferson is an infinitely better man; a wiser man, I am sure." Adams doubtless said more than he intended, but appearances notwithstanding, it is likely that Adams acted with calculation in choosing this moment to rid himself of these two unfaithful advisors. He sought to distance himself from the Ultra Federalists who were identified in the popular mind as pro-British warmongers who were responsible for the Alien and Sedition Acts. While he knew that discharging Pickering and McHenry might further split his fissured party, Adams gambled that his bold step, together with his peace initiative, would solidify his reputation as a nonpartisan chief executive. Like Washington before him, he hoped the populace would see him as a president above party who acted solely in the national interest. That his was not an impromptu act appears likely because of other steps that he took that spring. Against the wishes of the extremists in his party, President Adams pardoned John Fries, and two confederates, who had been sentenced to death for having led a rebellion in Pennsylvania against the taxes occasioned by Federalist military policies. The president also exercised his executive authority to demobilize the Provisional Army. He took these steps because he thought them proper, but also because he believed they offered the best hope—indeed, virtually his only hope—of winning reelection in 1800.[13]

This series of acts drove the wedge deeper between the president and the Ultras within his party. For instance, Sedgwick, who feared that Adams had paralyzed the party on the eve of the election, conspired that spring with Pickering and Wolcott to have the Federalist caucus dump the president in favor of Oliver Ellsworth, a delegate to the Constitutional Convention who had been appointed by Washington to be the chief justice of the Supreme Court.[14] Yet despite the abhorrence of the Ultras, Adams remained popular with many, perhaps most, Federalists. Marshall, Jay, and Harrison Gray Otis publicly endorsed his leadership, and in the course of that year Noah Webster authored a pamphlet that heaped abuse on party members who grumbled about the president. Many in the party firmly believed—as a stalwart from Massachusetts put it—that after "a Life of painful energies for the salvation of his country," Adams deserved their full support, and numerous faithful remained convinced that he possessed the skill and experience to be an effective chief executive. Others saw him as perhaps the only Federalist who could be elected president. Following Washington's demise, Adams was the most popular living Founder in the eyes of many. Furthermore, Adams enjoyed the solid backing of his party in New England, which controlled nearly one-quarter of the votes in the electoral college. Thus, that spring the Federalist congressional caucus nominated Adams and Charles Cotesworth Pinckney, whose brother had been on the national ticket four years earlier, and enjoined the party electors to support the two candidates equally. But because the caucus did not designate Adams as its clear-cut presidential nominee, dark rumors swirled immediately that Hamilton and his followers connived at what Jefferson called "hocus-pocus maneuvers." Allegedly, their intention was to secure all of New England's votes for Pinckney and Adams, but to betray the president in the middle or southern states, leaving the South Carolinian the winner by one or two votes. Given the well-known hatred that separated Adams and Hamilton, the stories resonated as truthful with contemporaries, a judgment that many historians have shared. Adams certainly believed the palaver. Indeed, as the firings of McHenry and Pickering came hard on the heels of the congressional caucus, it is likely that the timing of their dismissal was linked to Adams's belief that his two disloyal secretaries were involved in the machinations to deprive him of reelection.[15]

The Republican caucus met eight days after the Federalists acted. It renominated Jefferson and Burr, their ticket in 1796, but designated Jefferson as its choice to be president. Burr, who had not sought the nomination in 1800, evinced a nonchalance—one might even say a disinclination—at the prospect of serving four years in the dreary office of vice president. Burr had been humiliated four years earlier, when friends in Virginia had encouraged his candidacy, only to fail to support him, leaving him to finish dead last among the four party nominees, receiving but a scant few votes more than Samuel Adams, who had not been a contestant.[16] This was an especially bitter pill for a man such as Burr who already had enjoyed a lustrous career. The scion of an academic family—his father and grandfather were presidents of Princeton—Burr was orphaned while an infant. Raised by relatives, he went on to graduate from Princeton at age sixteen and two years later, in 1775, abandoned his legal studies to enlist in the Continental army. He soldiered with distinction for four years, enduring the agonizing march to Quebec, and fighting under Benedict Arnold in the disastrous attack on that citadel. He also fought in New York and New Jersey, and suffered through the bitter winter at Valley Forge. Health problems—he was troubled by chronic nausea and headaches—forced him to resign his commission in 1779. When he was well again, Burr briefly lived the life of a playboy before settling down and marrying the uncommonly well-educated widow of a British officer, a woman who was ten years his senior and already the mother of five children. The decade after he left the army

was a period of solid achievement for Burr. He completed his legal studies and emerged as an esteemed lawyer with a flair for winning over
juries. When he turned to politics, his glib and facile manner, as well as
his assertive intelligence, won others to his side. He rose steadily, winning election to the New York assembly in 1784 and appointment as attorney-general five years later. In 1791 he unseated General Schuyler,
Hamilton's father-in-law, to capture election to the United States Senate. Burr was attractive in many ways. Although slender and small of stature, eyewitnesses spoke of his well-proportioned physique. He remained
handsome in middle age, with thinning dark hair and penetrating hazel
eyes. Some commented on his elegant manner, and one observer concluded that his striking appearance and assured and lofty demeanor naturally granted him a "kind of dominion" over others. In 1800, Burr was yet
a young man, only forty-four years of age. Even if he served as vice president for eight years, he then would be five years younger than Washington, and ten younger than Adams, when those two had entered the
presidency. Given his enviable record of achievement and leadership, and
what appeared to have been a keen sense of political realities, Burr in 1800
seemed, next to Jefferson, to be the American politician with the most
golden prospects for a long, successful future in public life.[17]

In 1796 Jefferson had presented himself as a reluctant candidate.
There was no such posturing in 1800. While he never declared himself
an aspirant, in numerous letters that year Jefferson assayed the political
situation, ruminated on strategy, cultivated Republicans in the middle
states and New England, where the election could be won if the party
made inroads in traditional Federalist strongholds, and outlined his constitutional philosophy. Nor was this the real beginning of Jefferson's quest
to win election in 1800. When he learned that Adams had retained
Washington's cabinet, Jefferson concluded that Hamilton would check
the new president's independence. That belief was confirmed in
Jefferson's mind when, a few weeks later during the special session of
Congress in 1797, Adams made his first truculent speech regarding France.
From that moment forward, Jefferson was convinced that Adams was
more partisan than he had previously supposed. Now certain that the
president, and the Federalists who surrounded him, were "turned towards war" with France, Jefferson thereafter appears to have begun to
lay plans for a campaign for the presidency. His first object had been to
preserve the peace, but he also sought to blacken the reputations of
Hamilton and Adams. That summer he provided financial assistance to
James Callender, the scandalmongering pamphleteer who, as Jefferson
must have known, was gathering materials for an exposé of Hamilton's

extramarital affair with Maria Reynolds. Later, the vice president visited Callender at his residence to discuss the possibility of retaining his services. Eventually Jefferson not only paid Callender a modest retainer but lined up other party figures who provided what the writer later said was a handsome fee. Soon Callender pounded away at Hamilton, portraying him as corrupt and sordid. He also worked over Adams, denigrating him as "that scourge, that scorn, that outcast of America" and as "a repulsive pedant, a gross hypocrite, and an unprincipled oppressor [who] . . . in private Life . . . [was] one of the most egregious fools on the continent." Callender additionally blasted Adams as a deranged monarchist who, if reelected, planned to proclaim himself king of the United States.[18]

While Callender took the low road, Jefferson addressed philosophical issues. As the campaign of 1800 drew near, some of what he said bore a resemblance to the Anti-Federalist critique of the Constitution and hinted at constitutional revision. Overall, however, Jefferson spoke not of rewriting the Constitution but of applying what had been produced at the Philadelphia Convention in such a manner that the reach of the national government would be limited and its touch light, the system of governance that he believed had been intended by the Revolutionary generation. He saw his mission as one of rescuing the states from destruction by arousing them to defend the rights that in the recent "temporary frenzy" had slipped away. He spelled out his commitment to a strict construction of the Constitution, the preservation of the states, and state sovereignty in areas "unquestionably remaining with them." The "true theory of our constitution," he added, was that "the states are independent as to everything within themselves, & united as to everything respecting foreign nations." Confine the role of the national government largely to foreign affairs, he urged, but first disentangle "our affairs . . . from those of all other nations, except as to commerce." He specifically denounced two Federalist programs, Hamilton's fiscal system, which he believed had spawned a dangerous corruption, and the Provisional Army, which he feared threatened despotism. Jefferson obliquely proposed one actual change to the Constitution. The "object" of the American Revolution, he said, had been to establish a "government by representatives, elected by the people at *short* periods." The maxim in 1776 had been " where annual elections end, tyranny begins.'" The unhappy decade of Federalism, he said, had demonstrated the wisdom of the Founders.[19]

Adams and Jefferson are usually portrayed as remaining on the sidelines in this election, and in contrast with the candidates in presidential elections from 1896 onward they were inactive. However, unlike four years earlier, these two candidates actively sought to influence the out-come of the election. Adams wielded his presidential authority to shape events and opinion, reshuffling his cabinet and pardoning the tax rebels in Pennsylvania. Jefferson was equally active, and he too camouflaged political actions in the course of carrying out his duties as vice presi-dent. His shadow also loomed over the Republican press campaign, and he sought not only to mobilize key adherents but to arouse voters. At one point, for instance, he implored Governor James Monroe in Vir-ginia to organize "spontaneous" public demonstrations in his behalf along the route from the capital to Monticello during his trip home fol-lowing the spring adjournment of Congress. But neither formally cam-paigned, leaving that to others, who mostly sought to influence the congressional elections and selection of state assemblies. Burr, however, was active, characteristically approaching the election in a manner that soon would become habitual with nineteenth- and twentieth-century politicians. For example, over a three-day period he visited each ward in New York City, where he engaged in the unprecedented act of soliciting votes through addresses to large audiences.[20]

While Adams and Jefferson kept a low profile, their parties were busy. They aimed at establishing greater party discipline than had prevailed in the presidential contest four years earlier. The candidates were nomi-nated in congressional caucuses, which took the additional step of in-structing the electors how to cast their ballots. Activists in both parties also sought to secure the selection of party loyalists to serve in the elec-toral college, hopeful of preventing a repeat of 1796, when nearly one-fifth of all electoral votes had been cast for men who were not the nominee of either party. Both Federalists and Republicans additionally endeav-ored to cobble together national networks for sharing information. News-papers also sprang to life that year that were designed in part to remind the partisan faithful and their electors that they were "pledged" to sup-port the party's nominees.[21]

Each party had a discernible message that it presented to the public. The Federalists continued to capitalize on Washington, portraying him as committed to the party's program. Moreover, like a modern party, Federalists stressed that peace and prosperity had prevailed under their stewardship, and their speakers and editors savaged their foes. They por-trayed Jefferson as weak and cowardly for having avoided military ser-vice during the War of Independence and for having fled the approaching British soldiers who had descended on Monticello in June 1781. The Declaration of Independence, they said, was less the handiwork of Jeffer-son than the product of Congress and its committees. "Citizen Jefferson," as he was derisively labeled, was limned not merely as a "Jacobin" but as the puppet of France. He was branded an atheist, and the voters were told that God's wrath would be visited on a nation with such a leader.[22] Others portrayed him as an ignoble hypocrite. While he "writes and spouts incessantly about . . . the *danger of power*," it was said, Jefferson in fact was a "domestic monarch" who wielded absolute authority over a horde of slaves at his estate.[23] Whispers also abounded—the rumors did not appear in print, but John and Abigail Adams heard them—of a long-standing sexual relationship between Jefferson and one of his female chattel at Monticello.[24] The Federalists had long utilized fasts and feasts as a means of shaping opinion, and they had earlier seized on Washington's Birthday and the Fourth of July for festive celebrations filled with partisan oratory. They continued many of these practices in 1800, but what set this election apart was that the Republicans appropriated these tactics. They, too, held parades and barbecues near election time, staged rallies to celebrate the demobilization of the Provisional Army, and on Independence Day proclaimed Jefferson's authorship of the Declaration of Independence at numerous dinners and picnics.[25] The Republicans emphasized their commitment to small government, and depicted the Federalists as counterrevolutionaries who sought to decimate the gains of the American Revolution. According to the Republicans, the Federalists wished for nothing more than to reestablish monarchic and aristocratic rule across the land and to reconnect America with the former mother country.[26] They portrayed President Adams as a monarchist and broadcast the canard that he hoped to arrange the marriage of one of his sons to the daughter of George III, creating a dynasty that linked the United States and Great Britain.[27]

One activist who did not remain on the sidelines during this campaign was Hamilton. In October he published a *Letter from Alexander Hamilton, Concerning the Public Conduct and Character of John Adams, Esq., President of the United States*, a fifty-four-page diatribe that for scurrility rivaled anything that Callender had written about the president. Redolent with contempt, Hamilton maintained that Adams was unfit to be president: His vanity and jealousy distorted his judgment; his choleric temper was ungovernable; he was given to eccentric, unpredictable, and inexplicable behavior. Hamilton hinted at what others had said outrightly—President Adams was mentally unstable. Much of the pamphlet evaluated Adams's career after he left Congress in 1777. Hamilton charged that he was vastly overrated. He wrote that Adams had made only modest contributions in the negotiations that resulted in the Treaty of Paris and that many of the diplomatic choices he made as president had been impetuous, misguided, and potentially damaging to the nation. Whereas Washington's style had been to make decisions only after consultation and painstaking deliberation, Adams acted unilaterally. Washington's judgment had been unerring, but Adams had repeatedly blundered, and never more so than when he sent envoys to Paris in 1799. Hamilton's case against Adams boiled down to five charges. The president, he wrote, had mishandled America's relations with France, was wrong to dismiss McHenry and Pickering, erred egregiously in pardoning Fries and the anti-tax rebels in Pennsylvania, divided the Federalist Party, and by his "unfounded accusations" against leading Federalists had furnished the Republican Party with "deadly weapons" to use against its adversaries.[28]

Why had Hamilton taken the extraordinary step of publicly venting his grievances? He said he acted to defend his own character, which had been besmirched by Adams's scurrilous charges and by pamphleteers who had utilized the ammunition provided by the president. That was unconvincing. While Adams indeed had impugned Hamilton's character in private, he had never uttered any public criticism of the inspector general. Hamilton's explanation left unsaid why he chose to publish his philippic in the midst of the presidential campaign. It is tempting to think that Hamilton, a man of volatile passions, was overwrought and so bent on revenge against Adams that he acted irrationally, damaging his political party and ruining his most cherished ambitions.

Hamilton's hot-blooded nature can hardly be denied, but such an explanation is not entirely satisfying. While he sometimes acted capriciously, more often a calculating and cunning pragmatism shaped his behavior. His *Letter* more likely sprang from that same savvy propensity. While many Federalists exuded pessimism about the outcome of the election, Hamilton never gave up hope, and his vilification of Adams issued from his desire to lay the groundwork for Pinckney's eventual selection as president. The party caucus had instructed each Federalist elector to cast his two ballots for Adams and Pinckney, and Hamilton urged such a course in his *Letter*. If everything broke just right, Adams and Pinckney would deadlock with a majority of the electoral votes, throwing the issue to the House of Representatives. Thus, the audience that Hamilton addressed were the congressmen who might decide the election. Like a lawyer pleading a matter before a jury, Hamilton built a case that Adams was negligent, emotionally unstable, hopelessly churlish, and temperamentally ill-suited for the presidency. If Adams and Pinckney tied for the lead, and if his sulky accusations succeeded in winning over only one congressman, Hamilton would have helped engineer

Pinckney's election, and Major General Hamilton, the king maker, might once again exert sway within a Federalist administration. Furthermore, yet a young man of forty-three, Hamilton's political fortunes would be rehabilitated.

Voting began in some states as early as October, but when people spoke of "election day" in 1800, they referred to December 4, the date set for the electors to assemble in their respective capitals and cast their ballots. As the date for balloting in the electoral college drew near, President Adams once again was on the road, journeying south from Quincy. However, his destination on this journey was the new national capital, the Federal City, or Washington, as most had taken to calling it. The ten-year deadline imposed by the Residency Act for the completion of the capital had been met and the government had begun to move the previous spring soon after Congress adjourned. Adams had traveled to the muddy little village on the Potomac in June, his first trip into the South, and had been buoyed by the friendly crowds that greeted him as he journeyed into Maryland and twice crossed into Alexandria, Virginia. He stayed only long enough to look around a bit, then hurried to Massachusetts for his customary lengthy vacation. When he returned to Washington in November, Adams moved into the unfinished President's House, as the capital's designers referred to it.[29] On his first night there, the lonely president wrote to his wife, still in Quincy, about the prospect of living in a house that in time all knew would be an historic site. "May none but honest and wise Men ever rule under this roof," he said, a wish that subsequently was inscribed on one of the White House mantelpieces.[30] Two weeks following his arrival, President Adams delivered the first State of the Union Address to a Congress meeting in the North Wing—or Senate portion—of the domeless capitol.

The First Lady, who wished to see the new capital and to be with her husband during what both suspected would be the final 100 days of his long career of public service, arrived in mid-November. Her introduction to the area was inauspicious. Her driver became lost between Baltimore and Washington and spent hours riding in circles through the wooded moraine in search of the proper road. Once she saw Washington, an implacably shabby and mosquito-infested settlement, Abigail questioned the wisdom of having undertaken the arduous journey. Nor did her first glimpse of the President's House improve her spirits. The grounds looked like a war zone, with tall mounds of discarded building materials standing amidst ruts plowed by heavy wagons. Only six of the thirty rooms were more or less completed, and workmen were everywhere, hammering, sawing, plastering, and painting. The dust and noise were overwhelming, and she could not escape the smell of fresh cut wood mingled with wet mortar. What is more, the mansion, based on plans for an English gentryman's country estate, was too large, she concluded. It was twice the size of her church back in Quincy, she complained, and the capacious mansion swallowed her modest collection of furniture. The First Lady thought it a castle, and like most medieval strongholds it was poorly lighted and impossible to heat. Although she had nothing good to say about the new city of Washington, Abigail at least thought it preferable to nearby Georgetown, which she called the "dirtiest hole I ever saw."[31]

Jefferson arrived in Washington about the same time as the president and took up lodgings in Conrad and McMunn's boarding house, at the corner of New Jersey Avenue and C Street, a short walk from the Capitol. If the Adamses found their residence wanting, the vice president was not the least chagrined by his. Not only did a virgin forest border his neighborhood, but the capital's rusticity was hardly disappointing to a rural planter who professed a hearty dislike for cities. Jefferson lived simply. While he had a parlor and his own bedroom— roughly 300 square feet of private living space—he shared a dining table with up to thirty congressmen. All were Republicans, mostly old acquaintances, and some had been his comrades in earlier political battles.[32]

Until the electoral college met, no one could know the outcome of the election. After New York's canvass in May, the cloying smell of defeat dogged most Federalists, but to the very end Adams clung to the rapturous illusion that an upset was possible. Some party members also believed the president would squeak by, while others anticipated a narrow victory by Pinckney.[33] At least four states, New Jersey, Maryland, Pennsylvania, and South Carolina, were thought to be too close to call, but what made the outcome especially difficult to foretell was that each elector was to cast two ballots. Most observers could make a reasonable guess regarding each elector's first vote. The second vote, however, was tantamount to a wild card.

Rumors about the likely electoral college tally had eddied about the new capital throughout the autumn, but finally, eight days after the electors met, the *National Intelligencer* broke the news that Jefferson and Burr had triumphed. The newspaper based its call on the results from only thirteen states, but it seemed definitive, as the Federalists had little or no support in the three states yet to be heard from, Georgia, Kentucky, and Tennessee. "Mr. Jefferson may, therefore, be considered our future President," the newspaper exclaimed, an assessment that was confirmed a couple days before Christmas when the last of the results trickled in. Although the ballots remained sealed and would not be opened and officially tabulated for another six weeks, the outcome of this election was a secret that could not be kept. Jefferson and Burr had in fact won, in a manner of speaking. They had tied with seventy-three votes each. Adams had run third with sixty-five votes, one more than Pinckney received, for a Rhode Island elector had broken ranks and cast his second vote for John Jay, to ensure that Adams would not be nosed out by his fellow Federalist. The Federalist domination of Congress also ended. Their twenty seat majority vanished. The Republicans would control the Seventh Congress, which—given the odd rules that prevailed in those days—would not assemble until late autumn in 1801, a long year away.[34]

Discerning popular sentiment in 1800 is treacherous, especially with regard to the presidential race. Political parties were new, and their shape and organization primitive. Many freemen were disenfranchised for failing to meet the prescribed property qualifications, and women and free blacks everywhere were denied the vote. In addition, few electors were popularly elected. The Philadelphia Convention never intended that the presidency be the result of a national referendum, and if the election of 1800 mirrored popular opinion, it was more through accident than design. That said, it appears that the country renounced the Federalist Party more than it rejected President Adams. While the electoral college outcome in three-fourths of the states in 1800 was precisely as it had been four years earlier, Adams ran appreciably better in Pennsylvania and North Carolina than he had in 1796. Jefferson made a substantive gain in only one state, New York, where as expected he captured all twelve votes. Outside New York, Jefferson received seven fewer votes in 1800 than in 1796. He lost six votes in Pennsylvania and three in North Carolina, partially offsetting those losses by gaining one vote in both Maryland and Virginia. Thus, New York was the key, just as Abigail Adams had predicted when she learned in May that the Republicans had won control of the state assembly.[35]

In a country in which nearly everyone engaged in farming and 95 percent of the population lived in bucolic rural areas, this election turned on what transpired in New York City, where the full slate of thirteen Republican legislative candidates had won election, providing the party with a slim majority in the state assembly. This municipal clout not only presaged what would occur in many future presidential elections, but it was merely the latest example of the political weight of an urban center. The American Revolution would have been inconceivable without metropolitan protests, including the destructive attacks on Oliver's and Hutchinson's property, the bloody Boston Massacre, the carefully orchestrated Boston Tea Party, and the anti-tea demonstrations in Philadelphia, New York, and Charleston. Nor could the Constitution have been ratified without the solid support of the great urban ports. It was fitting, too, that the election hinged on the outcome in New York, for what occurred in the city was a harbinger of what was to come in the early years of the new century. Haughty gentility crashed under the weight of popular new democratic practices and techniques. With great clarity, the death knell sounded for those who were seen in the popular mind as roadblocks to the fulfillment of the American Revolution—for to most in this generation the Revolution was an epic undertaking to eradicate the political stranglehold of a small patronizing, privileged elite, enhance individual opportunity, thwart a central government that grasped at greater power and control, and permit ordinary people to structure their lives largely free of interference by the state.[36]

Paradox was evident, too, in that Adams, a city dweller during most of his adult life, lost the election to Jefferson, a ruralite who never hid his enmity for cities, as a result of an urban contest. Furthermore, Adams, who was neither beloved nor roundly despised, and who hoped above all to stand above partisanship, paid the price in New York City for his identification with the political party under whose banner he ran. Although Adams would have been the last to admit it, his defeat in 1800 was also the bitter harvest of his own shortcomings as a leader. However, in some respects he was simply unlucky, and in a race as tight as that of 1800 several factors beyond his control contributed to his loss. He was the first presidential candidate to fall prey to the winner-take-all policy of presidential electoral practices. In New York, the pivotal state, the electors were chosen by the combined votes of the two houses of the legislature, where the Republicans held a majority of eighty-five seats to sixty-four. Had New York's electoral votes been distributed proportionately, Adams would have edged Jefferson in the electoral college tally by seventy votes to sixty-eight. Furthermore, Adams was the first to be injured by the three-fifths clause in the Constitution. Had slaves not been counted in the allocation of electoral college seats, Adams would have nosed out Jefferson by a sixty-three to sixty-one margin.[37]

Adams also may have been damaged, perhaps badly, by not learning before election day of the success of his peace initiative. In large measure, he bore responsibility for this turn of events. He had failed to face down the Ultra Federalists and see to the embarkation of the commissioners before the autumn of 1799, eight long months after he announced the endeavor. Once the three commissioners reached France, the talks proceeded quickly and an accord was reached in October 1800. At the Chateau Mortefontaine north of Paris, the American envoys and the diplomats who served France's new ruler, Napoleon Bonaparte, signed the Convention of 1800, which established peace between the two nations by permitting the United States to trade in noncontraband items with all belligerents in the European war. The accord vindicated Adams's diplomacy. Believing that his peace initiative had spared the fragile nation a ruinous war, Adams thereafter referred to it as the "most splendid diamond in my crown" of achievements in a quarter century of public service. Had news of this diplomatic triumph arrived before election day, some electoral votes may have been changed. By the time the Senate began to consider the treaty, Hamilton at last understood the political value of the accomplishment. The Convention of 1800, he remarked, demonstrated that the "Foederal[ist] Administration" had successfully "steered the vessel through the storms raised by the contentions of Europe into a peaceable and safe port." Unfortunately for President Adams, word of the diplomatic achievement did not reach the United States until January 1801. In a sense, the surly Pickering had the last laugh on Adams. The secretary of state's stonewalling in the summer of 1799 had delayed the departure of the American envoys for nearly sixty days. The Senate ratified the treaty—with reservations—roughly sixty days after election day.[38]

From the moment when the war hysteria began to recede late in 1798, and certainly from the instant of the president's stunning announcement that he would pursue a diplomatic initiative, Federalist hegemony was imperiled. Not only had the party thrived on foreign policy crises since the middle of the decade, but as the French threat appeared to evaporate in the course of 1799, many seemed to see the Federalist program in sharper focus. New taxes, a standing army, the assault on civil liberties, and what now appeared to many to have been an unwanted enchantment with Great Britain and an overarching malevolence toward France, was the undisputed legacy of the past four years of Federalist rule. Even so, the Federalists emerged unscathed in many areas. The composition of seven congressional delegations went unchanged, and the Republicans gained merely one seat in New York and Pennsylvania. Indeed, truly great shifts occurred only in Massachusetts and Virginia.

The Bay State was a nationalist, then a Federalist, stronghold for a decade and a half beginning in the mid-1780s, if not earlier. In the Sixth Congress, the Federalists controlled twelve of the state's fourteen House seats, but in the forthcoming Seventh Congress, the Republicans, who picked up four seats, would comprise nearly half the delegation. The Republicans increased their vote total in the gubernatorial race by 100 percent over the previous election and Elbridge Gerry, their nominee, received 49 percent of the vote total, carrying even Boston. The Republican congressional candidates performed best in the commercial farming regions, where the party's Jeffersonian ideology of small, unobtrusive government resonated with the children of those who had protested British taxes, and among those who believed that the up and coming had a better chance of getting ahead in a more egalitarian society. Opposition to a strong central government was equally deep in Virginia, where the Republican assembly sometimes adopted resolutions that decried those "artificers of monarchy" and "an host of commercial and wealthy individuals" who were committed to the rapid removal of "every restraint upon federal power." It likely was a fair summation of what Virginians had come to believe, especially since the Ultra Federalist excesses of 1798. Given Virginia's deep attachment to limited government, it is startling that the Federalists had controlled roughly one-fifth of the state's seats in the Sixth Congress. However, the Federalists would form only one-tenth of Virginia's delegation in the Seventh Congress.[39]

The electoral college had met. Although it was clear that Adams had been defeated, the presidency remained undecided. Jefferson and Burr had tied. The Constitution stipulated that in the event of a tie the House of Representatives would settle the outcome, selecting the president by a majority vote "from the five highest on the List." Each state was to cast a single vote, and as sixteen states now were in the Union—Kentucky, Tennessee, and Vermont had joined the original thirteen states in the course of the decade—the votes of nine states were necessary to resolve the issue. The decision fell to the old Congress, elected in 1798 and 1799, and due to sit until March 4, 1801, Inauguration Day. A majority of the congressmen were Federalists, but the Republicans controlled eight delegations and the Federalists only six. The two remaining delegations were deadlocked. Vermont had one Federalist congressman and one Republican. Five of Maryland's eight congressmen were Federalists, but one announced his intention of voting for Jefferson, evenly dividing that delegation. Thus, the Republicans were one vote short of the magic number, and the door was ajar for designing men in both parties to artfully explore every imaginable opportunity for cutting a deal.

The Republican congressional caucus in May 1800 had designated Jefferson as its choice for president. However, if Burr wanted the office, the possibility existed that he might gain it by putting together a coalition consisting of New York Republicans, other party adherents who could be swayed by promises of favors, and a substantial bloc of Federalists. After a decade of intense rivalry and hyperbolic rhetoric, many Federalists so hated Jefferson that they were feverishly anxious to keep him out of the presidency. Many doubtless shared the outlook of Sedgwick, who despite believing that Burr was "ambitious—selfish— profligate," driven by "a mere love of power," and "unrestrained by any moral sentiment," nevertheless preferred him to Jefferson. Burr hailed from a mercantile-dominated state, Sedgwick remarked, which meant that he likely understood the needs of merchants and "justly appreciate[d] the benefits resulting from [the Federalist] commercial & other national systems." However, these Federalists also believed that Burr must first agree to terms they set, and as winter increased its hold on the new capital, some such as Sedgwick set to bargaining with Burr's New York friends.[40] They were engaged in a brazen undertaking. If successful, they would deliver to Burr states from which he had failed to gain a single electoral vote and in which—as they had to know—virtually no sentiment existed for his election to the presidency. What is more, they were betraying Hamilton, for so long their paladin. Not only did they know that their conduct was against his wishes, but Burr's election almost certainly would be a fatal blow to Hamilton's national political aspirations.

Not all Federalists were cut from the same cloth. It appears that a handful may have plotted to tie up the House proceedings so that no one would win, leaving the country without a chief executive or a vice president until the just-elected Republican Congress finally assembled late that year. Other Federalists preferred only a temporary deadlock. They could exploit the inevitable brawl between Burr and Jefferson, perhaps sowing deep, even lethal, divisions within the Republican Party. Hamilton, for instance, ruminated on having his party "throw out a lure [to Burr], in order to tempt him to start for the plate, & thus lay the foundation of dissension between the two chiefs." A brief deadlock was also attractive in that it could be the means to force concessions from the Jeffersonians. That was the strategy advocated by Hamilton. Having recently labeled Adams "unfit . . . for the office of Chief Magistrate," Hamilton now termed Burr "the most unfit man in the U. S. for the office of President." He was even less suited than Jefferson, whom Hamilton accused of being a lying, scheming, hypocritical fanatic. Nevertheless, Hamilton saw the prospect of a deal with Jefferson, with whom he had dealt previously while the Assumption Bill percolated. If Jefferson would agree to maintain the Hamiltonian fiscal program, American neutrality, the United States Navy, and some Federalist appointees in his cabinet, Hamilton indicated, he would do everything within his power to bring the members of his party around to the Virginian.[41]

No one understood the temptations for chicanery better than Jefferson. In mid-December, while a wet haze of wintry clouds clung to Washington, he took steps to head off a deadlock. He wrote a cryptic letter to his fellow Republican nominee in which he appeared to suggest that if Burr stepped aside, he would be given an expanded role as vice president. Burr responded reassuringly, writing about "your administration," and in veiled language he asked exactly what Jefferson was offering in return for his concession. Burr raised the possibility of assuming some position other than, or perhaps in addition to, the vice presidency. Jefferson did not thereafter pursue the matter in print, but it stretches credulity to imagine that further talks through intermediaries did not ensue, at the very moment that Federalists were conducting discussions both with Jefferson and Burr, either directly or through emissaries. By mid-January, a month after the election's outcome was known, no bargain had been struck, but the Federalists caucused and agreed to support Burr over Jefferson.[42]

Many haunting mysteries remain for historians who explore the fervid behavior of politicians of every shade during the passionate weeks between Christmas 1800 and the following February 17, when the issue at last was resolved, but no riddle is more unfathomable than the conduct of Burr. On its face, Burr appears not to have acted overtly to defeat Jefferson. Indeed, in mid-December he categorically "disclaim[ed] all competition" with Jefferson and proclaimed his fervent wish to see his running mate inaugurated as president.[43] However, once the wheeling and dealing commenced, Burr seems to have grown opportunistic. Whereas a public endorsement of Jefferson would have abruptly settled the issue, he instead waited and watched as others intrigued, doing nothing to stop the machinations, and leaving the inescapable impression that he hoped the conniving would redound to his benefit. By not conceding the presidency, he kept "the game perfectly in [his] hand," which was precisely what he had been advised to do on Christmas Eve by a Federalist who wished at all costs to keep Jefferson from becoming president.[44] What overt actions he took—or failed to take—during these tense weeks have been lost in the mists of time. Burr never came to Washington, that much is clear. However, early in January he came to Philadelphia, where he is known to have met with Samuel Smith, a Republican congressman from evenly divided Maryland, where a turnabout of one or two members of the delegation could resolve the election. An observer at the meeting later said Burr indicated that he planned to fight to win the presidency. Afterwards, Burr returned to New York City, then proceeded to Albany for the annual meeting of the New York legislature, where he remained until the election imbroglio was resolved.[45]

While much remains unclear, what now is apparent with crystal clarity is that the prudent choice for Burr would have been to simply step aside and, like Adams before him, patiently await his chance to become president. Given Jefferson's penchant for retiring to Monticello—he had already done so on three occasions, in 1776, 1781, and 1793—the chances were good that Burr might receive the Republican nomination as early as in 1804, before he celebrated his fiftieth birthday. Furthermore, Burr had to know that if he won the election through what was popularly perceived to be a wanton political bargain struck in a dark congressional corridor, his presidency would be derailed before he took the oath of office. Backed by neither a unified party nor the good will of the populace, his presidency would have been doomed to failure. But Burr did not act judiciously, and in the end his political future was ruined. In a sense, his fate was unsurprising. Many contemporaries discerned a lubricious quality about his character. His life was colored by excess, including an avaricious pursuit of power and glory. During this election crisis, Hamilton—hardly unbiased, but an observer who had watched Burr during their lengthy political rivalry in New York— characterized him as dishonest, unprincipled, morally bankrupt, and perpetually in pursuit of "permanent power and wealth."

Aaron Burr. Oil on canvas (detail) attributed to Gilbert Stuart, about 1792–1794.

Although Jefferson was a fanatical democrat, said Hamilton, he was preferable to Burr. According to Hamilton, Jefferson would stop short of actions that would prove ruinous to his class, but Burr would do anything to satisfy his "*extreme & irregular* ambition," including playing to the "floating passions of the multitude." Although tainted by bias, Hamilton's assessment more or less tallied with the appraisals of Gouverneur Morris and John Jay, New Yorkers who also had long observed Burr.[46]

A violent snowstorm lashed Washington on Wednesday, February 11, the day set for the Senate to officially count the votes of the electoral college. That took place at noon, and the results were announced by Vice President Jefferson, the presiding officer. Thereafter, the members of the House of Representatives, who had crowded in to observe, immediately trekked to their chamber to attempt to break the Jefferson-Burr deadlock. Anticipating this turn of events, the House two days earlier had agreed to remain in session until the election was resolved and to take up no other business in the interim, not even to receive a message from the president of the United States. The snowstorm notwithstanding, only 1 of the 105 congressmen was absent. Even Maryland's Joseph Nicholson, a thirty-year-old member of the House who was seriously ill, had arranged to be carried to the Capitol on a stretcher from a distance of more than two miles so that he might vote. A Jeffersonian, Nicholson knew that in his absence the Maryland delegation would ballot for Burr by a four-to-three division. Soon after noon, the session was called to order and the first vote taken. Nicholson, lying on a pallet in an anteroom, scribbled his vote on a ballot, which his wife hurriedly fetched to Speaker Sedgwick. The initial vote revealed that the deadlock remained unbroken. As expected, Jefferson won eight states. Burr took six. Burr captured South Carolina, from which he and Jefferson had each received eight electoral votes, and Delaware, whose lone representative, James Bayard, a Federalist, could not bring himself to vote for Jefferson. Burr also won the votes of four New England states—Massachusetts, New Hampshire, Rhode Island, and Connecticut—that had not awarded him a single electoral vote but which now conspired to deny Jefferson the presidency or to force the Virginian to bargain if he was to become the chief executive. Maryland and Vermont, in effect, did not vote. The House quickly voted a second time, with a similar result. Three other votes on that cold afternoon produced no change. Two, sometimes three, congressmen switched votes, but not enough changed from one to the other aspirant to alter their state's ballot. By nightfall, fifteen ballots had been taken, and the tally had not changed. Jefferson always carried eight states, Burr six. Maryland and Vermont remained deadlocked. Six hours after it started, the House recessed so that its members could scurry through the ice and slush to their boarding houses for a hurried supper. When they returned to the candlelit chamber, the voting resumed. The votes came more slowly that night, an indication that bargaining, and perhaps some arm-twisting, ensued between ballots. But it was to no avail. At 3 A.M., the nineteenth vote taken in the space of fifteen hours revealed no movement. Some congressmen were inflexibly linked to Jefferson. Others were intransigently opposed to him. Some felt bound by a sense of personal honor to adhere to the pledges they had made in their party caucuses. Utterly exhausted, the House members called a halt until noon, February 12, only nine hours away.[47]

Thursday's voting brought no change. Nor did the balloting on Friday or Saturday. Thirty-three votes had been taken by the evening of February 14. With Inauguration Day barely three weeks away, the House deadlock appeared to be irrevocable. Ominous signs of unrest now abounded. Some spoke openly of civil war should the machinations of the Federalists prevent one of the two Republicans from assuming office. Many Republican newspapers railed that the Federalists had plotted an unacceptable "legislative usurpation" of the executive branch. The Federalist attempt to thwart the popular will could not be tolerated, several editors protested. Party organs on both sides reported that men in every section were arming and that state militia units had been placed on alert. Although many of these alarming stories were untrue—some appear to have been contrived to coax the other side into a bargain—the governors of Virginia and Pennsylvania had covertly taken steps to ready their states for the possibility of armed conflict.[48]

The act that broke the deadlock occurred that weekend, and in part because of the talk of civil war and the threat to the existence of the Union. Delaware's Bayard announced that he would abandon Burr, but as he could not bring himself to vote for Jefferson, he would cast a blank ballot. His blank ballot would mean that with only fifteen states now participating in the poll, the winner would need to carry eight states, rather than nine, to receive a majority. Jefferson had won eight states on every previous ballot. Bayard's act would make Thomas Jefferson the third president of the United States.

Five weeks earlier, Bayard had indicated that Burr was his choice, in part because he wished to adhere to the decision of his party's caucus and—as he privately noted —because he viscerally disliked Virginians in general and Jefferson in particular.[49] But as Delaware's lone congressman, Bayard had the power to determine the next president. One can only guess at the pressures to which he must have been subjected and the temptations that may have been dangled before him in January and February. For instance, once the stalemate was evident, President Adams spoke with Bayard about an appointment as the United States minister plenipotentiary to France. Thinking that the president may have hoped to strike a deal that would lead to Jefferson's election, Bayard declined the appointment, lest the public think he had been manipulated into changing his vote. Subsequently, Bayard offered four explanations for having switched to Jefferson. He said that he had been swayed by public sentiment, which he believed leaned toward the election of Jefferson. He feared a civil war should Burr, with Federalist connivance, be elected. He turned against Burr, he later remarked, because the New Yorker would not actively campaign for the presidency, a comment that is open to numerous interpretations, including the notion that Burr would not offer enough—perhaps he offered nothing—to keep Bayard in line. Finally, Bayard said that he had concluded a deal with Jefferson. This was his most plausible explanation. Bayard said that he had conferred with Jefferson through an intermediary, Samuel Smith, the Maryland congressmen with whom Burr had conferred in Philadelphia just after New Year's Day. Bayard insisted that he had secured Jefferson's agreement to more or less the very terms that Hamilton had proposed six weeks earlier: In return for Delaware not casting a vote and making him the president, Jefferson allegedly agreed not to dismantle Hamilton's public credit scheme, reduce the size of the navy, or purge the federal bureaucracy of Federalists. Jefferson steadfastly denied having made such a bargain, and Congressman Smith repudiated Bayard's claim that he served as the broker for the deal. No written evidence confirming such a bargain ever surfaced, but the presumptive evidence points to the consummation of the very compact that Bayard said was arranged. Bayard initially made the claim in a letter composed on the evening that he announced his decision, and years later in a libel trial, he testified under oath that his action resulted from a mutual agreement between himself and Jefferson.[50] Furthermore, hours after the issue was settled, Burr reported that the "feds boast aloud that they have compromized with Jefferson."[51] Finally, despite having lashed out at the Federalist program for nearly a decade, once in office Jefferson neither warred on the Hamiltonian economic system nor purged the bureaucracy of Federalists. (He appointed Republicans as positions opened, but two years into his presidency nearly half of all federal offices were occupied by Federalists.) Jefferson did pursue naval reduction, but he acted within the discretionary limits left him by legislation passed near the end of the Adams administration.[52]

Bayard's bombshell decision was revealed at a stormy Federalist caucus on Sunday afternoon, February 15. Many of Bayard's colleagues were furious that he was breaking ranks. Cries of "Traitor! Traitor!" were heard, and a vexatious debate ensued. After an hour or so, the meeting adjourned, but the Federalist congressmen reconvened later in the day. It was a closed meeting, and those who attended carefully guarded their secrets. Some scholars believe that Bayard, under intense pressure, lost his resolve and agreed to continue to vote for Burr. However, as new letters from Burr in Albany were expected at any time, a better conjecture is that Bayard merely agreed not to abstain during the ensuing balloting until it was learned what Burr had written. At noon on Monday, another cold day in the new capital, the House reconvened and promptly cast two additional ballots, their thirty-fourth and thirty-fifth since Wednesday. Bayard voted for Burr on both occasions. After only an hour or so, the House adjourned. Clearly, the leadership had decided that it was futile to continue until word from Burr arrived.

Later in the day, Burr's letters finally reached Washington. Unfortunately, they disappeared—they probably were promptly destroyed, together (one suspects) with other missives that Burr wrote that January and February—and their contents have never been determined. Clearly, however, he offered nothing or too little. Late in the day Bayard told his fellow Federalists that on the morrow he would abandon Burr after thirty-five votes, prompting Speaker Sedgwick to sigh that "the gigg is up."[53] Bayard's decision could not be kept secret. When the House met on Tuesday, February 17, an air of anticipation prevailed. As with the previous thirty-five votes, everyone in the House knew the outcome in advance, only this time the vote would be conclusive and historic. Just after noon, six days after the process was initiated, the House voted for the thirty-sixth time. Bayard—and Delaware—did not vote. Nor did any of the Federalists from Maryland, Vermont, and South Carolina cast ballots. Jefferson captured the votes of ten states and the presidency.[54]

President-elect Jefferson breathed a sigh of relief. "In the event of an usurpation," he remarked a few days later, "I was decidedly with those who were determined not to permit it." In short, he had been committed to the use of force to assume the presidency that he believed he had fairly won after years of struggle, a quest that in some measure had begun on the day that Washington signed the Bank Bill into law, ten years earlier almost to the day. Like most, Jefferson had been rocked by the ordeal in the House, but he emerged filled with hope that the "weeks of ill-judged conduct" might prove to have been worthwhile. He was heartened because what he called the "patriotic part of the federalists" had joined with the Republicans to secure his election. This, he thought, might lead to greater respect, as well as to uncustomary cooperation, between the two factions. The lesson that he drew from this bruising battle, and from the errors of the Federalists throughout the 1790s, was that if his party sought "no intemperate measures," his administration might escape the dangerous partisan tempests that so often had brought the Union to the brink of destruction throughout the past decade.[55]

14

March 4, 1801

"An Age of Revolution and Reformation"

As was his custom, Jefferson arose early on the morning of March 4, 1801, before the first streaks of light touched the black night. Before dressing, he may have soaked his feet in a pail of ice water, a medicinal practice he long had pursued at the start of each day. He took breakfast at Conrad and McMunn's, occupying, as he had all winter, the "lowest and coldest seat at a table at which a company of more than thirty men sat," as an observer noted.[1] An air of unruffled calm prevailed through the lengthy meal. Indeed, the mood was lighthearted on this festive day. After a time, the vice president politely asked to be excused and returned to his room to reread the address he was scheduled to deliver at noon. He had written the speech himself, something that President Adams often had done but that Washington always turned over to a trusted advisor. Jefferson had always written with dispatch, and in this instance he had fourteen days between the resolution of the election and Inauguration Day, ample time to write and polish his remarks.

Late in the morning booming artillery and the clatter of the drum and fife of militia units could be heard. The time for the Inaugural ceremony was at hand. Jefferson, probably with the aid of a body servant, a slave, hurriedly finished dressing, and around 11 A.M. he departed his residence to take his place in the little processional that was forming nearby. The militia led the way, followed by United States marshals. The president-elect was next in line. Behind him were several dignitaries, including Republican congressmen and two members of Adams's cabinet.

Jefferson wore a plain suit, as had his two predecessors, but unlike them he had not powdered his hair or strapped on a sword. Also unlike

Washington and Adams, he eschewed riding in a fashionable carriage drawn by a team of prancing horses, preferring instead to walk the short distance to the Capitol, a distance of several hundred yards. By shunning pomp and every symbol of elitism (a carriage, for instance, was such an expensive item that not one American in 100 in 1801 owned such a conveyance), Jefferson hoped to underscore the revolutionary triumph of republican simplicity and equality.

As Washington was devoid of brick or cobblestone streets, Jefferson strolled along an unpaved thoroughfare, dotted with tree stumps and bare bushes. His lodging was in an untidy neighborhood, about a mile and a half from the spare village that had sprung up in the vicinity of the president's residence. Only a dozen or so houses had been built in the shadow of the Capitol, seemingly plopped down at random on land where tobacco and wheat had grown only a few years earlier. Boarding houses, a hotel, and the shops of a printer, tailor, and grocer stood there as well. Most were constructed of wood, and many were as yet unpainted. Vestiges of construction dotted the landscape. Scraps of lumber stood here, a kiln there, piles of sand and dirt in between. Fetid yellow mud was everywhere, and trees that had been felled, but not removed, were plentiful. Virtually everyone agreed that the busy little town was primitive. Albert Gallatin, soon to be Jefferson's secretary of treasury, said that living conditions in Washington were "far from being pleasant or even convenient."[2] Secretary Wolcott, whom Gallatin would succeed, thought the capital unfit for human habitation.[3] Jefferson, however, had lived with endless construction at Monticello since before the war. Furthermore, as Jefferson waited for the procession to move out, he must have relished the bucolic qualities in untidy Washington. An unspoiled forest yet stood to the north and east side of the capitol, while to the south, where much of the land had been cleared, the incoming president had an unobstructed view of the Potomac, blue and quiet and on this day dotted with sails. Ahead loomed Capitol Hill. The new Capitol was impressive, though it too remained under construction. The land about it, however, retained a pastoral look and was even fenced in, though for some reason a rough rail fence had been erected that, in the estimation of Secretary Wolcott, was "unfit for a decent barnyard."[4]

The festivity unfolding in the capital was not the only celebration on this day. Many communities throughout the land solemnized Jefferson's victory, but many also commemorated the fact that it had been achieved through an electoral process, and that power was being transferred peacefully from one party to another. Poems lauding the new president were published, and songs were sung that celebrated his election. "Jefferson and Liberty" was a popular ditty, while a variant, sung to the same tune, exulted that the "Election is Liberty's race, / By which noble charter our freedom we cherish / At the helm of the nation then Jefferson place." Killingsworth, Connecticut, found a novel means of re-creating the recent election struggle in the House of Representatives. Guns were fired and toasts raised to the eight states that had stuck with Jefferson from the initial ballot forward. Thirty-six minutes later—each minute coinciding with the number of ballots required to name a win-ner—two cannon boomed and a toast was offered to Maryland and Ver-mont, whose votes had ensured Jefferson's victory. After another pause of thirty-six minutes, more artillery fire and toasts recognized the roles of South Carolina and Delaware in the final House vote. Thirty-six min-utes later, the final shots were fired, and the last toasts were drunk, in honor of the four remaining states.[5]

In Jefferson's neighborhood, a large crowd had gathered along the muddy street. The spectators on this chilly day cheered excitedly for the incoming president. Anticipation filled the air. Virtually every observer realized that a "momentous crisis" had passed and that what was about to occur, as the president-elect soon would write to a friend, was some-thing "new under the sun." This was not merely a transition of power from Federalists to Republicans, Jefferson would remark, but a revolu-tionary "chapter in the history of man," a second American Revolution.[6] At last, he appeared to say, the leap in the dark—the anxious jump that had begun in 1774 when the First Continental Congress defied the Coer-cive Acts—had ended and the nation had landed safely. Jefferson soon would write to the surviving signers of the Declaration of Independence telling those whom he knew shared his views—such as Samuel Adams— that his election was the fulfillment of what most Americans in 1776 had believed the American Revolution was intended to achieve.[7]

When Jefferson reached the Capitol, he walked immediately to the Senate chamber, a circular room with galleries that splayed along the rear and sides. The president-elect, a naturally shy person, was uncom-fortable with the cheers from spectators and his Republican brethren as he marched to the platform. His distant cousin John Marshall, the chief justice of the Supreme Court, and Vice President Burr, who had been sworn in earlier in the morning, stood in the well to greet him. The pleasantries they exchanged were perfunctory. The recent election battle in the House had strained the relationship between the incoming presi-dent and vice president, and in fact before year's end Jefferson would block Burr's patronage recommendations for New York, signaling a de-cisive break between the two.[8] Despite their family ties through the Randolph clan, Jefferson and Marshall were old adversaries. Jefferson thought Marshall a traitor to republicanism for having joined up with the Federalists. Marshall, who had soldiered during the late war and had suffered through the terrible conditions at Valley Forge, burned with a feverish loathing for young, healthy Virginians—such as Jefferson—who had not borne arms during the young nation's great crisis.[9]

Sitting on the dais waiting to speak, Jefferson had a few moments to relish the occasion. He surely must have wished that Madison could have been in attendance on this happy occasion, but he was at Montpelier with his family and gravely ill father. However, he would be coming soon. In November, he had consented to serve as secretary of state should Jefferson win the election. If Jefferson knew beforehand that Madison would be absent, he was startled to discover that President Adams was not present. Not only had Washington attended Adams's inauguration, but the president's term did not end until noon on this day. But Adams was gone, having risen early in the still, cold darkness and caught the 4 A.M. stage out of town. Embittered by his recent defeat, and unwilling to witness his adversary's moment of triumph, Adams at noon likely was a score or more miles north of Washington, en route to a permanent retirement in Quincy that he equated with a maiming obscurity.

Once home, and enveloped in the isolation of Peacefield, Adams fought with melancholy for the next several years. With barely restrained vehemence, he lashed out at those whom he thought responsible for his undoing—Washington for making Hamilton the inspector general, his treacherous cabinet, Jefferson for having failed to be a nonpartisan vice president, and mostly Hamilton, who had sought both to wreck his peace initiative and to cause his defeat in the recent election. Time meliorated his rancor, and events ultimately extinguished it altogether. Mutual friends brought him together with Jefferson in 1812, and their old friendship was restored through a lively correspondence that left Adams feeling accepted, even vindicated. His daughter's agonizing death in 1813 was a transforming experience that caused him to want to appreciate whatever time was left. John Quincy's political and diplomatic career flourished, and Adams doubtless lived vicariously through his son. Above all, with the passage of time Adams increasingly exalted in the American Revolution and the Union, and in the realization that he had played a seminal role in the success of the former and the survival of the latter. Eventually, he found happiness. Retirement, he said with feeling, was the happiest phase of his life, for he delighted in the freedom to read and write, he was free at last of the terrible stress brought on by holding office, and he relished the comforts of home, including the company of his wife.[10]

Adams was not the only dignitary who was not present. Jefferson soon noticed that Speaker Sedgwick, the arch Federalist, also had skipped the proceedings. After serving for nearly a decade in Congress, Sedgwick had not sought reelection. In his final days in the House, he fought hard for Burr and could not bear to watch Jefferson, whom he hated, enter the presidency. Like Adams, Sedgwick started home early. Eleven years younger than Adams, Sedgwick hoped for a future in public life, and soon after arriving back in Massachusetts he was appointed to the state supreme court. He held that post until his death at age sixty-two in 1808.

As Jefferson glanced about the Senate and peered toward the corners and galleries into which most members of the House of Representatives had crowded, he saw few familiar faces from the war years or the days when he had served in the Congress under the Articles. He would have liked it had Benjamin Franklin, among the first to champion an American union, been present. But Franklin had died just as Jefferson arrived in New York in 1790 to become secretary of state. While the public venerated Franklin, giving him a place nearly alongside Washington in the American pantheon, virtually every American diplomat whose path crossed Franklin's in Europe after 1776 thought him treacherous and unprincipled.[11] Jefferson was the exception. He continued to view Franklin with admiration and respect. As Jefferson waited to speak, he may have noted how many others from bygone days were gone. Some had died, and some had aged and retired. But some of those "new men" of the 1780s—like Abraham Yates—been filtered out and replaced by those from a more exalted social class.

One individual that Jefferson wished could have been present was Samuel Adams, but he had not held national office for nearly twenty years, having left long before the new Constitution went into effect. Adams, who had served continuously since the First Continental Congress, resigned at age fifty-nine a few months prior to the triumphant siege at Yorktown in 1781. He sought reelection to the First Congress under the new Constitution, but was defeated by Fisher Ames, who outpolled him even within Boston. It was the price that Adams paid for having only given lukewarm support to the Constitution. He never again sought national office (save for the electoral college), and never left Massachusetts during the last twenty-two years of his life. However, he was active politically. Adams chaired Boston town meetings and sat in the state senate throughout much of the 1780s, frequently serving as its president. He fought for the preservation of republicanism, as he like Jefferson believed it was under siege. He especially battled for a free public education for all children, which he regarded as the linchpin of a republic. In

1789, as Washington was inaugurated, Adams's efforts were crowned with success. A public school system for boys in Boston was created (with some opportunities made available for girls), and the colonial educational system—which mandated that villages with more than fifty inhabitants must provide a town school—was reestablished throughout the state. That same year Adams was elected lieutenant governor. Later in the decade he served three terms as governor, in the course of which he became the unquestioned leader of the nascent Republican Party in Massachusetts. In 1797, just as John Adams—whom he had brought into politics—was inaugurated president of the United States, Samuel Adams retired from public office at age seventy-five. The last national campaign in which Samuel Adams played an active role was that which had just concluded, and he was delighted when he received the news that his cousin had lost to Jefferson. Soon thereafter, his health began to decline precipitously, and in October 1803 Samuel Adams passed away in Boston.[12]

Jefferson never again wished to see Hamilton, whom he knew to be involved in the Federalist machinations in the House election. Hamilton had not come to Washington for that battle, and he certainly did not come south to celebrate the installation of his bitter adversary. However, Hamilton was delighted that Burr had been kept from the presidency, and of course he was aware of the deal that Jefferson likely made to win the election. In light of this, it was not surprising that Hamilton characterized the incoming Republicans as offering "a ray of hope" both that a "retraction of past [Jeffersonian] misapprehensions" could be expected and that the new president would "not lend himself to dangerous innovations."[13] Hamilton never again held public office. He practiced law, was active in state politics, and from time to time published essays on contemporary affairs, keeping alive the flickering hope of a Federalist rebirth and of a better day for his own personal political ambitions. That golden day never dawned. In July 1804, before Jefferson's first term ended, Hamilton died at age forty-seven of a gunshot wound suffered in his famous duel with Burr at Weehawken, New Jersey.

Jefferson saw his Inauguration Day not just as a time for a muted celebration of his victory over his Federalist foes, such as Hamilton and Sedgwick, but as the culmination of the American Revolution and the climactic victory over all its enemies. Most who had stood against the Revolution were long gone. One example was Andrew Oliver, who for a time had avoided politics after the night his property was pillaged by a mob in August 1765. In fact, Oliver—together with other Tories—was purged from the Council by the assembly in the immediate aftermath of the Stamp Act disorders. However, in 1770 he became the lieutenant governor under Thomas Hutchinson. By this time, he was honeycombed with bitterness. He knew that most Bostonians despised him, and he was consumed with hatred for Samuel Adams, whom he blamed for the destruction of his residence. His enmity only swelled with the publication of the Hutchinson-Oliver Letters in 1773. In his final letter on public affairs, Oliver railed at Adams as the "pimp" of the common people and deplored the "spirit of persecution [that] still rages among us" in Boston. He did not live to witness the war that he believed Adams was fomenting. Oliver died of a stroke at age sixty-eight in March 1774. Even so, the American Revolution pursued him even beyond the grave. Most of the property that he left to his heirs was confiscated by Massachusetts in 1779 to pay for the war.[14]

Thomas Hutchinson witnessed the war from London, having gone into exile six months after the Boston Tea Party. He never returned to America. His years in England were bittersweet. He consorted for a while with ministerial figures, but after a time they largely abandoned him, as if he had been the cause of their innumerable imperial and diplomatic woes. Indeed, Governor Pownall shamelessly accused him of responsibility for the Revolution through his shortsighted policies. Hutchinson lived on unhappily for five years in the British homeland that he had so revered from his actual native land in Massachusetts. Each year he found himself treated more and more as an outsider, and when some former ministers with whom he had dealt while he held power could not even remember which colony he hailed from, Hutchinson was overwhelmed with the sense that he was residing in some faraway alien land. Thirty days after the loss of Charleston in 1780, at America's low ebb in its desperate war, Hutchinson died in London of a stroke at age sixty-nine.[15]

Joseph Galloway's American Revolution experience was equally sad. When the war erupted, he retired from politics at age forty-five, declining to serve in a congress or a colonial assembly that fostered hostilities with Great Britain. But he denied that he was a Loyalist, cloaking himself in the mantle of neutrality until the autumn of 1776 when, with New York City once again in British hands and Cornwallis closing in on Philadelphia, Galloway opportunistically offered his services to the British army. For the next twenty months he served the high command as an intelligence official and additionally acted as police commissioner of occupied Philadelphia after September 1777. Late in 1778, with his teenage daughter in tow, Galloway sailed for London. His wife, estranged from him at least in part because of poor choices he had made during the American rebellion which cost the family its wealth and status, stayed on in Philadelphia and fought unsuccessfully for retention of their property. They were never reunited. Galloway remained in London for the duration of the war, grinding out one pamphlet after another in a vain effort to maintain Britain's interest in suppressing the rebellion. At war's end, nine short years after he had battled in Congress for a compromise that might have prevented the conflagration, Galloway had lost everything—his wife, his power, his exalted standing, his wealth, and his property. He lived on in exile in England in what his daughter sulfurously portrayed as "a humiliating situation," existing on a pension provided by Parliament for his Tory activities. Late in life, he pleaded with Pennsylvania to permit him to return. If he came home, he was told, he must stand trial for alleged crimes that had occurred during the occupation of Philadelphia. Unhappily, Galloway remained in England; he was seventy years old and living in Watford on Jefferson's Inauguration Day. He died two years later, perishing thirty-five days before the death of Samuel Adams, his great rival in the pivotal First Congress.[16]

Galloway was bested in longevity as in politics by his rival John Dickinson, who lived to age seventy-five in 1808. Despite never embracing independence, Dickinson served in the state government in Pennsylvania throughout the 1780s, was a delegate to the Constitutional Convention, and helped write a new constitution for Delaware four years later. In 1793, in poor health, he retired from politics, although he reemerged briefly in 1796 to defend the Jay Treaty and again in 1798 to denounce Federalist belligerence in the Quasi-War with France. Although the positions that Dickinson had taken since 1775 often clashed with Jefferson's outlook, he welcomed the Virginian's election in 1800, thinking that a Republican president was most likely to refrain from war with France. He might have liked to make the relatively short trip from Wilmington to the capital for the inauguration, but at sixty-eight and infirm—and caring for a gravely ill wife—an arduous journey was out of the question.[17]

With perhaps the exception of Jefferson, many Americans felt that no one had done more than Thomas Paine to articulate the meaning of the American Revolution and the new republican world that was being celebrated on this festive day. But he, too, was absent. Paine had left the United States three weeks before the Constitutional Convention was to meet in 1787. He did not return until a few weeks after Jefferson entered office. Paine had spent most of the interim in France, where he had played an active role in that nation's Revolution, publishing tracts in which he publicly expressed radical ideas that Jefferson voiced in private. When he learned of Jefferson's victory in 1801, Paine quickly wrote from Paris: "I congratulate America on your election. There has been no circumstance, with regard to America, since the times of her revolution, that . . . has given more general joy" in France.[18]

The ceremonial rites on this Inauguration Day were unceremonious. Wishing to emphasize their clean break with the recent past, the Jeffersonians had carefully planned the amenities so that no hint of Federalist solemnity, pageantry, or grandiloquence was visible. After entering the Senate chamber, Jefferson had simply taken his seat and waited for Vice President Burr, his successor as the president of the Senate, to gavel the Congress to order. Thereupon Jefferson, who had not yet been sworn in—that would follow his address—rose to speak.[19] This would be his most difficult moment of this long day. He had never been comfortable as a public speaker, and he must have appeared nervous as he walked to the podium and extracted his speech from an inside coat pocket. Then he slowly began to read in a nearly inaudible voice that one observer described as "almost femininely soft."[20]

Jefferson began by reaching out to the opposition, especially to the "patriotic part of the Federalists," as he had privately called those in the opposition party who had not sought to block his election. While it was imperative that he act on the will of the majority, Jefferson reassured his listeners that the "minority possess their equal rights, which equal laws must protect." As he had privately vowed to avoid intemperate behavior, he now publicly promised to support only "reasonable" measures. He pledged that his would not be an administration of intolerance and persecution, for while "We have called by different names brethren of the same principle[,] We are all republicans—we are all federalists." Having not capitalized the words "republicans" and "federalists," he was referring to ideas, not parties, and to his presumption that all Americans embraced both republican government and a sharing of power by the states and the national government.

For a decade Jefferson had led the struggle against the consolidationist aspirations of the Federalists, and he now announced the triumph of a minimalist national government. Good government was sufficiently strong if it could "restrain men from injuring one another," encourage agriculture, and protect commerce, he said. Government must do nothing to inhibit freedom of religion or press, or interfere with the natural rights of a free citizenry. It must permit a free and open political process, leave the economy to its natural rhythm, and not burden the citizenry with excessive taxation or constraining regulations. Such a government would have sufficient strength. Indeed, it would be "the strongest government on earth," for unlike monarchies and oligarchies, America's republican government would have the support of its citizens, who "would fly to the standard of the law, and would meet invasions of the public order as [their] own personal concern."

The overarching theme of Jefferson's address was that his election had been about ideas, not personalities, and that the victory of the Republican Party heralded the consummation of the American Revolution. This would be true in foreign affairs as in domestic matters, he proclaimed. Independence, Franklin and Paine had said a quarter century earlier, would mean an escape from Great Britain's wars, an aim that Washington had reiterated in his Farewell Address, and that he and Adams had struggled to attain. Jefferson addressed that matter as well. Peace prevailed, he said, and while his administration could not ensure that it would continue, he would seek to avoid troubles through a policy of "friendship with all nations—entangling alliances with none."

As the new president continued, perhaps some in the audience reflected on America's amazing journey during the previous half century. In 1754, when Jefferson had been only eleven, American statesmen had been summoned by their imperial masters to a meeting in Albany. Those in attendance, including Franklin, had urged an American union, but their hopes had been shattered both by London, which had feared the American autonomy that might result from such a step, and the unwillingness of every American province to surrender its authority to a more centralized American government. Twenty years later, in 1774, imperial policy had driven the colonists to unite, and war in turn led them to fashion a national government. Thereafter, this American Revolutionary generation had striven for a quarter century, from 1776 when Congress began to draft the Articles of Confederation until this day of Jefferson's inauguration, to define the roles of the federal government and the states. Nor was the journey completed on this happy occasion, for subsequent generations would struggle to define the limits of national authority in halting slavery's expansion, in the regulation of the economy, and in the spread of civil rights.

Deep into his Inaugural Address, Jefferson sought to give meaning to the breathtaking years that had passed since the Stamp Act first roiled the imperial waters. The American people, he asserted, had passed through "an age of revolution and reformation." It had been a real revolution, Jefferson said, for the "blood of our heroes" had been shed to gain independence, to escape the inequality, dependency, and servility of a monarchical and aristocratical old regime, and to replace it with a republican government and society that held forth the promise of self-determination and individual liberty. Yet, he seemed to say, after 1776 some had stood in the way of the fulfillment of the American Revolution, and that had occasioned a second great struggle. This was the reformation to which he had alluded, a protracted battle against those who sought the consolidation of wealth and power and who had resisted loosening society's bonds and opening opportunities for advancement and personal fulfillment.

Federalists who listened to Jefferson, or subsequently read his speech, were no less interested in understanding what had occurred, and in particular they wished to comprehend their defeat in the recent election. Some concluded that they had been out politicked, and that they had been undone by having "neglected the cultivation of popular favour," as Hamilton reflected in a postmortem.[21] Hubris led to the Federalists' downfall, John Adams said. Success had gone to their head, he remarked soon after arriving in Quincy, leading to extremist policies that "wantonly destroyed them."[22] Both Adams and Hamilton were correct, but Jefferson saw things more broadly. He believed that the Federalists had not heeded the abiding expectations of the generation that made the American Revolution, a people willing to risk all to defy one of the world's greatest powers and to endure an endless war to give birth to what they envisioned as a new world. To too many, the Federalists had come to be seen as latter-day variations of Oliver and Hutchinson and Galloway, a party that wished to leave intact too much of the bitter past. One thing more, which can be seen more clearly retrospectively. The Federalists were victims of the new politics, the surprisingly modern politics, that were taking shape. Confronted with a popular party that was identified with a founder who had authored the Declaration of Independence, the Federalists were unable to overcome the lingering suspicion that behind their bellicosity toward France lay a hidden agenda. Their taxes to finance their military preparedness aroused enmity. Their repressive Alien and Sedition Acts fomented fear and anger. In addition, the Federalists were the first to be victimized by what successful politicians in the next two centuries discovered that they must never forget: To be seen as too elite, too remote from the people, too attached to old habits, and too tethered to a bygone time, especially what most believed to be an unhappy past, was to court political disaster in the slowly democratizing United States.

Though outsiders now, many of the conservative nationalists who composed the Federalist Party were proud of their achievements. They had, as Hamilton said soon after Inauguration Day, overcome the "degraded & ruinous state of our affairs under the old confederation." In its place, "a respectable & prosperous nation" had emerged, an embryonic modern state that one day would fulfill the aspirations voiced by Washington, Adams, and Hamilton, attaining such power that it never again would be the sport of European powers.[23] Furthermore, Washington's bold policies had truly opened the trans-Appalachian West, a burning but unrealized aspiration for half a century prior to his presidency. What is more, under the guardianship of two security-conscious Federalist presidents who understood the absolute necessity for the United States to maintain genuine independence from the great powers abroad, peace with Europe had been preserved, saving lives and treasure, and likely the Union as well. However, the longest lasting legacy of the conservative nationalists—and not just those who became Federalists, but of Madison and other Republicans as well—was their Constitution, a charter that perpetuated the Union and which, by design, brought into being a political system constructed in such a manner that even modest reforms could be had only with great difficulty and deep change was rendered virtually impossible.

After Jefferson had spoken for nearly twenty minutes, he told his audience that the "voice of the nation" had spoken in the recent election. Although he did not articulate the view in this speech, Jefferson then—and always thereafter—believed that the popular will expressed in the election was tantamount to a "revolution of 1800," a realization at last that the meaning of the American Revolution was that the voice of the people was to be heard. In 1800, Jefferson believed, they had spoken for a smaller, less threatening national government. Thus, the election of 1800 ushered in a revolution "in the principles of our government as [profound as] that of 1776 was in its form."[24] The route to this new day was the road chosen by America's patriots in 1776, for they had believed that the "blessings . . . necessary to make us a happy and prosperous people" included "a wise and frugal government" that rejected tyranny and was based on the popular will. The day now had arrived when the government they wished was being installed. Its promise was considerable. Indeed, said President Jefferson, it was "the world's best hope."[25]

Abbreviations

The following abbreviations are used in the notes to designate frequently cited publications, libraries, and individuals.

AA   Abigail Adams

AC   *Annals of the Congress of the United States.* Washington, 1847–51.

AFC   L. H. Butterfield et al., eds. *Adams Family Correspondence.* 4 vols. Cambridge: Harvard University Press, 1963–.

AFP   Adams Family Papers. Massachusetts Historical Society. Boston, 1954–59. Microfilm edition.

AH   Alexander Hamilton

AJL   Lester J. Cappon, ed. *The Adams-Jefferson Letters: The Complete Correspondence between Thomas Jefferson and Abigail and John Adams.* 2 vols. Chapel Hill: University of North Carolina Press, 1961.

BF   Benjamin Franklin

DAJA   L. H. Butterfield et al., eds. *The Diary and Autobiography of John Adams.* 4 vols. Cambridge: Harvard University Press, 1961.

DGW   Donald Jackson et al., eds. *The Diaries of George Washington.* Charlottesville: University Press of Virginia, 1976–79.

GW	George Washington
HSP	Historical Society of Pennsylvania
JA	John Adams
JCC	Worthington C. Ford et al., eds. *The Journals of the Continental Congress.* 34 vols. Washington, D.C.: Library of Congress, 1904–37.
JER	*Journal of the Early Republic*
JM	James Madison
LDC	Paul H. Smith. *Letters of Delegates to Congress, 1774–1789.* 29 vols. Washington, D.C.: Library of Congress, 1976–2000.
MHS	Massachusetts Historical Society
PAH	Harold C. Syrett and Jacob E. Cooke, eds. *Papers of Alexander Hamilton.* 26 vols. New York, 1961–79.
PBF	Leonard W. Labaree et al., eds. *The Papers of Benjamin Franklin.* New Haven, Conn.: Yale University Press, 1959–.
PGW: Col Ser	W. W. Abbot et al., eds. *The Papers of George Washington: Colonial Series.* 10 vols. Charlottesville: University Press of Virginia, 1983–95.
PGW: Ret Ser	W. W. Abbot et al., eds., *The Papers of George Washington: Retirement Series.* 4 vols. Charlottesville: University Press of Virginia, 1997–99.
PGW: Rev War Ser	Philander Chase et al., eds. *The Papers of Washington: Revolutionary War Series.* Charlottesville: University Press of Virginia, 1985–.
PGW: Confed Ser	W. W. Abbot et al., eds. *The Papers of George Washington: Confederation Series.* Charlottesville: University Press of Virginia, 1992–97.
PGW: Pres Ser	Dorothy Twohig et al., eds. *The Papers of George Washington: Presidential Series.* Charlottesville: University Press of Virginia, 1987–.
PJA	Robert J. Taylor et al., eds. *Papers of John Adams.* Cambridge: Harvard University Press, 1977–.

PJM	William T. Hutchinson et al., eds. *The Papers of James Madison.* Chicago and Charlottesville: University of Chicago Press and University Press of Virginia, 1962–
PTJ	Julian P. Boyd et al., eds. *The Papers of Thomas Jefferson.* Princeton, N.J.: Princeton University Press, 1950–.
SA	Samuel Adams
TJ	Thomas Jefferson
WJA	Charles Francis Adams, ed. *The Works of John Adams, Second President of the United States: With a Life of the Author.* 10 vols. Boston: Little, Brown, 1850–56.
WMQ	*William and Mary Quarterly*
WSA	Harry Alonzo Cushing, ed. *The Writings of Samuel Adams.* 4 vols. New York, 1904–8.
WTJ	Paul Leicester Ford, ed. *The Writings of Thomas Jefferson.* 10 vols. New York: Putnam, 1892–99.
WW	John C. Fitzpatrick, ed. *The Writings of Washington.* 39 vols. Washington, D.C.: Government Printing Office, 1931–34.

Notes

Chapter 1

1. Michael Kammen, *Colonial New York* (New York, 1975), 213; Roland van Zandt, *Chronicles of the Hudson: Three Centuries of Travelers' Accounts* (New Brunswick, N.J., 1971), 52–56; Arthur James Weise, *The History of the City of Albany, New York* (Albany, 1884), 1–9, 21–22, 304–11, 321–27, 402–5.

2. For GW's account of the journey, see "Journey to the French Commandant, 31 October 1753 to 16 January 1754," *DGW* 1:130–61.

3. Fred Anderson, *Crucible of War: The Seven Years' War and the Fate of Empire in British North America, 1754–1766* (New York, 2000), 57–59. On Washington's youth, see John Ferling, *The First of Men: A Life of George Washington* (Knoxville, Tenn., 1988), 1–26; John Ferling, *Setting the World Ablaze: Washington, Adams, Jefferson, and the American Revolution* (New York, 2000), 2–24; James T. Flexner, *George Washington* (New York, 1965–72), 1:9–92; Douglas Southall Freeman, *George Washington* (New York, 1948–57), 1:15–375.

4. Theodore Draper, *A Struggle for Power: The American Revolution* (New York, 1996), 146.

5. Anderson, *Crucible of War*, 35–37; Harry M. Ward, *"Unite or Die": Intercolony Relations, 1640–1763* (Port Washington, N.Y., 1971), 11.

6. Edmund S. Morgan, *Benjamin Franklin* (New Haven, Conn., 2002), 23.

7. Esmond Wright, *Franklin of Philadelphia* (Cambridge, Mass., 1986), 29–73; Benjamin Franklin, *The Autobiography of Benjamin Franklin*, introduction and notes by R. Jackson Wilson (New York, 1981), 151. On Franklin's life, see also H. W. Brands, *The First American: The Life and Times of Benjamin Franklin* (New York, 2000); Carl Van Doren, *Benjamin Franklin* (New York, 1938); and Morgan, *Franklin*.

8. Benjamin Franklin, *Observations concerning the Increase of Mankind, Peopling of Countries, &c.*, *PBF* 4:227–34.

9. Quoted in Walter LaFeber, "Foreign Policies of a New Nation: Franklin, Madison, and the 'Dream of a New Land to Fulfill with People in Self-Control,'" in William A. Williams, ed., *From Colony to Empire: Essays in the History of American Foreign Relations* (New York, 1972), 15.

10. Wright, *Franklin of Philadelphia*, 78–79; Benjamin Franklin, *Plain Truth*, *PBF* 3:200, 203; Benjamin Franklin, *Observations*, *PBF* 4:231; BF to James Parker, March 20, 1750/1751, *PBF* 4:119; Benjamin Franklin, *A Plan for Settling Two Western Colonies*, *PBF* 5:459, 462; Gerald Stourzh, *Benjamin Franklin and American Foreign Policy* (Chicago, 1954), 42–82.

11. Wright, *Franklin of Philadelphia*, 73–89; BF to Parker, March 20, 1750, *PBF* 4:118, 5:273–75.

12. Richard B. Morris, "Benjamin Franklin's Grand Design," *American Heritage* 7 (Feb. 1956): 106.

13. Lawrence Henry Gipson, *The British Empire Before the American Revolution* (15 vols., New York, 1935–70), 5:119–22; Anderson, *Crucible of War*, 78–79.

14. Patricia U. Bonomi, *A Factious People: Politics and Society in Colonial New York* (New York, 1971), 141–48, 175; Franklin, *Autobiography*, 175; Anderson, *Crucible of War*, 79.

15. Bernard Bailyn, *The Ordeal of Thomas Hutchinson* (Cambridge, Mass., 1974), 10–29. For an excellent analysis of Hutchinson's mind and thought, see William Pencak, *America's Burke: The Mind of Thomas Hutchinson* (Washington, D.C., 1982).

16. Jack P. Greene, "An Uneasy Connection: An Analysis of the Preconditions of the American Revolution," in Stephen G. Kurtz and James H. Hutson, eds., *Essays on the American Revolution* (Chapel Hill, N.C., 1973), 32–80.

17. John Ferling, *Struggle for a Continent: The Wars of Early America* (Arlington Heights, Ill., 1993), 74–75, 79; Anderson, *Crucible of War*, 81–82; Lawrence Henry Gipson, "Thomas Hutchinson and the Framing of the Albany Plan of Union, 1754," *Pennsylvania Magazine of History and Biography* 74 (1950): 5–35.

18. BF to James Alexander and Cadwallader Colden with Short Hints towards a Scheme for a General Union of the British Colonies on the Continent, June 8, 1754, *PBF* 5:337–38.

19. Ward, *"Unite or Die,"* 5–13.

20. Jack P. Greene, "The Problematic Character of the American Union: The Background of the Articles of Confederation," in Greene, *Understanding the American Revolution: Issues and Actors* (Charlottesville, Va., 1995), 139–40.

21. Oliver M. Dickerson, *American Colonial Government, 1690–1765: A Study of the British Board of Trade* (New York, 1912), 127, 212–13; James Henretta, *"Salutary Neglect": Colonial Administration under the Duke of Newcastle* (Princeton, N.J., 1972), 303, 335–36; Ferling, *Struggle for a Continent*, 108–9.

22. Ferling, *Struggle for a Continent*, 75–79; Ward, *"Unite or Die,"* 106.

23. Benjamin Franklin, "Reasons and Motives on Which the Plan of Union Was Formed" [July 1754], *PBF* 5:399–400.

24. Quoted in William A. Williams, *The Contours of American History* (New York, 1961), 110.

25. An excellent analysis of the evolution of the Albany Plan can be found in *PBF* 5:344–46, 357–60, 366–68, 374–87.

26. Albany Plan of Union [July 10, 1754], *PBF* 5:387–92.

27. Allison G. Olson, "The British Government and Colonial Union, 1754," *WMQ* 17 (1960): 22–34; Benjamin Franklin, "Fragments of a Pamphlet on the Stamp Act," *PBF* 13:76; Anderson, *Crucible of War*, 70.

28. Gipson, *British Empire*, 5:143–66.

29. Anderson, *Crucible of War*, 181–84.

30. Gipson, *British Empire*, 7:27, 59n, 69; GW to Robert Dinwiddie, Jan. 13, 1756, *PGW: Col Ser* 2:278; GW to John Forbes, Apr. 7, 1756, *PGW: Col Ser* 2:337.

31. Ward, *"Unite or Die,"* 116–17.

32. Ferling, *Struggle for a Continent*, 200; Douglas Edward Leach, *Arms for Empire: A Military History of the British Colonies in North America, 1607–1763* (New York, 1973), 416–19.

33. Anderson, *Crucible of War*, 373–74.

34. Franklin, *Autobiography*, 176.

Chapter 2

1. See "Andrew Oliver," in Clifford K. Shipton, ed., *Biographical Sketches of Those Who Attended Harvard College* (Cambridge, Mass., 1933–75), 8:383–413.

2. James K. Hosmer, *The Life of Thomas Hutchinson: Royal Governor of the Province of Massachusetts Bay* (reprint, New York, 1972), 313; James Henretta, *The Origins of American Capitalism: Collected Essays* (Boston, 1991), 135, 137; Andrew Oliver to Thomas Whatley, July 8, 1771, Andrew Oliver Letterbook, MHS; Andrew Oliver's Property Inventory, 1774, Hutchinson and Oliver Papers Coll., MHS.

3. Gary Nash, *The Urban Crucible: Social Change, Political Consciousness, and the Origins of the American Revolution* (Cambridge, Mass., 1979), 48–50, 103, 131, 221–23; William Pencak, *War, Politics, and Revolution in the Province of Massachusetts* (Boston, 1981), 95, 133; G. B. Warden, *Boston, 1689–1776* (Boston, 1970), 102, 117, 123; John J. Waters Jr., *The Otis Family in Provincial and Revolutionary Massachusetts* (Chapel Hill, N.C., 1968), 147; Stephen Patterson, *Political Parties in Revolutionary Massachusetts* (Madison, Wis., 1973), 50–51; David Conroy, *In Public Houses: Drink and the Revolution of Authority in Colonial Massachusetts* (Chapel Hill, 1995), 182.

4. *DAJA* 1:260; Pencak, *War, Politics, and Revolution*, 169.

5. "Crèvecoeur: From 'What Is an American?'" [1782], in Merrill Jensen, ed., *English Historical Documents: American Colonial to 1776* (London, 1953–75), 9:476–79.

6. Benjamin Franklin, "Examination before the Committee of the Whole of the House of Commons" [Feb. 13, 1766], *PBF* 13:135–36, 150. Excellent accounts of the state of the American colonies in 1763 can be found in Merrill Jensen, *The Founding of a Nation: A History of the American Revolution, 1763–1776* (New York, 1968), 7–35; Robert Middlekauff, *The Glorious Cause: The American Revolution, 1763–1789* (New York, 1982), 26–48; Colin Bonwick, *The American Revolution* (Charlottesville, Va., 1991), 12–30; Benson Bobrick, *Angel in the Whirlwind: The Triumph of the American Revolution* (New York, 1997), 30–64.

7. Nash, *Urban Crucible*, 247–63. The quotation can be found on 256.

8. BF to Lord Kames, Jan. 3, 1760, *PBF* 9:6–7.

9. Jack P. Greene, "The American Revolution: An Explanation," in Greene, *Understanding the American Revolution*, 52, 54. The quotation is on 49–50.

10. Carl Degler, *Out of Our Past: The Forces That Shaped Modern America* (New York, 1959), 49–50, 67–70.

11. Jack P. Greene, "An Uneasy Connection: An Analysis of the Preconditions of the American Revolution," in Kurtz and Hutson, eds., *Essays on the American Revolution*, 53–62.

12. Bernard to Lord Barrington, Nov. 23, 1765, in Edward Channing and Archibald Cary Coolidge, eds., *The Barrington-Bernard Correspondence, and Illustrative Matter, 1760–1770* (Cambridge, Mass., 1912), 93.

13. Anderson, *Crucible of War*, 560–63; John Alden, *A History of the American Revolution* (New York, 1969), 52.

14. Woody Holton, *Forced Founders: Indians, Debtors, Slaves, and the Making of the American Revolution in Virginia* (Chapel Hill, N.C., 1999), 5, 62; Bruce Ragsdale, *A Planters' Republic: The Search for Economic Independence in Revolutionary Virginia* (Madison, Wis., 1996), 48.

15. Alden, *American Revolution*, 58.

16. Holton, *Forced Founders*, 7–8, 30.

17. Bernard to Barrington, Nov. 23, 1765, in Channing and Coolidge, *Barrington-Bernard Correspondence*, 94–95.

18. Edmund S. Morgan, ed., *Prologue to Revolution: Sources and Documents on the Stamp Act Crisis, 1764–1766* (Chapel Hill, N.C., 1959), 36–38.

19. Merrill Jensen, *Founding of a Nation*, 99.

20. Edmund S. Morgan and Helen M. Morgan, *The Stamp Act Crisis: Prologue to Revolution* (Chapel Hill, 1953), 88; Petition of the Virginia House of Burgesses to the House of Commons, Dec. 18, 1764, in Jensen, *English Historical Documents*, 9:667–69; Ragsdale, *A Planters' Republic*, 52–53.

21. H. J. Eckenrode, *The Revolution in Virginia* (reprint, Hamden, Conn., 1964), 93; Richard Beeman, *Patrick Henry: A Biography* (New York, 1974), 1–33; Morgan and Morgan, *Stamp Act Crisis*, 88, 293.

22. "The French Traveller's Account," Morgan, *Prologue to Revolution*, 46.

23. Saul K. Padover, *The Complete Jefferson: Containing His Major Writings* (reprint, Freeport, N.Y., 1969), 903, 904, 1121; Jensen, *Founding of a Nation*, 103–5; Morgan, *Prologue to Revolution*, 48–49; Jensen, *English Historical Documents*, 9:669–70.

24. *A Report of the Record Commissioners of the City of Boston, Containing the Boston Town Records, 1759–1769* (Boston, 1886), 16:121–22. See also John K. Alexander, *Samuel Adams: America's Revolutionary Politician* (New York, 2002), 20; Jensen, *Founding of a Nation*, 83–84.

25. The quotations are from Jensen, *Founding of a Nation*, 108.

26. Jensen, *English Historical Documents*, 9:674; Account of Cadwalader Colden, Dec. 6, 1765, ibid., 9:683; William Bull to Board of Trade, Nov. 3, 1765, ibid., 9:681; Nash, *Urban Crucible*, 293–308; Edward Countrymen, *A People in Revolution: The American Revolution and Political Security in New York, 1760–1790* (Baltimore, 1981), 60–63; Richard A. Ryerson, *The Revolution Is Now Begun: The Radical Committees of Philadelphia, 1765–1776* (Philadelphia, 1978), 26–27; Douglass Adair and John A. Schutz, eds., *Peter Oliver's Origin and Progress of the American Rebellion* (Stanford, 1961), 54–55.

27. On rioting in early America, see Pauline Maier, *From Resistance to Revolution: Colonial Radicals and the Development of American Opposition to Britain, 1765–1776* (New York, 1972), 3–26. See also Jensen, *Founding of a Nation*, 145–53.

28. Nash, *Urban Crucible*, 185.

29. Oliver to Peter Oliver, May 19, 1765, Hutchinson and Oliver Papers, MHS; Hutchinson to Richard Jackson, June 4, Aug. 6, 1765, Thomas Hutchinson Letterbooks, MHS.

30. Hutchinson and Oliver Papers, MHS.

31. Oliver to John Spooner, Jan. 18, 1769, Hutchinson and Oliver Papers, MHS; Hutchinson to ?, Aug. 16, 1765, Hutchinson Letterbooks, MHS; Jensen, *Founding of a Nation*, 109; Hiller B. Zobel, *The Boston Massacre* (New York, 1970), 29–31; Dirk Hoerder, *Crowd Action in Revolutionary Massachusetts, 1765–1780* (New York, 1977), 92, 97–101.

32. Francis Bernard to earl of Halifax, Aug. 31, 1765, Jensen, *English Historical Documents*, 9:676; Hutchinson to Jackson, Aug. 30, 1765, Hutchinson Letterbooks, MHS; Hoerder, *Crowd Action*, 101–10.

33. Lawrence H. Gipson, *American Loyalist: Jared Ingersoll* (New Haven, 1920), 123; Jensen, *Founding of a Nation*, 98–125; Morgan and Morgan, *Stamp Act Crisis*, 119–58; Maier, *From Resistance to Revolution*, 67–68.

34. *DAJA* 1:263–64. The "Child Independence" quotation is from Richard B. Morris, *The American Revolution Reconsidered* (New York, 1967), 17.

35. John Pendleton Kennedy, ed., *Journals of the House of Burgesses in Virginia, 1761–1765* (Richmond, Va., 1907), 306, frontispiece; Morgan, *Prologue to Revolution*, 51; Jack P. Greene, "Origins of the American Revolution," in Greene, *Understanding the American Revolution*, 74–78.

36. Jensen, *Founding of a Nation*, 118; Clinton A. Weslager, *The Stamp Act Congress* (Newark, Del.), 92, 134.

37. James Otis, *The Rights of the British Colonies Asserted and Proved* (1764), in Bernard Bailyn and Jane Garrett, eds., *Pamphlets of the American Revolution, 1750–1776* (Cambridge, Mass., 1965), 1:408–82; James Otis, *A Vindication of the British Colonies* (1765), ibid., 2:558, 562; Jensen, *Founding of a Nation*, 106; JA to William Wirt, Jan. 5, 1818, AFP, reel 123; JA to F. A. Vanderkemp, Apr. 23, 1807, AFP, reel 118; JA to Jedediah Morse, Nov. 29, 1815, AFP, reel 122; JA to Morse, Dec. 5, 1815, *WJA* 10:190.

38. Morgan, *Prologue to Revolution*, 62–63; Morgan and Morgan, *Stamp Act Crisis*, 105–13.

39. Quoted in Jensen, *Founding of a Nation*, 108.

40. *Connecticut Courant,* Aug. 26, 1765, and *New York Mercury,* Oct. 21, 1765, in Morgan, *Prologue to Revolution*, 92–94.

41. Weslager, *The Stamp Act Congress*, 123, 149.

42. *DAJA* 1:263–64.

43. The quotations are taken from Gordon Wood, *The Radicalism of the American Revolution* (New York, 1992), 27. This section on social hierarchy draws extensively on Wood's assessment.

44. Fred Anderson, *A People's Army: Massachusetts Soldiers and Society in the Seven Years' War* (Chapel Hill, N.C., 1984), 99–101.

45. Quoted in ibid., 90.

46. The foregoing section on colonial politics and society is based primarily on Richard R. Beeman, "Deference, Republicanism, and the Emergence of Popular Politics in Eighteenth-Century America," *WMQ* 49 (1992): 401–30; Richard L. Bushman, *King and People in Provincial Massachusetts* (Chapel Hill, N.C., 1985), 80; Bernard Bailyn, *The Origins of American Politics* (New York, 1967), 95–105; Wood, *Radicalism of the American Revolution*, 11–92; Gary Nash, "The Transformation of Urban Politics, 1700–1765," *Journal of American History* 40 (1973): 605–32.

47. Oliver P. Chitwood, *Richard Henry Lee: Statesman of the Revolution* (Morgantown, W.Va., 1967), 7–52; Eckenrode, *The Revolution in Virginia*, 23.

48. Jensen, *Founding of a Nation*, 195.

49. James H. Hutson, *Pennsylvania Politics, 1746–1770: The Movement for Royal Government and Its Consequences* (Princeton, 1972), 131.

50. Ibid., 190–203; Benjamin Newcomb, *Franklin and Galloway: A Political Partnership* (New York, 1972), 5–36; John Ferling, *The Loyalist Mind: Joseph Galloway and the American Revolution* (State College, Pa., 1977), 7–14.

51. Quoted in Morgan, *Franklin*, 139.

52. Newcomb, *Franklin and Galloway*, 84–85, 86–98; Wright, *Franklin of Philadelphia*, 146–48.

53. Newcomb, *Franklin and Galloway*, 105–48; Hutson, *Pennsylvania Politics*, 192–203.

54. Franklin to Richard Jackson, Jan. 16, 1764, *PBF* 11:19, 13:127n.

55. Wright, *Franklin of Philadelphia*, 191; Samuel Wharton to BF, Oct. 13, 1765, *PBF* 12:315–16; Deborah Franklin to BF, Sept. 22, 1765, *PBF* 12:217; James H. Hutson, "An Investigation of the Inarticulate: Philadelphia's White Oaks," *WMQ* 38 (1971): 18.

56. Wright, *Franklin of Philadelphia*, 198.

57. "Examination before the Committee of the Whole of the House of Commons," *PBF* 13:135, 136, 143.

58. Peter D. G. Thomas, *British Politics and the Stamp Act Crisis: The First Phase of the American Revolution, 1763–1767* (London, 1975), 217–18, 221–22; BF to Thomas Cushing, June 10, 1771, *PBF* 18:122.

Chapter 3

1. Lester H. Cohen, ed., *The History of the American Revolution* (1789), by David Ramsay, M.D. (Indianapolis, 1990), 1:69; Adair and Schutz, *Peter Oliver's Origin and Progress of the American Rebellion*, 56.

2. Bernard to Lord William Barrington, Nov. 23, 1765, Jan. 26, 1768, in Channing and Coolidge, eds., *Barrington-Bernard Correspondence*, 96–97, 99, 132.

3. Gage to Henry Conway, Oct. 12, 1765, in Clarence E. Carter, ed., *The Correspondence of General Thomas Gage with the Secretaries of State, 1763–1775* (New Haven, Conn., 1931–33), 1:70.

4. Morgan and Morgan, *Stamp Act Crisis*, 285–86; *DAJA* 3:285.

5. BF to Joseph Fox, March 1, 1766, *PBF* 13:186–87.

6. *Gazetteer*, Dec. 28, 1765, in Verner Crane, ed., *Franklin's Letters to the Press, 1758–1775* (Chapel Hill, N.C., 1950), 43–44.

7. JA to Niles, Feb. 13, 1818, *WJA* 10:282; JA to TJ, Aug. 24, 1815, *AJL* 2:455.

8. *London Chronicle*, Apr. 9, 1767, in Crane, *Franklin's Letters to the Press*, 83–87; BF to Galloway, Apr. 14, May 20, 1767, *PBF* 14:125, 164.

9. Bernard to Barrington, Nov. 23, 1765, Channing and Coolidge, *Barrington-Bernard Correspondence*, 98–99.

10. Quoted in Draper, *A Struggle for Power*, 303.

11. Jensen, *English Historical Documents*, 9:701; Robert Chaffin, "The Townshend Duties of 1767," *WMQ* 27 (1976): 90–121.

12. Jensen, *Founding of a Nation*, 165–67, 179, 206–8, 227; John Tyler, *Smugglers and Patriots: Boston Merchants and the Advent of the American Revolution* (Boston, 1986), 71, 102–7.

13. Tyler, *Smugglers and Patriots*. 91, 111.

14. Quoted in Leonard W. Labaree, *Conservativism in Early America* (reprint, Ithaca, N.Y., 1959), 4.

15. Quoted in Jensen, *Founding of a Nation*, 194.

16. JA to AA, June 30, 1774, *AFC* 1:116.

17. *DAJA* 3:282, 287–89; Richard D. Brown, *Revolutionary Politics in Massachusetts: The Boston Committee of Correspondence and the Towns, 1772–1774* (Cambridge, Mass., 1970), 24.

18. Quoted in Patterson, *Political Parties in Revolutionary Massachusetts*, 43. See also Jensen, *Founding of a Nation*, 195, 197, 245; Labaree, *Conservatism in Early America*, 5, 25.

19. Thomas Hutchinson, *A History of the Colony and Province of Massachusetts-Bay*, ed. Lawrence S. Mayo (Cambridge, Mass., 1936), 2:155–56. See also Marc Egnal, *A Mighty Empire: The Origins of the American Revolution* (Ithaca, N.Y., 1988), 32, 35–36, 38, 40.

20. Alexander, *Samuel Adams*, 5–7; Nash, *Urban Crucible*, 140.

21. The definitive work on Adams is that of Alexander, *Samuel Adams*, 1–15. See also William M. Fowler, *Samuel Adams: Radical Puritan* (New York, 1997), 1–42, 54–55; John C. Miller, *Sam Adams: Pioneer in Propaganda* (Stanford, Calif., 1936), 3–47; Pauline Maier, *The Old Revolutionaries: Political Leaders in the Age of Samuel Adams* (New York, 1982), 34; John Ferling, *John Adams: A Life* (Knoxville, Tenn., 1992), 44.

22. Hutchinson, *History of the Colony and Province of Massachusetts*, 2:155–56.

23. Alexander, *Samuel Adams*, 8–12.

24. Fowler, *Samuel Adams*, 36.

25. JA to John Scollay, Dec. 30, 1780, *WSA* 4:238.

26. AA to Mary Cranch, July 15, 1776, *AFC* 1:54.

27. Ibid., 1:55–56.

28. Ibid.; Miller, *Sam Adams*, 84–85.

29. Jefferson is quoted in Miller, *Sam Adams*, 343. On JA's thoughts, see JA to William Tudor, June 5, 1817, *WJA* 10:263; JA to Jedidiah Morse, Dec. 5, 1815, *WJA* 10:190; *DAJA* 1:271; JA to Benjamin Rush, Aug. 1, 1812, in John Schutz and Douglass Adair, eds., *Spur of Fame: Dialogues of John Adams and Benjamin Rush, 1805–1813* (San Marino, Calif., 1966), 235.

30. Oliver to Richard Jackson, March 1, 1769; Oliver to Henry Bromfield, Apr. 20, 1771; Oliver to Bernard, Aug. 31, 1772, all in Andrew Oliver Letterbook, MHS; Hutchinson to Thomas Whatley, Apr. 30, 1770; Hutchinson to Bernard, March 10, 1773, both in Thomas Hutchinson Letterbooks, MHS.

31. Quoted in Maier, *Old Revolutionaries*, 38.

32. AA to Mary Cranch, July 15, 1766, *AFC* 1:54; *DAJA* 1:371.

33. JA to Tudor, June 5, 1817, AFP, reel 123.

34. Adair and Schutz, *Peter Oliver's Origin and Progress of the American Rebellion*, 39–40.

35. Alexander, *Samuel Adams*, 72.

36. *WJA* 2:144.

37. Quoted in Cass Canfield, *Samuel Adams's Revolution, 1765–1776* (New York, 1976), 32.

38. Alexander, *Samuel Adams*, 29; Miller, *Sam Adams*, 66, 69, 84; Maier, *Old Revolutionaries*, 28. On the role of the Sons of Liberty and "ordered resistance," see Maier, *From Resistance to Revolution*, 51–112.

39. Fowler, *Samuel Adams*, 78–79; Massachusetts Circular Letter, Feb. 11, 1768, in Jensen, *English Historical Documents*, 9:714–16.

40. Hillsborough to the Governors in America, Apr. 21, 1768, in Jensen, *English Historical Documents*, 9:716–17.

41. BF to Thomas Cushing, June 10, 1771, *PBF* 18:122; John Fiske, *The American Revolution*, 2 vols. (Boston, 1891), 1:48.

42. Robert Tucker and David Hendrickson, *The Fall of the First British Empire: Origins of the War of American Independence* (Baltimore, 1982), 258–59.

43. John Dickinson, *The Late Regulations respecting the British Colonies* (1765), in Bailyn and. Garrett, eds., *Pamphlets of the American Revolution, 1750–1776*, 1:683, 688–89.

44. John Dickinson, *Letters from a Farmer in Pennsylvania* (1768), in Merrill Jensen, ed., *Tracts of the American Revolution, 1763–1776* (Indianapolis, Ind., 1967), 133, 135, 139. On Dickinson's life, see Milton E. Flower, *John Dickinson: Conservative Revolutionary* (Charlottesville, Va., 1983), 1–70; Draper, *A Struggle for Power*, 305.

45. Dickinson, *Letters from a Farmer*, in Jensen, *Tracts of the American Revolution*, 140.

46. Jensen, *Founding of a Nation*, 82–83; George Wolkins, "The Seizure of John Hancock's 'Liberty,'" MHS, *Proceedings* 55 (1921–22): 239–84; Fowler, *Samuel Adams*, 81.

47. *Boston Gazette*, Aug. 8, 1768, in *WSA* 1:240; Fowler, *Samuel Adams*, 86–87.

48. *Boston Gazette*, Oct. 10, 17, Dec. 5, 19, 1768, Feb. 13, Apr. 24, 1769, *WSA* 1:250, 252, 256, 269, 309, 336.

49. Zobel, *Boston Massacre*, 110–11.

50. *Boston Gazette*, Apr. 11, Dec. 5, 1768, *WSA* 1:205–6, 258.

51. Oliver M. Dickerson, ed., *Boston under Military Rule, 1768–1769* (Boston, 1936); Andrew Eliot to Thomas Hollis, Sept. 27, 1768, MHS, *Collections*, 4th ser. (1858), 4:428.

52. Alfred F. Young, *The Shoemaker and the Tea Party: Memory and the American Revolution* (Boston, 1999), 37–38.

53. Zobel, *Boston Massacre*, 164–205.

54. Gage to Hillsborough, Apr. 10, 1770, Carter, *Correspondence of General Gage*, 1:249–50.

55. Quoted in Fowler, *Samuel Adams*, 106.

56. Quoted in Miller, *Sam Adams*, 186.

57. Peter D. G. Thomas, *The Townshend Duties Crisis: The Second Phase of the American Revolution* (Oxford, 1987), 180; Middlekauff, *The Glorious Cause*, 203.

58. Fowler, *Samuel Adams*, 103.

59. Maier, *From Resistance to Revolution*, 179, 183; Tyler, *Smugglers and Patriots*, 149–50.

60. Galloway to BF, Sept. 20, 1765, Oct. 17, 1768, *PBF* 12:269–70; 15:231; Hutson, *Pennsylvania Politics*, 220–21.

61. Hutson, *Pennsylvania Politics*, 224–43; Newcomb, *Franklin and Galloway*, 218; Ryerson, *Revolution Is Now Begun*, 27, 28, 32.

62. Benjamin Franklin, "Causes of the American Discontents before 1768," *PBF* 15:12–13; BF to the Massachusetts House of Representatives Committee of Correspondence, May 15, 1771, *PBF* 18:102.

63. BF to Galloway, Aug. 20, 1768, Jan. 9, 29, 1769, June 11, 1770, *PBF* 15:189–90; 16:15, 30; 17:168; Hutson, *Pennsylvania Politics*, 227.

64. Hutson, *Pennsylvania Politics*, 225–41; BF to Galloway, Aug. 20, 1768, March 21, 1770, *PBF* 15:189; 17:117; BF to Jean-Baptiste LeRoy, Jan. 31, 1769, *PBF* 16:33; BF to Charles Thomson and Thomas Mifflin, Jan. 5, 27, July 7, 1769, *PBF* 16:8–9, 27–28, 171–72; BF to Thomson, March 18, 1770, *PBF* 17:111–13.

65. TJ to Walter Jones, Jan. 2, 1814, *WTJ* 9:448–50.

66. *DGW* 1:338–40.

67. GW to Mason, Apr. 5, 1769, *PGW: Col Ser* 8:177–80. The section on Virginia speculators and the West draws on Holton, *Forced Founders*, 4–38, and Ferling, *First of Men*, 70–72, 91–93.

68. Mason to the Committee of Merchants of London, June 6, 1766, in Robert Rutland, ed., *The Papers of George Mason* (Chapel Hill, N.C., 1970), 1:69; GW to Mason, Apr. 5, 1769, *PGW: Col Ser* 8:177–80; Ragsdale, *A Planters' Republic*, 43–68; Holton, *Forced Founders*, 39–73.

69. Fowler, *Samuel Adams*, 86; Fiske, *American Revolution*, 1:45.

70. Florence D. Scull, *John Dickinson Sounds the Alarm* (Philadelphia, 1972), 82.

71. GW to Mason, Apr. 5, 1769, *PGW: Col Ser* 8:177–80; Scull, *John Dickinson Sounds the Alarm*, 82; H. R. McIlwaine and John Pendleton, *Journals of the House of Burgesses of Virginia, 1766–1769* (Richmond, Va., 1906), 216–19; *DGW* 2:143, 146–53.

72. BF to John Winthrop, July 25, 1773, *PBF* 20:330; BF to William Franklin, Dec. 29, 1767, *PBF* 14:349; BF to Galloway, June 11, 1770, *PBF* 17:168; Thomas, *Townshend Duties Crisis*, 152, 157.

73. Jensen, *Founding of a Nation*, 354–72.

74. BF to William Franklin, March 13, 1768, *PBF* 15:76. On the dilemma facing the imperial leadership, see Tucker and Hendrickson, *Fall of the First British Empire*, 267–75.

Chapter 4

1. BF to Galloway, Aug. 8, 1767, *PBF* 14:229; BF to Samuel Cooper, June 8, 1770, *PBF* 17:162; BF to New Jersey Committee of Correspondence, June 11, 1770, *PBF* 17:174; Peter D. G. Thomas, *From Tea Party to Independence: The Third Phase of the American Revolution* (Oxford, 1991), 217.

2. Thomas, *From Tea Party to Independence*, 258.

3. Ibid., 216, 245.

4. *PJA* 1:251–55; Draper, *Struggle for Power*, 378–79.

5. Alexander, *Samuel Adams*, 93.

6. SA to Charles Lucas, March 12, 1771, *WSA* 2:163; SA to Arthur Lee, Apr. 19, July 31, 1771, *WSA* 2:164–65, 190; *Boston Gazette*, Aug. 19, Sept. 23, 27, Oct. 7, 1771, *WSA* 2:201–2, 224–30, 233, 248–49.

7. Philip Davidson, *Propaganda and the American Revolution, 1763–1783* (Chapel Hill, N.C., 1941), 196–97; Fowler, *Samuel Adams*, 114.

8. Thomas P. O'Neill, *Man of the House: The Life and Political Memoirs of Speaker Tip O'Neill* (New York, 1987), 26.

9. James Henretta, "Families and Farms: *Mentalité* in Preindustrial America," in Henretta, *The Origins of American Capitalism*, 96–107; Robert J. Taylor, *Western Massachusetts in the Revolution* (Providence, R.I., 1954), 33–35.

10. Quoted in ibid., 59.

11. *Boston Gazette*, Aug. 13, Dec. 3, 10, 1770, *WSA* 2:36, 73, 78, 79, 80; Alexander, *Samuel Adams*, 94–95; Miller, *Sam Adams*, 234–35.

12. Massachusetts House of Representatives to BF, June 29, 1771, *WSA* 2:182; SA to A. Lee, July 31, 1771, *WSA* 2:190, 191; Edmund S. Morgan, "The Puritan Ethic and the American Revolution," *WMQ* 24 (1967): 3–43.

13. Holton, *Forced Founders*, 91; Jensen, *Founding of a Nation*, 331–32.

14. Miller, *Sam Adams*, 263–69; *Boston Gazette*, Dec. 10, 1770, *WSA* 2:79.

15. Brown, *Revolutionary Politics in Massachusetts*, 45–46, 47, 53.

16. Thomas Jefferson, *Autobiography*, in Padover, *Complete Jefferson*, 1122; SA to A. Lee, Sept. 27, 1771, *WSA* 2:234; SA to Elbridge Gerry, Oct. 27, 1771, *WSA* 2:340; Miller, *Sam Adams*, 271–72; Maier, *From Resistance to Revolution*, 224; Draper, *Struggle for Power*, 380–81.

17. Samuel Adams [?], *A State of the Rights of the Colonists* (1772), in Jensen, *Tracts of the American Revolution*, 235, 239.

18. Jensen, *Founding of a Nation*, 415–16.

19. *Boston Gazette*, Oct. 5, 1772, *WSA* 2:236; BF to Thomas Cushing, June 10, 1771, Jan. 13, 1772, Sept. 3, 1774, *PBF* 18:122; 19:23; 21:280; BF to James Bowdoin, Feb. 5, 1771, *PBF* 18:23; BF to Galloway, Apr. 20, 1771, *PBF* 18:77; BF to William Franklin, Aug. 19 [–22], 1772, *PBF* 19:258; BF to Samuel Cooper, July 7, 1773, *PBF* 20:269.

20. Jensen, *Founding of a Nation*, 437; Thomas, *Townshend Duties Crisis*, 246–54.

21. Holton, *Forced Founders*, 95–96.

22. Additional Queries, with Jefferson's Answers (to M. deMeunier), ca. Jan.–Feb. 1786, *PTJ* 10:27.

23. Jacob M. Price, *Capital and Credit in British Overseas Trade: The View from the Chesapeake* (Cambridge, Mass., 1980), 127–35; Thomas Jefferson, "Additional Queries," ca. Jan.–Feb. 1786, *PTJ* 10:27; Thomas Jefferson, *A Summary View of the Rights of British America* (Williamsburg, Va., 1774), *PTJ* 1:130; William J. Van Scribner et al., eds., *Revolutionary Virginia: The Road to Independence* (Charlottesville, Va., 1973–83), 1:116–18; Ragsdale, *A Planters' Republic*, 111–36.

24. Nash, *Urban Crucible*, 312–38; Marc Egnal and Joseph A. Ernst, "An Economic Interpretation of the American Revolution," *WMQ* 29 (1972): 3–36; Billy Smith, "The Material Lives of Laboring Philadelphians," *WMQ* 38 (1981): 163–202; Maier, *From Resistance to Revolution*, 171, 178–80, 184.

25. BF to Thomas Cushing, Dec. 2, 1772, *PBF* 19:412; *Copy of Letters Sent to Great Britain, by His Excellency Thomas Hutchinson, the Hon. Andrew Oliver, and Several Other Persons* (Boston, 1773); Jensen, *Founding of a Nation*, 420.

26. *DAJA* 1:264–65. Emphasis added.

27. *DAJA* 1:271, 274, 349, 352; 2:73–74; 3:290–91.

28. JA, "Replies to Philanthrop" (1766–67), in *PJA* 1:185; JA to AA, Jan. 29, 1774, *AFC* 1:114; *DAJA* 2:7, 35, 3:295.

29. *DAJA* 2:72, 74, 3:305; JA to William Tudor, March 8, 1817, *WJA* 2:311; *PJA* 1:311n; *Speeches of His Excellency Governor Hutchinson, to the General Assembly of the Massachusetts Bay . . . with the Answers* (Boston, 1773).

30. JA to Rush, Feb. 27, 1805, May 1, 21, 1807, Adair and Schutz, *Spur of Fame*, 35–36, 80, 88; *DAJA* 2:34–35, 55, 80, 119; John Adams, "The Letters of Novanglus" (Jan. 23–Apr. 1, 1775), in *PJA* 2:242, 256, 257, 277–78, 284, 370; John Adams, "Dissertation on the Canon and Feudal Law," *PJA* 1:106, 108, 103–4n. On the life of John Adams, see Ferling, *John Adams*. On his youth and emergence as a revolutionary, see also Ferling, *Setting the World Ablaze*.

31. JA to TJ, Nov. 15, 1813, *AJL* 2:402.

32. Thomas Jefferson, *A Summary View of the Rights of British America* (1775), in *PTJ* 1:122; TJ to Charles Bellini, Sept. 30, 1785, *PTJ* 8:568; John Adams, "Canon and Feudal Law" [1765], in *PJA* 1:113–14; John Adams, "The Earl of Clarendon to William Pym" [1766], *PJA* 1:163; John Adams, "Letters of Novanglus" [1774–75], *PJA* 2:242.

33. TJ to JA, March 25, 1826, *AJL* 2:614. The best and most detailed analysis of opportunity in colonial America, and often the lack thereof, can be found in Wood, *Radicalism of the American Revolution*, 95–212. See also Gordon Wood, "Afterword," in Milton Klein et al., eds., *The Republican Synthesis Revisited: Essays in Honor of George A. Billias* (Worcester, Mass., 1992), 143–51.

34. JA to Patrick Henry, June 3, 1776, *PJA* 4:235.

35. SA to Stephen Sayre, Nov. 23, 1770, *WSA*, 2:68.

36. Jensen, *Founding of a Nation*, 443–47, 462.

37. Ryerson, *The Revolution Is Now Begun*, 33–38.

38. Jensen, *Founding of a Nation*, 447–50; Miller, *Sam Adams*, 285–86.

39. Philip McFarland, *The Brave Bostonians: Hutchinson, Quincy, Franklin, and the Coming of the American Revolution* (Boulder, Colo., 1998), 2–3.

40. Hoerder, *Crowd Action*, 257–58.

41. Quoted in Brown, *Revolutionary Politics in Massachusetts*, 171.

42. On this Boston activist, see "Dr. Thomas Young and the Radicalism of Science and Reason," in Maier, *Old Revolutionaries*, 101–38.

43. Benjamin Labaree, *The Boston Tea Party* (New York, 1964), 138–41.

44. Brown, *Revolutionary Politics in Massachusetts*, 163; SA to A. Lee, Dec. 31, 1773, *WSA* 3:74, 76; DAJA 2:86.

45. BF to Thomas Cushing, Feb. 15 [–19], Sept. 3, 1774, *PBF* 21:90, 280; BF to Massachusetts House of Representatives Committee of Correspondence, Feb. 2, 1774, *PBF* 21:75; Thomas, *From Tea Party to Independence*, 30; Jack Sosin, "The Massachusetts Acts of 1774: Coercive or Preventive?" *Huntington Library Quarterly* 26 (1963): 235–52.

46. Benjamin Franklin, Draft of a Petition to the King, Feb. 17, 1775, *PBF* 21:496; Anon., *Advice from Philadelphia, Dated July 23, 1774* (New York, 1774); *DAJA* 2:96.

47. SA to A. Lee, Dec. 31, 1774, *WSA* 3:76, 78–79; Boston Committee of Correspondence to BF, March 31, 1774, *WSA* 3:85; Boston Committee of Correspondence to Marblehead Committee of Correspondence, March 24, 1774, *WSA* 3:80–81; Brown, *Revolutionary Politics in Massachusetts*, 178–209.

48. GW to George William Fairfax, Jan. 10 [–15], 1774, *PGW: Col Ser* 10:96.

49. BF to Massachusetts House Committee of Correspondence, Feb. 2, 1774, *PBF* 21:75–76; Hoerder, *Crowd Action*, 263.

50. Quoted in Fowler, *Samuel Adams*, 127.

51. Quoted in Labaree, *Boston Tea Party*, 220.

52. Jack Rakove, *The Beginnings of National Politics: An Interpretive History of the Continental Congress* (Baltimore, 1979), 23; Labaree, *Boston Tea Party*, 231–32; John Hancock, *An Oration, Delivered March 5, 1774* (Boston, 1774), 17–18.

53. Wood, *Radicalism of the American Revolution*, 12–16.

54. Ryerson, *The Revolution Is Now Begun*, 40–63.

55. *DAJA* 2:97–122; Alexander, *Samuel Adams*, 137; John Ferling, *John Adams*, 74–76.

56. JA to AA, Sept. 14, 1774, *AFC* 1:155.

57. JA to Joseph Palmer, Sept. 26, 1774, *PJA* 2:173.

58. Brown, *Revolutionary Politics in Massachusetts*, 61.

59. JA to William Tudor, Sept. 29, 1774, *PJA* 2:1777; Reed to ?, Sept. 4, 1775, Joseph Reed Papers, New York Historical Society; Rakove, *Beginnings of National Politics*, 45.

60. JA to Rush, June 12, 1812, Adair and Schultz, *Spur of Fame*, 225.

61. Alexander, *Samuel Adams*, 141; Miller, *Sam Adams*, 321; Joseph Galloway, *Historical and Political Reflections on the Rise and Progress of the American Revolution* (London, 1780), 67.

62. Edmund C. Burnett, *The Continental Congress* (New York, 1941), 33; *DAJA* 2:122; Robert Secor and John Pickering, *Pennsylvania 1776* (University Park, Pa., 1975), 274, 281, 301, 304, 322.

63. *DAJA* 2:151, 156; JA to AA, Oct. 9, 1774, *AFC* 1:166.

64. The text of Galloway's speech has not survived. Years later he attempted to recapitulate the speech in his pamphlet *Historical and Political Reflections on the American Rebellion* (London, 1780). It is even more likely that much of what he said was contained in a pamphlet that he published immediately following Congress's adjournment, *A Candid Examination of the Mutual Claim of Great Britain and the Colonies* (New York, 1775), although in all likelihood he was less temperate in those subsequent publications than in the course of remarks that he hoped would sway numerous congressmen. John Adams took notes during Galloway's presentation. See *DAJA* 2:141–44.

65. Galloway, *A Candid Examination*, in Jensen, *Tracts of the American Revolution*, 377–78, 387, 389.

66. Ibid., 384.

67. Ibid., 394. See also Ferling, *Loyalist Mind*, 25–30, 67–111.

68. Joseph Galloway, *The Examination of Joseph Galloway . . . before the House of Commons* (London, 1779), 48; Alexander, *Samuel Adams*, 140; Rakove, *Beginnings of National Politics*, 53; David Ammerman, *In the Common Cause: American Response to the Coercive Acts of 1774* (Charlottesville, Va., 1974), 58–59, 93; Jerrilyn G. Marston, *King and Congress: The Transfer of Political Legitimacy, 1774–1776* (Princeton, N.J., 1987), 101–2, 113.

69. Marston, *King and Congress*, 93–96; *JCC* 1:67–70.

70. *LDC* 1:231.

71. Maier, *From Resistance to Revolution*, 281–83; Marston, *King and Congress*, 108–10, 137; Ammerman, *In the Common Cause*, 109; *JCC* 1:54.

72. JA to Tudor, Oct. 7, 1774, *PJA* 2:188.

73. Silas Deane, Diary, *LDC* 1:139.

74. Ryerson, *The Revolution Is Now Begun*, 90–93; JA to AA, Oct. 7, 1774, *AFC* 1:164–66.

Chapter 5

1. Thomas, *From Tea Party to Independence*, 137–38, 143.

2. Gage to Dartmouth, Aug. 27, Sept. 2, 3, 25, 1774, in Clarence Carter, ed., *The Correspondence of General Thomas Gage with the Secretary of State, 1763–1775* (reprint, New York, 1969), 1:365–73, 376–77; Thomas, *From Tea Party to Independence*, 154.

3. George III to North, Nov. 18, 1774, W. B. Donne, ed., *Correspondence of George III with Lord North* (London, 1867), 1:214–15; Thomas, *From Tea Party to Independence*, 160, 165.

4. Dartmouth to Gage, Jan. 27, 1775, Carter, *Correspondence of Gage*, 2:179–83; McFarland, *Brave Bostonians*, 163–203.

5. Morgan, *Franklin*, 104–28.

6. Wright, *Franklin of Philadelphia*, 203–5, 211–13, 220–21; BF to Galloway, March 9, 1769, March 21, 1770, *PBF* 16:62–63; 17:117; BF to Thomas Cushing, Jan. 5, 1773, *PBF* 20:10.

7. BF to William Franklin, Oct. 6, 1773, *PBF* 20:437; BF to the printer of the *London Chronicle*, Dec. 25, 1773, *PBF* 20:515–16; Wright, *Franklin of Philadelphia*, 225.

8. BF to Deborah Franklin, Feb. 20, 1775, *PBF* 21:116.

9. BF to Cushing, Feb. 15 [–19], 1775, *PBF* 21:93; BF to William Franklin, Sept. 7, 1774, *PBF* 21:286.

10. For the solutions proposed by BF, and the counter of the intermediaries, see BF, " Hints,' or Terms for a Durable Union," Dec. 4 and 6, 1775, *PBF* 21:366–68, and "Answer to BF's 'Hints,'" Feb. 4, 1775, *PBF* 21:466–68. See also Van Doren, *Franklin*, 495–518; McFarland, *Brave Bostonians*, 143–52, 193–203.

11. BF to Galloway, Feb. 5 [–7], 1775, *PBF* 21:469; BF to Thomas Viny, Feb. 12, 1775, *PBF* 21:487; BF to Jonathan Shipley, Jan. 7, 1775, *PBF* 21:443; BF to Cushing, Oct. 6, 1774, Nov. 28, 1775, *PBF* 21:327, 457; BF to James Bowdoin, Feb. 25, 1775, *PBF* 21:507.

12. BF to Galloway, Feb. 25, 1775, *PBF* 21:509.

13. This account of this epic day is based on David Hackett Fischer, *Paul Revere's Ride* (New York, 1994). The two quotations (Pitcairn's order and SA's alleged comment) can be found on 191 and 183, respectively.

14. John Dickinson, "Notes for a Speech in Congress" [May 23–25, 1775], *LDC* 1:371–87; Flower, *Dickinson*, 128–29.

15. Thomas M. Doerflinger, *A Vigorous Spirit of Enterprise: Merchants and Economic Development in Revolutionary Philadelphia* (New York, 1986), 168. The following section on mercantile prowess in the mid-Atlantic provinces draws on Doerflinger's account, pages 70–196, as well as that in Labaree, *Conservatism in Early America*, 41, 46–49, 53.

16. Quoted in Doerflinger, *A Vigorous Spirit of Enterprise*, 194–95. On sectional interests, see Russell R. Menard, "Slavery, Economic Growth and Revolutionary Ideology in the South Carolina Lowcountry," in Ronald Hoffman et al., eds., *The Economy of Early America: The Revolutionary Period, 1763–1790* (Charlottesville, Va., 1988), 244–74; Peggy Liss, *Atlantic Empires: The Network of Trade and Revolution, 1713–1826* (Baltimore, 1983); Ralph Davis, *The Rise of the Atlantic Economies* (Ithaca, N.Y., 1973); John J. McCusker and Russell R. Menard, *The Economy of British America, 1607–1789* (Chapel Hill, N.C., 1985).

17. Dickinson, "Notes for a Speech" [May 23–25, 1775], *LDC* 1:371–83; John Dickinson, "Proposed Resolution" [May 23–25, 1775], *LDC* 1:383–86; James Duane, "Notes for a Speech" [May 23–25, 1775], *LDC* 1:391–95.

18. SA to Joseph Hawley, Apr. 15, 1776, *LDC* 3:528.

19. George W. Conner, ed., *The Autobiography of Benjamin Rush: His "Travels through Life" Together with His Commonplace Book for 1789–1813* (Philadelphia, 1948), 140.

20. JA to AA, Sept. 8, 1774, *AFC* 1:150.

21. JA to Tudor, March 29, 1817, *WJA* 10:245; JA to AA, Feb. 9, 1799, AFP, reel 393; JA to F. A. Vanderkemp, Apr. 18, 1815, AFP, reel 322; TJ to JM, Jan. 30, 1787, May 25, 1788, *PTJ* 11:94–95; 13:201–2.

22. Peter Shaw, *The Character of John Adams* (Chapel Hill, N.C., 1976), 95; Joseph Ellis, *Passionate Sage: The Character and Legacy of John Adams* (New York, 1993), 42–43.

23. "Character Sketches," in Padover, *Complete Jefferson*, 900, 902, 904; TJ to JM, Jan. 30, 1787, *PTJ* 11:94–95; Shaw, *Character of John Adams*, 95.

24. JA to Moses Gill, June 10, 1775, *PJA* 3:21; JA to James Warren, May 21, 1775, *PJA* 3:11; JA to AA, June 17, 1775, *AFC* 1:216; *DAJA* 3:318.

25. John Dickinson, "Notes of Debate" [May 23–25, 1775?], *LDC* 1:391; *JCC* 2:64–66; *DAJA* 3:321; Franklin to Jonathan Shipley, July 7, 1775, *PBF* 22:95.

26. Louis Birnbaum, *Red Dawn at Lexington* (Boston, 1986), 215; Christopher Ward, *The War of the Revolution* (New York, 1952), 1:54–56; *DAJA* 3:315.

27. Marston, *King and Congress*, 142–43, 158.

28. Merrill Jensen, *The American Revolution within America* (New York, 1974), 34, 35, 44–45.

29. Galloway, *A Candid Examination*, in Jensen, *Tracts of the American Revolution*, 371, 376, 387.

30. Charles Royster, *A Revolutionary People at War: The Continental Army and the American Character* (Chapel Hill, N.C., 1979), 35–43; Marston, *King and Congress*, 150–52; Eliphalet Dyer to Joseph Trumbull, June 17, 1775, *LDC* 1:499.

31. *DAJA* 3:321.

32. Silas Deane to Elizabeth Deane, June 16, 1775, *LDC* 1:494; Dyer to Trumbull, June 16, 1775, *LDC* 1:495–96; Deane to Trumbull, June 18, 1775, *LDC* 1:506; John Hancock to Elbridge Gerry, June 18, 1775, *LDC* 1:507; *DAJA* 3:323; JA to AA, June 17, 1775, *AFC* 1:215–16.

33. *JCC* 2:76–77, 87–90, 93, 97, 99, 103; JA to Gerry, June 18, 1775, *PJA* 3:25–26; Jonathan Rossie, *The Politics of Command in the American Revolution* (Syracuse, 1975), 17–30.

34. Samuel Ward to Henry Ward, June 22, 1775, *LDC* 1:535; JA to Timothy Pickering, Aug. 6, 1822, *WJA* 2:512.

35. Declaration of the Causes and Necessity for Taking Up Arms, *PTJ* 1:187–219; *JCC* 2:143–48.

36. JA to James Warren, July 6, 1775, *PJA* 3:62.

37. Dickinson to Arthur Lee, July ?, 1775, *LDC* 1:688; Thomas Johnson Jr. to Horatio Gates, Aug. 18, 1775, *LDC* 1:704; *JCC* 2:158–61; Marston, *King and Congress*, 209–16.

38. Richard Ketchum, *Decisive Day: The Battle for Bunker Hill* (New York, 1962), 181, 190–93; Ward, *War of the Revolution*, 1:46.

39. BF to Shipley, July 7, 1775, *PBF* 22:94–95; BF to Joseph Priestley, July 7, Oct. 3, 1775, *PBF* 22:92, 218; TJ to George Gilmer, July 5, 1775, *PTJ* 1:186; Henry Middleton to Arthur Middleton, July 6, 1775, *LDC* 1:695.

40. TJ to John Randolph, Aug. 25, 1775, *PTJ* 1:241.

41. Fowler, *Samuel Adams*, 134, 138; Edward Countryman, *A People in Revolution: The American Revolution and Political Society in New York, 1760–1790* (Baltimore, 1981), 141–42, 146, 155; Jackson Turner Main, *The Sovereign States, 1775–1783* (New York, 1973), 276; John Shy, *A People Numerous and Armed: Reflections on the Military Struggle for America* (New York, 1976), 168.

42. Galloway, *Mutual Claims*, in Jensen, *Tracts of the American Revolution*, 387; Janice Potter, *The Liberty We Seek: Loyalist Ideology in Colonial New York and Massachusetts* (Cambridge, Mass., 1983), 41, 46–50, 144.

43. Gordon S. Wood, *Creation of the American Republic, 1776–1787* (Chapel Hill, N.C., 1998), 67–70; TJ, *Summary View*, in *PTJ* 1:127.

44. Wood, *Creation of the American Republic*, 68–70; Ann Fairfax Withington, *Toward a More Perfect Union: Virtue and the Formation of the American Republic* (New York, 1991), 10–19.

45. Jensen, *English Historical Documents* 9:850–51; SA to James Bowdoin, Nov. 16, 1775, *LDC* 2:352; Samuel Ward to Henry Ward, Nov. 2, 1775, *LDC* 2:291; John DeHart to the New Jersey Assembly, Nov. 13, 1775, *LDC* 2:334; TJ to Randolph, Nov. 29, 1775, *PTJ* 1:269.

46. *JCC* 2:83–84; Jensen, *Founding of a Nation*, 640.

47. Jensen, *English Historical Documents* 9:863; Flower, *Dickinson*, 141–42.

48. Francis Lightfoot Lee to Landon Carter, Feb. 12, 1776, *LDC* 3:236; Thomas Nelson to Mann Page, Jan. 4, 1776, *LDC* 3:30; North Carolina Delegates to Samuel Johnson, Jan. 2, 1776, *LDC* 3:18–19; Hugh F. Rankin, *The North Carolina Continentals* (Chapel Hill, N.C., 1971), 23–25; Jensen, *Founding of a Nation*, 645.

49. Jensen, *English Historical Documents* 9:851–52; Hancock to Cushing, Feb. 13, 1776 *LDC* 3:244.

50. Quoted in Ferling, *Loyalist Mind*, 115.

51. On Paine's background and the creation of *Common Sense*, see David Freeman Hawke, *Paine* (New York, 1974), 7–41, and Eric Foner, *Tom Paine and Revolutionary America* (New York, 1976), 79–106. On the essay that first mentioned independence, see [Thomas Paine], "A Serious Thought," in Philip Foner, ed., *The Complete Writings of Thomas Paine* (New York, 1945), 2:19–20.

52. For a compilation of the American pamphlets in the imperial dispute prior to independence, see Thomas R. Adams, ed., *American Independence: The Creation of an Idea* (Providence, R.I., 1965).

53. [Thomas Paine], *Common Sense*, Foner, *Complete Writings of Paine*, 1:4–46. The quoted passages can be found in *Complete Writings of Paine*, 1:4, 17, 26, 27, 28, 31, 45. My analysis draws heavily on the brilliant assessment of *Common Sense* in Bernard Bailyn, *Faces of Revolution: Personalities and Themes in the Struggle for American Independence* (New York, 1990), 67–84.

54. SA to Warren, Jan. 13, 1776, *LDC* 3:87; SA to John Pitts, Jan. 12, 1776, *LDC* 3:84; SA to John Sullivan, Jan. 12, 1776, *LDC* 3:85.

55. John Dickinson, "Draft Address to the Inhabitants of North America" [Jan. 24?, 1776], *LDC* 3:139–44.

56. JA to Samuel Cooper [?], June 9, 1776, *PJA*, 4:242–43; GW to Philip Schuyler, Jan. 18, 1776, *PGW: Rev War Ser* 3:141; GW to Hancock, Jan. 19, 1776, *PGW: Rev War Ser* 3:147; Ward, *War of the Revolution*, 1:135–44.

57. Francis Lightfoot Lee to Landon Carter, Jan. 22, March 19, 1776, *LDC* 3:130, 407–8; William Whipple to Joshua Brackett, March 17, 1776, *LDC* 3:395–96; Paine, *Common Sense*, in Foner, *Complete Writings of Paine*, 1:31, 39.

58. *DAJA* 2:229–30; *JCC* 4:146; Flower, *Dickinson*, 144; Richard Smith, "Diary," Feb. 13, 1776, *LDC* 3:252.

59. *JCC* 4:146; JA to AA, Feb. 18, Apr. 12, 1776, *AFC* 1:348, 377.

60. Minutes of Proceedings, Committee of Secret Correspondence, March 2, 1776, *LDC* 3:320–23; *JCC* 4:257–59; JA to AA, Apr. 12, 1776, *AFC* 1:377; JA to Horatio Gates, *PJA* 4:59.

61. Thomas, *From Tea Party to Independence*, 286–89, 292–98; Jensen, *Founding of a Nation*, 650.

62. Flower, *Dickinson*, 150; Jensen, *EHD* 9:852; JA to John Winthrop, May 6, 1776, *PJA* 4:175.

63. GW to JA, Apr. 15, 1776, *PGW: Rev War Ser* 4:67; JA to Mercy Warren, Apr. 16, 1776, *PJA* 4:125; JA to Joseph Palmer, Apr. 2, 1776, *PJA* 4:103; Whipple to Joseph Whipple, May 6, 1776, *LDC* 3:634; Thomas Stone to Daniel of St. Thomas Jenifer, Apr. 24, 1776, *LDC* 3:580.

64. Jensen, *Founding of a Nation*, 672–81; Peter Force, comp., *American Archives*, 4th ser. (Washington, D.C., 1833–46), 6:1524; Pauline Maier, *American Scripture: Making the Declaration of Independence* (New York, 1997), 64.

65. Sullivan to Hancock, June 1, 1776, *PGW: Rev War Ser* 4:433–34n; GW to Schuyler, Apr. 19, June 7, 1776, *PGW: Rev War Ser* 4:90, 456; GW to John Augustine Washington, Apr. 29, 1776, *PGW: Rev War Ser* 4:172; GW to Hancock, June 9, 1776, *PGW: Rev War Ser* 4:470; Gerry to Warren, June 15, 1776, *LDC* 4:220; Lee to GW, Feb. 14, 1776, *LDC* 3:310–11; Hancock to Certain Colonies, June 4, 1776, *LDC* 4:136–37; Ward, *War of the Revolution*, 1:195–200.

66. JA to AA, June 17, 1775, *AFC* 1:216; Hancock to Certain Colonies, June 4, 1776, *LDC* 4:136; Joseph Hewes to James Iredell, May 17, 1776, *LDC* 4:27; Josiah Bartlett to John Langdon, May 19, 1776, *LDC* 4:39; Whipple to Joshua Brackett, June 2, 1776, *LDC* 4:119; Wolcott to Laura Wolcott, May 25, 1776, *LDC* 4:72.

67. TJ to Nelson, May 16, 1776, *PTJ* 1:292; SA to Warren, Dec. 5, 1775, *LDC* 2:439.

68. James Chalmers, *Plain Truth* (1776) in Jensen, ed., *Tracts of the American Revolution*, 485–87; Potter, *The Liberty We Seek*, 25–26; Wood, *Creation of the American Republic*, 94.

69. Wood, *Creation of the American Republic*, 71, 73; Elisha P. Douglass, *Rebels and Democrats: The Struggle for Equal Political Rights and Majority Rule during the American Revolution* (Chapel Hill, N.C., 1955), 15–17.

70. "Diary of James Allen, Esq., of Philadelphia," *Pennsylvania Magazine of History and Biography* 9 (1885): 186.

71. Landon Carter to GW, May 9, 1776, in *PGW: Rev War Ser* 4:236–37.

72. Wood, *Creation of the American Republic*, 66.

73. JA to AA, March 19, 1776, *AFC* 1:363.

74. JA to Mercy Warren, Apr. 16, 1776, *PJA* 4:124; JA to James Warren, Apr. 22, 1776, *PJA* 4:135.

75. John Adams, *Thoughts on Government* (1776), in *PJA* 4:86–93; Wood, *Creation of the American Republic*, 53–65.

76. Carter Braxton, *An Address to the Convention of the Colony and Ancient Dominion of Virginia* (1776), in Force, comp., *American Archives*, 6:748–52.

77. Lee to Henry, Apr. 20, 1776, *LDC* 3:564.

78. Wood, *Creation of the American Republic*, 101. See also Bernard Bailyn, *The Ideological Origins of the American Revolution* (Cambridge, Mass., 1967), 289–93; Jensen, *Founding of a Nation*, 664–65.

79. Shaw, *Character of John Adams*, 88.

80. John Hazelton, *The Declaration of Independence: Its History* (New York, 1906), 161–62; Shaw, *Character of John Adams*, 75, 87–88, 103–4; Page Smith, *John Adams* (New York, 1962), 1:237–43, 257; Edmund S. Morgan, *The Meaning of Independence: John Adams, George Washington, Thomas Jefferson* (New York, 1976), 15–17.

81. SA to Warren, Apr. 16, 1776, *LDC* 3:540; SA to Joseph Hawley, Apr. 15, 1776, *LDC* 3:528; Richard Henry Lee to Samuel Purviance Jr., May 6, 1776, *LDC* 3:632; Ryerson, *The Revolution Is Now Begun*, 166–75, 211.

82. The resolution can be found in *PJA* 4:185 or *JCC* 4:357–58. See also Flower, *Dickinson*, 151–52.

83. JA to Warren, May 15, 1776, *PJA* 4:186; Wolcott to Laura Wolcott, May 16, 1776, *LDC* 4:17n; Braxton to Landon Carter, May 17, 1776, *LDC* 4:19; Robert Livingston to John Jay, May 17, 1776, *LDC* 4:29; Gerry to Warren, May 20, 1776, *LDC* 4:43.

84. JA to AA, July 3, 1776, *AFC* 2:29–30.

85. *Pennsylvania Archives*, 8th ser., 8:7543; Ryerson, *The Revolution Is Now Begun*, 211–28; Joseph Illick, *Colonial Pennsylvania* (New York, 1976), 301–3; JA to Benjamin Hichborn, May 29, 1776, *PJA* 4:218.

86. JA to AA, July 10, 1776, *AFC* 2:42.

87. Morris to Deane, June 5, 1776, *LDC* 4:147.

Chapter 6

1. *Pennsylvania Gazette*, May 1, 1776.

2. JA to John Winthrop, June 23, 1776, *PJA* 4:332–33.

3. Paine, *Common Sense*, in Foner, *Complete Writings of Paine*, 1:45.

4. *JCC* 5:424.

5. JA to J. Warren, July 24, May 21, 1775, *PJA* 3:89, 11.

6. F. Lee to Carter, Jan. 22, 1776, *LDC* 3:130.

7. TJ, "Notes of Proceedings in Congress" [June 7–Aug. 1, 1776], *PTJ* 1:309–13.

8. Jensen, *Founding of a Nation*, 262. For profiles on the congressmen, see David Freeman Hawke, *Honorable Treason: The Declaration of Independence and the Men Who Signed It* (New York, 1976).

9. Quoted in Countrymen, *A People in Revolution*, 222.

10. JA to Pickering, Aug. 6, 1822, *WJA* 2:514; *DAJA* 3:336; 2:392; TJ to JM, Aug. 30, 1823, Ford, *WTJ* 10:267–69. Much of the above, as well as that which follows, draws on the splendid accounts in Pauline Maier, *American Scripture: Making the Declaration of Independence* (New York, 1997); Jensen, *Founding of a Nation*, 688–704. Also see Robert E. McGlone, "John Adams and the Authorship of the Declaration of Independence," *Journal of American History* 85 (1998): 411–38.

11. *DAJA* 3:336; Maier, *American Scripture*, 102–5; Joseph J. Ellis, *American Sphinx: The Character of Thomas Jefferson* (New York, 1997), 54–55. Also see Julian P. Boyd, *The Declaration of Independence: The Evolution of the Text as Shown in Facsimiles of Various Drafts* (Princeton, N.J., 1945), and Carl Becker, *The Declaration of Independence: A Study in the History of Political Ideas* (New York, 1922).

12. JA to Archibald Bulloch, July 1, 1776, *PJA* 4:352.

13. John Dickinson, "Notes for a Speech in Congress" [July 1, 1776], *LDC* 4:351–57; John Dickinson, "Notes on Arguments Concerning Independence" [July 1, 1776], *LDC* 4:357–58.

14. *DAJA* 3:396.

15. Quoted in Hazelton, *The Declaration of Independence: Its History*, 161–62. The Georgia congressman, Nathan Brownson, is quoted in Ferling, *John Adams*, 169.

16. The speech has not survived. Many years later, JA attempted to summarize its contents in his "Autobiography," See *DAJA* 3:396.

17. TJ, "To the Editor of the *Journal de Paris*, Aug. 29, 1787, *PTJ* 12:63.

18. Josiah Bartlett to John Langdon, July 1, 1776, *LDC* 4:351; Clark to Elisha Dayton, July 4, 1776, *LDC* 4:379.

19. Gerry to J. Warren, July 2, 1776, *LDC* 4:370.

20. JA to AA, July 3, 1776, *AFC* 2:27–28, 29–31.

21. Maier, *American Scripture*, 143–50.

22. *LDC* 4:157.

23. Flower, *Dickinson*, 175–79.

24. Dickinson, "Notes," July 1, 1776, *LDC* 4:354.

25. Maier, *American Scripture*, 228; Edmund S. Morgan, "The Great Political Fiction," *New York Review of Books*, March 9, 1978, 13–18.

26. Wood, *Creation of the Republic*, 356–57; Chase to Richard Henry Lee, July 30, 1776, *LDC* 4:571.

27. JA to Winthrop, June 23, 1776, *PJA* 4:332.

28. Chase to Lee, July 30, 1776, *LDC* 4:571; Wood, *Creation of the Republic*, 357.

29. Benjamin Rush, "Notes" [Aug. 1, 1776], *LDC* 4:600; TJ, "Notes," *PTJ* 1:325; TJ to JA, May 16, 1777, *PTJ* 2:19; Merrill Jensen, *The Articles of Confederation: The Interpretation of the Social-Constitutional History of the American Revolution, 1774–1781* (Madison, Wis., 1940), 144.

30. William Whipple to Joseph Whipple, July 29, 1776, *LDC* 4:565; Fleming, *1776*, 302.

31. *DAJA* 2:245–46; Witherspoon, "Speech to Congress," July 30, 1776, *LDC* 4:584–85; Jensen, *Articles of Confederation*, 145–48.

32. E. James Ferguson, *The Power of the Purse: A History of American Public Finance, 1776–1790* (Chapel Hill, N.C., 1961), 26–35.

33. Rush, "Notes of Debate," Feb. 14, 1777, *LDC* 6:274–77; Hancock to the States, Feb. 20, 1777, *LDC* 6:331–32; JA to J. Warren, Feb. 12, 1777, *PJA* 5:80–81; *JCC* 7:124–25.

34. Josiah Bartlett to John Langdon, Sept. 1, 1776, *LDC* 5:89.

35. GW to John Augustine Washington, [May 31–June 4, 1776], *PGW: Rev War Ser* 4:413; BF to GW, June 21, 1776, *PBF* 5:64; TJ to Edmund Pendleton, Aug. 13, 16, 1777, *PTJ* 1:493, 506; Freeman, *Washington*, 4:87.

36. Hooper to William Livingston, Sept. 2, 1776, *LDC* 5:93; Rush to Jacques Barbeu-Dubourg, Sept. 16, 1776, *LDC* 5:182–83; Francis Lightfoot Lee to Landon Carter, Sept. 15, 1776, *LDC* 5:173; Elbridge Gerry to ?, Dec. 12, 1776, *LDC* 5:602; Hooper to Samuel Johnson, Sept. 26, 1776, *LDC* 5:246; Robert Morris to Silas Deane, Sept. 12, 1776, *LDC* 5:149.

37. Ferling, *Setting the World Ablaze*, 138–42; Ferling, *First of Men*, 162–76, 260–66.

38. GW to John Augustine Washington, Dec. 18, 1776, *PGW: Rev War Ser* 7:369–71; Gerry to ?, Dec. 12, 1776, *LDC* 5:602; Samuel Chase to Maryland Council of Safety, Nov. 21, 1776, *LDC* 5:525; Morris to William Bingham, Dec. 4, 1776, *LDC* 5:574; Benjamin Rumsey to John Hall ?, Dec. 19, 1776, *LDC* 5:618; William Paca to Maryland Council of Safety, Dec. 7, 1776, *LDC* 5:586; Benjamin Harrison to R. Morris, Oct. 10, 1776, *LDC* 5:316n; JA to Henry Knox, *DAJA* 3:441–42.

39. GW to Reed, Dec. 23, 1776, *PGW: Rev War Ser* 7:423–24; Morris to GW, Dec. 26, 1776, *LDC* 5:676. On this campaign, see Ferling, *First of Men*, 182–94.

40. JA to Rush, March 19, 1812, in John Schutz and Douglass Adair, eds., *Spur of Fame*, 212.

41. GW to Congress, Sept. 2, 8, 1776, *PGW: Rev War Ser* 6:199–201, 248–52; N.C. Delegates to N.C. Council of Safety, Sept. 18, 1776, *LDC* 5:193; Committee of Secret Correspondence to Deane, Oct. 1, 1776, *LDC* 5:278; R. Morris to Deane, Jan. 8, 1777, *LDC* 6:62.

42. James Kirby Martin and Mark E. Lender, *A Respectable Army: The Military Origins of the Republic, 1763–1789* (Arlington Heights, Ill., 1982), 75–76; Royster, *A Revolutionary People at War*, 35–37.

43. Don Higginbotham, *The War of American Independence: Military Attitudes, Policies, and Practice, 1763–1789* (New York, 1971), 390; *DAJA* 3:388; JA to Col. Daniel Hitchcock, Oct. 1, 1776, *DAJA* 3:443; Hancock to GW, Nov. 9, 1776, *LDC* 5:460; Hancock to the States, Sept. 24, 1776, *LDC* 5:229.

44. SA to James Warren, Dec. 12, 1776, *LDC* 5:601; Gerry to ?, Dec. 12, 1776, *LDC* 5:602: Wolcott to Laura Wolcott, Dec. 13, 1776, *LDC* 6:606.

45. *DAJA* 2:257; Morris to GW, Jan. 1, 1777, *LDC* 6:12; William Hooper to Joseph Hewes, Jan. 1, 1777, *LDC* 6:5; Hancock to Robert T. Paine, Jan. 13, 1777, *LDC* 6:91; Benjamin Harrison to Morris, Jan. 8, 1777, *LDC* 6:57.

46. R. H. Lee to Henry, Apr. 15, 1777, *LDC* 6:584.

47. Richard Van Alstyne, *The Rising American Empire* (New York, 1960), 28–37; William Stinchcombe, *The American Revolution and the French Alliance* (Syracuse, N.Y., 1969), 9; Higginbotham, *War of American Independence*, 233; Edward Corwin, *French Policy and the American Alliance of 1778* (New York, 1916), 64–76.

48. *LDC* 4:157; Thomas Stone to James Hollyday ?, May 20, 1777, *LDC* 4:52; TJ to John Randolph, Aug. 25, 1776, *PTJ* 1:241–42; JA to James Warren, Oct. 7, 1775, *PJA* 3:189; "Plan of Treaties," *PJA* 4:260–302.

49. R. Morris to Deane, Dec. 20, 1776, *LDC* 5:624; Hooper to Morris, Dec. 28, 1776, *LDC* 5:688; Committee of Secret Correspondence to Committee at Paris, Dec. 21, 1776, *LDC* 5:633; Stinchcombe, *American Revolution and the French Alliance*, 9.

50. Rush to JA, Aug. 8, 1777, *PJA* 5:268; Laurens to John Rutledge, Aug. 12, 1777, *PJA* 7:471; Stinchcombe, *American Revolution and the French Alliance*, 8–9.

51. For a good treatment on the waning of support for monarchy, see Bushman, *King and People in Provincial Massachusetts*, 218–44.

52. Paine, *Common Sense*, in Foner, *Complete Writings of Paine* 1:6, 17, 18.

53. JA, "The Letters of Novanglus" (1775), in *PJA* 2:229, 314; JA, *Thoughts on Government* (1776), *PJA* 4:86–93; JA to William Heath, Apr. 15, 1776, *PJA* 4:120; Paine, *Common Sense*, in Foner, *Complete Writings of Paine*, 1:6, 7, 27; Bailyn, *Ideological Origins of the American Revolution*, 67–68. For an excellent analysis of Adams's evolving ideas of political theory, see C. Bradley Thompson, *John Adams and the Spirit of Liberty* (Lawrence, Kans., 1998), 44–87.

54. Main, *Sovereign States*, 143–85.

55. Ibid., 151; Colin Bonwick, *The American Revolution* (Charlottesville, N.C., 1991), 129–30; R. L. Brunhouse, *The Counter-Revolution in Pennsylvania, 1776–1790* (Harrisburg, Pa., 1942); Wood, *Creation of the American Republic*, 226–31.

56. Wood, *Creation of the American Republic*, 233; Hooper to Samuel Johnston, Sept. 26, 1776, *LDC* 5:248; Rush to Anthony Wayne, Sept. 24, 1776, *LDC* 5:235; William Williams to Jabez Huntington, Sept. 30, 1776, *LDC* 5:268; JA to AA, Oct. 5, 1776, *AFC* 2:138; JA to Francis Dana, Aug. 16, 1776, *PJA* 4:466.

57. Wood, *Radicalism of the American Revolution*, 176, 179, 200–204, 229, 230; Bonwick, *American Revolution*, 155, 157; Main, *Sovereign States*, 200.

58. JA to AA, Oct. 5, 1776, *AFC* 2:137–38.

59. Piers Mackesy, *The War for America, 1775–1783* (Cambridge, Mass., 1964), 121–23.

60. Francis Lightfoot Lee to Adam Stephen, May 3, 1777, *LDC* 8:232; William Duer to Philip Schuyler, June 19, 1777, *LDC* 7:230; SA to James Warren, June 23, 1777, *LDC* 7:241; Chase to Thomas Johnson, Aug. 23, 1777, *LDC* 7:534; JA to AA, July 20, Aug. 24, 1777, *AFC* 2:285–86, 327–28.

61. JA to AA, Sept. 30, *AFC* 2:349; *DAJA* 2:264–67.

62. JA to AA, Aug. 30, 1777, *AFC* 2:234; Mackesy, *War for America*, 129.

63. Thomas Burke's Notes of Debates, Feb. 12–19, 1777, *LDC* 6:263; Francis Lewis to New York Convention., Feb. 18, 1777, *LDC* 6:314; JA to Gen. Greene, March 9, 1777, *PJA* 5:108; JA to AA, Feb. 21, 1777, *AFC* 2:165; Rossie, *The Politics of Command*, 135–40.

64. SA to Warren, July 31, 1777, *LDC* 7:396; Paul David Nelson, *General Horatio Gates: A Biography* (Baton Rouge, La., 1976), 32, 81, 101; Calvin Jillson and Rick K. Wilson, *Congressional Dynamics: Structure, Coordination, and Choice in the First American Congress, 1774–1789* (Stanford, 1994), 197–98; Max Mintz, *The Generals of Saratoga: John Burgoyne and Horatio Gates* (New Haven, Conn., 1990), 178.

65. Henry Laurens to Gabriel Manigault, Aug. 15, 1777, *LDC* 7:486; Nathaniel Folsom to Josiah Bartlett, Aug. 12, 1777, *LDC* 7:465; James Duane to George Clinton, Aug. 25, 1777, *LDC* 7:548; R. H. Lee to John Page, Aug. 17, 1777, *LDC* 7:498; Mintz, *Generals of Saratoga*, 179.

66. Mintz, *Generals of Saratoga*, 180, 204, 225; Nelson, *Gates*, 94.

67. Dyer to Gates, Nov. 5, 1777, *LDC* 8:234; Duane to Gates, Dec. 16, 1777, *LDC* 8:421; Gerry to Thomas Gerry, Oct. 21, 1777, *LDC* 8:156; John Penn to Arthur Middleton, Oct. 21, 1777, *LDC* 8:158; Lovell to Whipple, Oct. 21, 1777, *LDC* 8:158; William Ellery to Nicholas Cooke, March 1, 1778, *LDC* 9:185; Lovell to SA, Feb. 19, 1778, quoted in Stinchcombe, *American Revolution and the French Alliance*, 12.

68. Stinchcombe, *American Revolution and the French Alliance*, 9.

69. Richard Van Alstyne, *Empire and Independence: The International History of the American Revolution* (New York, 1965), 135–54.

70. *LDC* 9:561n; Lovell to Massachusetts Council, May 3, 1778, *LDC* 9:587; GW to President of Congress, May 1, 1778, *WW* 11:332–33.

71. R. H. Lee to GW, May 6, 1778, *LDC* 9:615; Laurens to Steuben, May 11, 1778, *LDC* 9:647; Laurens to John Laurens, May 16, 1778, *LDC* 9:684–85.

72. Bobrick, *Angel in the Whirlwind*, 291; Marshall Smelser, *The Winning of Independence* (Chicago, 1992), 203; Ward, *War of the Revolution*, 2:546; Charles Lesser, ed., *The Sinews of Independence: Monthly Strength Reports of the Continental Army* (Chicago, 1976), 54–61; Higginbotham, *War of American Independence*, 213.

73. Lewis to New York Convention, March 30, 1778, *LDC* 9:354; Lawrence to Duane, Apr. 7, 1778, *LDC* 9:381; Laurens's Notes, Apr. 17–21, 1778, *LDC* 9:428; Laurens to William Livingston, Apr. 19, May 6, 1778, *LDC* 9:443, 613; Laurens to John Laurens, May 3, 1778, *LDC* 9:576.

74. Gerry to Warren, May 26, 1778, *LDC* 9:751; Ellery to Whipple, May 31, 1778, *LDC* 9:781; Lovell to Whipple, May 25, 1778, *LDC* 9:749; Connecticut Delegates to John Trumbull Sr., May 18, 1778, *LDC* 9:707.

75. GW to Conway, Nov. 9, 1777, *WW* 10:30; Rush to Henry, Jan. 12, 1778, in Jared Sparks, ed., *The Writings of George Washington* (Boston, 1833–37), 5:495–96.

76. Laurens to Laurens, Oct. 16, 1777, *LDC* 8:125; Sergeant to Lovell, Nov. 20, 1777, *LDC* 8:296; Gouverneur Morris to Robert Livingston, March 10, 1778, *LDC* 9:264; Lovell to SA, Dec. 20, 1777, Jan. 20, 1778, *LDC* 8:451, 618; JA to AA, Oct. 26, 1777, *AFC* 2:360–61; JA to Rush, Feb. 8, 1778, *PJA* 5:403.

77. Laurens to Benjamin Huger, Nov. 15, 1777, *LDC* 8:270, 271n; Lovell to JA, Feb. 8, 1778, *LDC* 5:55; Gerry to Knox, Feb. 7, 1778, *LDC* 9:45; Clark to William Alexander, Jan. 15, 1778, *LDC* 8:597; Richard Morris to Richard Peters, Jan. 25, 1778, *LDC* 8:649.

78. Laurens to Rawlins Lowndes, May 17, 1778, *LDC* 9:700; Reed to De Berdt, July 19, 1778, *LDC* 10:314; Laurens to Theveneau de Francy, July 26, 1778, *LDC* 10:353–54; Penn to Richard Casell, July 15, 1778, *LDC* 10:287; Laurens to John Rutledge, May 19, 1778, *LDC* 9:719.

Chapter 7

1. Lovell to Gates, Nov. 11, 1778, *LDC* 11:205; SA to Caleb Davis, Dec. 5, 1778, *LDC* 11:287–88.

2. JA to AA, May 17, 1776, *AFC* 1:410; JA to William Tudor, Sept. 29, 1774, *PJA* 2:176; JA to Joseph Hawley, Nov. 25, 1775, *PJA* 3:316; Rakove, *Beginnings of National Politics*, 247; Jillson and Wilson, *Congressional Dynamics*, 156.

3. Samuel Huntington's Proposed Resolution, [Apr. 22–23 ?], 1778, *LDC* 9:468; G. Morris's Draft Report, May 1, 1778, *LDC* 9:560; SA to Samuel Cooper, Apr. 29, 1779, *LDC* 12:402; John E. Selby, *The Revolution in Virginia, 1775–1783* (Williamsburg, Va., 1988), 190–91; Joseph L. Davis, *Sectionalism in American Politics, 1774–1787* (Madison, Wis., 1977), 17, 19.

4. Stinchcombe, *American Revolution and the French Alliance*, 62–63; William Henry Drayton's Notes of Proceedings, Feb. 15, 1779, *LDC* 12:171–73.

5. Stinchcombe, *American Revolution and the French Alliance*, 62, 64; Richard B. Morris, *The Peacemakers: The Great Powers and American Independence* (New York, 1965), 13, 17; Jonathan Dull, *A Diplomatic History of the American Revolution* (New Haven, Conn., 1985), 107–9.

6. *JCC* 13:239–44; John Fell's Diary, March 24, 1779, *LDC* 12:239.

7. Morris, *Peacemakers*, 14.

8. Davis, *Sectionalism*, 17.

9. Ibid., 16; Morris, *Peacemakers*, 11; Jonathan Dull, *The French Navy and American Independence: A Study of Arms and Diplomacy, 1774–1787* (Princeton, 1975), 359–76.

10. Fell's Diary, March 24, 1779, *LDC* 12:239.

11. Selby, *Revolution in Virginia*, 204–5.

12. North Carolina Delegates to Richard Caswell, Apr. 2, 1779, *LDC* 12:275–76; TJ to William Fleming, June 8, 1779, *PTJ* 2:288; H. James Henderson, *Party Politics in the Continental Congress* (New York, 1974), 197.

13. Lovell to Gates, Apr. 5[?], 1779, *LDC* 12:299; SA to Samuel Cooper, Apr. 29, 1779, *LDC* 12:402; Laurens's Notes of Debates, June 19, July 1, 1779, *LDC* 13:82–84, 133–343; John Armstrong to GW, June 25, 1779, *LDC* 13:108; G. Morris to Benjamin Towne, July 9, 1779, *LDC* 13:180; Daniel of St. Thomas Jenifer to Charles Carroll, June 30, 1779, *LDC* 13:129; Rakove, *Beginnings of National Politics*, 256–58; Stinchcombe, *American Revolution and the French Alliance*, 66–72; Davis, *Sectionalism*, 21.

14. *JCC* 13:363–68; JA to R. H. Lee, Aug. 5, 1778, *PJA* 6:354; Rakove, *Beginnings of National Politics*, 257.

15. JA to SA, Dec. 7, 1778, *PJA* 7:256; JA to Lovell, Feb. 20, 1779, *PJA* 7:420; JA to Thomas McKean, Sept. 20, 1779, *PJA* 8:162; *DAJA* 2:367, 391; 4:118–20; John Ferling, "John Adams, Diplomat," *WMQ* 51 (1994): 235.

16. Lovell to BF, Apr. 29, 1779, *LDC* 12:406; Laurens's Notes, Apr. 21 [?], 1779, *LDC* 12:364.

17. Lovell to A. Lee, June 13, 1779, *LDC* 13:63; Lovell to Warren, June 15, 1779, *LDC* 13:69–70; Lovell to JA, Sept. 29, 1779, *LDC* 13:581; Lovell to SA, Aug. 17, 1779, *LDC* 13:379; Lovell to Gates, Apr. 19, 1779, *LDC* 12:355; Nathaniel Peabody to Whipple, Nov. 1, 1779, *LDC* 14:141; Henderson, *Party Politics in the Continental Congress*, 187–213.

18. Freeman, *Washington*, 5:105.

19. Lesser, *Sinews of Independence*, 68–69, 116–18; Richard Buel Jr., *Dear Liberty: Connecticut's Mobilization for the Revolutionary War* (Middletown, Conn., 1980), 173, 176; John Miller, *Triumph of Freedom, 1775–1783* (Boston, 1948), 432; Royster, *A Revolutionary People at War*, 267–68, 270, 272.

20. E. Wayne Carp, *To Starve the Army at Pleasure: Continental Army Administration and American Political Culture, 1775–1783* (Chapel Hill, N.C., 1984), 55, 106, 109, 181–87.

21. John Ferling, *A Wilderness of Miseries: War and Warriors in Early America* (Westport, Conn., 1981), 96–97.

22. Ferguson, *Power of the Purse*, 45.

23. For a wonderful discussion of money and war, see the initial chapter in Niall Ferguson, *The Cash Nexus: Money and Power in the Modern World, 1700–2000* (New York, 2001).

24. Albert Bolles, *The Financial History of the United States* (New York, 1879), 1:159–60.

25. Flexner, *Washington*, 2:235–39; GW to Benjamin Harrison, Dec. 18 [–30], 1778, *WW* 13:467; Miller, *Triumph of Freedom*, 436, 474–76.

26. GW to Mason, March 27, 1779, *WW* 14:299–300; GW to Burwell Bassett, Apr. 22, 1779, *WW* 14:432; GW to Gouverneur Morris, May 8, 1779, *WW* 15:25; GW to John A. Washington, Nov. 26, 1778, May 12, 1779, *WW* 13:335; 15:60; GW to William Fitzhugh, Apr. 10, 1779, *WW* 14:365;

GW to Lund Washington, May 29, 1779, *WW* 15:180; GW to Joseph Reed, Dec. 12, 1778, *WW* 13:383.

27. Dickinson to Caesar Rodney, June 10, 1779, *LDC* 13:43; Cyrus Griffin to Burgess Ball, Aug. 10, 1779, *LDC* 13:345; Francis Lewis to Stephen Sayre, Aug. 10, 1779, *LDC* 13:351; Jenifer to Thomas Johnson, June 8, 1779, *LDC* 13:37; Cornelius Harnett to Burke, Oct. 9, 1779, *LDC* 13:50; Samuel Holton to William Gordon, Dec. 7, 1779, *LDC* 13:253; William Ellery to William Greene, Dec. 21, 1779, *LDC* 14:288; Root to Trumbull, Aug. 23, 1779, *LDC* 13:400.

28. Whipple to Langdon, June 1, 1779, *LDC* 13:10; Jenifer to Johnson, June 8, 1779, *LDC* 13:36; Gerry to GW, Jan. 12, 1780, *LDC* 14:336; Connecticut Delegates to Trumbull, March 20, 1779, *LDC* 14:519.

29. Whipple to Bartlett, Aug. 24, 1779, *LDC* 13:415.

30. Ellery to Greene, Dec. 21, 1779, *LDC* 14:288; Laurens to JA, Oct. 4, 1779, *LDC* 14:19.

31. Lovell to SA, Aug. 17, 1779, *LDC* 13:379; Laurens to John Laurens, July 23, 1779, *LDC* 13:286; Morris to Robert Livingston, Aug. 24, 1779, *LDC* 13:411; Main, *Sovereign States*, 245.

32. Quoted in Page Smith, *A New Age Now Begins* (New York, 1976), 2:1364.

33. Hawke, *Honorable Treason*, 41–44.

34. Sam Bass Warner Jr., *The Private City: Philadelphia in Three Periods of Its Growth* (Philadelphia, 1968); 29–43; John K. Alexander, "The Fort Wilson Incident of 1779: A Case Study of the Revolutionary Crowd," *WMQ* 31 (1974): 589–612; *LDC* 14:16n; Miller, *Triumph of Freedom*, 442.

35. Fell's Diary, Oct. 4, 1779, *LDC* 14:15; Fell to Morris, Oct. 5, 1779, *LDC* 14:24; James Forbes to Thomas Lee, Oct. 5, 1779, *LDC* 14:25; G. Morris to George Clinton, Oct. 7, 1779, *LDC* 14:44–45; Rakove, *Beginnings of National Politics*, 270; Main, *Sovereign States*, 245–46.

36. Ferguson, *Power of the Purse*, 34, 46, 50, 61, 100; John Mathews to Thomas Bee, Sept. 21, 1779, *LDC* 13:532; Fell to Morris, March 12, 1780, *LDC* 14:489; George Partridge to Samuel Freeman, Nov. 30, 1779, *LDC* 14:241; Rhode Island Delegates to Greene, June 1, 1779, *LDC* 13:10; Laurens to GW, Oct. 7, 1779, *LDC* 14:41–42.

37. Richard D. Brown, "The Confiscation and Disposition of Loyalists' Estates in Suffolk County, Massachusetts," *WMQ* 21 (1964): 534–50; Staughton Lynd, "Who Shall Rule at Home? Dutchess County, New York, in the American Revolution," *WMQ* 18 (1961): 352–53.

38. Main, *Sovereign States*, 234–68, 280–83; Miller, *Triumph of Freedom*, 458; Harry M. Ward, *Nationhood Achieved, 1763–1788* (New York, 1995), 265. On the depreciation of Continental money, see Ferguson, *Power of the Purse*, 31–32, 56n, and John J. McCusker, *How Much Is That in Real Money? A Historical Price Index for Use as a Deflator of Money Values in the Economy of the United States* (Worcester, Mass., 1992), 354–58. Generally, by late in 1779 $30 was required to purchase $1 in specie. Eighteen months later, $167 purchased $1 in specie.

39. GW to Mason, March 27, 1779, *WW* 14:300; GW to John Armstrong, May 18, 1779, *WW* 15:97; GW to Edmund Randolph, Aug. 1, 1779, *WW* 16:97.

40. Henry Laurens to JA, Oct. 4, 1779, *LDC* 14:18–19.

41. Lee to JA, Sept. 10, 1780, Adams Family Paper, reel 352, microfilm edition, MHS; Charles Thomson to Dickinson, Dec. 25, 1780, *LDC* 16:485–86.

42. Charles Royster, "The Nature of Treason': Revolutionary Virtue and American Reactions to Benedict Arnold," *WMQ* 36 (1979): 163–93; AH to Duane, Sept. 3, 1780, *PAH* 2:406; Lovell to JA, Jan. 2, 1781, *LDC* 16:537.

43. GW to Mason, *WW* 14:301.

44. Hancock to TJ, Sept. 30, 1776, *PTJ* 1:523–24; Lee to TJ, Sept. 27, Nov. 3, 1776, *PTJ* 1:522–23, 590; TJ to Hancock, Oct. 11, *PTJ* 1:524.

45. JA to TJ, May 26, 1777, *PJA* 5:204; GW to Harrison, Dec. 18–30, 1778, *WW* 13:467.

46. Lee to TJ, May 3, 1779, *PTJ* 2:262–63; Pendleton to TJ, May 11, 1779, *PTJ* 2:266; William Fleming to TJ, May 22, 1779, *PTJ* 2:269; John Page to TJ, Dec. 9, 1780, *PTJ* 4:192.

47. GW to Mason, March 27, 1779, *WW* 14:301.

48. Lovell to Holton, Sept. 12, 1780, *LDC* 16:58–59; *DAJA* 2:156; Rakove, *Beginnings of National Politics*, 198–205, 216–39; Miller, *Triumph of Freedom*, 434.

49. JM to TJ, March 27, 1780, *PTJ* 3:335.

50. Rakove, *Beginnings of National Politics*, 200, 222.

51. Duane to Clinton, Nov. 14, 1780, *LDC* 16:331, 333; John Witherspoon to William Livingston, Dec. 16, 1780, *LDC* 16:451–53; *JCC* 18:1032; Rakove, *Beginnings of National Politics*, 279–84.

52. John Ferling, "Jefferson's War," *American History* 35 (Feb. 2001): 36–44.

53. Selby, *Revolution in Virginia*, 243; Jensen, *Articles of Confederation*, 236–37; Forrest McDonald, *The Formation of the American Republic, 1776–1790* (Baltimore, 1967), 11, 15–16.

54. JM to TJ, Apr. 16, 1781, *LDC* 17:157; Duane to GW, Sept. 19, 1780, *LDC* 16:91; Varnum to William Greene, Apr. 2, 1781, *LDC* 17:115–17.

55. TJ to La Luzerne, Apr. 12, 1781, *PTJ*, 5:422; Lee Kennett, *The French Forces in America, 1780–1783* (Westport, Conn., 1977), 15, 77–91; Vergennes to Lafayette, Aug. 7, 1780, in Stanley J. Idzerda et al., eds., *Lafayette in the Age of the American Revolution: Selected Letters and Papers* (Ithaca, N.Y., 1977–), 3:129; 4:47.

56. *JCC* 20:614–15, 627; Stinchcombe, *American Revolution and the French Alliance*, 153–58.

57. Ferling, "John Adams, Diplomat," *WMQ* 51 (1994): 237–39; Reed to Gen. Greene, June 16, 1781, in Richard Showman et al., eds., *The Papers of Nathanael Greene* (Chapel Hill, N.C., 1976–), 8:399.

58. Rakove, *Beginnings of National Politics*, 289–90; Henderson, *Party Politics in the Continental Congress*, 283–86.

59. Cornell to William Greene, July 21, 1780, *LDC* 15:479; Varnum to Greene, March 16, Apr. 2, 1781, *LDC* 17:66, 115–17; Henderson, *Party Politics in the Continental Congress*, 246–50; Carp, *To Starve the Army at Pleasure*, 202–4; Stanley Elkins and Eric McKitrick, "The Founding Fathers: Young Men of the Revolution," *Political Science Quarterly* 76 (1961): 181–216.

60. Sullivan to Meshech Weare, Oct. 2, 1780, *LDC* 16:131;Varnum to Greene, Apr. 2, 1781, *LDC* 17:117; Lovell to Holten, Sept. 5, 1780, *LDC* 16:21; Cornell to William Greene, Aug. 28, 1780, *LDC* 15:626; Sullivan's Committee Notes [Nov. 7–23], 1780, *LDC* 16:306; Wolcott to Ellsworth, Jan. 2, 1781, *LDC* 16:543; Mathews to W. Livingston, Jan. 29, 1781, *LDC* 16:637; *JCC* 19:111; Henderson, *Party Politics in the Continental Congress*, 247, 273; Carp, *To Starve the Army at Pleasure*, 192; Stinchcombe, *American Revolution and the French Alliance*, 140.

61. Clarence Ver Steg, *Robert Morris: Revolutionary Financier* (Philadelphia, 1972), 3–7. The quotations in this paragraph are taken from Louis Potts, *Arthur Lee: A Virtuous Revolutionary* (Baton Rouge, La., 1981), 161 and Miller, *Triumph of Freedom*, 447.

62. Quoted in Ver Steg, *Morris*, 9, and Wood, *Radicalism of the American Revolution*, 211.

63. Thomas Paine, "The Affairs of Silas Deane," in Foner, *Complete Writings of Paine*, 2:135–37; Miller, *Triumph of Freedom*, 447, 449.

64. Samuel Osgood to John Lowell, Feb. 2, 1781, *LDC* 18:322; Duane to GW, Sept. 9, 1781, *LDC* 18:26; William Sharpe to Gen. Greene, Sept. 4, 1781, *LDC* 18:13; Rhode Islands Delegates to Wm. Greene, Dec. 6, 1781, *LDC* 18:239; Benjamin Hawkins to Abner Nash, Nov. 17, 1781, *LDC* 18:203.

65. Richard B. Morris, *The Forging of the Union, 1781–1789* (New York, 1987), 41–42; Rakove, *Beginnings of National Politics*, 300–306.

66. Henderson, *Party Politics in the Continental Congress*, 286–91.

67. Lee to SA, Aug. 6, 1782, *LDC* 19:25. The Joseph Reed quotations are from Merrill Jensen, *The New Nation: A History of the United States during the Confederation, 1781–1789* (New York, 1950), 60, 367.

68. Jensen, *New Nation*, 57; Richard Buel Jr., *In Irons: Britain's Naval Supremacy and the American Revolutionary Economy* (New Haven, Conn., 1998), 207–9, 238.

69. Boudinot to Hannah Boudinot, Oct. 21, 1781, *LDC* 18:152n; Mathews to Gen. Greene, Oct. 22, 1781, *LDC* 18:153; Boudinot to Elisha Boudinot, Oct. 23, 1781, *LDC* 18:154; Connecticut Delegates to Trumbull, Oct. 25, 1781, *LDC* 18:165; Henry P. Johnston, *The Yorktown Campaign and the Surrender of Cornwallis* (New York, 1881), 158.

70. Flexner, *Washington*, 2:429–30; Kennett, *French Forces in America*, 108; GW to Rochambeau, May 27, June 4, 13, 1781, *WW* 22:120, 157, 207–8; GW to Lafayette, May 31, 1781, *WW* 22:143; GW to Col. Laurens, Jan. 15, 1781, *WW* 21:108; GW to Daniel Webster, July 31, 1788, *PGW: Confed Ser* 6:415.

71. Virginia Delegates to Benjamin Harrison, March 19, 1782, *LDC* 18:413.

72. Rhode Island never ratified the amendments and several states attached what might have been insuperable conditions to their approval of a national impost.

73. Jensen, *New Nation*, 66.

74. *JCC* 22:429–47; 23:545–47, 604–6; Thomson's Notes, Aug. 5, 1782, *LDC* 19:21; Jacob Cooke, *Alexander Hamilton* (New York, 1982), 33; Ver Steeg, *Morris*, 123.

75. Morris to AH, Aug. 28, 1782, *PAH* 3:152.

76. Richard Brookhiser, *Alexander Hamilton* (New York, 1999), 14.

77. AH to Edward Stevens, Nov. 11, 1769, *PAH* 1:4.

78. GW to President of Congress, Oct. 16, 1781, *WW* 23:228.

79. On Hamilton, see Brookhiser, *Hamilton*, 13–50; Cooke, *Hamilton*, 1–20; John C. Miller, *Alexander Hamilton: Portrait in Paradox* (New York, 1959), 3–79; Richard B. Morris, *Seven Who Shaped Our Destiny: The Founding Fathers as Revolutionaries* (New York, 1973), 221–58; Adrienne Koch, *Power, Morals, and the Founding Fathers: Essays in the Interpretation of the American Enlightenment* (Ithaca, N.Y., 1961), 50–80; Ferling, *First of Men*, 256–57.

80. Sullivan to GW, March 6, 1781, *LDC* 17:30.

81. Alexander Hamilton, *The Continentalist, PAH* 2:649–50, 664, 665.

82. *PAH* 3:103, 106. See also AH to Duane, Sept. 3, 1780, *PAH* 2:400–418.

83. AH to GW, March 17, 1783, *PAH* 3:292. *PAH* 3:292.

Chapter 8

1. Theodorick Bland to St. George Tucker, Aug. 9, 1782, *LDC* 19:47.

2. William Blount to John Gray Blount, Jan. 7, 1783, *LDC* 19:555; Duane to George Clinton, Aug. 20, 1782, *LDC* 19:78; Virginia Delegates to Benjamin Harrison, Sept. 24, 1782, *LDC* 19:204.

3. Bland to Edmund Randolph, March 3, 1783, *LDC* 19:756; Osgood to John Lowell, Jan. 6, 1783, *LDC* 19: 548; Boudinot to Gen. Greene, Feb. 13, 1783, *LDC* 19:688; Gorham to John Lowell, Jan. 29, 1783, *LDC* 19:637; Montgomery to Robert Magaw, Feb.13, 1783, *LDC* 19:694.

4. AH to GW, Feb. 13, 1783, *PAH* 3:253–55.

5. Ibid., 3:253.

6. *JCC* 24:291–93.

7. *JCC* 24:294–95.

8. Lee to SA, Jan. 29, 1783, *LDC* 19:639.

9. AH to GW, Feb. 13, 1783, *PAH* 3:254.

10. Henderson, *Party Politics in the Continental Congress*, 328.

11. *JCC* 24:295–97.

12. GW, General Orders, March 11, 1783, *WW* 26:208–9.

13. Quoted in Flexner, *Washington*, 2:205.

14. GW, To the Officers of the Army, March 15, 1783, *WW* 26:222–27.

15. JA to F. A. Vanderkemp, Aug. 23, 1806, Apr. 23, 1807, Apr. 3, 1815, Gratz Collection, Historical Society of Pennsylvania; Richard Brookhiser, *Founding Father: Rediscovering George Washington* (New York, 1996), 43, 151–56.

16. *WW* 26:222n.

17. *JCC* 24:310–11; Higginbotham, *War of American Independence,* 411–12. On the Newburgh Affair see Richard H. Kohn, "The Inside History of the Newburgh Conspiracy: America and the Coup d'Etat," *WMQ* 27 (1970): 187–220; Paul David Nelson, "Horatio Gates at Newburgh, 1783: A Misunderstood Role," *WMQ* 29 (1972): 143–51, with Richard H. Kohn's reply, *WMQ* 29 (1972): 151–58.

18. Gunning Bedford Jr. to Nicholas Van Dyke, March 12, 1783, *LDC* 20:3; JA to AA, Jan. 22, 1783, Lyman H. Butterfield, ed., *The Book of Abigail and John: Selected Letters of the Adams Family, 1762–1784* (Cambridge, Mass., 1975), 337.

19. John Ferling, "John Adams, Diplomat," *WMQ* 51 (1994): 242–44; *JCC* 20:614–15, 618–19, 627, 648; Stinchcombe, *American Revolution and the French Alliance,* 153–62.

20. James H. Hutson, *John Adams and the Diplomacy of the American Revolution* (Lexington, Ky., 1980), 117–41; Morris, *Peacemakers,* 191–310; Dull, *A Diplomatic History of the American Revolution,* 137–51.

21. Richard Peters to Gates, March 13, 1783, *LDC* 20:27; John Taylor Gilman to Weare, March 12, 1783, *LDC* 20:10; Boudinot to GW, March 17, 1783, *LDC* 20:30; *DAJA* 3:52.

22. Martin and Lender, *A Respectable Army,* 195; *LDC* 20:329n.

23. Smith, *A New Age Now Begins,* 2:1777–79; Boudinot, "Draft Statement on the Mutiny," June 26, 1783, *LDC* 20:367–68.

24. Royster, *A Revolutionary People at War,* 352–53; Martin and Lender, *A Respectable Army,* 33; GW, General Orders, July 2, 1776, *GWP: Rev War Ser* 5:180.

25. James Tilton to Bedford, Dec. 25, 1783, *LDC* 21:232; James McHenry to Margaret Caldwell, Dec. 23, 1783, *LDC* 21:221; TJ to Benjamin Harrison, *PTJ* 6:419; GW, "Address to Congress," Dec. 23, 1783, *WW* 27:284–85.

26. Freeman, *Washington* 5:469–78; Garry Wills, *Cincinnatus: George Washington and the Enlightenment* (Garden City, N.Y., 1984), 13.

27. Mifflin to William Livingston, Jan. 4, 1784, *LDC* 21:258; Edward Carrington to James Madison, Dec. 18, 1786, *LDC* 24:54.

28. GW to TJ, March 29, 1784, *PGW: Confed Ser* 1:239; TJ to Edmund Pendleton, Jan. 18, 1784, *PTJ* 6:471.

29. Henderson, *Party Politics in the Continental Congress,* 384–85; Jensen, *New Nation,* 399.

30. Nathaniel Gorham to Caleb Davis, March 1, 1786, *LDC* 23:167; William Grayson to R. H. Lee, March 22, 1786, *LDC* 23:201; Charles Pettit to Jeremiah Wadsworth, May 27, 1786, *LDC* 23:316.

31. Henderson, *Party Politics in the Continental Congress,* 360–62; Rakove, *Beginnings of National Politics,* 337–39.

32. Jensen, *New Nation,* 125.

33. Ibid., 114–15.

34. Ibid., 133–34, 145–48.

35. Ibid., 192, 196, 200–202, 211, 215.

36. BF to Ferdinand Grand, Jan. 29, March 5, 1786, in A. H. Smyth, ed., *Writings of Benjamin Franklin* (New York, 1905–7), 9:482, 493; BF to David Hartley, Oct. 27, 1785, ibid., 9:472; BF to Jonathan Shipley, Feb. 24, 1786, ibid., 9:489; Thomson to TJ, Apr. 6, 1786, *PTJ* 9:380; AA to JA, May 2, 1784, *AFC* 5:330; Howell to William Greene, Jan.12, 1785, *LDC* 22:108; GW to La Luzerne, Aug. 1, 1786, *PGW: Confed Ser* 4:186.

37. See Cathy D. Matson and Peter S. Onuf, *A Union of Interests: Political and Economic Thought in Revolutionary America* (Lawrence, Kans., 1990), 31–100.

38. GW, Circular to the States, June 8, 1783, *WW* 26:484–89; GW to Henry Lee, Oct. 31, 1786, *PGW: Confed Ser* 4:318; GW to William Grayson, July 26, 1786, ibid., 4:169; GW to JM, Nov. 5, 1786, ibid., 4:360.

39. Thomson to TJ, May 19, 1785, *PTJ* 7:273; David Ramsay to Rush, Feb. 11, 1786, *LDC* 23:148; George Washington, "Address to Congress on Resigning His Commission," Dec. 23, 1783, *WW* 27:284.

40. On women and African Americans in this war, see the wonderful account in Ray Raphael, *A People's History of the American Revolution: How Common People Shaped the Fight for Independence* (New York, 2001), 135–81, 309–79.

41. Bailyn, *Ideological Origins of the American Revolution*, 283; Edward Rutledge to Ralph Izard, Dec. 8, 1775, *LDC* 2:463.

42. Quoted in Jensen, *The American Revolution within America*, 105.

43. Wood, *Creation of the American Republic*, 393–94.

44. *Boston Independent Chronicle*, March 1, 1787, in Seth Ames, ed., *Works of Fisher Ames* (Boston, 1854), 2:101; *The Federalist*, No. 62. For a more detailed treatment of these themes, see Wood, *Creation of the American Republic*, 471–83. The Randolph quote is from Jensen, *The American Revolution within America*, 105.

45. Alfred F. Young, *The Democratic Republicans of New York: The Origins, 1763–1797* (Chapel Hill, N.C., 1967), 9, 21, 29–30, 44, 62; E. Wilder Spaulding, *New York in the Critical Period, 1783–1789* (reprint, Port Washington, N.Y., 1963), 185; Roger Champagne, *Alexander McDougall and the American Revolution* (Schenectady, N.Y., 1975), 211–12; Thomas Cochran, *New York in the Confederation: An Economic Study* (reprint, Clifton, N.J., 1972), 136–37, 149, 170; E. Wilder Spaulding, "Abraham Yates," in *Dictionary of American Biography* (New York, 1929–37), 20:597–98; Abraham Yates to Robert Yates, June 9, 1787, *LDC* 24:320; Yates to Henry Oothoudt and Jeremiah Van Rensselaer, Aug. 29, 1787, *LDC* 24:411.

46. Yates to Oothoudt and Van Rensselaer, Aug. 29, 1787, *LDC* 24:411.

47. William Blount to Richard Caswell, Jan. 28, 1787, *LDC* 24:76; AH to Robert Morris, Aug. 13, 1782, *PAH* 3:139. The "cobbler" and "old booby" quotations are from Young, *Democratic Republicans of New York*, 44. The "little folks" quotation is from John P. Kaminsky, *George Clinton: Yeoman Politician of the New Republic* (Madison, Wis., 1994), 104. See also Wood, *Creation of the American Republic*, 487–88.

48. Quoted in Young, *Democratic Republicans of New York*, 572.

49. Curtis Nettles, *The Emergence of a National Economy, 1775–1815* (New York, 1962), 55–56; Frederick Marks, *Independence on Trial: Foreign Affairs and the Making of the Constitution* (Baton Rouge, La., 1973), 59, 69; Jensen, *New Nation*, 161–63, 198–200; Morris, *Forging the Union*, 134–47, 205–6; JA to Jay, Feb. 14, 1788, *WJA* 8:476.

50. Marks, *Independence on Trial*, 9.

51. Morris, *Forging of the Union*, 232–44.

52. Monroe to TJ, Aug. 19, 1786, *PTJ* 10:277; Monroe to JM, Aug. 14, Sept. 3, 1786, *PJM* 9:104, 113.

53. Quoted in Jack Rakove, *James Madison and the Creation of the Federal Republic* (Glenview, Ill., 1990), 44. On the mood of the moment, see Jack Rakove, *Original Meanings: Politics and Ideas in the Making of the Constitution* (New York, 1996), 35–36.

54. Joseph J. Ellis, *Founding Brothers: The Revolutionary Generation* (New York, 2000), 54.

55. Fisher Ames, quoted in Douglass Adair, "James Madison," in Douglass Adair, *Fame and the Founding Fathers: Essays by Douglass Adair* (New York, 1974), 128.

56. JM to TJ, Aug. 12, 1786, *PJM* 9:96–97; R. H. Lee to JM, Nov. 26, 1784, *PJM* 8:151; JM to R. H. Lee, Dec. 25, 1784, *PJM* 8:201; Lance Banning, *The Sacred Fire of Liberty: James Madison and the Founding of the Federal Republic* (Ithaca, N.Y., 1995), 13–75; Rakove, *Madison*, 1–43; Rakove, *Original Meanings*, 36.

57. Norman Risjord, *Chesapeake Politics, 1781–1800* (New York, 1978), 88.

58. Ibid., 148–56; JM, *The Federalist*, No. 10; Max Farrand, ed., *The Records of the Federal Convention of 1787* (reprint, New Haven, Conn., 1966), 1:423.

59. JM to Caleb Wallace, Aug. 23, 1785, *PJM* 8:350–52; JM to TJ, Oct. 24, 1787, March 18, 1786, *PJM* 8:501–2; 10:209–11; JM to GW, Apr. 16, 1786, *PJM* 9:383–84; JM, "Vices of the Political System of the United States" [Apr. 1787], *PJM* 9:349–50, 353–54; JM, *The Federalist,* No. 10; Banning, *Sacred Fire of Liberty,* 44, 98–102, 120.

60. JM to TJ, Aug. 12, 1786, March 19, 1787, *PJM* 9:94–95, 318; Wood, *Radicalism of the American Revolution,* 251. See also Gordon Wood, "Interests and Disinterestedness in the Making of the Constitution," in Richard Beeman et al., eds., *Beyond Confederation: Origins of the Constitution and American National Identity* (Chapel Hill, N.C., 1987), 69–77.

61. Quoted in Wood, *Radicalism of the American Revolution,* 230.

62. JM to GW, Dec. 7, 24, 1786, Feb. 21, 1787, *PJM* 9:200, 224, 286; JM to TJ, Dec. 4, 1786, Feb. 15, 1787, *PJM* 9:190, 267; JM to Edmund Randolph, Feb. 24, 25, 1787, *PJM* 9:295, 299; JM, "Vices," *PJM* 9:351, 353.

63. JM to Edmund Randolph, Apr. 8, 1787, *PJM* 9:369; JM to GW, Apr. 16, 1787, *PJM* 9:384; JM to Randolph, Apr. 8, 1787, *PJM* 9:370; Lance Banning, "The Practicable Sphere of a Republic: James Madison, the Constitutional Convention, and the Emergence of Revolutionary Federalism," in Beeman, *Beyond Confederation,* 167–70.

64. JM, *The Federalist,* No. 10.

65. Ibid. The literature on Madison's reflection of faction is considerable, but the classic pieces are Douglass Adair, " That Politics May Be Reduced to a Science': David Hume, James Madison, and the Tenth Federalist," *Huntington Library Quarterly* 20 (1957): 343–60, and Douglass Adair, "The Tenth Federalist Revisited," *WMQ* 8 (1951): 48–67. See also Garry Wills, *Explaining America: The Federalist* (Garden City, N.Y., 1981). Although published too late for utilization in this book, see Mark G. Spencer, "Hume and Madison on Faction," *WMQ* 59 (2002): 869–96, and Samuel Fleischacker, "Adam Smith's Reception among the American Founders, 1776–1790," *WMQ* 59 (2002): 897–924.

66. JM to TJ, March 19, 1787, *PJM* 9:318; Madison, "Views," *PJM* 9:355–57; JM, *The Federalist,* No. 10.

67. Forrest McDonald, *Alexander Hamilton: A Biography* (New York, 1979), 92; AH to Jay, July 25, 1783, *PAH* 3:417; Pettit to Wadsworth, Mary 27, 1786, *LDC* 23:315–17; Nathan Dane to John Choate, Jan. 31, 1786, *LDC* 23:122; Dane to SA, Feb. 11, 1786, *LDC* 23:141.

68. Matson and Onuf, *A Union of Interests,* 83–87. The quotation is on 87.

69. Henry Lee to GW, Feb. 16, March 2, 1786, *PGW: Confed Ser* 3:561, 578; Jay to GW, March 16, 1786, ibid., 3:601; Marks, *Independence on Trial,* 134.

70. Dane to Samuel Adams, Feb. 11, 1786, *LDC* 23:141; Fowler, *Samuel Adams,* 161–63.

71. Dane to John Choate, Jan. 31, 1786, *LDC* 23:122; Dane to Jacob Wales, Jan. 31, 1786, *LDC* 23:128.

72. Jensen, *New Nation,* 418–20.

73. Marks, *Independence on Trial,* 247–53. On Madison's role in the convening of the Annapolis Convention, see the editor's note in *PJM* 9:116–18.

74. JM to Monroe, March 14, 18, 1787, *PJM* 8:497–98, 505–6.

75. William Grayson to JM, May 28, 1786, *LDC* 23:320.

76. McDonald, *Hamilton,* 91; Annapolis Convention, "Address of the Annapolis Convention" [Sept. 14, 1786], *PAH* 3:686–90.

77. GW to James McHenry, Aug. 22, 1785, *PGW: Confed Ser* 3:197; GW to Henry Lee, Apr. 5, 1786, ibid., 4:4.

78. GW, Circular to the States, June 8, 1783, *WW* 26:489–90.

79. GW to JM, Nov. 30, 1785, *PGW: Confed Ser* 3:420; GW to Benjamin Harrison, Jan. 18, 1784, ibid., 1:56; GW, Circular to the States, June 8, 1783, *WW* 26:486.

80. GW to Knox, Feb. 3, 1787, *PGW: Confed Ser* 5:8–9; GW to Bushrod Washington, Nov. 15, 1786, ibid., 4:4.

81. Louis B. Wright and Marion Tinkling, eds., *Carolina to Quebec in 1785–1786* (San Marino, Calif., 1943), 50; GW to Randolph, March 28, 1787, *PGW: Confed Ser* 5:112–14.

82. Daniel P. Szatmary, *Shays' Rebellion: The Making of an Agrarian Insurrection* (Amherst, Mass., 1980); Morris, *Forging of the Union*, 258–66; Taylor, *Western Massachusetts in the Revolution*, 103–67; Gary Kornblith and John M. Murrin, "The Making and Unmaking of an American Ruling Class," in Alfred E. Young, ed., *Beyond the American Revolution: Explorations in the History of American Radicalism* (DeKalb, Ill., 1993), 53. Debtor agitation also occurred in the 1780s elsewhere in New England, Maryland, South Carolina, New Jersey, Virginia, and Pennsylvania. See Allan Kulikoff, "The American Revolution, Capitalism, and the Formation of the Yeoman Classes," in Young, *Beyond the American Revolution,* 100.

83. GW to David Humphreys, Dec. 26, 1786, *PGW: Confed Ser* 4:478; GW to Knox, Dec. 26, 1786, ibid., 4:481–83; GW to Benjamin Lincoln, Feb. 24, 1787, ibid., 5:51–52; GW to Lafayette, March 25, 1787, ibid., 5:106.

Chapter 9

1. For a profile of the delegates, see Clinton Rossiter, *1787: The Grand Convention* (New York, 1966), 138–56.

2. Forrest McDonald, *Novus Ordo Seclorum: The Intellectual Origins of the Constitution* (Lawrence, Kans., 1985), 220–22.

3. JM, *The Federalist,* No. 10.

4. Quoted in Jensen, *The American Revolution within America,* 169.

5. John P. Roche, "The Founding Fathers: A Reform Caucus in Action," *American Political Science Review* 55 (1961): 800–801.

6. JM, "Vices of the Political System," *PJM* 9:348–50, 355; JM, *Notes on the Debates in the Federal Convention of 1787, Reported by James Madison* (Athens, Ohio, 1966), 39, 42.

7. JA to AA, Apr. 28, 1776, *AFC* 1:399.

8. JM to GW, Apr. 16, 1787, *PJM* 9:383.

9. Farrand, *Records of the Federal Convention of 1787,* 1:18.

10. Ibid., 1:26–27; JM, *Notes on the Debates,* 35; "Virginia Plan," *PJM* 10:16–18; JM to TJ, March 19, 1787, *PJM* 9:318–19.

11. JM to Randolph, Apr. 8, 1787, *PJM* 9:369; JM to TJ, March 19, 1787, *PJM* 9:319.

12. Farrand, *Records,* 1:167.

13. JM, *Notes on the Debates,* 55, 57; Farrand, *Records,* 1:242n. For a different perspective, see Rakove, *Original Meanings,* 57–83, and Jack Rakove, "The Great Compromise: Ideas, Interests, and the Politics of Constitution Making," *WMQ* 44 (1987): 424–57.

14. Peter Kolchin, *American Slavery, 1619–1877* (New York, 1993), 63–92.

15. *PGW: Confed Ser* 4:16–17n.

16. Farrand, *Records,* 1:592, 596, 605; 2:95, 449–50; Earl M. Maltz, "The Idea of the Proslavery Constitution," *JER* 17 (1997): 57.

17. Paul Finkelman, "Slavery and the Constitutional Convention: Making a Covenant with Death," in Beeman, *Beyond Confederation,* 225; William M. Wiecek, "The Witch at the Christening: Slavery and the Constitution's Origins," in Leonard Levy and Dennis J. Mahoney, eds. *The Framing and Ratification of the Constitution* (New York, 1987), 167–84.

18. Farrand, *Records,* 1:567; 2:221–23. On Southern overrepresentation in Congress in the nineteenth century, see Wiecek, "Witch at the Christening," in Levy and Mahoney, *Framing and Ratification of the Constitution,* 180, and William W. Freehling, "The Divided South, Democracy's Limitations, and the Causes of the Peculiarly North American Civil War," in Gabor S. Boritt, ed., *Why the War Came* (New York, 1996), 148; William W. Freehling, *The*

Road to Disunion: Secessionists at Bay, 1776–1854 (New York, 1990), 147. For a more benign view of slavery and the Founders, see Thomas G. West, *Vindicating the Founders: Race, Sex, Class, and Justice in the Origins of America* (Lanham, Md., 1997), 1–36.

19. Matson and Onuf, *A Union of Interests*, 113–19; Finkelman, "Slavery and the Constitutional Convention," 217–18.

20. Farrand, *Records*, 2:449–50. Pinckney's statement to the South Carolina ratification convention is quoted in Finkelman, "Slavery and the Constitutional Convention," 193.

21. Farrand, *Records*, 1:529, 486, 400, 586, 533, 604, 402.

22. The notes of six delegates who listened to AH's speech have survived. Those of Robert Yates and JM are the most comprehensive. The quotations in this section are based on Yates's notes and can be found in *PAH* 4:201. For all the notes, see *PAH* 4:178–211.

23. Quoted in Alfred F. Young, "The Framers of the Constitution and the 'Genius' of the People," *Radical History Review* 42 (1988): 8–9.

24. McDonald, *Novus Ordo Seclorum*, 270.

25. The literature on the Constitutional Convention is vast. My interpretation draws heavily on the several sources cited above, and on Lance Banning, "The Constitutional Convention," and Michael P. Zuckert, "A System without Precedent: Federalism in the American Constitution," in Levy and Mahoney, *Framing and Ratification of the Constitution*, 112–31, 132–50; Charles Warren, *The Making of the Constitution* (Boston, 1928); Roche, "The Founding Fathers," *American Political Science Review* 55 (1961): 799–816; Donald Robinson, *Slavery in the Structure of American Politics, 1765–1820* (New York, 1971); Staughton Lynd, *Class Conflict, Slavery, and the Constitution* (Indianapolis, Ind., 1967); Wood, "Interests and Disinterestedness," in Beeman, *Beyond Confederation*, 69–109; William W. Freehling, "The Founding Fathers and Slavery," *American Historical Review* 77 (1972): 81–93; Morris, *Forging of the Union*, 267–97; McDonald, *Formation of the American Republic*, 155–208.

26. Farrand, *Records*, 1:26.

27. Ibid., 1:48.

28. Ibid.

29. Ibid., 1:58.

30. JM, *The Federalist*, No. 10; Jack Rakove, "The Structure of Politics at the Accession of George Washington," in Beeman, *Beyond Confederation*, 267.

31. JM, *The Federalist*, No. 10.

32. Roche, "Founding Fathers," *American Political Science Review* 55 (1961): 815.

33. Farrand, *Records*, 1:125.

34. Rossiter, *1787: The Grand Convention*, 297.

35. Merrill Jensen, "The Confederation Congress and the Constitution," in Merrill Jensen et al., eds., *Documentary History of the Ratification of the Constitution* (Madison, Wis., 1976–), 1:323–53. On the press campaign that commenced even before the Constitutional Convention terminated, see John K. Alexander, *The Selling of the Constitutional Convention: A History of News Coverage* (Madison, Wis., 1990), 176–204, 213–21.

36. Morris, *Forging of the Union*, 298–99; Robert Allen Rutland, *The Ordeal of the Constitution: The Anti-Federalists and the Ratification Struggle, 1787–1788* (Norman, Okla., 1966), 18–19; Jensen, "Confederation Congress."

37. For Rhode Island's official explanation for having not sent delegates to the Philadelphia Convention, see "Rhode Island's Reasons for Refusal to Appoint Delegates," Sept. 15, 1787, in Jensen, ed., *Documentary History of Ratification*, 1:225–29.

38. Paine, *Common Sense*, in Foner, ed., *Complete Writings of Paine*, 1:4, 6, 19, 27.

39. Saul Cornell, *The Other Founders: Anti-Federalism and the Dissenting Tradition in America, 1788–1828* (Chapel Hill, N.C., 1999), 72, 81, 89, 119.

40. SA to R. H. Lee, Dec. 3, 1787, *WSA* 4:325.

41. Letters of "Centinel," No. 1, in Cecelia M. Kenyon, ed., *The Antifederalists* (Indianapolis, Ind., 1966), 14; Letters of "Cato," No. 4, ibid., 305; Debates in the South Carolina Legislature and Convention, ibid., 187.

42. Debates in the Virginia Convention, ibid., 255–56.

43. SA to R. H. Lee, Dec. 3, 1787, *WSA* 4:324–25.

44. Debates in the Virginia Convention, Kenyon, *Antifederalists,* 256, 248.

45. Letters of "A Republican Federalist," No. 3, Kenyon, *Antifederalists,* 118; SA to R. H. Lee, Dec. 3, 1787, *WSA* 4:325. On the Anti-Federalist viewpoint, see also Lance Banning, *The Jeffersonian Persuasion* (Ithaca, N.Y., 1978), 106–11; Cornell, *The Other Founders,* 29, 31, 54, 69–71, 90–91, 100; Wood, *Creation of the American Republic,* 484–85, 519–32; Rakove, *Original Meanings,* 146–47, 273; Jackson Turner Main, *The Antifederalists: Critics of the Constitution* (Chapel Hill, N.C., 1961), 174, 175, 177, 181, 183, 184; Rossiter, *1787: The Grand Convention,* 283.

46. Main, *Antifederalists,* 203.

47. SA to R. H. Lee, Dec. 3, 1787, *WSA* 4:324.

48. "Candidus" [Samuel Adams], *Boston Independent Chronicle,* Dec. 1787/Jan. 1788, in Herbert J. Storing, ed., *The Complete Anti-Federalist* (Chicago, 1981), 4:125–32. Storing attributes the two "Candidus" essays to Adams or his acolyte Benjamin Austin, a Boston mechanic, as well as a series of additional essays written under the pseudonym "Helvidius Priscus." The literary style of "Candidus" closely resembles that of Adams.

49. Quoted in Main, *Antifederalists,* 97.

50. Jensen, ed., *Documentary History of Ratification,* 15:290–95. Also see Gary Kornblith, "Partisan Federalism: New England Mechanics and the Political Economy of the 1790s," in Ronald Hoffman and Peter J. Albert, eds., *Launching the "Extended Republic": The Federalist Era* (Charlottesville, Va., 1996), 259–61.

51. Jonathan Elliot, ed., *The Debates in the Several State Conventions on the Adoption of the Federal Constitution* (Philadelphia, 1866), 2:131.

52. Main, *Antifederalists,* 200–210; Rutland, *Ordeal of the Constitution,* 66–88.

53. Main, *Antifederalists,* 249, 273–74, 285–86; Rutland, *Ordeal of the Constitution,* 182–234.

54. Main, *Antifederalists,* 233–42, 249; Rutland, *Ordeal of the Constitution,* 255–65; JM to AH, July 20, 1788, *PAH* 5:184–85.

55. David Waldstreicher, *In the Midst of Perpetual Fetes: Nationalism, 1776–1820,* (Chapel Hill, N.C., 1997), 90–103; Rutland, *Ordeal of the Constitution,* 97, 211, 262.

56. Cornell, *Other Founders,* 20–21; Freeman, *Washington,* 6:134–35; Rakove, *Original Meanings,* 57–58; JM, *The Federalist,* No. 37.

57. Morris, *Forging of the Union,* 308.

58. This paragraph draws on, and quotes from, *The Federalist,* Nos. 3, 6, 9, 11, 15, 22, 34, 62. See also Gottfried Dietze, *The Federalist: A Classic on Federalism and Free Government* (Baltimore, 1960), 177–254.

59. Rutland, *Ordeal of the Constitution,* 208–9.

60. *JCC* 31:494–98; Jensen, *New Nation,* 400–421; Waldstreicher, *In the Midst of Perpetual Fetes,* 55.

61. On the Anti-Federalists and national security, see Richard Henry Lee, *Letters from the Federal Farmer* in Kenyon, *The Antifederalists,* 207; "Letters of 'Montezuma,'" ibid., 64; "Letters of 'Philadelphiansis,'" ibid., 72; Speeches of Patrick Henry in the Virginia State Ratifying Convention, in Storing, *Complete Anti-Federalist,* 5:219.

62. In addition to the works previously cited, my assessment of ratification and the Anti-Federalists draws heavily on Murray Dry, "The Case Against Ratification: Anti-Federalist Constitutional Thought," and David Epstein, "The Case for Ratification: Federalist Constitutional Thought," in Levy and Mahoney, *Framing and Ratification of the Constitution,* 271–91, 292–304; and McDonald, *Formation of the American Republic,* 209–36. Anti-Federalist tracts can be found

in Kenyon, *The Antifederalists;* Storing, *Complete Anti-Federalist;* and Jensen, *Documentary History of Ratification.*

63. See Ferling, *Loyalist Mind,* especially 30, 70–99, and John Ferling, "The American Revolution and American Security: Whig and Loyalist Views," *The Historian* 40 (1978): 492–507. See also *WJA* 2:378n; *DAJA* 2:138.

64. GW to Benjamin Lincoln, Oct. 26, 1788, 1:6, 72; GW to William Gordon, Sept. 24, 1788, 1:1–2; GW to Lincoln, Sept., 24, 1788, 1:6; Robert Livingston to GW, Oct. 21, 1788, 1:56; Trumbull to GW, Oct. 28, 1788, 1:80; Samuel Vaughn to GW, Nov. 4, 1788, 1:165–66; John Armstrong to GW, Jan. 27, 1789, 1:254; Benjamin Harrison to GW, Feb. 26, 1788, 1:345; AH to GW, Sept. [?], 1788, 1:23–24; GW to AH, Oct. 3, 1788, 1:32, all in *PGW: Pres Ser.*

65. McDonald, *Hamilton,* 127; JA to James Lloyd, Feb. 11, 1815, in *WJA* 10:119.

66. John Ferling, "School for Command: George Washington and the Virginia Regiment," in Warren R. Hofstra, ed., *George Washington and the Virginia Backcountry* (Madison, Wis., 1998), 195–222.

67. Ibid., 214–20; Ferling, *First of Men,* 257–66; Flexner, *Washington,* 2:3–5, 42–43, 199–201, 490–91, 550–52; Richard Brookhiser, "A Man on Horseback," *Atlantic Monthly* (Jan. 1996), 50–64; Claude Blanchard, *Journal* (Albany, N.Y., 1876), 67.

68. GW to JA, May 10, 1789, *PGW: Pres Ser* 2:245–47, 247–50n.

69. Kenneth R. Bowling and Helen E. Veit, eds., *The Diary of William Maclay and Other Notes on Senate Debates* (Baltimore, 1988), 342, 349.

70. AH to GW, May 5, 1789, *PGW: Pres Ser,* 2:211, 248n; Joanne B. Freeman, *Affairs of Honor: National Politics in the New Republic* (New Haven, Conn., 2001), 45–46; Worthington C. Ford, *The True George Washington* (Philadelphia, 1896), 174.

71. David Stuart to GW, July 14, 1789, 3:199; GW to Stuart, July 26, 1789, 3:323; GW to JM, May 12, 1789, 2:282, all in *PGW: Pres Ser.*

72. Stanley Elkins and Eric McKitrick, *The Age of Federalism* (New York, 1993), 65–68.

73. *PJM* 12:57–59n. On the Bill of Rights, a good starting place is Robert Allen Rutland, *The Birth of the Bill of Rights, 1776–1791* (Chapel Hill, N.C., 1955) and Robert A. Rutland, "Framing and Ratifying the First Ten Amendments," in Levy and Mahoney, *Framing and Ratification of the Constitution,* 305–16.

74. *PAH* 5:412n; GW to Catherine Sawbridge Macaulay Graham, Jan. 9, 1790, *PGW: Pres Ser* 4:552–53.

Chapter 10

1. Jacob E. Cooke, *Alexander Hamilton* (New York, 1982), 74–75.

2. Hamilton, "The Continentalist," *PAH* 2:673–74; Ver Steeg, *Morris,* 78–96; Ferguson, *Power of the Purse,* 117–24.

3. *DGW* 5:477–92; 6:113–22.

4. AH, *The Farmer Refuted . . .* (New York, 1775), *PAH* 1:129; Hamilton, "The Continentalist," *PAH* 3:106.

5. Hamilton, *The Federalist,* Nos. 6, 8, 12, 30, 34; Hamilton, Report on the Subject of Manufactures [Dec. 5, 1791], *PAH* 10:291; Gerald Stourz, *Alexander Hamilton and the Idea of Republican Government* (Stanford, Calif., 1970), 126–70.

6. Alexander Hamilton, Report Relative to a Provision for the Support of Public Credit [Jan. 9, 1790], *PAH* 6:65–110.

7. Ferguson, *Power of the Purse,* 281.

8. Paul A. Gilje, "The Rise of Capitalism in the Early Republic," *JER* 16 (1996): 162, 171; Brookhiser, *Hamilton,* 86.

9. Wood, *Radicalism of the American Revolution,* 326.

10. AH to GW, Sept. 15, 1790, *PAH,* 7:52; John C. Miller, *The Federalist Era, 1789–1801* (New York, 1960), 40–41; McDonald, *Hamilton,* 167; Elkins and McKitrick, *Age of Federalism,* 124, 131; Ferguson, *Power of the Purse,* 292.

11. AH to Edward Carrington, May 26, 1792, *PAH* 11:426–45. Historians have debated Madison's turnabout for generations. Most have insisted that he was appalled by the injustice of funding. See Ferguson, *Power of the Purse,* 298–99; McDonald, *Hamilton,* 173–81; Rakove, *Madison,* 89, 94–96; Cooke, *Hamilton,* 81; Elkins and McKitrick, *Age of Federalism,* 137–38. It has also been argued that he had supported a stronger national government in order to save the Union but that he had always insisted on tightly circumscribing the powers of the central government. See Banning, *Sacred Fire of Liberty,* 297, 307–15.

12. JM to AH, Nov. 19, 1789, *PJM* 12:449–51; JM to TJ, Jan. 24, 1790, *PJM* 13:4; James Madison, Speeches to Congress, Feb. 16, 18, 1790, *PJM* 13:34–38, 47–56; JM to Rush, March 7, 1790, *PJM* 13:93.

13. James Morton Smith, ed., *Republic of Letters: The Correspondence between Thomas Jefferson and James Madison, 1776–1826* (New York, 1995), 1:37, 207, 439, 442, 445, 639, 643.

14. Herbert E. Sloan, *Principle and Interest: Thomas Jefferson and the Problem of Debt* (New York, 1995), 131, 147.

15. Rakove, *Madison,* 89; James Roger Sharp, *American Politics in the Early Republic: The New Nation in Crisis* (New Haven, Conn., 1993), 36; Elkins and McKitrick, *Age of Federalism,* 147–51; Cooke, *Hamilton,* 81.

16. JM to Henry Lee, Apr. 13, 1790, *PJM* 13:147–48.

17. "Slave Trade Petitions" [Feb. 12, 1790], *PJM* 13:39n; "Public Credit," Apr. 26, 1790, *PJM* 13:177; "Navigation and Trade," May 13, 14, 17, 1790, *PJM* 13:198–214, 216–20; *AC* 1:1478–80; H. W. Brands, *The First American,* 298, 789, 701–4.

18. JM to Monroe, June 1, 1790, *PJM* 13:234; JM to JM Sr., June 13, 1790, *PJM* 13:242.

19. Elkins and McKitrick, *Age of Federalism,* 159; Kenneth R. Bowling, *Creating the Federal City, 1774–1800: Potomac Fever* (Washington, D.C., 1988), 7–78; McDonald, *Hamilton,* 181–82.

20. TJ to James Monroe, June 20, 1790, *PTJ* 16:536.

21. "Jefferson's Account of the Bargain on the Assumption and Residence Bills" [1792?], *PTJ* 17:206–7.

22. TJ to Monroe, June 20, 1790, *PTJ* 16:537.

23. TJ to Francis Eppes, July 4, 1790, *PTJ* 16:598.

24. Kenneth R. Bowling, *The Creation of Washington, D.C.: The Idea and Location of the American Capital* (Fairfax, Va., 1991), 173–95; Jacob E. Cooke, "The Compromise of 1790," *WMQ* 27 (1970): 523–45; Kenneth R. Bowling, "Dinner at Jefferson's: A Note on Jacob E. Cooke's 'Compromise of 1790,'" *WMQ* 28 (1971): 629–48; Norman Risjord, "The Compromise of 1790: New Evidence on the Dinner Table Bargain," *WMQ* 33 (1976): 309–14; Banning, *Sacred Fire of Liberty,* 321; *PJM* 13:244–46n; Ferguson, *Power of the Purse,* 321.

25. JM to Monroe, July 24 [25?], 1790, *PJM* 13:282; Ferguson, *Power of the Purse,* 325n; GW, To the U.S. Senate and House of Representatives, Jan. 8, 1790, *PGW: Pres Ser* 4:544; *PAH* 6:209n.

26. Freeman, *Washington,* 6:279; Cooke, *Hamilton,* 86; Dumas Malone, *Jefferson and His Time* (Boston, 1948–81), 2:321; Richard Miller, "The Federal City, 1783–1800," in Russell F. Weighley, ed., *Philadelphia: A 300-Year History* (New York, 1982), 172–73.

27. James Monroe to TJ, July 3, 1790, *PTJ* 16:596–97.

28. TJ to GW, Sept. 9, 1792, *PTJ* 24:352–54.

29. Smith, *Republic of Letters,* 1:11–12.

30. Elkins and McKitrick, *Age of Federalism,* 233–44, 257–90; Banning, *Sacred Fire of Liberty,* 334–65; Ellis, *American Sphinx,* 123.

31. The foregoing draws on Ferling, *Setting the World Ablaze,* 36–39, 49–54, 150–59, 206–13, 229–36, 244–46. Also see Ferling, "Jefferson's War," *American History,* 35:36–44.

32. TJ to Edward Randolph, Sept. 15, 1781, *PTJ* 6:116–17; TJ to Chevalier de Chastellux, Nov. 26, 1782, *PTJ* 6:203.

33. TJ to Maria Cosway, Oct. 12, 1786, *PTJ* 10:445–49; Fawn Brodie, *Thomas Jefferson: An Intimate History* (New York, 1974), 252–92.

34. TJ to Carlo Bellini, Sept. 30, 1785, *PTJ* 8:568–69; TJ to JM, Oct. 28, 1785, Jan. 30, 1787, *PTJ* 8:681–82; 11:92–93; TJ to David Ramsay, Aug. 4, 1787, *PTJ* 11:687; TJ to John Rutledge, Aug. 6, 1787, *PTJ* 11:701; TJ to Jay, Oct. 8, 1787, *PTJ* 12:218; TJ to George Wythe, Aug. 13, 1786, *PTJ* 10:244–45; TJ to GW, May 2, 1788, *PTJ* 13:128; Jefferson, *Notes on the State of Virginia,* ed. William Peden (reprint, New York, 1972), 165.

35. On the changing face of Great Britain, see John M. Murrin, "The Great Inversion; or, Court versus Country: A Comparison of the Revolution Settlements in England (1688–1721) and America (1776–1816)," in J.G.A. Pocock, ed., *Three British Revolutions: 1641, 1688, 1776* (Princeton, N.J., 1980), 379–81. An excellent analysis of Jefferson's outlook on the iniquities inherent in an urban manufacturing society can be found in Peter Onuf, *Jefferson's Empire: The Language of American Nationhood* (Charlottesville, Va., 2000), 69–79. For an overview see Drew McCoy, "Political Economy," in Merrill D. Peterson, ed., *Thomas Jefferson: A Reference Biography* (New York, 1986), 106–12.

36. TJ to GW, Dec. 4, 1788, *PTJ* 14:330.

37. TJ to Jay, Aug. 6, 1787, *PTJ* 11:698.

38. TJ to Paine, July 11, 1789, *PTJ* 15:268; TJ to Jay, May 23, 1788, *PTJ* 13:190.

39. TJ to JM, Jan. 12, 1789, *PTJ* 14:437.

40. TJ to William Short, Jan. 8, 1825, *WTJ* 10:332–33.

41. On TJ's gathering of information, see the wonderful essay in Freeman, *Affairs of Honor,* 74–85. See also Banning, *Jeffersonian Persuasion,* 120–23. Few scholars today believe that Adams was a monarchist. The scholar who has most recently closely scrutinized JA's thought found him to be "squarely within the mainstream of Federalist thought." On JA and republicanism, monarchy, and Federalist thought, see Thompson, *John Adams and the Spirit of Liberty,* 107–25, 183–84, 264.

42. JA to Jay, Jan. 26, 1785, *WJA* 8:274–75; TJ, Report [Dec. 17, 1790], *PTJ* 18:301–3; GW to Benjamin Harrison, Oct. 10, 1784, *PGW: Confed Ser* 2:92; Banning, *Jeffersonian Persuasion,* 156.

43. TJ to JM, Aug. 28, 1789, *PTJ* 15:366; TJ to Mason, Feb. 4, *PTJ* 19:241. On TJ's hatred of England, see Elkins and McKitrick, *Age of Federalism,* 314–17, 338.

44. TJ to George Mason, Feb. 4, 1791, *PTJ* 19:241–42; Bowling and Veit, *Diary of Maclay,* 364; McDonald, *Hamilton,* 200; Elkins and McKitrick, *Age of Federalism,* 229; Miller, *Federalist Era,* 56; Sharp, *American Politics in the Early Republic,* 39; Sloan, *Principle and Interest,* 171.

45. TJ, "Opinion on the Constitutionality of the Bill for Establishing a National Bank," Feb. 15, 1791, *PTJ* 19:275–80; AH, "Opinion on the Constitutionality of an Act to Establish a Bank," Feb. 23, 1791, *PAH* 8:63–134.

46. TJ to John Taylor, June 1, 1798, Ford, *WTJ* 7:263–66; TJ to JM, Sept. 21, 1795, *PTJ* 28:475–76; TJ to Mason, Feb. 4, 1791, *PTJ* 19:241–42; Elkins and McKitrick, *Age of Federalism,* 228; Joseph Charles, *The Origins of the American Party System* (New York, 1956), 21, 37–38.

47. TJ to GW, May 3, 1792, *PTJ* 22:536–39; Charles, *Origins of the American Party System,* 31–33.

48. The best succinct statement of this view can be found in Joseph J. Ellis, "The Big Man: History vs. Alexander Hamilton," *New Yorker* (Oct. 29, 2001), 76–84.

49. TJ to GW, May 23, 1792, *PTJ* 22:536–39.

50. JM, "A Candid State of Parties," *PJM* 14:370–72.

51. TJ to Freneau, Feb. 28, 1791, *PTJ* 19:351; TJ to JM, May 9, July 21, 1791, *PTJ* 20:293, 657; TJ to GW, Sept. 9, 1792, *PTJ* 24:356–57; Malone, *Jefferson*, 2:423–28; Noble E. Cunningham, *The Jeffersonian Republicans: The Formation of Party Organization, 1789–1801* (Chapel Hill, N.C., 1957), 17.

52. TJ to Edward Rutledge, Aug. 25, 1791, *PTJ* 22:74; TJ to Robert Livingston, Feb. 4, 1791, *PTJ* 19:241; TJ to Mason, Feb. 4, 1791, *PTJ* 19:241–42; TJ to Henry Innes, March 13, 1791, *PTJ* 19:542–43; Livingston to TJ, Feb. 20, 1791, *PTJ* 19:296.

53. TJ, "Journal of the Tour," May 21–June 10, 1791, *PTJ* 20:453–56, 434–53n; Elkins and McKitrick, *Age of Federalism*, 241; Smith, *Republic of Letters*, 2:671.

54. Thomas Paine, *The Rights of Man* (1791), in Moncure Daniel Conway, ed., *The Writings of Thomas Paine* (reprint, New York, 1967), 2:278, 304; Foner, *Paine and Revolutionary America*, 98–106; Jeffrey L. Pasley, "'A Journeyman, Either in Law or Politics': John Beckley and the Social Origins of Political Campaigning," *JER* 16 (1996): 546–48; Michael Durey, "Thomas Paine's Apostles: Radical Émigrés and the Triumph of Jeffersonian Republicanism," *WMQ* 44 (1987): 661–88; Roland M. Baumann, "John Swanwick: Spokesman for 'Merchant Republicanism' in Philadelphia, 1790–1798," *Pennsylvania Magazine of History and Biography* 97 (1973): 131–82.

55. Cunningham, *Jeffersonian Republicans*, 33–49, 73.

56. Donald H. Stewart, *The Opposition Press of the Federalist Era* (Albany, N.Y., 1968), 8–9, 42–45; Freeman, *Affairs of Honor*, 85, 127.

57. On the use of print media and the shaping of public opinion, see Freeman, *Affairs of Honor*, 105–58.

58. *PJM* 14:370–72.

59. Ibid. Although its publication came too late for utilization in this book, those interested in Madison's polemics in 1791–1792 should see Colleen A. Sheehan, "Madison and French Enlightenment: The Authority of Public Opinion," *WMQ* 59 (2002): 925–56.

60. TJ to GW, May 23, 1792, *PTJ* 22:536–39.

61. GW to AH, July 29, 1792, *PAH* 12:129; *PTJ* 23:540n.

62. GW to AH, July 29, 1792, *PAH* 12:129–34; Robert Troup to AH, June 15, 1791, *PAH* 8:478; AH to Edward Carrington, May 26, 1792, *PAH* 11:428.

63. AH to GW, Aug. 18, Sept. 9, 1792, *PAH* 12:228–58, 348.

64. Ellis, *American Sphinx*, 132.

65. Gordon S. Wood, "Launching the 'Extended Republic': The Federalist Era," in Ronald Hoffman and Peter J. Albert, eds., *Launching the "Extended Republic"* (Charlottesville, Va., 1996), 6–8; John Adams, *The Defence of the Constitutions of Government of the United States of America, WJA* 4:585; 5:473; 6:186–87; John Adams, "Discourses on Davila," *WJA* 6:241, 248, 252, 254, 256, 323; Ralph Ketchum, *Presidents above Party: The First American Presidency, 1789–1829* (Chapel Hill, N.C., 1984), 57–68, 93–99.

66. TJ to Charles Clay, Jan. 27, 1790, *PTJ* 16:129.

67. Herbert E. Sloan, "Hamilton's Second Thoughts: Federalist Finance Revisited," in Doran Ben-Atar and Barbara B. Oberg, eds., *Federalists Reconsidered* (Charlottesville, Va., 1998), 62.

68. Joyce Appleby, *Capitalism and a New Social Order* (New York, 1984), 53–54.

69. Hamilton, Report on the Subject of Manufactures, *PAH* 10:230–340; Miller, *Hamilton*, 289.

70. Hamilton, Report on the Subject of Manufactures, *PAH* 10:303; TJ, "Memoranda of Conversations with the President," March 1, 1792, *PTJ* 23:187; TJ, "Notes on the Constitutionality of Bounties to Encourage Manufacturing" [Feb. 1792], *PTJ* 23:172–73.

71. Cooke, *Hamilton*, 101–2.

72. *PAH* 12:163–64, 381, 383–85, 393–401, 499, 504; Elkins and McKitrick, *Age of Federalism*, 286–88; Cooke, *Hamilton*, 109–20; Ellis, *American Sphinx*, 130; GW to Mason, March 27, 1779, *WW* 15:26; GW to Benjamin Harrison, Dec. 18 [–30], 1778, *WW* 13:464.

73. On GW's health, see Ferling, *First of Men*, 378, 383, 390, 411, 421, 445–57. See also James E. Guba and Philander Chase, "Anthrax and the President, 1789," in the *Papers of George Washington: Newsletter*, no. 5 (spring 2002): 4–6.

74. Freeman, *Washington*, 6:384; TJ to GW, May 23, 1792, *PTJ* 23:539; AH to GW, July 30 [–Aug. 3], 1792, *PAH* 12:137.

75. Freeman, *Washington*, 6:355–57, 371–72.

76. Ames to G. R. Minot, May 3, 1792, in Ames, *Works of Fisher Ames*, 1:114–15, 118–19; TJ to Thomas Pinckney, Dec. 3, 1792, *PTJ* 24:697; Malone, *Jefferson*, 2:448; McDonald, *Hamilton*, 258; Sharp, *American Politics in the Early Republic*, 56–59; Cunningham, *Jeffersonian Republicans*, 35–45.

77. Sharp, *American Politics in the Early Republic*, 59–60; Cunningham, *Jeffersonian Republicans*, 45–49; TJ to Pinckney, Dec. 3, 1792, *PTJ* 24:696; TJ to Thomas Mann Randolph Jr., March 3, 1793, *PTJ* 25:314.

78. Eugene R. Sheridan, "Thomas Jefferson and the Giles Resolutions," *WMQ* 49 (1992): 589–608; TJ, "Notes on the Giles Resolutions" [n.d.], *PTJ* 25:311; TJ to Thomas Mann Randolph Jr., March 3, 1793, *PTJ* 25:314; Elkins and McKitrick, *Age of Federalism*, 293–302. The text of the Giles Resolutions can be found in *PTJ* 25:294–96.

79. TJ to John Syme, Aug. 17, 1792, *PTJ* 24:388; Miller, *Portrait in Paradox*, 359; GW to G. Morris, Oct. 20, 1792, *WW* 32:189.

Chapter 11

1. Freeman, *Washington*, 7:8; Flexner, *Washington*, 4:16; Malone, *Jefferson*, 3:56.

2. Flexner, *Washington*, 4:13–15.

3. TJ, "Anas," Ford, *WTJ* 1:214–16; Freeman, *Washington*, 7:5–6.

4. GW to TJ, Jan. 25, 1793, *PTJ* 25:95; Freeman, *Washington*, 7:22–33.

5. GW to Henry Lee, Jan. 20, 1793, *WW* 32:310; GW, Second Inaugural Address, March 4, 1793, *WW* 32:374–75; Freeman, *Washington*, 7:41–42.

6. Alexander Hamilton, "The French Revolution" (1794), *PAH* 17:586; JA to TJ, Oct. 9, 1787, *AJL* 1:202–3; JA, "Discourses on Davila," *WJA* 6:275; JA to John Jackson, Dec. 30, 1817, *WJA* 19:270; TJ, "Notes on JA and the French Revolution" [1793], *PTJ* 25:63–64; TJ to John F. Mercer, Dec. 10, 1792, *PTJ* 24:757; Thompson, *John Adams and the Spirit of Liberty*, 103–5. Adams's views on constitutionalism, published prior to the frenzy in France, were important in defining and shaping the ideological debate among the early French reformers. See C. Bradley Thompson, "John Adams and the Coming of the French Revolution," *JER* 16 (1996): 361–87.

7. John Howe, *The Changing Political Thought of John Adams* (Princeton, N.J., 1966), 171; Fisher Ames, "[Untitled] Against Jacobins," [1794], Ames, *Works of Ames*, 2:974–84; Ames to Theodore Dwight, Aug. 1793, ibid., 2:964; David Waldstreicher, "Federalism, the Style of Politics, and the Politics of Style," in Doran Ben-Atar and Barbara B. Oberg, eds., *Federalists Reconsidered* (Charlottesville, Va., 1998), 115–16; Goodrich to Oliver Wolcott, Feb. 17, 1793, in George Gibbs, ed., *Memoirs of the Administrations of Washington and Adams, Edited from the Papers of Oliver Wolcott* (New York, 1946), 1:88; AH, "French Revolution," *PAH* 17:586–87.

8. Monroe to TJ, May 9, 1793, *PTJ* 25:697; JM to TJ, Apr. 12, 1793, *PTJ* 25:533.

9. TJ to William Short, Jan. 3, 1793, *PTJ* 25:14; TJ to Thomas M. Randolph Jr., Jan. 7, 1793, *PTJ* 25:30.

10. GW to Humphreys, March 23, 1793, *WW* 32:398–99; GW to G. Morris, March 25, 1793, *WW* 32:402.

11. Freeman, *Washington*, 7:27–29, 33, 35; Cooke, *Hamilton*, 127; TJ, "Anas," Ford, *WTJ* 1:224, 226–27. For AH's views on the French treaties, see *PAH* 14:367–408. For TJ's views, see *PTJ* 25:607–18.

12. Robert W. Tucker and Daniel C. Hendrickson, *Empire of Liberty: The Statecraft of Thomas Jefferson* (New York, 1990), 53–54.

13. Elkins and McKitrick, *Age of Federalism*, 330–36.

14. Freeman, *Washington*, 7:44–51; TJ to JM, Apr. 28, 1793, *PTJ* 25:619; Harry Ammon, *The Genet Mission* (New York, 1975), 54–59.

15. TJ to Monroe, May 5, 1793, *PTJ* 25:661.

16. Genet to TJ, June 22, 1793, *PTJ* 26:339–41; TJ to JM, Aug. 11, 1793, *PTJ* 25:652.

17. TJ to T. M. Randolph Jr., Jan. 7, 1793, *PTJ* 25:30; TJ to Short, Jan. 3, March 23, 1793, *PTJ* 25:14, 436; TJ to JM, May 5, 1793, *PTJ* 25:660.

18. Quoted in Cornell, *Other Founders*, 198.

19. Matthew Schoenbachler, "Republicanism in the Age of Democratic Revolution: The Democratic-Republican Societies of the 1790s," *JER* 18 (1998): 245–46; Philip S. Foner, ed., *The Democratic-Republican Societies, 1790–1820: A Documentary Sourcebook* (Westport, Conn., 1976), 5; Eugene Link, *Democratic-Republican Societies, 1790–1800* (New York, 1942), 44–70.

20. Foner, *Democratic-Republican Societies*, 19.

21. Ibid., 22; Appleby, *Capitalism and a New Social Order*, 57–60.

22. Cunningham, *Jeffersonian Republicans*, 62–66; Richard Hofstadter, *The Idea of a Party System: The Rise of Legitimate Opposition in the United States, 1780–1840* (Berkeley, 1964), 92.

23. Quoted in Schoenbachler, "Republicanism in the Age of Democratic Revolution," *JER* 18:241.

24. Ibid., 18:243; Albrecht Koschnik, "The Democratic Societies of Philadelphia and the Limits of the American Public Sphere, circa 1793–1795," *WMQ* 58 (2001): 630–31.

25. Nathaniel Chipman to AH, [June] 9, 1794, *PAH* 16:465–70; AH, "No Jacobin" [1793], *PAH* 15:269.

26. Sharp, *American Politics in the Early Republic*, 90; Gordon Wood, "Early American Get-Up-and-Go," *New York Review of Books* (June 29, 2000), 50–53; Cornell, *Other Founders*, 204.

27. TJ, "Anas," Ford, *WTJ* 1:203–4, 256–57; TJ to JM, Aug. 11, 1793, *PTJ* 26:651–52; JM to TJ, Sept. 2, 1793, *PTJ* 27:16.

28. JM to Monroe, Sept. 15, 1793, *PJM* 15:111; TJ to JM, Aug. 11, 1793, *PTJ* 26:652; TJ, "Report on Commerce," Dec. 16, 1793, *PTJ* 27:567–78; Miller, *Federalist Era*, 143.

29. Quoted in Smith, *Republic of Letters*, 2:824. Also see TJ to JM, Apr. 3, 1794, *PTJ* 28:49–50.

30. Cooke, *Hamilton*, 136.

31. Malone, *Jefferson*, 3:18.

32. Alexander Hamilton, "The Reynold's Pamphlet" [Aug. 1797], *PAH* 21:238.

33. McDonald, *Hamilton*, 286–87; Cooke, *Hamilton*, 137–38; Freeman, *Washington*, 7:173.

34. JM to TJ, March 2, 1794, *PJM* 15:269–70; Elkins and McKitrick, *Age of Federalism*, 388.

35. JM to TJ, March 12, 14, 26, 1794, *PJM* 15:279, 284, 294–95; Ames to ?, March 19, 1794, Ames, *Works of Ames*, 2:1036.

36. Freeman, *Washington*, 7:159–60; AH to GW, Apr. [14], 1794, *PAH* 16:266; Sedgwick to Ephraim Williams, March 10, 1794, Sedgwick Family Papers, MHS; GW to the Senate, Apr. 16, 1794, *WW* 33:332.

37. JM to TJ, May 11, 1794, *PJM* 15:327–28.

38. Elkins and McKitrick, *Age of Federalism*, 396; Stewart, *Opposition Press*, 190; Richard Buel Jr., *Securing the Revolution: Ideology in American Politics, 1789–1815* (Ithaca, N.Y., 1972), 60; Resolution of the Democratic Society of Pennsylvania, May 8, 1794, Foner, *Democratic-Republican Societies*, 105; Resolution of the Democratic Society of the County of Washington, in Pennsylvania, June 23, 1794, ibid., 134.

39. Link, *Democratic-Republican Societies*, 54; Foner, *Democratic-Republican Societies*, 18, 36.

40. Thomas P. Slaughter, *The Whiskey Rebellion: Frontier Epilogue to the American Revolution* (New York, 1986), 67, 88, 106–7; Elkins and McKitrick, *Age of Federalism*, 471.

41. TJ to GW, May 23, 1792, *PTJ* 23:536; Smith, *Republic of Letters*, 2:850.

42. TJ to GW, May 23, 1792, *PTJ* 23:536; Slaughter, *Whiskey Rebellion*, 109–24, 156, 163–64.

43. Slaughter, *Whiskey Rebellion*, 151–52; GW to Governors of Pennsylvania, North Carolina, and South Carolina, Sept. 29, 1792, *WW* 32:169; Cooke, *Hamilton*, 147, 149, 150.

44. Freeman, *Washington*, 7:191; Slaughter, *Whiskey Rebellion*, 133–39, 144–57; Morris, *Forging of the Union*, 50; AH to GW, Aug. 2, 5, 1794, *PAH* 17:16, 17–18, 58; GW to AH, Aug. 21, 1794, *PAH* 17:126; GW to H. Lee, Aug. 26, 1794, *WW* 33:475–79.

45. Slaughter, *Whiskey Rebellion*, 217–20; Miller, *Federalist Era*, 159.

46. GW, Sixth State of the Union Address, Nov. 19, 1794, *WW* 34:29–35; GW to Jay, Nov. 1 [–5], 1794, *WW* 34:17–18.

47. JM, Speech to Congress, Nov. 27, 1794, *PJM* 15:391; JM to TJ, Nov. 30, 1794, *PJM* 15:396–97; TJ to JM, Dec. 28, 1794, *PJM* 15:426–28; Smith, *American Politics in the Early Republic*, 101–2; *AC*, 3d Cong., 921–32. Some historians have contended that the Federalists took their name in 1795 during the battle over the Jay Treaty. This view was advanced in Leonard D. White, *The Federalists: A Study in Administration History* (New York, 1948), 51n.

48. Robert Kelley, *The Cultural Pattern in American Politics: The First Century* (New York, 1979), 114.

49. JM to Monroe, Dec. 4, 1794, *PJM* 15:406; TJ to JM, Dec. 28, 1794, *PJM* 15:428; Smith, *American Politics in the Early Republic*, 104; Elkins and McKitrick, *Age of Federalism*, 487–88.

50. GW to AH, Feb. 2, 1795, *WW* 34:110.

51. Sloan, "Hamilton's Second Thoughts," 61–76. The quotations can be found on pages 62 and 76.

52. Quoted in Flexner, *Washington*, 4:193.

53. GW to Jay, Dec. 18, 1794, *WW* 32:61; Freeman, *Washington*, 7:235.

54. Freeman, *Washington*, 7:236–37.

55. Elkins and McKitrick, *Age of Federalism*, 403–7. Whether Jay could have done better has been the subject of considerable scholarly debate. For a succinct view, see ibid., 410–14.

56. Alexander De Conde, *Entangling Alliances: Politics and Diplomacy under George Washington* (Durham, N.C., 1958), 108–9; Stewart, *Opposition Press*, 190–94; Elkins and McKitrick, *Age of Federalism*, 416–18.

57. Elkins and McKitrick, *Age of Federalism*, 416; Stewart, *Opposition Press*, 194.

58. Jerald Combs, *The Jay Treaty: Political Background of the Founding Fathers* (Berkeley, Calif., 1970), 161; Miller, *Federalist Era*, 167; De Conde, *Entangling Alliance*, 112.

59. GW to AH, July 3, 13, 29, 1795, *WW* 34:226–28, 237–40, 262–64; GW to Randolph, July 22, 31, 1795, *WW* 34:244, 266; GW to Knox, Sept. 20, 1795, *WW* 34:310–11; Todd Estes, "Shaping the Politics of Public Opinion: Federalists and the Jay Treaty Debate," *JER* 20 (2000): 393–422.

60. The quotation is from Rudolph M. Bell, *Party and Faction in American Politics: The House of Representatives, 1789–1801* (Westport, Conn., 1973), 191. Also see Miller, *Federalist Era*, 172. For a shading of difference on the shaping of the parties, see Sharp, *American Politics in the Early Republic*, 135.

61. Buel, *Securing the Revolution*, 52.

62. Stewart, *Opposition Press*, 195, 211–13, 215–17.

63. The scholarly literature on the ideology of the Republican Party is extensive, but excellent appraisals can be found in Appleby, *Capitalism and a New Social Order*, 25–87; Banning, *Jeffersonian Persuasion*, 179–245; Miller, *Federalist Era*, 70–98; Elkins and McKitrick, *Age of Federalism*, 195–208, 263–70, 354–65.

64. Fisher Ames, "No Revolutionist" (1801), in Ames, *Works of Ames*, 1:5; Samuel Eliot Morison, *Harrison Gray Otis, 1765–1848: The Urbane Federalist* (Boston, 1969), 87.

65. Max Mintz, *Gouverneur Morris and the American Revolution* (Norman, Okla., 1970), 186; Ames, "The Republican," 11 (Sept. 10, 1804), in Ames, *Works of Ames*, 1:116.

66. David Hackett Fischer, *The Revolution of American Conservatism: The Federalist Party in the Era of Jeffersonian Democracy* (New York, 1965), 7.

67. Fischer, *Revolution of American Conservatism,* 23; Robert Ernst, *Rufus King: American Federalist* (Chapel Hill, N.C., 1968), 86, 83.

68. Morison, *Harrison Gray Otis,* 88; Ames, "The Republican," 10 (Aug. 30, 1804), in Ames, *Works of Ames,* 1:264.

69. AH, *The Federalist,* No. 85; Joyce Appleby, *Inheriting the Revolution: The First Generation of Americans* (Cambridge, Mass., 2000), 27.

70. Fischer, *Revolution of American Conservatism,* 5, 3.

71. Estes, "Shaping the Politics of Public Opinion," *JER* 20:399–422.

72. Ernst, *Rufus King,* 55; Fischer, *Revolution of American Conservatism,* 3–4, 246, 249, 253, 255.

73. Alan Taylor, "From Fathers to Friends of the People: Political Personae in the Early Republic," in Ben-Atar and Oberg, eds., *Federalists Reconsidered,* 225–45.

74. Ronald Formisano, *The Transformation of Political Culture: Massachusetts Parties, 1790s– 1840s* (New York, 1983), 131; Taylor, *Western Massachusetts in the Revolution,* 72–73.

75. Sedgwick to Williams, Dec. 12, 1794, Sedgwick Family Papers, MHS.

76. Sedgwick to Pamela Sedgwick, June 24, 1786, Sedgwick Family Papers, MHS; Taylor, *Western Massachusetts in the Revolution,* 73.

77. Richard E. Welch Jr., *Theodore Sedgwick, Federalist: A Political Portrait* (Middlebury, Conn., 1965), 7–42.

78. Sedgwick to Pamela Sedgwick, June 24, 1787, in Shays's Rebellion Collection, MHS.

79. Welch, *Sedgwick,* 136.

80. Pamela Sedgwick to Sedgwick, Jan. 15, 1799, Sedgwick Family Papers, MHS.

81. Sedgwick to Henry Van Schaack, Dec. 13, 1787, Sedgwick Family Papers, MHS; Welch, *Sedgwick,* 61.

82. Sedgwick to Henry Van Schaack, July 10, 1789, Sedgwick Family Papers, MHS; Welch, *Sedgwick,* 96, 97.

83. Sedgwick to Williams, Dec. 26, 1790, Feb. 23, Dec. 16, 1791, Jan. 31, 1793, March 3, 10, 20, 29, Apr. 18, 25, May 28, 1794, Feb. 10, 24, 1795, Jan. 1, 1796, Jan. 7, 1797; and Sedgwick to Peter Van Schaack, Dec. 12, 1794, all in Sedgwick Family Papers, MHS.

84. Buel, *Securing the Revolution,* 118–21; AH, "The Defence," *PAH* 19:89, 102.

85. The contents of "The Defence" can be found in volumes 18–20 of *PAH.* For an excellent introductory essay on Hamilton's efforts, see *PAH* 18:475–79.

86. TJ to JM, Sept. 21, 1795, *PTJ* 28:475.

87. Walt Brown, *John Adams and the American Press: Politics and Journalism at the Birth of the Republic* (Jefferson, N.C., 1995), 43.

88. Samuel Flagg Bemis, *Pinckney's Treaty: America's Advantage from Europe's Distress, 1783– 1800* (Baltimore, 1926); Arthur P. Whitaker, *The Spanish-American Frontier, 1783–1795: Westward Movement and the Spanish Retreat in the Mississippi Valley* (Boston, 1927).

89. JM to TJ, Dec. 27, 1795, *PJM* 16:173.

90. Smith, *Republic of Letters,* 2:887–90.

91. JM to TJ, Dec. 27, 1795, Jan. 31, March 6, 1796, *PJM* 16:173, 208, 247.

92. Cunningham, *Jeffersonian Republicans,* 82.

93. JM to Monroe, Apr. 18, 1796, *PJM* 16:333; JM to TJ, Apr. 23, 1796, *PJM* 16:335.

94. Larry Tise, *The American Counterrevolution: A Retreat from Liberty, 1783–1800* (Mechanicsburg, Pa., 1998), 173. Sedgwick's biographer labeled the speech his "finest hour." See Welch, *Sedgwick,* 145.

95. *AC* 5:514–30; Welch, *Sedgwick,* 149.

96. TJ to Thomas M. Randolph, Nov. 16, 1792, *PTJ* 24:623.

97. On Ames's life and the impact of his speech, see the modern introduction by William B. Allen in Ames, *Works of Ames,* xix–xxxii.

98. Andrew Burstein, *Sentimental Democracy: The Evolution of America's Romantic Self-Image* (New York, 1999). The historian Gordon S. Wood has declared that the eighteenth century, once thought of as the "Age of Reason," has come to be seen as the "Age of Sensibility," and that many scholars have concluded that it was a time when "feelings seem to have been more important than thought." See Wood, "The American Love Boat," *New York Review of Books* (Oct. 7, 1999): 40–42.

99. Adams is quoted in Miller, *Federalist Era,* 174.

100. Fisher Ames, speech of Apr. 26, 1796, in Ames, *Works of Ames,* 2:1143–82. The quotations from Ames's address can be found on 2:1174–75.

101. Robert Rutland, *James Madison: The Founding Father* (New York, 1987), 141.

102. JM to TJ, May 22, 1796, *PJM* 16:364.

103. GW to Carrington, May 1, 1796, *WW* 35:32–33; GW to Jay, May 8, 1796, *WW* 35:36–37.

104. The quotations are taken from James Tagg, *Benjamin Franklin Bache and the Philadelphia Aurora* (Philadelphia, 1991), 252, 278, 283, 287; Harry M. Tinkcom, *The Republicans and Federalists in Pennsylvania, 1790–1801* (Harrisburg, Pa., 1950), 143; and Brown, *John Adams and the American Press,* 54–55.

105. GW to Landon Carter, Oct. 5, 1798, *WW* 36:484; GW to Thomas Erskine, July 7, 1787, *WW* 36:489–90; Ferling, *First of Men,* 411, 421, 445–47, 491, 504.

106. GW to Jay, May 8, 1796, *WW* 35:37; GW to AH, May 15, Aug. 25, Sept. 2, 6, 1796, *WW* 35:48–51, 190–92, 199–201, 204–20; TJ, "Anas," Ford, *WTJ* 1:175, 199; AH, "Draft of GW's Farewell Address, *PAH* 20:265–88; "Introductory Note," *PAH* 20:169–73.

107. GW, Farewell Address, Sept. 19, 1796, *WW* 35:214–38.

108. Ibid., 35:220–23, 225–26, 228, 230–33, 235, 237.

109. JM to Monroe, Sept. 29, 1796, *PJM* 17:403; Tazewell to JM, Oct. 3, 1796, *PJM* 17:406; Stewart, *Opposition Press,* 532–33; Hofstadter, *Idea of a Party System,* 99.

110. Ames to Wolcott, Sept. 26, 1796, Ames, *Works of Ames,* 2:1192; JA to AA, Jan. 5, 1796, AFP, reel 381; Freeman, *Washington,* 7:377.

111. JA to Trumbull, Nov. [?], 1805, AFP, reel 118; AA to Abigail Adams Smith, July 16, 1788, Caroline Smith De Windt, ed., *Journal and Correspondence of Miss Adams* (New York, 1841), 2:89.

112. Sedgwick to Williams, Jan. 28, 1795, and Sedgwick to Van Schaack, Dec. 30, 1796, both in Sedgwick Family Papers, MHS; Sedgwick to Rufus King, March 12, 1797, Sedgwick Letterbook, MHS; Linda Dudek Guerrero, *John Adams's Vice Presidency, 1789–1797: The Neglected Man in the Forgotten Office* (New York, 1982), 128.

113. Maier, *American Scripture,* 169–70.

114. JM to TJ, March 23, 1795, *PJM* 15:493; JM to Monroe, February 26, 1796, *PJM* 16:232; TJ to JM, Apr. 27, 1795, *PTJ* 28:338–39; Noble E. Cunningham, *In Pursuit of Reason: The Life of Thomas Jefferson* (Baton Rouge, 1987), 199–200; Sharp, *American Politics in the Early Republic,* 143–45.

115. TJ to Edward Rutledge, Dec. 27, 1796, Ford, *PTJ* 29:232–33; TJ to Mary Jefferson Eppes, March 3, 1802, in Edwin M. Betts and James A. Bear, Jr., eds., *The Family Letters of Thomas Jefferson* (Columbia, Mo., 1966), 219.

116. Joanne B. Freeman, "The Presidential Election of 1796," in Richard Alan Ryerson, ed., *John Adams and the Founding of the Republic* (Boston, 2001), 150–51; Freeman, *Affairs of Honor,* 213–27. On the "state of politics" in 1796, see also Elkins and McKitrick, *Age of Federalism,* 513–28.

117. Sedgwick to King, March 12, 1797, Sedgwick Letterbook, MHS; TJ to JM, Jan. 22, 1797, *PJM* 16:473; in Ames to Christopher Gore, Dec. 3, 1796, Ames, *Works of Ames,* 2:1203, 1208; Ames, "[Untitled] Against Jacobins" [1794?], ibid., 2:975.

118. Sedgwick to Rufus King, March 12, 1797, Sedgwick Letterbook, MHS; AH to ?, Nov. 8, 1796, *PAH* 20:377. On the election, see Freeman, "Presidential Election of 1796," in Ryerson, *John Adams and the Founding of the Republic,* 142–67; John Ferling, "1796: The First Real Election," *American History* (Dec. 1996): 24–28, 66–68; Sharp, *American Politics in the Early Republic,* 145–49. On the notion of honor, see the extensive treatment throughout Freeman, *Affairs of Honor.*

119. Sedgwick to Williams, Jan. 9, 1797, Sedgwick Family Papers, MHS.

120. Charles, *Origins of the American Party System,* 58.

121. JA to AA, Apr. 9, Dec. 8, 12, 1796, AFP, reels 381, 382; JA to Knox, March 30, 1797, AFP, reel 117; Fowler, *Samuel Adams,* 174–75. Samuel Adams had sought election as a Republican elector in 1796. See Alexander, *Samuel Adams,* 217–18.

122. Freeman, "Presidential Election of 1796," in Ryerson, *John Adams and the Founding of the Republic,* 154.

123. Ferling, *John Adams,* 332.

124. TJ to JM, Jan. 1, 22, 1797, *PTJ* 29:249–51, 270–71.

125. Sedgwick to Peter Van Schaack, Dec. 29, 1796, Sedgwick Family Papers, MHS; GW to Knox, March 2, 1797, *WW* 35:409; GW to George Washington Parke Custis, Feb. 27, 1797, *WW* 35:403; GW to Trumbull, March 3, 1797, *WW* 35:412; Freeman, *Washington* 7:436.

126. Sedgwick to King, March 12, 1797, Sedgwick Letterbook, MHS; JA to AA, March 5, 1797, Charles Francis Adams, ed., *Letters of John Adams Addressed to his Wife* (Boston, 1841), 2:244; David McCullough, *John Adams* (New York, 2001), 468–69.

Chapter 12

1. JA to Richard Cranch, March 25, 1797, AFP, reel 117.

2. Quoted in Tagg, *Benjamin Franklin Bache,* 297.

3. TJ to Adet, Oct. 14, 1795, quoted in Malone, *TJ* 3:249–50. Also see Malone, *TJ* 3:286–87.

4. JA to A. Lee, Apr. 12, 1783, AFP, reel 360; JA to William Lee, Apr. 6, 1783, AFP, reel 108.

5. Gerald Clarfield, *Timothy Pickering and the American Republic* (Pittsburgh, Pa., 1980); AH to GW, March 5, 1796, *PAH* 20:374.

6. In the absence of a good modern biography of Wolcott, see Gibbs, ed., *Memoirs of the Administrations of Washington and John Adams,* and James Wettereau, "Oliver Wolcott," in *Dictionary of American Biography* (New York, 1921–37), 20:443–45. An excellent brief sketch of Wolcott can also be found in Elkins and McKitrick, *Age of Federalism,* 627–28.

7. Bernard Steiner, *The Life and Career of James McHenry* (Cleveland, Ohio, 1907); AH to GW, Nov. 5, 1795, *PAH* 19:397.

8. TJ to Gerry, May 13, 1797, *PTJ* 29:362–63; TJ to JA, Dec. 28, 1796, *PTJ* 29:235.

9. JA to Rush, March 19, June 12, 1812, Schutz and Adair, *Spur of Fame,* 214, 226.

10. Sedgwick to Henry Van Schaack, Jan. 7, 1798, Sedgwick Family Papers, MHS; Sedgwick to AH, Feb. 7, 1799, *PAH* 22:471.

11. JA, *Defence, WJA* 4:289–91, 585; 5:473; 6:73, 97–99, 186–87; JA, "Davila," *WJA* 6:241–48, 252, 254, 256, 323; Ketchum, *Presidents above Party,* 57–68, 93–99. See also John Ferling, " Father and Protector': President John Adams and Congress in the Quasi-War Crisis," in Kenneth R. Bowling and Donald R. Kennon, *Neither Separate nor Equal: Congress in the 1790s* (Athens, Ohio, 2000), 294–332.

12. TJ, "Anas," Ford, *WTJ* 1:272–73; JA, "Correspondence Originally Published in the *Boston Patriot,*" *WJA* 9:285; Wolcott to AH, March 31, 1797, *PAH* 20:571; Elkins and McKitrick, *Age of Federalism,* 543.

13. JA to Knox, March 30, 1797, AFP, reel 117; JA to John Quincy Adams, March 31, 1797, AFP, reel 117; Pickering to AH, March 26, 1797, *PAH* 20:549.

14. Pickering to AH, March 22, 1797, *PAH* 20:545, 549; Wolcott to AH, March 31, 1797, *PAH* 20:569; AH to Pickering, March 29, 1797, *PAH* 20:556; AH to Wolcott, March 30, 1797, *PAH* 20:567; AH to McHenry, March ?, 1797, *PAH* 20:574.

15. JA, Speech to the Special Session of Congress, May 16, 1797, in James D. Richardson, ed., *A Compilation of the Messages and Papers of the Presidents* (New York, 1897–1917), 1:223–29.

16. TJ to JM, May 18, 1797, *PTJ* 29:371–73; TJ to Horatio Gates, May 30, 1797, *PTJ* 29:407; Elkins and McKitrick, *Age of Federalism,* 554–55; Sharp, *American Politics in the Early Republic,* 168.

17. Alexander De Conde, *The Quasi-War: The Politics and Diplomacy of the Undeclared War with France, 1797–1801* (New York, 1966), 28–29; JA, "Correspondence Originally Published in the *Boston Patriot,*" *WJA* 9:286–87; Ferling, *John Adams,* 345; Sharp, *American Politics in the Early Republic,* 164–65.

18. Manning J. Dauer, *The Adams Federalists* (Baltimore, 1953), 135.

19. Ferling, *John Adams,* 318, 320; Shaw, *Character of John Adams,* 240, 242, 244.

20. See John Ferling and Lewis Braverman, "John Adams's Health Reconsidered," *WMQ* 55 (January 1998): 83–104.

21. John Quincy Adams to JA, Sept. 21, 1797, AFP, reel 385.

22. McHenry to AH, Jan. 26, 1798, *PAH* 21:339; AH to McHenry, Jan. 27–Feb. 11, 1798, *PAH* 21:341–46; McHenry to JA, Feb. 15, March 14, 1798, APM, reel 387; Lee to JA, March 8, 14, 1798, APM, reel 387.

23. De Conde, *Quasi-War,* 62; Gerald H. Clarfield, *Timothy Pickering and American Diplomacy, 1795–1800* (Columbia, Mo., 1969), 194.

24. William Stinchcombe, *The XYZ Affair* (Westport, Conn., 1980), 54–58; Elkins and McKitrick, *Age of Federalism,* 565–67, 569–71.

25. JA, "Message," AFP, reel 387; AH to Pickering, March 17, 1798, *PAH* 21:365–66; JA, "Message to Congress," March 19, 1798, in Richardson, ed., *Messages of the Presidents,* 1:264–65.

26. TJ to JM, March 21, 29, Apr. 5, 26, May 3,1798, Smith, *Republic of Letters,* 2:1029, 1030–31, 1033, 1042, 1045; JM to TJ, Feb. 18, Apr. 2, 1798, Smith, *Republic of Letters,* 2:1021, 1032.

27. *AC,* 5th Cong., 2d sess., 1357–58; TJ to JM, Apr. 6, 1798, Ford, *WTJ* 7:235; Ames to Christopher Gore, July 28, 1798, in Ames, *Works of Ames,* 2:1293.

28. TJ to JM, Apr. 6, 12, 19, 1798, Ford, *WTJ* 7:236, 237, 242; TJ to Peter Carr, Apr. 12, 1798, *WTJ* 7:240; TJ to Archibald Rowan, Sept. 26, 1798, *WTJ* 7:281.

29. Stewart, *Opposition Press,* 287–89, 302, 308, 311, 317; Richard Rosenfeld, *American Aurora: A Democratic Republican Returns* (New York, 1997), 142; Tagg, *Benjamin Franklin Bache,* 324–25; Smith, *Republic of Letters,* 2:1003; TJ to JM, Apr. 12, 1798, *WTJ* 7:237.

30. Stewart, *Opposition Press,* 393, 423–25, 428, 441.

31. TJ to JM, Apr. 12, 1798, Smith, *Republic of Letters,* 2:1035.

32. De Conde, *Quasi-War,* 90–91, 96.

33. JA to Rush, Aug. 23, 1798, Schutz and Adair, *Spur of Fame,* 36; JA to TJ, May 11, 1794, *AJL* 1:255; JA to Gerry, May 3, 1793, AFP, reel 117; JA to McHenry, Oct. 22, 1798, AFP, reel 391.

34. GW, Address to Congress, Aug. 26, 1783, *WW* 27:116–17; Ferling, *First of Men,* 316; Richard H. Kohn, *Eagle and Sword: The Federalists and the Creation of the Military Establishment in America, 1783–1802* (New York, 1975), 47–48, 73–88, 91–127, 139–57, 174–89.

35. Quoted in James Morton Smith, *Freedom's Fetters: The Alien and Sedition Laws and American Civil Liberties* (Ithaca, N.Y., 1956), 7n.

36. Elkins and McKitrick, *Age of Federalism,* 598–99.

37. Benjamin Rosseter to Sedgwick, March 30, 1798, Sedgwick Family Papers, MHS.

38. Sedgwick to Williams, Jan. 4, 1798, Sedgwick Family Papers, MHS.

39. Ames to Wolcott, Apr. 22, June 8, 1798, in Ames, *Works of Ames,* 2:1272–73, 1281; Ames to Otis, Apr. 23, 1798, 2:1275; Ames to Pickering, June 4, 1798, 2:1278.

40. AH, "The Stand," No. I, VI, and VII, *PAH* 21:383, 437, 447.

41. AA to Abigail Adams Smith, Apr. 11, 1798, in De Windt, ed., *Journal and Correspondence of Miss Adams,* 2:151; AA to Cotton Tufts, Apr. 14, 1798, AFP, reel 388.

42. Many of JA's seventy-one addresses can be found in AFP, reels 388–90. His address to the New York Society of the Cincinnati of July 9, 1798, can be found in the Myers Collection, New York Public Library. See also Smith, *Freedom's Fetters,* 16, 18–19.

43. Kohn, *Eagle and Sword,* 227–29.

44. Sedgwick to King, Apr. 9, 1798, Sedgwick Letterbook, MHS; Peter Van Schaack to Sedgwick, Dec. 6, 1797; Daniel Dewey to Sedgwick, June 16, 1798; and Henry Van Schaack to Sedgwick, Feb. 5, 1799, all in Sedgwick Family Papers, MHS.

45. Sedgwick to Van Schaack, Dec. 14, 1797, and Sedgwick to Williams, Jan. 29, 1798, Sedgwick Family Papers, MHS; Smith, *Freedom's Fetters,* 8–9, 13–16; Smith, *Republic of Letters,* 2:1005; TJ to JM, May 10, 1798, *WTJ* :251.

46. TJ to JM, May 3, Apr. 26, 1798, Ford, *WTJ* 7:246–47, 244.

47. TJ to JM, Apr. 26, 1798, *WTJ* 7:244–45; TJ to James Lewis Jr., May 9, 1798, *WTJ* 7:250; JM to TJ, May 13, 1798, Smith, *Republic of Letters* 2:1048.

48. JA to TJ, June 14, 1813, *AJC* 2:329; JA to Rush, Dec. 25, 1811, Schutz and Adair, *Spur of Fame,* 201; AH to Wolcott, June 5, 29, 1798, *PAH* 21:485, 522; AH to Pickering, June 7, 1798, *PAH* 21:495; AH to GW, May 19, 1798, *PAH* 467.

49. Sedgwick to ?, March 7, 1798, Sedgwick Family Papers, MHS; Welsh, *Sedgwick,* 194, 194n; Ames to Wolcott, Apr. 22, 1798, in Ames, *Works of Ames* 2:1273; Ames to Pickering, June 4, 1798, ibid., 2:1277–78.

50. TJ to Gerry, Jan. 26, 1799, Ford, *WTJ* 7:331.

51. Waldstreicher, *In the Midst of Perpetual Fetes,* 129, 131, 136–37, 140, 145, 158, 204, 239–40; Waldstreicher, "Federalism, the Style of Politics, and the Politics of Style," in Ben-Atar and Oberg, *Federalists Reconsidered,* 99–117; Link, *Democratic-Republican Societies,* 179; Simon P. Newman, *Parades and the Politics of the Street: Festive Culture in the Early American Republic* (Philadelphia, 1997), 57, 89, 94, 125, 160–63, 176, 180–81. On liberty caps, liberty trees, and liberty poles, see Bobrick, *Angel in the Whirlwind,* 63; Peter Shaw, *American Patriots and the Rituals of Revolution* (Cambridge, Mass., 1981), 12, 14, 180–84.

52. The foregoing is based primarily on Appleby, *Capitalism and a New Social Order,* 41–105; Wood, *Radicalism of the American Revolution,* 305–47.

53. Ames to Pickering, June 4, 1798, in Ames, *Works of Ames,* 2:1278–79; and Ames to Gore, Dec. 18, 1798, 2:1303.

54. John C. Miller, *Crisis in Freedom: The Alien and Sedition Acts* (Boston, 1951), 59, 61, 67–70; Elkins and McKitrick, *Age of Federalism,* 593; TJ to Samuel Smith, Aug. 22, 1798, Ford, *WTJ* 7:277.

55. Ralph Adams Brown, *The Presidency of John Adams* (Lawrence, Kans., 1975), 125–26; Miller, *Crisis in Freedom,* 221–22.

56. Cornell, *Other Founders,* 253–73.

57. TJ to JM, Apr. 26, May 3, 1798, Smith, *Republic of Letters,* 2:1042, 1045; TJ to John Taylor, June 1, 1798, Ford, *WTJ* 7:265, 266; TJ to GW, Sept. 9, 1792, *PTJ* 24:353.

58. TJ to Taylor, June 1, 1798, Ford, *WTJ* 7:263–64.

59. TJ to Smith, Aug. 22, 1798, *WTJ* 7:277; TJ to Taylor, Nov. 26, 1798, *WTJ* 7:311; Onuf, *Jefferson's Empire,* 94.

60. Cornell, *Other Founders,* 229; TJ to Monroe, Sept. 7, 1797, *PTJ* 29:526–27; TJ, Petition to the Virginia House of Delegates, Aug. 3, 1797, *PTJ* 29:493–98; TJ, Revised Petition to the Virginia House of Delegates, Aug. 7–Sept. 7, 1797, *PTJ* 29:499–504; Smith, *American Politics in the Early Republic,* 169–71.

61. TJ to Smith, Aug. 22, 1798, Ford, *WTJ* 7:298; TJ to Gerry, Jan. 26, 1799, *WTJ* 7:327; TJ to JM, Nov. 17, 1798, *WTJ* 7:288; TJ to Stevens Thompson Mason, Oct. 11, 1798, *WTJ* 7:283; Onuf, *Jefferson's Empire,* 95.

62. TJ, draft of the Kentucky Resolution of 1798 [Nov. 1798], Ford, *WTJ* 7:289–309.

63. Madison, "Virginia Resolutions," Dec. 21, 1798, *PJM* 17:185–88n, 188–90; JM to TJ, Dec. 29, 1798, *PJM* 17:191; TJ to Gerry, Jan. 26, 1799, Ford, *WTJ* 7:733; Sharp, *American Politics in the*

Early Republic, 199. On what JM did and did not write in late 1798, see the editorial comment, "Notes on the . . . Address of the General Assembly to the People of the Commonwealth of Virginia," in *PJM* 17:199–206.

64. AH to GW, May 19, 1798, *PAH* 21:466–68; GW to AH, May 27, 1798, *PAH* 21:470–74; JA to GW, June 22, 1798, *WJA* 8:573; McHenry to GW, June 26, 1798, *PGW: Ret Ser.*

65. GW to JA, July 4, 1798, *WW* 36:312–15; GW to McHenry, July 4, 1798, *WW* 36:304–312.

66. GW to JA, July 13, 1798, *WW* 36:329.

67. JA to McHenry, Aug. 29, Sept. 30, 1798, *PAH* 22:8n, 16n; GW to JA, Sept. 25, 1798, *WW* 36:453–62.

68. The quotation is from Kohn, *Eagle and Sword*, 254. Somewhat similar interpretations can be also found in Cooke, *Hamilton*, 199–203, and Brookhiser, *Hamilton*, 140–42. For the argument that AH did not seek the military command, but was offered the post as a result of GW's demands, see McDonald, *Hamilton*, 339–41.

69. Kohn, *Eagle and Sword*, 253; JA to Rush, Dec. 4, 1805, Schutz and Adair, *Spur of Fame*, 45; TJ to Thomas M. Randolph, Feb. 2, 1800, *WTJ* 7:423; TJ to Rush, Jan. 16, 1811, *WTJ* 9:296.

70. Kohn, *Eagle and Sword*, 204–18.

71. AA to Mary Cranch, May 10, 1798, in Stewart Mitchell, *New Letters of Abigail Adams, 1788–1801* (Boston, 1947), 170–71; JA to TJ, June 30, 1813, *AJC* 2:347.

72. AH to Rufus King, Oct. 2, 1798, *PAH* 22:192; AH to Harrison G. Otis, Jan. 26, 1799, *PAH* 22:440–41.

73. JA to McHenry, Aug. 29, Sept. 13, 1798, *WJA* 8:588, 594; JA to Trumbull, July 23, Nov. [?], 1805, AFP, reel 118; JA to Vanderkemp, Aug. 23, 1806, Apr. 3, 1815, Simon Gratz Coll., *HSP*; JA to Rush, Aug. 23, Sept. 30, 1805, Sept. 2, Nov. 11, 1807, Apr. 18, 1808, Schutz and Adair, *Spur of Fame*, 35, 42, 94–95, 98–99, 113; JA to Benjamin Waterhouse, July 12, 1811, in Worthington C. Ford, ed., *Statesman and Friend: Correspondence of John Adams and Benjamin Waterhouse, 1784–1822* (Boston, 1927), 65; Ferling, *John Adams*, 392; AA to William Smith, July 232, 1798; Smith-Townsend Coll., MHS; AA to Smith, July 7, 1798, Smith-Carter Coll., MHS.

74. JA to Rush, Aug. 23, Sept. 30, Dec. 4, 1805, Jan. 25, 1806, Aug. 28, 1811, Jan. 25, 1806, Schutz and Adair, *Spur of Fame*, 34–35, 42, 45, 47–48, 192; JA to William Cunningham, Oct. 15, 1808, in *Correspondence between the Hon. John Adams . . . and the Late William Cunningham* (Boston, 1823), 44; McHenry to AH, May 31, 1800, *PAH* 24:552–65.

75. AA to Elizabeth Peabody, June 22, 1798, Shaw Papers, Library of Congress; Wolcott to JA, Nov. 26, 1798, AFP, reel 392; McHenry to JA, Nov. 25, 1798, AFP, reel 392; Pickering to JA, Nov. 27, 1798, AFP, reel 392; Stoddert to JA, Nov. 25, 1798, AFP, reel 392; Jacob E. Cooke, "Country above Party: John Adams and the 1799 Mission to France," in Edward P. Willis, ed., *Fame and the Founding Fathers* (Bethlehem, Pa., 1967), 58n.

76. TJ to JM, Jan. 3, 1799, Ford, *WTJ* 7:313.

77. De Conde, *Quasi-War*, 147–48, 162, 191; Samuel Flagg Bemis, *John Quincy Adams and the Foundations of American Foreign Policy* (New York, 1956), 99–101; JA to David Sewall, Dec. 22, 1806, AFP, reel 118; TJ to JM, Jan. 16, 1799, Ford, *WTJ* 7:318; *Correspondence of the Late President Adams in the Boston Patriot* (Boston, 1809), 10; Stephen G. Kurtz, *The Presidency of John Adams: The Collapse of Federalism, 1795–1800* (Philadelphia, 1957), 341; Murray to JA, July 1, 17, 22, Aug. 3, 20, Oct. 7, 1798, *WJA* 8:677–91.

78. Barlowe to GW, Oct. 2, 1798, in Jared Sparks, ed., *The Writings of Washington* (Boston, 1834–37), 11:560; GW to JA, Feb. 1, 1799, *WW* 37:119–20.

79. De Conde, *Quasi War*, 178; TJ to Archibald Stuart, Feb. 13, 1799, Ford, *WTJ* 7:352; John Adams, State of the Union Address, Dec. 8, 1798, in Richardson, ed., *Messages of the Presidents*, 1:261–65.

80. AH to King, Aug. 22, 1798, *PAH* 22:154–55; AH to Francisco de Miranda, Aug. 22, 1798, *PAH* 22:155–56; King to AH, May 12, July 31, 1798, *PAH* 21:458–59; 22:44–45; Miranda to AH, Feb. 7, Apr. 6–June 7, 1798, *PAH* 21:348–49, 399–402; Sharp, *American Politics in the Early Republic*,

214–15; Miller, *Federalist Era*, 220; Charles, *American Party System*, 132–35; Brookhiser, *Hamilton*, 140–41.

81. TJ to JM, Feb. 5, 1799, Ford, *WTJ* 7:342; Malone, *Jefferson*, 3:416; AH to H. G. Otis, Dec. 27, 1798, Jan. 26, 1799, *PAH* 22:394, 441; AH to Sedgwick, Feb. 2, 1799, *PAH* 452–53; Elkins and McKitrick, *Age of Federalism*, 615–17.

82. Adams, "Correspondence Originally Published in the *Boston Patriot*," *WJA* 9:305–6.

83. JA to TJ, Dec. 6, 1787, *AJC* 1:213; Adams, *Defence*, in *WJA* 4:585, 5:473, 6:186–87; Adams, "Davila," *WJA* 6:241–48, 252, 254, 256, 323. The best scholarly work on JA as a political theoretician is Thompson, *John Adams and the Spirit of Liberty*. On JA's reflections on the role of the executive within a system that featured a separation of powers, see pages 212–22.

84. Morison, *Harrison Gray Otis*, 159; De Conde, *Quasi-War*, 182–83.

85. Sedgwick to King, Jan. 20–27, March 20, 1799, Sedgwick Letterbook, MHS; Peter Van Schaack to Sedgwick, March 12, 1799, Sedgwick Family Papers, MHS.

86. Sedgwick to King, March 20, Dec. 29, 1799, Sedgwick Letterbook, MHS; Sedgwick to Hamilton, Feb. 7, 1799, *PAH* 22:471.

87. Brown, *Presidency of Adams*, 97; Pickering to McHenry, Feb. 3, 1799, Steiner, *Life and Career of James McHenry*, 568; Sedgwick to AH, Feb. 22, 25, 1799, *PAH* 22:494, 503; De Conde, *Quasi-War*, 182; Sedgwick to Van Schaack, Feb. 26, 1799, Jan. 4, 1800, Sedgwick Family Papers, MHS; Sedgwick to John Rutherford, March 1, 1799, Sedgwick Family Papers, MHS; JA to AA, Feb. 27, 1799, AFP, reel 393.

88. Elkins and McKitrick, *Age of Federalism*, 620.

89. JA to Pickering, Aug. 6, Sept. 14, 1799, AFP, reel 120; Pickering to JA, Sept. 14, 1799, AFP, reel 120; Stoddert to JA, Aug. 29, Sept. 13, 1799, *WJA* 9:18–19, 26–29; JA to Stoddert, Sept. 21, 1799, *WJA* 9:34; Gerald Clarfield, *Timothy Pickering and the American Republic*, 208; Stephen G. Kurtz, "The French Mission of 1799–1800: Concluding Chapter in the Statecraft of John Adams," *Political Science Quarterly* 80 (1965): 556.

90. JA to AA, Oct. 24, 1799, AFP, reel 396; Cooke, "Country above Party," in Willis, *Fame and the Founding Fathers*, 68–69.

91. *WJA* 9:255–56n; JA, "Letters to the *Boston Patriot*," *WJA* 9:253–55; Cunningham, *Correspondence*, 47–48; AA to Mary Cranch, Dec. 30, 1799, Mitchell, *New Letters of Abigail Adams*, 224–25.

92. Miller, *Portrait in Paradox*, 503.

93. AH to GW, Oct. 21, 1799, *PAH* 23:545; TJ, "Anas," Ford, *WTJ* 1:279; JA to Rush, March 19, 1812, Nov. 11, 1807, Schutz and Adams, *Spur of Fame*, 214, 99; Kohn, *Eagle and Sword*, 257.

94. TJ to Pendleton, Apr. 22, 1799, Ford, *WTJ* 7:375; TJ to Thomas Lomax, March 12, 1799, Ford, *WTJ* 7:373–74.

Chapter 13

1. Ferling, *John Adams*, 322, 386, 395, 402, 405.

2. Peter Henriques, *He Died as He Lived: The Death of George Washington* (Mount Vernon, Va., 2000), 27–36.

3. Ibid., 60–61.

4. Dauer, *Adams Federalists*, 233–34; Miller, *Federalist Era*, 255.

5. TJ to JM, May 12, 1800, Smith, *Republic of Letters*, 2:1135; Sharp, *American Politics in the Early Republic*, 222–23.

6. Cunningham, *Jeffersonian Republicans*, 134, 139; AH to King, Jan. 5, 1800, *PAH* 24:168; Elkins and McKitrick, *Age of Federalism*, 731, 905n; Miller, *Federalist Era*, 255.

7. AH to King, Jan. 5, 1800, *PAH* 24:168; AH to Sedgwick, May 10, 1800, *PAH* 24:475; AH to McHenry, June 6, 1800, *PAH* 24:573; Elkins and McKitrick, *Age of Federalism*, 728, 732.

8. AA to Mary Cranch, May 5, 1800, in Mitchell, ed., *New Letters of Abigail Adams*, 251.

9. Quoted in Noble Cunningham, "Election of 1800," in Arthur M. Schlesinger Jr., ed., *The Coming to Power: Critical Presidential Elections in American History* (New York, 1972), 1:109.

10. AA to Thomas B. Adams, Nov. 13, 1800, Charles F. Adams, ed., *Letters of Mrs. Adams, the Wife of John Adams* (Boston, 1841), 2:238; Milton Lomask, *Aaron Burr*, vol. 1 (New York, 1979), 238–46.

11. AH to King, May 4, 1796, *PAH* 20:158.

12. William Merrill and Sean Wilentz, eds., *The Key of Liberty: The Life and Democratic Writings of William Manning, "A Laborer," 1747–1814* (Cambridge, Mass., 1993), 59, 63–64, 73–74, 112, 126; Gordon Wood, "The Enemy Is Us: Democratic Capitalism in the Early Republic," *JER* 16 (1996): 293–308; Cunningham, "Election of 1800," in Schlesinger, ed., *The Coming to Power*, 1:61–63; Joanne B. Freeman, "The Election of 1800: A Study in the Logic of Political Change," *Yale Law Journal* 108 (1999): 1975–76; Brown, *Presidency of Adams*, 193; Miller, *Hamilton*, 510, 512–13; Sharp, *American Politics in the Early Republic*, 233; Elkins and McKitrick, *Age of Federalism*, 732–33.

13. McHenry to AH, May 31, 1800, *PAH* 24:552–65; JA to Pickering, May 10, 12, 1800, AFP, reel 120; JA to Lloyd, March 31, 1815, AFP, reel 122; Kohn, *Eagle and Sword*, 266–67.

14. Sedgwick to King, May 11, Sept. 26, 1800, Sedgwick Letterbook, MHS; Ames to Sedgwick, Dec. 14, 1800, Sedgwick Family Papers, MHS; Welch, *Sedgwick*, 208–18.

15. Joseph Lyman to Sedgwick, Dec. 25, 1800, Sedgwick Family Papers, MHS; Sedgwick to AH, *PAH* 24:467; AH to Charles Carroll of Carrollton, July 1, 1800, *PAH* 25:2; Samuel Eliot Morison, ed., *Life and Letters of Harrison Gray Otis* (Boston, 1913), 1:189; Miller, *Federalist Era*, 263; Malone, *Jefferson*, 3:475; Elkins and McKitrick, *Age of Federalism*, 734–36.

16. Freeman, *Affairs of Honor*, 227.

17. Lomask, *Burr*, 36–69, 89–90, 271–79.

18. TJ to Gerry, May 13, 1797, *PTJ* 29:362; TJ to Monroe, Jan. 12, 1800, Ford, *WTJ* 7:401–2; TJ to JM, March 4, 1800, *WTJ* 7:433–34; TJ to Philip Nicholas, Apr. 7, 1800, *WTJ* 7:439–40; TJ to Edward Livingston, Apr. 3, 1800, *WTJ* 7:443–44; TJ to Robert Livingston, Apr. 30, 1800, *WTJ* 7:445–46; TJ to Pierce Butler, Aug. 11, 1800, *WTJ* 7:449–50; TJ to Gideon Granger, Aug. 13, 1800, *WTJ* 7:452; TJ to French Strother, June 8, 1797, *WTJ* 7:138; Malone, *Jefferson*, 3:332–33, 469–71; Smith, *Freedom's Fetters*, 358; Joseph Ellis, "The First Democrats," *U.S. News and World Report* (Aug. 21, 2000), 34–39.

19. TJ to SA, Feb. 26, 1800, Ford, *WTJ* 7:425; TJ to Granger, Aug. 13, 1800, *WTJ* 7:450–52.

20. Freeman, *Affairs of Honor*, 230–32.

21. Ibid., 232–34, 237–38.

22. David Waldstreicher and Stephen R. Grossbart, "Abraham Bishop's Vocation; or, The Mediation of Jeffersonian Politics," *JER* 18 (1998): 636–37; Cunningham, "Election of 1800," in Schlesinger, ed., *The Coming to Power*, 46–47, 51–53; Cunningham, *In Pursuit of Reason*, 221–37; Brodie, *Jefferson*, 430; Miller, *Federalist Era*, 264–65; JA to Ward, Jan. 8, 1801, AFP, reel 118.

23. The quotations are from Finkelman, "Problem of Slavery in the Age of Federalism," in Ben-Atar and Oberg, *Federalists Reconsidered*, 145.

24. Ferling, *John Adams*, 399.

25. Waldstreicher, *In the Midst of Perpetual Fetes*, 153–55, 186.

26. Malone, *Jefferson*, 3:480.

27. Brown, *Presidency of Adams*, 187.

28. Hamilton's *Letter* can be found in *PAH* 25:186–234. The quotation is on 233.

29. JA to AA, June 13, 1800, AFP, reel 398; William Shaw to AA, June 5, 8, 1800, AFP, reel 398.

30. Quoted in Smith, *John Adams,* 2:1056. Also see Brown, *Presidency of Adams,* 195.

31. Ferling, *First of Men,* 396–98, 422; AA to Cotton Tufts, Nov. 28, 1800, AFP, reel 399; AA to Mary Cranch, Nov. 21, 1800, in Mitchell, ed., *New Letters of Abigail Adams,* 257, 259; AA to Abigail Adams Smith, Nov. 21, 1800, Adams, *Letters of Mrs. Adams,* 2:242; Amy L. Jensen, *The White House and Its Thirty-four Families* (New York, 1958), 8–10.

32. Malone, *Jefferson,* 3:491–92.

33. H. G. Otis to ?, 1800, Otis Papers, MHS; Welch, *Sedgwick,* 217.

34. Malone, *Jefferson,* 3:492; Miller, *Federalist Era,* 268.

35. AA to Mary Cranch, May 5, 1800, in Mitchell, ed., *New Letters of Abigail Adams,* 251. The best succinct study of the election remains Noble E. Cunningham, "Election of 1800," in . Schlesinger, ed., *The Coming to Power,* 1:111–34.

36. Appleby, *Inheriting the Revolution,* 26–55.

37. Freehling, *The Road to Disunion,* 146–48; Sharp, *American Politics in the Early Republic,* 247.

38. De Conde, *Quasi War,* 223–58; Ferling, *John Adams,* 407–9; JA to Lloyd, Feb. 6, 1815, *WJA* 10:115; AH to G. Morris, Jan. 10, 1801, *PAH* 25:307.

39. George A. Billias, *Elbridge Gerry: Founding Father and Republican Statesman* (New York, 1976), 301; Dauer, *Adams Federalists,* 246–61.

40. Sedgwick to AH, Jan. 10, 1801, *PAH* 25:311; James Bayard to AH, March 8, 1801, *PAH* 25:345; Sedgwick to Sedgwick Jr., Feb. 15, 1801, Sedgwick Family Papers, MHS; Ames to Sedgwick, Dec. 31, 1800, MHS.

41. AH to Wolcott, Dec. 16, 1800, *PAH* 25:258; AH, *Letter, PAH* 25:186; AH to James Bayard, Dec. 27, 1800, Jan. 16, 1801, *PAH* 25:277, 319; AH to McHenry, Jan. 4, 1801, *PAH* 25:292–93; "The Electoral Tie of 1801," in Mary-Jo Kline et al., eds., *Political Correspondence and Public Papers of Aaron Burr* (Princeton, N.J., 1983), 1:485.

42. TJ to Burr, Dec. 15, 1800, Ford, *WTJ* 7:466–68; G. Morris to AH, Dec. 19, 1800, *PAH* 25:267; Harper to Burr, Dec. 24, 1800, Kline, *Political Correspondence of Burr,* 1:474; Sharp, *American Politics in the Early Republic,* 254–55; Malone, *Jefferson,* 3:497–99.

43. Burr to Samuel Smith, Dec. 16, 1800, in Kline, *Political Correspondence of Burr,* 1:471; Burr to John Taylor of Caroline, Dec. 18, 1800, 1:473.

44. Robert Goodloe Harper to Burr, Kline, *Political Correspondence of Burr,* 1:474.

45. Lomask, *Burr,* 270–71, 276–77, 285–86.

46. AH to James Ross, Dec. 29, 1800, *PAH* 25:280; AH to Gouverneur Morris, Dec. 24, 1800, *PAH* 25:272; AH to McHenry, Jan. 4, 1801, *PAH* 25:320–24; AH to Wolcott, Dec. ?, 1800, *PAH* 25:287; Miller, *Federalist Era,* 270.

47. Bernard A. Weisberger, *America Afire: Jefferson, Adams, and the Revolution of 1800* (New York, 2000), 272; Freeman, "Election of 1800," *Yale Law Journal* 108 (1999): 1988–89. On the sense of honor that led most of the congressmen to remain true to their earlier commitments, see Freeman, *Affairs of Honor,* 241–61.

48. TJ to JM, Feb. 18, 1801, Ford, *WTJ* 7:494; Sharp, *American Politics in the Early Republic,* 265–71.

49. Bayard to AH, Jan. 7, 1801, *PAH* 25:300–301.

50. Lomask, *Burr,* 292, 322. Joanne Freeman has argued persuasively that these men were able to delude themselves into believing that they had never made a bargain. See Freeman, *Affairs of Honor,* 252.

51. Burr to Albert Gallatin, Feb. 25, 1801, Kline, *Political Correspondence of Burr,* 1:509.

52. Cunningham, *In Pursuit of Reason,* 244, 261; Malone, *Jefferson,* 4:102–3.

53. Sedgwick to Sedgwick Jr., Feb. 16, 1801, Sedgwick Family Papers, MHS.

54. Sharp, *American Politics in the Early Republic,* 271–72; Elkins and McKitrick, *Age of Federalism,* 749–50; Lomask, *Burr,* 293; Malone, *Jefferson,* 503–4.

55. TJ to Thomas McKean, March 9, 1801, Lipscomb and Bergh, *WTJ* 10:221; TJ to Lomax, Feb. 25, 1801, Ford, *WTJ* 7:500.

Chapter 14

1. Quoted in Merrill D. Peterson, *Thomas Jefferson and the New Nation* (New York, 1970), 654.

2. Quoted in Weisberger, *America Afire*, 7.

3. Brown, *Presidency of John Adams*, 196.

4. Quoted in Albert J. Beveridge, *The Life of John Marshall* (Boston, 1929), 3:1–2, 5.

5. Waldstreicher, *In the Midst of Perpetual Fetes*, 187–93.

6. TJ to Joseph Priestley, March 21, 1801, Ford, *WTJ* 8:22.

7. TJ to SA, March 29, 1801, Ford, *WTJ* 8:38–40.

8. Cunningham, *In Pursuit of Reason*, 271.

9. Beveridge, *Life of Marshall*, 1:125–26.

10. Ferling, *John Adams*, 417–44.

11. Wright, *Franklin of Philadelphia*, 294.

12. Alexander, *Samuel Adams*, 167–72, 191–221.

13. AH, "An Address to the Electors of the State of New York" [March 21, 1801], *PAH* 25:365.

14. Oliver to Francis Bernard, Aug. 9, 1773, Andrew Oliver Letterbook, MHS; "Memorial of Daniel Oliver to the Office of American Claims, ca. 1787, Hutchinson and Oliver Papers, MHS; "Andrew Oliver," in Clifford Shipton, ed., *Biographical Sketches of Those Who Attended Harvard College* (Cambridge, Mass., 1933–75), 8:401–12.

15. Bailyn, *Ordeal of Thomas Hutchinson*, 273–373; Mary Beth Norton, *The British Americans: The Loyalist Exiles in England, 1774–1789* (New York, 1972), 71–73, 124–25, 259.

16. Ferling, *Loyalist Mind*, 35–64. The remark by Elizabeth Galloway can be found in Norton, *British-Americans*, 60.

17. Flower, *Dickinson*, 230–303.

18. Paine to TJ, June 9, 1801, in Foner, *Complete Writings of Paine*, 2:1419.

19. *National Intelligencer*, March 6, 1801, quoted in Esther Singleton, *The Story of the White House* (New York, 1907), 29.

20. Sarah N. Randolph, *The Domestic Life of Thomas Jefferson* (reprint, Charlottesville, Va., 1978), 275–76.

21. AH to Bayard, Apr. 16–21, 1802, *PAH* 25:606.

22. JA to Stoddert, March 31, 1801, *WJA* 9:582.

23. AH, "Campaign Speech," Apr. 10, 1801, *PAH* 25:377.

24. TJ to Priestly, March 21, 1801, Ford, *WTJ* 8:22; TJ to Spencer Roan, Sept. 6, 1819, Ford, *WTJ* 10:140.

25. Thomas Jefferson, First Inaugural Address, March 4, 1801, in Richardson, ed., *Messages of the Presidents*, 1:321–24.

Index

Stamp Act: Adam's response to, 98; Assembly Party's indifference to, 78; denounced by Dickinson, 70; denounced by Franklin, 51; effects of crisis, 25, 32–40,.45, 50, 53–55, 122, 141, 429; enactment of, 31–32; repealed, 51, 54; stamp agents, 46; Virginia Resolves, 34, 57, 67

Stamp Act Congress, 41, 43, 69, 109, 120

"The Stand" (Hamilton), 423–24

State House in Philadelphia, 282

states. *See also individual states*: assumption plan, 316, 318, 319, 320–21, 322–24, 325, 326, 327, 338, 382, 387, 399, 469; bill of rights, 195; confiscation of property by, 315; debts of, 238, 239, 278, 315–16; economic responsibilities, 224–25, 230; expropriation by, 315; financing war, 238, 258; governors, 195, 290; Kentucky Resolutions, 433–35; liberties, 195; Madison on, 269–70; national government and, 232, 291, 293; powers of, 234, 291, 297; raising revenue, 315; ratification of Constitution, 294–303; responsibilities to army, 217; royal charters, 193; sovereignty of, 181–82, 269–70, 271, 274, 291; state constitutions, 193, 195, 285; taxation, 196, 225, 258; Washington on, 278

Steuben, Frederich von, 330

stockjobbers, 336–37

Stockton, Richard, 162, 173

Stoddert, Benjamin, 446

Stone, Michael Jenifer, 337

suffrage rights: in colonies, 101; demands for, 159; Dickinson on, 178; Federalists on, 384; Madison on, 270; in Paine's model of government, 194; in Pennsylvania, 196; qualifications for, 195, 261, 400, 465; voter turnout, 45

Sugar Act, 30–31, 34

Sullivan, John, 158, 234, 235

A Summary View of the Rights of British America (Jefferson), 145, 329, 434

Superintendent of Finance post, 235, 238–41

Susquehanna River, 325

Talleyrand-Périgord, Charles-Maurice de, 416

taxation. *See also* Stamp Act; Tea Act; Townshend Duties: Adam's response to, 98; Albany Plan of Union on, 18; Articles of the Confederation on, 180; on British shipping proposed, 324, 367, 368, 375–76; Congressional powers, 232, 251, 268, 296; debates on, 181, 182; denounced by assemblies, 68; effect of reconciliation on, 152; in Europe, 333; federal taxes, 362;

Federalists' implementation, 467, 487; Hamilton on, 319, 336, 337, 376; on imports, 235; impost amendment, 242, 252, 256, 262, 268, 319; increases in, 279; Jefferson on, 371; Madison on, 268; Morris on, 242; Mutiny Act (Quartering Act), 31, 86; plans for, 93; property taxes, 196, 262; public reaction to, 442; Quasi-War Crisis, 422; reduction of, 30; representation and, 40–41; resistance to union, 15; revenues, 86, 212, 220; slavery, 180, 181, 288; by states, 196, 224, 258, 315; Sugar Act, 30–31, 34; war financing, 260; on whiskey, 352, 371–72

Tea Act: goals of, 94; news of, 102; reaction to, 102, 103–7, 108, 126; repealed, 202; trade embargo, 120

tea duty: boycotts of, 86; protests and demonstrations, 101–2, 103; revenues from, 88; violations of boycott, 91–92, 93–94

Tennessee, 264, 336, 464, 468

Thomas, Peter D. G., 77

Thomson, Charles, 81, 111, 258

Thoughts on Government (Adams), 161, 194

tobacco, 95, 116, 192, 207, 263, 290

Tories: assisting deserters, 204; charges of, 159; on civil discord, 148; exile of, 257, 386; Federalists and, 382; in military forces, 200; as minority, 113; as political party, 344; political process of, 178; in public office, 196, 257; redistribution of land, 224, 225, 253, 257, 262; warnings of, 260

Townshend, Charles, 55–56

Townshend Duties: Adams's resolution denouncing, 67; Dickinson on, 70; effectiveness of, 109, 121; enactment of, 56; enforcement of, 184; Massachusetts Circular Letter, 57; partial repeal, 86, 87; reaction to, 57, 59, 76, 78, 79

trade and commerce. *See also* economy: Albany Congress on, 18; American Prohibitory Act, 150, 157, 163; in the Caribbean, 368, 410–11; Dickens' emphasis on, 71; effect of Constitution on, 300; effect of reconciliation on, 152; embargoes (*see main entry for* trade embargo); foreign conflicts' effects on, 356; framers involved in, 282; with France, 170, 191–92, 207, 237; Franco-American treaties, 203; French attacks on, 410–11; with Great Britain, 257–58, 298, 316, 320, 365–66, 375, 379; imperial trade regulation, 29, 56–57, 84, 120, 202; international trade, 257–58; interstate trade, 349; Madison on, 276;